THE RAMAYANA OF VALMIKI

BA

14

by the same author

THE HEART OF THE EASTERN MYSTICAL TEACHING
(Shri Dada Sanghita)

THE SEARCH FOR A GURU

WISDOM FROM THE EAST

MEDITATION — ITS THEORY AND PRACTICE

YOGA (Foyles Handbook)

A PATH TO GOD-REALIZATION

ECHOES OF JAPAN

SCIENTIST AND MAHATMA (Swami Rama Tirtha)

SPRING SHOWERS

VEDANTA LIGHT

Translations

THE WORLD WITHIN THE MIND (Yoga Vasishtha)

THE PHILOSOPHY OF LOVE (Narada Sutras)

THE AVADHUT GITA

THE ASHTAVAKRA GITA

TEACHINGS FROM THE BHAGAVAD GITA

PANCHADASI

INDIAN MYSTIC VERSE

SELF-KNOWLEDGE, a quarterly journal including articles by Dr. Shastri, and all the above publications, are obtainable from Shanti Sadan 29 Chepstow Villas, London, W.11.

THE

RAMAYANA

OF

VALMIKI

Translated by

HARI PRASAD SHASTRI

Vol. III.

YUDDHA KANDA

UTTARA KANDA

SHANTI SADAN
29 CHEPSTOW VILLAS
LONDON, W.11

First published 1959
Second impression 1970
Third impression 1976
Fourth impression 1985

ISBN 0-85424-017-9

Originally printed in Great Britain
at the Burleigh Press, Bristol
Reprinted by Biddles Ltd, Guildford, Surrey

CONTENTS

BOOK VI—YUDDHA KANDA

CHAPTER | PAGE
1. Rama felicitates Hanuman. His Perplexities - - 3
2. Sugriva consoles Rama - - - - - - - 4
3. Hanuman describes the Strength of Lanka to Rama - 6
4. The Army reaches the Shores of the Sea - - - 8
5. Rama is afflicted when thinking of Sita - - - 15
6. Ravana consults his Subjects - - - - - - 16
7. The Titans persuade Ravana to make War and remind him of his former Exploits - - - - - 18
8. The boasting of Ravana's Generals - - - - 19
9. Bibishana advises Ravana to send back Sita - - 21
10. Bibishana insists that Sita should be given back to Rama 23
11. Ravana summons his Assembly - - - - - 25
12. The Discourse between Ravana and Kumbhakarna - 27
13. Ravana tells the Story of the Nymph Punjikasthala - 30
14. Bibishana blames the attitude of Ravana's Courtiers - 31
15. Bibishana reproaches Indrajita for his boasting - - 33
16. Ravana rebukes Bibishana who takes his departure - 34
17. Words of the leading Monkeys regarding Bibishana - 36
18. Rama listens to the Advice of the Monkeys about receiving Bibishana - - - - - - - 40
19. Bibishana is brought before Rama - - - - - 43
20. Ravana sends Shuka to Sugriva - - - - - 46
21. Rama looses his Arrows on Sagara - - - - 48
22. The Army crosses the Sea - - - - - - 51
23. Rama sees diverse Portents - - - - - - 56
24. Shuka describes his reception by the Monkeys to Ravana 57
25. Ravana sends out Shuka and Sarana to spy on the Monkeys - - - - - - - - - 60
26. Sarana tells Ravana of the principal Leaders of the Monkeys - - - - - - - - - 62
27. Sarana continues his Deposition - - - - - 65
28. Shuka in his turn enumerates the Enemy - - - 68
29. Ravana sends out fresh Spies - - - - - - 71
30. Shardula gives an Account of his Mission to Ravana - 73
31. Ravana deceives Sita about the Death of Rama - - 75
32. Sita's Despair - - - - - - - - - 78
33. Sarama consoles Sita - - - - - - - - 81
34. Sarama spies on Ravana's Plans - - - - - 83

CONTENTS

CHAPTER   PAGE

35. Malyavan advises Ravana to make peace - - - 85
36. Ravana directs Lanka's Defences - - - - - 87
37. Rama makes his Plans for the Attack - - - - 89
38. The Ascent of Mount Suvela - - - - - - 91
39. Description of Lanka - - - - - - - - 92
40. The extraordinary Combat between Sugriva and Ravana 94
41. Rama sends Angada to Ravana - - - - - 96
42. The Titans make a Sortie - - - - - - 102
43. The Conflict between the Monkeys and the Titans - 104
44. Angada's Exploit - - - - - - - - 107
45. Rama and Lakshmana are struck down by Indrajita - 110
46. The despair of Sugriva and his Army. Bibishana re-
     assures Him - - - - - - - - 112
47. Sita sees Rama and Lakshmana lying on the Battlefield 115
48. Sita's Lamentations - - - - - - - - 116
49. Rama returns to consciousness and weeps over Lakshmana 119
50. Garuda liberates Rama and Lakshmana - - - 121
51. Dhumraksha goes out to fight the Monkeys - - 125
52. Dhumraksha fights and is slain by Hanuman - - 127
53. Vajradamshtra enters the Lists - - - - - 130
54. Angada slays Vajradamshtra - - - - - - 132
55. Akampana goes out to fight against the Monkeys - 134
56. Akampana is slain by Hanuman - - - - - 138
57. Prahasta goes out to fight - - - - - - - 139
58. The Death of Prahasta - - - - - - - 141
59. Ravana's prowess. Rama overcomes him but grants
     him his Life - - - - - - - - - 145
60. The Titans rouse Kumbhakarna - - - - - 156
61. The Story of Kumbhakarna - - - - - - 162
62. The Meeting between Kumbhakarna and Ravana - 164
63. Kumbhakarna consoles Ravana - - - - - 166
64. Mahodara's Speech - - - - - - - - 170
65. Kumbhakarna enters into combat - - - - - 172
66. Angada reproaches the Monkeys for flying from
     Kumbhakarna - - - - - - - - 176
67. Kumbhakarna's Exploits. He is slain by Rama - 178
68. Ravana weeps for Kumbhakarna - - - - - 189
69. Narantaka is slain by Indra - - - - - - 191
70. The Death of Devantaka, Trishiras, Mahodara and
     Mahaparshwa - - - - - - - - 197
71. Lakshmana slays the Titan Atikaya - - - - 201
72. Ravana, overcome by anxiety, makes further Plans - 208
73. Indrajita, making himself invisible, puts the Monkey
     Army out of action - - - - - - - 209
74. On Jambavan's Instructions, Hanuman goes to the
     Mountain of Medicinal Herbs - - - - 214

CONTENTS

CHAPTER   PAGE

75. Lanka is set on fire by the Monkeys - - - - 220
76. The Prowess of Angada and Kumbha : Kumbha is slain 224
77. The Fight between Nikumbha and Hanuman - - 229
78. Maharaksha goes out to meet Rama and Lakshmana - 231
79. Maharaksha falls under Rama's Blows - - - - 232
80. Indrajita sets out to fight once more - - - - 235
81. Indrajita's Stratagem. Sita's Apparition - - - 238
82. Hanuman rallies His Forces : Indrajita's Sacrifice - 240
83. Lakshmana's Speech - - - - - - - - 242
84. Bibishana consoles Rama - - - - - - - 245
85. Lakshmana goes to the Nikumbhila Grove to fight Indrajita - - - - - - - - 246
86. Indrajita breaks off his Sacrifice to fight with Lakshmana 249
87. Indrajita and Bibishana denounce each other - - 251
88. The Combat between Lakshmana and Indrajita - 253
89. Lakshmana and Indrajita continue to fight - - - 255
90. Indrajita loses his Charioteer, Chariot and Horses - 258
91. The Death of Indrajita - - - - - - - 261
92. Rama commends Lakshmana who is cured of His Wounds by the Monkey Sushena - - - - 266
93. Ravana's Grief on hearing of his Son's Death - - 268
94. Rama's Exploits - - - - - - - - - 272
95. The Lamentations of the Titan Women - - - 275
96. Ravana goes out to fight and encounters ill Omens - 277
97. The Fight between Virupaksha and Sugriva : Virupaksha's Death - - - - - - - 281
98. Mahodara is slain by Sugriva - - - - - - 283
99. The Combat between Angada and Mahaparshwa - 285
100. Rama and Ravana fight with magic Weapons - - 287
101. Ravana flees from Rama - - - - - - - 290
102. Lakshmana's miraculous Recovery - - - - - 294
103. Rama and Ravana renew their Combat - - - - 297
104. Rama arraigns Ravana and reproaches him for his Misdeeds - - - - - - - - - 301
105. Ravana reproaches his Charioteer - - - - - 303
106. The Sage Agastya instructs Rama in the Hymn to the Sun - - - - - - - - - - 305
107. Sinister Portents appear - - - - - - - 308
108. The Fluctuations of Combat - - - - - - 310
109. The Duel continues - - - - - - - - 312
110. The Death of Ravana - - - - - - - 314
111. The Lamentations of Bibishana - - - - - 316
112. The Lamentations of Ravana's Consorts - - - 318
113. The Lamentations of Mandodari : Ravana's Funeral Rites - - - - - - - - - - 320
114. Bibishana is installed as King of Lanka - - - 328

CONTENTS

CHAPTER   PAGE

115. Hanuman carries Rama's Message to Sita - - - 329
116. Rama sends for Sita - - - - - - - - 332
117. Rama repudiates Sita - - - - - - - - 334
118. Sita's Lamentations. She undergoes the Ordeal by Fire 336
119. Brahma's Praise of Rama - - - - - - - 338
120. Sita is restored to Rama - - - - - - 341
121. Dasaratha appears to Rama - - - - - - 342
122. On Rama's Request, Indra restores the Army - - 345
123. Bibishana places the Chariot Pushpaka at Rama's disposal - - - - - - - - - 346
124. Rama sets out for Ayodhya - - - - - - 348
125. Rama tells Sita of the Places over which they are passing 350
126. Rama's Meeting with the Sage Bharadwaja - - 353
127. Rama sends Hanuman to seek out Bharata - - - 355
128. Hanuman tells Bharata of all that befell Rama and Sita during their Exile - - - - - - - 358
129. Bharata sets out to meet Rama - - - - - 361
130. Rama is installed as King. The Benefits that accrue from the Recitation and Hearing of the "Ramayana" 365

CONTENTS

BOOK VII—UTTARA KANDA

CHAPTER   PAGE

1. The Sages pay homage to Rama - - - - - 375
2. The Birth of Vishravas - - - - - - - 377
3. Vishravas becomes the Protector of Wealth - - 379
4. Origin of the Rakshasas and of the Boons they received 382
5. The Story of the three Sons of Sukesha - - - 384
6. Vishnu goes to the defence of the Gods - - - 387
7. The Combat between Vishnu and the Rakshasas - 392
8. The Combat between Vishnu and Malyavan - - 395
9. The Birth of Dashagriva and His Brothers - - 397
10. Concerning the Penances practised by Dashagriva and
His Brothers - - - - - - - - - 401
11. Dhanada cedes Lanka to Dashagriva - - - - 404
12. The Marriages of the Rakshasas - - - - - 407
13. Ravana's Crimes - - - - - - - - - 410
14. The Combat between Ravana and the Yakshas - - 412
15. The Combat between Ravana and Dhanada. Ravana
seizes Pushpaka - - - - - - - - 414
16. The Origin of Ravana's Name - - - - - 417
17. The Story of Vedavati - - - - - - - 420
18. The Gods assume a thousand Forms in fear of Ravana 423
19. Ravana fights with Anaranya who dies prophesying the
Rakshasa's End - - - - - - - - 425
20. Ravana's Meeting with the Sage Narada - - - 427
21. Ravana goes to the Nether Regions to challenge Yama 430
22. The Duel between Ravana and Yama : Brahma inter-
venes - - - - - - - - - - - 433
23. Ravana's Struggle with the Sons of Varuna - - - 436
First of the Interpolated Chapters. 1st Series. Ravana's
Meeting with Bali - - - - - - - 439
Second of the Interpolated Chapters. 1st Series
Ravana challenges the Sun-god - - - - 445
Third of the Interpolated Chapters. 1st Series.
Ranvana's Encounter with the King Mandhata - 446
Fourth of the Interpolated Chapters, 1st Series
Ravana visits the Moon Region and is given a Boon
by Brahma - - - - - - - - - 449
Fifth of the Interpolated Chapters. 1st Series.
Ravana and the Maha-Purusha - - - - 453

CONTENTS

CHAPTER   PAGE

24. Ravana carries off a number of Women and is cursed
    by them - - - - - - - - - - 457
25. Dashagriva allies himself to Madhu - - - - 460
26. Nalakúvara curses Ravana - - - - - - 463
27. The Fight between the Gods and the Rakshasas. The
    Death of Sumali - - - - - - - 467
28. The Duel between Indra and Ravana - - - - 470
29. Ravani takes Indra captive - - - - - - 472
30. Telling of the Curse pronounced by the Sage Gautama
    on Shakra - - - - - - - - - 475
31. Ravana goes to the Banks of the Narmada River - 479
32. Arjuna captures Ravana - - - - - - - 481
33. Arjuna releases Ravana at the request of Poulastya - 486
34. Bali hangs Ravana on his Girdle - - - - 487
35. The Story of Hanuman's Childhood - - - - 490
36. The Boons bestowed on the Child Hanuman and how
    he was cursed by the Ascetics - - - - 494
37. Homage is paid to Shri Rama - - - - - 499
    First of the Interpolated Chapters. 2nd Series - - 500
    Second of the Interpolated Chapters. 2nd Series - 503
    Third of the Interpolated Chapters. 2nd Series - - 505
    Fourth of the Interpolated Chapters. 2nd Series - 507
    Fifth of the Interpolated Chapters. 2nd Series - 507
38. Rama takes leave of His Allies - - - - - 511
39. Rama loads His Allies with Gifts - - - - - 513
40. Rama takes leave of the Bears, Monkeys and Titans - 515
41. Rama dismisses the Pushpaka Chariot - - - - 517
42. The Felicity enjoyed by Rama and Sita - - - 518
43. Rama informs Himself concerning current Rumours
    from His Friends - - - - - - - 521
44. Rama summons His Brothers - - - - - - 522
45. Rama commands Lakshmana to take Sita to the
    Hermitage - - - - - - - - - 524
46. Lakshmana takes Sita away - - - - - - 525
47. Lakshmana tells Sita she has been repudiated - - 527
48. Lakshmana leaves Sita on the Banks of the Ganges - 529
49. Valmiki offers Sita His Protection - - - - - 530
    Traditional Verses - - - - - - - - 532
50. Sumantra seeks to console Lakshmana - - - - 533
51. Vishnu is cursed by Bhrigu - - - - - - 535
52. Lakshmana seeks out Rama - - - - - - 537
53. Rama tells Lakshmana the Story of Nriga - - - 538
54. The End of the Story of Nriga - - - - - 539
55. The Story of Nimi - - - - - - - - 541
56. The Cursing of the Nymph Urvashi - - - - 542
57. The End of the Story of Vasishtha and Nimi - - 544

CONTENTS

CHAPTER   PAGE

58. Shukra curses Yayati - - - - - - - 545
59. Puru takes the place of His Father cursed by Shukra 547
     First of the Interpolated Chapters. 3rd Series - - 549
     Second of the Interpolated Chapters. 3rd Series - 550
     Third of the Interpolated Chapters. 3rd Series - 554
60. The Ascetics seek out Rama - - - - - - 558
61. The Story of Madhu - - - - - - - 559
62. Shatrughna asks permission to fight Lavana - - 561
63. The Installation of Shatrughna - - - - - 562
64. Shatrughna sets out to meet Lavana - - - - 564
65. The Story of Saudasa who is cursed by Vasishtha - 565
66. The Birth of Kusha and Lava - - - - - 568
67. The Story of Mandhata - - - - - - 569
68. Shatrughna encounters Lavana - - - - - 571
69. The Death of Lavana - - - - - - - 572
70. Shatrughna establishes Himself in the City of Madhu 574
71. Shatrughna seeks out the Sage Valmiki - - - 576
72. Shatrughna returns to see Rama - - - - - 577
73. The Death of a Brahmin's Son - - - - - 579
74. Narada's Discourse - - - - - - - 580
75. Rama makes a Tour of Inspection of His Kingdom - 582
76. Shambuka is slain by Rama - - - - - - 583
77. The Story of Swargin - - - - - - - 586
78. Shveta tells His Story - - - - - - 588
79. The hundred Sons of Ikshvaku - - - - - 589
80. Danda insults Aruja - - - - - - - 591
81. The destruction of Danda's Kingdom - - - - 592
82. Rama takes leave of Agastya - - - - - - 593
83. Bharata persuades Rama not to perform the Rajasuya
     Sacrifice - - - - - - - - - 595
84. The Story of Vritra - - - - - - - 596
85. The Death of Vritra - - - - - - - 597
86. Indra is liberated by means of the Ashvamedha Sacrifice 599
87. The Story of Ila - - - - - - - - 600
88. Budha encounters Ila - - - - - - - 602
89. The Birth of Pururavas - - - - - - 604
90. Ila regains her natural state through the Performance
     of the Ashvamedha Sacrifice - - - - - 605
91. Rama gives the command for the Ashvamedha Sacrifice
     to be performed - - - - - - - - 607
92. Description of the Ashvamedha Sacrifice - - - 609
93. Valmiki commands Kusha and Lava to recite the
     Ramayana - - - - - - - - - 610
94. Kusha and Lava chant the Ramayana - - - - 611
95. Rama sends for Sita - - - - - - - 613
96. Valmiki leads Sita before Rama - - - - - 615

CONTENTS

CHAPTER PAGE

97. Sita descends into the Earth - - - - - - 616
98. Rama's Anger and Grief, Brahma appeases Him - 618
99. The Death of the Queens - - - - - - 619
100. Rama sends Bharata to conquer the Gandharvas - 621
101. The slaying of the Gandharvas and the conquest of
     Their Country - - - - - - - - 622
102. Rama bestows Kingdoms on Lakshmana's Sons - 623
103. Death is sent to seek out Rama - - - - - 625
104. Death delivers his Message - - - - - 626
105. The Sage Durvasa comes to visit Rama - - - 627
106. Rama banishes Lakshmana - - - - - - 628
107. Rama installs Kusha and Lava on the Throne - - 630
108. Rama issues His last Commands - - - - - 631
109. Rama's Departure for the Mahaprasthana - - 633
110. Rama ascends to Heaven with the other Beings - - 635
111. The Supreme Virtue of the Ramayana - - - 636

BOOK VI.
YUDDHA KANDA

CHAPTER I

Rama felicitates Hanuman.—His Perplexities

HEARING Hanuman's faithful narrative, Rama, full of joy, said :
" The mission that Hanuman has carried out is of great
significance and the most arduous in the world ; none other
could have achieved it, even in thought ! Other than Garuda
and Vayu, verily I know of no being able to cross the mighty
ocean save Hanuman himself. Neither Gods, Danavas, Yakshas,
Gandharvas, Uragas nor Rakshasas could enter Lanka which is
protected by Ravana and, did any in his presumption enter
it, would he return alive ? Who is able to capture that citadel
by assault, that has been rendered inaccessible by its rampart
of titans, but one whose courage and valour are equal to
Hanuman's ? Hanuman has carried out this important service
for Sugriva by manifesting a strength equal to his audacity.
That servant to whom his master confides a difficult task and
who acquits himself with zeal is said to be a superior man. The
one who is ready and capable but who yet does no more than
his sovereign exacts from him, in order to render himself
agreeable, is called an ordinary man, but he who is well and
able and yet does not carry out the command of his king, is
said to be the least of men. Hanuman has fulfilled the task
confided to him unfalteringly, to the satisfaction of Sugriva; in
consequence, through the discovery of Vaidehi's retreat by
this faithful messenger, the House of Raghu, the valiant
Lakshmana and I have been saved. Yet even so my heart is
heavy, since I am not able to requite the bearer of these good
tidings in a fitting manner. Let me at least embrace the magnanimous Hanuman since, in the present circumstances, this
is all that is permitted to me ! "

Having spoken thus, Rama, trembling with joy, clasped
Hanuman in his arms, who, master of himself, his mission
fulfilled, had returned.

Then the great Scion of the House of Raghu, after reflecting awhile, added in the presence of Sugriva, King of the Monkeys :

" Though the discovery of Sita has been accomplished, yet when I behold that vast ocean, I am plunged in despondency. How will the army of the monkeys be able to reach the southern shore, crossing over that impassable stretch of water ? Having received these tidings of Vaidehi, what can now be done to take the monkeys to the further side of the ocean ? "

In the anguish that possessed him, the mighty Rama, scourge of his foes, having spoken to Hanuman, was filled with apprehension and became absorbed in thought.

CHAPTER 2

Sugriva consoles Rama

RAMA, the son of Dasaratha, being plunged in despair, the fortunate Sugriva spoke to him in consoling accents, saying : " Why dost thou give way to sorrow like a common man, O Hero ? Shake off this melancholy as do ungrateful men the recognition of favours accorded to them. After the tidings thou hast received and now that the haunt of thine enemy is known to thee, I see no cause for thine anxiety, O Raghava. Prudent and versed in the scriptures, intelligent and cultured as thou art, do thou as one master of himself, banish these unworthy fears that are the obstacles to success. We shall cross the sea where monstrous crocodiles abound, take Lanka by assault and slay thine adversary ! The pusillanimous and despondent man, whose mind is agitated by grief, accomplishes nothing worth while and rushes towards destruction.

" In order to please thee, these monkey warriors who are brave and skilled are ready to enter a blazing fire ! Observing their martial ardour I am filled with confidence ; do thou test my courage by suffering me to bring back Sita to thee after having slain thine adversary Ravana of evil exploits. But first construct a bridge for us that we may approach that city of the Lord of the Titans. The instant we behold Lanka, built on the summit of Trikuta, Ravana is slain as it were, but unless a bridge is thrown over that formidable domain of Varuna, the sea, the Gods and Asuras themselves with their leaders cannot force an entry into Lanka.

" When that dyke on the waters in the vicinity of Lanka is constructed and all the troops shall have passed over it, Ravana is, as it were, already defeated, so valiant are these monkey warriors who are able to change their form at will.

" Enough of this faint-hearted attitude, fatal to any enterprise, O King. In this world, man is unbraced by sorrow ; that which must be done should be accomplished with resolution, it is assuredly expedient to act swiftly ! For this enterprise, O Great Sage, unite energy with virtue, for, if it be a question of loss or death, the great warriors, thy peers, see grief as the consumer of their resources. Thou art the foremost of the wise and versed in all the scriptures ; with allies such as I am, thy victory is assured ! In sooth I see none in the Three Worlds able to withstand thee in combat when thou art armed with thy bow ! With the success of thine enterprise in the hands of the monkeys, thou canst not fail. When thou hast crossed the imperishable ocean thou shalt see Sita ere long. Desist from this melancholy that thou hast allowed to invade thee and yield to thy legitimate indignation, O Prince. Unadventurous warriors never win honour but all fear the wrathful. It is for the purpose of crossing the formidable ocean, the Lord of Rivers, that thou hast come hither with us ; now with thy resourceful mind ponder on it. Once the ocean has been crossed by my forces, know victory to be certain ; verily when the whole army has passed over the sea, our triumph is assured !

" The monkeys, those courageous soldiers, who are able to change their form at pleasure, will crush their opponents with an avalanche of rocks and trees. Whatever the means employed, once we have crossed Varuna's domain, Ravana is as dead in mine eyes, O Destroyer of Thy Foes ! But of what use are all these words ? Thy victory is assured and the portents, which I perceive, fill my heart with joy."

CHAPTER 3

Hanuman describes the Strength of Lanka to Rama

THESE words of Sugriva, judicious and full of good sense, pleased Kakutstha who said to Hanuman :—

" By the power of mine austerities, I am well able to cross the ocean by throwing a bridge over it or even drying it up. What are the fortifications of this inaccessible Lanka ? Describe them fully to me, I wish to hear all about them as if I had myself beheld them, O Monkey. How are its gates manned ; what is the strength of the army ; what kind of moats surround it and how are the retreats of the titans constructed ? Thou didst explore Lanka at thy leisure when opportunity arose, now in the light of thine observations give me exact and complete information thereon."

Thus interrogated by Rama, Hanuman, the Son of Maruta, the most eloquent of narrators, said :—

" Hear, O King, I will tell thee the extent of the defences, of the moats and the number of troops guarding that city. I will describe to thee the opulence of those titans and the great prosperity of their capital due to Ravana's austerities ; I will tell thee also of the formidable ocean and the many regiments of infantry and the strength of the cavalry ".

After this preamble, the foremost of monkeys began to relate lucidly everything he knew and said :—

" Filled with happy people, Lanka abounds in elephants intoxicated with Mada juice and is swarming with chariots and titans. It has four immense gateways that are extremely high and furnished with strong doors which are closed with massive iron bars. Catapults, darts and stones are placed near at hand, capable of repelling the assaults of the enemy and the valiant titans have heaped in readiness, formidable spears in their hundreds.

" The city is encircled by a high golden wall difficult to scale, lined within with precious gems, coral, emerald and pearl.

6

On all sides awe-inspiring moats of great splendour, filled with icy water, have been dug, which are deep and abounding in crocodiles and fishes. At the entrance to these dykes there are four long draw-bridges furnished with innumerable weapons and five great cannons are placed round about 'which defend the entries against the approach of the enemy, whose battalions would be flung by these engines of war into the moats on every side. The most important of these bastions, impossible to force, is of unsuperable strength and dazzling with its pillars and fulcrums of gold.

" Endowed with great physical strength, O Prince, Ravana is avid for combat, ever on the alert and constantly reviewing his forces. Lanka is therefore impregnable, it is a celestial citadel that inspires terror. Surrounded by water, built on a mountain with its fourfold defences[1], it is situated on the other side of the impassable ocean, O Rama, where no vessel can approach it, as it offers no harbourage anywhere. Built on the summit of an inaccessible rock, Lanka, where horses and elephants abound, resembling the City of the Gods, is extremely difficult to conquer. With its moats and Shataghnis, its engines of war of every kind, that capital of the wicked Ravana is unique.

" The eastern gate is defended by ten thousand men, all skilled warriors armed with spears, the foremost of swordsmen ; the southern gate is guarded by a hundred thousand warriors, there a whole army of seasoned fighters is assembled ; ten thousand troops armed with swords and shields, all accustomed to the wielding of weapons, defend the western gate ; the northern gate is protected by a million men who are mounted in chariots or who ride on horses ; they are the sons of distinguished families. Titans to the number of hundreds and thousands occupy the centre of the city with one million tested troops in addition.

" I have destroyed the ramparts and filled up the moats and, having torn down the walls, have set fire to the town, therefore, if we can find some means of crossing Varuna's domain, the city is ours ; let the monkeys deliberate on the matter.

"Angada, Dvivida, Mainda, Jambavan, Panasa, Nala and the General Nila will fall upon Ravana's capital with its hills,

[1] See glossary under fourfold . . .

7

woods, moats, archways and ramparts and bring Sita back to thee, O Raghava, what need is there of the rest of the monkeys ? Come, give the command quickly to the whole army of these valiant monkeys and, at a propitious hour, let us set out ! "

CHAPTER 4

The Army reaches the Shores of the Sea

HAVING listened to the judicious and well-reasoned speech of Hanuman, the illustrious Rama, a true hero, spoke saying :—

" Now that thou hast told me everything concerning Lanka, that dread citadel of the terrible demons, I shall make preparations to destroy it without delay, this is the truth !

" O Sugriva, be gracious enough to order our departure; the sun is in mid-heaven and has entered the constellation of victory[1]. As for Sita's abductor, he shall not escape, wherever he may go ! When Sita learns of my approach, her hopes will revive, as one who, having drunk poison and on the point of death, quaffs the nectar of immortality.

" The northern planet Phalguni is in the ascendent and will be in conjunction with the Hasta Star to-morrow. Let us depart, O Sugriva, and let all the troops accompany us; every portent is favourable ! Having slain Ravana, I shall return with Sita, the daughter of Janaka. My right eye-lid is twitching which is an indication that victory is near and that my purpose will be accomplished."

At these words, King Sugriva and Lakshmana, bowing low, paid obeisance to Rama, who, full of faith and versed in the moral law, spoke once more, saying :—

" Let General Nila with a guard of a hundred thousand intrepid warriors go before the army to explore the way. He should lead his forces speedily by the path where fruit, roots, shade, fresh water and honey abound. In their wickedness, the demons are capable of destroying the roots and fruits and

[1] Abhijit. (See Glossary.)

8

vitiating the water on the way. Keep them at a distance and be on your guard ! Let those dwellers of the woods search the ravines and dense thickets in the forest in order to discover the ambushes of the enemy.

" Those who are weak should remain here for your task is formidable and demands endurance; therefore let the foremost of the monkeys gifted with prodigious prowess lead the vanguard, composed of hundreds and thousands of monkeys, resembling the waters of the sea. Let Gaja who is like unto a hill and the exceedingly powerful Gavaya and Gavaksha go ahead like proud bulls leading the kine. The leader of monkeys, Rishabha, skilled in leaping, should protect the right flank of the army and the fiery Gandhamadana, resembling an elephant in mustha, should defend the left flank. I myself, mounted on the shoulders of Hanuman, like Indra on Airavata, will march in the centre of my troops in order to encourage them. Lakshmana who resembles death itself, will ride on the shoulders of Angada, as Kuvera, the Lord of Creatures and God of Wealth on Sarvabhauma. Let the mighty Lord of the Bears, Jambavan with Sushena and the monkey Vegadarshin, all three, protect the rear of the army."

Hearing Raghava's words, Sugriva, commander of the forces, gave his orders to the monkeys. Thereupon a multitude of monkeys, eager to fight, issued from the caves and mountain peaks, leaping on all sides. Honoured by the King of the Monkeys, as also by Lakshmana, the virtuous Rama, accompanied by hundreds and thousands of monkeys resembling elephants, set out in a southerly direction and under Sugriva's command, that great army in high spirits, betraying its delight, escorted him.

Guarding the flanks of the army and pressing forward, they ran towards the south, leaping on all sides, emitting leonine roars, growling and shouting, feeding on honey and delicious fruits, brandishing great trees and flowering shrubs. In their pugnacity, some lifted their fellows up and threw them down or climbed on each others backs vying with one another in turning somersaults.

" We will slay Ravana with all his nocturnal rangers ! " Thus did those monkeys roar in the presence of Rama.

Going in advance of the army, Rishabha, the valiant Nila and also Kumuda cleared the way with the assistance of innumerable monkeys. In the centre, the King Sugriva, Rama and Lakshmana, scourges of their foes, were surrounded by countless redoutable warriors. The courageous monkey, Shatabali, at the head of ten kotis, was, in himself, sufficient to protect the entire host of monkeys! With an escort of a hundred kotis, Kesarin and Panasa, Gaja and Arka with their battalions protected the flanks of that army, whilst Sushena and Jambavan surrounded by a multitude of bears, having placed Sugriva at the head, formed the rearguard. The valiant General Nila, a lion among monkeys, who excelled in marching, constantly inspected the ranks, and Valimukha, Prajangha, Jambha and the monkey Rabhasa went about everywhere encouraging the Plavamgamas.

Whilst those lions among monkeys advanced on every side proud of their strength, they beheld the great Mountain Sahya crowned with hundreds of trees and lakes and lovely pools covered with flowers.

Under the command of Rama of searing wrath, skirting the precincts of cities and public highways, that vast and terrible army of monkeys, like the ocean tide, surged forward with a thunderous sound. At the side of the son of Dasaratha, those heroic monkeys bounded forward with agility, like swift steeds urged on by the spur. And those foremost of men, borne on the shoulders of the monkeys, appeared beautiful like the sun and moon, in conjunction with those two great planets, Rahu and Ketu, and honoured by the King of the Monkeys and Lakshmana, Rama accompanied by his army, proceeded towards the south.

Then Lakshmana, mounted on Angada's shoulders, spoke to Rama who was accomplishing his design, in sweet accents, saying :—

" Having regained Vaidehi and slain Ravana her abductor, thus fulfilling thy purpose, thou wilt return to Ayodhya, who,[1] too, will be gratified. I perceive auspicious omens in the heavens and on the earth, O Descendant of Raghu, indicating the success of thine enterprise ! A favourable wind blows

---

[1] That is the presiding Deity of the City.

behind the army, that is soft, health-giving and auspicious ; birds and beasts emit cheerful and sonorous sounds ; all the quarters are serene and the sun shines clearly. Ushanas, Bhrigu's son, too, wears an auspicious aspect for thee, and the pole star is unaccompanied by adverse planets; the seven Rishis, pure and brilliant, circumambulating it. Before us shines the grandsire of the high-souled Ikshvakus, the immaculate Trishanku accompanied by his priest; and the twin Vishakas, our racial star, gleam free from obstruction.

" Nairrita, the ruling star of the titans, is badly aspected and in opposition to the rising planet Dhumaketu, presaging the overthrow of the titans. Those about to die, in their last hour, become a prey to Graha. The water of the lakes is fresh and tastes sweet, the woods are laden with fruit, fragrant breezes blow softly and the trees are flowering out of season, O Lord ! The army of the monkeys looks splendid in its formations, like the Celestial Host at the destruction of Taraka. Surveying the whole scene, O Noble One, thou shouldst experience supreme delight ! "

Thus did Saumitri speak in gay tones to his elder brother in order to console him and meantime the army of the monkeys advanced, covering the earth. The dust raised by those mighty bears and monkeys, furnished with nails and claws, enveloped the whole earth and the splendour of the sun was obscured. Like a mass of cloud enveloping the sky, that monkey army advanced in solid formation encompassing the southern region. As they pressed on mile on mile, crossing the rivers and streams against the current, they traversed many leagues in one stretch. Resting by lakes of pure water, passing over mountains covered with forests, across plains, through woods laden with fruit, skirting them or passing through the centre, they went on, covering the entire earth, and their countenances manifesting joy, they ran with the swiftness of the wind.

All those monkeys were zealous in Rama's service, each vying with the other in high spirits, vigour and prowess. Some, proud of their youth and supple limbs, increased their pace, running with extreme speed and executing handsprings and some of those rangers of the woods shouted ' Kila ! Kila ! ' lashing their tails and stamping on the earth whilst others with upraised arms broke off the trees and rocks here and there or climbed to the summit of the mountains like true mountaineers. Emitting loud cries and roaring, they frequently tore down handfuls of creepers with their thighs. In their energy, with their jaws set, some juggled with rocks and trees. It was by hundreds and thousands and millions that these formidable monkeys covered the earth with their splendour ; and that great army of monkeys, full of energy, proceeding under Sugriva's orders, eager for battle and anxious to deliver Sita, did not linger even for an instant.

Then Rama, seeing the Sahira and Malaya Mountains with their dense woodlands frequented by various kinds of wild animals and marvellous forests, streams and rivers, went towards them, and the monkeys broke down Champaka, Tilaka, Cuta, Praseka, Sindubaraka, Tinisha, Karavira, Ashoka, Karanja, Plaksha, Nyagrodha, Jambuka and Amlaka Trees, and, seated on those enchanting plateaus, the forest trees shaken by the wind covered them with flowers.

A soft breeze, fresh and perfumed with sandal, blew while the bees hummed in the nectar scented woods. From this mountain, rich in ore, the dust raised by those monkeys enveloped that immense army on all sides.

On the smiling mountain slopes, Ketaka Trees, Sinduvara, charming Vasanti, scented Madhavi, clumps of Jasmine, Shiribilva, Madhuka, Vanjula, Vankula, Ranjaka, Tilaka Nagavriksha, all in flower, with Cuta, Patalika, Kovidara, Muchulinda, Arjuna, Shimshapa, Kutaja, Hintala, Tinisha, Shurnakha, Nipaka, the blue Ashoka, Sarala, Ankola and Padmaka Trees bloomed and teemed with monkeys disporting themselves there. Enchanting lakes and pools, frequented by waterfowl, ducks and herons, were to be found on that mountain, which was the haunt of boars, deer, bears, hyenas, lions and tigers inspiring terror, and innumerable venomous snakes infested it. Kumudas, Utpalas and many other flowers embellished the lakes, and flocks of birds of various kinds sang on that mountain side.

Having bathed in those waters and quenched their thirst, the monkeys began to disport themselves and splashing one another, climbing the mountain, they plucked the delicious fruits as fragrant as ' Amrita ' and the roots and flowers from the trees. Yellow as honey themselves, they, delighted, feasted on the combs, a ' drona ' in size, which were suspended from the trees, and, shaking the lovely branches and letting them spring back again, they tore down the creepers,; some drunk with nectar, dancing joyfully as they continued on their way ; some climbed the trees, others quenched their thirst and the whole earth, covered with monkeys, resembled a field of ripe corn.

Reaching the Mahendra Mountain, the long-armed Rama, whose eyes resembled lotus petals, climbed to the summit adorned with various trees and from that peak, the elder son of King Dasaratha beheld that vast sea with its rising waves full of fish and turtle.

Having crossed the Sahya and Malaya Mountains, the army halted in their ranks along the shores of the sea with its thundering waves. Then that foremost of men, Rama, descended from the heights and accompanied by Lakshmana and Sugriva, quickly entered a lovely wood on the shores of the ocean and reaching that immense strand strewn with boulders, washed by the billowing waves, he spoke thus :—

" O Sugriva, we have reached the abode of Varuna ; now we should consider the matter with which we were formerly preoccupied. This ocean, the Lord of Rivers, with its vast expanse, is impossible to cross unless some special course be adopted. Let us camp here therefore and deliberate on the means by which we can transport the army to the further shore."

Speaking thus, that long-armed hero, who had been rendered desolate by Sita's abduction, approached the sea and issued orders for the troops quartering.

" Let the whole army pitch their camp on the shore, O Lion among Monkeys ! The time has come to take counsel and devise some way to cross the main ; let every leader remain with his forces and, under no pretext whatever, shall he leave them ; meantime they should find out if any ambush has been laid by the enemy."

At Rama's command, Sugriva, assisted by Lakshmana, caused his forces to camp on the shore which was covered with trees and the monkey host looked resplendent like a second ocean whose waves were yellow as honey. Reaching that wooded shore those lions of monkeys encamped, eager to reach the further side of the ocean; and the tumult caused by those forces pitching their tents could be heard above the roaring of the sea. That vast army of monkeys, commanded by Sugriva, ranged in three divisions, were deeply concerned with the accomplishment of Rama's mission and, from the shore where they were stationed, the monkey host gazed with delight on the vast ocean lashed by the tempest. Then those leaders of monkeys surveyed that abode of Varuna of limitless expanse, whose distant shore was inhabited by titans. Rendered formidable by the ferocity of its sharks and crocodiles, that ocean, with its foaming waves at the close of day and the approach of night, appeared to laugh and dance. When the moon rose, whose image was reflected limitlessly in its bosom, the ocean surged, swarming with gigantic sharks, whales and great fish, strong like the tempest, and it was fathomless, abounding in serpents of flaming coils and many aquatic animals and reefs. In that ocean, difficult to cross, whose ways were impassable, haunted by titans, the waves, in which sharks and sea monsters swarmed, rose and fell joyfully, whipped into motion by the breeze.

Emitting sparks and turbulent with its gleaming reptiles, the ocean, that dread refuge of the enemies of the Gods, the eternal region of hell, resembled the sky and there seemed no difference between them. The waters simulated the firmament and the firmament the waters, both manifesting the same appearance with the stars above and the pearls below with which they were filled and, one with its racing clouds and the other with its squadrons of waves, caused the sea and sky to look identical.

As wave clashed against wave without pause, the King of Rivers emitted a terrific clamour like the sound of the beating of great gongs in the sky. With its murmuring waves, its innumerable pearls and its monsters as it were pursuing it like a pack of hounds, the ocean, in the grip of a hurricane, seemed to leap excitedly.

And the magnanimous monkeys surveyed that ocean lashed by the winds and the waves which, whipped by its blast, seemed to groan. Struck with astonishment, those monkeys regarded the sea with its dashing waves, rolling on and on.

CHAPTER 5

Rama is afflicted when thinking of Sita

ON the northern shore, the army under the command of Nila halted and the two generals, Mainda and Dvivida, foremost among the monkeys, patrolled up and down and on all sides in order to protect the monkey host.

The army being thus encamped on the shores of the Lord of the Waters, Rama, observing Lakshmana standing at his side, said to him :—

" Sorrow invariably decreases with the passing of time but in the absence of my beloved, mine increases daily ! Not that my sufferings are caused by separation from my companion nor my misfortune by her abduction, what I deplore is that her youth is slipping away. O Breeze, speed to that place where my beloved is and, having caressed her, touch me, thus causing me the same delight that a weary traveller experiences when gazing on the moon ! That which consumes my limbs as though I had swallowed poison, is the cry of my dear one, while being borne away, ' Help, O Thou who art my defender ! ' With my separation from her as the coals and my thoughts of her as the shimmering flames, the fire of my love consumes my body day and night !

" O Lakshmana, remain here while I plunge into the sea ere I sleep, so that the fire of my distress shall cease from tormenting me. It is enough that she and I sleep on the same earth. As dry land draws nourishment for its vegetation from marshy ground, so do I exist in the knowledge that Sita still lives ! O When shall I, having overcome mine enemies, behold her of graceful limbs, whose eyes resemble lotus petals, the equal of Shri herself ? When, gently raising her lotus-like face with its ravishing lips and teeth, shall I drink in her glances, as a sick man the nectar of immortality ? When will that playful maiden embrace me, her round and quivering breasts like unto Tala fruits pressed against my body, like sovereignty united with prosperity?

" Alas! Though I am her support, that dark-eyed princess, who has fallen among the titans, resembles an orphan! How can it be that the daughter of Janaka, my beloved, is now in the midst of titans, she, the daughter-in-law of Dasaratha?

" When I have put those demons to flight, Sita will live anew as the autumnal moon shines forth again when the clouds are scattered. By nature slender, Sita, on account of grief, fasting and circumstance, is now a shadow of her former self.

" When, with my shafts piercing the breast of that King of Titans, shall I empty my heart of sorrow? When shall I behold the virtuous Sita, resembling a daughter of the Gods, her arms encircling my neck, shedding tears of joy? When, like a soiled garment, shall I discard the pain born of my separation from Maithili? "

As the sagacious Rama was thus lamenting, the day declined and the disc of the sun, diminishing slowly, disappeared below the horizon. Thereupon Rama, whom Lakshmana sought to console, his mind still engaged in the thought of Sita, whose eyes were as large as lotus petals, distracted by grief, performed his evening devotions.

CHAPTER 6

Ravana consults his Subjects

IN the face of the terrible and awe-inspiring feat executed in Lanka by Hanuman who was the equal of Indra in prowess, the King of the Titans, discomfited, with bowed head addressed his subjects, saying :—

" Lanka, hitherto inaccessible, has been laid waste by a mere monkey who has had converse with the daughter of Janaka, Sita. Overthrowing the palaces and slaying the foremost of the titans, he has turned the city upside down, such is Hanuman's achievement! What should I do now? May prosperity attend you! What plan do you consider fitting for me to adopt first ? Say what you hold to be proper for us to do and which will be to our advantage !

" The wise affirm that good counsel is the root of victory, that is why, O Brave Ones, I desire to consult you concerning Rama.

" There are three kinds of men in the world, the good, the bad and the mediocre. I will describe the qualities and defects of them all to you :—

" He, who in his deliberations consults experienced counsellors, his friends with whom he shares common interests, his relatives and his superiors and then pursues his design with energy and the help of God, is considered to be the foremost of men.

" He, who enters into deliberation and pursues his duty by himself single-handedly, accomplishing that which should be accomplished, is considered a mediocre man.

" He, who fails to weigh the advantages and disadvantages of a matter and refuses God's aid, merely saying ' I shall do it ', disregards his duty and is considered the least of men !

" Just as there are always those who are superior, those who are mediocre and those who are inferior among men, so there exists also good, bad and indifferent counsel.

" That judgement which is given after a clear-sighted examination of the question and to which, re-inforced by scriptural authority, the counsellors agree, is considered excellent.

" Those deliberations, where unanimity is finally reached after innumerable discussions, are considered mediocre, and those in which each person continues to stand by his own opinion and opposes those of others and where no conclusion can be reached, are considered pernicious. Therefore an undertaking that follows on wise deliberation will succeed.

" You, who are all eminently sagacious, must decide what should be done and I will subscribe to it. Rama, surrounded by thousands of heroic monkeys, is advancing on Lanka to exterminate us. Undoubtedly Raghava will cross the ocean with ease by virtue of his natural powers and be followed by his younger brother and the monkey host. He is able to dry up the sea through his valour or he may use some other means (to bridge the ocean). In view of Rama's attack on you with those monkeys, do you devise some plan to protect the city and the army ! "

CHAPTER 7

The Titans persuade Ravana to make War and remind him of his former Exploits

HEARING the words of Ravana, their lord and master, all those powerful titans, in their ignorance, instilled him with contempt for the enemy and with joined palms, offered him ill-considered advice, saying :—

" O King, we possess a vast army furnished with maces, spears, swords, lances, harpoons and barbed darts, why art thou apprehensive ? Didst thou not enter Bhogavati, having overcome the Serpent Race in war ? Didst thou not subdue Dhanada, who inhabited the summit of Mt Kailasha, surrounded as he was by Yakshas, creating a terrible carnage amongst them ? Though he regarded himself as the Lord of Men and prided himself on his friendship with Mahadeva, in thy wrath thou didst vanquish him on the field of battle.

" O Foremost among the Titans, Maya, the Lord of the Danavas in fear gave his daughter to thee in wedlock and thou didst also subjugate the powerful and arrogant giant, Madhu, the joy of Kumbhinasi ! Descending into the nether regions thou didst defeat the Serpents Vasuki, Takshaka, Shankha and Jati despite their irresistible power, courage and the boons conferred on them, O Lord ! After fighting for a whole year, confident though they were in their own strength, thou didst force them to submit to thy yoke and learnt the science of magic from them, O King of the Titans, Vanquisher of thyFoes!

" O Great Hero, the valiant sons of Varuna were defeated by thee in the open field as also the fourfold army attending on them, and thou didst descend into the vast ocean, that dark region, whose sceptre is the aquatic world, his crown the Shalmali Tree, his noose the great billows, his serpents the attendants of Yama, who is irresistible in his feverish and fearful motion and thou didst win a glorious victory there, overcoming Death and filling all thy subjects with joy.

18

The earth was peopled with innumerable and valiant warriors, equal to Indra in prowess, resembling giant trees, yet thou didst destroy those invincible heroes! Raghava is neither their equal in courage, virtue nor in might! Yet do thou remain here, O Great King, why fatigue thyself? Indrajita is able to exterminate those monkeys single-handed. That prince, O Great Sovereign, returning from a sacrifice to Maheshwara, who is surpassed by none, received a boon from him not easily obtainable in this world and, approaching that divine sea, whose fish are lances and spears, which abounds in weapons for its trees, whose turtles are the elephants and whose frogs are the teeming horses, whose cetaceans are the Adityas and Maruts, its great serpents the Vasus, its waters the chariots, steeds and elephants, the sandy banks its infantry, that vast ocean of the Celestial Hosts, Indrajita approached; in order to bear away their king and bring him to Lanka. Thereafter that Monarch was liberated by the command of the Grandsire of the World and the Vanquisher[1] of Shambara and Vritra returned to his abode where all the Gods paid homage to him.

"Therefore let thy son, Indrajita, go forth and destroy the army of the monkeys and Rama also, O King; it is not worthy of thee to imagine harm can come from common persons, such thoughts should not even enter thy mind for assuredly thou shalt bring about Rama's end!"

CHAPTER 8

The boasting of Ravana's Generals

THEN the heroic general, the Titan Prahasta, who resembled a dark cloud, joined his palms together and expressed himself thus :—

"We are able to overcome the Devas, Danavas, Gandharvas, Pisachas, Patagas and Uragas in the open field, how much more those two mortals!

"Under the influence of liquor and trusting in our own strength, we suffered ourselves to be deceived by Hanuman but as long as

[1] Indra, King of the Gods.

I live, that ranger of the woods will not enter here again alive, I shall sweep the land surrounded by the sea clean of monkeys together with its hills, forests and jungles ; thou hast but to issue the command ! I shall rid thee of that monkey, O Ranger of the Night and thou shalt not have to suffer on account of thine offence.[1]"

Thereafter Durmukha, in his turn, spoke in measured tones, saying :—

" Assuredly we shall not tolerate this outrage that he has committed against us all. The devastation of the city and the palaces and the insult offered to our sovereign by this monkey shall be avenged by me. Setting out alone, I shall exterminate those monkeys, whether they have taken refuge in the dreadful deep, in heaven or in hell ! "

Then the powerful Vajradamshtra, in a transport of rage, began to speak, brandishing a huge mace stained with flesh and blood, and said :—

" What is that puny and miserable monkey, Hanuman, to us as long as the mighty Rama, Sugriva and Lakshmana exist? This very day, I shall return, having slain Rama, Sugriva and Lakshmana single-handed with the blows of my mace and routed that army of monkeys, or, if it pleaseth thee, hear this further plan of mine ; he, who is resourceful, may easily overcome his adversaries.

" Thousands of titans, able to change their shape at will, courageous, invincible, of terrifying aspect, are devoted to thee. Let them, assuming human form, present themselves before Kakutstha, foremost of the Raghus, and, full of confidence, say to him :—

" ' We are here on behalf of Bharata, thy younger brother ', whereupon Rama, summoning his forces will instantly come hither ; then armed with lances, picks and maces, carrying bows, arrows and swords in our hands, we will set out with speed from here and meet him. Thereafter, stationed in battalions in the air, we will exterminate that army of monkeys under a hail of rocks and shafts and send them to the region of Yama. Should they fall into the trap, it will prove disastrous for them and Rama and Lakshmana will inevitably lose their lives."

[1] The abduction of Sita.

Then the son of Kumbhakarna, the valiant and powerful Nikumbha, in the height of anger, said in the presence of Ravana, the destroyer of the worlds :—

" Let all of you remain here with our great king ; by myself I shall slay Raghàva, Lakshmana, Sugriva and also Hanuman and all the monkeys."

Thereafter in his turn, a titan named Vajrabanu, as tall as a mountain, who, in his wrath, was licking his lips, took up the tale, saying :—

" Free from all anxiety, occupy yourselves with those things which afford you entertainment, single-handed I shall consume the entire monkey host. Remain here at ease and drink wine[1]; alone I shall slay Sugriva, Lakshmana and also Hanuman, Angada and all the monkeys."

CHAPTER 9

Bibishana advises Ravana to send back Sita

THE Generals Rabhasa, the mighty Suryashatru, Saptaghna, Yajnakopa and Mahaparshwa, Mahodeva, the irrespressible Agniketu and the Titan Rashiketu, the lusty Indrashatu, son of Ravana, also Prahasta, Vimpaksha and the exceedingly powerful Vajradamshtra, Dhumraksha, Nikumbha and the Titan Durmukha, brandishing maces, harpoons, lances, darts, spears, axes, bows furnished with arrows and swords shining like a great expanse of water, all of whom were blazing with anger addressed Ravana saying :—

" To-day we shall slay Rama, Sugriva and Lakshmana as also that wretch Hanuman who laid Lanka waste ! "

Then Bibishana, restraining those who had seized hold of their weapons, persuaded them to be seated and spoke thus with joined palms :—

" My Dear Brother, the wise affirm that when the end which is sought cannot be attained by the three means[2], the conditions

---

[1] Varuni—See Glossary.
[2] Conciliation, gift and sowing dissension.

when force should be employed are determined by the tacticians. O Friend, deeds of valour which have been tested according to prescribed injunctions, succeed against those who are careless when attacked, or who are in opposition to the divine power. Now, Rama is on his guard, he is eager for victory, he is upheld by divine power, he has subdued his passions and is invincible, yet you seek to defeat him.

" When Hanuman crossed the ocean, that formidable Lord of Streams and Rivers, who could have conceived or even imagined the path he would take ? Our adversary has immense resources and troops at his disposal O Rangers of the Night, you should in no way disregard him ! What wrong has the illustrious Rama ever done to the King of the Titans that he should go to Janasthana and bear away the consort of that great One ?

" If Khara, who had trespassed into a region that was not his own, was slain in combat by Rama, is it not legitimate for everyone to defend his life ? It is on account of Vaidehi's abduction that we are in this great peril and we should therefore yield her up. What advantage is there in continuing the quarrel ? Nay, it is not proper to enter into hostilities with that powerful and virtuous prince, who would never initiate warfare without a definite cause. Therefore do you give back Maithili to him ere he, by means of his arrows, destroys this city abounding in wealth of every kind with its horses and elephants ! Before that formidable and mighty monkey host attack this, our Lanka, do you give back Sita. Lanka with all her heroic titans will perish unless the beloved consort of Rama is voluntarily returned to him.

" I adjure you by the blood that unites us to follow my counsel, which is salutory. Return Maithili to Rama ere he looses his shafts for your destruction, which are freshly sharpened, steely, infallible, plumed and bright as the autumnal sun. Give back Maithili to the son of Dasaratha without delay ; renounce a resentment which destroys all felicity and virtue and pursue righteousness which increases well-being and glory. Be pacified, that we may live in tranquillity with our sons and kinsfolk. Give back Maithili to Dasaratha's son ! "

Thus spoke Bibishana, and Ravana, the Lord of the Titans, dismissing them all, entered his private apartments.

CHAPTER 10

Bibishana insists that Sita should be given back to Rama

As the day dawned, Bibishana, renowned for his exploits, fixed in the knowledge of what was just and profitable, entered the palace of the King of the Titans which resembled a mass of crags like unto the peak of a mountain.   That vast area was the resort of the great ; well ordered and divided, it was inhabited by learned persons and guarded by loyal and vigilant titans on all sides.   Re-echoing to the sound of the wind blended with the trumpeting of intoxicated elephants, the blare of conches and the blasts of trumpets, groups of lovely girls filled the alleys with their chattering.   Its gates were of pure gold enriched by magnificent decorations resembling the abode of the Gandharvas or the mansions of the Maruts, and it contained heaps of gems like unto the Serpents[1] dwellings.

Then that One of exceeding energy and renown entered the palace of his elder brother, as the sun of sparkling rays enters a cloud, and he heard the blessings invoked on his brother for his victory uttered in a loud voice by those versed in the Veda. And he beheld those priests instructed in the science of ' Mantras ' and the Veda, worshipped with vessels of curds, clarified butter, flowers and hulled rice.   Thereafter the mighty-armed Bibishana, duly honoured by the titans, observed the younger brother of the Bestower of Riches[2], who was seated there.

Approaching the throne that was covered with gold, embellished by the person of the king, he paid homage, extending fitting courtesies to him and took the seat indicated by Ravana's glance. Thereafter he addressed the mighty Dashagriva in the presence of his ministers alone and, standing before him, with soothing speech sought to pacify him, manifesting his knowledge of time and place, and expressed himself thus :—

" O Subduer of thy Foes, ever since Vaidehi was brought here, inauspicious omens have been observed !   The sacrificial fire emits sparks and its brightness is dimmed by smoke ;

---

[1] Serpents, the Nagas or the Serpent Race.
[2] The Bestower of Riches, the God Kuvera, brother of Ravana.

23

impure vapours arise therefrom even after the oblations have been poured to the accompaniment of sacred formulas nor does it burn in a proper manner. In the kitchens, sacred pavilions and the halls, where the Vedas are recited, reptiles are to be found and ants are discovered in the sacrificial offerings. The milk of the kine has dried up, ichor no longer flows from the strongest of the elephants, horses find no satisfaction in their fodder and neigh incessantly, while the asses, buffalo and mules, their hair standing on end, shed tears, and, though ministered to by experts, do not behave normally, O King.

" Fierce crows gather together from all sides, emitting harsh cries and are seen swarming on the roofs of the temples. Vultures plane mournfully over the city and at dusk, jackals appear howling lugubriously. Wild beasts and deer assemble at the gates of the city, setting up an ominous noise to the accompaniment of growls. These omens indicate that thy fault should be expiated as the Lord thinks proper by returning Vaidehi to Raghava.

" If, through error or expediency, I have given cause for offence, thou shouldst not condemn me, O Great Monarch! All thy people, both male and female and thy court affirm that the fault is thine! It is through fear that thy ministers dare not counsel thee but I feel compelled to inform thee of what I have seen and heard. Judge what thou considerest to be right and act accordingly."

Thus spoke Bibishana in measured words to his brother, Ravana, Lord of the Titans, in the presence of the ministers, and, hearing that judicious, reasonable, moderate and logical speech, productive of great good for the past, present and future, Ravana, who had conceived a passion for Sita, answered with mounting anger, saying :—

" I see no cause for fear anywhere! Rama shall never regain Maithili! Even were Lakshmana's elder brother upheld by the Gods with Indra at their head, how could he withstand me in the field ? "

Having spoken thus, that destroyer of Celestial Hosts, Dashagriva, who was endowed with terrific strength and extreme prowess in combat, dismissed his brother Bibishana of frank speech.

CHAPTER 11

Ravana summons his Assembly

THAT unrighteous monarch, a slave to his passion, disregarding his real friends, in consequence of his evil act began to suffer decrease.

His lustful desire exceeding all bounds, his thoughts constantly occupied with Vaidehi, though the occasion for war was lacking, with his ministers conceived that the time for entering into hostilities had come. Thereupon, sallying forth, he ascended his mighty chariot plated with gold, encrusted with coral and pearl and harnessed to well-trained horses. Seated in that excellent car, which reverberated like thunder, Dashagriva, the foremost of titans drove to the place of assembly.

Titans with swords, bucklers and every kind of weapon preceded their king on the highway, some garbed in strange attire covered with every kind of gem marched at his side or followed in his wake, and they surrounded him on all sides. The foremost of the car-warriors speedily precipitated themselves in his vanguard with their chariots or on great elephants intoxicated with Mada juice or horses which they caused to rear. Brandishing maces and crowbars, they held picks and darts in their hands.

As Ravana approached the assembly, the sound of innumerable musical instruments could be heard and the blare of trumpets broke forth to the accompaniment of the rolling of vehicles whilst the great chariot of that Indra of Demons passed along the splendidly decorated highway. The canopy, that was held over his head, shone with an immaculate purity, resembling the king of the stars at his full, and two fans of Yaks tails with crystal handles and golden fringes were waved to and fro from left to right. All the titans having alighted, stood with joined palms and bowed heads in homage to their king who was seated in his car.

Amidst acclamations and cries of triumph from those titans, that scourger of his foes made his solemn entry into the assembly hall that had been constructed by Vishvakarma.

The floor was of refined gold and six hundred evil spirits guarded it. Into that excellent audience hall, a masterpiece of Vishvakarma, Ravana made his entry sparkling with magnificence and seated himself on a gorgeous throne wrought of emeralds, carpeted with skins of deer and furnished with thick cushions.

Thereupon he issued his orders imperiously to exceedingly fleet messengers, saying :—

" Summon the titans hither with all speed ! " thereafter adding, " A great blow is about to be struck by the enemy ! "

Hearing this command, his envoys dispersed to search throughout Lanka, entering every house and scouring the highways and pleasure resorts, assembling the titans without ceremony. Some started out in excellent chariots, some on swift and mettlesome horses or elephants and some on foot. The city was thronged with cars, elephants and horses and resembled the sky filled with birds.

Then they abandoned their mounts and chariots of every kind in order to enter the audience chamber and they resembled lions penetrating into a rocky cavern.

Having, each in turn, paid homage to the feet of the king, they took up their positions, some on seats, some on cushions, some on the ground, and gathering in that hall at his command they grouped themselves according to rank round their sovereign, the Lord of the Titans.

They came in hundreds ; ministers distinguished for their skill in dealing with affairs and talented sagacious counsellors able to view all with the eye of understanding ; warriors also in great numbers gathered in the hall that sparkled with gold, in order to prepare for the success of their campaign.

At that moment, arriving in a magnificent chariot, its various parts encrusted with gold, Bibishana appeared in the assembly presided over by his elder brother and, announcing himself by name, he paid obeisance to the feet of the king, whereafter Shuka and Prahasta, in their turn, did homage to that monarch, who conferred special places upon them befitting their rank.

26

The titans were adorned with fine gold and every kind of ornament, arrayed in rich vestures, and the fragrance of aloes and rare sandalwood from their garlands perfumed the hall on every side.

Neither harsh accents nor ill-advised utterances nor loud whisperings could be heard in the assembly and, their desires crowned, all those titans of extreme prowess fixed their eyes on the face of their sovereign.

In the midst of those skilled warriors full of energy, the intelligent Ravana appeared resplendent in that assembly like unto the God with the Thunderbolt amongst the Vasus.

CHAPTER 12

The Discourse between Ravana and Kumbhakarna

THEN Ravana, the conqueror of hostile armies, let his gaze wander over the assembly and addressing himself to the General of his forces, Prahasta, said :—

" O General, it is for thee, who art conversant with the four branches of strategy, to dispose of thy forces in the way that the defence of the city demands."[1]

Thereupon Prahasta, alert to his sovereign's behests and eager to carry them out, distributed the whole of his troops within and without the fortress and, having disposed of his entire army in the city's defence, he returned to his seat in front of the king and said :—

" O Mighty Lord, I have stationed thy forces within and without the city, now accomplish that which thou hast resolved to do speedily and without anxiety ! "

At these words of Prahasta's, that monarch, who aspired to happiness and who was devoted to the public welfare, expressed himself thus amidst his followers :—

" Should duty, pleasure or self-interest endanger whatever is pleasant or unpleasant, whether it be in prosperity or adversity,

[1] According to whether they were in chariots, on elephants, horses or on foot.

gain or loss, whether useful or disadvantageous, you are bound to point it out. No undertaking of mine, that I have engaged in with you, re-inforced by the recitation of sacred formulas, has ever proved fruitless ! As the Maruts, the moon, the stars and the planets follow in Vasava's wake, so do you all follow me in a splendid procession assuring me of victory !

"In truth I intended to mobilize you all but, on account of Kumbhakarna being asleep, I have not pressed this matter ! After sleeping for six months, the foremost of those bearing arms, has just risen. As regards the beloved consort of Rama, the daughter of Janaka, I brought her here from the solitudes of the Dandaka Forest which is frequented by titans. That princess of languid pace does not wish to share my bed, though in the Three Worlds, I see none to compare with her. Slender-waisted, with well developed hips, her countenance resembling the autumnal moon, she is like an image made of gold created by Maya.[1] Her palms are rosy, her feet are delicate and well set, her nails coppery and, seeing her, I am overcome with desire. Shining like the flame of the sacrificial fire she rivals the brightness of the sun ; her face with its arched nose is flawless and fair, her eyes beautiful. On beholding her I am no longer master of myself and become the slave of love. Torn between anger and delight, this passion has proved my undoing, the cause of ruin and the eternal source of pain and suffering. In anticipation of the advent of her lord, Rama, that lovely large-eyed lady has solicited a year's grace of me and I have looked with favour on the request of that one of tender glances but, like unto a spent steed on the highway, I am weary of the pricks of passion.

"How will those inhabitants of the woods cross the impassable ocean with the innumerable monsters that inhabit it and how can those two sons of Dasaratha traverse it ? The outcome of this enterprise is impossible to predict. Say what you think in this matter ! A mere man causes no apprehension ; yet ponder on it carefully !

"Formerly, in the war between Gods and Titans, thanks to your support I was victorious and you are still ready to stand by me.

---

[1] Maya—The Artificer of the Gods.

" Having ascertained where Sita is, those two princes, preceded by the monkeys with Sugriva at their head, have reached the shores of the sea. It is not for us to return Sita but to destroy the two sons of Dasaratha, therefore deliberate on this and adopt a judicious line of conduct. In truth, I know of none in the world who can overcome us, even should he cross the water with the monkeys; victory is therefore indubitably mine."

Hearing the ramblings of that bashful lover, Kumbhakarna flew into a transport of rage and said :—

" On first seeing Sita, the consort of Rama, who is accompanied by Lakshmana, she who was brought here by force, thy mind was wholly possessed by her as the waters of the lake are filled by the Yamuna. O Great King, this conduct is not worthy of thee ! Thou shouldst have consulted us at the outset of this affair. The king who acquits himself of his obligations punctiliously, O Ten-faced One, and whose mind is concentrated on what he is about, has not to repent later ! Those undertakings that are carried out carelessly and against the scriptural law turn out badly, like unto impure offerings poured into the sacrificial fire by those who are heedless. To seek to end where one should begin or to begin where one should conclude is to ignore what is proper and what is not. If an adversary examines the defects of one who is unrestrained, he soon discovers his weak points, as birds the fissures in the Krauncha Mountains. Thou didst make this assault without forethought and it is fortunate that Rama did not slay thee, as poisoned food the eater thereof ! Nevertheless I shall do my part in this campaign that thou dost contemplate launching against thine enemies, O Irreproachable One ! I shall destroy thine adversaries, O Ranger of the Night, even as Indra, Vivasvat, Pavaka, Maruta, Kuvera or Varuna themselves, I shall fight against them !

" Entering the combat with my enormous body, the size of a mountain and my sharp teeth, roaring the while and brandishing my immense mace, I shall strike terror into Purandara himself !

" Ere the foe can deliver a second blow, I shall drink his blood, therefore take comfort, for by slaying Dasaratha's son I shall bring thee an auspicious victory ! Having destroyed Rama as also Lakshmana, I shall devour all the monkey leaders ! Enjoy thyself therefore and drink the most excellent of wines to the extent of thy desire without anxiety ; do what thou judgest to be best !

"When ı have despatched Rama to the region of death, Sita will be at thy disposal for ever."

CHAPTER 13

Ravana tells the Story of the Nymph Punjikasthala

SEEING Ravana wrought up with ire, the mighty General Mahaparshwa reflected a moment and, with joined palms, spoke thus :—

"He who, having penetrated into a wood frequented by wild beasts and serpents, does not partake of the honey he finds there, is a fool !

"Who is thy master ? Thou art the master, O Scourge of Thy Foes ! Enjoy thyself with Vaidehi, having placed thy foot on the head of thy foe ! Act in the manner of a cock, O Valiant Prince ! Approach Sita again and again in order to enjoy her and pass the time in dalliance with her. Having sated thy passion, what is there to fear ? Whether taken unawares or no, thou art well able to meet every exigency ! Without support Kumbhakarna and Indrajita of immense energy, would be capable of challenging the God who bears the Thunderbolt armed with his mace !

"Bestowal of gifts, conciliation and sowing dissension in the ranks of the enemy are the means of subduing them, according to the wise, but in the present circumstances, I incline to the use of the fourth ! O Lord, we shall subdue thy foes by the strength of our arms, do not doubt it ! "

Thus spoke Mahaparshwa and the king, thanking him, replied thus :—

"O Mahaparshwa, I will answer thee by recounting a strange adventure that befell me a long time ago.

"While she was going to worship the Grandsire of the World, I came upon the nymph, Punjikasthala, flashing through the sky like a flame. I stripped her of her attire in order to deflower her, after which like a faded lotus she reached the abode of Swyambhu. The magnanimous Ordainer of the World, learning of the matter, addressed me in anger, saying :—

"'O Ravana, from to-day, if thou dost violence to any other woman, thy head will be split into a hundred pieces, this is certain !'

"This curse alarmed me and it is for this reason that I have not forced Sita, the Princess of Videha, to ascend the nuptial couch. My fury is like unto the sea and my speed resembles the wind but the son of Dasaratha is unaware of it and it is on this account he has set out to fight me. Who would seek to waken a lion lying asleep in a hidden mountain den whose anger resembles the God of Death himself ?

"Ramachandra has not seen my arrows in combat that resemble snakes with forked tongues, wherefore he is considering marching against me. From my bow, loosing my shafts that are like unto lightning on him from a myriad sides, I shall speedily consume Rama, as a forest is set on fire by flaming brands. I shall wipe out his army with mine, as the rising sun blots out the light of the stars. Neither Vasava of a thousand eyes nor Varuna can withstand me in battle ! It was by the strength of mine arms that I conquered the city defended by Kuvera ! "

CHAPTER 14

Bibishana blames the Attitude of Ravana's Courtiers

PRINCE BIBISHANA listened to the boasting of Ravana and the thundering of Kumbhakarna and addressed the king in words that were profitable and sagacious, saying :—

"O King, why hast thou brought that great serpent in the form of Sita hither, her breasts its coils, her anxieties its poison, her laughter its sharp fangs, her five fingers its five hoods ? While Lanka is yet not assailed by those monkeys, armed with their teeth and nails, who are as high as hills, give back Maithili to the son of Dasaratha !

"Neither Kumbhakarna nor Indrajita, O King, neither Mahaparshwa nor Mahodara neither Nikumbha nor Kumbha nor yet Atikaya are able to withstand Rama on the field of battle ! Thou wouldst never escape from Rama alive even wert thou protected by Savitar or the Maruts or if thou didst take refuge in the region of Yama or plunge into the lowest hell ! "

Thus spoke Bibishana and Prahasta answered him saying :—

" We do not know what it is to fear the Gods or titans whoever they may be, nor do we stand in awe of Yakshas, Gandharvas nor great Serpents, gigantic birds nor great snakes in the field. Why then should we tremble to enter into combat with Rama, that son of a mortal king ? "

Hearing this injudicious speech of Prahasta's, Bibishana, who sought to save the king and whose intellect was rooted in the values of virtue, profit and expediency, uttered these words full of good sense, saying :—

" O Prahasta, the intrigues proposed by the King, Mahodara, thee and Kumbhakarna against me, born with qualities such as Rama possesses are as unlikely to succeed as the entry into heaven of one of perverse soul. It is impossible for me or thee or Prahasta or all the titans to slay Rama, who is supremely experienced. It is as if we sought to cross the sea without a boat ! In the presence of such a hero, essentially pious, that Prince of the Great Car, the issue of the Ikshvaku Race who is capable of any exploit, even the Gods themselves are confounded ! It is because those sharp arrows, irresistible and furnished with heron's plumes, that are loosed by Raghava, have not as yet pierced thy limbs, that thou art still able to boast, O Prahasta ! It is because those pointed shafts that Rama discharges, which quench the vital breaths and are equal to the lightning in their velocity, have not penetrated thy body, that thou dost still bluster in this wise ! Neither Ravana nor the exceedingly powerful Trishiras nor the son of Kumbhakarna, Nikumbha nor Indrajita, nor even thou thyself, are able to overcome the son of Dasaratha in combat, who is equal to Indra himself. Neither Devantaka nor Narantaka, neither Akampana, the magnanimous Atiratha nor Atikaya are capable of resisting Raghava in battle.

" You, the friends of this monarch who is dominated by passion, violent by nature and whose acts are thoughtless, flatter him, as though you were his foes, to the destruction of the titans ! Rescue and deliver that king who is held fast in the illimitable coils of a serpent possessed of a thousand hoods and who is formidable and of exceeding energy. It is for the sovereign's friends, whose desires have been gratified by him, to save him, even were it by dragging him by the hair of his head, like one who has fallen a prey to fiends of immeasurable power. It is for you unitedly to rescue that monarch from the surging waters of the ocean Rama, he who is sinking into the mouth of the Kakutstha hell !

"I will here repeat those words that are to the advantage of the city, the titans, the king and the host of courtiers ! I repeat them loyally and candidly ' Let Maithili be given back to that Prince ! '

"He who, having estimated the strength of his foes, his own resources, the situation and the loss and gain of his undertaking and, after mature reflection, expresses himself frankly and judiciously to his master, is a true counsellor."

CHAPTER 15

Bibishana reproaches Indrajita for his boasting

THIS speech of Bibishana's, who was equal to Brihaspati in wisdom, displeased the great Indrajita, Leader of the Nairrita Hosts, who replied to him thus :—

"What do these idle words fraught with fear signify, O Youngest of my Uncles ? None other, even were he the issue of another race than our own, would speak thus or even conceive such thoughts ! Valour, courage, endurance, steadfastness, audacity and strength are lacking in Bibishana alone, the youngest brother of my sire.

"Who are, in fact, these two sons of a king of men ? One of us single-handed, were he the least of the titans, would suffice to exterminate them both ! O Coward, from whence springs thy fear ? Was I not able to cast the Protector of the Three

Worlds to the ground, the Lord of the Devas himself? Struck with terror, the Hosts of the Gods scattered in all directions and the loudly trumpeting Airavata was brought down by me, whose tusks I rooted out, dispersing the celestial armies by my valour. I who humbled the pride of the Gods themselves and afflicted the Daityas, am I in mine immeasurable energy not able to subdue these two princes, insignificant mortals as they are?"

At this speech of that invincible and powerful rival of Indra, Bibishana the foremost of warriors answered him in words fraught with good sense, saying:—

"My Child, thy reflections are worthless! Thou art young and thine intellect is not yet ripe; further, to our ruin, thou art incapable of ascertaining what is expedient and inexpedient.

"Under the guise of a son, O Indrajita, thou art in truth a hidden foe to Ravana and, hearing him prate of slaying Raghava, thou dost support him. Thou dost merit death, as also he who had the grievous idea of bringing thee here this day and introducing a youthful, rash and arrogant warrior into an assembly of counsellors! O Indrajita, thou art thoughtless, imprudent, feeble of intellect, thy mind ruined by folly and extreme frivolity and thou speakest thus from childishness. Who can withstand the shock of those shining arrows which Raghava looses in combat resembling the Rod of Brahma, like unto fate or the Sceptre of Yama? Do thou give back Sita to Rama with treasure, pearls, rich ornaments, celestial attire and gems, so that we may dwell here without anxiety, O King."

CHAPTER 16

Ravana rebukes Bibishana who takes his Departure

BIBISHANA, having uttered these words that were reasoned and full of good sense, Ravana replied in harsh accents, saying:—

"It were better to live as a declared enemy or with a venomous serpent than to dwell with one who, under the guise of a friend, is in league with the foe. The disposition of relatives who ever rejoice in others' misfortunes is well known, O Titan. Kinsfolk ever seek to bring down the one who is endowed with authority, energy, learning and loyalty and, should he be a hero, he is the more condemned by them. Constantly finding delight in the discomfiture of one another, their bows ready to strike each other down, their hearts full of deceit, they are both formidable and dangerous.

" Those verses formerly recited by the elephants in the Padma Forest, on seeing men with snares in their hands, are well known ; I will repeat them to thee :—' Neither fire nor weapons nor traps strike terror into us but those of our own kind who are cruel and self-interested, it is they whom we fear ! They alone, undoubtedly divulge the means of making us captive ! '

" Of all perils, those that spring from relatives are the worst, this is known to us. From cows we have milk, from relatives malice, from women capriciousness, from brahmins asceticism. That I am held in honour by my subjects and have been called to rule over an empire by descent and have set my foot on the heads of mine enemies, will certainly not have found favour with thee ! As drops of water are unable to remain on the lotus leaves, so does friendship slip from the hold of worthless persons. As in autumn the thunderclouds, which empty themselves, fail to saturate the earth, so does friendship fail with the vicious. As bees fly away after they have sucked out the honey they have found, so do the unworthy relinquish a friendship after it has served their purpose. As the honey stealer in its greed, feeding on the Kusha Flowers, does not exhaust their nectar neither do the wicked savour friendship to the full.

" If any other had addressed such a speech to me, O Ranger of the Night, he would have ceased to breathe at that very instant ! As for thee, a curse upon thee, O Obloquy of thy Race ! "

At this affront, Bibishana, who ever spoke what was true, rose up mace in hand with four other titans and, filled with indignation, that fortunate one, standing in space, said to his brother, the King of the Titans :—

" Thou hast lost thy reason, O King, but say what thou wilt, an elder brother is the equal of a father and must be reverenced even if he leave the path of equity ; nevertheless I am unable to tolerate these outrageous utterances of thine ! Words of wisdom that are dictated by a desire for the welfare of others, O Ten-necked One, are not acceptable to those who are not masters of themselves and have fallen under the sway of death ! Those who make flattering speeches are easy to find but rare are they who utter salutary though unpleasing words or those who will listen to them ! I could not brook seeing thee caught in the noose of death, who bears away all beings, neither did I desire to see thee pierced by the sharp and golden arrows of Rama resembling flaming torches. Even stout-hearted persons full of skill and courage fall in combat and are carried away like walls of sand if death overcomes them. Thou shouldst accept this counsel on account of its import for thine own good ! By every means defend thyself as well as this city and the titans ! In thine own interest I sought to restrain thee but my words have not found favour with thee, O Ranger of the Night. Fare-thee-well, I go ; thou wilt be happier without me ! At the point of death, those whose life has run its course do not listen to the advice of their friends ! "

CHAPTER 17

Words of the leading Monkeys regarding Bibishana

HAVING spoken thus severely to Ravana, Bibishana went away and almost immediately reached the place where Rama and Lakshmana were.

Resembling the peak of Mount Meru, like a flash of lightning in the sky, he was seen by the leaders of the monkeys who were stationed on the ground.

Accompanied by four titans of renowned courage, furnished with armour and arrows, adorned with marvellous jewels, he resembled a mass of cloud, the equal of the God who wields the Thunderbolt and that hero was bearing excellent weapons and was covered with celestial gems.

Beholding him with his four companions, Sugriva, the sagacious King of the Monkeys, who was invincible, standing amidst his forces became thoughtful and, after reflecting a moment, addressed the monkeys with Hanuman and others anxiously, saying :—

" Without doubt, this titan, armed with weapons and accompanied by four of his kind, is coming to slay us ! "

Hearing these words of Sugriva, all the leading monkeys brandishing great trees and rocks, said to him :—

" Do thou speedily order us to slay these evil doers, O King ! Let us strike these weaklings down so that they fall on the earth ! "

As they were speaking thus, Bibishana, who was master of himself, had reached the northern shore and halting there, that highly intelligent and powerful titan, who was fully self-subdued, on perceiving Sugriva and the monkeys, said aloud to them :—

" Ravana is the name of a wicked titan and their lord, and I am his younger brother, my name is Bibishana. It is Ravana who, having killed Jatayu, carried off Sita from Janasthana. That unfortunate one is held captive against her will amidst the female titans who guard her jealously. I have tried to persuade them by diverse arguments, continually repeated, to return Sita to Rama but Ravana impelled by fate will not listen to my sage advice. Reviled by him and treated like a slave, I, abandoning my consort and my son, have come to take refuge with Rama. Do thou inform the high-souled Raghava, that magnanimous protector of the worlds, that I, Bibishana, have come hither."

At these words, the swift-footed Sugriva, full of indignation, ran to find Rama and, in the presence of Lakshmana, said to him :—

" Having belonged to Ravana's forces, here is an adversary taking us unawares, who without warning has come hither to slay us at the first opportunity, like an owl destroying crows ! Thou knowest all concerning the plans, organization, distribution of troops and the secret service of the monkeys, as also of thy foes, O Thou who art their scourge ! May good betide Thee ! These titans, who are able to change their forms at will, conceal their designs ; they are bold and inventive in strategy, assuredly one may not trust them !

" This must be an emissary of the Lord of the Titans who, undoubtedly has come to sow dissension amongst us or to dis-cover our weak points ; having first gained our confidence by

D

craft, he himself intends to attack us one day. Assistance that is provided by a friend or an inhabitant of the woods like ourselves or by a compatriot or a servant, may be accepted but one should eschew that offered by a foe, O Lord! This deserter who has come to us is a titan by nature and the brother of thine adversary, how can we trust him on first sight? He is Bibishana, the younger brother of Ravana and he has come with four titans to ask for thy protection. Nay, it is Ravana who has sent this Bibishana; it is essential that thou satisfy thyself regarding him, O Thou, the most circumspect of persons! This titan of deceitful soul has come hither for the purpose of treacherously striking thee down when thou dost least expect it, O Irreproachable Hero! Let him and his confederates die in extreme torture, this brother of the wicked Ravana!"

Having given vent to his fury in the presence of the eloquent Rama, the King of the Monkeys, a skilled orator, became silent!

Hearing Sugriva's words, the mighty Rama said to the monkeys headed by Hanuman who stood near:—

"You have heard for yourselves what your Sovereign has expressed in judicious words of deep significance regarding the younger brother of Ravana; in times of crisis one should always receive the counsel of one who desires the welfare of his friends, and who is intelligent and prudent."

Thus addressed by Rama, all those monkeys, ardently desiring his success, hastened to express their opinion, saying :—

"Nothing is unknown to thee in the Three Worlds, O Raghava; it is in deference to us that thou dost consult us as friends! Thou art loyal, brave, pious, established in heroism and dost act only after thou hast considered the matter in accord with tradition with full confidence in thy friends. Let all the intelligent and experienced ministers debate this matter thoroughly, each in his turn."

Thus spoke those monkeys and first the sagacious Angada suggested to Raghava that he should enquire into Bibishana's intentions, saying :—

"One should sound a deserter who presents himself in every way. It would not befit us to put full trust in Bibishana at once. It is in concealing their real nature that these perfidious beings act, and further they attack unexpectedly, which would prove

38

fatal to us. Examine him to discover what is right or wrong before taking any decision and, if it prove to our advantage, form an alliance with him ; if to our disadvantage, reject it. If it be fraught with danger, then renounce it, but if it should bring us real benefit, let us give him a fitting welcome ! "

Thereafter Sharabha, having reflected awhilè, gave his opinion, revealing his motives, saying :—

" Without delay, O Lion among Men, send out a spy and, having by means of a wary agent, undertaken a thorough investigation, deal with him in a suitable manner."

Then Jambavan, inspired by his knowledge of the scriptures and his own experience, expressed himself in irreproachable and lucid terms saying :—

" Bibishana has come to us from a declared enemy, the wicked Lord of the Titans, and he has arrived here without any regard for time and place ; let us be on our guard against him ! "

In his turn, Mainda, skilled in the matter of truth and error, a fluent speaker, uttered these prudent words :—

" Bibishana is the younger brother of Ravana, let us interrogate him gently and progressively, O King of Kings ! When thou hast informed thyself of his feelings, then act according to whether his intentions are honest or no, O Prince of Men ! "

Thereafter, Hanuman, the foremost of beings versed in the scriptures, spoke in sweet accents in words fraught with integrity, saying :—

" Even Bibishana himself cannot excel thee who art of an exalted intellect and the foremost of those skilled in speech. It is not from a desire to speak nor out of emulation nor a sense of superiority nor from a love of debate that I open my mouth, O my Lord Rama, but on account of the importance of the matter in hand. That which thy counsellors have said seems to me erroneous and the real question does not lie there. If one does not interrogate this titan, it is impossible to discover why he has come hither but to make use of him has its disadvantages also. Concerning the sending out of a spy to make investigations as thy minister advises, I regard it as unwise nor will it succeed. It has been said that Bibishana had no regard for time and place when he came hither, I reserve my judgment here ; it appears to me that the time and place are appropriate, his fault or merit

consists in leaving one for another. Knowing the wickedness
of Ravana and thy true value, Bibishana has, by his arrival,
shown his tact and intelligence. Further it was said, O Prince,
' Let emissaries in disguise question him ' and this speech
suggested several thoughts to me. He who is suddenly interrogated, if he be wise, becomes cautious and refuses to speak ;
the most amiable of those, who come as friends, will change
after such an useless enquiry. It is not possible, O King, to
discover the character of a stranger immediately but only after
frequent conversations when words may escape him that will
betray any perfidy. The speech of this titan does not indicate
an evil nature and further he has an open countenance and I have
no doubts concerning him. He is in no way embarrassed and is
master of himself, he does not appear to be a knave. His
language is not that of a perverse being and I do not feel any
suspicion regarding him. Inevitably people's real nature is
only gradually revealed. When an undertaking is suited to the
time and place, O Most experienced of Men, and it is a practical
proposition, it will meet with speedy success. Bibishana is
aware of thy magnanimity and also of Ravana's baseness. He
has heard of the slaying of Bali and the crowning of Sugriva
and what is more he has a desire to rule the kingdom ! If this
is what has determined him to come hither and these are
apparently his motives, then this is what his alliance is worth to
us. I have said what I had to say to prove the upright character
of this titan ; thou hast listened to me and the rest depends on
thee, O Prince of the Wise."

CHAPTER 18

Rama listens to the Advice of the Monkeys about receiving Bibishana

HEARING the words of the Wind-god's son, the invincible Rama,
versed in the scriptures, answered him and, expressing his own
conclusions, said :—

"I also have reflected on Bibishana and wish to make the result
known to thee, O Thou who art established in virtue ! I shall

never refuse to receive one who presents himself as a friend, even were I mistaken no honest man could reproach me for it."

At these words, Sugriva, that lion among monkeys, reflecting carefully, replied in more reasonable words and in eloquent terms addressed Rama, saying :—

" What matters it if this ranger of the night be well or ill-intentioned, if in time of peril he abandons his brother, whom will he not betray subsequently ? "

At these words of the King of the Monkeys, Kakutstha looked round on that company and, smiling gently, said to Lakshmana, distinguished for his saintly characteristics :—

" He who has not studied the scriptures nor possessed reverence for authority could not utter such words as have been expressed by the Lord of Monkeys ! There is however something peculiar in these circumstances, it seems to me, which is particularly to be seen in monarchs. Kings have two avowed enemies, their kinsmen and their neighbours, who turn against them in times of adversity ; this is what brings this titan here !

" Relatives who are not of a perverse nature, honour those of their own family who have treated them well but in the case of kings even a virtuous relative is suspect ! As to the fault that you point out which consists in accepting the assistance of a foe, I will tell you what the scriptures say on this, hear me !

" We are not related to the titans and it is not our kingdom that he covets. It is certain his compatriots are informed about Bibishana's departure and for this reason we should receive him. They will have assembled with joy and without anxiety and thereafter the cry ' This one or that is afraid ', will have created a division amongst them ; this is what has brought about Bibishana's arrival here.

" All brothers, O Dear One, do not resemble Bharata nor all sons what I was to my sire nor do all friends resemble each other."

Thus spoke Rama, and Sugriva rising, as also Lakshmana, bowed low and thereafter that exceedingly sagacious monkey said :—

" Know that it is Ravana who has sent out this ranger of the night ! I regard it as imperative that we should make an end of him, O Thou, the most circumspect of persons ! This demon under the order of a perverse creature has come hither to make an assault on thee, myself and Lakshmana, when we are unprepared for it, O Irreproachable Warrior. He merits death, this Bibishana, brother of that inhuman Ravana, as well as his accomplices."

Having spoken thus to the eloquent prince of the House of Raghu, Sugriva, the leader of the army, a fluent speaker became silent and Rama, having listened to Sugriva, that lion among monkeys, reflected awhile and then addressed that foremost of monkeys in measured terms, saying :—

" Whether this titan be ill-intentioned or no, what does it matter, he cannot do me the least mischief. On earth, Pisachas, Danavas and Yakshas, as also the titans can be slain by me with the tip of my finger, if I so desire it, O King of the Monkeys.

" It is related how a pigeon with whom his adversary had taken refuge entertained him and invited him to partake of his own flesh, even though he was the ravisher of his mate. Such was the hospitality offered by a pigeon ; what should therefore a man like myself not do ? Hearken to these verses, pre-eminently sacred, sung aforetimes by the son of Kanva, that great ascetic of truthful speech, Kandu :—

" ' A miscreant who approaches with joined palms, seeking refuge, should not in the name of humanity be slain even if he be a foe, O Parantapa ! The unfortunate or the fearful who plead for shelter or throw themselves on the mercy of their enemy, should be protected by him who is master of himself. If, conforming to the tradition, one does not render assistance according to one's capacity, either for reasons of fear, delusion or anger, one is reproached by all and the suppliant, who perishes before the eyes of the one of whom he has sought help in vain, carries away all his merit ! '

" Therefore it is a heinous crime not to give shelter to those who petition it on this earth ; it is to deprive oneself of heaven and glory and to lose one's strength and prowess ! Consequently I shall follow the excellent counsel of Kandu, which is pious, honourable and leads to heaven as the fruit of merit. Any being who has sought refuge with me, saying—' I am thine ' is assured of my protection, I swear it ! Bring this stranger

42

to me, O Monkey, I shall offer him security whether he be Bibishana or Ravana himself ! "

Thus did Rama speak and Sugriva, the King of the Monkeys, answered that son of Kakutstha, whom he held in deep affection, thus :—

" What wonder is it that thou who art loyal, virtuous and established in righteousness, thou who shinest like a jewel in the head of kings, shouldst speak thus ? I, also, in my heart, am convinced of Bibishana's integrity. Deduction, feeling, everything has been used to probe this matter thoroughly ; let him be admitted immediately amongst us on equal terms, O Raghava ! Let Bibishana, who is full of wisdom, join our alliance ! "

At these words of Sugriva, the King of the Monkeys, Rama immediately joined Bibishana as Purandara the King of the Birds.

CHAPTER 19

Bibishana is brought before Rama

RAGHAVA having accorded him protection, the younger brother of Ravana, the highly intelligent Bibishana bowed to him, looking down on the earth.

Thereafter he descended joyously from the sky to the ground with his faithful companions and that virtuous one ran towards Rama and, falling at his feet with the four titans, addressed him in words full of loyalty and discretion, fitting the occasion :—

" I am Ravana's younger brother and I have been greatly affronted by him. I have therefore come to seek refuge with thee, the protector of all beings ! Abandoning Lanka, friends and possessions, I place my kingdom, life and happiness at thy disposal ! "

At these words, Rama, in soothing tones, while seeming to consume him with his gaze, said :—

" O Bibishana, tell me truly what is the strength and weakness of the titans ? "

Thus questioned by Rama of imperishable exploits, that titan described the might and extent of Ravana's power, saying :—

" By virtue of a special boon conferred on him by Swyambhu, Dashagriva is invulnerable to all beings, Gandharvas, Serpents and Birds, O Prince. I have also another brother older than myself, the valiant Kumbhakarna, the illustrious rival of Indra in war.

" O Rama, Ravana has Prahasta commanding his forces, who is perhaps known to thee. It is he who vanquished Manibhadra in combat on Mount Kailasha ! When clad in armour that no arrow can pierce, furnished with his archer's gloves, Indrajita, taking up his bow, makes himself invisible, and on the battle-field, having propitiated the God of Fire, that fortunate one sows carnage amongst the foe, O Raghava. Mahodara, Mahaparshwa and the Titan Akampana, who are his lieutenants, resemble the Lokapalas on the field of battle.

"Ten thousand kotis of titans, able to change their form at will, feeding on flesh and blood, inhabit Lanka. At their head, their sovereign the wicked Ravana made war on the supporters of the earth as also the Gods who were all overcome by him."

Having listened to Bibishana and weighed his words carefully, Rama expressed himself thus :—

" These exploits of Ravana's that thou hast faithfully described are well known to me ; I shall slay Dashagriva as also Prahasta and his sons; thereafter I shall install thee as king; believe me, this is the truth ! Were he to plunge into the region of Rasatala or even Patala or take refuge with the Grandsire of the World, he would not escape alive ! Before I have annihilated Ravana with his sons, his kinsfolk and his allies in battle, I shall not return to Ayodhya, I swear it by my three brothers ! "

Thus did Rama of imperishable exploits speak and the venerable Bibishana bowing unto him, said :—

" In the slaying of the titans and the capture of Lanka, I will assist thee with all my strength ; I will break through the enemy's ranks."

As he spoke thus, Rama embraced him and thereafter he commanded Lakshmana saying :—" Do thou bring water from the sea and anoint the sagacious Bibishana as King of the Titans under my direction, O Noble Brother ! "

Thereupon Saumitri, in accord with Rama's behest, performed the royal anointing in the midst of the leading monkeys and immediately those monkeys, beholding Bibishana raised to that supreme rank, acclaimed that magnanimous titan, crying : " Excellent ! Excellent ! ".

Meanwhile Hanuman and Sugriva enquired of Bibishana, saying :—

" How shall we, with the mighty army of monkeys who surround us, cross the ocean, that indestructible empire of Varuna ? What means should we employ to traverse the refuge of the Lord of Streams and Rivers speedily with our troops ? "

At this question, the virtuous Bibishana answered :—" That Prince, the offspring of the Race of Raghu, should approach the ocean that was excavated by Sagara[1] and he will assuredly help one of his own race ".

Thus spoke Bibishana, that sagacious titan, and Sugriva instantly went away with Lakshmana to join Rama.

Thereafter the thick-necked Sugriva conveyed to him this salutory counsel of Bibishana's to take refuge with Sagara and it found favour with the virtuously minded Rama. Then that illustrious prince replied to Sugriva, the King of the Monkeys, who was accompanied by Lakshmana Full of respect for that monkey, who sought to gratify him in every way, he smiled upon him as also on his brother Lakshmana and said :—

" This plan of Bibishana's pleases me, O Sugriva and Lakshmana. Sugriva is sagacious and was ever a prudent counsellor : do ye both reflect on the matter and say what you consider to be best."

Having spoken thus to them, those two warriors Sugriva and Lakshmana answered in respectful tones, saying :—

" How should the counsel of Bibishana not find favour with us in these circumstances ? He brings us the means to success. Without throwing a bridge over the sea, that redoubtable dominion of Lanka will remain inaccessible even to the Gods and titans with their leaders. Let us carry out the suggestion of the virtuous Bibishana scrupulously ; enough time has been lost. Let us approach Sagara, so that with our army we may reach Lanka of which Ravana is the support."

[1] Sagara being one of Rama's ancestors. His story is told in Balakanda.

At these words, Rama proceeded to the shore that was covered with Kusha Grass belonging to the Lord of Streams and Rivers as the God of Fire ascends the altar.

CHAPTER 20

Ravana sends Shuka to Sugriva

Now the titan, Shardula by name, who had gone out to reconnoitre, beheld the army encamped under Sugriva's command, and that spy belonging to the wicked Ravana, King of the Titans, having inspected those troops, returned and, regaining Lanka with all speed, said to his sovereign :—

" Behold a multitude of monkeys and bears, immeasurable and boundless as the sea, approaching Lanka. The sons of Dasaratha, the brothers Rama and Lakshmana, who are illustrious and endowed with beauty, have come to search for Sita. Having reached the shores of the sea, they have encamped there, O Illustrious Prince. These forces cover ten leagues in extent in every direction ! O Great King, it behoves thee to inform thyself of the true state of affairs immediately ! Let thine emissaries enquire into the matter speedily ; restitution, conciliation or sowing dissension are involved here."[1]

Hearing Shardula's words, Ravana, the Lord of the Titans became perturbed and, reflecting on the matter, instantly gave orders to Shuka, the most skilled of negotiators, saying :—

" Go and seek out Sugriva on my behalf and say to that prince in persuasive and ingratiating tones :—

"Assuredly thou, the offspring of a race of great monarchs, the mighty son of the King of the Bears, art exceedingly powerful ! Thou hast nothing to fear ; thou art to me as a brother, O Lord of the Monkeys. If I bore away the consort of that crafty prince, what is it to thee ? Do thou return to Kishkindha ; Lanka cannot be conquered by these monkeys by any means nor by the united efforts of the Gods with the Gandharvas, how much less by men or apes ?' "

---

[1] The Three means of dealing with an enemy.

At this command of the King of the Titans, that Night-ranger Shuka, rising into the air, rapidly passed through space and, having journeyed for some time high over the waters, halted and, standing in the sky, repeated all he had been told by the wicked Ravana to say to Sugriva. As he was still speaking, the monkeys bounded into the air and, smiting him with their fists, prepared to tear him to pieces and fling him to the ground.

Thus maltreated by the monkeys, Shuka spoke in this wise :—

" One does not assault an ambassador, O Kakutstha, therefore send away these monkeys. He who withholds the message of his master and gives voice to that which he has not been authorized to utter, merits death."

Hearing Shuka's complaints, Rama issued a command to those monkeys, who were assaulting that titan, saying :—" Do not slay him ! " and Shuka having received immunity from the attacks of the monkeys, steadying himself in the air with his wings, spoke again, saying :—

" O Sugriva, Thou who art endowed with magnanimity, O Hero, who art full of energy and valour, what shall I say to thee on the part of Ravana, the Scourge of the World ? "

Being thus addressed, that mighty King of the Monkeys, the foremost of all the apes, interrupted that Ranger of the Night, Shuka, and made the following proud reply, characteristic of his nature :—

" Thou art not my friend nor art thou worthy of my pity, thou art neither my benefactor nor dost thou find favour with me ! Thou and thy kinsfolk are the enemies of Rama, thou shalt perish like Bali and thou meritest death ! I shall annihilate thee, thy sons, thy relatives as also Lanka to which I shall lay siege at the head of my great army and reduce it to ashes !

" Nay, thou insensate Ravana, thou shalt never escape Raghava even if thou wert protected by the Gods themselves with their leaders. Wert thou to make thyself invisible in the sun's path or enter into hell or take refuge at the lotus feet of the King of the Mountains,[1] thou with thy followers wilt succumb to Rama's blows. In the Three Worlds, I see none whether be it Pisacha, Rakshasa, Gandharva, or Asura, who is able to

---

[1] Mt. Kailasha.

protect thee ! Thou hast slain the aged King of the Vultures and carried off the large-eyed Sita in the presence of Rama and Lakshmana and, having made her captive, dost not recognize her for what she is ! Thou art unaware how strong, powerful and irresistible to the Gods themselves is this Prince of the Race of Raghu, who shall deprive thee of thy life."

Thereafter the foremost of monkeys, the son of Bali, Angada, took up the discourse and said :—

"O Virtuous King, this is no ambassador, he has the appearance of a spy ; he is only here to count our forces, let him be arrested, do not allow him to return to Lanka. Such is my opinion."

Thereupon at a sign from the king, the monkeys flung themselves on that titan, whom they seized and bound, whilst he, without defence, wailed loudly.

Ill-treated by those furious monkeys, Shuka began to cry upon the magnanimous Rama, born of Dasaratha, saying :—

" They are tearing out my wings ruthlessly and putting out my eyes, may the consequences of all the evil deeds that I have done since the day I was born till the night I die, fall on thee if I lose my life ! "

Hearing his cries, Rama would not sanction his death and ordered the monkeys to release him.

CHAPTER 21

Rama looses his Arrows on Sagara

THEREAFTER, spreading the Darbha Grass on the shore of the sea, Rama with joined palms, his face turned towards the east, made obeisance in honour of the ocean and laid himself down.

That Scourge of his Foes pillowed his head on his arms that resembled the coils of a serpent and were adorned with ornaments of gold, their habitual decoration ; those arms that formerly were perfumed with sandal and aloes, saffron of the hue of the dawn lending them lustre ; those arms on which Sita leant on the nuptial couch causing them to shine as do the waters of the

Ganges the body of Takshaka ; those arms, resembling the shafts of a chariot, that increased the distress of his foes and the delight of his friends, were stretched out on the shore of the sea.

The tightening of the bow-string had rubbed the skin off the left arm of that skilful archer and the right, that bestower of thousands of kine in charity, resembled a great mace. Leaning on his powerful elbow, the mighty-armed Rama said :—

" Sagara will grant me a passage or he shall be slain by me ! "

Having thus resolved, he lay down by the ocean, restraining his speech and with a concentrated mind in accord with tradition. There, following the scriptural injunction, Rama lay on the ground spread with Kusha Grass and slept peacefully for three nights. For three nights Rama, endowed with learning and piety, remained beside Sagara, the Lord of the Waters. Nevertheless that indolent one did not appear to that hero, who had yet paid him honour as was his due. Thereupon, his eyes suffused with wrath, Raghava, enraged against him, said to Lakshmana, the bearer of auspicious marks, who stood near :—

" It is from contempt that the Ocean does not appear to me in person ! Deference and forbearance, integrity and friendly speech, these qualities belonging to virtuous men are not valued by those who are deprived of them, who regard them as weakness, whereas the braggart, the dissolute and the arrogant who boast openly and commit every kind of excess, are overwhelmed with regard ! Meekness will never bring victory on this earth, O Lakshmana, any more than in the forefront of battle ! To-day, pierced by my shafts, thou shalt behold aquatic monsters by their leaping churn up the waters where they dwell on every side ! See, O Lakshmana, how I shall sever the serpents' coils and the limbs of the great fish like unto the trunks of elephants. To-day I shall dry up the ocean with its multitudinous waves, shells, pearls, fish and monsters. Because I have manifested patience, the Ocean, the abode of whales, regards me as power-less ! Away with forbearance to such persons ! It is on account of my mildness that he manifests his true nature ! Bring me my bow, O Saumitri and mine arrows resembling venomous snakes, I shall dry up the sea and the monkeys may then cross it on foot ! To-day, indomitable though he be, I shall yet overthrow Sagara with my shafts ; he who is bounded by the shore and who is filled with a myriad waves! I shall wipe out that Ocean, the Abode of Varuna, that is inhabited by great giants."

Speaking thus, bow in hand, his eyes dilated with anger, Rama appeared exceedingly terrible, like unto the Fire at the end of the world cycle. Grasping his formidable bow with its barbed and fearful shafts more firmly, he caused the earth to tremble as does Shatakratu with his thunderbolts. His flaming and impetuous arrows, unrivalled in power, penetrated the waters of the sea and struck terror in the serpents. And those waves of the sea with their sharks and monsters, were extremely agitated, so that with the roaring of the wind, a formidable clamour arose. In a trice, the ocean became a mass of clashing waves, throwing up spray, shells and fragments of mother of pearl, and panic spread among the Pannagas of flaming jaws and brassy eyes and amidst the mighty Danavas in their abode, the depths of hell. Waves in their millions as high as the Vindhya and Mandara Mountains rose from that Lord of Waters with his crocodiles and great fish and the Ocean emitted a loud roaring, amidst the breaking billows, with the terrified serpents, demons and great crocodiles in flight.

Then Saumitri rushed towards Rama, who, in his burning ardour, was stretching his incomparable bow with loud mutterings, crying:—"Stay! Stay!" and thus speaking, he took hold of that weapon, saying :—

"Thou hast no need to act in this wise to accomplish thine end and bring Sagara to subjection, O Foremost of Heroes! Thy peers do not permit themselves to be overcome by anger! Call to mind the forbearance of virtuous men!"

At that instant, the Brahmarishis and celestial Rishis, who, invisible, were stationed in the sky, cried out :—"Hold! Hold! do not act thus!"

CHAPTER 22

The Army crosses the Sea

THEREAFTER the Prince of the Raghus addressed the Ocean in menacing tones, saying :—

" To-day I shall dry up the sea with the nether regions ! O Sagara, with thy waters consumed by my shafts, thy denizens slain by my blows, a great cloud of dust will arise from thy drained bed and the monkeys will cross to the other shore on foot !

" Thou hast sought to oppose me but art unaware of my valour or my strength ! O Abode of the Danavas, being full of pride, thou canst not foresee thy fate ! "

Thereafter, fixing an arrow resembling the Rod of Brahma and placing it on his excellent bow, Raghava stretched that weapon, and heaven and earth seemed to be riven, as it were, and the mountains trembled, darkness covered the earth and all the regions were obscured. Tremors ran through the lakes and rivers ; the sun, moon and stars swerved in their course and though the sky was lit by the sun's rays, it was enveloped in darkness and blazed with a hundred meteors, whilst thunder reverberated with an unparalleled sound in the firmament. The five celestial Maruts blew and like massed legions tore up the trees, dispersing the clouds in the twinkling of an eye, breaking off the points of the rocks and shattering the mountain peaks. In the sky, loud thunder claps resounded with immense power and tumult. The invisible beings emitted cries of fear and, lying prostrate on the earth in their agony, shook with terror, convulsed and unable to move. Thereafter the Ocean with its mass of water, serpents and demons surged beyond its confines to the extent of a league, though the time of the final deluge was not yet at hand ; nevertheless Rama, the descendant of Raghu, scourge of his foes, did not retreat before the disordered heavings of that Lord of Rivers and Streams !

Sagara himself rose out of the waves, like the day's orb rising over the eastern mountain, Meru, and that Ocean appeared with the Pannagas of flaming jaws and he was of the hue of emerald, adorned with gold ; wreaths of pearls festooned his attire and on his head he bore a diadem of every kind of flower ; ornaments of refined gold and pearls from his domain were his decoration. Covered with gems and metals of every kind, resembling the Himavat Mountain, the waters surging round him, he was encircled by the clouds and winds, while the rivers Gunga and Sindhu were his escorts.

Rising, the noble Sagara, escorted by the rivers with the Gunga and Indus at their head, approached Rama with joined palms, who stood arrows in hand, and, reflecting awhile the Ocean said:—

" Earth, wind, air, water and light, O Beloved Raghava, remain fixed in their own nature. Neither from desire nor ambition nor fear, O Prince, nor from affection am I able to solidify my waters inhabited by sharks ; nevertheless I will make it possible for thee to cross over them ! This is my resolve—the sharks will remain inactive while the army makes its way across and, for the monkeys, I shall become like the earth ! "

On this, Rama said to him :—"Hear me, O Thou who art the refuge of Varuna ! This arrow of mine must accomplish its intended end ! Where shall I let this mighty shaft fall ? "

Hearing Rama's words and seeing that formidable missile, the exceedingly powerful Ocean replied :—

" To the north of this place is a sacred region, Drumakulya, a name as renowned in the world as thine own ! There innumerable robbers of fearful aspect and deeds, having Abhiras as their chief, drink my waters. The vicinity of those perverse beings is intolerable to me ; it is there, O Rama, that thou shouldst loose thy shaft that never misses its target."

Thus spoke the magnanimous Sagara and Rama, in accord with his wish, let fly that marvellous dart in his presence. And the place, where that arrow resembling a flash of lightning fell, is known in the world as the desert of Maru[1]. The earth pierced by that dart emitted a loud cry and from its gaping wound the waters of hell gushed forth. As the arrow fell, it created a thunderous sound and the deep crater which is known as Vrana[2]

[1] Maru—Malwar in Ragasthan.
[2] Vrana—The Wound.

was filled with the water of the deeper springs ; it seemed as if the earth was riven and wells and ponds appeared there. This place became known as Marukantara and is famous in the Three Worlds. Thereafter Rama, the son of Dasaratha, having dried up the waters of the ocean, conferred a boon, saying :—

" This place shall be rich in pasturage and free from disease ; it will abound in fruit, roots, honey, ghee and milk and be fragrant with aromatic herbs ; thus it will remain retaining those excellent qualities ! "

In this way the Desert of Maru came to possess these manifold features and by the grace of Rama's liberality, assumed a pleasant aspect. When the waters had been dried up, Samudra, the Lord of Streams and Rivers, said to Raghava, who was skilled in the use of weapons :—

" My Friend, there stands Nala, the son of Vishvakarma, whose father has overwhelmed him with gifts ; he is generous and devoted ; great are the powers of that monkey ; let him construct a bridge over my waters, I will uphold it ; Nala is as skilled as his sire ! "

At these words the Ocean disappeared and Nala, that prince of monkeys spoke to the valiant Rama thus :—

" Resorting to the skill I have inherited from my sire, I shall build a bridge over the spacious and vast domain of aquatic monsters ; what the Ocean has said is true !

" When one has to do with the ungrateful, in my opinion the rod is the most salutary method for men ! A plague on forbearance as also on generosity and kindness ! Assuredly Sagara, that formidable mass of water, in fear of punishment, wished to see a bridge constructed and out of fear was willing to suffer Raghava to pass over it.

" My mother received a boon on the Mandara Mountain from Vishvakarma, who said to her :—' A son will be born to thee who will resemble me, O Goddess ! '

" No one having questioned me, I have not spoken of my powers but I can assuredly construct a causeway over Varuna's domain ; from to-day let all the leading monkeys set to work ! "

At Rama's command, those lions among the monkeys entered the mighty forest with alacrity in hundreds and thousands on every side and those leaders of the simian tribes, tearing up the rocks, which in size they resembled, and the trees also dragged them to the sea and they covered the ocean with Sala, Ashvakarna, Dhava, Vamsha, Kutaja, Arjuna, Tala, Tilaka, Tinisha, Balalaka, Saptaparna and Karnikarna Trees in full flower, as also Cutas and Ashokas. Those foremost of monkeys transported those trees, with or without roots, bearing them like so many standards of Indra and they heaped Talas and piles of Dadina, Narikela, Bibhitaka, Kanya, Bakula and Nimba Trees here and there. With the aid of mechanical devices, those powerful colossi dug up stones as big as elephants and rocks, and the water suddenly spouted into the air only to fall instantly. Thereafter those monkeys churned up the sea by rushing into it on all sides or pulling on the chains.

That immense causeway constructed by Nala in the bosom of the sea was built by the arms of those monkeys of formidable exploits and it extended over a hundred leagues.

Some brought trunks of trees and others set them up ; it was by hundreds and thousands that those monkeys, like unto giants, made use of reeds, logs and blossoming trees to construct that bridge, rushing hither and thither with blocks of stone resembling mountains or the peaks of crags, which, flung into the sea, fell with a resounding crash.

The first day those monkeys resembling elephants, of immense energy, full of high spirits and exceedingly merry, erected fourteen leagues of masonry. The second day, those highly active monkeys of formidable stature set up twenty leagues. Bestirring themselves, those giants threw twenty-one leagues of structure over the ocean on the third day and on the fourth, working feverishly, they built up twenty-two leagues in extent. The fifth day, those monkeys, industrious workers, reached to twenty-three leagues distance from the further shore.

That fortunate and valiant son of Vishvakarma, leader of monkeys, constructed a causeway worthy of his sire over the ocean and that bridge erected by Nala over the sea, the haunt of whales, dazzling in its perfection and splendour, was like the constellation of Svati in space.

Then the Gods, Gandharvas, Siddhas and supreme Rishis assembling, stood in the sky, eager to see that masterpiece and the Gods and Gandharvas gazed on that causeway, so difficult of construction that was ten leagues in width and a hundred in length built by Nala.

Those monkeys thereafter dived, swam and shouted at the sight of that unimaginable marvel that was almost inconceivable and caused one to tremble ! And all beings beheld that causeway thrown over the ocean and by hundreds and thousands of kotis, those monkeys, full of valour, having built that bridge over the immense repository of waters, reached the opposite shore.

Vast, well-constructed, magnificent with its wonderful paved floor, solidly cemented, that great causeway like unto a line traced on the waves, resembled the parting of a woman's hair.

Meanwhile Bibishana, mace in hand, held himself ready at his post with his companions in case of an enemy attack. Thereafter Sugriva addressed Rama, who was valiant by nature, saying :—

" Mount on the shoulders of Hanuman and Lakshmana on those of Angada. O Hero, vast is this ocean, the abode of whales ; those two monkeys who freely range the sky will transport you both ! "

Then the fortunate Rama and Lakshmana advanced thus and that magnanimous archer was accompanied by Sugriva. Some monkeys strode forward in the centre, some threw themselves into the waves, some sprang into the sky, others marched on the bridge, some ranged through space like birds, and the terrific tumult of the tramping of that formidable army of monkeys, drowned the roar of the ocean.

When those simian troops had passed over the sea by the grace of Nala's causeway, the king ordered them to camp on the shore which abounded in roots, fruits and water.

At the sight of that masterpiece that had materialized under the command of Raghava, despite the difficulties, the Gods, who had drawn near with the Siddhas and Charanas as also the great Rishis, anointed Rama in secret there, with water from the sea and said :—

" Mayest thou be victorious over thy foes, O Thou, who art a God amongst men ! Do thou rule over the earth and the sea eternally ! "

Thus in various auspicious words did they acclaim Rama in the midst of the homage offered to him by the brahmins.

CHAPTER 23

Rama sees diverse Portents

THE elder brother of Lakshmana beheld certain portents and as their significance was known to him, he embraced Saumitri and said :—

" O Lakshmana, occupying this region provided with fresh water, and woods abounding in fruit, let us speedily divide these innumerable forces and form ourselves into battalions ! Great is the danger I foresee, boding destruction to the world and the slaughter of the valiant bears, monkeys and titans.

"A dust storm is blowing up, the earth trembles and the peaks of the mountains shake; trees fall, clouds resembling wild beasts emit a terrible roaring and let loose dreadful showers mingled with blood; there is an awe-inspiring twilight, lurid like unto red sandalwood; from the blazing sun, a circle of fire falls; filled with terror, wild beasts and birds with harsh voices are raising mournful cries to the sun on every side. In the night, the moon, bereft of brilliance, burning with a black and red halo as it rises, resembles the destruction threatening the world. A dark stain appears on the solar disc which is diminished, sombre, without radiance and coppery. Behold, O Lakshmana, a thick dust blots out the stars and seems to foreshadow the end of the world ! Crows, eagles and vultures fall wheeling, whilst jackals inspiring the greatest terror emit sinister howls. Rocks, maces and spears, hurled by the monkeys and demons, cover the earth which has become a morass of flesh and blood.

"Without delay, attended by all the monkeys, let us, this very day, attack this city difficult of access of which Ravana is the support ! "

Thus spoke the Archer Rama, the subduer of the foe in conflict, and, bearing his bow and arrows, he set forth in the direction of Lanka.

Thereupon all the valiant monkeys with Bibishana and Sugriva at their head rose up crying destruction on their powerful foe and the boisterous demonstration of those heroic monkeys, made with the object of pleasing Rama, filled that son of the House of Raghu with delight.

CHAPTER 24

Shuka describes his Reception by the Monkeys to Ravana

THAT army of warriors in well-ordered formations looked splendid with the radiance Rama conferred on it which resembled the full moon on a starry night, and the earth, pressed under foot by the energetic tread of that multitude like unto the sea, trembled with fear.

Meanwhile those inhabitants of the woods heard a great tumult arising in Lanka and the formidable rolling of drums and clashing of gongs caused their hair to stand on end. This clamour filled the leaders of the monkeys with joy and, in their ardour, they emitted shouts that surpassed that uproar, and the cheering of the Plavamgamas, resembling the rumble of thunder in the skies, reached the ears of the titans.

Seeing Lanka dressed with many coloured banners, the son of Dasaratha bethought himself of Sita and his heart was filled with grief. He reflected—' It is there that that youthful woman, whose eyes resemble a gazelle's, is held captive by Ravana, like Rohini when she is overpowered by the red-bodied planet'[1].

Heaving long and burning sighs, that hero looked at Lakshmana and spoke words fitting to the occasion to him :—

" See, O Lakshmana, this marvellous city, built by Vishvakarma on the summit of the mountain, set aloft so that it appears to lick the skies, where innumerable palaces cluster like unto the aerial abode of Vishnu covered with white clouds ; Lanka with its blossoming groves looks magnificent like Chaitaratha which is filled with the song of birds of every kind and glowing with fruit and flowers ! See how a gentle breeze

[1] Mars.

sways the branches from which the birds dart, where bees swarm and where cuckoos abound."

Thus did Rama, the son of Dasaratha address Lakshmana and thereafter ranging his forces according to the traditional methods, he issued the following commands to that army of monkeys.

" Let the valiant and invincible Angada place his troops in the centre with the General Nila. Surrounded by the simian battalions, Rishabha should establish himself on the right wing of the army, and he who resembles an elephant in mustha, the indomitable and courageous Gandhamadana, should place himself at the head of the left flank. I shall go to the forefront of the army with Lakshmana as mine aide-de-camp and Jambavan, Sushena and Vegadarshin to spy out the land.

" Those three high-souled ones, the leaders of the bears, should protect the centre of the forces and the rearguard be under the command of the Lord of Monkeys, as the western region is dominated by the sun of brilliant rays."

The innumerable divisions being thus skilfully distributed, that army, led by the foremost of monkeys armed with boulders and huge trees, resembled the heavens with its mass of clouds ; and those monkeys advanced on Lanka that they were eager to destroy.

" It is with the peaks of mountains that we shall demolish Lanka or if need be with our bare fists ! " such was the resolve of those powerful monkeys.

At that instant the exceedingly valiant Rama said to Sugriva :—

" Our forces are properly marshalled, now let Shuka be released ! "

Under the order of that Indra of Monkeys, who was full of energy, Ravana's agent was set at liberty. Released on Rama's command and harassed by the monkeys, Shuka, in a frenzy of terror went to seek out the King of the Titans, whereupon Ravana with a sneer enquired of him :—

" What is the meaning of thy fettered wings ? Why are thy flanks torn ? Hast thou fallen into the power of those capricious monkeys ? "

Thereupon Shuka, wrought up with fear, pressed by his exceedingly powerful sovereign, made this reply :—

" Repairing to the northern shore of the sea in order to deliver thy message faithfully by employing gentle and soothing tones, those barbarous Plavamgamas, barely having caught sight of me, hurled themselves upon me and began to beat and pound me with their fists.   It was quite impossible to enter into any form of mediation with them or discuss anything ; those monkeys are ferocious and violent by nature, O Lord of the Titans ! The slayer of Viradha, Kabandha and Khara, Rama, however, who is accompanied by Sugriva, is searching for Sita.   Having thrown a bridge over the sea and traversed the salty waves, that archer, Raghava, has come hither and sets the titans at nought.

" The bears and monkeys, gathering in thousands of divisions equal to mountains or clouds, cover the earth.   There is no more possibility of an alliance between the monkeys and the titans than between a God and a demon !   Before they reach the ramparts decide quickly how thou wilt act ; either restore Sita to Rama or enter into conflict with him ! "

Thus spoke Shuka and Ravana, his eyes red with anger, looked at him as if he would consume him with his glance and said :—

" Even had I to enter into conflict with the Devas, Gandharvas and Danavas, I would not restore Sita, were the whole earth to shake !   When will my shafts fall on Raghava as the intoxicated bees fall on the blossoming trees in Spring ?   When, with mine arrows, shall I consume his body flowing with blood as flaming torches destroy an elephant.

" His forces will suffer eclipse before my powerful army as the brilliance of the stars at the rising of the sun.   That son of Dasaratha is not aware that I possess the strength of Sagara and the swiftness of Maruta, that is why he desires to meet me in combat.   Rama has not yet seen the shafts resembling venomous serpents that repose in my quiver ; that is why he wishes to enter into combat with me !   That Raghava is not yet conversant with my great might nor with the Vina in the form of my bow that I pluck with mine arrows, the bow-string producing a formidable sound, the cries of the wounded its terrible accompaniment, the darts its innumerable notes and which, when I enter the river of the enemy ranks as into a vast arena, I shall cause to resound on the field of battle !

"Neither the thousand-eyed Vasava in person nor Yama of the fiery missiles nor Vaishravana himself is able to overcome me in battle!"

CHAPTER 25

Ravana sends out Shuka and Sarana to spy on the Monkeys

RAMA, the son of Dasaratha, having traversed the ocean with his army, the boastful Ravana addressed his counsellors Shuka and Sarana, saying :—

"The entire army of monkeys has crossed the impassable ocean on a bridge constructed by Rama, an unprecedented exploit! I never deemed it possible to throw a causeway over the sea!

"Introduce yourselves into their ranks without being discovered and inform me exactly regarding the number and prowess of those monkey leaders, the counsellors who customarily attend on Sugriva and Rama and the scouts and warriors among them ; further how the dyke was constructed over the waters of the sea ; how the army advances, of their plans and of the strength and weapons used by Rama and the courageous Lakshmana."

At this command, the two Titans, Shuka and Sarana, assuming the form of monkeys, boldly entered into the simian ranks but they were unable to count the monkey host which was endowed with unimaginable energy causing the hair to stand on end and which amidst the caves and waterfalls spread over the summits of the mountains. From every side those divisions came, some having crossed, some crossing and some still to cross, and those who were arriving or had still to come, emitted loud roars and, to those rangers of the night, resembled the infinite sea.

Now the illustrious Bibishana recognized Shuka and Sarana under their disguise and arresting them denounced them to Rama, saying :—

"Here are two followers of the King of the Titans who have come to spy out conditions, O Conqueror of Hostile Citadels!"

Terrified at the sight of Rama and despairing of their lives, the two demons, with joined palms, said to him in great fear :—

" O Most Cherished Issue of the House of Raghu, we have been sent by Ravana to find out about the whole army ! "

Hearing these words, Rama, the son of Dasaratha, who delighted in the welfare of all beings, smiling, answered them, saying :—

" If you have inspected the whole army and examined their positions carefully and fulfilled the mission entrusted to you, then return in peace. But if there is anything you have not investigated and you still wish to see, then Bibishana will show it to you fully. Your arrest should not cause you any apprehension with regards your lives, you are envoys and, having laid aside your arms, have been taken captive ; you do not merit death !

" O Bibishana, set these two rangers of the night free, who have come in disguise to spy on us with the intention of creating division amongst their foes. And you, when you return to the great City of Lanka, repeat my words faithfully to the King of the Titans, saying :—

" ' That force on which thou didst rely when taking Sita away from me, employ freely with the aid of thy troops and allies. To-morrow at break of day, thou shalt see mine arrows demolish the City of Lanka with its ramparts and arches as well as the army of titans ! My dreadful ire will fall on thee and thy forces at dawn, O Ravana, as the God bearing the Thunderbolt, Vasava, discharges it on the Danavas ! ' "

Receiving this command, the two Titans, Shuka and Sarana, admiring his justice, cried out :—" Mayest thou be victorious ! " and paid obeisance to Rama.

Returning to Lanka, they said to the Lord of the Titans :—

" Bibishana took us captive with the intention of slaying us, O King, but Rama, he whose valour is immeasurable, seeing us, let us go !

" In that place four of the foremost monkey leaders are assembled who are equal to the Protector of the Worlds. Their warriors, skilled in the use of weapons, of proved prowess, are Rama the son of Dasaratha, the fortunate Lakshmana, Bibishana and the highly energetic Sugriva, whose strength is equal to the great Indra's.

"Even without the monkeys themselves taking part, they are able to penetrate into this City of Lanka with its walls and arches and tear up the foundations and transplant them elsewhere. Such is Rama's capacity and such his weapons that he could overthrow the city single-handed, his three companions standing by! Under Rama, Lakshmana and Sugriva's protection that army is completely invincible even against the Gods and Asuras combined! Now that army of powerful and aggressive monkeys, dwellers in the woods, is breathing war; it is useless to dispute with them. Make peace and restore Maithili to the son of Dasaratha!"

CHAPTER 26

Sarana tells Ravana of the principal Leaders of the Monkeys

HEARING the sincere and courageous utterance of Sarana, the King Ravana, answered :—

"Even did the Gods, Gandharvas and Danavas unitedly seek to attack me and were all beings to tremble, I would not restore Sita; O Friend, having been roughly handled by the monkeys thou dost fear them and for this deemest it opportune for me to give up Sita! What adversary is able to overcome me in war?"

Having uttered this arrogant speech, Ravana, the Lord of the Titans, in order to survey the horizon, proudly went up to his palace that was as white as snow and as high as innumerable palm trees. Accompanied by his ministers, Ravana, who was transported with anger, swept the mountains, forests and ocean with his glance and he beheld the entire region covered with Plavamgamas.

Seeing that illimitable and invincible army of monkeys, Ravana enquired of Sarana, saying :—

"Who are the leaders of these monkeys? Who are their warriors? Who their princes? Who are those marching at their head in order to demonstrate their valour? Who are

Sugriva's counsellors and his generals ? Tell me all, O Sarana !
What is the strength of these monkeys ? "

Sarana, thus interrogated by that Sovereign of the Titans
being well-informed, pointed out the leaders of those dwellers
in the woods to him.

He said : " That monkey who stands before Lanka roaring
amidst a hundred thousand leaders who escort him, whose
powerful voice shatters the whole city with its walls, gates and
arches, its rocks, forests and jungles and who is in command of
the army of the magnanimous Sugriva, Lord of all the Deer of
the Trees, is the valiant General Nila.

" He who holds his arms high and who tramples the earth under
his feet as he marches, that hero whose face is turned towards
Lanka and who, in fury, yawns convulsively, who resembles
the peak of a mountain in stature and the filaments of a lotus in
hue, who, in an excess of anger, continuously lashes out with
his tail, the swish of which is heard in the ten regions, that
warrior whom Sugriva, the King of the Monkeys, installed as
heir-apparent, is named Angada and he is challenging thee to
combat. That warrior, the equal of his sire, Bali, is beloved of
Sugriva and as devoted to Raghava's interests as Varuna is to
Shakra's. That Janaka's daughter has been seen by Hanuman,
who is as swift as the wind and the servant of Raghava, is all due
to the advice of Angada. Having formed innumerable battalions
with the foremost of monkeys, that warrior is marching against
thee at the head of his army in order to destroy thee.

" Close to Bali's son and himself surrounded by a considerable
number of troops, the valiant Nala, the builder of the bridge,
stands ready on the battlefield.

" Those soldiers clad in saffron colour, who are stretching their
limbs, roaring and gnashing their teeth, are following the one
who boasts that he will overthrow Lanka with his forces : it is
Shveta of silver hue, who is exceedingly agile and brave ; that
intelligent monkey, a warrior renowned in the Three Worlds
has come to take his orders from Sugriva and will leave at once
to place the army of monkeys in strategic positions and inspire
enthusiasm amongst his divisions.

" That one who formerly ranged the Mountain Ramya, that is
also called Samrocana on the borders of the Gaumati River and

which is covered with trees of varying fragrance, ruled over a kingdom there, is the General Kumuda and that other, who joyfully draws in his train hundreds and thousands of warriors with long hair and immense tails hanging down, who are coppery-coloured, yellow, black, white and matted, hideous to look upon, is the intrepid Monkey Kanda. He yearns to fight and boasts that he will destroy Lanka with his forces.

"The third, who resembles a tawny lion with a great mane and whose gaze is fixed attentively on the city as if he wished to consume it with his glances, who dwells mostly on the Mountains Krishna and Sahya of the Vindhya Range of pleasing aspect, is the General Rambha, O King. Three hundred kotis of the most valiant of monkeys who are formidable, impetuous, burning with ardour surround him and follow in his steps for the purpose of causing the destruction of Lanka by their blows.

"The one who is shaking his ears and yawning continuously, who, when facing death remains immoveable and who never retreats in the face of a hostile army but eyeing them askance foams with rage ; he who lashes out with his tail and gnashes his teeth, that hero of immense energy, wholly devoid of fear, O King, has his abode on the ravishing Mountain of the Salveyas and the name of that leader is Sharabha ; to him belong forty hundred thousand monkeys named Viharas[1].

" The one who is like unto a great cloud enveloping space and who, surrounded by monkey warriors, resembles Vasava amidst the Gods, whose voice like the roll of a drum, can be heard from the midst of the monkeys, who is eager to fight, dwells in Pariyatra, a mountain that is exceeded by none in height ; that general ever invincible in combat is named Panasa. That commander with fifty lakhs of lieutenants, each of whom leads his own battalion, who shines resplendent amidst the host of monkeys of terrifying bounds, who are encamped on the seashore like unto a second ocean, he who resembles Dardura[2] is called General Vinata. In his wanderings he drinks the waters of the Vena, that most excellent of rivers. His army is composed of sixty thousand Plavamgamas and that monkey, named Krathana,

---

[1] Viharas—'Those who roam about at will'.
[2] Dardura—A mountain in the south, sometimes associated with Mount Malaya.

challenges thee to combat. His lieutenants are full of daring and vigour and each commands a battalion. That monkey whose body is well nourished and who is of the colour of red ochre, who, in the pride of his strength ever holds the other monkeys in contempt, is the illustrious Gavaya. He is advancing towards thee full of fury and seventy hundred thousand warriors accompany him ; he also boasts that he will lay Lanka waste with his troops.

"Those invincible heroes may not be numbered and the flower of their captains are each at the head of his own particular force."

CHAPTER 27

Sarana continues his Deposition

"I shall describe these valiant leaders that thou art able to see, who are devoted to Raghava, full of prowess and who count their lives as nought. That one, the hairs adhering to whose enormous tail are coppery, yellow, black, white and hideously matted and that stand on end, a tail that brilliant as the sun's rays brushes the earth as he advances, is the Monkey Hara. He is followed by hundreds and thousands of monkeys brandishing trees, awaiting the moment to attack Lanka ; they are the leaders of the Monkey King and in the service of the Simian government.

"Those warriors, whom thou perceivest in such incalculable numbers, that are no more able to be counted than the sands on the limitless shores of the sea and who cover the mountains, plains and rivers, ranged like sombre clouds, black as collyrium, extremely ferocious and valiant fighters, are the bears ; observe how they are advancing to confront thee, O King. In their midst, surrounded on every side by them, like Parjanya by storm clouds, is their sovereign of dreadful glance and fearful aspect ; he inhabits Rikshavat, a very high mountain and goes to slake his thirst at the Narmada River ; he is the lord of all the bears and his name is Dhumra ! He has a brother, younger than he, who resembles him in stature but who far surpasses him in valour ; behold him, Jambavan, like unto a mountain ! Of controlled senses, he is full of reverence for his spiritual superiors and implacable in combat. His intelligence greatly assisted Shakra in the war between the Gods and the titans and he was the recipient of many boons. These giants hurl down great rocks as large as clouds from the mountain heights, which they have scaled, nor do they tremble in the face of death. Shaggy, resembling Rakshasas or Pisachas, those warriors of surpassing energy roam about in great numbers. And that commander on whom the eyes of the monkeys are fixed, who now leaps up in fury and then stands motionless, that foremost of monkeys, O King, dwells on the Sahasraksha Mountain, and the name of that exceedingly valiant leader is Rambha.

" He who, walking on all fours touches the mountain a league away with his flanks, whose chest is a league in height, who is not surpassed by any quadruped in beauty is the renowned Samnadana, the Grandsire of the Monkeys. Extremely skilful, he formerly entered into combat with Shakra on the battlefield, who was unable to defeat him, such is that superior leader.

" Another whose valour equals Indra's on the battlefield was born of a youthful Gandharva maiden and Krishnavartman. In the struggle between the Devas and Asuras he brought help to the Celestials. That illustrious one sits beneath the Jambhu tree on that mountain, the King of Peaks,[1] frequented by Kinneras, which constantly affords delight to thy brother, O Lord of the Titans. It is near there that that fortunate one, that powerful Lord of the Monkeys, General Krathana, whose prowess is not confined to words and who ever eschews defeat, sports. He is standing surrounded by thousands of monkeys ; he also undertakes to crush Lanka !

" The one who usually roams by the Ganges, sowing terror among the elephants, remembering, as he does, the old quarrel between elephants and monkeys, that leader with a voice of thunder, who dwells in the mountain caves, subduing the tuskers in the woods and uprooting the trees, that Prince of Monkeys, like unto Indra himself, passes his life happily at the head of a

[1] Kailasha.

host of monkeys by the river that issues from the Himalayas or Ushirabija, otherwise Mandara, the highest of mountains. Hundreds and thousands and millions of monkeys, proud of their strength and agility, full of prowess and fire, roaring loudly, follow that indomitable warrior, their leader, named Pramathin. It is he, resembling a great cloud propelled by the wind, whom thou hast pointed out, surrounded by a furious band of intrepid monkeys who stir up a cloud of yellow-coloured dust which the wind carries in all directions. Those formidable and powerful black-snouted Golangulas, numbering a hundred times a hundred thousand, who, having assisted in the construction of the causeway, have gathered growling round the General of the Golangulas, named Gavaksha, threaten to demolish Lanka themselves. There where, frequented by bees, the trees yield fruit in every season, on that mountain encircled by the sun, the brightness of which it equals, the radiance of which shed on beast and bird, lends them the same brilliance, whose plateaus are never forsaken by the magnanimous and great Rishis, whose trees are laden with fruit possessed of every desirable savour, where exceedingly rare honey abounds ; on that golden and ravishing mountain, the General Kesharin lives amidst those delights, O King.

" 'There are sixty thousand wonderful golden mountains in the midst of which Savarnimeru stands out, as thou amongst the titans, O King ! It is on that mountain, that brown, white and copper-coloured monkeys or those yellow as honey dwell, who possess pointed teeth and nails and who resemble lions ; they are as indomitable as tigers, the equals of Vaishvanara, with their long coiled tails like unto serpents vomiting poison or like elephants intoxicated with ichor as high as great hills, and they roar like thunder ; their eyes are grey and round and when they are on the march they create an appalling uproar ; all of them stand looking on Lanka as if they were about to destroy it. In their midst is the powerful leader who ever faces the sun ; he is eager to conquer thee ; his name is renowned in the world, it is Shatabali, O King, and he swears to destroy Lanka with his troops. Courageous, powerful, full of daring, he prides himself on his personal valour. In his devotion to Rama that monkey will not spare his life.

" Gaja, Gavaksha, Gavaya, Nala, Nila, all those monkeys are surrounded by ten kotis of fighters each, as also other leading monkeys impossible to count, so great is their number, agile inhabitants of the Vindhya Range. All, O Great King, are exceedingly powerful, their stature is equal to high hills and all are capable of levelling the earth by uprooting and razing its mountains to the ground."

CHAPTER 28

Shuka in his turn enumerates the Enemy

SARANA having described the forces of the enemy to Ravana, the Lord of the Titans, Shuka, in his turn, took up the tale, saying :—

" Dost thou observe those resembling elephants intoxicated with ichor, rising up like banian trees on the banks of the Ganges or Sala Trees on the Himalayas ?

" O King, those warriors, able to change their form at will, are irresistible, equal to the Daityas and Danavas and, in war, are endowed with the valour of the Gods. They number twenty-one million or more ; they are Sugriva's companions and Kishkindha is their accustomed abode ; those monkeys born of the Gods and Gandharvas are capable of assuming different shapes at will.

" The two who stand there, who resemble each other and have the appearance of Gods, are Mainda and Dvivida, none is their equal in combat. Sanctioned by Brahma, they have drunk the water of immortality and they boast that they will demolish Lanka by their own prowess.

" As for that monkey whom thou seest there, resembling an intoxicated elephant, who in strength and fury is able to churn up the ocean itself, it is he who came to Lanka to find Vaidehi and spy on thee, O Lord. That monkey whom thou perceivest, has returned, he is the eldest son of Kesarin and his sire is said to be Vayu ; he is Hanuman, who crossed the ocean. Able to change his shape at will, that handsome and courageous warrior is no more able to be stayed in his course than Satataga[1] himself.

---

[1] Satataga—The God of the Wind.

"While yet a child, seeing the sun rise, he desired to eat it and, springing up, followed it to a distance of three thousand leagues, reflecting :—' I shall seize hold of Aditya and my hunger will be appeased forever ! ' In this thought, intoxicated with his own strength, he leapt into the air but was unable to reach that God, who is invincible even to the Celestials, Rishis and Demons, and he fell on the mountain where that radiant orb rises. In his fall he fractured his jaw slightly on a rock and on account of the strength of his jaw he was called Hanuman !

" By associating with those monkeys I was enabled to learn his history, yet I am quite unable to describe his prowess, beauty and vigour adequately. He plumes himself on being able to destroy Lanka single-handed ; it was he who formerly set fire to the city ; how is it that thou dost not remember him ?

" Nearby is a warrior, dark of hue with eyes like lotuses, the Atiratha[1] among the Ikshvakus ; his heroism is well known in the world ; his sense of duty never wavers nor does he ever swerve from righteousness ; he knows how to loose Brahma's weapon and is conversant with the Veda ; indeed he is the most learned of Vedic scholars ; he shatters the firmament with his arrows and rends the earth; his ire is equal to Mrityu's and he resembles Indra in valour ; his consort is Sita, whom thou didst bear away from Janasthana ; he is Rama, who has come to wage war on thee, O King.

" He who stands on his right, radiant as gold refined in the crucible, with a broad chest, reddened eyes and dark curly locks, is Lakshmana, who is devoted to his brother's interests and fortune; a general and a seasoned soldier, he knows better than any how to handle every weapon. Full of ardour, invincible, victorious, brave, accustomed to success and powerful, he has ever been Rama's right hand and his very life's breath. Where it concerns Raghava he would never be the one to seek to preserve his life. He has also sworn to exterminate all the titans in battle.

" He who stands on Rama's left and who is surrounded by a group of titans, is Bibishana, whom that king of kings has installed as sovereign of Lanka ; he, filled with ire, is advancing in order to enter into conflict with thee !

[1] Atiratha—Chief warrior.

" The other whom thou seest standing in the centre like an immoveable rock, rules over the foremost of those deer of the branches ; his prowess is immeasurable ; for energy, glory, intelligence, strength and nobility, he stands out among those monkeys as Himavat amongst the mountains. He dwells with the principal monkey leaders in Kishkindha with its groves and trees, an inaccessible citadel of impenetrable approaches, excavated from the mountains. He wears a golden chain, wrought with a hundred lotuses in which Lakshmi, who symbolises prosperity, beloved of Gods and men, dwells. That chain, his consort Tara and the eternal empire of the monkeys, were conferred on Sugriva by Rama after he had slain Bali.

" O King, a hundred thousand multiplied by a hundred, is called a koti and a hundred thousand such kotis make one shanku. A hundred thousand shankus make one maha-shanku, a hundred thousand maha-shankus make one vrinda. A hundred thousand vrindas make a maha-vrinda and a hundred thousand maha-vrindas make a padma. A hundred thousand padmas make a maha-padma and a hundred thousand maha-padmas make a kharva. A hundred thousand kharvas make a samudra and a hundred thousand samudras make an ogna. A hundred thousand ognas make a maha-ogna. That Lord of the Monkeys as also Bibishana with his counsellors are surrounded by a hundred thousand shankus, plus a hundred thousand maha-vrindas, a hundred padmas, a hundred thousand maha-padmas, a hundred kharvas, a samudra and a maha-ogna. a koti of maha-ognas and a thousand samudras, and that Sugriva has come to make war on thee !

"Powerful is that army following the King of the Monkeys, who is ever strong and brave. In the presence of those forces that resemble a blazing meteor, O Great King, prepare thyself to vanquish the enemy and take measures to avoid defeat ! "

CHAPTER 29

Ravana sends out fresh Spies

BEHOLDING those foremost of monkey leaders pointed out by Shuka—the valiant Lakshmana, Rama's right arm, his own brother Bibishana standing close to Raghava, the King of all the Monkeys, Sugriva, of exceeding prowess, the heroic Angada, grandson of the Bearer of the Thunderbolt, the powerful Hanuman and the invincible Jambavan, Sushena, Kumuda, Nila and Nala, those paragons among the monkeys, Gaja, Gavaksha, Sharabha, Mainda and Dvivida—Ravana, his heart agitated, became enraged and began to inveigh against those two heroes, Shuka and Sarana, who had completed their report.

In a voice strangled with fury, he overwhelmed them with reproaches as they stood with bowed heads before him, saying :—

" In sooth it is scarcely fitting that such unpleasing words should be uttered by loyal servants to their king who has the power to mete out punishment or reward. That you should both hymn the praises of the foe belonging to an alien race who has come here to attack me, is unbecoming ! In vain have you sat at the feet of your elders, spiritual preceptors and the aged, since the essential traditions of the scriptures do not rule your lives or, if you have imbibed them, you have not remembered them ; you are over-burdened with ignorance ! Having such unintelligent servants as you are, it is a miracle that I am still able to wield the sceptre. Have you no fear of death that you dare address me thus insolently, I, whose tongue dispenses good and evil ?

"Even in contact with fire, the forest trees may remain standing but an evil-doer cannot escape the condemnation of his sovereign ! Did the remembrance of your past services not moderate mine ire, I should certainly punish you miserable wretches by death, who thus hymn the praises of mine adversaries.

"Begone! Go hence, leave my presence! Having regard for your past services I shall not put you to death. You are already

71

dead, ungrateful creatures, since you have no devotion for me ! "

Hearing these accusations, which covered them with confusion, Shuka and Sarana paid obeisance to Ravana, saying :—" Be thou victorious ! " and withdrew.

Then Dashagriva said to Mahodara who stood beside him :—" Bring me other emissaries quickly ! "

At this command, that Ranger of the Night, Mahodara, without delay summoned spies and these presenting themselves in all haste before the king, hailed him with joined palms and expressed their desire to see him victorious.

Thereupon Ravana, the Lord of the Titans, said to those agents who were full of confidence, courage and zeal and were fearless :—

" Go and find out Rama's plans, who are his ministers and who stand nearest to him in counsel and friendship, what are his hours of sleeping and waking and what he intends to do next.

"A wise monarch who discovers all that concerns his adversary through his spies, needs to exert himself only to a moderate degree to overcome his enemy on the field of battle."

" May it be so!" answered the emissaries full of joy and, placing Shardula at their head, they honoured their sovereign by circumambulating him. Having paid obeisance to that powerful Lord of the Titans, those spies set out for where Rama and Lakshmana were to be found.

Leaving in disguise they observed Rama, Lakshmana, Sugriva and Bibishana near the Mountain Suvela. Beholding that army they were seized with terror and as they stood there, the righteous Prince of the Titans, Bibishana, recognized them and arrested them but Shardula alone was held captive, Bibishana saying :—" This one is the traitor ! "

Rama however released Shardula also, who was being harassed by the monkeys, having already in his compassion given the other titans their freedom.

Beaten by those impetuous and agile monkeys, they returned to Lanka, groaning and beside themselves : and those emissaries, valiant rangers of the night, who were wont to penetrate into enemy territory, returned to Dashagriva and informed him that Rama's army was camping in the neighbourhood of the Suvela Mountain.

CHAPTER 30

Shardula gives an Account of his Mission to Ravana

THE King of Lanka's spies informed him that Rama was camping with his great army near Mount Suvela and, hearing from them of Rama's approach at the head of a vast host, he was perturbed and said to Shardula :—

" Thou appearest to be unmanned which is alien to thy nature, O Ranger of the Night ! Can it be that thou hast fallen a victim to those savage monkeys ? "

Thus questioned by that tiger among the titans, Shardula, trembling with fear, answered in a faint voice, saying :—

" O King, it is impossible to spy on those lions among the monkeys, who are full of energy and prowess and protected by Raghava nor can one interrogate them in order to find out anything ! On all sides the approaches are guarded by monkeys as big as hills.

" Scarcely had I penetrated into their ranks when I was recognized and forcibly seized and myself interrogated in every way by those monkeys, who attacked me with their knees, fists, teeth and the palms of their hands ; thereafter I was led through the entire army by those pitiless monkeys who, having paraded me everywhere, brought me into Rama's presence, exhausted and bewildered, my limbs covered with blood and wounds. They wished to murder me despite my supplications made with joined palms, when, fortunately I was saved by Rama who cried ' Stay ! ' ' Stay ! '

"'That prince who has filled the sea with boulders and crags is encamped at the gates of Lanka, well equipped with weapons, his forces arranged in the form of Garuda[1] and he is surrounded on all sides by monkeys. Having set me free, he is there full of energy advancing on Lanka ! Ere he reaches the ramparts, do one thing or the other with all speed, either return Sita to him immediately or give him battle ! ' "

[1] In spread eagle formation.

Having reflected on what he had just heard, the King of the Titans, Ravana, made this significant reply :—

" Even were the Gods, Gandharvas and Danavas to arraign themselves against me and were the whole world in peril, I would not restore Sita."

Then that exceedingly powerful one added :—

" Thou hast explored the ranks of their army, who are the warriors among the Plavamgamas ? What is the measure of their prowess ? Who are these invincible monkeys ? Whose sons and grandsons are they ? Tell me the truth, O Faithful Friend ! "

Thus interrogated, Shardula, the most skilled of envoys, began to speak thus in Ravana's presence :—

" First there is the son of Riksharajas, invincible in war, O King, and the son of Gadgada. There follows another son of Gadgada and the son of the spiritual preceptor of Shatakratu, the father of the monkey who slew so many titans. Thereafter comes the virtuous Sushena, the valiant son of Dharma, then Saumya born of Soma, O King, and the monkey Dadimukha and Sumukha, Durmukha and Vegadarshin, the equals of Mrityu, whom Swyambhu formerly begot in the form of monkeys, and further there is the great Nila himself, the son of the Bearer of the Sacrificial Offerings[1] and the son of the Wind, Hanuman. Then there is the grandson of Shakra, the youthful, invincible and courageous Angada, and Mainda and Dvivida who are both valiant and equal to the Ashvins. Five are the sons of Vivasvata who resembles Time as the Destroyer, Gaja, Gavaya, Gavaksha, Sharabha and Gandhamadana.

" There are ten kotis of monkeys full of prowess and martial ardour and I was unable to count the rest of those fortunate children of the Gods.

" That son of Dasaratha with the body of a lion, that youth, Rama, to whom none in the world can be compared for valour, slew Dushana, Khara, Trishiras and Viradha who fell under his blows, as also Kabandha, the equal of Antaka. No one is able to describe Rama's qualities by whom the titans who went to Janasthana were slain.

" There too is the virtuous Lakshmana like unto the foremost

---

[1] The God of Fire.

of elephants, Matanga, in the path of whose shafts Vasava himself could not survive ! There are also Shveta and Jyotirmukha, both born of Bhashkara and the son of Varuna, the monkey Hemaketu. The heroic son of Vishvakarma, the foremost of monkeys Nala, and the impetuous son of Vasu, Durdhara.

" Finally there is that prince of the titans, thy brother Bibishana, on whom Rama has conferred the City of Lanka as the reward for his devotion. Thus I have described the entire army of monkeys stationed on the Mount Suvela ; it is for thee to decide what remains to be done ! "

CHAPTER 31

Ravana deceives Sita about the Death of Rama

MEANWHILE the king's spies spread the tidings in Lanka that Raghava was encamped with his powerful forces on Mount Suvela.

Ravana, who knew, through his emissaries, of Rama's arrival at the head of a vast army, somewhat perturbed, said to his attendants :—

" Let all the ministers assemble here immediately ! O Titans, the time has come to take counsel together ! "

On this command, his counsellors instantly came together and he entered into conference with those loyal titans, then, having duly deliberated with them concerning the immediate measures to be taken, Durdharsha[1] dismissed them all and returned to his abode.

Taking with him the Titan Vidyujjihva, a powerful and skilled magician, he turned his steps towards the place where Maithili was to be found. Thereafter the King of the Titans said to Vidyujjihva, who was proficient in magic :—

" With thy spells, create an illusion in order to deceive Janaka's daughter ! Do thou produce a head resembling

---

[1] Durdharsha—A name given o Ravana meaning 'Dreadful, Unapproachable '.

Raghava's and a mighty bow, its arrows set, and then present thyself before me ! "

On this command, that Ranger of the Night, Vidyujjihva, answered " Be it so " and displayed his powers as a magician, whereupon Ravana, satisfied, bestowed rich attire upon him.

In his impatience to behold Sita once again, that mighty monarch of the Nairritas entered the Ashoka Grove and the younger brother of Dhanada beheld that unfortunate One who did not deserve her fate, her head bowed, plunged in grief, lying on the ground in the Ashoka Grove where she had been banished, absorbed in the thought of her lord, hideous titan women seated not far distant from her.

Then Ravana, approaching, manifested his gratification and addressed that daughter of Janaka in confident tones, saying :—

" O Beautiful One, he in whom thou didst trust at the time when thou didst repel me when I sought to console thee, that murderer of Khara, thy consort Raghava, has been slain in combat. Thy roots are completely severed and thy pride humbled by me ; in consequence of the calamity that has over-taken thee, thou art mine ! Give up thy resolution therefore, what wilt thou do with one dead ? O Beautiful One, become the chief Queen over all my consorts, thou who till now hast enjoyed so little happiness, thou who art without resources ! O Foolish One, who deemest thyself wise, hear how, like unto the destruction of Vritra, thy lord was slain !

" In order to destroy me, Raghava alighted on the shore of the sea surrounded by a vast army assembled by the King of the Monkeys. Having ranged the northern shore with his great legions, Rama struck camp when the sun set. Sending out my spies to reconnoitre, they came upon that host stationed there overcome with fatigue, fast asleep at midnight.

" Under the command of Prahasta, my great forces destroyed them during the night and Rama and Lakshmana were amongst them. The titans, wielding harpoons, maces, discus, daggers, sticks, great arrows, spears, shining Kutamudgaras, picks, lances, darts, millstones, massed weapons and a hail of missiles, made use of them again and again in order to strike down the monkeys. Thereafter the impetuous Prahasta with a steady hand severed the head of the sleeping prince with his sword.

"Bibishana, who was wandering about aimlessly, was taken captive whilst Lakshmana and the monkey warriors fled in all directions. Sugriva, the King of the Plavagas had his neck broken, O Sita ; Hanuman of the fractured jaw was slain by the titans. Jambavan, while attempting to rise from his knees perished in the mêlée like an axed tree pierced by innumerable harpoons. Mainda and Dvivida, those two great scourgers of their foes, the foremost of monkeys, groaning and breathless, their limbs bathed in blood were cut to pieces by the sword, and Panasa, crying for help, was stretched on the earth under a tree of the same name. Pierced by countless Narachas, Darimukha is lying in a pit and the exceedingly valiant Kumuda died shrieking, under a hail of missiles. Angada, assailed on all sides by titans, pierced by innumerable shafts, vomiting blood, fell on the earth and the monkeys themselves were crushed by elephants and mowed down like clouds before the wind.

"The enemy fled in terror under the blows of the titans, who followed on their heels like lions pursuing great elephants. Some flung themselves into the sea, others took refuge in the sky ; the bears with the monkeys climbed the trees whilst the titans of fierce glance brought about a great carnage amongst the Pingalas in the midst of the rocks and woods on the shores of the ocean. It was thus that thy consort perished with his forces ! Here is his head, which was gathered up, dripping with blood and besmeared with dust ! "

Thereafter that abominable Ravana, the Lord of the Titans, said to the titan women in the hearing of Sita :—

"Bring hither Vidyujjihva of cruel deeds, who himself brought back Raghava's head from the field ! "

Then Vidyujjihva, holding the head and the bow, bowed before Ravana, whereupon the King said to that Titan Vidyujjihva of the long tongue, who stood before him :—

" Let Sita speedily behold the head of Dasaratha's son so that she may see clearly the sad end of her lord. "

On this command, the titan threw the cherished head at Sita's feet and immediately went away. Ravana, however, brandishing that great and brilliant bow, cried out :—

" Here is Rama's bow famed in the Three Worlds ! This is the bow with its cord stretched belonging to Rama that Prahasta brought back from the field after he had slain that hero in the night!"

Speaking thus, he cast the bow on the ground near the head, which had been thrown down by Vidyujjihva, and thereafter he addressed that illustrious daughter of the King of Videha, saying :—

"Now submit thyself to my desire!"

CHAPTER 32

Sita's Despair

BEHOLDING that head and the marvellous bow and remembering the alliance with Sugriva of which Hanuman had spoken; seeing those eyes and the hue of the countenance resembling that of her lord and the locks at the fringe of which a jewel shone on the brow, all those signs that convinced her of her misfortune, that wretched woman began to inveigh against Kaikeyi and cry out like an osprey, exclaiming :—

"Rest content, O Kaikeyi! He, who was the delight of his House is dead and, through thee, the entire race has perished, O Sower of Discord! What had the noble Rama ever done to Kaikeyi that she should have presented him with a robe of bark and sent him to the forest?"

Speaking thus, Vaidehi began to tremble and that young ascetic fell to the ground like a plantain cut to the roots. After a time the youthful large-eyed woman, regaining her breath and consciousness, approached the head and gave herself up to lamentation, crying :—

"Alas! I am undone! O Great-armed Warrior, faithful to thine heroic vow, bereft of thee, I have fallen into the lowest depth of calamity. It is said that for a woman, the death of her husband is the greatest of misfortunes! Virtuous consort of a faithful companion, thou hast preceded me in death! I have fallen into the last extremity and am swallowed up in an ocean of grief, since thou hast been struck down, thou who else had risen to deliver me! My mother-in-law, Kaushalya, who

78

cherished thee tenderly, thou, her son Raghava, now resembles a cow that has lost its calf. Those who boast that they can foretell the future prophesied a long life for thee ; false were their words, for thou hast barely lived, O Rama, or does prudence perchance sometimes desert those who are usually prudent as thou wert, for time, the master of all beings brings all to maturity? How has death been able to steal upon thee unawares, O Thou, versed in the law of polity and the science of expediency, who wert so skilled in warding off evil ? For having clasped me in thine arms, that cruel and inhuman night of death has robbed thee of existence by force, O Lotus-eyed One. Here art thou, lying on the ground, O Long-armed Warrior, having deserted me for the earth, thy more cherished love, O Lion among Men ! O Hero, here lies thy golden bow so dear to me, which I anointed with perfumes and decorated with garlands ! Thou art now re-united in heaven with thy Sire Dasaratha, my father-in-law and all thine ancestors, O Irreproachable Prince !

" Thou dost disdain to rejoin the saintly race of Rajarishis, who through the merit of their virtuous conduct have taken their places amongst the constellations. Why dost thou not look on me, O King ? Why dost thou not speak to me, I, thy spouse, who joined my youth to thine ? Dost thou not recall the promise made to me when, taking my hand in thine, thou didst say ' I shall be thy companion ? ' O Kakutstha, take me with thee, wretched as I am!

" Why, leaving this world for the other hast thou abandoned me in mine affliction, O Thou, the wisest of Sages ? Wild beasts are tearing that beautiful body, now a corpse, which was formerly perfumed by my hands with divine essences. Having performed the Agnihotra and other sacrifices, accompanied by the bestowal of splendid gifts in charity, how is it that thou art not honoured by the performance of that same ceremony ?

Kaushalya, a prey to grief will see Lakshmana alone return of the three who went into exile On her enquiry he will inform her of the destruction of thine allies and how thou wert slain while asleep, whilst I was taken into the abode of the titans, whereupon her heart will break ; Kaushalya will not survive,

O Raghava ! Miserable creature that I am, it is on my account that the irreproachable Rama who is full of valour, having crossed the ocean has perished in the footprint of a cow. It was in an ill-judged moment that the son of Dasaratha wedded me, I, the obloquy of my race, for thus did the illustrious Rama wed death. Without doubt in a previous existence I refused a rare gift,[1] I who to-day weep for my lord, who here was dear to all.

" O Ravana, unite the wife with the husband and, without delay, let me die near Rama. Join my head with his head and my body with his body ; O Ravana, let me follow in the path of my magnanimous lord ! "

Thus in her burning grief did that large-eyed princess, born of Janaka, lament on seeing the head and bow of her lord and, as Sita was thus bewailing, a titan, who was standing guard at the gate, ran to his master with joined palms, crying :—

" Mayest thou be victorious, O Noble Lord ! " thereafter, approaching, he informed him of the arrival of Prahasta, the leader of the army, saying :—

" Prahasta, accompanied by all the ministers, has come hither to find thee ! O Mighty Monarch, thou whom the burden of royalty has rendered forbearing, accord him audience for some urgent decision must be taken ! "

Hearing these words of the titan, Dashagriva left the Ashoka Grove and went to join his counsellors. Then, having deliberated with them as to what action to pursue, he entered the council chamber and issued his commands in accordance with the knowledge he possessed of Rama's forces.

Meanwhile the instant Ravana had departed, the illusory head and bow vanished.

Then the King of the Titans, in consultation with his highly powerful ministers, decided on the measures he would adopt against Rama. All the generals devoted to his interests stood near and Ravana the Lord of the Titans resembled Death the Destroyer while he addressed them, saying :

" With the beating of drums, summon all the forces without further explanation ! "

[1] Refused a rare gift—Some Commentators interpret this as having obstructed a marriage.

" So be it ! " they answered obedient to his commands and instantly gathered the vast army together and, when they were all assembled, informed the king who was burning to fight.

CHAPTER 33

Sarama consoles Sita

SEEING Sita in distress, that dear Vaidehi whom she loved so tenderly, a female titan named Sarama approached her and, with gentle words, sought to console her, overwhelmed as she was with the grief and anguish into which that Indra among the titans had plunged her.

The affectionate Sarama, beholding Sita distraught, resembling a mare, who having rolled in the dust has just risen, reassured her and, in her deep devotion for that virtuous princess, said to her :—

" That which Ravana uttered and what thou thyself didst reply was overheard by me as I stood concealed in the solitary grove, for where thou art the cause, I have no fear of Ravana, O Lady of Large Eyes ! And I have also learnt, through my perspicacity, why that Lord of the Titans has gone hence in fear, O Maithili.

" It is not possible to take the prudent Rama by surprise during sleep nor can one slay the foremost of those conversant with the Self nor is it possible to wipe out the monkeys who fight with trees and who are under Rama's protection like the Gods under the King of the Celestials. With his long rounded arms, that broad-chested powerful archer, full of fire, clad in mail, who is essentially virtuous and renowned in the world, has, with the support of his brother Lakshmana, ever known how to defend himself and others ; he, that illustrious warrior versed in the science of politics and warfare, the exterminator of hostile battalions, of inconceivable courage, nay that fortunate Raghava, the scourge of his foes, has not perished, O Sita.

" Perverse in thought and action, that tyrant who oppresses all beings, made use of magic to deceive thee. Banish thy grief, great happiness awaits thee ! Assuredly thou art beloved of Lakshmi ; now hear some pleasant tidings, O Blessed One !

" Having crossed the ocean with his army of monkeys, Rama has come to the southern shore where he has encamped. I perceive that Kakutstha, who is accompanied by Lakshmana, has fully attained his purpose, he is secure in the midst of innumerable allies who have halted on the shores of the sea.

" Zealous titans sent out to reconnoitre by Ravana have brought him news of Raghava's crossing the ocean. Learning of this, O Large-eyed Princess, he held a council of his ministers."

While Sarama, the titan woman, was conversing thus with Sita, a terrifying clamour issuing from the full-throated titans came to her ears and a great din of gongs struck with sticks could be heard. Thereupon the gentle-speaking Sarama said to Sita :—

" Listen to that formidable clang of gongs struck with sticks which resembles thunder. Intoxicated elephants are saddled and steeds harnessed to chariots ; hosts of combatants are to be seen with darts in their hands mounted on their horses, fully equipped, rushing hither and thither in their thousands. The royal highways are choked with soldiers wonderful to behold, leaping and roaring like the waves of the sea. Glittering armour, breast-plates, shields, chariots, horses and elephants belonging to the titans full of fire and courage, surging forward, follow in the wake of their king. See how they send forth shafts of light of every hue. That multitude of titans indicates that a terrible calamity is about to descend on them causing the hair to stand on end.

" Rama, thy consort, whose eyes resemble lotus petals, like unto Vasava the Vanquisher of the Daityas, will win thee back by slaying Ravana in combat by his unimaginable prowess, whereupon, his anger appeased, he will take thee away. Thy lord with Lakshmana will fall on the titans as Vasava with Vishnu on his enemies the Daityas. I shall soon see thee in the lap of Rama who has come hither, all thy desires fulfilled and the tyrant fallen. Tears of joy will fall from thine eyes, O Janaki, when thy lord, re-united with thee, will hold thee clasped to his breast. Ere long, O Divine Sita, that mighty

Rama will loosen the plait that hangs down thy back which thou hast worn these many months.

" Beholding his radiant countenance resembling the full moon, O Queen, thou wilt renounce thy tears, born of grief, as the female snake casts off its slough.

" Having destroyed Ravana in combat, he will assuredly not delay in rejoicing thee, O Maithili, thou, his beloved, so that he may enjoy the felicity he merits. Embraced by the magnanimous Rama, thou shalt be happy, even as the open field bringing forth a harvest under plenteous showers. Do thou now seek refuge with him, O Queen, that sun, thine haven, which spreads from here to the highest of mountains, like a steed that courses rapidly in its path, he is the Lord of all beings ! "

CHAPTER 34

Sarama spies on Ravana's Plans

SITA, who had been overwhelmed with misery on hearing Ravana's words, was comforted and rendered happy by Sarama, as the parched earth by rain. Desiring to be of further service to her friend, the affectionate female titan, skilled in the knowledge of time and place, smiling, began to speak in apposite terms, saying :—

" O Dark-eyed Lady, I am able to carry a message of goodwill from thee to Rama and return secretly, for when I am journeying in the sky, that is extended without support, not even Pavana or Garuda can follow in my wake."

Thus spoke Sarama, and Sita, her voice no longer charged with grief, answered in gentle and caressing tones, saying :—

" Thou art capable of ascending to heaven itself or descending into the nethermost regions. Learn what is best for thee to do, if thine intention is to please me and thy resolve is fixed. I wish to know what Ravana is doing now. That powerful magician, the ruthless Ravana, a real Ravana[1] to his foes, has bemused me with his wickedness as wine recently imbibed ;

[1] Ravana—One who causes others to roar or cry out.

he threatens me continually and insults me unceasingly while
titans of frightful aspect surround me ; I am a prey to terror and
my spirit is uneasy. He causes me to tremble with fear in this
Ashoka Grove where I am confined. If in the assembly there
be any talk of delivering me or keeping me captive, then communicate the decision taken to me and thou wilt render me a
great service."

Thus spoke Sita and Sarama answered in gentle tones, wiping
the tears from her face the while :—

" If this be thy wish, I will go at once and when I have
discovered his design, I will return, O Maithili, O Daughter of
Janaka ! "

With these words she returned to where Ravana was to hear
what decision he had taken with his ministers.

Having listened secretly and learnt of the plans that perverse
wretch had made, she returned to the enchanting Ashoka Grove.
On entering there, she beheld the daughter of Janaka waiting
for her, like unto Lakshmi bereft of her lotus.

Thereupon Sita ardently embraced Sarama who had returned
and addressed her in friendly tones, offering her her own seat,
saying :—

" Rest at ease and tell me exactly all that the ruthless Ravana
of perverse soul has resolved to do."

Then Sarama described the whole interview of Ravana with
his ministers to the trembling Sita, saying :—

" The mother of the King of the Titans, through an aged
counsellor, who is devoted to her, insisted again and again that
they should let Vaidehi go, saying :—

" ' Let them return Maithili honourably to that King of Men !
His astonishing exploits in Janasthana should be a lesson to
thee ; what mortal could have accomplished the crossing of the
ocean, the discovery of Sita by Hanuman and the carnage of
the titans in combat ? '

" Thus did the elderly minister and his mother exhort him
but he is no more capable of giving up his treasure than a miser
his gold. He will never set thee free unless he is slain in combat,
O Maithili ; such is the resolve of that wicked wretch made with
his counsellors ; impelled by death his determination is fixed.
Fear will never cause Ravana to let thee go ; nor will he do so

till he is struck down by weapons or all the titans and he himself have succumbed. When he has destroyed Ravana with his sharp arrows in combat, Rama will take thee back to Ayodhya, O Dark-eyed Lady ! "

At that moment the cheering of the whole army blended with the roll of drums and the blare of trumpets arose and the earth shook. That tumult raised by the monkey forces was heard by the adherents of the King of the Titans, who were assembled in Lanka, and their spirits fell. Seeing no hope on account of their sovereign's offence they were plunged in despondency.

CHAPTER 35

Malyavan advises Ravana to make peace

IT was to the beating of gongs and the blare of trumpets that the long-armed Rama, the conqueror of hostile cities, approached Lanka and, on hearing this tumult, the Lord of the Titans paused a moment to reflect and then addressed his ministers.

The mighty Ravana, in a voice that resounded through the hall, began to decry Rama, his valour, the strength of his arms and his crossing of the ocean, saying :—

" I have heard all that is reported of Rama ; I know too of your courage in the field, yet, on beholding that valiant warrior, you now look on each other in silence ! "

Thereupon hearing the words of Ravana, whose maternal grandfather he was, the highly intelligent Titan Malyavan answered him thus :—

" O King, that monarch who is versed in the fourteen sciences, who follows polity, rules an empire over a long period and overcomes his adversaries, who concludes peace or wages war at a fitting time, advances his own party and attains great power. A monarch should ally himself to one stronger than himself or to an equal ; he should never underrate a foe and if he is more powerful, should make war on him. On this account I counsel an alliance with Rama and the return of Sita who is the actual cause of the dispute. Devas, Rishis, Gand-harvas, all desire him to triumph ; do not wage war but resolve to make peace with him !

" The blessed Grandsire created two paths that rest either on righteousness or unrighteousness, the path of the Gods and the path of the titans. Righteousness is the path of the magnani-mous Immortals and unrighteousness that of the demons and titans. When virtue consumed evil, it was the Krita Age and when wrong-doing swallowed up virtue, the Tishya planet was in the ascendant and thou, adopting unrighteousness, didst range the worlds destroying virtue ; it is on account of this that thy foes have waxed powerful ! The serpent of evil, nourished by thy folly, is now consuming us, while those allied with the Gods are fortified by their practice of virtue. A slave of the senses, all that thou undertakest excites the wrath of the ascetics, those personifications of the Fire-God whose power is as irresistible as the glowing flames. They purify their souls through austerities and find satisfaction in the performance of their duty. In truth, those Twice-born offer innumerable and excellent sacrifices, kindling the sacred fire in accordance with prescribed rituals ; they recite the Vedas in a loud voice and utter sacred texts while subduing the titans. Scattered in all directions, like the stormy waves during the hot season, the smoke, arising from the Agnihotra performed by those Rishis, the equals of Agni, spreads over the ten cardinal points and diminishes the titans' energy. In the various regions sanctified by their religious observances, the burning austerity of those ascetics torments the titans.

" Thou hast received the boon of invincibility from Devas, Danavas and Yakshas but these are men, bears and powerful Golangulas who, full of energy and prowess, are coming hither roaring like lions. Beholding these sinister and formidable portents of every kind, I foresee the total extermination of the titans. With a terrifying clamour, monstrous clouds, inspiring horror, rain hot blood on Lanka on every side. Those beasts drawing the chariots are shedding tears. Discoloured with dust, the four quarters no longer shine ; serpents, jackals and vultures are invading Lanka, gathering in the public squares with frightful cries ; standing before us in dream, coal black women with white teeth resembling Kali burst into loud laughter, pillaging the dwellings and chattering incoherently ; in the houses, dogs devour the sacred offerings and donkeys are born of cows, rats of mongoose ; cats mate with tigers, pigs with dogs and Kinneras with demons and men. Red-footed and white pigeons, messengers of death, by their flight foretell the extermination of the titans ; domesticated parrots, falling under the attack of other birds, call ' Chichikuchi ' ! Birds and wild beasts, their eyes fixed on the sun, cry out ! Death in the shape of a human monster, deformed, bald and tawny-coloured, visits the dwellings in turn. These and other omens equally sinister appear. Raghava of fixed prowess is, I deem, Vishnu in human form ; he is undoubtedly no mere man ; he who built a bridge over the deep is an exceedingly wonderful being ! Therefore, O Ravana, for thine own good, conclude peace with Rama who is the king of men."

Having spoken thus, Malyavan, the bravest of warriors, aware of what was passing in Ravana's mind, eyeing him, became silent.

CHAPTER 36

Ravana directs Lanka's Defences

Dashanana[1] could not brook Malyavan's salutory utterances and, scowling, a prey to anger, rolling his eyes in fury, answered him thus :—

" I have closed mine ears to the speech thou hast made, albeit with good intentions ; how canst thou hold a mere man like Rama, who is single-handed, without any support but that of the deer of the trees, cast off by his sire and exiled to the forest, to be of my stature, I, the Lord of the Titans, the terror of the Gods ? Dost thou then consider me to be destitute of power ?

" I am at a loss to determine if it be envy of my prowess or predeliction for the foe that has brought thee to address such

[1] Ten-faced One.

87

hard words to me, unless it be that thou desirest to spur me on ! In truth, what man learned in the science of the Shastras would speak thus harshly to a seasoned warrior, were it not to incite him ?

" Having borne Sita away from the forest, she who resembles Shri bereft of her lotus, why, through fear, should I return her to Raghava ? Thou shalt see him fall under my blows in the midst of the innumerable monkeys who surround him. How should Ravana, whom the Deities themselves dare not meet in single combat, experience fear in this encounter ? Rather would I be cut in twain than bend before any ! Such was I from birth, it is my nature and unalterable ! Even if Rama by some happy chance has been able to throw a bridge over the sea, what great marvel is there in that, that thou shouldst give way to terror ? It is true he has crossed the ocean with an army of monkeys but I swear to thee he will not return alive."

Beholding Ravana to be highly provoked and speaking with such fury, Malyavan, abashed, did not reply and duly invoking his success as courtesy demanded, he begged permission to retire.

Meanwhile Ravana, assisted by his ministers, having deliberated on what ought to be done, set about planning the defence of Lanka.

Thereafter he gave over the eastern gate to the Titan Prahasta and that of the south to the warriors Mahaparshwa and Mahodara. At the western gate he placed his son Indrajita, a powerful magician, with a considerable force of titans and he established Shuka and Sarana at the northern gate, saying :—

" I myself shall take up that position also ! "

Finally he commanded the Titan Virupaksha, who was full of energy and courage, to occupy the centre of the city with a large number of soldiers.

Taking every precaution for the safety of Lanka, that bull among the titans, under the sway of destiny, deemed his purpose accomplished. Having made provision for the defence of the city, he dismissed his ministers and received the acclamations of the assembly, after which he entered his sumptuous inner apartments.

CHAPTER 37

Rama makes his Plans for the Attack

MEANWHILE that King of Men, the Sovereign of the Monkeys, the Son of the Wind, Jambavan the King of the Bears, the Titan Bibishana with Bali's son Angada and Saumitri, the Ape Sharabha, also Sushena and his kinsfolk Mainda and Dvivida, Gaja, Gavaksha, Kumuda, Nala and Panasa, all having reached the enemy's territory, assembled to take counsel together.

They said :—" Yonder under our very eyes is the City of Lanka defended by Ravana, impregnable even to the Gods and Asuras together or the Uragas and Gandharvas. Let us take counsel as to what means to adopt that will ensure the success of our expedition in order to penetrate into the eternal retreat of Ravana, the King of the Titans."

At this, the younger brother of Ravana, Bibishana, uttered these words that were both just and irreproachable :—

" Anala, Panasa, Sampati and Pramati have been to Lanka from whence they have returned. Assuming the form of birds, all four entered that hostile citadel and studied the measures taken by Ravana closely. I will give a detailed report as it was given to me of the defences organized by that perverse wretch ; O Rama, hear me !

" At the eastern gate, Prahasta is stationed with his division; at the southern gate are the warriors Mahaparshwa and Mahodara ; Indrajita is at the western gate where he is in command of a considerable force armed with harpoons, swords, bows, spears and hammers. Ravana's son has thousands of warriors under his command, holding lances in their hands, furnished with weapons of every kind.

" Apprehensive, a prey to great anxiety, Ravana, versed in the sacred formulas, is himself stationed with the titans at the northern gate. As for Virupaksha, he, with a strong detachment armed with spears, clubs and bows occupies the centre of the city.

"Having seen these hosts thus distributed, my spies have set out in all haste and returned again. The elephants number some ten thousand, the cavalry twenty thousand and there are more than a million foot soldiers. Hardy and vigorous, these intrepid warriors have ever been their sovereign's favourites; each of the titan generals, when on campaign, commands a million soldiers, O Lord of Men."

Having conveyed this information concerning the city, the mighty Bibishana brought his envoys before Rama and those titans confirmed all that was known regarding Lanka. Thereafter the younger brother of Ravana, in his desire to please Raghava, addressed that Lotus-eyed One further, saying :—

" O Rama, when Ravana made war on Kuvera, seven million soldiers accompanied him. For vigour, daring, energy, extreme power of endurance and pride, they equalled their wicked king. There is no question here of my wishing to agitate thee by what I have said but a desire to rouse thine indignation, not thy fears, for in knightly valour, thou art equal to the Gods themselves. Having set out these monkey forces in battle array, thou shalt destroy Ravana with thy great army composed of four angas[1] which surround thee."

Bibishana having spoken thus, Raghava gave his orders for the attack, saying :—

" At the eastern gate, Nila, that lion among monkeys, should oppose Prahasta with his innumerable infantry and let Bali's son, Angada, at the head of a strong division, drive away Mahaparshwa and Mahodara from the southern gate ; that son of the Wind, whose valour is immeasurable, will penetrate into the city with his great forces.

" I reserve the right to slay the wicked King of the Titans, who owing to the boon he has received enjoys oppressing the Daityas and Danavas as also the magnanimous Rishis and who ranges the worlds persecuting all beings. With the aid of Saumitri I shall force an entry through the northern gate and follow in the wake of Ravana and his army. Let the mighty Indra among Monkeys, the valiant King of the Bears and the younger brother of the Lord of the Titans occupy the central position.

[1] Angas—lit. limbs, probably divisions.

" The monkeys should not assume human form in the fray for, when we are fighting in the ranks, the monkey shape should serve as a sign of recognition amongst us. Seven will attack the foe in human form, I, my brother Lakshmana, who is full of valour, my friend Bibishana and his four companions."

Having said this to Bibishana for the success of the enterprise, Rama, in the role of a wise leader, decided to stay on Mount Suvela whose ravishing slopes he had observed.

Thereafter at the head of his great army which spread over the earth, the magnanimous Rama set out for Lanka with a joyous and exultant air, resolved to destroy his enemy.

CHAPTER 38

The Ascent of Mount Suvela

HAVING resolved to stay on Mount Suvela, Rama, followed by Lakshmana, addressed Sugriva and also Bibishana the night-ranger, who was full of integrity, devotion, sagacity and experience and, in tones of great sweetness and nobility, said :—

" Let us ascend the Mount Suvela, that king of peaks and plateaus, filled with hundreds of metallic veins, in order to pass the night there. Then we shall be able to survey Lanka, the haunt of that titan, that wretch who has borne away my consort to his own destruction ! He has neither regard for justice, virtue nor the honour of his House, he, who, in consequence of his base nature, has committed this heinous deed."

Thus reflecting and censuring Ravana, Rama approached Mount Suvela with its ravishing slopes and began the ascent. Behind him came Lakshmana, proud of his great valour, alert, bearing his bow and arrows and Sugriva, who with his ministers and Bibishana scaled the mountain also. Those rangers of the hills bounded with the speed of the wind scrambling from a hundred sides at once in the steps of Raghava and did not take long to reach the summit.

From there they observed that splendid city with its marvellous gates enclosed in magnificent ramparts, as if suspended in the air ; thus did Lanka, filled with warriors, appear to those monkey leaders and, standing on those wonderful ramparts, the dark-hued titans resembled a second wall in the eyes of the foremost monkeys. Beholding them, the monkeys, in Rama's presence, burning to fight, redoubled their cries.

Meanwhile the sun, dyed with the fires of dusk, moved towards the west, and the night, illumined by the full moon, drew on. Then Rama, the leader of the monkey army, having exchanged salutations with Bibishana, established himself happily on the breast of Mount Suvela with the leaders of the monkeys.

CHAPTER 39

Description of Lanka

HAVING passed the night on Mount Suvela, the valiant monkey generals surveyed the woods and groves of Lanka and observing them to be so extensive, agreeable, pleasant, vast and wide, marvellous to behold, they were seized with admiration.

Champakas, Ashokas, Bakulas, Salas and Talas abounded ; Tamalas, Hintalas, Arjunas, Nipas, Saptaparnas in full flower, Nagas, Tilakas, Karnikaras and Patalas grew on every side. The trees with their flowering crests, round which magnificent creepers twined, gave Lanka a brilliant appearance which she owed also to the borders planted with diverse flowers and red and tender buds as also innumerable shady avenues. The blossom and fragrant fruit with which the trees were laden caused them to resemble men adorned with jewels or the ravishing Chaitaratha, the equal of the Nandana Gardens, a grove resplendently green in all seasons, filled with swarming bees and sparkling with beauty. Then the valiant monkeys able to change their shape at will penetrated into those groves frequented by waterfowl intoxicated with love and with honey bees where the branches of the trees were filled with cuckoos and resounded to the notes of the shrike and the cry of the osprey and, as they entered there, a breeze redolent with the scent of flowers blew like a soft breath.

Meanwhile some of the leaders broke away from the monkey ranks and, with the permission of their prince, approached that paved city. Terrifying the birds, deer and elephants, they shook Lanka with their roaring, excelling as they did in shouting and, in their immense ardour, they trampled down the earth so that the dust rose in clouds under their feet.

Bears, lions, buffalo, wild elephants, antelopes and birds, alarmed by the noise, spread over the ten points of the horizon.

The Trikuta Mountain had an exceedingly lofty summit that appeared to touch the skies; it was covered with blossom, sparkling like gold, a hundred leagues in extent, stainless, graceful to behold, smooth, inaccessible in height even to birds and could not be scaled even in thought, much less in reality; it was on this promontory that Lanka was built of which Ravana was the highway.

Ten leagues wide, twenty in length, with its tall gates which resembled white clouds and its ramparts of gold and silver, it was a very marvel! Palaces and temples were the splendid decoration of that city, as clouds at the end of summer are to the region of Vishnu that is found between earth and heaven.

In Lanka, a building of a thousand pillars artistically constructed, resembling the peak of Kailasha which seemed to lick the firmament, was to be seen. This was the retreat of the Indra of the Titans and the ornament of the city, guarded constantly by a hundred titans. Ravishing with its gold, the mountains served as its decoration and it was dazzling with its rich parks and many squares re-echoing to the song of birds of every kind, frequented by deer, covered with various flowers, inhabited by titans of every degree, and that opulent city of immense resources resembled the celestial regions.

Beholding that auspicious capital, the valiant elder brother of Lakshmana was seized with astonishment and Rama with his vast army contemplated that citadel filled with treasure, abundantly provisioned, garlanded with palaces, exceedingly strong, with its powerful engines of war and solid gates.

CHAPTER 40

The extraordinary Combat between Sugriva and Ravana

THEN Rama, accompanied by Sugriva and his monkey leaders, ascended the summit of Mount Suvela that had a circumference of two leagues; there he halted awhile, surveying the ten cardinal points and his gaze fell on Lanka which was ravishing with its enchanting groves that had been built by Vishvakarma on the summit of the Trikuta Mountain.

There above a gateway stood the invincible Lord of the Titans, white chanwaras being waved above him and the triumphal parasol indicating his rank. Anointed with red sandal-paste, adorned with scarlet ornaments, he was attired in raiment embroidered with gold and resembled a dark cloud. The scars of the wounds, inflicted on him by Airavata with his tusks, pitted his breast, and he was wrapped in a cloak of the colour of hare's blood so that he appeared like unto a cloud dyed with the tints of sunset.

The Indra of the Monkeys beheld him as Raghava also and, on seeing him, Sugriva, gathering up his strength, in an impulse of fury suddenly bounded from the summit of the mountain and descended at the gate. For a moment he paused, then with a fearless soul he eyed that titan whom he regarded as a mere straw and thereafter addressed him harshly, saying :—

" I am the friend of the Protector of the Worlds, Rama ; by the grace of that King of Kings thou shalt not escape me to-day."

Speaking thus he suddenly leapt upon him and, snatching off his brilliant diadem, threw it on the earth.

Seeing him about to rush upon him again, that Ranger of the Night said to him :—

" Sugriva thou wert unknown to me, now thou shalt be Hinagriva !¹ "

Speaking thus, he threw himself upon him and with his two arms flung him to the ground. Bouncing up like a ball, that monkey struck his adversary in his turn and perspiration broke

¹ Sugriva meaning ' handsome-necked ' and Hinagriva ' neckless '.

out on the limbs of both and their bodies were red with blood ; each clung to the other, paralysing his opponent's movements and they resembled the Shalmali and Kimshuka Trees.

Then followed blows and slaps with hands and arms and an indescribable struggle arose between the two powerful kings, the Lords of the Titans and Monkeys. Hard and long was the combat between these two doughty champions in the gateway, each in turn lifting the other up, crouching and changing their positions, tripping each other and throwing each other down, crushing one another, bruising each other's limbs, and, falling between the Sala Trees and the moat, they would leap up again, pausing an instant to regain their breath. Then, with arms interlaced like ropes, they remained locked together, struggling and furious, full of skill and energy, moving to and fro. Like a lion and a tiger or two young elephants, that have just grown their tusks, scrutinising each other, with arms interlaced and grappling with one another, they fell on the earth together. Thereafter, rising, they hurled themselves on each other afresh, circling round the arena again and again, like skilled and mighty wrestlers nor were they easily fatigued. Like unto great tuskers, with their enormous arms resembling the trunks, they gripped each other tightly. Circling round and round in that duel which was long and fierce, they trampled down the earth and, approaching each other, like two wild cats fighting over a piece of meat, each tried to kill his adversary. Taking up diverse postures, describing innumerable evolutions, running like an ox's urine, halting, coming and going, they executed a myriad different movements; stepping sideways, making feints, twisting to avoid a blow, turning about, darting to the attack, each hurling himself on his opponent, standing firm and erect, disengaging themselves, presenting back and flank, preparing to leap, letting go or stealing away, thus Sugriva and Ravana, to their utmost satisfaction, multiplied such feats in which they excelled.

Meanwhile the titan had recourse to magic and when the King of the Monkeys perceived it, he flew into the sky triumphant, shaking off all fatigue whilst Ravana, overcome with exhaustion, breathing heavily, baffled by the King of the Monkeys, stood confounded.

Thus the Lord of the Monkeys, acquiring fame as a warrior, having wearied Ravana in combat, ascended into the infinite blue with the swiftness of thought, and that offspring of the Sun, having accomplished this feat, delighted, rejoined the army, honoured by the monkey leaders, thereby increasing the joy of the foremost of the Raghus.

CHAPTER 41

Rama sends Angada to Ravana

SEEING him bearing the marks of valour, the elder brother of Lakshmana, Rama, embracing him, said to Sugriva :—

" Without consulting me thou hast acted thus imprudently ; such rashness is not seemly in a king. By thy recklessness thou hast caused me great anxiety as also the army and Bibishana! O Warrior, thou art enamoured of deeds of daring ! Do not act thus in the future, O Vanquisher of thy Foes ! If thou hadst come by some misfortune, what would Sita or Bharata or my younger brothers, Lakshmana or Shatrughna have availed me ?

" O Valiant Scourge of Thy Foes, if thou hadst not returned, though I am conversant with thy valour, this was my fixed resolve ; having destroyed Ravana in fight with his sons, forces and chariots, I should have installed Bibishana as King of Lanka, suffered Bharata to ascend the throne and renounced my life, O Great Prince."

At these words of Rama, Sugriva answered, saying :—

" Seeing the one who had borne away thy consort, O Brave Descendant of Raghu, conscious of mine own strength, how could I have acted otherwise ? "

Thus spoke that warrior, and Raghava, having commended him, addressed Lakshmana who was endowed with auspicious marks, saying :—

" Beside these cool waters and trees laden with fruit, let us divide and marshal our forces, O Lakshmana ! I foresee a terrible calamity boding universal destruction and death to the intrepid bears, monkeys and titans. Harsh winds blow, the earth trembles and the mountains quake ; trees crash to the earth, sinister clouds resembling birds of prey roar in terrifying wise and let fall rain mixed with blood ; the dusk, red as sandal, is full of horror and from the sun, a flaming circle falls. Wild beasts and birds emit frantic cries and are ill at ease ; their voices and fierce aspect deprive them of their beauty. In the night, the moon, shorn of its radiance, surrounded by black and fiery rays, burns red, as at the time of the destruction of the world. A thin, dark, sinister rim of coppery hue is seen round the sun and on its surface a black mark appears nor does that orb approach any other planets as is usual, all of which prefigures the final dissolution of the world.

" Behold, O Lakshmana, how crows, eagles and vultures are flying low, circulating rapidly, emitting piercing and lugubrious cries ! The earth changed to mud and gore will be covered with rocks, javelins and darts hurled by the monkeys and titans ! This very day, surrounded by the monkeys on all sides, let us make an attack on that citadel defended by Ravana."

Having spoken thus to Lakshmana, his younger brother, that mighty warrior rapidly descended from the summit of the mountain and coming to the bottom of that hill, the virtuous Raghava inspected his army which was invincible to the foe. Then, the time having come, Rama, who was conversant with the fitting moment to act, gave the signal to advance and, at an auspicious moment, bow in hand, turned towards Lanka.

Bibishana, Sugriva, Hanuman, Nala, Jambavan the King of the Bears, as also Nila and Lakshmana followed, and behind them the mighty host of bears and monkeys, covering a vast stretch of earth, threw themselves in Raghava's wake. Hundreds of rocks and enormous trees served as weapons to those monkeys, verily the vanquishers of their foes, who resembled elephants.

Soon the two brothers, Rama and Lakshmana, those subduers of the foe, reached the city of Ravana, garlanded with banners, enchanting with the pleasure gardens which adorned it, inaccessible with its many gateways, high walls and arches. Then those denizens of the forests, encouraged by the sound of Rama's voice and obedient to his commands, halted before Lanka, which was impregnable, even to the Gods.

Thereafter Rama, accompanied by his younger brother, bow

in hand, surveyed the northern gate, which was as high as the peak of a mountain and took up his position there. That valiant son of Dasaratha, followed by Lakshmana, advanced under the walls of Lanka, whose highway was Ravana. None but Rama could have approached and examined the northern gate where Ravana stood, which was formidable and guarded by him as the ocean by Varuna and which was defended on all sides by titans, as the Danavas, who sow terror in the hearts of the weak, guard Patala. And Rama observed innumerable weapons and armour of every kind heaped there for the combatants.

Meanwhile Nila took up his position with Mainda and Dvivida at the eastern gate at the head of a host of monkeys.

Angada with his vast forces, assisted by Rishabha, Gavaksha, Gaja and Gavaya, occupied the southern gate. Hanuman, that virtuous monkey, was stationed at the western gate with Prajangha, Tarasa and other warriors grouped round him, whilst Sugriva, personally occupied an observation post in the centre. At the head of all those leading monkeys, the equals of Suparna and Pavana, thirty-six kotis of renowned warriors were grouped round Sugriva.

Meanwhile, under Rama's command, Lakshmana, assisted by Bibishana, distributed his innumerable divisions at each gate. Behind Rama, Sushena and Jambavan, those lions among the monkeys, possessing the teeth of tigers, furnished with trees and rocks, waited delightedly for the signal to fight. Lashing their tails feverishly, they used their jaws and nails as weapons ; trembling in every limb, their faces were set grimly and they were extremely strong, some having the strength of ten elephants, some ten times more powerful, some equalling a thousand elephants in might and there were some who had the vigour of a million elephants and even more, for the might of those monkey leaders was immeasurable ! Marvellous and astonishing was the gathering of those monkey forces resembling a cloud of locusts ! The earth and the air were filled with monkeys rushing towards Lanka or already stationed beneath its walls. By hundreds and hundreds of thousands, bears and monkeys poured towards the gates of Lanka that others assailed on every side. The hills disappeared completely under that host of Plavamgamas, numbering millions, who were ranging round the city and those heroic monkeys, with tree trunks in their hands, surrounded the whole of Lanka that even the winds were unable to penetrate.

Then the titans, who in their valour rivalled Shakra, seeing themselves besieged by those monkeys like massed clouds, were struck with a sudden terror, and, as they broke rank, a tremendous clamour arose from that host of combatants which resembled the roar of the ocean beating against the shore ! At this tumult, the whole of Lanka with its ramparts, arches, hills, woods and forests, began to tremble.

Under the direction of Rama, Lakshmana and Sugriva, that army became even more invincible than the hosts of the Gods and titans. Raghava, however, having ranged his forces in order to wipe out the demons, took counsel with his ministers and pondered deeply again and again. Desiring to act without delay and with circumspection, he, in his consummate experience with Bibishana's approbation, calling to mind the duty of kings[1], summoned Bali's son, Angada and said to him :—

" Go My Friend on my behalf and, passing through the City of Lanka without fear, say to Dashagriva :—' Thou hast sacrificed thy renown, destroyed thy kingdom and, in thine haste to die, hast lost thy wits ! Rishis, Devas, Gandharvas, Apsaras, Nagas, Yakshas and kings, O Ranger of the Night, have been oppressed by thee in thy reckless pride. O Titan, from now on, that arrogance, begot of the boon thou didst receive from Swyambhu, shall be subdued ! I shall inflict a fitting penalty for thy ruthless abduction of my consort ; it is with the Rod of Chastisement, that I have stationed myself at Lanka's gates.[2] Having displayed thy martial valour, slain by me thou shalt attain the region of the Gods ! Do thou demonstrate the same courage that thou didst employ in bearing Sita away from me, having first deceived me by magic arts. O Most Vile of Titans, I shall rid the earth of titans with my pointed shafts, if thou dost not make an appeal to my clemency by returning Maithili to me.

[1] Duty of Kings—If a king is able to accomplish his purpose by conciliation, he must not use force.
[2] That is, in the form of Dandadhara, a name of Death as the Bearer of the Rod of Retribution.

" ' That virtuous prince of the titans, the illustrious Bibishana, who is here, will undoubtedly reign in Lanka without opposition. Nay, it is not fitting that, even for an instant, the crown should belong to one as perfidious as thou art, a wicked creature who surroundest thyself with fools and who is not conversant with the Self!

" ' Enter into combat with me, O Titan, exert thy strength and valour in the fight, mine arrows will chasten thee and thou wilt be subdued! Even shouldst thou range the Three Worlds in the form of a bird, O Night-ranger, my glance would follow thee and thou wouldst not return alive. I give thee this salutary counsel—prepare for thine obsequies, let Lanka regain her splendour, thy life is in my hands! ' "

Furnished with Rama's instructions, the son of Tara ascended into the air, like unto the God bearing away a sacrificial offering, and in an instant arrived at Ravana's palace where he beheld him seated at ease amidst his ministers.

That youthful Prince of the Monkeys, Angada of golden bracelets, like a flaming torch descended close to the king and having made himself known, addressed the whole of Rama's exceedingly significant speech, without adding or subtracting anything, to him in the presence of his court, saying :—

" I am the messenger of the King of Koshala, Rama of imperishable exploits. I am the son of Bali, Angada is my name ; perchance thou hast heard of me ? The descendant of Raghu, Rama, the increaser of Kaushalya's delight, speaks thus to thee :—

" ' Come forth and enter into combat with me! Manifest thy valour! I shall destroy thee, thy counsellors, thy sons, relatives and allies. Thou being dead, the Three Worlds will cease to be troubled, O Thou whose enemies are the Devas, Danavas, Yakshas, Gandharvas, Uragas and Rakshasas ; thou thorn in the side of the ascetics! Bibishana will become king when thou art slain by me, if thou dost not return Vaidehi, having paid her every homage, and cast thyself at my feet! ' "

Hearing these harsh words from that lion among the monkeys, the Lord of the Titans, infuriated, issued the following command repeatedly to his attendants, saying :—" Seize him and put him to death! "

On this order being given by Ravana, Angada, who in his splendour resembled a blazing torch, was seized by four terrible titans and the son of Tara suffered himself to be made captive, without offering any resistance, for that valiant warrior desired to display his prowess to the host of: Yatudhanas. Thereafter, seizing three of the titans, like unto serpents in his arms, he leapt on to the palace that resembled a mountain. Shaken by his impetuous bound the three titans fell to the ground under the eyes of their king. Then the powerful son of Bali scaled the palace up to its roof, which equalled the summit of a mountain in height, and the impact of his bounds caused it to crumble before Dashagriva's gaze as a peak in the Himalayas is shattered by lightning.

Having destroyed the roof of the palace, Angada proclaimed his name and with a triumphant roar rose into the air. To the exceeding terror of the titans and the great delight of the apes, he alighted in the midst of the monkeys beside Rama.

Thereupon Ravana, transported with anger, giving himself up for lost began to sigh heavily. Meanwhile Rama, who was surrounded by Plavamgamas emitting joyful cries, eager to destroy his adversary, advanced to meet him in combat.

Now Sushena was at the head of innumerable monkeys who were able to change their form at will and, under the order of Sugriva, he patrolled the gates and that invincible warrior resembled the moon moving amidst the stars.

Seeing the hundreds of divisions encamped under the walls of Lanka and marshalled on the shores of the sea, the titans were amazed whilst some were terror-struck and others, overjoyed at the prospect of fighting, leapt in exultation. Beholding those hosts occupying the whole space between the walls and the moat, however, and seeing the monkeys like unto a second rampart, those rangers of the night, cast down, cried out :— " Woe ! Alas ! " in their terror.

In the midst of that appalling tumult, the soldiers of Ravana seized hold of their powerful weapons and advanced like the winds that blow at the dissolution of the worlds.

CHAPTER 42

The Titans make a Sortie

THEN those titans approached the abode of Ravana and informed him that Rama and the monkeys had laid siege to the city.

This news enraged that Ranger of the Night, who, repeating his former commands went up into the palace. From there he surveyed Lanka with its hills, woods and groves, which was besieged on all sides by countless divisions of monkeys, eager to fight. Beholding the earth all brown with innumerable Plavagas, in great perplexity he reflected : " How can they be exterminated ? "

Having pondered long, Ravana regained his confidence and, opening his great eyes wide, he gazed on Raghava and the simian battalions.

Meanwhile Rama, at the head of his army was rapidly advancing on Lanka which was guarded on all sides and thronged with titans. Thereafter the son of Dasaratha, seeing that city furnished with flags and banners, remembered Sita and was filled with anguish. He reflected " That daughter of Janaka whose eyes resemble a young doe's, will be a prey to anxiety on my account ! Consumed with grief and emaciated, she is pining away, the bare ground her bed ! "

Reflecting on the sufferings of Vaidehi, the virtuous Raghava speedily issued a command to the monkeys to prepare for the enemy's destruction.

Hearing the order of Raghava of imperishable exploits, the Plavagas, urging each other on, filled the air with their roaring.

" Let us demolish Lanka with rocks and stones or with our fists alone " was the resolve of the monkey leaders and, under the eyes of the King of the Titans, in order to accomplish Rama's cherished desire, those troops divided themselves into columns and began to scale the heights of Lanka. Hurling themselves on that city with rocks and trees, those golden-hued Plavamgamas of coppery countenance, willing to lay down their lives in

Rama's service, destroyed innumerable battlements, ramparts and arches with blows from trees, rocks and fists and filled the moats and trenches of clear water with sand, stones, grass and logs.

The commanders led their divisions by thousands and hundreds of millions of thousands to attack Lanka and the Plavamgamas tore up the golden arches, broke down the gates, that equalled the peak of Kailasha in height and from the sides and the centre, hurled themselves on the city like great elephants with cries of " Victory to the mighty Rama and the valiant Lakshmana ! " " Victory to Sugriva protected by Raghava ! " Shouting thus, the monkeys, who were able to change their form at will, roaring, rushed to attack the city.

Virabahu, Subahu, Nala and Panasa, having demolished some of the outposts, reached the foot of the walls and assigned each column to a post of attack. The eastern gate was besieged by the valiant Kumuda surrounded by ten kotis of triumphant monkeys ; his lieutenants were Prasabha and the long-armed Panasa, who were at the head of those forces.

At the southern gate was the warrior Shatabali, a monkey of proved valour, who was stationed with twenty kotis to obstruct the exit. Sushena, the father of Tara, full of courage and strength, with a hundred thousand monkeys surrounded the western gate. The northern gate was blockaded by the mighty Rama assisted by Saumitri and Sugriva, the King of the Monkeys.

The colossal Golangula, Gavaksha, of grim aspect and immense energy, supported one of Rama's flanks with a koti of warriors and the valiant Dhumra, scourger of his foes, supported the other flank with a koti of bears of redoubtable fury.

The intrepid Bibishana, attended by his loyal ministers, followed his ally, the heroic Rama, everywhere, whilst Gaja, Gavaksha, Gavaya, Sharabha and Gandhamadana patrolled every side in defence of the simian army.

Meanwhile, his heart filled with rage, the King of the Titans ordered his troops to make a rapid sortie. At this command falling from Ravana's lips, a tremendous clamour arose among the rangers of the night and the sound of kettledrums, their discs white as the moon, on which the titans beat with sticks of gold, broke out on every side, while hundreds and thousands of trumpets blared forth, blown by the titans with their cheeks extended to the full. With their dark limbs adorned with ornaments and their conches, those rangers of the night resembled clouds bordered with lightning or rows of cranes; and their battalions advanced gaily under Ravana's imperious commands as, at the time of Pralaya, the tumultuous sea overflows.

At that moment from every side, a clamour arose from the army of the monkeys which filled Malaya with its plains, valleys and chasms, and the sound of the trumpets and drums and the leonine roars of those warriors re-echoed over the earth, sky and sea, as also the trumpeting of elephants, the neighing of horses, the clatter of chariot wheels and the thunder of the titans marching.

Thereafter a terrible struggle ensued between the monkeys and the titans as, in former times between Gods and Asuras. With their flaming maces, their spears, harpoons and axes, the titans, demonstrating their native prowess, struck the army of the monkeys and from their side, those gigantic apes attacked their adversaries ferociously with blows from trees, rocks, teeth and nails.

" Victory to King Sugriva ! " yelled the monkeys, " May our Sovereign prevail ! " shouted the titans and each proclaimed his name, while other demons, standing on the walls, hacked at the monkeys below with hooks and harpoons and they, infuriated, leapt into the air and dragged down those soldiers stationed on the walls by seizing them with their arms, and that conflict between demons and monkeys was appalling and the earth was covered with mud and flesh in that astonishing fight.

CHAPTER 43

The Conflict between the Monkeys and Titans

THOSE high-souled monkey troops fought with terrible ferocity whilst the titans wakened the ten regions as, mounted on steeds with golden trappings or elephants bright as fire or in cars flashing like the sun, they issued forth clad in marvellous suits of mail, eager to triumph in Ravana's name.

On their side, the mighty army of monkeys, burning for victory, hurled themselves on those demons of formidable exploits and extraordinary duels arose between titans and monkeys who rushed upon each other.

As Tryambaka fought against Andhaka, so did the son of Bali, Angada, fight with Indrajita, who was endowed with immense energy. Prajangha was attacked by the ever indomitable Sampati and the Monkey Hanuman measured his strength with Jambumali. A prey to violent anger, Bibishana, the younger brother of Ravana, entered into a furious combat with the exceedingly impetuous Shatrughna. The valiant Gaja fought with the Titan Tapana and the powerful Nila with Nikumbha. That Indra of Monkeys, Sugriva, attacked Praghasa with violence and the fortunate Lakshmana engaged in combat with Virupaksha. The unapproachable Agniketu with the Titan Rashmiketu, Mitraghna and Yajnakopa unitedly entered into combat with Rama, Vajramushti fought against Mainda and Ashanipratha against Dvivida, those two foremost of monkeys with the greatest of titans. The valiant son of Dharma, Sushena, that great monkey of illustrious name, grappled with Vidyunmalin and, from every side, other monkeys heroically engaged in countless duels with other titans. Then an appalling battle, causing the hair to stand on end, took place between titans and monkeys who were full of prowess and eager to triumph.

From the bodies of those monkeys and rangers of the night, torrents flowed, their hair being the grass, their blood the water bearing away heaps of corpses.

As Shatakratu with his thunderbolt, so Indrajita, with his mace, in fury, struck at Angada but that intrepid destroyer of enemy hosts shattered his chariot, the framework of which being encrusted with gold, and slew his horses and driver. Sampati, wounded by Parjangha with three arrows, struck him over the head with an Ashvakarna Tree; Jambumali, standing in his chariot, full of strength and fury tore open Hanuman's breast in the fight with the force of his driving, but he, who was born of the Wind-god, approaching that car, soon overthrew it with the palm of his hand. The redoubtable Pratapana, yelling, rushed on Nala, who with his limbs pierced by the pointed shafts of that skilful titan, suddenly scratched out his eyes.

As Praghasa appeared to be consuming the hosts of the King of the Monkeys, Sugriva hastily struck him with a Saptaparna Tree, while Lakshmana, overwhelmed by a hail of missiles by Virupaksha, that titan of ferocious aspect, struck him down with a single blow. Thereafter the indomitable Agniketu, the Titans Rashmiketu, Mitraghna and Yajnakopa sought to consume Rama with their arrows, whereupon he, in fury, with four formidable shafts, resembling tongues of fire, severed the heads of all four in the struggle. Vajramushti, struck by a blow from Mainda's fist in the fight, was overthrown with his chariot, driver and horses, which resembled an aerial car belonging to the Gods ; Nikumbha battling against Nila, who was like unto a piece of collyrium, pierced him with his whetted shafts as the sun with its rays pierces a cloud ; and, again and again that deft-handed ranger of the night Nikumbha, with a hundred arrows wounded Nila in the fray whereupon that monkey began to laugh and seizing the wheel of his adversary's chariot, he who resembled Vishnu on the battlefield, severed the head of that titan and that of his charioteer.

Dvivida, whose impact was like unto a flash of lightning, struck Samaprabha with a great rock at which the titans stared in amazement and that foremost of monkeys, Dvivida, who fought with blows of trees, was pierced in his turn with arrows resembling lightning and his limbs being lacerated by those shafts, that monkey grew enraged and with a single blow from a Sala Tree struck down the titan, his chariot and his horses.

Thereafter Vidyunmalin repeatedly emitting loud cries, standing in his car, wounded Sushena with gold encrusted arrows and seeing him, that foremost of monkeys suddenly overthrew the chariot with a great rock. Vidyunmalin however, that agile night ranger, sprang down from his car and, mace in hand, stood ready on the field whereupon that lion among monkeys, infuriated, seizing a great rock, rushed at the titan but as he precipitated himself upon him, Vidyunmalin with a deft stroke, wounded him in the belly with his mace. Then the excellent Plavaga, receiving that terrible and unexpected blow dealt by his opponent, immediately turned and, in a desperate encounter, hurled a rock upon him. Struck by that missile, Vidyunmalin, that prowler of the night, his chest crushed, fell lifeless on the earth. Thus, under the blows of the simian warriors, the heroic titans perished in a series of hand to hand encounters as the Daityas under the blows of the inhabitants of the Celestial Region. Bhallas and other weapons, maces, lances, darts, shattered chariots, war-horses that had been slain, as also elephants from whose temples ichor exuded and the bodies of monkeys and titans, with wheels, axles, yokes and shafts strewed the earth; the carnage was fearful, a veritable jackal's feast. The headless trunks of monkeys and titans lay in heaps everywhere in the midst of that appalling conflict which resembled the war between Gods and Asuras.

In that stubborn engagement, decimated by the foremost of monkeys, the rangers of the night as the day ended, maddened by the smell of blood, in desperation made preparations for the morrow, and those titans, their limbs covered with blood, desired nothing so greatly as that night should fall.

CHAPTER 44

Angada's Exploit

DURING the combat between monkeys and titans, the sun sank below the horizon, giving place to a night of carnage. In their mutual hostility, monkeys and titans, burning for victory, continued to fight in the gathering gloom.

" Art thou a titan ? " asked the monkeys—" Art thou a monkey ? " questioned the titans and struck at each other in the darkness. " Strike ! " " Kill ! " " Come hither ! " " Why fleest thou ? " could be heard in that appalling struggle.

Clad in mail, the titans, their dark hue intensified by the impenetrable gloom, resembled hills covered with woods abounding in phosphorescent herbs and, transported with anger, they bounded forward in order to fall on the Plavamgamas and devour them, but these hurled themselves on the horses with golden plumes and the banners, like unto tongues of fire, and with indescribable fury tore them down with their sharp claws. Thus did those mighty monkey warriors sow confusion amongst the titans and they clawed the elephants and those mounted upon them and the chariots from which the banners streamed, breaking them to pieces with their teeth.

Full of fury, Lakshmana and Rama, with their arrows resembling venomous snakes pierced the foremost of the titans, both those who were visible and those who were invisible, and the dust rising from the hooves of the horses and the wheels of the chariots filled the ears and eyes of the combatants, whilst rivers of blood flowed in dreadful torrents in that ghastly tumult which caused the hair to stand on end.

Meanwhile the sound of gongs and drums, marvellous to hear, joined to the blare of conches and the rattle of wheels, and a terrible clamour arose of horses neighing mingling with the cries of the wounded. The corpses of great monkeys, spears, maces and the bodies of the titans, who were able to change their form at will, lay in heaps as high as a mountain on the battlefield. And those weapons appeared to be offered up as a profusion of flowers by the earth, which was entirely hidden and rendered impassable by rivers of blood. That fatal night was as calamitous to the monkeys and titans as the night of dissolution wherein no being survives.

Meanwhile the titans, aided by that impenetrable darkness, with great ferocity showered a hail of weapons on Rama and, yelling, advanced upon him in fury like the ocean at the time of the destruction of all creatures. And Rama, in the twinkling of an eye, with six shafts resembling tongues of flame struck down six titans—the indomitable Yajnashatru, Mahaparshwa, Mahodara, Vajradamshtra of colossal stature and the two emissaries, Shuka and Sarana. With his innumerable shafts, Rama thereafter pierced them all in their vital parts, so that under that shower of arrows they fled from the field, barely escaping with their lives. In an instant, that warrior of the great car lit up the cardinal points with his formidable missiles resembling tongues of fire so that every quarter became luminous. All those titans, who dared to challenge Rama, perished like moths in a flame, and those arrows, whose points were of fine gold, flying everywhere, illumined the night as do the fireflies in autumn. The cries of the titans and the roll of drums increased the horrors of that night beyond imagining and, in that terrible uproar which re-echoed on every side, it seemed as if the Mount Trikuta was emitting confused murmurs from its innumerable caves.

The gigantic Golangulas, black as night, crushed the rangers of the night in their arms in order to devour them and Angada destroyed his foes with savagery in the struggle.

Then Indrajita, after that monkey had slain his steeds and charioteer, overcome with fatigue, made himself invisible and vanished.

For this feat, Bali's son, worthy of being honoured, was lauded by the Gods and Rishis as also by the brothers, Rama and Lakshmana. All beings aware of the prowess of the mighty Indrajita in war, witnessing his discomfiture and, beholding that high-souled one, were elated and, in the height of joy, the monkeys with Sugriva and Bibishana, seeing the enemy's defeat, cried out " Excellent ! Excellent ! "

Meanwhile Indrajita, who had been overcome in the duel with Bali's son of redoubtable deeds, was seized with violent wrath Rendering himself invisible by virtue of the boon he had received from Brahma, that wicked wretch, who was exhausted by the fight, transported with anger, loosed some sharp arrows bright as lightning on Rama and Lakshmana. On the field of battle, in his rage, he pierced the limbs of those two Raghavas with formidable shafts resembling serpents. Enveloped by illusion, he sought to confuse them in the struggle and, invisible to all beings through his magic arts, that ranger of the night bound those two brothers Rama and Lakshmana with a network of arrows. Then the monkeys beheld the two warriors, those lions among men, enmeshed by the serpentine darts of that furious titan. Not being able to overcome those two princes in his manifest form, the son of the King of the Titans, in his perversity, had recourse to magic in order to make them captive.

CHAPTER 45

Rama and Lakshmana are struck down by Indrajita

ANXIOUS to ascertain what had become of Indrajita, Rama, that illustrious and mighty prince sent out ten monkey leaders in his pursuit ; the two sons of Sushena, the monkey, General Nila, Angada the son of Bali, the valiant Sharabha, Dvivida, Hanuman, the exceedingly courageous Sanuprastha, Rishabha and Rishabaskandha.

Those monkeys flung themselves joyfully into the air brandishing huge trunks of trees in order to explore the ten regions, but Ravani[1], by means of his arrows, loosed with force from the most excellent of bows, arrested their impetuous flight and those monkeys of terrific bounds, who were cruelly pierced by those shafts, were unable to discern Indrajita in the darkness, as the sun is obscured when veiled in cloud. With those darts, that lacerated the flesh, the titan transfixed Rama and Lakshmana and remained master of the field and there was no part of Rama or Lakshmana's body that was not pierced by those serpentine shafts so that streams of blood flowed from their gaping wounds, and they appeared like two Kimshuka Trees in flower.

At that instant, his eyes inflamed, Ravana's son, who resembled a mass of collyrium mixed with oil, though still invisible, said to those two brothers :—" When I, making myself invisible, enter into combat, even the Chief of the Gods, Shakra himself, is not able to discern or approach me, how much less you two! O Descendants of Raghu, having imprisoned you in this network of plumed darts, I, yielding myself up to the violence of my wrath, am about to dispatch you to the region of Yama ! "

Thus addressing those virtuous brothers, Rama and Lakshmana, he pierced them afresh with his pointed arrows shouting exultantly.

Resembling a heap of antimony, the swarthy Indrajita, stretching his immense bow, let fly an even thicker shower of

---

[1] Ravani—Ravana's son, Indrajita.

formidable arrows in the fight. That warrior, who knew how to make his darts pierce Rama and Lakshmana's vital parts, set up a continual shouting and the two princes in the forefront of battle, imprisoned in the net of arrows and darts, in the twinkling of an eye, became incapable of distinguishing anything. Paralysed, pierced in their vital parts, exhausted, those two mighty and courageous archers fell to the earth, they who were her lords! Lying on that heroes' bed, those two warriors, covered with blood, their limbs bristling with arrows, swooned away in their extremity. And there was not a hair's breadth on their bodies from the tips of their fingers to the end of their feet that was not lacerated, pricked and pierced by those irresistible darts and from both those warriors who had been struck down by that ferocious titan, able to change his shape at will, the hot blood gushed forth as water from a spring. And Rama fell first, his vital parts pierced by the shafts of the wrathful Indrajita, who had formerly vanquished Shakra, and Ravana's son riddled Raghava's body with smooth and polished darts as thick as dust clouds. Naracas, Demi-naracas, Bhallas, Anjalis, Vatsadantas, Sinhadantas,[1] and those shafts like unto razors fell on that warrior, who lay on the earth like a hero, allowing his golden bow, which was severed, to sink from his grasp.

Beholding Rama, that lion among men, fall under a hail of arrows, Lakshmana gave up all hope of living and he was overcome by grief on beholding the lotus-eyed Rama, his refuge, who ever delighted in battle, lying on the earth.

The monkeys too, witnessing this, suffered extreme distress and, their eyes full of tears, overcome with despair, emitted mournful cries; and while those two warriors lay unconscious on that heroes' bed, the monkeys surrounded them and, assembling there, with the son of the Wind at their head, remained inconsolable and a prey to despair.

[1] See Glossary of weapons.

CHAPTER 46

The despair of Sugriva and his Army. Bibishana
reassures him

MEANWHILE those inhabitants of the woods, surveying the earth
and the sky, beheld the brothers, Rama and Lakshmana, covered
with arrows and the titan resting, like unto Indra having loosed
the rains. Accompanied by Sugriva, Bibishana, lamenting,
came to that place in haste, and Nila, Dvivida, Mainda, Sushena,
Kumuda, Angada and Hanuman approached, weeping for the
sons of Raghu.

Breathing but faintly, bathed in blood, riddled with innumerable darts, motionless, they lay stretched on a bed of
arrows sighing like serpents, washed in blood, resembling two
golden standards, and those warriors, lying on a hero's couch,
were surrounded by monkey leaders whose eyes were suffused
with tears.

Beholding the two Raghavas pierced with darts, a profound
emotion stirred those monkeys, who were accompanied by
Bibishana, and they surveyed the four quarters without being
able to discover Ravani, who had veiled himself in his magic
during the fight. But while he was hidden by his occult
power, Bibishana, also having recourse to magic arts, looking
round, beheld his nephew of incomparable exploits, who was
invincible in battle, standing nearby. Although that warrior,
who had no peer in the field, had made himself invisible by
virtue of the boon he had received, he was recognized by
Bibishana, who was full of energy, glory and prowess.

Indrajita, however, contemplating his own feat, gazed on
those two warriors stretched on the earth and, in an excess of joy,
wishing to share it with all the titans, said :—

" Those two mighty brothers, Rama and Lakshmana, the
slayers of Khara and Dushana, are now struck down by my
darts ! Even were they aided by the Gods and Asuras with the

hosts of Rishis, they would never be able to release themselves from those arrows that paralyse them! I have overcome Rama for the sake of my sire, who is a prey to anxiety and fear, passing the three watches of the night without allowing his limbs to rest on his couch. I have subdued that wretch, who destroys all beings to their very root, on account of whom the whole of Lanka is agitated like a river in the rainy season. As clouds are dispersed in the autumn, so have the exploits of Rama and Lakshmana and all the inhabitants of the woods been rendered void."

Having spoken thus to all the titans, who had witnessed the scene, Ravani began to assail all the monkey leaders. First he struck down Nila with nine exceedingly powerful javelins, thereafter he wounded Mainda and Dvivida with three more and that mighty bowman, having pierced Jambavan in the breast with an arrow, loosed ten shafts on the impetuous Hanuman. Then Ravani, in the fight, full of ire, with twin arrows pierced Gavaksha and Sharabha, those two of immeasurable prowess, and the leader of the Golangulas and the son of Bali, Angada, were overcome by innumerable darts by the swift-coursing Ravani. Transfixing the leading monkeys with shafts resembling tongues of fire, that mighty and colossal son of Ravana began to shout in triumph and, having overwhelmed and routed the monkeys with a hail of weapons, that long-armed hero burst into loud laughter, exclaiming :—

" Behold, O Titans, with a formidable net I have bound those two brothers in the presence of their forces ! "

Thus did he speak and all those titans, versed in magic, were exceedingly delighted by his exploit and cheered him unanimously with a roar like unto thunder, crying :— " Rama is dead ! " and hearing these tidings and beholding the two brothers, Rama and Lakshmana, lying on the earth without breath or movement, they all paid homage to Ravana's son, reflecting " They are slain ! " In a transport of joy, Indrajita, victorious in conflict, returned to Lanka spreading happiness among the Nairritas.

A great fear however had taken possession of Sugriva, who was overcome with terror on beholding Rama and Lakshmana riddled with arrows and pierced in every limb and bone, whereupon Bibishana said to the King of the Monkeys, who was afflicted, his face bathed in tears, his eyes wild with terror :—

" Have no fear, O Sugriva, stay this rain of tears ; these are the fortunes of war ; the titan's victory is not assured ; fate may still smile upon us, O Warrior. These two heroes, full of prowess will recover from their swoon. Take courage and inspire me with courage also, who am bereft of a protector, O Monkey ! Death cannot strike terror in those who find their felicity in truth and justice."

Thus speaking, Bibishana, dipping his hand in water, washed Sugriva's beautiful eyes and, after taking water and uttering a sacred formula, the virtuous Bibishana then dried the face of that intelligent King of the Monkeys and addressing him in words full of good sense and comfort, said :—

" This is not the moment, O Greatest of Monkey Kings, to manifest agitation, excessive emotion in such a situation leads to death, therefore abandon this faint-heartedness that will prove thine undoing and consider how thou canst best serve the troops. Keep watch over Rama so long as he has not regained consciousness, for when they come to themselves, the two Kakutsthas will remove all fear from us. This is nothing to Rama nor is he dying, and Lakshmi[1], who is inaccessible to those who are doomed, has not abandoned him. Therefore pluck up thy courage and call on thy prowess while I seek to inspire the ranks with renewed confidence. Those monkeys, their eyes dilated, trembling and discouraged by the rumours whispered from ear to ear, on seeing me cheerfully going about amongst the ranks of the army, will abandon their fears like a discarded garland, O King of the Monkeys ! "

Having reassured Sugriva, that Indra among the Titans, Bibishana, passed through the monkey lines reviving their confidence.

Meanwhile Indrajita, that great magician, surrounded by all his forces re-entered the City of Lanka and sought out his sire. Approaching Ravana with joined palms, he imparted the pleasant tidings to him, saying :—

" Rama and Lakshmana are slain ! " Then Ravana joyfully springing up in the midst of the titans, on hearing that his two

---

[1] Goddess of prosperity.

enemies had succumbed, smelt the head of his son and in great delight questioned him concerning the matter.

Being interrogated by his sire regarding what had taken place, Indrajita related how the two brothers, bound by his shafts, were lying without strength or movement. On hearing those tidings from that warrior of the great car, joy flooded Ravana's inmost being and Dashagriva, banishing his fears regarding the son of Dasaratha, warmly felicitated his offspring who stood beside him.

CHAPTER 47

Sita sees Rama and Lakshmana lying on the Battlefield

THE son of Ravana having returned to Lanka, his purpose accomplished, the leading monkeys surrounded Raghava in order to watch over him, and Hanuman, Angada, Nila, Sushena, Kumuda, Nala, Gaja, Gavaksha, Panasa, Sanuprastha and the mighty Jambavan with Sunda, Rambha, Shatabali and Prithu, having re-organized their ranks, alert, armed with trees surveyed the quarters of the sky up and down and on every side and, even if a grass stirred, they exclaimed " It is a titan ! "

Ravana, meanwhile, full of joy dismissed his son Indrajita and thereafter summoned the female titans who guarded Sita and they with Trijata, having hastened there at his command, were addressed by that monarch in his delight who said to them :—

" Inform Vaidehi that Indrajita has slain Rama and Lakshmana ! Compel her to enter the Pushpaka Plane and show them to her lying on the field of battle ! Her consort, the One depending on whom rendered her so proud that she refused to be united with me, lies there struck down with his brother in the presence of his army ! From now on, free from anxiety, grief and expectation of re-union, Maithili, adorned in all her jewels, will submit herself to me. To-day, beholding Rama with Lakshmana fallen under the sway of death on the battlefield, seeing no other haven and hoping for nought else, the large-eyed Sita will voluntarily seek refuge with me ! "

At these words of that wicked monarch, they all replied—
" Be it so ! " and went to where the Pushpaka Chariot was,
thereafter ascending it. Taking that aerial car, the female
titans, in obedience to Ravana's behests, rejoined Maithili in
the Ashoka Grove.

There they found her overcome with the grief that separation
from her lord caused her, nevertheless they placed her in the
Chariot Pushpaka and when they were seated therein with
Trijata, Ravana took her round the city garlanded with flags
and banners and at the same time the delighted Monarch of
the Titans caused a proclamation to be made in Lanka announcing
that Rama as also Lakshmana had been slain by Indrajita in
combat.

Sita, transported with Trijata in that car, beheld the monkey
troops who had been slain and witnessed the joy exhibited by
those eaters of flesh and the monkeys afflicted with grief standing
round Rama and Lakshmana. And she beheld those two
warriors also, lying pierced with arrows, unconscious, riddled
with weapons, their armour shattered, their bows broken,
transfixed by darts. Those two brothers, who were filled with
valour, the foremost of heroes were lying stretched on the earth
resembling two youthful sons of Pavaka.

And when the unfortunate Maithili beheld those two intrepid
lions among men, pierced with spears, she broke into piteous
lamentations, and the dark-eyed Sita, the daughter of Janaka,
of faultless limbs, beholding her lord and Lakshmana lying on
the earth, burst into sobs. Exhausted with weeping and grief
on seeing those two brothers resembling the offspring of the
Gods and, believing them to be dead, overwhelmed with
affliction, she spoke thus :—

CHAPTER 48

Sita's Lamentations

SEEING her lord lying on the earth as also the valiant Lakshmana,
Sita, in the grief that overwhelmed her, gave voice to her
complaint, saying :—

" The soothsayers, reading the lineaments of my body, prophesized thus :—

' Thou shalt bear sons and never be widowed ! '—now that Rama has been slain, their words have proved to be untrue ! Since Rama is slain, those who predicted that I should be the companion and consort of the performer of great sacrifices, have uttered a falsehood ! Now that Rama has been slain, those soothsayers, who told me I should be highly honoured by the wives of warriors and kings, are proved not to have spoken truly ! Now that Rama has been slain, the astrologers among the brahmins, who openly foretold happiness for me, are proved to have spoken falsely !

" Yet I bear the marks of the lotus on my feet by which high-born women receive the supreme consecration with their lords at their coronation nor do I find in myself any marks of ill-fortune which betoken widowhood in those who are ill-starred, yet all the auspicious signs appear to be rendered void for me ! These marks of the lotus, said to be of good augury by the Pundits, have no meaning for me, now that Rama is slain !

" My locks are fine, of even length and dark, my eyebrows meet, my legs are round and smooth, my teeth evenly separated, the corners of my eyes are shaped like the conch, my breasts, hands, feet and thighs well proportioned, my nails smooth and polished, my fingers well-shaped, my breasts touch each other and have depressed nipples, my navel too is deeply indented, my bosom well-formed, my complexion has the sheen of a pearl, the down on my skin is soft. It is said I possess the twelve auspicious signs : my feet and hands are without hollows and marked with the barley corn[1] and my smile is langorous. Thus did those, who interpret the marks of youthful maidens, speak of me.

" Having purified Janasthana[2], received the tidings of my fate and crossed the impassable ocean, those two brothers have perished in the imprint of a cow's hoof. Did they not recollect (that they possessed) the arrows of Varuna, Agni, Indra and Vayu, as also the Brahmashira weapon ?

---

[1] A natural line crossing the thumb at the second joint resembling a barley corn, which is considered auspicious.
[2] Purified Janasthana—that is—' Rid Janasthana of the titans '.

" By means of magic arts, an invisible foe has slain those two,
Rama and Lakshmana, my protectors, who are equal to Vasava
in combat and I am now bereft of any support.   Nay, if he had
come into Rama's presence, he would not have returned alive
even were he possessed of the swiftness of thought but since
Rama and his brother are lying struck down on the battlefield,
there is no burden too heavy for death to shoulder !   Fate is
inexorable.   I do not weep so much for Rama and Lakshmana
or for myself or my mother but for my unfortunate mother-in-
law, Kaushalya, who dwells constantly on her son's return after
fulfilling his vows, she who asks herself, ' When shall I behold
Lakshmana and Sita with Raghava once more ? ' "

Thus did Janaki lament and Trijata said to her :—" Do not
despair, O Goddess, thy lord lives !   I will tell thee what
powerful considerations have convinced me that those two
brothers, Rama and Lakshmana still live, O Queen.   They are,
that resolution and martial ardour do not animate the faces of
soldiers who have lost their leader, neither would the celestial
car, Pushpaka, have brought thee hither, O Vaidehi, if those two
heroes had succumbed.   An army that sees its valiant commander
fall is bereft of courage and wanders aimlessly about on the
battlefield like a ship which has lost its rudder.   Yet there is
neither confusion nor disorder among the intrepid forces that
mount guard over the two Kakutsthas.   I am pointing this out
to thee on account of mine affection for thee.   These auspicious
omens should re-assure thee fully, for know well, the two
Kakutsthas are not dead, I hasten to tell thee this out of love
for thee.

" I have never spoken what is not true to thee nor shall I
ever do so, O Maithili, for by thy conduct and natural gaiety
thou hast found a place in my heart !   Nay, those two warriors
are not able to be vanquished even by the Gods and Asuras
with their leaders.   This is what I have observed and communicate to thee.   Yea, there is a great marvel to be seen, O
Maithili ; behold how, fallen under those shafts and deprived
of their senses, their beauty has not deserted them.

" In the natural course, when men have lost their lives, their
features exhibit appalling alteration, it is therefore impossible
that these two do not still live.   Banish thy grief on account of

Rama and Lakshmana, abandon thy sorrow, O Daughter of Janaka ! "

At these words, Sita, who resembled a daughter of the Gods, with joined palms, exclaimed " May it be so ! "

Meanwhile the Chariot Pushpaka, swift as the wind, had returned and the plaintive Sita re-entered the city with Trijata, whereupon descending from the car, she entered the Ashoka Grove with the female titans.

Having returned to the royal enclosure planted with innumerable trees, Sita, recalling the two princes whom she had just seen, became a prey to extreme grief.

CHAPTER 49

Rama returns to consciousness and weeps over Lakshmana

BOUND by those formidable weapons, the two sons of Dasaratha, breathing like serpents, lay bleeding on the earth.

Those foremost of monkeys, the valiant companions of Sugriva, plunged in grief, were all standing round the two illustrious warriors.

Then the mighty Raghava, by virtue of his hardihood and native strength, awoke from his swoon despite the shafts that held him captive. Beholding his brother bleeding, unconscious, tightly bound and his features changed, Rama, full of grief, lamented thus :—" Of what use to me is the recovery of Sita or even life itself, since my brother, now lying before mine eyes, has been struck down in the fight ? It were possible for me to find a consort equal to Sita in this world of mortals but not a brother, friend and comrade in arms such as Lakshmana ! If he has returned to the five elements, he, the increaser of Sumitra's joy, I will yield up my life breaths in the presence of the monkeys !

" What shall I say to my mother, Kaushalya, or to Kaikeyi ? If I return without Lakshmana, how shall I console Sumitra trembling and crying out like an osprey, who sighs for her son's return from whom she has been separated so long ? What answer shall I give to Shatrughna and the illustrious Bharata when I return without the one who followed me to the forest ? Nay, I should not be able to endure Sumitra's reproaches ; I will leave my body here ; I am unable to continue living. Woe unto me and to my lack of nobility, since, through my fault, Lakshmana has fallen and lies on a bed of arrows as one who has yielded up his life !

"O Lakshmana, thou didst ever console me in my great misfortune ; now that thou art slain, thou wilt no longer be able to allay my sufferings by thy words. Thou, who, in this battle, struck down innumerable titans, art fallen, pierced by darts, like a hero on the selfsame field. Lying on a bed of arrows, bathed in blood, thou art nought but a heap of weapons ! It appears as if the sun has set behind the Astachala Mountains ! Pierced with spears, thy limbs express thine agony without the aid of words. I shall follow that illustrious warrior to the region of Yama, as he accompanied me when I retired to the forest ; he, who ever loved his own and was filled with devotion for me, lies in the state to which my misdeeds have brought him, wretch that I am !

" Even when deeply provoked, that valiant hero never uttered an unpleasant or harsh word ; he who was able to loose five hundred arrows in one shot and who excelled Kartavirya himself in the science of archery ; Lakshmana, who was accustomed to a rich couch and who, with his arrows could sever those of the mighty Shakra, is lying slain on the earth.

" Those vain words, which I uttered, will undoubtedly consume me since I have not enthroned Bibishana as King of the Titans ! Return at once, O Sugriva, since bereft of my support thou and thy leaders will be overcome by Ravana. Recross the sea accompanied by thine army led by Angada with Nila and Nala, O King. I am fully satisfied by the great military exploit of Hanuman, impossible to any other and by that accomplished by the King of the Bears and the General of the Golangulas. That which Angada, Mainda and Dvivida did, the terrible combat that Kesarin and Sampati sustained, the formidable struggle in which Gavaya, Gavaksha, Sharabha, Gaja and other monkeys, who are willing to sacrifice their lives for me, took part, are sufficient for me. Nay, it is not possible for mortals to avoid their destiny. O Sugriva, fearing to fail in thy duty, thou hast done all that a friend and comrade could do; all that is due to friendship, thou hast accomplished, O Foremost of Monkeys! I take leave of you all; go where it seems best to you!"

Hearing Rama lament thus, the monkeys allowed tears to fall from their reddened eyes, when, at that moment, Bibishana, having established order in the ranks, mace in hand hurried to rejoin Raghava. Seeing him, who resembled a mass of collyrium, hastening towards them thus, the monkeys thinking him to be Ravani, fled away.

CHAPTER 50

Garuda liberates Rama and Lakshmana

MEANWHILE the illustrious and powerful King of the Monkeys enquired saying:—"What does this stampede signify? The army resembles a ship amidst the waves struck by a tempest!"

Hearing Sugriva's speech, Angada, the son of Bali, answered:

"Dost thou not see Rama and Lakshmana of the Great Car, those two valiant and illustrious sons of Dasaratha, covered with darts lying all bloody on a bed of arrows?"

Thereupon that Indra among monkeys, Sugriva, said to his son:—"To my mind there is some other cause why the monkeys, bewildered, their eyes distended with terror, are throwing down their arms in order to flee in all directions without shame and without looking behind them, jostling each other and leaping over those who have fallen!"

In the midst of this turmoil, the warrior Bibishana came there, a great mace in his hand and said "Victory to Rama! Victory to Rama!" and Sugriva observed that it was this titan who had caused the panic among the monkeys whereat he addressed the illustrious King of the Bears, who stood near, and said:—

"It is Bibishana who has come hither! On seeing him the monkeys, seized with terror, have fled, deeming him to be

Ravana's son; do thou rally those fugitives immediately, who, in fear, have scattered in all directions and inform them that it is Bibishana who has come!'"

In obedience to Sugriva's command, Jambavan perceiving it to be Bibishana and recognizing his voice, re-assured the monkeys and arrested the stampede, whereupon freed from anxiety they all retraced their steps.

Meanwhile the faithful Bibishana, on beholding Rama's body as also Lakshmana's covered with arrows, was overcome with distress in his turn. Dipping his hand in water, he washed their eyes, but, anguish seizing his heart, he began to weep and lament, saying :—

" Behold to what a pass these two powerful and valiant warriors have been brought by that titan with his crafty ways ! The son of my brother, that wicked youth of perverse soul, in his demoniacal cunning, has deceived those two honourable fighters. Pierced by arrows, covered with blood, they are lying on the earth like two porcupines. Those two gallant beings, those two lions among men, on whom depended the position to which I aspired, to my destruction are lying here insensible. I am as one dead and, deprived of the hope of becoming king am lost, whilst my rival Ravana sees his vow fulfilled and his desires realised ! "

Thus did Bibishana lament, whereupon Sugriva embraced him and that magnanimous King of the Monkeys spoke to him in this wise :—

" O Virtuous Prince, thou shalt certainly reign over Lanka ; Ravana and his son will not achieve their purpose ; the injury done to Rama and Lakshmana is not grave, they will both emerge from their swoon and destroy Ravana and his hordes in battle. "

When he had thus consoled and comforted the titan, Sugriva issued his commands to Sushena, his stepfather, who stood before him, saying :—

" Take these two brothers, Rama and Lakshmana with the foremost of the monkey divisions to Kishkindha, till these two scourgers of their foes have recovered consciousness. As for me, I shall slay Ravana with his son and his relatives and bring back Maithili as did Shakra the prosperity he had lost."

Thus did that King of the Monkeys speak and Sushena answered him saying :—

" Formerly a great war took place between the Devas and Asuras and, by making themselves invisible again and again, the Danavas overcame the Gods despite their skill in bearing arms. Experienced warriors though they were, wounded, unconscious and almost deprived of life, yet Brihaspati revived them by the aid of remedies accompanied by the recitation of sacred formulas.

" Let the monkeys, Sampati, Panasa and others go in haste to gather those simples by the ocean of milk ; undoubtedly those monkeys are conversant with the two mountain herbs, the celestial Samjivakarana and Vishalya, which were created by a God. From the bosom of the milky ocean rise the Mountains Chandra and Drona, where the divine ' Amrita ' emerged after the churning,[1] it is there that these miraculous herbs are to be found. Let the Son of the Wind, Hanuman go to those two mountains placed in that vast sea by the Gods."

As he was speaking, a great wind arose accompanied by massed clouds and lightning, whipping up the salty waves and causing the mountains to tremble as from an earthquake. Under the mighty stroke of Vata's wing the great trees fell headlong into the briny waters of the sea, their branches broken, whilst terror seized the great snakes who inhabited these regions and those monsters plunged into the depths.

Suddenly Garuda, the valiant son of Vinata like unto a blazing torch appeared to all those monkeys and, on beholding him, the serpents who bound those two warriors in the form of mighty arrows, fled away. Thereafter Suparna, touching the two Kakutsthas and offering them his good wishes, with his hands wiped their faces that shone like the moon.

Under Vainateya's touch, the wounds of both were closed and their bodies immediately assumed a brilliant and glowing hue. Their valour, vigour, strength, endurance and resolution, those great qualities, also perspicacity, intelligence and memory were redoubled.

Having raised up those equals of Vasava, the exceedingly valiant Garuda embraced them warmly and Rama said to him :—

[1] Referring to the churning of the Ocean by Gods and Asuras.

" Thanks to thy beneficence and grace we have both been delivered from the strange evil that Ravana brought upon us and our strength has returned. As in the presence of my father Dasaratha, or my grandfather Aja, in thy presence also my heart is filled with felicity. Who art thou endowed with a beauty which distinguishes thee, thou bearing crowns, divine perfumes and celestial ornaments, the raiment which clothes thee being free from dust ? "

Then the extremely illustrious Vainateya, who was full of valour and the Lord of Winged Creatures, his heart enraptured, addressed Rama, whose eyes sparkled with delight, and said :—

" I am thy dear friend, O Kakutstha, thy very breath, Garuda, who have come hither to assist you both. The mighty Asuras and exceedingly energetic monkeys as also the Gandharvas with Shatakratu at their head or the Gods themselves would not have been able to sever these formidable bonds wrought with arrows, woven with the aid of great magic by Indrajita of ruthless deeds. These offspring of Kadru of sharp fangs and subtle poison, which the potent arts of the titan had changed to arrows, had fettered thee. Fortunate art thou, O Virtuous Rama, thou true hero, as also Lakshmana, thy brother, the destroyer of his foes in combat.

Hearing of thy plight, summoning up mine energy in affection for you both, giving ear to the call of friendship alone, I came hither with all speed. Now that you are liberated from these formidable bonds let both of you be constantly on your guard ! All titans by nature have recourse to treachery in war, whilst for you, O Chivalrous Warriors, honour is your only weapon. Never trust the titans on the battlefield for such perfidious means are ever employed by them."

Having counselled him in this wise, the mighty Suparna embraced Rama tenderly and craved his permission to depart, saying :—

" Dear and Virtuous Raghava, thou art a friend to thy foes, allow me to take my leave. Do not enquire indiscreetly into the cause of my friendship, O Raghava, who am as near to thee as thy breath, though external to thee. Thou shalt know of it when thou hast achieved success in battle, O Hero ! When, under the rain of thy missiles, Lanka has been destroyed save for the aged and the children and thou hast slain Ravana, thine adversary, thou shalt bring back Sita ! "

Having said this, Suparna of swift flight, who had just healed Rama's wounds in the presence of the monkeys, having paid obeisance to him and taken him into his arms, mounted into the sky with the speed of the wind.

Seeing the two Raghavas healed of their wounds, the leaders of the monkeys, lashing their tails, roared like lions. Thereafter gongs were beaten and drums resounded, whilst conches were blown amidst general rejoicing. Some manifested their strength by breaking down the trees which they used as maces and, in their warlike frenzy, those Plavamgamas hurled themselves on the gates of Lanka.

Thereafter a terrible and appalling clamour arose amongst the foremost of monkeys as, at the end of summer, the roaring of thunderclouds in the night.

CHAPTER 51

Dhumraksha goes out to fight the Monkeys

THAT formidable clamour, set up by the monkeys who were full of martial ardour, arrested the attention of Ravana and his titans, and he, hearing the joyful and spirited acclamations and the distant tumult, said to his ministers who surrounded him :—

" A great uproar, resembling the muttering of clouds, has arisen from that horde of delighted monkeys. Undoubtedly their joy is great, their mighty shouts are agitating the ocean itself. Nevertheless whetted shafts have rendered the two brothers, Rama and Lakshmana, insensible, therefore this tremendous outcry almost alarms me ! "

Having spoken thus to his ministers, the Lord of the Titans said to his Nairritas, who stood round him :—

" Do ye speedily discover from what cause this general rejoicing among those forest dwellers proceeds in their present painful situation ! "

At this command, the titans hastily climbed the ramparts

from where they beheld the army and its leader the illustrious Sugriva with the two Raghavas also, freed of their bonds, seated in noble ease, whereupon the titans were thunderstruck. With terror in their hearts, those fierce warriors jumped down from the walls and, deadly pale, returned to their king. With downcast mien, those titans, skilled in speech, faithfully informed Ravana of those unpleasant tidings, saying :—

" The two brothers, Rama and Lakshmana, whom Indrajita had bound with his benumbing shafts and whose arms he had pinioned, are freed from the arrows which paralysed them and now appear on the field of battle in their native vigour, resembling two elephants who have snapped their fetters."

At these words, the powerful King of the Titans, full of anxiety and highly incensed, grew pale and said :—

" If mine adversaries, having thus been bound, are now free despite those formidable arrows, those rare boons resembling serpents bright as the sun, that were infallible and with which Indrajita secured them after overcoming them in combat, then mine entire authority is in jeopardy ! Verily those darts, bright as fire, which in battle deprived mine enemies of life have been rendered void."

Having uttered these words in furious tones, hissing like a snake, he addressed one named Dhumraksha who was seated amidst the titans and said :—

" Taking with thee a considerable force of titans go without delay and slay Rama and Lakshmana."

At the command of that crafty monarch, Dhumraksha circumambulated him and immediately left the palace, thereafter having crossed the threshold he said to the General of the Forces:

" Mobilize the army, what need is there for delay when the battle is joined ! "

Thus spoke Dhumraksha and the General gathered together a large number of troops in accord with Ravana's command.

Thereafter those prowlers of the night, who were valiant and of a formidable aspect, with girdles of bells round their waists, shouted exultantly and ranged themselves round Dhumraksha.

Furnished with every kind of weapon, brandishing spears, hammers, maces, harpoons, sticks, iron cudgels, bars, hooks, picks, nooses and axes, those terrible titans sallied forth with the noise of thunder. Clad in mail and mounted on chariots that were magnificently dressed with flags and decorated with bands of pure gold, harnessed to mules of many heads or steeds of exceeding fleetness or elephants maddened with Mada juice, some of those titans bounded forward like veritable tigers.

And Dhumraksha, with a great clatter set out in a celestial car to which mules with golden harness and the heads of deer and lions were hitched ; and that valiant general surrounded by the titans set forth amidst mocking laughter through the western gate, where Hanuman was stationed. As he advanced in his excellent car harnessed to mules, whose voices he emulated, birds of ill-omen planed above him and on the top of his chariot a terrible vulture alighted while those devourers of corpses clustered on the point of his standard. Streaming with blood a huge decapitated and livid trunk fell to earth emitting inarticulate cries at Dhumraksha's approach and the sky rained down blood, the earth shook, the wind blew adversely with the roar of thunder and darkness obscured every quarter.

Beholding those terrible portents that appeared in all their horror, boding ill-fortune to the titans, Dhumraksha was filled with alarm, and terror seized all the soldiers who accompanied him. At the moment when, full of fear, amidst his countless titans, eager to enter into combat, that valiant general set out, he beheld the vast army of the monkeys resembling a great flood, protected by the arms of the Raghavas.

CHAPTER 52

Dhumraksha fights and is slain by Hanuman

SEEING Dhumraksha of redoubtable courage set forth, all the monkeys in their martial ardour emitted loud cries and a terrific struggle ensued between those forest dwellers and the titans, who attacked each other with huge trees, spears and maces.

On all sides ferocious monkeys were massacred by titans and titans felled to the earth by monkeys employing trees. The titans struck their opponents with pointed arrows furnished with heron's plumes, fearful to behold, which never missed their target and terrible maces, harpoons, axes, formidable bars and tridents of all kinds, which, brandished by them, mutilated those powerful monkeys, while they, exasperated, redoubled their efforts and, without flagging, continued the fight. Their limbs pierced with arrows, their bodies transfixed with spears, those foremost of the monkeys armed themselves with trees and rocks and, with terrific bounds, having proclaimed their names to the accompaniment of yells, crushed those intrepid titans.

Thereafter the battle waxed exceedingly furious between monkeys and demons and the former amidst shouts of triumph seized hold of stones of every kind and trees with countless branches and rocks in order to destroy the enemy; the titans, who fed on gore, fell in heaps, vomiting blood, their sides slashed open by the trees, whilst others were crushed by the stones and yet others torn to pieces by the monkeys' teeth.

Their standards broken, their swords snapped, their chariots overturned, they wandered about blindly and the earth was covered with the corpses of great elephants resembling hills and horses with their riders crushed by the great rocks hurled on them by those dwellers in the woods; and the monkeys of exceeding valour rushed on the titans, flinging themselves upon them with great bounds and scratching their faces with their sharp nails.

Mutilated, their hair torn out, maddened by the smell of blood, the titans fell in great numbers; some of those fierce warriors however, in a paroxysm of fury hurled themselves on the monkeys and struck them with the palms of their hands, which resounded like the clap of thunder, and the monkeys, receiving that sharp shock, with an even greater ferocity crushed the titans with blows of their feet, teeth and trees.

Seeing his army routed, Dhumraksha, that lion among the titans, in his rage, began to create carnage among those bellicose apes and some pierced with spears lost rivers of blood whilst others, struck down by the blows of the axe, fell to earth.

Here some were crushed by iron bars, others torn by harpoons or pierced by javelins, stumbled and fell, yielding up their vital breaths. Mowed down, covered with blood, put to flight, those inhabitants of the woods fell dying under the furious onslaught of the titans in the struggle. Their breasts torn open they lay on their side or, slashed with tridents, their entrails gushed forth.

Then that mighty conflict took on fearful proportions by virtue of the number of monkeys and titans who took part and the innumerable darts, stones and trees that were used. With the bowstrings as the tuneful lute, the neighing of the horses, the clapping of the hands and the trumpeting of the elephants as the melody, the whole battle resembled a symphony.

Meanwhile Dhumraksha, armed with his bow, in the forefront of battle, under a hail of missiles, dispersed the monkeys as in sport on every side, and Maruti, beholding the monkey army being exterminated and put to flight by that titan, hurled himself upon him in fury, a great rock in his hand. His eyes inflamed with anger, the equal of his sire in courage, he flung the rock on the chariot of his foe and seeing the stone fall, Dhumraksha, brandishing his mace, in his agitation leapt quickly from the car to the ground. Then that rock rolled on the earth, having shattered the chariot with its wheels, its pole, its shafts, banner and Dhumraksha's bow.

Thereafter Hanuman, born of Maruta, leaving the car lying, slew the titans with the trunks of trees furnished with their branches, and their heads crushed, covered with blood, mangled by those trees, they fell to the earth.

Having routed the army of the enemy, Hanuman, born of Maruta, breaking off the peak of a mountain hurled himself on Dhumraksha, who, brandishing his mace, rushed on his adversary and he advanced with haste towards him shouting. Then Dhumraksha, in his rage, brought down that weapon studded with countless points on the head of the infuriated Hanuman and assailed by that violent and fearful stroke, the monkey, who was endowed with the strength of Maruta, was in no wise disturbed but struck the titan full on the skull with his rocky peak which shattered all his limbs, whereupon Dhumraksha suddenly fell to the earth like a mountain crumbling.

Beholding him slain, the night-rangers who had survived the

slaughter, terrified, re-entered Lanka, harassed by the Plavamgamas.

The illustrious son of Pavana, however, having destroyed his enemies, causing rivers of blood to flow, weary of slaughter, with delight received the cordial felicitations of the monkey leaders.

CHAPTER 53

Vajradamshtra enters the Lists

HEARING of the death of Dhumraksha, Ravana the King of the Titans fell into a transport of fury and began to hiss like a serpent. Wrought up with ire, with long and burning sighs he addressed the exceedingly powerful Vajradamshtra, saying :—

" O Warrior, go forth at the head of the titans and triumph over the son of Dasaratha, Rama, as also over Sugriva and the monkeys ! "

" Be it so ! " answered the general who was versed in the art of magic, and he departed speedily with the innumerable divisions that surrounded him.

With the utmost care he assembled teams of elephants, horses, donkeys and mules, adorning them with countless flags of different colours, and that titan, wearing bracelets and a diadem of great price, set out immediately, bearing his bow and, having circumambulated his chariot dressed with pennants, which dazzled the gaze with its facings of pure gold, he ascended it.

Thereafter infantry of every kind issued forth, furnished with weapons, such as cutlasses, innumerable darts, gleaming maces, harpoons, bows, lances, spears, swords, discus, hammers and sharp axes. All those illustrious lions among the titans in their resplendent and many-coloured uniforms, full of ardour mounted on elephants intoxicated with ichor, resembled moving hills. Their mounts equipped for combat, driven by mahouts bearing lances and goads, were headed by those distinguished for their trappings and great strength.

And the whole army of titans filed out, looking as brilliant as the clouds riven by lightning in the rainy season and they emerged from the northern gate where the General Angada was stationed.

Thereafter, as they set forth, fearful portents appeared and, from a cloudless yet burning sky, meteors fell while jackals, emitting fearful howls, belched forth flames and fire. Hideous beasts foretold the destruction of the titans who entered into the combat stumbling miserably.

Yet despite those ill-omens, the mighty Vajradamshtra, full of energy and prowess, went forward eager to meet the foe and, seeing their adversaries advancing, the monkeys, burning for victory, set up tremendous shouts which echoed in every quarter.

Thereafter a furious struggle ensued between the monkeys and the titans and those redoubtable warriors of ferocious aspect sought to bring about each other's destruction. Some of those warriors, their heads and bodies severed, fell to the earth bathed in blood, whilst others, whose arms resembled steel, approached one another, attacking with various weapons, neither giving ground. Trees, stones and javelins clashed with a tremendous noise, striking terror in the heart of the listeners and the appalling clatter of chariot wheels, the twanging of bow-strings, the blare of trumpets, the roll of drums, the booming of gongs, created an indescribable uproar.

Then, throwing away their weapons, they wrestled with one another in hand-to-hand combat, striking each other with the palms of their hands, their feet, their knees and even with trees. Some of the titans had their bodies torn open, some were crushed by rocks and some were beaten down by the blows of the monkeys in the fight.

Now Vajradamshtra, having surveyed the scene, began to sow terror among the monkeys, as Antaka, noose in hand, at the destruction of the worlds.

Full of vigour, those skilled warriors, the titans, transported with rage, decimated the monkey forces with every kind of weapon and, on his side the audacious son of Vayu struck down all those titans in the fight, fury re-doubling his strength, so that he appeared like the Fire of Dissolution. Then the valiant Angada, the equal of Shakra in valour, brandishing a tree, his eyes red with anger, like a lion amidst defenceless deer, caused a terrible carnage. By the force of his blows, the titans of redoubtable courage, their skulls crushed, fell like trees under the blows of the axe and the earth, strewn with chariots of every kind, standards, horses, bodies of monkeys and titans and rivers of blood, was fearful to behold. Strings of pearls, bracelets, raiment, and parasols decorated the battlefield, which glowed like an autumnal night and the tempestuous Angada scattered the great army of the titans as the wind dispels the clouds.

CHAPTER 54

Angada slays Vajradamshtra

THE extermination of his army through Angada's prowess filled the valiant Vajradamshtra with fury. Stretching his formidable bow, like unto Shakra's thunderbolt, he assailed the monkey battalions with a hail of shafts whereupon the foremost of the titans mounted on chariots, armed with every kind of weapon and full of courage, entered the lists whilst the monkeys, those powerful bulls among the Plavagas, assembling on all sides, fought with rocks.

Thousands of weapons were hurled in that desperate encounter by the titan and monkey leaders and, from their side, the great monkeys with the ardour of elephants in rut, showered down giant trees and huge lumps of rock on the demons so that between those intrepid warriors, the titans and the monkeys, who never retreated in battle, a tremendous struggle ensued.

Monkeys and titans, still possessing heads but bereft of arms and legs, lay on the earth bathed in blood and bristling with arrows, a prey to herons, vultures and crows or devoured by troops of jackals.

Monkeys and night-rangers fell on the battlefield; headless trunks leapt up to the terror of all, their arms, hands and heads severed and their limbs hacked to pieces in the fight.

Meanwhile the army of Vajradamshtra, overcome by the monkeys, broke up under his eyes, whereupon that leader, seeing the titans terrorised and decimated by the Plavamgamas, his eyes red with anger, bow in hand, penetrated the enemy ranks, sowing panic amongst them. Thereafter he dispatched those monkeys with arrows furnished with heron's plumes that flew straight to their target and pierced seven, eight, nine or five of his·opponents simultaneously, thus destroying them in his fury. Put to flight, those simian battalions, their limbs crippled by those darts, sought refuge with Angada as all creatures with Prajapati ; and when he beheld those monkey divisions fleeing in disorder, the son of Bali exchanged glances of hatred with Vajradamshtra and, in a paroxysm of rage, they entered into a terrible duel one with the other so that it seemed a lion and an elephant intoxicated with ichor fought together. And the son of Bali full of valour, was struck in his vital parts by a hundred thousand arrows resembling tongues of fire and all his limbs were besprinkled with blood. Then that exceedingly energetic monkey of redoubtable courage hurled a tree at Vajradamshtra but that intrepid titan, seeing it fall, cut it into innumerable pieces which fell in heaps on the earth.

Witnessing the strength of his rival, that lion among the Plavagas seized hold of a huge rock which he spun round, emitting a shout and, as it descended, that hero leaping down from his chariot, armed with his mace, stood waiting unperturbed. Meanwhile that rock discharged by Angada fell on the forefront of the battle where it shattered the chariot with its wheels, shafts and horses.

Then the monkey broke off a great crag from the mountain once more and it was covered with trees and he brought it down on the head of his adversary so that Vajradamshtra, seized with a sudden giddiness, faltered and began to vomit blood, clenching his mace convulsively and breathing heavily. Thereafter, coming to his senses, in a transport of fury he hit the son of Bali full on the chest with his mace and, letting it fall, began to fight with his fists whereupon a hand-to-hand struggle ensued between monkey and titan. Exhausted by the blows, spitting blood, those valiant warriors resembled the planets Mars and Mercury.

Meanwhile the exceedingly powerful Angada, that lion of Plavagas stood waiting and he seized hold of a shield covered with the hide of a bull and a great sword decorated with golden bells enveloped in a leathern sheath.

In the midst of innumerable graceful evolutions, the monkey and the titan attacked each other, roaring and thirsting for victory. With their gaping wounds, they shone like two Kimshuka Trees in flower and the struggle robbed them of their breath so that they sank to their knees on the earth. Thereafter in the twinkling of an eye, Angada, that elephant among monkeys, rose up, his eyes inflamed like a serpent that has been struck with a stick and, with his stainless sword that was well sharpened, the son of Bali who was full of vigour, struck off the huge head of Vajradamshtra, whose limbs were bathed in blood. Under the stroke of that sword, his beautiful head fell, cleft in twain, the eyes rolling.

Beholding Vajradamshtra slain, the titans, wild with terror, fled panic-stricken towards Lanka, harassed by the Plavamgamas, their faces woe-begone, their heads bowed in shame.

Having struck down the enemy with his powerful arm, the mighty son of Bali experienced great joy amidst the monkey army, honoured by them for his high courage and he resembled the God of a Thousand Eyes surrounded by the Celestials.

CHAPTER 55

Akampana goes out to fight against the Monkeys

HEARING that Vajradamshtra had been slain by the son of Bali, Ravana addressed the General of his forces who, with joined palms, stood near him and said :—

" Let the invincible titans of irresistible courage go forth immediately with Akampana at their head, who is conversant with the use of every weapon and missile; he excels in vanquishing the foe and in preserving and leading his own forces ; he has ever desired my welfare and loved war ; he will prove victorious over the two Kakutsthas and the exceedingly energetic Sugriva. The rest of the monkeys too are formidable but without doubt he will exterminate them all."

At this command from Ravana, the valiant titan, in great haste, mobilized an entire division of the army. Furnished with every kind of weapon, those foremost of titans of terrifying aspect, fearful to look upon, rushed into the fray where their general had despatched them.

Akampana of the stature and colour of a cloud, whose voice resembled thunder, ascended his car decorated with fine gold and set out surrounded by dreadful demons. He, who was incapable of trembling in battle even before the Gods themselves, seemed to the monkeys to be as splendid as the sun. As he sped on his way, furious and eager to enter into combat, the horses drawing his chariot were suddenly deprived of their energy and the left eye of that one who delighted in warfare began to twitch. His countenance grew pale, his voice trembled, the day which had seemed so fair became threatening and a bitter wind began to blow. Birds and beasts uttered mournful cries but that titan, who had the shoulders of a lion and the agility of a tiger, disregarding those portents, rushed towards the battlefield and, as he went forward with his troops, an immense tumult arose that seemed to convulse the ocean and the sound appalled the simian army, who, furnished with trees, prepared to enter into combat.

Thereafter a fearful struggle ensued between monkeys and demons and, ready to sacrifice their lives in the cause of Rama and Ravana, those monkey and titan warriors of exceeding valour, who resembled hills, contended with each other and, the yells they emitted in the thick of the fight and the shouts of defiance that they let forth in their rage created an indescribable clamour. A thick coppery dust, raised by the monkeys and the titans enveloped the whole horizon and, in the midst of that yellow cloud resembling silk which covered them, the combatants could no longer distinguish each other on the field. Neither standard, banner, shield, weapon nor chariot could be discerned in that pall of dust and the terrific clamour of warriors challenging and rushing upon each other was appalling to hear, yet in the confusion no form was visible.

In that fight monkeys fell under the blows of enraged monkeys, titans massacred titans in the darkness ; Plavagas and demons slew foe and friend, and the earth drenched with gore was thick with mud.

Under the rain of blood the dust was laid, revealing the

earth covered with corpses. Then the monkeys and titans assailed each other with blows from trees, spears, maces, javelins, stones, bars and picks, wrestling with their adversaries who resembled mountains. In that encounter those monkeys slew the titans of dreadful deeds and they, transported with rage, bearing darts and javelins in their hands, destroyed the monkeys with their cruel weapons.

Thereafter Akampana, the leader of the titans, full of ire, consoled all those fierce and valiant soldiers; the monkeys however, leaping upon them, shattered their weapons and crushed those titans with blows from trees and stones.

At that instant, the courageous monkey Leaders, Kumuda, Nala and Mainda, in a paroxysm of rage, as in sport, with mighty bounds and blows of trees created a great carnage amongst the titans and all those lions among the monkeys brought about complete disorder in the enemy ranks with their countless missiles.

CHAPTER 56

Akampana is slain by Hanuman

WITNESSING this great exploit executed by the monkey leaders, Akampana was seized with violent anger and his features became distorted. Brandishing his powerful bow, he addressed his charioteer in these words :—

" Drive the chariot with all speed to that place, for those warriors are slaying countless titans on the battlefield. Those arrogant monkeys of exceeding ferocity, armed with trees and rocks, dare to affront me ! I shall exterminate those audacious warriors who are seen sowing confusion in the ranks of the titans ! "

Thereupon, in his chariot drawn by fast-moving horses, Akampana, the most skilful of car-warriors, with a hail of darts, overwhelmed the monkeys so that they were no longer able to maintain their formation nor for this reason could they fight and, crushed under the shafts of the titan, the confusion became general.

Then the valiant Hanuman, seeing them fall under the sway of death, pursued by Akampana's darts, went to the rescue of his companions and, beholding that great Plavaga, those lions among the monkeys rallied and, in the field, grouped themselves boldly round him. Observing his courage, those foremost of the monkeys took heart in the shelter of his valour.

Meanwhile Akampana, like unto a second Mahendra, caused a hail of arrows to descend on Hanuman who remained as firm as a rock, heedless of the weapons that fell upon his body, and that exceedingly courageous monkey resolved to slay his adversary and, with peals of laughter, the impetuous son of Maruta leapt on the titan, causing the earth to shake as it were, while burning with energy he emitted yells, so that it was impossible to look upon him as it is impossible to gaze on a fire in a brazier.

Finding himself without weapons, that foremost one among the monkeys, in the fury that possessed him, tore up a rock and seizing a huge crag with one hand, Maruti, letting forth a roar, began to spin it rapidly thereafter hurling it at the Titan Leader Akampana, as formerly in the encounter, Purandara hurled his thunderbolt at Namuchi.

Akampana, however, seeing that crag flying towards him, shattered it from a distance by means of great crescent-shaped darts. Beholding that rocky peak shattered in the air by the titan's arrows and falling in pieces, Hanuman became mad with anger and observing an Ashvakarna Tree as large as a mountain, in the transport of rage that possessed him, that monkey uprooted it with violence and taking hold of that tree of immense branches, in his great strength, brandished it exultantly. Then he began to run with great strides, breaking down the trees in his haste and, in the excess of his fury, tearing up the earth with his feet; and he struck down elephants as also those who rode upon them and charioteers with their cars and the formidable titan infantry.

Seeing Hanuman, like unto Antaka, the Destroyer of Vital Breaths, full of wrath, armed with a tree, the titans took to flight. Thereupon the valiant Akampana beholding that enraged monkey

sowing terror amongst his soldiers, greatly perturbed, set up a
mighty shout and, with fourteen pointed arrows that tore the
flesh, he pierced the exceedingly powerful Hanuman.

Riddled with sharp-pointed iron shafts, that simian warrior
resembled a mountain covered with forests and, like unto a
flowering Ashoka Tree, he shone like a smokeless flame. Uprooting another tree, with a prodigious bound he struck the
head of the Titan General a fearful blow and, by that stroke with
which that Indra among Monkeys smote him in his fury,
Akampana fell dead.

Seeing their leader lying lifeless on the earth, all the titans
trembled as trees when the earth quakes. Put to flight, all those
warriors, throwing away their arms, escaped in the direction of
Lanka, terrified, pursued by the monkeys. Their hair loosened,
panic-stricken, their pride broken by defeat, their limbs dripping
with sweat, in their bewilderment, they fled in confusion.
Thereafter, mad with fear, looking back continually, crushing
each other in their haste, they entered the city.

And when those titans had entered Lanka, those exceedingly
powerful monkeys surrounded Hanuman in order to pay
homage to him and the mighty Hanuman, of noble nature,
honoured them all in accord with their rank.

Then the triumphant monkeys shouted with might and main
and once more pursued the titans with the intention of slaying
them while that great Plavaga, born of Maruta, returning to his
own companions, having slain the titan, enjoyed the same
renown in battle as Vishnu when he overcame the mighty Asura
of immense power in the forefront of the fight.

Thereafter that monkey received the homage of the Gods and
of Rama himself as also that of the exceedingly valiant Lakshmana
and the Plavamgamas led by Sugriva and the great-souled
Bibishana.

CHAPTER 57

Prahasta goes out to fight

HEARING of Akampana's death, the irascible Lord of the Titans with a downcast mien, took counsel with his ministers and, having reflected awhile and deliberated with them, Ravana, the Lord of the Titans, passed the forenoon in inspecting the defences ; and the King passed through that city, decorated with banners and flags, guarded by the titans and filled with innumerable troops.

Seeing Lanka beseiged, Ravana, the Sovereign of the Titans, said to the devoted Prahasta, a skilled soldier :—

" This city thus beleaguered and hard pressed, O Skilful Warrior, may only be delivered by myself, Kumbhakarna, thou, who art in command of the army, Indrajita or Nikumbha ; none else could undertake such a task !

" Taking a company of warriors, do thou speedily place thyself in their midst and set forth in order to triumph over those inhabitants of the woods. In this sortie, as soon as the army of monkeys hear the uproar created by the titans, they will disperse. Volatile, undisciplined and fickle, the monkeys will not be able to endure thy cry, any more than an elephant can endure the roaring of a lion. His army routed, Rama with Saumitri, robbed of further authority, will fall into thy power, O Prahasta.

"A hypothetical misfortune is preferable to one that is certain ! Whether it be unpleasing to hear or no, say what thou considerest to be to our advantage ! "

Thus addressed by that Indra among Titans, Prahasta, the leader of the army, answered him as Ushanas the King of the Asuras, saying :—

" O King, formerly we discussed this matter with the wise and, after examining the different points of view, a disagreement arose between us. To return Sita was what I considered the most advantageous course, not to do so, meant war ; we forsaw this.

" I have ever been heaped with gifts and honours by thee as also with every mark of friendship. When the opportunity arises, is it not for me to render thee a service ? Nay, I shall neither spare life, children, wife nor wealth ! Know me to be ready to sacrifice my life in thine interest in battle ! ''

Having spoken thus to his brother, the General Prahasta said to his leading officers who stood before him :—

'' Gather a large army together immediately ; to-day the flesh-eating birds and beasts shall feed on the enemy that I strike down on the battlefield with my swift arrows ! ''

At this command those highly powerful leaders assembled the forces in the abode of the King of the Titans. In an instant, Lanka was filled with redoubtable warriors like unto elephants, furnished with weapons of every kind.

While they propitiated the God who feeds on offerings[1] and paid homage to the brahmins, a fragrant breeze, bearing the scent of clarified butter, began to blow and the titans, all ready for battle, taking hold of garlands of every kind, adorned themselves with delight. Thereafter, armed with bows and mail, they set out in their chariots at a brisk pace, their eyes turned towards their King, Ravana. And they ranged themselves round Prahasta whilst he paid obeisance to his Sovereign to the beating of a gong of dreadful sound, whereafter, with his weapons, that general ascended his chariot that was furnished with all that was needful, harnessed to exceedingly swift steeds, skilfully driven and in perfect condition.

Rumbling like a great cloud, shining like the moon itself, unapproachable as the serpent that served as its standard, solidly and artistically constructed, decorated with a net of pure gold, smiling as it were in its magnificence, such was the car in which Prahasta, having received Ravana's command, stood.

Then the titan set out from Lanka immediately in the midst of a powerful army and, at his departure, a rolling of drums, resembling the roar of Parjanya, and a blast of fanfares arose that seemed to fill the earth and, with the blare of conches, the titans advanced, creating a terrible uproar.

Narantaka, Kumbhahanu, Mahanada and Samunata, colossal giants, his adjutants, surrounded Prahasta who emerged from the eastern gate in the midst of an immense, formidable and powerful army resembling a herd of elephants and, in the centre

[1] The Fire-god, Agni.

of that force, vast as the sea, Prahasta in his fury appeared like Death at the end of the world, whilst the uproar, that arose on his setting forth with his titans raising their war cries, drew a sinister answering call from all creatures.

In a cloudless sky, birds of prey advancing to meet the chariot, circled from left to right ; fearful jackals vomited forth fire and flames, howling lugubriously ; a meteor fell from heaven and the wind blew chill ; planets, in opposition to each other, lost their brilliance whilst clouds with a raucous sound showered blood on Prahasta's car with which his attendants were bespattered ; a croaking vulture, facing the south, alighted on the top of his standard depriving that titan of his lustre. His charioteer, who never turned back in battle, despite his skill, again and again allowed the goad to fall from his hand. The brilliance of that sortie of incomparable pomp vanished in an instant and the horses stumbled on the even ground.

Beholding Prahasta, renowned for his martial valour, advancing to give battle, the army of monkeys, furnished with weapons of every kind, went forward to meet him and a formidable clamour arose amongst them as they tore up the trees and seized hold of great rocks.

Thereafter the titans yelled and the monkeys roared, both armies being filled with ardour and, in their fury and zeal and their impatience to slay each other, they challenged one another with tremendous shouts.

Meanwhile Prahasta advanced on the forces of the monkeys whom in his folly he imagined he would destroy and, with an impetuous bound, he hurled himself upon that army as a grasshopper falls into a flame.

CHAPTER 58

The Death of Prahasta

BEHOLDING Prahasta setting out with martial ardour, the Conqueror Rama, smiling, enquired of Bibishana, saying :—

" Who is this colossus surrounded by an immense army,

who with such speed, valour and courage, advances so swiftly ? Make known to me this brave ranger of the night."

On this enquiry, Bibishana answered :—

" Prahasta is the name of this titan ; he is the leader of the army ; a third of the forces belonging to the King of the Titans accompanies him. He is courageous, a master of the science of weapons and a warrior renowned for his prowess."

While the terrible Prahasta of formidable exploits advanced roaring, that colossus, surrounded by his troops, was observed by the great and powerful army of the monkeys who began to emit cries of defiance.

Swords, lances, daggers, spears, darts, maces, bludgeons, bars, javelins and axes of every kind with many different bows glittered in the hands of the titans who, desirous of victory, fell upon the monkeys.

Trees in flower, rocks, huge and heavy stones were the weapons of the Plavamgamas, who were burning to fight and, as they approached each other, a formidable struggle arose between those innumerable combatants, who showered down a hail of stones and arrows. In the conflict, countless titans caused the death of thousands of mighty monkeys and countless monkeys destroyed as many titans. Some of the combatants fell under the lances, others under great arrows, some were struck down by the blows of bars, others cloven by axes. Deprived of their life's breath they lay on the earth their hearts transfixed or cut to pieces by the avalanche of missiles. And those monkeys fell on the earth cut in two by the strokes of swords, their sides torn open by those bold titans and they, on their part, full of fury, overthrew the enemy ranks, heaping the earth with them, and they struck at them with trees and crags, administering thundering slaps and terrific blows with their fists, so that the titans, blinded, their faces ashen, vomited blood.

Thereafter an appalling clamour arose and, amidst cries of pain and leonine roars, the monkeys and titans, each maddened, their features distorted, following the path of heroes, conducted themselves with great courage. Narantaka, Kumbhahanu, Mahanada and Samunnata, Prahasta's companions, decimated those inhabitants of the woods, hurling themselves on the monkeys in rage, destroying them ; and Dvivida struck down

one of them named Narantaka ; then the ape Durmukha, leaping
up in his turn, with a ready hand, struck Samunnata with a
great tree; Jambavan, in the height of anger, seizing a huge stone
hurled it with force on Mahanada's chest and, on his side, the
valiant Kumbhahanu, having attacked the General Tara, who
was armed with a huge tree, received a blow that cost him his
life.

Infuriated by the quadruple murder, Prahasta, who stood in
his chariot, with the bow held in his hand, caused a dreadful
havoc amongst the monkeys and the two armies became a vortex,
resembling a roaring tempest over a vast ocean. In that great
battle, the titan, intoxicated with combat, in his fury annihilated
the monkeys under an immense avalanche of arrows. The
corpses of monkeys and titans heaped the ground and covered it
like hideous mountains and the earth, running with the blood
which inundated it, shone as in the month of Spring when
covered by the blossoming Palasha Trees.

With the heaps of warriors for its banks, the broken weapons
its trees, the torrents of blood its huge waves, death appeared
like an ocean receiving its floods ; livers and spleens its mire,
entrails its moss, severed heads and trunks the fish, and morsels
of flesh the grass, innumerable vultures its lovely swans, herons
its geese, covered as it was with fat for the foam, the tumult the
sound of its waters, the battlefield resembled a river, incapable of
being crossed, visited by waterfowl at the end of the rainy
season. And the foremost of the titans and the monkeys crossed
over that impassable river as elephants lead their herds across
a lake that the lotuses have covered with pollen.

Meanwhile Prahasta, standing in his chariot, letting fly
countless shafts scattering the Plavamgamas, was observed by
Nila and, like unto a violent wind, the General of the Titans
beheld Nila advancing on him like a mass of clouds in the sky.

Directing his chariot bright as the sun towards him, that
foremost of archers, stretching his bow in the midst of the fray,
covered Nila with his barbed shafts, which, piercing him in their
rapid flight, passed through his body and, like furious serpents,
buried themselves in the earth with great spurts. When Nila
was wounded by those pointed shafts resembling tongues of fire,
that huge and mighty monkey, brandishing a tree, struck that

exceedingly redoubtable Prahasta who had set upon him with such fury.

Roaring with anger under his blows, that lion among titans overwhelmed the monkey chief with a rain of arrows and the shower of missiles loosed by that cruel demon was received by the monkey with closed eyes. Like a bull standing under a sudden autumnal downpour, so under that intolerable rain of darts, Nila immediately closed his eyes, suffering it, though it was scarce to be endured. Mad with rage, under the hail of arrows, that great and mighty monkey, arming himself with a Sala Tree, struck down Prahasta's horses and thereafter his heart surging with anger he severed the bow of that barbarian, shouting again and again.

Deprived of his bow, Prahasta, the leader of the army, seizing a formidable mace, leapt down from his chariot, and those two generals, facing each other, adversaries full of courage, their limbs covered with blood, like unto two elephants with broken tusks, tore each other with their sharp teeth. Lion and tiger in gait, lion and tiger in prowess, those two warriors, vanquishers of other heroes, intrepid combatants, thirsting for fame, resembled Vritra and Vasava.

Meanwhile Prahasta with a supreme effort struck Nila on the forehead with his mace, causing the blood to flow, whereupon that powerful monkey, his limbs covered with gore, seized a great tree and struck Prahasta full in the chest with fury. He, however, not heeding the impact, brandishing an enormous iron bar, hurled himself on the valiant Plavamgama. Seeing him advancing towards him with terrific bounds, full of rage, the mighty monkey Nila, snatched up a great rock which he swiftly threw at the head of his bellicose opponent armed with a mace. Loosed by that monkey chief, that immense and formidable stone broke into several pieces on Prahasta's head and the titan, deprived of breath, lustre, strength and consciousness instantly fell on the earth, like a tree severed at the root.

From his riven head and body the blood flowed, so that it resembled a torrent falling from a mountain. Prahasta being slain by Nila, the invincible and mighty army of the titans bereft of joy, fled to Lanka, their leader having succumbed, nor could they be stayed, as the waters of the sea may not be stemmed by a broken dyke.

Their leader slain, the titans disconsolate regained the abode of their sovereign. Dumb and dispirited, plunged in an ocean of burning grief, they appeared to have lost their wits.

The triumphant warrior Nila, however, on his return, was honoured by Rama with Lakshmana who accompanied him, and experienced supreme joy.

CHAPTER 59

Ravana's Prowess. Rama overcomes him but grants him his Life

THEIR General having succumbed in the fight against the foremost of the monkeys, the heavily armed forces of the King of the Titans took to flight with the speed of the tide.

Coming before their lord, they apprised him of the death of their leader who had fallen under the blows of the Fire-god's offspring, and at these tidings, the king was transported with anger. Learning that Prahasta had perished in the fight, his heart was filled with grief and he addressed the foremost of his leaders, as Indra those who never grow old[1] and said :—

"That foe is not to be despised, under whose blows the destroyer of Indra's host, the leader of my army with his followers and elephants, fell. I myself shall enter this strange battlefield without hesitation in order to obtain victory and destroy the enemy. As a forest is consumed by fire, so shall I to-day with a myriad arrows burn up the simian army with Rama and Lakshmana."

Speaking thus, that enemy of the Lord of the Celestials ascended his chariot which shone like a flame and was yoked to a team of horses, its brilliance increased by the splendour of his person.

The sound of trumpets, gongs, drums and leonine roars accompanied by the clapping of hands, acclamations and hymns

---

[1] The Gods, who are said to remain young.

of praise, frenziedly greeted the departure of the Sovereign of the Titans. Those eaters of flesh, resembling mountains or clouds, whose glances flashed like torches, surrounded the supreme Leader of the Titans as he marched out, like unto the Bhutas escorting Rudra, the Lord of the Immortals. Issuing from the city, that monarch observed the army of ferocious monkeys with trees and rocks in their hands, ready for combat, roaring like a vast ocean or a mass of thunder clouds.

Seeing the demon divisions seething with fury, the incomparably illustrious Rama, whose arms resembled great serpents, accompanied by his forces, said to Bibishana :—

" Who is in command of this army furnished with every kind of standard, banner and canopy, armed with javelins, swords, stakes and other weapons and missiles, that is indomitable and composed of intrepid soldiers and elephants as high as the Mahendra Mountain ? "

Thus interrogated, Bibishana, the equal of Shakra in valour, pointed out the principal leaders of those courageous lions among the titans to him and said :—

" That hero of coppery hue mounted on the back of an elephant, causing its head to sway, the rival of the rising sun, know, O Prince, to be Akampana.

" He who, standing in his chariot, brandishes his bow which resembles Shakra's, whose standard bears the image of a lion and who is like unto an elephant with its long curved tusks, is Indrajita, who is renowned for the boons he has received from Brahma.

" That archer yonder, like unto the Vindhya, Asta or Mahendra Mountains, standing in his car, a mighty warrior, who wields a bow of unequalled size, is called Atikaya on account of his immense stature.

" The tawny-eyed warrior resembling the dawn, riding a wild elephant with its bells jangling, who is shouting aloud, is Mahodara.

" The rider of the brilliantly caparisoned steed he, who is armed with a gleaming javelin and resembles a mass of evening clouds, whose fury rivals the lightning and possesses the velocity of a well-directed thunder-bolt, who is seated on the foremost of bulls and shines like the moon, is Trishiras. The other, resembling a thunder-cloud, of large and well-developed chest, who is twanging his bow and has the King of the Snakes as his standard, is Kumbha.

" The one who carries a mace decorated with gold and diamonds from which flames and smoke issue; who advances as a standard bearer to the titan army, is Nikumbha of prodigious exploits.

" That warrior in a chariot adorned with flags, gleaming like a glowing brazier, who is furnished with bows, swords and arrows, is Narantaka, who, in combat, fights with mountain peaks.

" Finally the one who appears surrounded by spectres of dreadful form with heads of tigers, buffalo, mighty elephants, deer and horses, riding under a white canopy with a slender handle, his diadem resembling the moon, he who is the humbler of the Gods themselves, like unto Rudra amidst the Bhutas is the mighty Lord of the Titans himself. His countenance is graced by swinging earrings, his formidable stature equals the Vindhya, that Lord of Mountains, he who brought Mahendra and Vaivasvat low, is the King of the Titans, equal to the sun in splendour."

Then Rama, the subduer of his foes answered Bibishana and said :—

" Ah ! What glory, what exceeding majesty is Ravana's, the Lord of the Titans ! As one cannot gaze on the sun, neither can the eye rest on him, such is the blinding strength of his magnificence ! Neither Devas, Danavas nor heroes possess a body equal to his ! Who can rival the brilliance of the King of the Titans ? All are as high as hills, all have crags as their weapons, all are furnished with fiery darts. The Lord of the Titans stands out among those ardent warriors as Antaka amidst the impetuous Bhutas of strange form. It is to his destruction that that wretch comes to-day within my sight ! To-day I shall slake my wrath born of Sita's abduction ! "

At these words, the valiant Rama who was accompanied by Lakshmana, took up his bow and, standing erect, placed an arrow, the most powerful of all, upon it.

Meanwhile the haughty Monarch of the Titans said to his brave troops :—

"Take up your positions unfalteringly at the gates and principal exits, the outposts and fortifications. Learning of my presence amongst you, these savages will try and profit by this opportunity to take this heretofore impregnable city by surprise, it being now denuded of its defenders, and they will then immediately put it to the sword with their united forces."

Thereafter Ravana dismissed his escort and the titans left on his orders, whereupon he plunged into the sea of monkeys, agitating it as a great fish the waters of the ocean.

As soon as that Indra of the Titans with his bow and burnished arrows had thrown himself into the fray, the leader of the monkeys rushed out to meet him, tearing up a great mountain peak. Seizing that rock covered with innumerable trees, he hurled it at that prowler of the night, who, seeing it flying towards him, broke it in pieces with his golden-stemmed arrows. That huge and high peak covered with trees being shattered, fell on the earth, and the Lord of the Titans, like unto another Antaka, selected a dart resembling a great serpent. Taking up that arrow, which rivalled Anila in velocity and possessed the brilliance of fire and the force of lightning, he loosed it with fury on Sugriva in order to slay him, and that weapon, equal to Shakra's thunderbolt, loosed by Ravana's arm, penetrated Sugriva's breast in its flight as formerly Guha's spear when he discharged it at the Krauncha Mountain.

Wounded by that missile which bereft him of consciousness, that warrior fell moaning to the earth. Beholding him stretched on the ground deprived of his senses, the Yatudhanas raised a shout of triumph.

Thereupon Gavaksha, Gavaya, Sushena as well as Rishabha, Jyotirmukha and Nala, of exceeding corpulence, tearing up rocks, hurled themselves on the King of the Titans. Then that Lord of the Titans, with hundreds of arrows possessed of sharp points, rendered their projectiles fruitless and pierced those leaders of the monkeys with a hail of marvellous golden-shafted arrows.

Under the blows with which the Enemy of the Gods assailed them, those generals of terrifying stature were overcome, whereupon he covered that formidable army of monkeys with a shower of arrows.

Assailed and wounded, those warriors emitted cries of terror and pain, and those deer of the branches, whom Ravana was destroying with his darts, fled for refuge to the intrepid Rama, whereupon that mighty and skilful archer, Raghava, seizing a weapon, set out at once. Lakshmana however, approaching him with joined palms, addressed him in moving tones, and said :—

" Truly, O Noble Brother, I am able to slay this wretch ! It is I who will destroy him, do thou give me leave, O Lord ! "

Then the exceedingly powerful Rama, a true hero, answered him saying :—

" Go, O Lakshmana, and in this duel may thy valour prevail ! Without doubt Ravana is endowed with great strength, he is a warrior of outstanding prowess ; the Three Worlds themselves could not withstand his fury ; seek out his weak points and guard against thine own ; be ever vigilant and defend thyself with eye and bow ! "

Thus spoke Raghava and Saumitri embraced him, thereafter offering obeisance to him and bidding him farewell, he entered the lists. There he beheld Ravana with arms as large as the trunks of elephants, who was brandishing his dread and fiery bow, covering the monkeys, whose limbs he had severed with a close rain of darts.

Beholding this, the exceedingly energetic Hanuman, born of Maruta, in order to bring that rain of arrows to an end, rushed on Ravana and, approaching his chariot, lifted his right arm and threatened him ; thereafter the sagacious Hanuman addressed him, saying :—

" Thou hast obtained the boon of invulnerability to Devas, Danavas, Gandharvas, Yakshas and also Rakshasas but the monkeys are a danger to thee ! This five-branched hand of mine,[1] which I now raise, will rob thee of the life that has long been resident in thy body ! "

At these words of Hanuman, the exceedingly valiant Ravana, his eyes inflamed with anger, answered :—

" Strike swiftly without fear ! Win eternal renown, having measured thy strength with mine, I shall destroy thee ! "

[1] Four fingers and the thumb.

Then the son of the Wind answered Ravana who spoke thus, saying :—

" Recollect that I have slain thy son Aksha already ! "

At this, the powerful Lord of the Titans struck the son of Anila a violent blow with the palm of his hand and the monkey reeled ; thereafter the mighty and illustrious Hanuman recovered his balance and, steadying himself, struck that enemy of the Immortals in fury. Under the violent impact of the monkey's blow, Dashagriva shook like a mountain when the earth trembles.

Seeing Ravana struck in the fight, Rishis, Siddhas and monkeys raised a great shout, as also the Devas, Suras and Asuras.

Then the extremely spirited Ravana, having regained his breath, said :—

" Well done ! Well done ! O Monkey, thou art an adversary worthy of praise ! "

Thus did he speak, and Maruti answered him, saying :— " Cursed be that strength since thou dost still survive, O Ravana ! Now come, enter into a decisive struggle with me, O Perverse Wretch ! Why this boasting ? My fist is about to despatch thee to the abode of Yama ! "

Hearing Hanuman's words, the powerful Ravana, enraged, his eyes red with fury, whirling his fist with force brought it down violently on the monkey's chest and, under the shock, Hanuman reeled once more, whilst the King of the Titans, Dashagriva, that exceedingly fiery warrior, seeing his valiant opponent bereft of strength, turned his chariot towards Nila. With his arrows, like unto great serpents, he pierced the vital parts of his enemy overwhelming the Monkey General, but Nila, the leader of the monkey army, assailed by that hail of weapons, with one hand flung a great rock at the King of the Titans.

Meanwhile Hanuman, burning with courage, having recovered his senses, in his martial ire cried out furiously :— " O Ravana, King of the Titans, who art engaged in combat with Nila, to attack one already fighting with another is unjust ! "

The titan, however, shattered the crag, hurled by Nila, with seven pointed darts so that it fell in pieces and, seeing the rock riven asunder, the leader of the monkey army, Nila, destroyer of hostile forces, who resembled the Fire of Time, glowed with fury and began to hurl Asvakarna, Sala, Cuta and other flowering trees of varying fragrance in the fight, whereupon Ravana caught them in his arms and snapped them, showering a formidable rain of shafts, as from a cloud, on Pavaki[1] but that colossus, assuming a diminutive form, leapt on to the point of Ravana's standard.

Beholding the offspring of Pavaki thus installed on the point of his standard, the King blazed with fury, whilst Nila let forth a shout, and sometimes the monkey leapt on to the apex of the banner and sometimes on to the end of the bow and sometimes on to the peak of the diadem, so that Lakshmana, Hanuman and Rama also, were astonished.

The intrepid titan too was amazed at the monkey's agility and took up a marvellous and flaming arrow but the Plavamgamas shouted joyously at Nila's tactics, being amused to see Ravana disconcerted by his leaping about in combat and the shouts of the monkeys infuriated Dashagriva, who, in his confusion, did not know how to act.

Taking up an arrow charged with sacred formulas, that prowler of the night aimed at Nila, who had climbed to the tip of his standard and, at that instant, the King of the Titans, said :—

" O Monkey, thine agility proceeds from a rare power of magic ; do thou save thyself if thou canst by these innumerable tricks with which thou art familiar and constantly employest ! This mantra-propelled weapon of mine, that I am about to loose, will sever the existence thou seekest to retain ! "

Speaking thus, the long-armed Ravana, Lord of the Titans, having placed Agni's shaft on his bow, struck Nila, the General of the monkey army, with that weapon and he, pierced through the breast by that shaft charged with sacred mantras, was suddenly overcome and fell to the earth, yet by virtue of his sire's powerful aid and his own native vigour, though brought to his knees he was not deprived of life.

Beholding the monkey unconscious, Dashagriva, insatiable in combat, in his chariot, whose rattling resounded like thunderclouds, rushed on Lakshmana and coming to the centre of the field, halted, standing there in his glory.

Thereafter the majestic Lord of the Titans lifted up his bow,

---

[1] Pavaki—The name of Nila as son of the God of Fire.

whereupon Saumitri, of indomitable courage, said to him as he prepared to loose his powerful shaft :—

" O King of the Night-rangers, now enter into combat with me ; cease from fighting with the monkeys ! "

Hearing that marvellously modulated voice that resounded like the twanging of a bow-string, the King, drawing near to his adversary, who stood close to his chariot, answered in anger :—

" O Son of Raghu, it is my good fortune that brings thee within my range to-day, thou who, in thy folly, advancest to meet thy death ! This very instant thou shalt descend to the region of Mrityu under a rain of missiles loosed by me."

Then Saumitri, unmoved, spoke to that boastful titan of sharp and protruding teeth, saying :—

" O King, stout hearts eschew bragging ! O Greatest of Evil Doers, thou art sounding thine own praises ! I am well acquainted with thy strength, prowess, vigour and audacity, O King of the Titans ! Approach ! Here I stand with bow and arrows in my hand ; of what use are vain boasts ? "

Thus accosted, the Lord of the Titans, infuriated, let fly seven marvellously plumed arrows which Lakshmana shattered with his golden-shafted darts. Observing his shafts resembling great serpents, whose coils had been crushed in an instant, the Lord of Lanka was transported with anger and let fly further sharp arrows. The younger brother of Rama, however, caused a well-aimed rain of missiles from his bow to fall on Ravana, but he, with the aid of weapons in the forms of knives, crescents and long-eared arrowheads, severed them, without allowing them to disturb him.

Seeing that the succession of his shafts proved useless, the King of those hostile to the Gods, astonished at Lakshmana's skill, let fly more whetted shafts upon him anew and, from his side, Lakshmana, the equal of Mahendra, placing some sharpened darts on his bow that were formidable, swift as lightning and of blazing effulgence, loosed them on the Titan King in order to strike him down, whereupon Ravana shattered those pointed darts and struck his rival in the forehead with a shaft as bright as the Fire of Time, which had been bestowed on him by Swyambhu. Then Lakshmana, struck by that missile, reeled a little, scarcely able to retain his bow but coming to himself with difficulty, he shattered that weapon belonging to Indra's foe. Having broken his bow, the son of Dasaratha struck him with three pointed darts and the king, pierced by those arrows, swooned, regaining his senses with difficulty. Wounded by those shafts, his bow wholly demolished, his limbs spattered with flesh and streaming with blood, the Enemy of the Gods, himself of formidable energy, seized a spear which had been given him in war by Swyambhu. That smoking lance, as bright as fire, the terror of the monkeys in the fray, the powerful guardian of the titan empire, was hurled on Saumitri the younger brother of Bharata, who received that spear falling upon him with arrows and darts, as if it were a sacrificial fire ; nevertheless that weapon entered his broad chest.

The powerful Raghu, struck by that spear, lay on the earth, breathing fire and the King of the Titans rushing on him suddenly, while he was yet insensible, seized him brutally in his two hands, yet though he was able to lift up Himavat, Mandara, Meru and the Three Worlds with the Gods, he could not raise the younger brother of Bharata, for Lakshmana, though wounded in the breast by Brahma's weapon, recollected that he was of the substance of Vishnu Himself, and that thorn in the side of the Gods, though overcoming Saumitri, was unable to bear him away.

At that instant, the son of Vayu, enraged, threw himself in anger on Ravana like a flash of lightning and struck him with his fist on the chest. Under that blow, the Lord of the Titans was brought to his knees and stumbling, fell. From his ten mouths, eyes and ears, blood streamed in torrents and, rolling unconscious, he slid under the body of the chariot; there he remained deprived of his senses, stupified, not knowing where he was. Beholding Ravana, despite his redoubtable strength swoon on the battlefield, Rishis and monkeys began to shout in triumph as did also the Gods and Asuras, whilst the courageous Hanuman lifting up Lakshmana in his arms, who had been wounded by his adversary, returned to Raghava. In his friendship and extreme devotion to him, the son of Vayu found Lakshmana, whom foes were unable to move, as light as a feather. Thereafter the spear, that had overcome Saumitri, returned to the titan's chariot.

Meanwhile Ravana who was full of energy in combat, having recovered consciousness, selected some steel-pointed arrows and armed himself with an enormous bow.

On his side, healed and freed from that lance, Lakshmana recollected that he was part of Vishnu, and Rama, seeing the innumerable army of powerful monkeys overthrown on the battlefield, rushed on Ravana, but Hanuman, following him, said :—

" Climb on my shoulders in order to overcome the titan ! "

Hearing those words from the son of Vayu, Raghava climbed on the shoulders of that great monkey, as Vishnu on Garuda, in order to fight with the Enemy of the Gods.

Standing in his chariot, Ravana appeared before that Lord of Men and, seeing him, that mighty hero rushed upon him, like unto Vishnu with his mace upraised rushing furiously on Virochana. Thereupon Rama drew the cord of his bow and, like unto the roll of thunder, said in a deep voice to the Lord of the Titans :—

" Stay ! Stay ! Thou hast evoked my displeasure ! Where, O Tiger among the Titans, wilt thou flee to escape me ? Even if thou seekest refuge in the region of Indra or Vaivaswata or Bhaskara or Swyambhu, Vaishnavara, Shankara or in the ten regions, even in those abodes thou shalt not elude me from now on. The one who, struck by the spear, fell swooning this day only to recover consciousness immediately, shall now, assuming the form of death, claim thee, thy sons, and grandsons in battle. O King of the Titan People, here is he under whose blows, fourteen thousand titans of terrible form perished, who had established themselves in Janasthana and were furnished with excellent weapons."

Hearing Raghava speak thus, the exceedingly powerful Lord of the Titans full of rage, hurled himself on the son of Vayu, who was bearing Rama with extreme velocity through the fray and, recollecting his former hostility, he smote him with flaming arrows resembling the tongues of the Fire of Dissolution. Struck by that titan as also pierced by his darts, the native strength of which Hanuman was possessed increased still further. Nevertheless the extremely illustrious Rama, seeing the wound that Ravana had just inflicted on that lion among the Plavagas, was transported with anger and, approaching his chariot with his slender and pointed shafts, shattered it with its wheels, horses, banner, canopy, great standard, charioteer, darts, spears and swords; thereafter, with great force, he hurled a weapon like unto a thunderbolt falling on Mount Meru so that that valiant monarch, whom neither thunder nor lightning could cause to tremble, stumbled, letting fall his bow at the violent impact of Rama's missile, which created a deep wound.

Seeing him swooning, the magnanimous Rama took up a flaming arrow shaped like a crescent moon and used it to shatter the crown of the supreme Lord of the Titans, which was as bright as the sun.

Then Rama said to that Indra of the Titans, whose splendour was dimmed, the setting of his diadem riven, and who resembled a venomous snake robbed of its poison, or the sun, its rays extinguished, bereft of lustre :—

" Thou hast accomplished a great feat and my brave soldiers have succumbed beneath thy blows; now thou art weary; in this condition I shall not put thee under Mrityu's power with my shafts. Leave the fray and return to Lanka; I grant thee this reprieve, O King of the Rangers of the Night! Having regained thy breath, return in thy chariot with thy bow and, standing on thy car, thou shalt once more bear testimony to my prowess ! "

At these words, his joy and boasting subdued, his bow shattered, his horses and charioteer slain, pierced with arrows, his great diadem broken, the king instantly returned to Lanka.

After the departure of that powerful Indra of Night Rangers, Lakshmana drew out the arrows from the monkeys, which they had received while fighting in the forefront of that vast battle-field, and the adversary of the King of the Gods being vanquished, all the Celestials, Asuras and creatures of the ocean and other regions with the great serpents, as also all beings on earth and in the waters, rejoiced.

CHAPTER 60

The Titans rouse Kumbhakarna

RETURNING to the City of Lanka, afflicted with the fear of Rama's arrows, his pride humbled, the king's mind was troubled. Like an elephant by a lion or a snake by Garuda, that monarch had been overcome by the great-souled Rama, and the Lord of the Titans was maddened by the mere recollection of Rama's shafts possessed of the splendour of lightning, resembling the Rod of Brahma.

Seated on his magnificent and elevated throne made of gold, he let his gaze wander over the titans and said :—

" Since I, the equal of the mighty Indra, have been defeated by a mere man, all the rigorous asceticism I have practised has been in vain. I asked to be rendered invulnerable to Devas, Danavas, Gandharvas, Yakshas, Rakshasas and Pannagas, but of man I made no mention. Rama, the son of Dasaratha is the one, I deem, of whom Anaranya,[1] born of the race of Ikshvaku spoke, saying :—

" 'O Lord of the Titans, in my House will be born a man who will slay thee in battle with thy sons, ministers, army and charioteer, O Vilest of Thy Race, O Perverse Wretch ! '

" I was further cursed by Vedavati for a former outrage and perchance she has been born as the high-souled daughter of Janaka and what was predicted by Uma, Nandishwara, Rambha and Punjikasthala, the daughter of Varuna, has come to pass ! The words of the sages never prove false, it is on account of all this therefore that you should exert yourselves to the uttermost.

" Let the titans go to the summit of the Charyapura Mountain and awaken Kumbhakarna on whom the curse of Brahma rests, he who is without equal in prowess and who humbles the pride of the Gods and Danavas themselves."

---

[1] The stories of Anaranya, Vedavati and Punjikasthala are told in Uttarakanda.

Prahasta being slain and the king himself defeated in the fight, that monarch issued his commands to the dreadful host, saying :—

" Guard the gates and man the ramparts, rouse Kumbhakarna who is slumbering soundly. He is sleeping peacefully oblivious of all that is passing, his senses overcome by lust, and he remains unconscious for periods of two or three or nine days and sometimes for six, seven or eight months. Having met in consultation with me nine days ago, he has since fallen asleep. In combat, that warrior is the rampart of all the titans ; he will soon strike down all the monkeys and those two sons of a king. He is the very banner of the titans in battle but that insensate one, intent on vulgar pleasures, still slumbers. Though overcome by Rama in this terrible struggle, my fears will be dissipated when Kumbhakarna wakes ; of what use is this rival of Indra to me, if, in so pressing a danger, he is not ready to assist me ? "

Hearing their sovereign's words, the titans ran in great haste to Kumbhakarna's abode. At Ravana's command, those eaters of flesh and drinkers of blood took perfumes, garlands and a great store of food and left immediately. They entered that cave with its gates measuring a league in extent, the wonderful refuge of Kumbhakarna, from which issued the fragrance of flowers. And with his breathing, Kumbhakarna pressed those titans back despite their strength who, with difficulty, had penetrated into the cave.

When they had entered into that ravishing underground dwelling paved with precious stones and gold, those lions among the Nairritas beheld that redoubtable giant lying there, and that monster, wrapt in profound slumber, resembled a crumbling mountain and together they sought to waken him.

His limbs covered with down which stood on end, Kumbhakarna, he of irresistible valour, was breathing like a serpent, and, as he slept, he emitted dreadful snores, his nostrils being horrible and his mouth a gaping hell. Stretched to his full length on the earth, he gave forth an odour of marrow and blood ; his limbs were adorned with golden armlets and he wore a diadem as bright as the sun ; thus did that lion among the Nairritas, Kumbhakarna, the slayer of his foes, appear !

Then those powerful titans, in order to satisfy him, placed a heap of venison as high as Mount Meru before him and piled up a great mass of viands, antelope, buffalo and bear and a prodigious mound of victuals, leathern bottles of blood and meats of every kind before Kumbhakarna, the Enemy of the Gods. Thereafter they rubbed that scourge of his foes with the most rare sandalwood and covered him with celestial garlands, and sweet smelling perfumes, and they burnt incense and hymned the praises of that warrior who proved fatal to his foes.

The voices of the Yatudhanas burst forth on every side like thunder and with full cheeks they blew impatiently on their conches as bright as the moon, causing a terrible uproar, and those rangers of the night clapped their hands and shook Kumbhakarna, creating a great clamour, in order to awaken him, so that the birds passing through the air fell down at the sound of the conches, drums, gongs, clapping of hands and leonine roars.

As the illustrious Kumbhakarna did not waken from his slumber despite the great uproar, all those troops of titans seized hold of bars, pestles, maces, rocks, clubs, hammers, and with these and blows from their fists, those titans beat the chest of Kumbhakarna violently as he was sleeping peacefully on the ground. And Kumbhakarna's breathing prevented those titans from standing upright so that they had to seat themselves round him and, with all their strength, which was considerable, they began to beat drums, cymbals and gongs and to blow their myriad conches and trumpets. Ten thousand demons surrounded that colossus who resembled a heap of antimony, and tried in every way to rouse him by their blows and cries; nevertheless he did not wake.

As they were unable to rouse him by these means, they had resort to more energetic and ruthless methods, causing horses, camels and elephants, whom they beat with sticks, whips and thongs, to trample upon him, while gongs, conches and trumpets blared forth as they crushed his limbs under piles of heavy logs. The noise of the hammers and pestles they wielded with all their strength and the shouts they raised filled the whole of Lanka with its hills and woods but still he did not wake.

Then they beat a thousand drums simultaneously with sticks of refined gold but yet he did not stir from his profound slumber, being under the spell of the divine curse.

Finally those powerful rangers of the night, growing enraged, redoubled their efforts in order to rouse the titan and some beat drums, some shouted, some tore out his hair and others bit his ears, pouring hundreds of pitchers of water into them, but Kumbhakarna, plunged in deep sleep, did not stir. Some armed with daggers struck that mighty titan on the head, chest and limbs but that monster did not wake, though smitten by Shataghnis fastened with ropes, and at last a thousand titans ran up and down his body, till Kumbhakarna, becoming aware of that pressure, he who had remained insensible to the violent blows of crags and trees, under the prompting of extreme hunger suddenly emerged from sleep, yawning, and with one bound, stood up. Waving his two arms resembling serpent's coils or the peaks of mountains, hard as cut diamonds, that ranger of the night opened his monstrous mouth, like unto Vadavamukha and yawned horribly, and when he yawned, his mouth resembled hell and glittered like the sun rising over the high peak of Mt. Meru.

That extremely powerful ranger of the night, being awake, yawned, heaving a sigh like unto a tempest that shatters a mountain ; and Kumbhakarna, rising up, resembling Time at the dissolution of the world, prepared to devour all beings and his two great eyes, like glowing braziers, glittering like lightning, resembled two huge flaming planets.

Then they pointed to those victuals of every kind, boar and buffalo and the giant devoured them. Thereafter that enemy of Shakra's satisfied his hunger with flesh and his thirst with blood, and he swallowed pitchers full of fat and wine, whereupon he, having feasted, those rangers of the night approached him and, surrounding him, paid obeisance to him.

Raising his eyelids that were heavy with sleep, his gaze still veiled, he let his glance fall on the night rangers on every side and, in a voice of authority, that lion among the Nairritas, surprised at being roused, enquired of them, saying :—

" For what reason have you thus wakened me so suddenly ? Is all well with the king or is he in some peril ? In truth there must be some pressing and serious danger from an external source since you have come in haste to awaken me. I shall drive every misfortune away from the King of the Titans this very day even if I have to cut Mahendra himself to pieces or freeze Anala! Nay, it is certain that one does not interrupt the slumbers of one, such as I, for any trivial motive. Tell me frankly for what reason you have roused me, Kumbhakarna, the vanquisher of my foes ? "

At these words, that were tinged with wrath, Yupaksha, the king's confidential minister, with joined palms, answered him saying :—

" It is not the Gods who threaten us in any way but a man who has placed us in this evil case, O Prince ! It is not the Devas or Danavas who have put us in this peril ; it comes to us from a mortal. Monkeys as large as hills are besieging Lanka ! Furious on account of Sita's abduction, Rama is pressing us heavily. Recently a single monkey set fire to our great city and slew the youthful Prince Aksha with his escort of elephants. ' Get thee hence ! ' were the words addressed by Rama to the King of the Titans in person, the offspring of Poulastya, that thorn in the side of the Gods, he who is equal to Aditya in splendour. That which this monarch never suffered at the hands of the Gods or Daityas or Danavas, he has had to endure from Rama, who spared his life."

Hearing from Yupaksha that his brother had been defeated in combat, Kumbhakarna, rolling his great eyes, said :—

" This very day, O Yupaksha, the whole army of monkeys with Lakshmana and Raghava will be destroyed by me on the field of battle after I have presented myself before Ravana. I shall gorge the titans on the blood of monkeys and, as for Rama and Lakshmana, I shall drink their blood myself ! "

Hearing these bold words from that titan, whose anger increased his ferocity, Mahodara, the Leader of the Nairrita warriors, having offered him obeisance with joined palms, said to him :—

" When thou hast listened to Ravana and weighed the advantages and disadvantages of the matter, then, O Long-armed Warrior, set out immediately and destroy the foe on the battle-field."

Thus spoke Mahodara and Kumbhakarna, surrounded by titans, full of energy and prowess, prepared to depart. Thereupon the titans, having succeeded in rousing that prince of dreadful aspect and formidable valour, returned to the king's palace in all haste. Approaching Dashagriva who was seated on the throne, all those night-rangers with joined palms said to him :—

" Thy brother, Kumbhakarna, has wakened, O King of the Titans, and now is it thy will that he should enter the battlefield or dost thou desire him to come hither ? "

Thereupon Ravana answered those titans who stood before him and, with a glad heart, said :—

" I desire to see him here ; let him receive the honours due to his rank ! "

" Be it so ! " answered all the titans and they returned to Kumbhakarna in order to apprise him of Ravana's command and said :—

" Do thou go to the king, that lion of all the titans desires to see thee ; go and gratify thy brother ! "

Then Kumbhakarna, that indomitable and mighty warrior, hearing what was his brother's wish, cried :—" So be it ! " and leapt up from his couch. Washing his face and bathing, refreshed and delighted, he desired them to bring him to drink with speed, whereupon they brought him a soothing draught and those titans hastened to carry out Ravana's commands and presented him with wines and meats of every kind.

Having swallowed two thousand full pitchers, Kumbhakarna prepared to set out and, slightly inebriated and flushed, he was exhilarated and filled with energy. Impatiently, he marched away like Yama at the end of the World period, and approaching his brother's palace, he caused the earth to tremble with his tread. His body illumined the royal highway, like unto that orb of a thousand rays which gives light to the earth and, as he advanced, surrounded by a circle of titans paying him obeisance, he resembled Shatakratu approaching Swyambhu's abode.

Seeing that slayer of his foes on the royal highway, that monster as high as the peak of a mountain, the inhabitants of the woods, stationed outside (the city) as also their leaders, were seized with a sudden panic.

Some rushed to Rama for refuge, others fled away in fear,

some, terrified, stampeded in all directions, others, paralysed with fright, lay on the ground.

Beholding that giant like a great peak, adorned with a diadem. who seemed to quench the sun with his brilliance, the inhabitants of the woods were seized with terror and, at the sight of that prodigy, fled in all directions.

CHAPTER 61

The Story of Kumbhakarna

MEANWHILE the illustrious and valiant Rama, bow in hand, beheld that giant Kumbhakarna adorned with a diadem and, seeing that Indra among Titans with golden armlets, who resembled a mountain and was like unto a cloud charged with rain, or Narayana[1] when formerly taking the three strides, the monkeys scattered once more.

In view of the stampede of his forces and that titan, who appeared to be increasing in size, Rama, astonished, enquired of Bibishana :—

" Who is this hero with a diadem and yellow eyes, resembling a mountain, who is to be seen in Lanka like unto a cloud riven by lightning or a great and strange meteor which has fallen to earth ; he, at whose sight, the monkeys flee away on all sides ? Tell me, who is this colossus ? Is it a Rakshasa or an Asura ? Never have I seen such a being ! "

Thus questioned by Prince Rama of imperishable exploits, Bibishana, in his great wisdom, answered :—

" It is he by whom Vaivasvata and Vasava were defeated in battle ; it is the illustrious Kumbhakarna, the son of Vaishravas ! There is no titan equal to him in stature, he routed the Devas, Danavas, Yakshas, Bhujamgas, Pishitashanas, Gandharvas, Vidyadharas and Pannagas in their thousands, O Raghava ! The Gods themselves are not able to slay Kumbhakarna, who, spear in hand, is of monstrous aspect. ' It is the God of Death himself ' they cry.

[1] See glossary.

" The mighty Kumbhakarna is innately powerful, whilst the foremost of the titans owe their strength to the boons they have received. As soon as that monster was born and while yet an infant, urged on by hunger, he devoured thousands of beings. Seeing their kind consumed, those creatures, mad with fear, took refuge with Shakra and told him all that had taken place. Enraged, Mahendra struck Kumbhakarna with his mighty thunderbolt and, at the impact of Indra's weapon, that giant reeled howling with terror.

" When the cries of the titan were heard, the fear of those beings increased, and in his anger, the mighty Kumbhakarna tore out one of Airavata's tusks in order to pierce Vasava's breast and, under the blows of that monster, Indra appeared like a flame. Seeing this, the Devas, Brahmarishis and Danavas were thunderstruck and Shakra with those Celestials went to Swyambhu's abode and informed Prajapati of Kumbhakarna's wickedness ; he also described to the inhabitants of the heavenly region, how he had devoured all those creatures, laid waste the hermitages and carried off others wives and said ' If he continues to devour those beings, in a short time the whole world will become a desert'.

" Hearing Vasava's words, the Grandsire of the Worlds summoned that titan, who appeared before him. On beholding Kumbhakarna, Prajapati was troubled but, recovering himself, said to him :—

" 'Assuredly Poulastya begot thee to the destruction of the worlds ! From to-day thou shalt sleep like the dead ! ' Struck by the Lord's curse that titan fell down before him.

" Meanwhile Ravana, exceedingly perturbed, said to Brahma:—

" 'Thou hast hewn down the golden tree which was about to bear fruit! It does not behove thee to curse thine own grandson, O Prajapati ; nevertheless thy words may never prove vain ; assuredly he must slumber but at least appoint a time for sleeping and a time for waking ! '

" On Ravana's request, Swyambhu answered :—' He shall sleep for six months and wake for a single day ; for one day that warrior shall range the earth in order to appease his hunger, otherwise with his huge mouth he will consume the worlds like a great fire.'

" It is in fear of thy prowess that the King Ravana, beset with peril, has now awakened Kumbhakarna, and that warrior of exceeding valour has emerged from his retreat transported with anger and is rushing upon the monkeys in order to devour them and appease his hunger. Seeing Kumbhakarna they have taken to flight; how can those monkeys withstand him in combat ? Let them be told that he is merely a mechanical device created to frighten them ; at these tidings they will take heart and remain here."

Hearing Bibishana's eloquent and persuasive speech, Raghava said to the General Nila :—

" Go, rally thy forces and, having occupied the outposts of Lanka, the highways and bridges, let them strike camp, O Pavaki ! See that the monkeys, furnished with rocks, trees and stones, arm themselves with these weapons."

At Rama's command, Nila, the leader in chief, a prince of monkeys, issued his orders to the army and thereafter armed with boulders, Gavaksha, Sharabha, Hanuman and Angada, like unto hills, advanced to the gates.

Having listened to Rama, the monkeys, those valiant apes, fell upon the enemy's army with shouts of triumph, battering it with trees and that ferocious company of monkeys, brandishing crags and trees, appeared as resplendent as a lowering mass of clouds spreading over a mountain.

CHAPTER 62

The Meeting between Kumbhakarna and Ravana

MEANWHILE that Lion among the Titans, resplendent in glory, still heavy with sleep, advanced with great strides along the royal highway ; titans in their thousands surrounded that most invincible of warriors and, from the houses, a rain of flowers fell upon him as he passed.

Thereafter he beheld the vast and enchanting residence covered with gold of that Indra of the Titans which shone like the sun, resembling that orb when it enters a mass of clouds, and he penetrated into the palace belonging to the King of the Titans, observing him from afar on his throne, like unto Shakra approaching Swyambhu seated in state.

Coming to Ravana's abode with his escort of titans, Kumbhakarna, pacing the earth, caused it to tremble. Having crossed the threshold of the palace, he passed through the courtyard and perceived his elder brother, who appeared troubled, seated in the Chariot Pushpaka. Full of anxiety, Dashagriva, beholding Kumbhakarna, immediately rose up joyfully and motioned him to approach.

Then that mighty warrior, bowing to the feet of his brother, who was reclining on a couch, enquired of him :—" What dost thou desire of me ? "

With renewed delight, Ravana rose and embraced him whereupon with brotherly salutations and traditional courtesies, Kumbhakarna ascended the celestial and shining throne, and that giant being seated, his eyes red with anger, enquired of Ravana :—

" Why hast thou forcibly torn me from my slumber, O King ? Say from whence springs thy fear and whom dost thou wish me to slay this day ? "

Then Ravana answered the enraged Kumbhakarna seated beside him, who was rolling his inflamed eyes, and said :—

" Thou hast slumbered for some time, O Warrior, and, in thy profound oblivion, wert indifferent to the peril in which Rama has plunged me. This glorious and mighty son of Dasaratha accompanied by Sugriva, having crossed the sea without hindrance, is destroying our race. Alas ! See how by means of a bridge, these monkeys have made an ocean of the woods and groves of Lanka !

" The foremost of the titans have been slain by them in combat, nor do I see how these monkeys can be destroyed in battle by any means. Save us from this great peril, O Mighty Hero, and exterminate them to-day ! It is on this account that thou hast been awakened ; all my resources are exhausted ! Help me to save the City of Lanka, in which the children and the aged alone remain. O Long-armed Warrior, for thy brother's sake, accomplish this feat, impossible to another. I have never before spoken thus to any of my brothers, O Scourge of Thy

Foes ! I have placed my supreme hopes and affections on thee ! O Bull among the Titans, how often, in the wars between Devas and Asuras, hast thou overcome the Gods and Celestial Beings ranged against thee ! Call upon thy valour, assuredly among all creatures none is equal to thee in strength, O Redoubtable Hero ! Render me this great service, O Thou, the lover of combat ; do this for me, O Thou who art devoted to thy friends ! By thy personal prowess scatter these hostile forces as the wind scatters the autumnal clouds."

CHAPTER 63

Kumbhakarna consoles Ravana

HEARING the lament of the King of the Titans, Kumbhakarna said with a mocking laugh :—

" As an evil doer falls into hell as a result of his misdeeds, a swift retribution has followed on the error of judgment we saw thee commit formerly in council through lack of trust in thy ministers ! Firstly, O Great King, thou didst not reflect on what might happen and, in the pride of thine own strength, overlooked the consequences. He, who trusting in his own power, leaves until last that which should be done first or who does first, that which should follow, is unable to distinguish between what is wise and what is foolish. As offerings poured into an unsanctified fire so are those actions disastrous which are performed without regard to time and place or in opposition to them. He goes straight to the goal, who, in consultation with his ministers, has examined the three kinds of action and their five aspects[1]. A king who makes his decisions according to the traditional laws, and allows himself to be advised by his counsellors and consults his friends, pursuing duty, profit and

[1] Three kinds of action—Trivial, common or ordinary, important and urgent.
Five aspects—The consideration of (*a*) Time, (*b*) Place, (*c*) Of persons or things concerned, (*d*) Provision against mischance, (*e*) Consideration of the possibility of success.

pleasure[1] at the proper season or following two of them or all of them combined, is a wise monarch and has a sound understanding, O Lord of the Titans.

" But the sovereign or heir-apparent, who, having heard what is best for the cultivation of these three means and yet does not comprehend them, has spent his time listening to instruction in vain. The king who consults his ministers regarding the bestowal of gifts, conciliation, sowing dissension, taking action or uniting himself with the foe as also the consideration of what should or should not be done and the questions of duty, profit and pursuit of pleasure, dealing with them in conformity with circumstances, and is master of himself, is not visited by misfortune !

" He verily is a king, who, with experienced and sagacious counsellors, having studied the advantages he desires to reap from an undertaking and the wisdom of entering into it, takes action.

" One should never follow the advice of those admitted to council who are not conversant with the meaning of the scriptures, whose intelligence is equal to the beasts and who, in their conceit, prate continuously ! Neither should one follow the advice of those who, in their ignorance of the tradition and the works of political science, merely seek to amass wealth. And those counsellors who, in their complacency, hold specious but sinister debates, should be excluded from any deliberation, for they mar every transaction. Those in the pay of well-informed enemies, who, in order to betray their master, advise him to act contrary to his interests, will be recognized by the king when they are in the assembly, and a monarch will soon discover those who, under the mask of devotion hide their treachery, by studying their conduct in their deliberations when they are met together. Those foolish ones, who rush precipitately into action like birds entering a hole in the Krauncha Mountain, are overwhelmed by the enemy and he who, disregarding the foe, fails to protect himself, experiences nothing but reverses and loses his status.

---

[1] Duty, profit and pleasure—The Three Ends of Life should be pursued in the following order :—Duty or devotion in the morning, profit or affairs in the afternoon and the pursuit of pleasure in the evening.

" The advice that the beloved Mandodari and my younger brother, Bibishana, formerly gave thee, I now repeat for thine own good ; do what thou considerest best ! "

Hearing Kumbhakarna's words, Dashagriva frowned and replied angrily :—

" One should pay the same respect to one's elder brother as to one's spiritual preceptor ! Of what interest to me are thy counsels ? Why fatigue thyself ? Consider what is fitting at the moment ; whatever has impeded success, whether it has been folly or too great a confidence in the strength of mine army, it is useless to discuss it now ! Advise me as to what should be done in the present circumstances. Let thy valour remedy the evil that mine imprudence has brought about if thou art truly devoted to me and hast confidence in thine own prowess and if thine heart is in this great struggle and thou considerest it to be of supreme moment. He is a friend who rescues one in distress ; a kinsman he, who helps one who has failed."

Thus spoke Ravana in imperious and harsh accents and Kumbhakarna reflecting within himself ' he is enraged ', answered him mildly in soothing tones, Looking fixedly at his brother, whose mind was agitated, he spoke comforting words to him in a quiet voice, saying :—

" Listen carefully, O King, O Scourge of Thy Foes, O Leader of the Titan Princes, banish thy grief, renounce thine anger and be thyself again ! There is no reason for thine heart to be troubled as long as I live, O Lord ! I will slay him who is the cause of thy distress but, in any circumstances, I had, of necessity, to speak for thine own good because of kinship and brotherly affection for thee, O Monarch.

" It is on account of this that I will show myself to be a friend and a brother and, in combat, annihilate the enemy under thine eyes. To-day, O Long-armed Warrior, thou shalt see me in the forefront of battle, having slain Rama and his brother and put the monkey army to flight. Seeing me bring back Rama's head from the battlefield this day, thou wilt be happy, O Warrior, and Sita overwhelmed with despair.

" To-day all the titans of Lanka, whose kinsfolk have perished, will witness the death of Rama who is the object of men's desires ! By striking down the foe in battle, I shall dry the tears of those who are overcome with sorrow and have been rendered desolate by the loss of their relatives. To-day thou shalt see Sugriva, the leader of the Plavagas, who resembles a mountain illumined by the sun, lying on the earth. The titans, and I also, are eager to slay Dasaratha's son ; this should fill thee with confidence, how is it that thou art still trembling, O Irreproachable Hero ? Should he slay me, Raghava will assuredly slay thee also but I have nothing to fear, O Lord of the Titans ! Now command me, O Scourge of Thy Foes, do not seek another for this encounter, O Incomparable Hero ! I shall destroy thy foes despite their strength ! Even were it Shakra or Yama or Pavaka or Maruta, I should enter into combat with them or with Kuvera or Varuna themselves ; I, who in stature am like unto a mountain, with a sharpened spear as my weapon, my war-cry, my pointed teeth, at the sight of which Purandara himself trembles, throwing away my arms, shall strike down the foe with blows of my fists. None will be able to withstand me, no matter how much they may cling to life, nor have I need of lance, mace, sword or whetted dart ; with my bare hands alone, I will kill Raghava, were he accompanied by the God who bears the Thunderbolt himself ! If he is able to withstand the force of my fists then mine arrows will drink his life's blood ! O King, I stand here, why art thou overwhelmed with despair ? Here I wait ready to exterminate the slayers of titans, by whom Lanka has been set on fire, and also the monkeys, in the struggle that is about to take place. I shall confer a rare and great glory upon thee ! Did the danger come from Indra or Swyambhu or the Gods themselves, I should make them measure their length on the field of battle, O King ! I shall overcome Yama, consume Pavaka, hurl down Varuna, pulverize the mountains and shatter the earth ! After my long sleep, let those beings I am about to consume, witness the prowess of Kumbhakarna this day ! Nay, the Three Worlds shall not be able to glut mine appetite ! In order to please thee I will slay the son of Dasaratha! Having struck down Rama and Lakshmana, I shall devour all the foremost of the monkey leaders. Rejoice therefore, O King and drink wine, do what thou hast to do and banish grief ; to-day I shall send Rama to the abode of death and Sita will become thine for ever ! "

CHAPTER 64

Mahodara's Speech

HEARING this speech of the colossal and valiant Kumbhakarna, Mahodara replied :—

" Kumbhakarna, thou art an offshoot of an illustrious race, thou art courageous but thou hast two vulgar characteristics and, in thy conceit, art unable to anticipate the course of events in all its aspects.

" It is not true that the king does not understand what is politic and impolitic, O Kumbhakarna, but thou, in thy youthful impetuosity, knowest only how to prate ! The Lord of the Titans, who is conversant with the laws of time and place, is also aware of increase and loss as well as our situation and the state of the enemy.

" What man of sense would attempt that which an old thick-headed soldier with no respect even for his elders plumes himself on accomplishing ? When thou dost assert that duty, profit and pleasure are essentially opposed to each other, it is a proof that thou art unaware of their real nature. Action is undoubtedly the source of all experiences and here below, happiness is the fruit we seek even in our most evil acts. Apart from pleasure, duty and profit yield felicity, but the fruit reaped from injustice and unrighteousness is calamitous. Men of strong character undertake those acts, the consequences of which they reap in another world, whilst those who give themselves up to the pursuit of pleasure reap the consequences here.

" Why should that which the king has so much at heart and which we approve, namely the chastising of his enemies, be set aside in any way? As for the motives thou hast given for marching against Rama single-handed, I will point out to thee what is ill-considered and reprehensible about them ! How canst thou defeat Rama alone, he who formerly destroyed innumerable exceedingly powerful titans in Janasthana ? Those rangers of the night whom he overcame in Janasthana were valiant warriors also and dost thou not behold them in the city,

170

stricken with fear? By rousing Rama, the son of Dasaratha, who resembles a wounded lion, alas thou art waking a sleeping serpent! Burning with valour and unapproachable in his fury, inaccessible as Mrityu, who would dare to challenge him? This entire army cannot face that foe without being imperilled, therefore it in no wise recommends itself to me that thou shouldst go out to meet him alone, O Child. Who, bereft of resources would be eager to meet with an adversary, ready to sacrifice his life and furnished with every pre-requisite! Rama has no equal among men, O Best of the Titans, how canst thou plume thyself on entering into combat with him who is the rival of Indra and Vaivasvata?"

Having spoken thus to the enraged Kumbhakarna, Mahodara said to Ravana, the Destroyer of the Worlds, who was surrounded by the titans :—

"Having formerly borne Vaidehi away, why dost thou delay? If thou desirest Sita to submit to thy will, I see a means of bringing her to thy feet. If it pleases thee, O Indra among the Titans, then hear me!

"Let it be proclaimed that I, Dvijihva, Samhradin, Kumbhakarna and Vitadarna, all five, are going forth to slay Rama! We shall engage him in a fierce struggle and, if we triumph over thine enemy, we need resort to no other means, but, if thy rival survive and we escape from the fight, then we will adopt the measures I have planned.

"We shall return from the battlefield and come hither covered with blood, our limbs pierced by darts on which are engraved Rama's name, and relate how we have destroyed Raghava and Lakshmana! Thereafter we shall press thy feet and thou wilt cover us with honour, after which, mounted on an elephant thou wilt publish the tidings throughout the city, relating how Rama, his brother and his army were entirely destroyed. Simulating an extreme satisfaction, O Subduer of Thy Foes, thou wilt promote feasting and rejoicing and bestow gold and slaves on thy servants and distribute garlands, raiment and perfumes on thy warriors, thou thyself manifesting thy delight by drinking. Thereupon a rumour will spread everywhere that Rama and his friends have been devoured by the titans; such will be the report!

" Then shalt thou repair secretly to where Sita is, in order to offer her consolation and tempt her with grain, diamonds and entertainment in order to seduce her. By this deceit, O King, Sita's grief will be increased and she, bereft of felicity, without a protector, will accede to thy desire. Learning that her charming lord is slain, Sita, in despair and on account of womanly frailty, will submit to thy will !

" Brought up in the lap of prosperity, this woman who is worthy of felicity and who is afflicted with misfortune, realising her happiness depends on thee, will surrender herself wholly to thee.

" This is the best course for thee to follow. Even to behold Rama may prove disastrous ; have no anxiety ! Great happiness awaits thee here without entering into combat ! Neither losing thy forces nor courting danger, triumph over thine enemy, O Monarch ! Glory, felicity, prosperity and renown will long be the lot of thy sovereign majesty ! "

CHAPTER 65

Kumbhakarna enters into Combat

REPLYING to Mahodara's reproaches, Kumbhakarna said to his brother, Ravana, the King of the Titans :—

' " Forsooth I shall dispel the immediate peril this day by slaying that wretch, Rama ! Freed from thine adversary, be happy ! Heroes do not thunder in vain like clouds bereft of rain ! Do thou mark how my threats find fulfilment in mine exploits ! Warriors do not need to boast, and accomplish the most difficult of feats without bluster ! Cowardly monarchs, devoid of intelligence, who plume themselves on being wise, will ever find thy speech acceptable, O Mahodara !

" All you effeminate creatures, agreeable talkers, who flatter the king, have always ruined any martial enterprise. Nothing is left in Lanka save its sovereign ; its wealth is exhausted, its army destroyed and that monarch is beset by foes in the guise of friends ! I shall go out and fight, determined to triumph over the foe and, in this wise, redeem thy calamitous policy in this great struggle."

Hearing these words of the intelligent Kumbharkarna, the King of the Titans answered laughing :—

"In sooth, Rama has terrorized Mahodara! Assuredly he does not relish battle, O Dear Friend! O Sagacious Warrior, I have none equal to thee in devotion and prowess ; go, slay mine adversary, O Kumbhakarna and speed towards victory !

"Thou wast sleeping and it was for mine enemy's destruction that I had thee wakened ; this hour is of extreme significance to the titans, O Vanquisher of thy Foes ! Go, arm thyself ; let those two princes, the equals of Aditya in splendour, be thy pasture ! Beholding thee, the monkeys will take to flight and the hearts of Rama and Lakshmana will cease to beat."

Having spoken thus to the exceedingly powerful Kumbhakarna, that illustrious lion of the titans felt he had received new life. Aware of Kumbhakarna's prowess and knowing his valour, the king expanded with joy like unto the immaculate moon.

Hearing his words, which filled him with delight, that warrior went away and, having listened to the king's speech, prepared for battle. Then that scourge of his foes vigorously brandished his iron spear decorated with fine gold that shone brightly and was as renowned as Indra's thunderbolt and equally heavy. The scourge of the Devas, Danavas, Gandharvas, Yakshas and Pannagas, wreathed in garlands, festooned with crimson flowers, emitting flames, that great spear, stained with the blood of his enemies, was taken up by the illustrious Kumbhakarna, who addressed Ravana, saying :—

"I shall set out alone ; let thy powerful army remain here ! To-day in mine hunger and fury, I shall devour the monkeys ! "

At these words of Kumbhakarna, Ravana answered :—

" Do thou go out accompanied by troops furnished with picks and hammers ; those monkeys are brave and exceedingly energetic ! He who is rash enough to meet them alone will be torn to pieces by their teeth, yet, though they are extremely difficult to overcome, surround thyself with warriors and setting out, utterly destroy that enemy host so fatal to the titans ! "

Thereafter, descending from the throne, the mighty Ravana placed a diadem, the interior of which was encrusted with pearls, on Kumbhakarna's brow and decked out that hero with bracelets, rings, precious gems and a necklace as bright as the moon, covering his limbs with celestial and fragrant garlands and setting earrings in his ears. With the bracelets, anklets and golden coins[1], with which he was adorned, the large-eyed Kumbhakarna shone like the sacrificial fire.

Resplendent with his great dark-blue girdle, he resembled the Mandara Mountain encircled by the snake at the time of the churning of the water of immortality. Clad in golden armour that no arrow could penetrate, which in its natural brilliance seemed to project flames, he was rendered as radiant as the King of the Mountains encircled by evening clouds. His entire body was covered with ornaments of every kind and, spear in hand, that titan called to mind Narayana, when, in his might, he took the three strides.

Thereafter that warrior embraced his brother and paid obeisance to him by circumambulating him in the traditional manner and, inclining his head to him, set out to the sound of conches and gongs.

Then Ravana, dismissing him with good wishes, caused an escort of well-equipped soldiers to accompany him with elephants, horses and chariots, emitting a sound like thunder-clouds. Valiant fighters accompanied that prince of warriors mounted on serpents, buffalo, donkeys, lions, elephants antelopes and birds.

It was under a prodigious shower of blossom, a parasol over him, bearing a pointed spear in his hand, full of daring, that the enemy of Devas and Danavas, intoxicated with the smell of blood, set forth. And innumerable titans followed him on foot, full of energy and prowess, fierce of aspect, bearing weapons in their hands, their eyes red ; and their ranks measured many leagues in extent and they resembled heaps of antimony and brandished maces, swords, sharp axes, javelins, bars, ramrods, hammers, great Sala Trees and were furnished with nets.

Meanwhile Kumbhakarna, assuming another terrible and ferocious form, advanced impetuously, measuring a hundred bows in breadth and six hundred in height, formidable, full of power and energy with eyes like unto chariot wheels. And,

[1] Lit. Nishkas—See glossary.

having assembled the titans, that colossus with his large mouth, who looked like a flaming crag said with a mocking laugh :—

"To-day the foremost of the monkey divisions will be consumed by me in my wrath one after the other like moths in a flame. Yet those inhabitants of the woods have never given offence and their race adorns the gardens of our dwellings.

"The cause of the city being beseiged is Raghava, and Lakshmana who accompanies him ; he being slain, all will be slain ; I shall therefore destroy him in fight."

At these words of Kumbhakarna, the titans emitted a great shout that seemed to agitate the ocean.

Then the crafty Kumbhakarna went forth and sinister portents appeared on every side ; dark and fearful clouds accompanied by meteors were seen, and the earth, the sea and the forests trembled. Jackals of ferocious aspect, with flames darting from their mouths, began to howl and birds wheeled from left to right. A vulture alighted on the titan's spear as he advanced, and his left eye and arm twitched ; a flaming meteor fell with a terrible crash ; the sun lost its brilliance and no favourable wind blew.

Without heeding these threatening portents, causing the hair to stand on end, Kumbhakarna set out, urged on by the force of destiny. Having crossed the ramparts, that giant, equal to a mountain, beheld the vast army of the monkeys resembling a cloud and, seeing that most powerful of the titans, as high as a mountain, those monkeys fled in all directions, like clouds driven before the wind. At the sight of that tremendous host of monkeys scattering to the four quarters like a mass of cloud melting away, Kumbhakarna joyfully redoubled his shouts resembling thunder.

Hearing those terrible shouts, like unto the roar of clouds in the sky, countless Plavagas fell to the earth like great Sala Trees whose roots have been severed and, as Kumbhakarna hurled himself on the enemy with his huge mace in order to destroy him, he filled the ranks of the monkeys with extreme fear as does the Lord of Death accompanied by his minions at the end of the World Period.

CHAPTER 66

Angada reproaches the Monkeys for flying from Kumbhakarna

HAVING leapt over the wall, Kumbhakarna, that giant, like unto the peak of a mountain, full of valour, set out from the city in haste and emitted a great shout which agitated the waters, drowned the thunder claps and appeared to shatter the mountains.

Seeing that warrior of fierce glance, as invincible as Maghavat, Yama or Varuna, the monkeys stampeded, and Prince Angada, beholding them fleeing, addressed the mighty Nala, Nila, Gavaksha and Kumuda, saying :—

" Forgetting your native valour and noble lineage, where are you fleeing in terror like common monkeys ? Come back, O Companions, return ! Is it thus that you defend your lives ? Nay, this titan is not able to fight against you all ; he is here to create panic amongst you. This great fear, that the titan inspires in you, will be dispelled by our prowess ; return, O Plavamgamas ! "

Rallied with difficulty from here and there and re-assured, those monkeys, armed with trees, halted in the field, and those dwellers in the woods stayed there ready to advance in fury on Kumbhakarna, like elephants intoxicated with Mada juice. Thereafter they attacked him valiantly with blows from mountain peaks, rocks and trees with their flowering crests but were unable to overthrow him. Innumerable stones, and trees with blossoming tops fell shattered on the earth, having come in contact with his limbs and that hero, enraged, on his side, struck down the ranks of those energetic monkeys by exercising his great strength, like unto a fire which suddenly blazes forth in the forest. Their limbs be-spattered with blood, those lions among the monkeys, overcome and cut down, lay there in great numbers resembling trees with coppery flowers. Thereafter, those monkeys bounded away without looking in which direction and some threw themselves into the sea and some leapt into the air. Overcome by that titan, who was disporting himself, some, despite their valour, fled over the sea by the way by which they had come and some, pale and distraught, escaped to the valleys. The bears climbed into the trees and some took refuge in the mountains ; others being no longer able to stand, fell down and remained lying on the earth insensible as if asleep or dead.

Seeing the monkeys routed, Angada called out to them :—

" Stay ! Let us fight ! Return, O Plavamgamas ! Were you to range the whole earth in your flight I see no refuge for you anywhere ! Why do you seek to preserve your lives ? If you fly, leaving your weapons, lest they impede your course, your wives will deride you for this cowardice, which is death to men of honour, O Warriors ! Whither are you fleeing filled with fear like common monkeys, you who are born in rich and illustrious families ? Where are those deeds of valour and prowess of which you boasted in the assembly ? The reproach of cowardice will be heard by you ; he, who seeks to save his life by fleeing, is despised ! Follow the path chosen by men of courage and overcome your fears. If, after a brief existence, you lie stretched on the earth dead, you will attain Brahmaloka, inaccessible to cowards. We shall acquire glory by striking down the foe in fight and, if we succumb, we shall enjoy the treasures of heaven in the region of heroes, O Monkeys ! Nay, Kumbhakarna will never return alive, having come before Kakutstha, as a moth that draws near to a glowing brazier. If one, despite our numbers, is able to disperse us and we preserve our lives by fleeing, then there is an end to our renown ! "

Such was Angada's speech, he of the golden bracelets, and the fugitives replied to that hero's reproaches, saying :—

" That Titan Kumbhakarna, has caused a terrible carnage amongst us ; it is not the moment to stay ; life is dear to us ! "

With these words the leaders of the monkeys, beholding that giant of fearful glance advancing, scattered in all directions.

Nevertheless Angada, by his exhortations and arguments, succeeded in rallying them and, re-assured by that sagacious son of Bali, they submitted to his commands and those foremost of monkeys returned to the field.

CHAPTER 67

Kumbhakarna's Exploits.   He is slain by Rama

RETRACING their steps on hearing the voice of Angada, all those huge-bodied monkeys, resolutely taking their stand, desired nothing more than to join issue in the fight.

Their confidence restored by the words of the valiant Angada, those monkeys, feeling their energy revived and their courage mounting, advanced, resolving to die and sacrifice their lives. Then those giants, arming themselves with trees and enormous crags, which they spun with great rapidity, hurled themselves on Kumbhakarna, whereupon, full of ire and vigour, that warrior of immense stature, brandishing his mace, dispersed the enemy on every side.   Seven hundred and eight thousand monkeys lay scattered on the earth struck down by Kumbhakarna and, like unto Garuda consuming serpents, he seized hold of seven, eight, ten, twenty and thirty in his arms, crushing and devouring them in his extreme fury as he ran.

Re-assured with exceeding difficulty, those monkeys rallied here and there and, armed with trees and rocks, took up their stand in the forefront of the battle.   At that instant, Dvivida, that lion among monkeys, resembling a threatening cloud, tearing up a rock, hurled himself on the enemy who was like unto a mountain peak ; and that monkey, breaking off the crag, flung it at Kumbhakarna, missing him, so that the missile fell on the titan force, crushing horses, elephants and chariots harnessed to excellent steeds.   Another rock created further victims and, under that avalanche of stones, the titans wounded, their horses slain, their charioteers struck down, streaming with blood and mounted in their cars, suddenly let forth terrible cries and with the aid of death-dealing arrows, severed the heads of those foremost of monkeys who were roaring.

On their side, the monkeys, full of valour, uprooted great trees in order to crush the chariots, horses, elephants, buffalo and titans and, from the air where he was stationed, Hanuman showered rocks, stones and trees of every kind on the head of Kumbhakarna but that mighty one split and evaded that rain of trees. And he hurled himself upon that great army of monkeys brandishing his sharp pick and, as he rushed forward Hanuman placed himself in the way armed with the peak of a mountain, and, in fury struck Kumbhakarna a violent blow, who, in his appalling corpulence, appeared like a hill! Then he whose limbs were dripping with fat and streaming with blood, stumbled under the shock and the titan hurled his spear, which was as bright as lightning and like a mountain spouting forth flames, striking Maruti between the arms, as Guha formerly struck the Krauncha Mountain with his formidable lance. His breast pierced by that spear, beside himself, vomiting blood, Hanuman, in fury, let forth a terrible cry in the midst of the battle, like the roar of a thundercloud at the end of the World Period, and a great cheer arose from the ranks of the titans as they beheld his plight, whilst the monkeys, distraught and terrified, fled from the field.

At that instant, summoning up his courage, the valiant Nila discharged a crag against that crafty titan, who, seeing it approaching, struck it with his fist and, on the impact, that rock broke and fell on the earth emitting sparks of fire. Then Rishabha, Sharabha, Nila, Gavaksha and Gandamadhana, those five tigers among the monkeys, hurled themselves on Kumbhakarna and, in the struggle, showered him with blows from stones, trees, the palms of their hands, feet and fists, attacking that giant on every side. Kumbhakarna, however, scarcely felt those blows and, unheeding, seized the impetuous Rishabha in his two arms. Crushed in this embrace, that bull among the monkeys fell to the ground, his mouth filled with blood.

Thereafter, in the fight, that enemy of Indra struck Sharabha with his fist, Nila with his knee and Gavaksha with the palm of his hand. Dazed by the blows they had received, terrified, covered with blood, they fell on the earth like Kimshuka Trees that have been uprooted. Those powerful leaders of the monkeys being overcome, the rest hurled themselves in thousands on Kumbhakarna and, flinging themselves upon him and climbing about him as if he were a rock, those bulls among the

Plavagas, who themselves resembled hills, attacked and bit him. With their nails, teeth, fists and arms, those foremost of monkeys assailed the valiant Kumbhakarna, a veritable tiger in stature, and that titan, covered by thousands of apes, resembled a mountain overgrown by trees.   Crushing all those monkeys in his arms, that giant devoured them, as Garuda the serpents. Cast into Kumbhakarna's mouth, that resembled the pit of hell, the monkeys issued from his ears and nostrils.   As high as a mountain in his rage he devoured those monkeys, and that prince of titans crushed them covering the earth with their flesh and blood and ranging through their ranks which he overran, so that he appeared like the Fire of Time itself. Resembling Shakra bearing the thunderbolt in his hand or Death with the noose, so did that powerful titan appear, armed with his spear, in the fight.   As in the summer season, fire destroys the dry forests, so did Kumbhakarna consume the simian ranks.

Thus decimated, their leaders struck down, the Plavamgamas, wild with terror, emitted dreadful cries and, overpowered again and again by Kumbhakarna, those monkeys fled for refuge to Raghava.   Witnessing the massacre of those monkeys, Angada, born of the son of the Bearer of the Thunderbolt, hurled himself in rage upon Kumbhakarna in the struggle.   Seizing hold of a great crag, he roared again and again, putting all the titans, who accompanied Kumbhakarna, to flight ; thereafter he struck the head of his adversary with the rock, and that enemy of Indra inflamed with anger on receiving the blow, leapt with one bound upon the irascible son of Bali.   Emitting loud cries, that titan struck terror among the monkeys and, in his anger, threw his spear with extreme force at Angada, but with a light bound, that valiant lion among the monkeys, an experienced warrior, avoided the impact and leapt on his opponent, striking his chest with the palm of his hand.   That violent blow dazed the giant, who resembled a mountain, but regaining his senses that most powerful of titans, doubling his fist, with a mocking laugh, struck, Angada who fell insensible to the earth.

As that lion among the Plavagas lay stretched unconscious on the ground, Kumbhakarna, brandishing his spear, rushed on Sugriva and, seeing that colossus running towards him, the courageous King of the Monkeys went out to meet him whereupon, beholding that Indra among the Monkeys advancing, Kumbhakarna halted and stood facing him with braced limbs.

Beholding Kumbhakarna standing still, his body streaming with the blood of the great monkeys whom he had devoured, Sugriva said to him :—

" In slaying these warriors thou hast accomplished a most difficult feat and, by devouring my soldiers, hast acquired immense renown ; now let the army of monkeys be, what hast thou to do with common folk ? Do thou seek to bear the weight of this rock I am about to hurl on thee, O Titan ! Find thy satisfaction in slaying me, O Titan, thou who resemblest a mountain ! "

At these words of the King of the Monkeys, who was possessed of courage and fortitude, that lion among the titans, answered :—

" Thou art the grandson of Prajapati and the son of Riksharajas, thou art energetic and brave, hence thine arrogance, O Monkey ! "

At these words of Kumbhakarna, Sugriva, taking up a stone, hurled it at him suddenly and struck his breast with that missile resembling a thunderbolt. The rock broke on the huge chest of that giant and the titans were appalled, whilst from the ranks of the monkeys rose shouts of joy. Struck by that rocky peak, Kumbhakarna, enraged, roared ; opening his huge mouth wide and brandishing his spear, that resembled lightning, he hurled it at the King of the Monkeys and the Bears in order to slay him. As it fell, the son of Anila, Hanuman, with his two hands seized hold of that sharp spear and its gold-encircled shaft loosed by the titan's arm and, in play as it were, broke that powerful weapon across his knee.

Seeing his lance shattered to pieces by Hanuman, the army of monkeys, in a transport of delight, began to cheer. Meanwhile hearing those rangers of the woods emitting leonine roars and lauding Maruti in their joy, on beholding his spear shattered, that titan became enraged and, pale with fear, tore off a peak of the Malaya Mountain nearby, in the vicinity of Lanka, hurling it on Sugriva in order to strike him down. Struck by that crag, the Indra of the Monkeys fell on the earth insensible and the Yatudhanas let forth a roar of triumph.

Thereafter Kumbhakarna, approaching that powerful King of the Monkeys, lifted him up and bore him away like unto a violent wind driving away a cloud and, as he ranged the battle-field dragging Sugriva with him, who resembled a great cloud, Kumbhakarna, with his lofty stature, appeared like Mount Meru of exceedingly high peaks. Having laid hold of Sugriva, the mighty Lord of the Titans turned towards Lanka amidst the acclamations of his own people and the wailing of the Inhabitants of the Celestial Region, who were inconsolable on account of the capture of the King of the Plavamgamas and, having overcome the King of the Monkeys, that enemy of Indra and his rival in power, reflected :—' He being dead, the entire simian host is destroyed together with Raghava ! '

Then Hanuman, the sagacious son of Maruta, seeing Sugriva borne away by Kumbhakarna and the monkeys fleeing, thought to himself : ' Now that Sugriva has been made captive what ought I to do ? Assuredly I shall accomplish that which is fitting ; in order to slay this titan, I shall assume the shape of a mountain ! When I have destroyed the extremely powerful Kumbhakarna in combat by pounding his body with blows and have delivered the king, the delight of the monkeys will be general ! Yet that great monkey is well able to free himself though meseems, that, struck by Kumbhakarna with a rock in the struggle, the Chief of the Monkeys is not yet conscious of his plight. Presently, when Sugriva recovers consciousness, he will know how to save himself and the monkeys in this great conflict. That warrior will not be pleased if I deliver him, for his fair name would be tarnished and irretrievably lost. That is why I shall delay a while so that he may extricate himself from this predicament by his own prowess and I shall confine myself to rallying the scattered forces.'

Reflecting thus, Hanuman, born of Maruta, sought to instil courage into the simian army.

Meanwhile, bearing the great and quivering form of the monkey in his arms, Kumbhakarna returned to Lanka, and from the temples, highways, dwellings and city gates, the people honoured him with a rain of flowers. Under the shower of roasted grain and the fragrance of the blossoms with which he was drenched and also on account of the coolness of the royal highway, little by little the valiant Sugriva recovered consciousness. Borne in the arms of his powerful rival and, beholding the great highway of the city, that warrior was assailed by innumerable thoughts—'Taken captive in this way, what can I do now? I shall act in such a way that it is to the advantage of the monkeys.'

Then with his sharp nails, the King of the Monkeys, instantly attacked the enemy of the Gods and tore off his two ears with his teeth, biting off his nose and splitting his thighs with his feet.

With his nose and ears torn off by Sugriva's teeth and nails, Kumbhakarna, transported with anger, his limbs covered with blood, threw the monkey down in order to crush him. Flung to the ground with fearful violence and struck by the Enemy of the Gods, Sugriva bounced into the air like a ball and with all speed flew to rejoin Rama.

Kumbhakarna, his ears and nose severed, drenched in gore, shone like a mountain with its torrents and, covered with blood, vomiting blood, that gigantic titan of fearful aspect, the younger brother of Ravana, blazed with anger. Like unto a mass of dark collyrium or an evening cloud, that formidable Ranger of the Night resolved to enter into combat once more and, Sugriva having escaped, that enemy of Indra, furious, immediately threw himself into the struggle but reflecting 'I have no weapon' that ferocious warrior seized hold of a huge hammer. Issuing from the city, the valiant titan began to consume the redoubtable army of the monkeys with the violence of Fire at the destruction of the worlds. Famished and avid for flesh, Kumbhakarna entered the ranks of the monkeys and, in his rage, like unto Mrityu at the end of the world period, indiscriminately ate up titan, monkey, Pisacha and bear. Thereafter in his fury, he consumed the monkeys, seizing one, two, three or more in one hand and titans also, thrusting them greedily into his mouth so that he streamed with flesh and blood and, though struck by the peaks of mountains, continued to feast on those monkeys, whilst they, seeing their companions being devoured, took refuge with Rama, whereupon Kumbhakarna, in a transport of rage, pursued them in order to consume them. Seizing them in his arms, in the chase, he took hold of them in groups of seven, eight, twenty, thirty and a hundred ; his limbs were covered with fat, flesh and blood, while wreaths of tangled entrails hung over his ears, and that colossus, of sharp teeth, began to discharge his weapons so that he appeared like Time at the end of the world.

At that instant, the son of Sumitra, the scourge of enemy hosts and the destroyer of hostile citadels, enraged, entered the fight and the courageous Lakshmana loosed seven darts into Kumbhakarna's body, aiming a hail of other missiles on him but Kumbhakarna shook off those falling shafts. Then the valiant son of Sumitra was provoked beyond measure and covered the shining armour of that titan, that was made of gold, with his shafts, as a mountain is overlaid with clouds by the wind at evening. Like unto a mass of dark collyrium, that titan, riddled with golden darts, blazed like the sun shining amidst the clouds. And that terrible monster, whose voice equalled the crash of countless thunder-clouds, spoke scornfully, increasing Saumitri's delight, saying :—

" Thou hast manifested thy courage by entering into combat fearlessly with me, I who have overcome Antaka himself without difficulty in the field ! He who is able to face the rival of Mrityu himself, armed for combat, is worthy of honour, how much more so if he should enter into conflict with him ! Mounted on Airavata surrounded by the Gods, Shakra, their king, has never dared to challenge me to battle. This courage from a youth is gratifying to me ; now go hence, O Saumitri, I wish to meet Raghava !

" In sooth thy valour, energy and martial prowess are pleasing to me but my only desire is to slay Rama, when he is slain, all are slain ! When Rama has fallen under my blows, I shall fight with all my might against all those who remain on the battlefield ! "

Thus boastfully did the titan speak and Saumitri, with a mocking smile, answered in dread accents saying :—

" That thy prowess renders thee invincible to Shakra and the other Gods is true, O Warrior, and to-day thou dost manifest the same valour ! Yonder is the son of Dasaratha immoveable as a rock ! "

Hearing these words, that ranger of the night, the mighty and powerful Kumbhakarna, disregarding Lakshmana, passed him by and, causing the earth to tremble, rushed on Rama.

The son of Dasaratha, Rama, however, loosed some pointed arrows with Indra's weapon on Kumbhakarna's breast and, wounded by Rama in his furious course, flames mixed with embers shot from his mouth! Pierced by Rama's arrow, that lion among the titans, emitting a terrible cry, hurled himself full of rage upon Raghava, throwing off the monkeys. With his breast pierced with darts, adorned with peacock's plumes, his mace fell shattered from his hand and all his weapons were scattered on the earth. Finding himself disarmed, that colossus created a great carnage with his fists and hands.[1] Covered with blood, that streamed from his wounds, like a torrent falling from a mountain, his limbs riddled with arrows, maddened by the smell of blood, he rushed about in his violent rage devouring the monkeys, titans and bears. Brandishing a huge crag, that mighty and formidable giant, the equal of Antaka, hurled it at Rama but before it reached him, that hero struck it in the centre with the aid of seven infallible darts.

The virtuous Rama, elder brother of Bharata, shattered it with arrows encrusted with gold and, like unto the peak of Meru, that crag, shining with splendour, fell, crushing two hundred monkeys.

At that instant, the virtuous Lakshmana, after reflecting deeply on the various means of destroying Kumbhakarna, said to Rama:

" O Prince, that monster is no longer able to distinguish between monkeys and titans ; drunk with the smell of blood, he devours friends and foes alike ! Let the foremost of the monkeys climb upon him courageously and let their officers and leaders hang upon him on every side ; under the heavy load that will crush him as he is rushing over the ground, that insensate one will annihilate the titans and not the monkeys."

At these words of that intelligent prince, the valiant monkeys all flung themselves on Kumbhakarna with alacrity and he, full of ire against the monkeys, who had climbed on his back, shook them violently as a fierce elephant his keepers. Seeing the titan shaking himself thus, Rama said to himself : ' He is incensed ' and rushed upon him with his excellent bow. His eyes red with anger, the intrepid Raghava, consuming him with his glance as

[1] He having many arms.

it were, bounded quickly forward, re-assuring the leaders, who were tormenting the mighty Kumbhakarna and, in order to encourage the monkeys, taking hold of his great bow encrusted with gold, that with its cord resembled a serpent, Rama advanced with his huge quiver full of arrows.

Surrounded by the monkey host, that warrior went forward full of valour, followed by Lakshmana and he beheld the illustrious and mighty Kumbhakarna, the vanquisher of his foes, surrounded by titans, his eyes inflamed, adorned with golden bracelets, pursuing all those monkeys with fury like unto one of the elephants of the four quarters; and he resembled the Vindhya or Mandara Mountains and was vomiting blood like a great cloud pouring down rain. With his tongue he licked the corners of his mouth that were wet with blood while he continued to destroy the simian army like Death at the end of the world.

Beholding that Prince of the Titans shining like a glowing brazier, that lion among men stretched his bow, and the sound of that weapon infuriated that foremost of the titans, who, highly provoked, hurled himself on Raghava.

Meanwhile Rama, whose arms were like unto the great coils of the King of the Serpents, said to Kumbhakarna who, possessing the splendour of a mountain, was rushing to attack him like a cloud driven by the tempest :—

" Come, O Prince of the Titans, tremble not, I await thee bow in hand and in an instant will deprive thee of life ! "

' It is Rama ! ' reflected Kumbhakarna and, bursting forth into hideous laughter, rushed forward in fury, scattering the monkeys on the battlefield. By his monstrous and terrible laughter, like unto the muttering of a thundercloud, he seemed to cleave the hearts of the inhabitants of the woods, and Kumbhakarna, in his great splendour, said to Raghava :—

" Take me not for Viradha, Kabanda or Khara, Bali or Maricha ; it is I, Kumbhakarna, who stand here ! Behold my dreadful and mighty mace wrought of iron ; with this, Devas and Danavas were formerly struck down by me ! Do not hold me in contempt in that I possess neither nose nor ears, I do not feel the least discomfort or pain on account of their loss ! Manifest the strength of thy limbs, O Tiger among the Ikshvakus ;

having displayed thy prowess and might, I shall devour thee, O Irreproachable Prince ! "

Hearing him speak thus, Rama loosed one of his plumed arrows at Kumbhakarna that struck him with the force of lightning but that enemy of the Gods was neither shaken nor moved and those shafts, which had pierced seven Sala Trees and slain that bull among the monkeys, Bali, cut into the body of the titan that was as hard as a diamond.

Then, as though they were drops of water, that enemy of the mighty Indra, drank up those arrows through his body, thus quenching their fury, whilst he whirled his mace in a fine frenzy. And that weapon covered with blood, the terror of the celestial hosts, brandished by that titan with formidable energy, created panic in the simian ranks.

Then Rama, taking up another arrow named the Vayavya,[1] loosed it against that ranger of the night and cut off the arm with which he held the mace. With his arm severed, he let out a terrible cry and his arm, cut off by Raghava's shaft, fell with its mace, like unto the peak of a mountain on the army of the King of the Monkeys, crushing it. Thereafter, beside themselves, the monkeys who had escaped the massacre caused by that fall, their limbs lacerated, took refuge in the vicinity and became the witnesses of the terrific struggle between that Indra among men and the Prince of the Titans.

His arm severed by that arrow, Kumbhakarna resembling the King of the Mountains its peak cloven by a great sword, struck down a tree with his remaining hand and rushed upon that lord of men, but Rama, with a shaft decorated with gold joined to Indra's weapon, cut off his upraised arm like the coiled body of a snake and the Tala Tree also.

Beholding the titan with two arms severed who, roaring, was rushing upon him, Rama took out two whetted and crescent-shaped arrows and severed his two feet, whereupon the intermediary regions, the four quarters, the caves of the mountain, the vast ocean, the City of Lanka and the ranks of the monkeys resounded with the thunder of his fall.

His arms and legs severed, that titan opened his mouth like Vadavamukha and suddenly rushed howling on Rama like

---

[1] Vayu's weapon. See glossary of weapons.

Rahu on the moon in the sky. Thereupon Rama filled his mouth with steel-pointed and plumed shafts decorated with gold and, with his mouth thus filled, he was unable to speak and, emitting inarticulated sounds with extreme difficulty, fell senseless.

Thereupon Rama selected an arrow bright as the rays of the sun, which resembled the Rod of Brahma at the time of the final dissolution and was fatal to his foes, the weapon of Indra, well-plumed and sharpened, the rival of Maruta in speed, and Rama discharged that arrow, the shaft of which was admirably inlaid with diamonds and gold, brilliant as the flames of a blazing sun, swift as Mahendra's thunderbolt, against that ranger of the night.

Loosed from Raghava's arm, that missile, which lit up the ten regions with its brilliance and which, in its formidable aspect, resembled a smokeless flame, struck that Prince of the Titans, the equal of Shakra and severed his head with its prominent teeth and swinging earrings, like unto the peak of a high mountain, as formerly Purandara severed the head of Vritra. The enormous head of Kumbhakarna with the curls that adorned it, looked like the moon floating in the sky at the time of the sun's rising, when the night has passed. Severed by Rama's shafts, the head of the titan resembling a mountain, fell on the earth crushing the highways, residences, gates and edifices of the city, bearing down the high walls also ; and that gigantic body of great resplendence belonging to the titan, fell into the sea where it crushed the great sharks, huge fishes and serpents, and plunged into the depths below.

When Kumbhakarna, that great enemy of the brahmins and the Gods, was slain in combat, the earth shook as all the mountains also and the Celestials shouted for joy. Thereafter Gods, Rishis, Maharishis, Pannagas, Suras, Bhutas, Suparnas, Guhyakas and the hosts of Yakshas and Gandharvas, who ranged the skies, loudly extolled Rama's exploit.

But on beholding that valiant Prince of the House of Raghu, the adherents and kinsfolk of the Lord of the Nairritas emitted loud cries at Kumbhakarna's fall, as do elephants in the presence of a lion. Having overcome Kumbhakarna in the field, Rama, amidst the simian host, resembled the sun emerging from the jaws of Rahu when it drives away the darkness from the celestial region.

In their delight, the countless monkeys, whose faces resembled opening lotuses, lauded Prince Raghava, who saw the fulfilment of his desires in the death of his formidable adversary, and the elder brother of Bharata rejoiced that he had slain Kumbhakarna, the Scourge of the Gods, who had never been overcome in any great encounter, as the King of the Celestials rejoiced at the death of the great Asura, Vritra.

CHAPTER 68

Ravana weeps for Kumbhakarna

SEEING Kumbhakarna fall under the blows of the exceedingly courageous Raghava, the titans brought the tidings to their King, Ravana, and said :—

" O King, the rival of Kala is dead ! Having overthrown the monkey ranks and devoured the Plavagas, he, for a space, displayed his prowess which has now been extinguished by Rama's unconquerable strength and half his body lies submerged in the vast ocean. Streaming with blood, his nose and ears severed, his head obstructing Lanka's gateway, he who resembled a mountain, Kumbhakarna, thy brother, struck down by Kakutstha's arrow, is now but a naked and mutilated corpse, like unto a tree consumed by fire ! "

Hearing this report of the mighty Kumbhakarna's death on the battlefield, Ravana, overwhelmed with distress, swooned away.

Learning that their paternal uncle had been slain, Devantaka, Narantaka, Trishiras and Atikaya, a prey to grief, groaned aloud, and Mahodara and Mahaparshwa, on hearing that their brother had perished under the blows of Rama of imperishable exploits, were seized with anguish.

Thereafter, regaining his senses with extreme difficulty, that lion among the titans, tormented by the death of Kumbhakarna, his senses troubled, began to lament, saying :—

" O Hero, O Humbler of the pride of thy foes, O Mighty Kumbhakarna, urged on by destiny, thou hast left me for the abode of death ! To go whither hast thou deserted me without having extracted that thorn from my side or from the side of my kinsfolk ? O Thou powerful warrior, destroyer of hostile ranks, from henceforth I no longer exist since I have lost my right arm, the support that delivered me from the fear of the Gods and Asuras. How has such a warrior, who quelled the pride of the Gods and Danavas, who resembled the Fire of Time, fallen to-day in the fight with Raghava ? How has Rama been able, with a single arrow, to stretch thee on the ground, thou, whom the descent of the thunderbolt could not overwhelm? Seeing thee succumb in combat, the Hosts of the Gods, standing in the heavens with the Rishis, emit shouts of joy. Assuredly this very day the Plavamgamas, making use of a favourable occasion, will scale the gates and fortifications of Lanka on every side, which heretofore were impregnable ! I have no further need for a kingdom and what shall I do with Sita ? Bereft of Kumbhakarna, I no longer wish to live. Since I am unable to kill Raghava, the slayer of my brother in combat, would it not be better to die, for life is empty to me ? To-day I shall go where my brother has gone, nay, far from my brother I cannot live for an instant ! Witnessing my plight, the Gods, who were formerly wronged by me, will certainly mock me ! O Kumbhakarna, now that thou art dead, how shall I vanquish Indra ? Bibishana's prudent speech, that great soul whom I disregarded in my blindness, has proved true ; the cruel end of Kumbhakarna and Prahasta has justified his words ! This is the disastrous consequence of that deed of mine, the banishment of the virtuous and fortunate Bibishana."

Such were the many burning lamentations to which the Ten-necked Ravana gave voice in the anguish of his soul on account of Kumbhakarna, his younger brother, the enemy of Indra, and, knowing him to have perished in combat, he swooned away.

CHAPTER 69

Narantaka is slain by Angada

HEARING the lamentation of the wicked Ravana who was overcome with grief, Trishiras addressed him thus :—

" O King, brave men do not give way to sorrow even at the death of so valiant a warrior as thy younger brother, our uncle. Since thou art able to conquer the Three Worlds, O Lord, why, like a common man, dost thou suffer thy courage to falter? Brahma bestowed on thee a spear, mail, a dart, a bow and a chariot harnessed to a thousand mules, sending forth a rumble like unto a thundercloud ; furnished with all these weapons, thou wilt vanquish Raghava ! Yet if it please thee, O Great King, I myself will descend into the arena and bear away thy foes, as Garuda the serpents. As Shambara fell under the blows of the King of the Gods and Naraka under those of Vishnu, so shall Rama fall this day, struck down by me on the battlefield."

At these words of Trishiras, Ravana, the Lord of the Titans, under the sway of destiny, felt himself to be born anew and, hearing Trishiras speak thus, Devantaka, Narantaka and Atikaya, burning with martial ardour, desired nothing more than to enter into combat. "Away! Away!" roared those valiant sons of Ravana, the foremost of the Nairritas, the equals of Shakra in prowess.

All were able to fly in the air, all were skilled in magic, all had humbled the pride of the Gods, all were invincible warriors, all were endowed with great strength, all enjoyed great renown, of none was it recounted that they had been defeated in battle even by the Gods, Gandharvas, Kinneras or great Serpents. All were expert in the use of weapons, all were courageous and able fighters, all were highly learned and all had been the recipients of great boons.

Surrounded by his sons, the king, radiant as the solar orb, the destroyer of the power and glory of his foes, shone like Maghavat amidst the Gods, the humbler of the pride of the great Danavas.

Embracing his sons, he covered them with ornaments and sent them out to fight, heaping blessings upon them. Nevertheless Ravana sent his brothers Yuddhonmatta and Matta to accompany those youthful warriors and watch over them in the struggle. Then those heroes of immense stature paid obeisance to the mighty Ravana, the destroyer of creatures, and, circumambulating him, departed. Thereafter the foremost of the Nairritas, furnished with every kind of medicinal herb and perfume, went away, eager to fight, and Trishiras, Atikaya, Devantaka, Narantaka, Mahodara and Mahaparshwa, under the sway of destiny, set out.

A magnificent elephant, like unto a dark cloud, offspring of Airavata's race, named Sudarshana, served as Mahodara's mount and that hero, furnished with every weapon, armed with a quiver, seated on his elephant, shone like the sun on the peak of the Astachala Mountain.

Trishiras, born of Ravana, was seated in an excellent car drawn by the foremost of steeds and it was filled with weapons of every kind. Standing in his chariot, armed with his bow, he looked as resplendent as a storm cloud on the peak of a mountain, attended by lightning, thunder, meteors and Indra's bow.[1] With his triple crown, Trishiras shone in his chariot like Himavat, the Lord of Mountains with its golden crests.

Then the exceedingly war-like Atikaya, son unto that Lord of the Titans, most skilful of archers, ascended a superb chariot with excellent wheels, stout axles, magnificent steeds, carriage and yoke, rich in quivers and bows, filled with missiles, swords and maces, and that warrior wore a diadem encrusted with gold and covered with gems so that he looked like Meru shining in its own splendour. That mighty Prince of the Titans, surrounded by the foremost of the Nairritas, glowed in his chariot like the God who bears the thunderbolt amidst the Immortals.

And Narantaka, mounted on a white steed, as swift as thought, harnessed with gold, resembling Ucchairavas, was armed with a javelin like unto a thunderbolt and appeared exceedingly resplendent, resembling the illustrious Guha, the offspring of Shikhin riding on his peacock.

Devantaka, bearing a gilded iron bar, looked like an incarnation

[1] Indra's bow—The Rainbow.

of Vishnu holding the Mandara Mountain in his arms and Mahaparshwa, full of strength and energy, brandished a mace like unto Kuvera armed for combat.

Thereafter those intrepid warriors set out from Lanka like the Gods leaving Amaravati and powerful titans on elephants, horses and in chariots thundering like clouds, followed, armed with excellent weapons; and those youthful beings shone like the blazing sun with their brows encircled with diadems, sparkling in splendour like planets flaming in the heavens and, in the brightness of the raiment in which they were attired, that brilliant cavalcade resembled an autumn cloud or a flock of cranes in the sky.

Determined to die or vanquish their foe, they went forward in this courageous resolve, eager to fight, boasting, shouting and uttering threats, and those invincible heroes set out furnished with arrows amidst the clamour and clapping of hands, causing the earth to tremble as it were.

As the roars of their troops seemed to rend the heavens, those mighty titan princes, full of joy, increased their pace and beheld the simian host brandishing rocks and trees, whilst from their side, the courageous leaders of the monkeys observed the titan army with its mass of elephants, horses and chariots advancing like unto a thunder cloud to the sound of hundreds of gongs and, furnished with huge weapons, encompassed on all sides by the resplendent Nairritas, resembling blazing torches or suns.

Beholding that company approaching, the desire of the Plavamgamas was realised and, armed with huge rocks, they redoubled their cries in their eagerness to fight the titans, who responded with their shouts. Hearing the roars that the monkeys and their leaders let forth, the titan ranks, provoked by the joyous cheering of the enemy, roared with an even greater fury in their extreme valour.

Thereafter, as they joined issue with that formidable host of titans, the monkeys with their leaders hurled themselves upon them, brandishing sharp rocks like unto mountains and those Plavamgamas, armed with crags and trees, threw themselves upon the titan forces, some fighting in the air and some on the ground. Some amongst those foremost of monkeys fought with heavily-branched trees and the struggle between the titans and the monkeys became desperate.

Those monkeys of redoubtable courage let an unequalled shower of trees, stones and rocks fall on the enemy who overwhelmed them with a hail of missiles. Titans and monkeys roared like lions on the battlefield ; the Plavamgamas crushed the Yatudhanas with blows from stones and, in fury struck those warriors covered in mail and jewels, mounted in chariots, and on elephants and horses in the fray. Then the Plavamgamas redoubled their attacks against the Yatudhanas with crags that they tore up with their hands. Their bodies tense, their eyes starting from their heads, shouting, they stumbled and fell, whilst those lions among the titans, on their side, pierced those elephants among the monkeys with sharp arrows, striking them with spears, mallets, swords, javelins and lances and they mowed each other down in their desire to triumph. The limbs of monkeys and titans were streaming with the blood of their enemies, and rocks and swords, thrown by the monkeys and titans, covered the blood-stained earth in an instant, so that the ground was smothered with titans like unto mountains, who, mad with martial ardour, had been crushed and mangled by their foes.

Thereafter the monkeys, giving and receiving blows, their rocks shattered, engaged in a fresh and dreadful fight, using the severed limbs as weapons. And the Nairritas struck the monkeys with their own corpses and the apes struck the titans with the titan dead. Tearing the rocks from the hands of their foes, the titans broke them on the heads of the monkeys who shattered the arrows of the titans, using the pieces to destroy them. And they overwhelmed each other with crags in the battle and monkeys and titans set up a roaring like unto lions.

Then, their armour and shields pierced, those titans, attacked by the monkeys, dripped blood as trees their sap, and some monkeys in the conflict, destroyed chariots with chariots, elephants with elephants, horses with horses, whilst the titans employed weapons like razors or half moons and Bhallas and pointed shafts in order to shatter the rocks and trees of those intrepid monkeys. In that encounter, the earth became impassable, covered as it was with monkeys and titans mangled and crushed under the rocks and trees in the fight.

Full of audacity and ardour, the monkeys, engaged in the struggle, casting aside all fear, fought the titans with a light heart and various kinds of weapons.

Witnessing that appalling mêlée, the joy of the monkeys and the massacre of the titans, the great Rishis and hosts of Celestial Beings emitted shouts of triumph.

Narantaka however, mounted on his steed, that was as swift as the wind, with a pointed lance plunged into the thick of the simian ranks like a fish into the sea and that warrior pierced seven hundred monkeys with his effulgent spear and that enemy of Indra, of exceeding courage, in an instant, single-handed, overthrew the army of the foremost of monkeys under the eyes of the Vidhyadharas and Maharishis, hacking a pathway for himself through the simian ranks, the bleeding flesh its mire, and which was covered with heaps of monkey corpses as high as hills.

Whenever those lions among the monkeys sought to bar his way, so often did Narantaka cleave their ranks by mowing them down. As a fire burns up a forest, so did he consume those simian battalions and each time those inhabitants of the woods tore up the trees and rocks, they fell under his lance like mountains riven by lightning.

Brandishing his glittering spear in the forefront of battle, the valiant Narantaka ranged the entire welkin, overthrowing everything in his course as the wind in the rainy season and, whether they stayed at their post or went out to meet him, those courageous monkeys could neither stand against him nor escape from him so that all fell, pierced by that warrior.

That unique javelin resembling Death itself,[1] bright as the sun, was able, by itself, to destroy the ranks of the monkeys and leave them stretched on the earth, and the impact of that pike resembled the stroke of lightning so that the monkeys were unable to endure it and emitted loud cries. Those high-souled and intrepid monkeys, falling, resembled the peaks of mountains crumbling away, struck by lightning.

Meanwhile the powerful leaders of the monkeys, who had previously been put to flight by Kumbhakarna, having regained their vigour, were ranged round Sugriva and he, looking about

[1] The Reaper Death.

him, observed the army of the monkeys fleeing before Narantaka, terror-stricken and scattering in all directions.

Witnessing this stampede, he beheld Narantaka, spear in hand, who was advancing, mounted on his steed. At this, the illustrious Sugriva, King of the Monkeys, addressed the youthful Prince Angada, a warrior whose valour equalled Shakra's, and said :—

" Go out against that bold titan, who, riding on a horse, is consuming the army I have sent against him and speedily deprive him of his life's breaths."

At this command from his sovereign, the intrepid Angada, the foremost of monkeys resembling a rocky mass, broke away from that company like the sun emerging from a cloud and, with the bracelets he wore, he glittered like a mountain with its metallic veins. Without any weapons save his nails and teeth, that son of Bali, in his great strength, rushed out to meet Narantaka and said to him :—

" Why dost thou strive with common monkeys ? Do thou with thy spear, the impact of which is equal to lightning, strike my breast which I now present to thee ! "

The words of Angada, son of Bali, angered Narantaka, who bit his lip with his teeth hissing like a serpent, and hurled himself upon him in fury. Brandishing his spear, which glittered like fire, he struck at Angada but the weapon broke against the breast of that son of Bali, that was as hard as diamond, and fell to the earth.

Seeing his lance shattered, like a snake whose powerful coils are sundered by Suparna, the son of Bali raised his hand and struck the head of the steed of his adversary. Sinking to its knees, its eyeballs starting from their sockets, its tongue hanging out, that horse, as high as a hill, fell to the earth, its head crushed by the blow from the palm of his hand.

Then Narantaka, beholding his steed lying dead, grew enraged and, clenching his fist, struck the son of Bali on the forehead with energy so that the hot blood gushed forth from his injured brow. Now he flared up with wrath and then swooned away and, having lost consciousness awhile, on coming to himself was confused.

Thereafter Angada, Bali's mighty son, clenching his fist,

which equalled Mrityu's in strength and resembled a great rock, brought it down on Narantaka's breast.

His chest crushed, broken by the shock, vomiting flames, his limbs streaming with blood, Narantaka fell on the earth like a mountain struck by lightning : and when the mighty Narantaka fell in the struggle with Bali's son, from the sky, the foremost of the Celestials and the monkeys emitted a great shout of triumph ! And Angada filled Rama's heart with joy and he was astonished at his exceedingly difficult achievement. Thereafter that warrior of illustrious exploits eagerly prepared for fresh encounters.

CHAPTER 70

The Death of Devantaka, Trishiras, Mahodara and Mahaparshwa

SEEING that Narantaka was slain, those lions among the Nairritas, Devantaka, Trishiras and Mahodara, the son of Poulastya, wept bitterly.

Thereafter Mahodara, mounted on that Indra of elephants like unto a cloud, rushed impetuously on the exceedingly energetic son of Bali.

Then the valiant Devantaka, distressed on account of the calamity that had visited his brother, arming himself with a formidable mace, also ran on Angada and, in his turn, the energetic Trishiras, standing in his chariot, that was as bright as the sun and harnessed to excellent steeds, advanced on the son of Bali.

Attacked by three of the foremost of titans, who had humbled the pride of the Gods, Angada tore up a many-branched tree, and as Shakra his flaming thunderbolt, hurled that huge trunk with its immense branches at Devantaka. Thereupon Trishiras severed it with his arrows which resembled venomous snakes and Angada, beholding the tree shattered, darted forward and that elephant among monkeys caused a shower of trees and rocks to fall upon the titans.

Enraged, Trishiras broke them with his whetted shafts and, with the head of his mace, Mahodara crushed them, while

Trishiras pursued the valiant Angada with his darts. Thereafter Mahodara urged his elephant to advance on the son of Bali and, in his anger, pierced his breast with Tomaras that were equal to lightning, and Devantaka, provoked, approaching Angada, struck him with his mace and swiftly turned away. The combined assault of those three Nairritas left that illustrious warrior unmoved; that agile and invincible hero however hurled himself in great fury on the colossal elephant belonging to Mahodara and, with the palm of his hand, struck it down.

Its eyes starting from their sockets, the elephant fell dead and that powerful son of Bali tore out one of its tusks, thereafter, rushing on Devantaka, he dealt him a blow in that struggle which caused him to stumble like a tree buffeted by the wind, and he vomited blood profusely which was the colour of lac. Breathing with difficulty, the energetic and mighty Devantaka, brandishing his mace, struck Angada a violent blow. At the impact, the son of that Indra among Monkeys fell to his knees but soon rose up again and, as he did so, Trishiras, with three infallible and formidable darts, pierced that son of the simian king.

Meanwhile Hanuman and Nila, beholding Angada assaulted by three of the foremost of the titans, came to his aid, and Nila struck Trishiras with a rock which the skilful son of Ravana broke with his sharp darts. Shattered by a hundred arrows, its surface broken to pieces, that rocky peak, from which sparks and flames spurted, fell.

Witnessing their astonishment, the courageous Devantaka, full of joy, in the fight flung himself with his mace on the son of Maruta and, as he rushed upon him, that lion among the monkeys leapt to meet him and with his fist struck him a thunderous blow on the head. Thereafter the heroic son of Vayu, that great and powerful monkey, battered in his skull and his roaring caused the titans to tremble. Devantaka, the son of the King of the Titans, gasping from the blow, his skull shattered, his teeth protruding, his eyes starting from their sockets, his tongue hanging out, fell to the earth instantly bereft of life.

Enraged by the death of the foremost of the titan warriors, that mighty enemy of the Gods, Trishiras, let fall a fearful shower of whetted shafts on Nila's breast and Mahodara, in fury, quickly mounted a second elephant as high as a hill. As the sun scales the Mandara Mountain, so did he let fall a rain of arrows on Nila as, under a rainbow, a cloud lets loose a shower on a mountain amidst the muttering of thunder. Covered with those darts, with which the valiant titan overwhelmed him, the leader of the monkey army, his limbs pierced, faltering, swooned away; then coming to himself, Nila tore up a rock covered with many-branched trees and, with a terrific bound leapt on Mahodara and struck him on the head. Crushed by the impact with which that elephant among monkeys had just overwhelmed him, Mahodara fell to earth deprived of life, like a rock riven by lightning.

Beholding his uncle slain, Trishiras seized hold of his bow and, full of ire, pierced Hanuman with his sharp arrows. Thereupon the son of the Wind, provoked, flung a crag at the valiant Trishiras who broke it to pieces with his whetted shafts. Seeing that his missile was useless, the monkey let fall a rain of trees on the son of Ravana in the struggle and he, observing that shower of trees falling through the air upon him, severed them in fury with his sharp arrows, emitting shouts of triumph. Then Hanuman, leaping upon his steed, tore at it violently with his nails, as the King of the Beasts claws a great elephant.

Thereafter, from his side, the son of Ravana, as Death with his noose, arming himself with a spear hurled himself on the son of Anila. As a meteor falls from the skies, so did that lance descend unobstructed and that lion among the monkeys caught it and snapped it, emitting a great shout.

Beholding that weapon of formidable aspect destroyed by Hanuman, the monkey forces raised joyful roars like unto the rumble of thunder, and Trishiras, the foremost of the titans, drawing his sword, pierced the breast of that Indra of the Monkeys.

Wounded by the thrust of his sword, the mighty Hanuman, born of Maruta, struck that Three-headed One on the breast with the palm of his hand. Smitten by the blow from Hanuman's palm, the illustrious Trishiras let his gauntlet fall and dropped swooning to the ground, and as he fell, the great monkey, who resembled a mountain, broke his sword letting out a roar which struck terror in all the titans. Unable to endure the terrible cry of triumph, that ranger of the night rose up

and struck Hanuman with his fist. The blow infuriated the
great monkey who, in anger, seized hold of the titan by his
crown and, as formerly Shakra severed the head of Tashtri's
son,[1] so Hanuman, with a terrific stroke of his sharp sword, cut
off his three heads each encircled with a diadem and decorated
with earrings. The heads of that enemy of Indra with their
large eyes resembling stones, their glances like unto a glowing
brazier, fell to the earth like stars falling from the sky. When
the enemy of the Gods, Trishiras was slain by Hanuman, who
was equal to Shakra in valour, the monkeys shouted in triumph
and the earth shook, whilst the titans scattered on all sides.

Beholding Trishiras, Yuddhonmatta and the irresponsible
Devantaka and Narantaka slain, the fury of Matta knew no
bounds. Seizing a mace, plated with gold, stained with flesh,
blood and foam, immense, glittering, saturated with the enemy's
gore, its point effulgent, festooned with scarlet garlands, the
terror of Airavata, Mahapadma and Sarvabhauma,[2] he armed
himself with that weapon. In his fury, Matta, that lion among
the titans, scattered the monkeys like the Fire at the end of the
World Period.

Meanwhile the monkey, Rishabha, rushed towards Mattanika,[3]
the younger brother of Ravana, and stood courageously facing
him. Beholding that monkey, as high as a hill, standing before
him, Matta, enraged, struck him violently on the chest with his
mace that resembled lightning. Under the impact of that
weapon, the lion among monkeys, his chest riven, stumbled,
blood flowing in streams from the wound. Regaining consciousness after a long time, that prince of the monkeys, his lips
trembling, threw a savage glance at Mahaparshwa and, with a
bound, hurled himself on that titan; thereafter the impetuous
leader of the intrepid monkeys, of the size of a mountain in
stature, clenched his fist and struck him full on the chest and,
like a tree whose roots have been severed, the titan suddenly
fell to the earth, his limbs streaming with blood. Thereupon,
Rishabha, tore that terrible mace which resembled the Rod of
Death, from his grasp, shouting in triumph. For an instant

---

[1] Tashtri's son. The son of Vishvarupa.
[2] The Elephants supporting the Quarters.
[3] Another name of Matta.

that enemy of the Gods appeared to be dead but, regaining his senses, his colour that of an evening cloud, he threw himself on the son of the Lord of Waters and struck him.

Dazed' by the shock, the monkey sank to the ground, but, having regained consciousness, quickly rose again, and, brandishing the mace resembling a huge rock, he struck the titan a violent blow. When that terrible mace fell on the powerful breast of the enemy of the Gods, hostile to sacrifice and the priests, from his riven breast, blood fell in torrents, as mineral-charged waters flow from a mountain. Thereafter Rishabha, still armed with that formidable weapon, advanced upon him rapidly, striking his mighty adversary again and again and that hero felled Mattanika in the forefront of the battle and, crushed by his own mace, his teeth and eyes pressed in, Matta sank to the earth bereft of life and strength like a rock shattered by lightning.

At his fall, all those titan warriors fled and, Ravana's brother being slain, the whole army of the Nairritas, which was as vast as the sea, throwing away their weapons, seeking only to preserve their lives, scattered in all directions like the sea bursting its banks.

CHAPTER 71

Lakshmana slays the Titan Atikaya

WITNESSING the rout of his great army, causing the hair to stand on end, and the death of his brothers the equals of Shakra in prowess and, beholding his two uncles Yuddhonmatta and Matta, the foremost of the titans, struck down in the fight, the illustrious Atikaya, who resembled a rock, the humbler of the pride of Devas and Danavas, he who had been favoured by Brahma, fell into a transport of rage.

Ascending his chariot, glittering like a hundred suns, that enemy of Indra hurled himself on the monkeys and, stretching his bow, that titan, wearing a diadem and adorned with sparkling earrings, proclaimed his name, emitting a tremendous shout. The proclaiming of his name, the leonine roar and the fearful twanging of his bow-string struck terror in those monkeys and they, beholding that gigantic warrior, reflected:—'Kumbhakarna has come again' and, in their panic, took shelter one with the other. At the sight of that apparition, like unto Vishnu taking the three strides, the simian warriors, seized with fear, fled in all directions and in the presence of Atikaya, those monkeys, bewildered, sought refuge with the one who is the refuge of all, the elder brother of Lakshmana.

At that instant, Kakutstha beheld the titan, like unto a mountain, standing in his chariot, afar off, armed with a bow and roaring like a cloud at the time of the dissolution of the worlds. Seeing that monster, Raghava, struck with astonishment, re-assuring the monkeys, enquired of Bibishana, saying:—

"Who is that archer, as high as a hill, with yellow eyes, standing in his vast chariot, harnessed to a thousand horses amidst sharp picks, javelins, gleaming and pointed darts, who shines like Maheshwara among the Bhutas and who is surrounded by glittering spears that fill his car like tongues of the Fire of Death, blazing like a cloud riven by lightning, his best and golden-backed bow illumining his marvellous car on all sides, as Shakra in the heavens? This tiger among titans diffuses a brilliant light over the battlefield as he, the prince of warriors, advances in a chariot reflecting the sun's rays. On the point of his standard, Rahu has lent him his splendour[1] and his arrows like unto the rays of the sun light up the ten regions; his triply-curved bow, inlaid and backed with gold, resounding like thunder, is as resplendent as Shatakratu's! With its standard, banner, carriage and the four outriders who escort it, that vast chariot thunders like a storm cloud. Eight and thirty quivers lie in the car with dreadful bows furnished with yellow cords! Two shining swords illumine its sides, their hafts measuring four palms and they are assuredly ten palms in length. With his red garlands, this hero of the size of a mountain, dark of hue, his great mouth like unto death, resembles the sun veiled by cloud! Who is this titan leader with his arms loaded with golden bracelets?"

Thus questioned by Rama, the descendant of Raghu of immense energy, the extremely illustrious Bibishana answered:—

"It is the valiant son of that king who is without equal in

[1] Rahu being his emblem.

might, Dashagriva of great splendour, the younger brother of Vaishravana of terrible exploits, the mighty Ravana, Lord of the Titans. Full of reverence for his elders, renowned for his strength, the most skilful of those versed in the science of arms, he is able to fight on horseback or on the back of an elephant, either with a spear or bow and, whether it be a question of destruction or of sowing dissension or of making peace, of bestowing gifts, of using diplomacy or of strategy, he is highly esteemed. His mother was Dhanyamalini and he is named Atikaya.

" Having found favour with Brahma through his chastity and austerity, he has obtained possession of marvellous weapons with which he has overcome his enemies and Swyambhu granted him invulnerability to Gods and Danavas and bestowed this celestial armour on him and a chariot reflecting the sun's rays. A hundred times has he triumphed over Gods and Danavas, rescued the titans and exterminated the Yakshas. In battle, that intrepid warrior stayed Indra's thunderbolt with his darts and repelled the noose belonging to the Lord of the Waters, Varuna. He, Atikaya, the most powerful of the titans is the intelligent son of Ravana and the subduer of the pride of Devas and Danavas. Speedily direct thine efforts against him, O Lion among Men, lest, with his arrows, he annihilate the monkey race ! "

At that instant, the mighty Atikaya, shouting again and again, stretching his bow, hurled himself on the monkey host.

Beholding that fearful monster, standing in his chariot, the greatest of car warriors, the foremost of the illustrious monkey leaders advanced to meet him, and Kumuda, Mainda, Nila and Sharabha, coming together, also went out with trees and rocks.

Then that mighty titan, prince of warriors, broke those rocks and trees and all the monkeys resisted him, but that virtuous hero of appalling stature, pierced them with iron darts. Overwhelmed by that hail of missiles, their limbs dislocated, demoralized, they were unable to endure the furious assaults of Atikaya and that hero sowed terror amidst the hosts of the valiant monkeys, as a lion, proud of its youth and strength, stands amongst a herd of deer ; nevertheless that Indra among the titans desisted from striking any who were defenceless.

Thereafter with his bow and quiver, he rushed on Rama and addressed him proudly, saying :—

" Here I stand in my chariot with my bow and arrows in my hand ! I do not contend with common soldiers but he, who desires it and is willing, I challenge, here and now, to combat ! "

This speech incensed Saumitri, the slayer of his foes, and, in his rage, he sprang forward with a smile of disdain, bow in hand. Provoked, he advanced, taking an arrow from his quiver and placing himself before Atikaya, stretching his great bow so that the earth, the sky, the sea and the four quarters resounded with the formidable thrumming of the bowstring and terror seized those rangers of the night.

Hearing that dreadful twanging of Saumitri's bow, the powerful and valiant son of that Indra of Titans was astounded and, enraged on beholding Lakshmana advancing towards him, he took out a sharp dart and spoke thus :—

" Go hence, O Saumitri, thou art but a child without any experience of warfare ; why dost thou seek to measure thy strength with mine, who am the equal of Death ! Nay, assuredly the force of these arrows loosed by mine arm may not be withstood by Himavat himself nor the earth nor the heavens. Thou art seeking to rouse the Fire of Dissolution which, to thy good fortune, is now sleeping. Throw away thy bow and go hence ! Do not sacrifice thy life by advancing to meet me ! Nevertheless if thou art determined not to turn back then stay and, yielding up thy life, enter Yama's abode ! Behold my whetted shafts, which wrought of refined gold, subdue the boasting of mine adversaries and resemble Shiva's trident. This arrow also, resembling a serpent, shall this instant quaff thy blood as the king of the beasts drinks the blood of the lord of the elephants. "

Speaking thus, in rage, the titan placed an arrow on his bow and that speech of Atikaya's, full of wrath and threats, infuriated Lakshmana who was brave and virtuous by nature so that he answered him proudly and with dignity, saying :—

" Superiority is not measured by speech nor is bragging indulged in by men of worth ! Here I am armed with my bow, an arrow in mine hand, manifest thy prowess, O Wretch ! Reveal thyself in deeds and cease to blow thine own trumpet !

He who conducts himself with courage is said to be a warrior !
Thou art furnished with every kind of weapon, art mounted on
thy chariot and hast a bow ; now manifest thy valour either
with arrows or with magic darts ! I shall cut off thine head
with my whetted shafts as the wind detaches the ripe fruit of the
palm from its stem ! Soon mine arrows, decorated with refined
gold, shall drink thy blood, that their points will cause to flow by
piercing thy limbs. Thou hast said ' He is but a child ' but
let not this thought cause thee to underestimate me. Old or
young, know that it is death who is about to enter into combat
with thee. Vishnu, while yet a child, covered the Three
Worlds in his three strides ! ''

These words of Lakshmana, fraught with sense and reason,
exasperated Atikaya, who laid hold of an excellent dart. At
this, Vidyadharas, Bhutas, Devas, Daityas, Maharishis and
Guhyakas of great soul, gathered to witness the duel.

Thereafter Atikaya, provoked, placed an arrow on his bow
and loosed it on Lakshmana and it ate up space, as it were,
but that sharpened arrow like unto a venomous snake, in the
form of a crescent, as it flew was severed by that slayer of his
foes and, seeing his dart broken, Atikaya, in a paroxysm of
rage took out five arrows at once, and that ranger of the night
loosed them on Lakshmana, but before they reached him, the
younger brother of Bharata shattered them with his whetted
shafts.

Having severed those missiles with his sharpened darts,
Lakshmana, the slayer of his foes, selected a pointed arrow, the
brilliance of which sent forth flames and placed it on his excellent
bow, then bending it with force, he struck the forehead of that
prince of the titans.

That shaft, sinking into the brow of the terrible titan with the
blood that covered it, resembled the King of the Serpents
entering a mountain and, as the formidable gateway of Tripura
shook, when struck by Rudra's shaft, so did that titan falter
at the impact of Lakshmana's weapon. Breathing heavily, that
colossus reflected ' Assuredly the arrow thus loosed proves to
me that thou art a worthy adversary ! ' Thinking thus, he
opened his mouth and, stretching his great arms, leaning on his
seat, urged his chariot forward.

One, three, five and seven were the arrows selected by that lion among the titans and, placing them on his bow and drawing it, he let them fly and those shafts, bright as the sun, seemed as it were to set the firmament ablaze. Meantime, unmoved, the younger brother of Raghava severed them with the aid of innumerable whetted darts. Seeing those arrows broken, the son of Ravana, enemy of the Lord of the Gods, incensed, took hold of a sharp weapon and, placing it on his bow, he loosed it with great force against Saumitri, who was advancing towards him, striking him on the breast. Wounded in the breast by Atikaya, Saumitri began to bleed profusely, like an elephant discharging its temporal juices, and that prince plucked out the shaft and threw it away ; thereafter he selected a sharp dart to which he joined a mantra-charged arrow and set Agni's weapon on his bow whereupon both bow and arrow spat forth flames. Thereupon Atikaya, endowed with great strength, took up Rudra's weapon and fixed an arrow with a golden haft, resembling a serpent, on his bow.

Then Lakshmana loosed that powerful weapon, his flaming and redoubtable missile on Atikaya like Antaka wielding the Rod of Death. Seeing that shaft joined to the Agneya dart the Ranger of the Night loosed Rudra's shaft joined to Surya's weapon, and those two missiles rushed towards each other in space and their flaming points made them appear like infuriated serpents. Devouring each other, they fell on the earth, their fire extinguished, reduced to ashes and bereft of their splendour, and having set the sky ablaze, they lay without lustre on the earth.

Thereafter Atikaya, enraged, discharged the Aishika Reed joined to Twashtar's Weapon, but the mighty Saumitri severed it with Indra's shaft. Seeing the reed broken, that prince born of Ravana, enraged, joined a spear to Yama's Weapon and that ranger of the night hurled it at Lakshmana who destroyed it with the Vayavya Weapon.

Then, like a mass of cloud letting loose its rain, Lakshmana, in anger, covered the son of Ravana with a rain of missiles and those shafts coming in contact with Atikaya's coat of mail which was encrusted with diamonds, had their points shattered and fell on the earth. Seeing them rendered fruitless Lakshmana, the slayer of hostile warriors, covered his adversary with a thousand arrows. Inundated by that hail of shafts, Atikaya, that mighty warrior, whose cuirass could not be pierced, remained unmoved and that hero was unable to inflict a wound on the titan.

Thereafter the Wind-god approached him and said :— " Because of the boon received from Brahma, that warrior is clothed in impenetrable armour, do thou therefore strike him with the Brahma Weapon, else he may not be slain, his mail being proof against aught else ! "

On hearing Vayu's words, Saumitri, the equal of Indra in prowess, instantly took up a dart of incredible velocity and joined it to Brahma's Weapon. Having placed that excellent weapon with the foremost of arrows furnished with sharp points on his bow, every region, the sun, moon and the great planets were struck with terror and the heavens and earth also shook. Then, having fixed the Brahma Weapon on his bow, that missile, the stem of which being like death's messenger and equal to lightning, Saumitri let it fly on the son of Indra's foe. And Atikaya beheld that shaft loosed by the mighty-armed Lakshmana, swift as the tempest, with its haft encrusted with gold and diamonds, falling upon him and beholding it, immediately struck at it with his innumerable shafts but that arrow, swift as Suparna himself, flew towards him with extreme velocity and seeing it draw near, like Death at the time of dissolution, Atikaya struck at it with lances, spears, maces, axes, picks and arrows with unrelenting energy, but those weapons of marvellous aspect were rendered fruitless by that flaming dart, which, striking him, severed his head with its diadem.

Cut off by Lakshmana's arrow, the head instantly fell on the earth with its crown like unto the peak of Himavat. Then those rangers of the night, who had escaped the slaughter, beholding the body lying on the ground, its raiment and adornments in disarray, were thunderstruck and, their features distored, those unfortunate beings, exhausted with fighting, suddenly began to emit piercing and inarticulate cries. Thereafter those titans, who surrounded their dead leader, terrified, without paying him honour, fled towards the city.

The monkeys, however, their faces shining like full-blown

lotuses, in their delight, all paid homage to Lakshmana on account of the success he had won in striking down that formidable adversary who was renowned for his prowess and theretofore invincible.

CHAPTER 72

Ravana, overcome by anxiety, makes further Plans

HEARING that Atikaya had been slain by the mighty Lakshmana, Ravana became extremely anxious and spoke as follows :—

" Dhumraksha, who is full of ardour and the most skilled in the use of arms, Akampana, Prahasta, and Kumbhakarna, those valiant titan warriors eager for combat, the destroyers of hostile forces, ever invincible, brave titans of immense stature who were versed in the use of every weapon, have fallen with their troops under the blows of Rama of imperishable exploits. Yet many powerful warriors were struck down by my son Indrajita, who is renowned for his strength and prowess ; those two brothers were fettered by his formidable shafts bestowed on us as a boon. All the Gods and Asuras combined, despite their power, could not have broken those fearful bonds, nor the Yakshas, Gandharvas or Pannagas ! I do not know by what force, magic or supernatural means, those bonds were severed by those two brothers, Rama and Lakshmana.

" Those courageous titans, who went out to fight at my command, have all perished in combat with the exceedingly valiant monkeys. Henceforth I do not see who, on the battlefield, will be able to slay Rama and Lakshmana or the powerful Sugriva and his forces.

" Ah ! How mighty is Rama ! How great is the range of his shafts ! Those titans, who challenged this warrior, have all been destroyed ! Now, on his account, let defences be set up everywhere, both in the city and round the Ashoka Grove where Sita is being guarded. Let the entries and exits be patrolled continuously by our sentinels, wherever they are posted ! Establish yourselves with the foremost battalions everywhere in order to observe the movements of the monkeys, O Night-rangers! In the evening, at midnight or at dawn, no matter when, do not relax your vigilance in regard to the simian army. Observe what troops are placed in the line by the enemy, how they advance and where they halt; let the gateways and turrets be barricaded at once!"

All the titans listened to the commands of the mighty Lord of the Titans and went away to carry them out. Ravana, the King of the Titans, however, having issued these orders, exceedingly despondent, entered his abode, the fire of his anger smouldering within him, and that powerful monarch of those rangers of the night, reflecting on the misfortune that had befallen his son, sighed without ceasing.

CHAPTER 73

Indrajita making himself invisible puts the Monkey Army out of action

The titans, who had escaped the slaughter, hastened to apprise Ravana of the death of their leaders, Devantaka and others, as also Trishiras and Atikaya.

Hearing these mournful tidings, great tears immediately filled the king's eyes and for a long time he remained absorbed in the melancholy thought of the death of his sons and brothers.

Beholding the wretched monarch plunged in an ocean of grief, Indrajita the son of that Lord of the Titans, the foremost of warriors, addressed him thus:—

" O My Dear Father, since Indrajita still lives, do not give thyself up to despair! O Prince of the Nairritas, he whom the enemy of Indra strikes with his shafts in the fight is not able to preserve his life. To-day thou shalt see Rama and Lakshmana lying stretched on the earth, their bodies pierced, torn to pieces by mine arrows, their limbs riddled with my whetted shafts. Bear witness to the well-considered vow of Shakra's enemy re-inforced by my prowess and the divine power! This very day I shall overwhelm Rama and Lakshmana with arrows that never miss their target. Let Indra, Vaivasvata, Vishnu, Rudra, the Sadhyas, Vaishvanara, Chandra and Surya this day witness mine immeasurable prowess as redoubtable as that of Vishnu at Bali's place of sacrifice ! "

Having spoken thus, that rival of the Lord of the Celestials, craved permission of the king to depart and with fearless soul ascended his chariot, that was as swift as the wind, harnessed to excellent steeds and furnished with weapons, resembling the car of Hari himself. Then he set out for the battlefield immediately and that magnanimous hero was escorted by innumerable warriors, full of ardour, bearing great bows in their hands.

As they advanced, some on the backs of elephants, others on prodigious mounts such as tigers, scorpions, cats, mules, buffalo, serpents, boars, cheetahs, lions and jackals, as large as hills, crows, herons and peacocks, those titans of redoubtable courage were armed with javelins, hammers, sabres, axes and maces. To the sound of conches and the rolling of drums, that valiant enemy of the King of the Gods rushed out to fight. With his parasol, pearly like the moon, that slayer of his foes shone like the firmament when that orb is full. Fanned by marvellous chowries with elegant handles, that warrior, adorned with golden ornaments, the foremost of archers, Indrajita, blazed like the solar disc and he, whose strength was irresistible, illumined Lanka like the burning sun in the sky. Then that intrepid subduer of his foes, on reaching the battlefield, ranged the titans round his chariot and, according to the traditional rites, that Prince of the Titans prayed to the God who feeds on sacrificial offerings,[1] whose brilliance he possessed, reciting the most auspicious mantras, and, offering libations of Soma and roasted grain, with garlands and perfumes, that resplendent leader of the titans invoked Pavaka.

Thereafter he brought there weapons such as Sharapatras, Samidhs and Bibhitakas with red robes and an iron spoon and, heaping the fire with Sharapatras and Tomaras, he seized hold of a live goat by the neck.

Blazing up suddenly the fire gave off no smoke but manifested the signs betokening victory and, having been lit, the flames

[1] The God of Fire, Pavaka or Agni.

bright as gold, whirling in a southerly direction, passed through the crucible and instantly consumed the offerings.

Thereafter Indrajita, who was skilled in handling arms, took out the Brahma-weapon and pronounced a mantram on his bow, his chariot and on all. Then he, having uttered the sacred formula and invoked Pavaka, the firmament, the sun, the planets, the moon and the stars, trembled. Having called on the God of Fire, whose brilliance he possessed, he, the equal of Indra in power, whose strength was unimaginable, disappeared in the sky with his bow, arrows, sword, chariot, horses and spear.

Then the army of titans, abundantly furnished with horses and chariots, flags and pennants, burning to fight, set out emitting war cries and, in the struggle, those titans, full of rage, attacked the monkeys with darts of different kinds which were sharp, swift and beautifully wrought, and with spears and hooks. Beholding them, the son of Ravana, addressing those rangers of the night, cried out :—" Attack the foe speedily whom you are burning to destroy ! Be of good cheer ! "

At these words, the titans, in their anxiety to triumph, roared aloud and caused a hail of missiles to descend on those redoubtable monkeys. Arming himself with arrows,[1] maces and clubs, Indrajita, on his side, in the midst of the titans, assaulted the monkeys from where he stood invisible in the sky.

Then those monkeys, struck down in the fight, instantly began to assail Ravani with blows from stones and trees and, full of anger, Indrajita, born of Ravana, that hero full of power, smote the monkeys with a single lance and, in fierce fury, pierced five, seven and nine monkeys at one time to the great delight of the titans. Thereafter that invincible warrior crushed those monkeys under his shafts that glittered like the sun and were decorated with gold.

Their limbs pierced, the monkeys, overwhelmed by those arrows, fell like great Asuras destroyed by the Gods. Before this second Aditya who consumed them with those formidable weapons as his rays, those lions among the monkeys fled away, filled with terror. Their bodies mutilated, their senses confused, they stampeded, bathed in blood and terrified but, in their

---

[1] Different kinds of arrows such as Nalikas and Navachas. See Weapons Glossary.

devotion to Rama, those monkeys, willing to sacrifice their lives. suddenly halted and returned shouting, armed with rocks, and, closing their ranks, showered down a hail of trees, crags and stones on Ravani.

That murderous and fearful avalanche of trees and rocks was however dispersed by the mighty Indrajita, who was ever victorious in combat and, with his arrows as bright as fire, resembling serpents, that prince pierced the ranks of his foes. With eighteen penetrating darts he wounded Gandhamadana; with nine others he struck Nala, who stood some way off, and, in his great strength, he assailed Mainda with seven arrows, tearing out his entrails, and Gaja with seven blunted shafts. Thereafter he pierced Jambavan with ten arrows, Nila with thirty and Sugriva, Rishabha, Angada and Dvivida with dreadful flaming arrows that had been received as boons, thus rendering those foremost of the monkeys insensible, who, struck by innumerable shafts fell under his furious onslaught so that he appeared like the Fire of Death itself.

With the aid of arrows as bright as the sun, loosed with skill, that were exceedingly swift, he scattered those monkey divisions in that great fight and, with transports of the keenest joy, that renowned warrior, born of the Indra of the Titans, witnessed the entire simian army, bathed in blood, overwhelmed with that rain of missiles.

Under that shower of arrows and cruel hail of weapons with which he assailed them, the valiant Indrajita ranged the monkey ranks spreading destruction. Then, leaving his army behind, he speedily flung himself on the monkey forces in that great fight, covering them with a huge wave of formidable shafts like the downpour from a dark cloud.

Victims of his magic arts, their bodies crushed by those missiles loosed by that vanquisher of Shakra, the monkeys, who were as large as rocks, emitted piteous cries, falling in the fray like great hills struck by Indra's thunderbolt, and they could see nothing but those sharp arrows decimating their ranks, whilst the enemy of the King of the Gods, that titan, veiled in his magic power, remained invisible. Then that illustrious Prince of the Titans let fly his whetted shafts that shone like the sun in all directions covering the foremost of the monkeys and destroying them;

and he caused spears, swords and axes resembling fire, shooting forth flames like a glowing brazier from which sparks fly, to fall on the ranks of the foremost of the Plavagas. Under the arrows and flaming darts, with which the vanquisher of Indra overwhelmed them, the monkey leaders resembled Kimshuka Trees in full flower.

As they looked upwards, some, struck in the eyes were blinded, and jostling one another, fell to the earth. With the aid of javelins, spears and whetted shafts charged with mantras, Indrajita, the Prince of the Titans, crushed all those warriors, Hanuman, Sugriva, Angada, Gandhamadana, Jambavan, Sushena, Vegadarshin, Mainda, Dvivida, Nila, Gavaksha, Gavaya, Kesarin, Hariloman, Vidyuddamshtra, Suryanana, Jyotimukha, Dadhimukha, Pavakaksha, Nala and Kumuda and, having disarmed those monkey leaders, he caused a shower of glittering darts, like unto the rays of the sun, to fall on Rama, and Lakshmana who accompanied him.

Under the wave of arrows, which he heeded as little as though they were drops of rain, Rama, of prodigious splendour began to ponder within himself and said to his brother :—

" O Lakshmana, having overwhelmed the simian army, that Indra among the Titans, the enemy of the Gods, trusting in his powerful weapon, now attacks us afresh with his sharp darts ! In virtue of the boon he has received from Swyambhu, that hero, full of energy and prowess, has made himself invisible despite his formidable size. How may Indrajita, who has taken up arms against us, be struck down in combat when his body is invisible ?

" I recognize this to be the weapon and power of Swyambhu, the Beneficent and Incomprehensible One ! With a tranquil heart, O Sagacious Lakshmana, bear the fall of this shaft with me to-day ! Let this Indra of Titans, the leader of them all, cover us with a rain of darts ! The entire army of the Monkey King, his greatest warriors having been struck down, appears to have lost its splendour, yet when Ravani beholds us lying stretched insensible and impotent, manifesting neither joy nor anger, he will certainly rejoin Ravana, the enemy of the Gods, in his abode, having gained a great victory."

Thereafter Indrajita, overwhelmed them both with a hail of

missiles and, having reduced them to a state of impotence, that Indra among the Titans set up a shout of triumph.

In this way, having overcome the simian army in battle, as also Rama and Lakshmana, he returned at once to the city ruled by Ravana's hand where, extolled by the Yatudhanas and filled with delight, he related all to his sire.

CHAPTER 74

On Jambavan's Instructions, Hanuman goes to the Mountain of Medicinal Herbs

SEEING the two Raghavas lying unconscious on the field, the army of monkeys and their leaders lost courage, nor did Sugriva, Nila, Angada or Jambavan dare to take any action.

Thereupon Bibishana, foremost among the wise, seeing the general despondency, with his sagacious words re-assured those warriors belonging to the simian king, saying :—

" Although those two princes are lying here without consciousness, have no fear, you have no cause to despair ; it is in order to honour Swyambhu's pledge that they have allowed themselves to be struck down by Indrajita with his rain of missiles ! Indrajita received that excellent weapon that is not to be withstood from Brahma. It is in order to render homage to that God that the two princes have fallen in the fight ; it is therefore not the moment to lose heart ! "

Having paid honour to Brahma's weapon, Maruti answered Bibishana, saying :—

" Let us console those who still live among the army of the monkeys, which has been decimated by that celestial shaft."

Thereupon, with torches in their hands, those two heroes, Hanuman and the foremost of the titans, began to range the battlefield together during the night, and they beheld the earth covered with tails, hands, breasts, feet, fingers, necks and severed limbs, scattered here and there, from which the blood flowed, and monkeys as large as hills fallen on the field, their weapons still glowing.

Thereafter Bibishana and Hanuman beheld Sugriva, Angada, Nila, Sharabha, Gandhamadana, Jambavan, Sushena, Vegadarshin as also Mainda, Nala, Jyotimukha, Dvivida and all those monkeys lying on the battlefield. Seventy-six kotis of brave monkeys had been overthrown in the fifth and last period of the day by Brahma's cherished weapon.

While looking on that formidable army, that had fallen under the blows of the enemy and that resembled the waters of the sea, Hanuman, accompanied by Bibishana, began to search for Jambavan and, beholding that aged one, bowed with the weight of years, riddled with a hundred arrows, the valiant son of Prajapati, like unto an extinguished brazier, the grandson of Poulastya[1] rushed towards him and said :—

" O Hero, is it possible that those penetrating shafts did not cut off thine existence ? "

Hearing the voice of Bibishana, Jambavan, the foremost of the bears, who was scarcely able to speak, answered saying :—

" O Indra among the Nairritas, thou who art full of valour, I recognize thy voice, O Pious One, say whether he, on account of whom Anjana and Matarishwan are happy parents, that hero, Hanuman, still lives ? "

On this enquiry from Jambavan, Bibishana replied :—

" Why dost thou remain silent concerning the two princes and question me on the subject of Maruti ? How is it that King Sugriva, Angada or even Raghava do not inspire thee with an affection as great as that which thou bearest for the son of Vayu, O Venerable One ? "

Hearing Bibishana's words, Jambavan answered :—" Hear, O Tiger among the Nairritas, as to why I enquire concerning Maruti ; it is, that should the valiant Hanuman still live, even if the army has been destroyed, it is not destroyed ! If Maruti yet lives, O Dear Friend, he, the rival of Maruta, the equal of Vaishvanara in power, then there is still the possibility of survival ! "

At that moment the son of Maruta approached that venerable one with reverence, paying obeisance to him and touching his

---

[1] POULASTYA—Ravana and his younger brother Bibishana were descended from the Sage Poulastya.

feet and the voice of Hanuman moved his heart, so that the
Prince of the Plavagas felt new life had been bestowed on him.

Thereafter the illustrious Jambavan said to Hanuman :—

" Come hither, O Mighty One, it is for thee to deliver the
monkeys, none other has the power and thou art their best
friend. This is the moment to demonstrate thy prowess, I
see no other ; do thou bring joy to those brave troops of bears
and monkeys ! Heal those two unfortunate beings, Rama and
Lakshmana of their wounds. Prepare to cross far above the
great path of the ocean in order to reach Himavat, the highest of
mountains, O Hanuman, and there direct thy course to that
golden Peak Rishabha, difficult to scale and of an extreme
altitude. There the summit of Mount Kailasha will be seen
by thee, O Slayer of Thy Foes ! Between the peaks of these
two mountains, thou wilt behold the mountain of medicinal
herbs rising in unparalleled splendour, where every kind of
healing plant abounds. O Foremost of the Monkeys, thou wilt
discover four plants growing on the summit, the radiance of
which illumines the ten regions. They are—Mritasamjivani,
Vishalyakarani, Suvarnakarani and Sandhani,[1] herbs of rare
value. Gather all four, O Hanuman, thou the son of the Bearer
of Fragrance, and return to aid the monkeys by reviving them."

At these words of Jambavan, Hanuman, born of Maruta, felt
himself infused with tremendous power, as the ocean heaves
with the force of the wind. Standing on the summit of the
high mountain which he crushed with his weight, the valiant
Hanuman looked like a second mountain. Trodden down by
the monkey's feet, the mountain sank, unable to endure the load
that pressed so heavily upon it, and the trees fell to the ground
and caught fire on account of the rapid course of the monkey,
whilst the peaks, trampled down by him, were shattered. Thus
crushed, its trees, rocks and soil torn up, it became impossible
for the monkeys to stand erect on that high mountain which was
shaking, and Lanka, with its great gateways destroyed, its
dwellings and bastions crumbling, full of terror-stricken titans,
appeared to be reeling. Then the son of Maruta, like unto a

[1] MRITASAMJIVANI   Reviver of the Dead.
VISHALYAKARANI.   Healer of wounds inflicted by darts.
SUVARNAKARANI.   That which heals the skin.
SANDHANI.   That which produces a salve for wounds.

mountain, trod that support of the earth under foot, causing the earth and sea to quake ; pressing the mountain under his feet, he opened his mouth like the fearful jaws of Vadava and began to roar with all his might in order to strike terror into the titans and, when they heard that formidable clamour, those lions among the titans in Lanka were paralysed with fear.

Thereafter, paying obeisance to Samudra, Maruti, the scourge of his foes, possessed of redoubtable courage, for Raghava's sake prepared himself for the undertaking.

Raising his tail which resembled a serpent, flattening his ears and opening his mouth wide, like unto the entry to Vadava, he sprang into the air with an impetuous bound, drawing trees with their branches, stones and a rabble of monkeys in his wake and, borne away by the force of the wind produced by the movement of his arms and thighs, deprived of resistance, they all fell into the ocean.

Then the son of Vayu, stretching his two arms that resembled the coils of serpents, with a strength equal to the enemy of reptiles,[1] set out in the direction of that celestial peak of the Lord of the Mountains, displacing all the cardinal points as it were. And he observed the ocean that rolled on and on with its garlands of waves and all the creatures moving in its depths while he coursed on like the discus loosed by the fingers of Vishnu. Mountains, flocks of birds, lakes, rivers, ponds, vast cities, crowded provinces, passed under his gaze as he journeyed on with the swiftness of his sire, the Wind-god. And the agile and courageous Hanuman, the rival of his father in valour, strove to follow the orbit of the sun and, in extreme haste, the foremost of monkeys went on with the speed of the wind and all the quarters re-echoed to the sound.

Then Maruti, that great monkey, full of energy, remembered Jambavan's words and suddenly Himavat appeared with its many streams, its great number of caves and waterfalls, the many kinds of trees that adorned it and its peaks like a mass of white clouds lovely to look upon. Thereafter he approached that King of Mountains and, as he drew near that Indra of high mountains with its golden peaks of great altitude, Hanuman beheld those illustrious and holy retreats of the ascetics,

---

[1] Garuda.

frequented by the foremost of the Gods, Rishis and Siddhas, and he saw Brahmakosha,[1] Rajatalaya, Shakralaya, Rudrashara-pramoksha, Hayanana and the blazing Brahmashiras and he recognized the servants of Vivasvat.

Thereafter he beheld the Vahnyalaya and the Vaishravanalaya, Suryaprabha and the Suryanibandhana, Brahmalaya and Shanka-rakarmukha, thus did he perceive the centre of the earth ; and Hanuman also discovered the steep Mountain Kailasha and the Rock of Himavat and Vrisha, that sublime and golden mountain, illumined by the radiations of all the curative herbs, the King of Mountains, where all the simples grow. Astonished on beholding that mountain wreathed in phosphorescent fires, the son of Vasava's messenger descended on that Lord of Hills covered with medicinal herbs, in order to gather them.

Then the great monkey, born of Maruta, covered a thousand leagues, ranging that mountain where those specifics grew on that most elevated of peaks ; nevertheless, those sovereign remedies, knowing that Hanuman had come to gather them, made themselves invisible. Thereupon that hero, not being able to see them, grew angry and, in his ire, began to emit loud cries. Impatient, his glances inflamed, he questioned that mountain, the support of the earth, saying :—

" What impels thee, thou who art of such strength, to show thyself (to be) without pity for Raghava ? O King of the Mountains, the hour having struck, overcome by the power of mine arms, thou shalt see thyself shattered to pieces ! "

Thereupon, seizing hold of the crest with its trees, elephants, gold and many kinds of ore that adorned it, with its summit of

---

[1] BRAHMAKOSHA. The Place of Hiranyagarbha.
RAJATALAYA. The Place of the Silver-navelled One. A mountain near Kailasha.
SHAKRALAYA. The Abode of Shakra.
RUDRASHARAPRAMOKSHA. The place where Rudra discharged the arrow at Tripura.
HAYANANA. The Place of the Horse-necked One. (See Hayagriva).
BRAHMASHIRAS. The Abode of the Deity presiding over the Brahma Weapon.
VIVASVAT. The God of Death.
VAHNYALAYA. The Abode of the Fire God.
VAISHRAVANALAYA. The Abode of Kuvera.
SURYAPRABHA—SURYANIBANDHANA. The Place where the suns meet.
BRAHMALAYA. The Abode of the Four-faced Brahma.
SHANKARAKARMUKHA. The Place of Shankara's bow.
ROCK OF HIMAVAT. The rock on which Rudra sat to practice asceticism.
VRISHA. The name literally means—The Bull of Shiva.

jagged peaks and sublime and radiant plateaus, he broke it off roughly.

Having thus uprooted it, he flew into the air to the great terror of the worlds, the Gods and their leaders and to the acclamations of innumerable inhabitants of the sky. Thereafter he flew away with the speed of Garuda, carrying that rocky peak which shone like the luminous orb and he too was filled with radiance as he followed the path of the sun. Coursing thus in the vicinity of that orb, he appeared to be its very image, and that peak spread a great light over the son of the God, who is the bearer of fragrance, so that it appeared as if Vishnu Himself, armed with his discus of a thousand fiery rays, were in the sky.

Then the monkeys, observing him, shouted with delight and he also on beholding them, emitted tremendous roars.

Hearing those cries of triumph, the inhabitants of Lanka set up a dreadful clamour and Hanuman alighted on a high rock in the midst of that host of monkeys.

Thereafter he bowed to the chief monkeys and embraced Bibishana.

Then the two sons of that King of Men, having inhaled those wonderful herbs, were instantly healed of their wounds and the others, those valiant monkeys, rose up in their turn and all the brave Plavagas were instantly cured of their wounds and sufferings, having inhaled those wonderful herbs and those who had been slain returned to life like sleepers waking when the night is over.

From that moment the monkeys and titans fought in Lanka itself, and thereafter on Ravana's command and out of perversity, all the titans struck down in the fight by the valiant monkeys, both wounded and dead were thrown into the sea.

Meantime the son of the Bearer of Fragrance, Hanuman, of formidable bounds, carried the peak of medicinal herbs back to Himavat and returned with speed to rejoin Rama.

CHAPTER 75

Lanka is set on fire by the Monkeys

AT that moment, Sugriva, the illustrious King of the Monkeys, addressed Hanuman in words fraught with wisdom, saying :—

" Now that Kumbhakarna has been slain and the youthful princes have perished, Ravana can no longer harm us ! Therefore let those valiant and agile Plavamgamas, who are able to do so, hurl themselves on Lanka with torches in their hands ! "

Meanwhile the sun had withdrawn behind the Astachala Mountains and at the dread hour of night, the foremost of the monkeys approached Lanka with flaming torches and those simian ranks, furnished with fiery brands, rushed in on all sides so that the grim-visaged titan sentinels instantly fled away. Then the monkeys joyfully set fire to gates, pavilions, highways and byways and buildings of every kind, and the dwellings were consumed by thousands, and the public monuments, as high as mountains, toppled down and fell to earth ; all was consigned to the flames ! Sandal of great price, pearls, brilliant jewels, diamonds and coral, woollen cloths, rich silks, carpets of many kinds made of lambs wool, vases and weapons of gold, countless rare objects, harness and horse cloths, collars and girths for elephants, chariots with their furnishings and decorations, warrior's armour, trappings for their mounts, swords, bows and bow-strings, arrows, spears, goads and lances, cloths of wool and horsehair, tiger skins, innumerable perfumes, palaces enriched with pearls and precious gems, with stores of arms of every kind, all were burnt to ashes. And the fire consumed all the buildings with their ornamentation and devoured the dwellings of the titans who inhabited them.

Clad in armour encrusted with gold, decorated with garlands and other ornaments, their eyes wild with inebriation, wine caused those inhabitants of Lanka to reel as they walked, whilst courtesans clung to their apparel, and they were incensed with fury against their foes. Armed with maces, picks and swords, they were gorging themselves with meat and drink or sleeping on sumptuous beds with the objects of their desire. Full of terror they fled distracted, carrying their sons with them in all haste, whilst their luxurious and splendid mansions, which combined every comfort, were consumed by fire in hundreds and thousands on every side. Those golden buildings that seemed to touch the skies constructed like moons and crescents with their magnificent upper galleries, their trellised windows and terraces decorated with pearls and crystal, re-echoed to the cries of herons, peacocks and the tinkling of ornaments.

Asleep in the many-storied residences, the lovely courtesans, awakened by the flames that scorched them, threw off the jewels that impeded their flight, crying:—'Ah! Alas!' in piercing tones.

Meanwhile the palaces crumbled in the fire that consumed them, and those flaming mansions spread their light afar, like unto the summits of high mountains when struck by Indra's thunderbolts, so that it appeared as if the Peak of Himavat itself were ablaze.

The houses on all sides, wreathed in fire, resembled blossoming Kimshuka Trees; thus did Lanka appear that night! Elephants and horses that had broken loose from their keepers gave the city an appearance of the ocean with its maddened sharks and crocodiles at the time of the end of the world! Here a horse was seen running unchecked or an elephant standing motionless in terror. Lanka in flames illumined the sea, the waters of which, streaked with shadows, seemed to flow with blood.

In an instant, the monkeys had set fire to the city and it looked as if the whole earth were aflame, as at the dread destruction of the world.

Seeing the smoke, the women began to shriek and, when the flames reached them, their cries could be heard at a hundred leagues distance. The titans rushed out of the city, their limbs covered with burns, whereupon the monkeys, eager to come to blows, fell upon them. Monkeys and titans set up such a clamour that it caused the ten regions, the ocean and the whole earth to re-echo.

Meantime, healed of their wounds, the two brothers, Rama and Lakshmana, intrepid warriors, took up their marvellous bows and, when Rama drew that excellent weapon, the dreadful thrumming thereof struck terror in the titans and, whilst he bent his great bow, Raghava shone in glory, as Bhava in his fury when he stretches the bow of the Vedas.[1]

Under the shafts loosed by that warrior, one of the gates of the city, resembling the peak of Mount Kailasha, fell shattered on the earth, and beholding Rama's arrows falling on temples and mansions, those Indras among the titans made a supreme effort and, while they closed their ranks, they emitted leonine roars so that it appeared as if the Night of Final Dissolution was at hand.

Then the leaders of the monkeys received orders from the magnanimous Sugriva, who said :—

" Enter the nearest gate and begin to fight, O Plavagas ! If any amongst you acts contrary to my orders, let him be slain ! "

Thereupon the monkey leaders bearing torches in their hands, took up their positions at the entrance of the city and, beholding them, Ravana, transported with fury yawned and the ten regions were thrown into confusion so that it seemed as if Rudra were manifesting his wrath. In his rage he sent out Kumbha and Nikumbha, both born of Kumbhakarna, with innumerable titans and, at his command, Yupaksha, Shonitaksha, Prajangha and Kampana set out with the two sons of Kumbhakarna.

Then with the roar of a lion, Ravana said to those valiant warriors :—

" Go forth immediately, O Titans ! "

At his command, those brave titans, with their shining weapons, left Lanka emitting a continuous clamour and, with the splendour of their ornaments and persons they illumined the whole firmament as did the monkeys also with their torches.

Then the light of the moon and stars and the brilliance of the two armies irradiated the heaven whilst the rays of the moon, their ornaments and the planets lit up the ranks of monkeys and titans on all sides and the light from the half-demolished mansions projected lurid flames over the flowing and tumultuous waves.

[1] A bow having the characteristics proper to bows as laid down in the Veda of Archery (Dhanur Veda.)

With their flags and pennants, their swords and excellent axes, their formidable cavalry, chariots and elephants, their innumerable hosts of infantry, their spears, maces, sabres, javelins, darts and shining bows, that terrible army of titans of redoubtable valour and ardour seemed to be furnished with flaming missiles and, amidst the clash of hundreds of gongs, their arms, encased in golden sheaths, were brandishing axes, and the javelins of the titans rang as they struck with their arrows and their great bows, whilst the air was permeated with the fragrance of their garlands and the aroma of wine.

Beholding that formidable army of titans that was not to be withstood, emitting the muttering of a great cloud, the Plavamgamas were agitated and, whilst their terrible opponents advanced towards them they let forth loud cries.

Thereafter the enemy forces hurled themselves upon them like moths into a flame and, their maces whirling in their fevered hands, emitted lightning flashes which increased the exceeding splendour of that host of excellent titans.

Meanwhile, as if a prey to intoxication, the monkeys rushed forward eager to fight, striking those rangers of the night with blows from trees, rocks and fists, whilst they advanced on them loosing their sharp arrows. Then those titans of immense energy, cut off the heads of the monkeys who tore off their ears with their teeth and battered in their skulls with their fists, crushing their limbs with stones as they moved about. Other rangers of the night, of grim aspect, struck the foremost of the monkeys here and there with their sharp swords and the slayer was slain in his turn, cursing and biting as they massacred each other. Then one cried ' Strike ! ' and was struck in his turn, whilst another called ' It is for me to deal the blow ' and yet others called in chorus ' Why trouble thyself ? Stay ! '

Amidst the stained missiles, armour and shattered weapons, long spears were thrust forward and blows from fists, maces, sabres, javelins and ploughshares were given. Then the encounter between monkeys and titans assumed terrifying proportions and, in the conflict, the rangers of the night slew their enemies in tens of sevens and, in their turn, the army of titans, their raiment in disorder, their armour and standards shattered, were assaulted and hemmed in on all sides by the monkeys.

CHAPTER 76

The Prowess of Angada and Kumbha : Kumbha is slain

AT the height of that appalling struggle in which so many valiant soldiers perished, Angada advanced on the heroic Kumbha ; and the impetuous Kampana, in anger, challenged Angada and, forestalling him, struck him a violent blow causing him to reel. Thereafter that warrior, coming to himself, hurled a rock on his adversary, who, crushed under the blow, fell to the ground.

Seeing Kampana slain, Shonitaksha drove his chariot boldly at the monkey and, in his fury, struck him with his sharp and fiery arrows, tearing his flesh ; then, like unto the Fire of Death, he loosed innumerable flaming Kshuras, Kshurapras, Narachas, Vatsadantas, Shilimukhas, Karnis, Shalyas and Vipathas[1] on him, and that valiant and energetic son of Bali, his limbs pierced, in his might, snapped the formidable bow of that titan and shattered his chariot with its shafts also.

Thereupon Shonitaksha instantly took up his sword and shield and, without hesitation, sprang forward with an impetuous bound but the courageous Angada, receiving the violent impact, with a shout, broke that weapon with his hand. Thereafter that lion among monkeys, as if following the line of the sacred thread, let the blade fall on the titan's shoulder, cutting it in two and, raising his great sword, the son of Bali, shouting again and again, ran to the forefront of the battle to seek out further opponents.

Now, in company with Prajangha, the courageous Yupaksha drove his car furiously against that valiant monkey and, at that instant, Shonitaksha, breathing heavily, rushed on that warrior of the golden bracelets.[2] Full of energy, Prajangha, the intrepid companion of Yupaksha, hurled himself on the mighty Angada, mace in hand and, between Shonitaksha and Prajangha

---

[1] See Glossary of Weapons.
[2] Angada.

the Prince of Monkeys resembled the full moon between two Vishakhas.[1] Then Mainda and Dvivida went to Angada's aid and stood on guard near him, whilst the titans of immense stature, their battalions drawn up, full of vigour, threw themselves furiously on the monkeys with swords, arrrows and maces and the encounter between those Indras among the monkeys, in the grip of those bulls of titans, was desperate, causing the hair to stand on end. In that fight, the former, seizing trees and stones, discharged them, but Prajangha, who was exceedingly powerful, broke them with his sword. Stones and trees fell thick and fast on his chariot but were all severed by the countless shafts of the mighty Yupaksha, while the trees that, on their side, were thrown by Dvivida and Mainda, were crushed and destroyed by Shonitaksha, who was full of ardour and courage.

Thereafter the infuriated Prajangha, brandishing his great sword with which he severed the limbs of his adversaries, leapt on Angada and, seeing him close beside him, that Indra among the monkeys, in his great strength struck him a violent blow with an Ashvakarna Tree and, with his fist, hit out at the arm holding the sword which fell at the impact. Beholding his sword lying on the earth, like unto an iron bar, that powerful titan raised his fist and, like unto lightning, brought it down with great force on the brow of the intrepid Angada, foremost among the monkeys, who reeled for an instant but, having regained his senses, that courageous son of Bali, boiling with rage, struck Prajangha's head from his shoulders.

Then Yupaksha, seeing his paternal uncle lying on the field, quickly alighted from his chariot, his eyes full of tears and, as his quiver was empty, drew his sword.

Beholding Yupaksha rushing towards him thus, Dvivida, with a mighty blow, struck him on the breast and, in his ire, seized hold of him with force. Perceiving his valiant brother made captive, the exceedingly energetic Shonitaksha struck Dvivida on the chest, and the blow caused the intrepid Dvivida to stumble, but he clung to the mace that his rival sought once more to raise against him. Meanwhile Mainda joined Dvivida, and Shonitaksha and Yupaksha, burning with courage, engaged

[1] Asterisms, (see Nakshatras.)

the two Plavagas in a terrible struggle. The mighty Dvivida tore the face of Shonitaksha with his nails and, dragging him to the ground, crushed him, whilst Mainda, fired with wrath, pressed Yupaksha in his arms so that he fell lifeless on the earth.

Then the army of those foremost among the titans, discouraged by the death of their leaders, turned and fled in order to rejoin the sons of Kumbhakarna ; and Kumbha, seeing those soldiers fleeing in all haste, rallied them and, perceiving those valiant warriors to have been cruelly used by the highly powerful monkeys, and their leaders being slain, Kumbha, full of ardour, began to execute difficult feats in the encounter.

Taking up his bow, he, the foremost and most skilled of archers, let fly a series of arrows like unto venomous serpents able to pierce the limbs and, with his shafts and marvellous bow, shining with a great lustre he appeared like a second Indra illumined by the effulgence of Airavata! Thereafter he stretched that bow up to his ear and struck Dvivida with a golden-hafted and plumed arrow and, as soon as it pierced that foremost of the Plavagas, who resembled the Trikuta Mountain, his legs stiffened and, trembling, he stumbled and fell.

Mainda, however, beholding his brother succumb in that great combat, rushed towards his adversary with a huge rock and that hero hurled it at the titan, but Kumbha shattered it with five whetted shafts and, taking hold of another dart with a sharp point, resembling a poisonous snake, he struck the breast of Dvivida's elder brother with violence.

Under the blow, Mainda, the General of the Monkeys, his chest torn open, fell unconscious on the earth. Thereupon the fiery Angada, seeing his maternal uncles overcome despite their prowess, hurled himself on Kumbha who was stretching his bow and, as he advanced, Kumbha pierced him with five whetted darts, then with a further three, and again with three spears, as if he were attacking an elephant. Thus Angada was struck by the mighty Kumbha with innumerable shafts but, though his limbs were pierced by a succession of penetrating darts, that were flaming and adorned with gold, yet he remained immoveable and let fall a shower of rocks and trees on the head of that warrior born of Kumbhakarna, who cut off and severed all the weapons that the son of Bali loosed upon him.

Seeing that leader of monkeys, Kumbha cut off his two eyelids with twin arrows, as one blinds an elephant with torches, so that the blood flowed and his eyes were veiled; thereupon Angada, with one hand protected his bloody lids and with the other seized hold of a Sala Tree that stood near and, propping it on his chest, he stripped that leafy tree of its branches, and, having bent it a little, discharged it in the fight in the sight of all the titans, and that Sala Tree, that resembled the banner of Indra, appeared like unto Mount Mandara. Thereafter Kumbha cut that tree to pieces and pierced his adversary with seven pointed and murderous shafts so that Angada suddenly fell down, unconscious.

Beholding the invincible Angada stretched on the ground, like unto the sea when its waters recede, the leaders of the monkeys carried the tidings to Raghava. Then Rama, hearing that the son of Bali had fallen and been overcome in the course of a desperate struggle, issued his orders to the simian leaders who were led by Jambavan. At Rama's command, those lions among the monkeys, full of rage, their eyes red with anger, rushed on Kumbha, who was stretching his bow, and flew to the aid of Angada.

Then Jambavan, Sushena and Vegadarshin, enraged, threw themselves on that warrior born of Kumbhakarna, and seeing them advance, the titan cut short the impetuous onslaught of those foremost of monkeys with a hail of arrows, as a rock obstructs the course of a torrent and, in the path sown with arrows, the intrepid monkeys were unable to discern anything, nor, as the sea cannot overstep its shores, were they able to pass.

Beholding the simian ranks overwhelmed by the rain of shafts, the King of the Monkeys, Sugriva, placing his nephew, Angada, behind him, fell upon the son of Kumbhakarna in the fight, as an impetuous lion on an elephant who is wandering on the slopes of a mountain, and that powerful monkey tore up huge trees, Ashvakarnas and others of varying fragrance, in great numbers, which he hurled at his adversary. Then the illustrious son of Kumbhakarna, with his sharp arrows, shattered that irresistible avalanche of trees that covered the whole sky and scattered those forest giants that shone like Shataghnis.

Beholding the rain of missiles dispersed by Kumbha, the valiant Monarch of the Monkeys, full of glory and majesty, remained unmoved and, suddenly struck by an arrow, he seized hold of Kumbha's bow that was equal to Indra's and broke it, throwing that weapon on the ground with violence. Then, having accomplished that incredible feat, he angrily addressed Kumbha, who resembled an elephant whose tusks are broken, and said :—

" O Elder Brother of Nikumbha, thy strength and prowess in loosing thine arrows are admirable as are thy filial piety and courage and Ravana's also. O Thou who art equal to Prahlada or Bali or the Slayer of Vritra or Kuvera or Varuna, thou alone art like unto thy mighty Sire. Thou only, O Long-armed Warrior, armed with thy mace, the slayer of thy foes, cannot be overcome by the Gods any more than misfortune can overwhelm him who is master of his senses ! Advance, O Most Intelligent Prince and witness me in action !

" On account of a boon, thy paternal uncle is able to withstand Devas and Danavas and, full of prowess, Kumbhakarna, in his turn, defied the Suras and Asuras ! With thy bow thou art equal to Indra and in valour Ravana's peer ! In the world thou art now the foremost of the titans in strength and power ! Let all beings witness the mighty and prodigious duel between us to-day resembling the combat between Shakra and Shambara! By striking down those valiant monkeys, who were possessed of extreme courage, thou hast accomplished a feat without equal and manifested thy skill in the use of weapons. O Hero, it is from fear of incurring reproach that I have not slain thee, for thy great exploits have wearied thee ; rest awhile therefore, reflecting on my prowess ! "

Thus flattered by Sugriva with fair words, the ardour of that warrior was redoubled, as the sacred fire flames up when butter is poured therein. Then Kumbha seized Sugriva in his two arms, whereupon, like two elephants intoxicated with ichor, those two, breathing heavily again and again, their limbs interlaced, crushed each other, wrestling, and from their mouths emitting flames mingled with smoke. Under the trampling of their feet, the earth sank and the waters of Varuna's abode, overflowed on every side.

Finally Sugriva, having thrown Kumbha down with violence, cast him into the salty waves, thus causing him to become acquainted with the depths of the ocean. Nevertheless Kumbha rose again and leapt on Sugriva, with his fist delivering a furious blow like unto lightning upon his breast, and the armour of the monkey was shattered and blood gushed forth. That violent blow from the titan's fist struck against the bones of his adversary and, from the impact, a flame shot forth resembling the fire that bursts from the Mountain Meru when struck by lightning. Thereafter Sugriva, that mighty lion among the monkeys, effulgent like the solar disc of a thousand rays, parrying the thrust, lifted up a fist resembling a thunderbolt and brought it down with force on his opponent's breast. At the impact, which shattered him, Kumbha, bereft of his senses, sank like a brazier, the brightness of which is extinguished. Under this blow of the fist, the titan suddenly fell down, like unto the Lohitanga of brilliant rays expelled from heaven by the force of destiny. And Kumbha falling, his chest crushed by Sugriva, resembled the flaming body of a meteor shooting from the sky !

Thereupon Kumbha being struck down in the fight by that Monarch of the Plavamgamas of formidable valour, the earth with its mountains and forests trembled and a great fear seized the titans.

CHAPTER 77

The Fight between Nikumbha and Hanuman

NIKUMBHA, seeing his brother slain by Sugriva, gazed on the King of the Monkeys as if he would consume him with the fury of his glance, and that warrior took hold of his brilliant and terrible mace as large as the peak of the Mahendra Mountain, like unto the Rod of Death, the support of the titans, which was festooned with garlands, plated with gold and embellished with diamonds and coral.

Brandishing that weapon of a splendour equal to Indra's standard, the fortunate Nikumbha, who was endowed with redoubtable courage, opening his mouth wide, emitted loud cries. With his breast adorned with golden pieces, his arms encircled with bracelets, his charming earrings and graceful garlands, his jewels and his mace, Nikumbha shone like a cloud shot with lightning and charged with thunder to which the bow of Indra is added. The tip of his weapon shattered the conjunction of the seven winds and that loud-voiced hero glowed like a smokeless flame, whereupon the firmament with the City of Vitapavati, the most lovely palaces of the Gandharvas, the clusters of stars and planets, the moon and great luminaries seemed to be spinning round with the whirling of Nikumbha's mace! Unapproachable in ardour, Nikumbha was like unto the Fire at the destruction of the worlds, his mace and his ornaments the flames, his wrath the fuel, and, in their terror, neither titans nor monkeys dared to move.

Hanuman, however, baring his breast, stood fearlessly before him, and that titan, with arms as thick as iron bars which shone like the star of day, brought his weapon down on the breast of that mighty one so that it broke into a hundred pieces like a meteor suddenly exploding in space. But the great monkey remained unmoved under the impact of that weapon like a mountain in an earthquake. Thus assailed by his adversary, Hanuman, the foremost of the Plavagas, swinging his fist round with extreme force and lifting it up, with a swift bound struck Nikumbha a violent blow on the chest so that his armour was shattered and blood shot forth like lightning from a cloud.

The shock caused Nikumbha to stumble but, steadying himself, he seized hold of the energetic Hanuman, whereupon a great cheering broke out amongst the inhabitants of Lanka, witnessing that combat.

Though lifted up in this wise by the titan, the mighty Hanuman struck him a violent blow with his fist and, freeing himself from Nikumbha's grasp, leapt to the ground, thereafter, with a supreme effort, in his rage he struck him down, crushing him and then, leaping into the air, he fell heavily on his chest and taking hold of his neck, pressed it with his two hands while he cried out, whereupon he tore off his head which was of an appalling size.

Amidst the shrieks emitted by Nikumbha, who had fallen under the blows of the son of Pavana, the armies of the son of

Dasaratha and the son of that Indra of the Titans, both filled with fury, entered into a desperate struggle. And Nikumbha being slain, the Plavagas emitted cries of joy that re-echoed in all the quarters of the horizon and the earth seemed to tremble and the heavens crumble, whilst the hosts of the titans were filled with terror.

CHAPTER 78

Maharaksha goes out to meet Rama and Lakshmana

SEEING Nikumbha slain and Kumbha also laid low, Ravana, in extreme wrath, appeared like unto a raging fire, and that Nairrita, mad with anger and grief, spoke with urgency to the son of Khara, the large-eyed Maharaksha, saying :—

" Go, O My Son, and, at my command, strike down Raghava and Lakshmana with all the dwellers in the woods."

On this behest, the son of Khara, Maharaksha, who was proud of his courage, answered :—

" It is well ! I shall obey thee ! " Thereafter, having paid obeisance to Ravana by circumambulating him, that valiant warrior emerged from his sumptuous abode. Then Khara's son addressed the commander of the army, who stood near, saying :—

" Let my chariot be brought hither immediately and assemble the troops at the earliest moment ! "

On this, that night-ranger brought his chariot and assembled the army, whereupon Maharaksha, having paid obeisance to the car and circumambulated it, caused it to be driven forward urging on his charioteer with the words : ' Drive on ! '.

Thereafter Maharaksha issued this order to all the titans :—

" Do ye precede me, O Soldiers ! As for myself, the magnanimous Ravana has commanded me to slay those two brothers, Rama and Lakshmana, in combat ! Today I shall lay them low with my whetted shafts, O Night Rangers, as also the deer of the trees and Sugriva. Today, under the blows of my mace, the great host of monkeys will be destroyed as dry wood by fire ! "

Hearing Maharaksha's words, the rangers of the night, furnished with all sorts of weapons, full of valour, closed their ranks. Able to change their shape at will, ferocious, endowed with sharp claws, their eyes inflamed, emitting the roar of elephants, causing the hair to stand on end, inspiring terror, those giants surrounded the huge son of Khara, shouting joyfully, shattering the vault of heaven. Then conches and drums sounded by thousands in all the quarters whilst they, leaping and clapping their hands, caused a great tumult.

Thereafter Maharaksha's charioteer suddenly let the goad drop from his hand, and the standard fell to the ground, whilst the horses, harnessed to his chariot, slackened their pace and stumbled as they advanced, mournfully shedding tears, and, as the illustrious Maharaksha set forth, a sinister and biting dust storm arose.

Nevertheless the titans, having witnessed those portents, set out unheeding and full of courage to meet Rama and Lakshmana and their hue was like unto herds of elephants or buffalo and they bore the marks of the blows from maces and swords received in the forefront of battle.

"Here stand I! Here stand I!" cried those seasoned warriors beginning to range to and fro on the battlefield.

CHAPTER 79

Maharaksha falls under Rama's Blows

SEEING Maharaksha approach, the foremost among the monkeys rushed forward burning to fight. Thereupon a desperate struggle ensued between the rangers of the night and the Plavagas, like unto that combat formerly waged between Devas and Danavas, causing the hair to stand on end.

Blows from trees and swords, clashes of maces and iron bars were exchanged, whilst monkeys and night-rangers assailed each other and the titans created carnage among the foremost of the monkeys with swords, maces, lances, javelins, harpoons, goads and arrows, nets, hammers, sticks and other weapons with which they struck out on every side.

Overwhelmed by a mass of missiles which the son of Khara hurled upon them, all the monkeys, distracted, fled full of terror and, seeing their enemies routed, the titans emitted leonine roars and triumphant shouts, while the monkeys scattered in all directions. Then Rama covered the titans with a hail of arrows and, beholding them overpowered in this wise, Maharaksha, that ranger of the night, consumed with the fire of his wrath, challenged Rama in these words, saying :—

" Stay ! It is with me, O Rama, that thou shouldst measure thy strength ! With whetted shafts loosed from my bow, I am about to relieve thee of thy life ! Since, in the Forest of Dandaka, thou didst slay my sire, remembering thine iniquity, my wrath has increased ! O Wicked Raghava, a violent fire consumes my limbs since I failed to meet with thee in that great forest ! By good fortune thou art now before me ; as a hungry lion desires to see its prey, so did I seek this encounter ! Soon shall my swift arrows despatch thee to the region of the dead where thou shalt rejoin the warriors thou hast slain ! Of what use are further words ? O Rama, let all the worlds witness our combat ; let us fight with darts, maces, fists or whatever weapon thou preferest ! "

Thus spoke Maharaksha and the son of Dasaratha, smiling, interrupted that flow of words, saying :—" O Titan, of what use is this prating ? It is in no wise worthy of thee ! On the battlefield one does not triumph by strength of words but by fighting ! Fourteen thousand titans and thy sire, Trishiras and Dushana himself, fell under my blows in the Dandaka Forest ! Today vultures, jackals and crows shall feed on thy flesh with their beaks, nails and claws, O Wretch ! "

Hearing these words of Raghava's, Maharaksha loosed innumerable shafts on him with great violence, but Rama, with a shower of darts, severed those golden-hafted and richly bejewelled arrows again and again so that they fell in pieces on the earth. Thereafter, as they joined issue, a desperate struggle ensued between the son of the demon, Khara, and the son of Dasaratha, and the clanging of their bow-strings and the clash of their gauntlets was like the muttering of thunderclouds.

Then Devas, Danavas, Gandharvas, Kinneras and great Serpents stood in the sky eager to witness that prodigious conflict. Each wound inflicted on the combatants redoubled their ardour as they exchanged blow for blow, and the countless shafts loosed by Rama were destroyed by the titan whilst those of the titan were severed by Rama again and again.

Innumerable missiles covered all the regions and space itself and the earth was heaped on every side so that it could not be distinguished. Finally the long-armed Raghava, enraged, broke the bow of his adversary and with eight Narachas wounded his charioteer; with his shafts he demolished the chariot and slew the horses who fell to the ground.

Deprived of his car, Maharaksha, that prowler of the night, stood on the ground and, armed with his spear, he shone like Fire at the dissolution of the worlds; and he was irresistible with his great lance, a gift from Shiva, that glittered in the air like unto the weapon of destruction.[1]

Beholding that great spear that emitted flames, the Gods, struck with terror fled on all sides whilst that ranger of the night, lifting it up, hurled it with fury against the magnanimous Raghava. As it fell flaming from the hand of the son of Khara, Raghava, with four arrows, severed it in its flight and, broken at many points, that spear with its celestial gilding, having been destroyed by Rama's shafts, fell to earth like a great meteor.

Beholding that weapon shattered by Rama of imperishable exploits, the Bhutas cried out in the sky :—" Well done ! Well done ! " and observing his spear to be broken, Maharaksha, that, ranger of the night, raising his fist, called out to Kakutstha, " Stay ! Stay ! "

Seeing him advancing, Rama, the joy of the House of Raghu, smiling disdainfully, took the Fire-weapon from his quiver whereupon, struck by Kakutstha's shaft, the titan, his heart transfixed, fell down and perished.

Witnessing the fall of Maharaksha, all the titans, terrified of Rama's arrows, fled to Lanka. Thereafter the Gods rejoiced at the death of that night ranger, born of Khara, who had been stricken by the violent blows of Dasarathi and shattered like a mountain struck by lightning.

---

[1] The weapon Shiva is said to wield at the destruction of the universe.

YUDDHA KANDA

CHAPTER 80

Indrajita sets out to fight once more

HEARING of the death of Maharaksha, Ravana, hitherto victorious in war, became a prey to violent anger, grinding his teeth and, enraged, he reflected on what ought to be done. Having considered the matter, in his wrath he sent his son, Indrajita, out to fight, saying :—

" Having triumphed over those two powerful brothers, Rama and Lakshmana, return, O Hero ! Visible or invisible, thou art superior in every way. Wert thou not victorious in the struggle with Indra of incomparable exploits, therefore why shouldst thou not succeed with these two mortals ? "

At this command of the King of the Titans, Indrajita, in obedience, proceeded to the place of sacrifice to offer oblations to Pavaka according to the traditional rites. During the ceremony female titans carrying red turbans also came there and took part in sacrificing to the fire. Thereafter titans came up hurriedly to that place where Ravani was, and, in that sacrifice, weapons such as Sharapatras, Bibhitakas, with fuel, red robes and iron ladles were placed there, then, having heaped the fire with Sharapatras and Tomaras, Indrajita seized hold of a living black buck by the neck. And that smokeless brazier devoured the sacred grass, oblations and fuel, whereupon many auspicious omens, indicative of victory, appeared. With its flames, bright as the moon, whirling in a southerly direction, the fire, having been kindled, seized hold of the offerings.

Thereafter, having offered oblations to Agni and gratified the Devas, Danavas and Demons, Indrajita ascended his marvellous car which he had rendered invisible. In his magnificent vehicle harnessed to four horses, that hero, furnished with whetted shafts and armed with his great bow, appeared resplendent. The chariot with its decorations of refined gold, carved with figures of gazelles, moons and crescents shone with beauty ; and Indrajita possessed a standard that, with its golden rings and encrustations of emerald, glowed like a brazier.

Under the protection of the Rod of Brahma, like unto the sun, the mighty Ravani was invincible. Setting out from the city, having invoked Agni and acquired the power to make himself invisible by the aid of sacred formulas lawful to titans, the triumphant Indrajita spoke thus :—

" Today I shall slay those two who have passed their exile in the forest in vain and, in combat, win a decisive victory for my Sire, Ravana. Today, having destroyed Rama and Lakshmana, I shall enjoy the supreme felicity of ridding the earth of monkeys!"

Having spoken thus, he made himself invisible and thereafter rushed furiously into the fray, whither Ravana had despatched him. Effulgent, with bow and shafts, that ardent adversary of Indra, beholding those two valiant heroes like unto a serpent with three heads, who were loosing a stream of arrows in the midst of the monkeys, reflected :—' These are those two ! ' and stretching his bow he covered those warriors with a shower of darts, as Parjanya lets loose his rain. Standing in his aerial car, invisible to the eye, he overwhelmed Rama and Lakshmana with whetted shafts.

Enveloped by those swift darts, Rama and Lakshmana placed celestial arrows on their bows and those two valiant warriors covered the sky with a rain of missiles as bright as the sun, without striking Indrajita.

Thereupon that powerful titan filled the sky with darkness and smoke, blotting out the cardinal points and shrouding himself in a dense fog; and, during his airy flight, neither the twanging of his bow-string nor the sound of the wheels nor the clattering of the horses' hoofs could be heard nor could he himself be seen.

In the midst of that fearful darkness, that long-armed warrior loosed a shower of Narachas so that it appeared like an avalanche of rocks and, with his golden shafts, bestowed on him as a boon, the furious Ravani wounded Rama and Lakshmana grievously in every limb.

Then those two lions among men, overcome by Narachas, like unto mountains under a deluge, loosed their whetted and golden-hafted arrows and those darts, adorned with heron's plumes, struck the son of Ravana in the sky and pierced him in his course, whereupon they fell on the earth covered with blood.

Thereafter, those two princes, with the aid of innumerable shafts, sought to sever the mass of missiles in their flight that burned them cruelly, and the two sons of Dasaratha aimed their excellent shafts in the direction whence those whetted darts fell. Ravani, however, a skilled driver, coursing on every side in his chariot, struck the two sons of Dasaratha with swift arrows and sharp shafts. Riddled by the golden-hafted arrows that rained upon them incessantly, the two sons of Dasaratha appeared like Kimshuka Trees in flower.

None could follow the rapidity of the titan's course; none catch a glimpse of him nor his chariot nor his arrows so that he resembled the sun obscured by heavy cloud.

Struck down, wounded and slain by him, the monkeys lay stretched on the earth in hundreds, whereupon Lakshmana, enraged, addressed his brother, saying :—

" Shall I loose the Brahma Weapon in order to exterminate all the titans ? " But Rama, who bore the marks of royalty, answered him :

" Nay, it doth not behove thee to rid the earth of titans ! No one may strike him who has withdrawn from the fight, or who has sought protection or has hidden himself or stands before thee with joined palms or who is fleeing or intoxicated ! O Long-armed Hero, we will strive to slay Indrajita by employing those exceedingly fiery arrows resembling serpents. That magician, that insignificant titan with his invisible chariot will be overthrown by the monkey leaders should he reveal himself. Whether he penetrate heaven or hell or range the firmament, my shafts will consume him wheresoever he may take refuge and he will fall, deprived of life ! "

Having spoken these significant words, that hero of the House of Raghu, who was surrounded by the Plavagas, in his great might, reflected on how he should destroy that barbarian, the perpetrator of evil deeds.

CHAPTER 81

Indrajita's Stratagem. Sita's Apparition

INDRAJITA, having divined the mighty Raghava's intention, withdrew from the fight in order to re-enter the city. Thereafter, remembering the death of those brave titans, his eyes red with anger, the valiant Ravani set forth once more, leaving by the western gate surrounded by titans; and the extremely energetic Indrajita, the descendant of Poulastya, that thorn in the side of the Gods, seeing those warriors, the two brothers, Rama and Lakshmana burning to fight, resorted to magic and caused the illusory figure of Sita to appear in the chariot encircled by a large force and he made seeming preparations to slay her.

For the purpose of deceiving the monkeys, that wretch conceived this design and, advancing to meet them, resolved to slay Sita as it were. Then the monkeys, beholding him approaching, enraged, rushed upon him with rocks in their hands, burning to fight. At their head marched Hanuman, that elephant among monkeys, armed with an enormous mountain peak. And he beheld in the chariot of Indrajita the unfortunate Sita, with a single tress, sorrowful, her features wasted on account of fasting; and the beloved of Raghava wore only a soiled garment nor had she washed her countenance and the limbs of that lovely woman were covered with dust and mud.

Seeing Maithili, Hanuman stood a moment as if stupefied, for, but a little while since, he had beheld the daughter of Janaka and, at the sight of that unfortunate being standing sorrowfully in the car, under the sway of that Indra of Titans, Hanuman thought to himself ' What does this titan intend to do ? ' Having reflected thus, that great monkey, the foremost of the Plavagas, rushed forward to meet Ravani.

Beholding that simian army, the son of Ravana, transported with rage, drew his sword from its sheath and brandished it over Sita's head in their presence, and he struck that woman in the chariot, who was created by illusion, whilst she cried out,

238

" O Rama, O Rama ! " Then Hanuman, born of Maruta, seeing the titan seize her by her attire, became greatly afflicted and tears of grief fell from his eyes as he beheld the cherished consort of Rama, who was so divinely beautiful. Thereafter, in his anger, he addressed the son of the King of the Titans harshly, saying :—

" O Wretch, it is to thy destruction that thou hast laid hands on her hair ! O Offspring of a family of Brahmarishis, thou hast fallen into the womb of a female demon. Cursed art thou for thine infamous conduct in cherishing such a desire ! Cruel and ruthless scoundrel, vile and puerile warrior, art thou not ashamed to perpetrate such an infamous deed ? O Pitiless One, without a heart, what has Maithili done, torn as she is from her home, her kingdom and the arms of Rama, that thou shouldst seek to slay her without mercy ? Sita being slain, thou shalt undoubtedly not survive long, since, deserving death for such a crime, thou hast fallen into my hands ! When thou hast yielded up thy life's breath, thy fate will be the lowest hell to which the slayers of women descend and which is eschewed by the most infamous of evil-doers ! "

Speaking thus, Hanuman, attended by armed monkeys, hurled himself in fury on the son of that Indra of Titans who opposed the powerful army of monkeys that surged towards him with his titans of redoubtable ferocity. And he himself assailed that simian host with thousands of arrows and thereafter addressed Hanuman, that monkey leader, saying :—

" I am about to slay Vaidehi before your eyes, who is the cause of Sugriva, thee and Rama, coming hither ! She being slain, I shall destroy Rama, Lakshmana, thou thyself, O Monkey, and Sugriva, as also the vile Bibishana. Thou hast said ' One must not slay a woman ', O Plavagama, but assuredly one is justified in doing that which will injure a foe ! "

Speaking thus, with his sword furnished with a sharp blade, he struck Sita, that illusory phantom, who was sobbing and, having slain her, Indrajita said to Hanuman :—

" Behold how the beloved of Rama has fallen under my sword ! Vaidehi is dead, thine arduous undertaking has been in vain ! "

Having thus slain her with his great sword, Indrajita, full of joy, standing in his chariot, began to shout aloud, and the monkeys, ranged before him at no great distance, heard him roaring full throatedly, stationed in his aerial citadel.

Having slain the illusory Sita, the perfidious Ravani manifested great delight and, beholding him fully satisfied, the monkeys, a prey to despair, took to flight.

CHAPTER 82

Hanuman rallies his Forces : Indrajita's Sacrifice

HEARING that formidable clamour and beholding Ravani, whose voice resembled Indra's thunder, the monkeys immediately fled in all directions.

Then Hanuman, born of Maruta, called to those who, with a downcast mien, sorrowful and fearful, were fleeing on all sides and said :—

" Why are you fleeing with a cheerless mien in all directions, O Plavamgamas ? Where is your courage ? Do not turn your back on the foe but follow me into battle ! "

At this reprimand from the virtuous son of Vayu, the monkeys, re-assured, armed with rocks and trees, advanced and, in a transport of fury, challenged the titans. Thereafter those lions among the monkeys encircled Hanuman who accompanied them in the great fight and, as the Consumer of Offerings burns up the east with his rays, so did Hanuman, surrounded on all sides by the foremost of monkeys, consume the enemy host. Creating carnage among the titans, that most powerful monkey, attended by the simian battalions, resembled Yama on the day of the final dissolution and, smarting with grief and anger, Hanuman hurled a huge rock on Ravani's chariot.

Seeing that missile descending, the driver, master of his horses, turned his car aside so that neither Indrajita nor the charioteer were struck by that rock which split the earth, burying itself after a fruitless flight.

Then those inhabitants of the woods, shouting, rushed on the enemy in their hundreds and those giants brandished trees and mountain peaks so that Indrajita was covered by a fearful hail of trees and stones by those Plavamgamas of redoutable valour. And they created havoc in the ranks of the enemy causing a great tumult and, under the ferocious blows of those terrible monkeys, the hideous rangers of the night fell, overwhelmed by trees on the battlefield.

Beholding his forces thus roughly handled by the monkeys, Indrajita, enraged, surrounded by his divisions, advanced towards them loosing a quantity of arrows and that intrepid warrior struck down the foremost of the monkeys in great numbers.

Furnished with spears, rocks, swords, harpoons, picks and maces, the monkeys, on their side, annihilated his companions in the struggle, and the exceedingly valiant Hanuman made use of huge trunks and branches of trees, stones and rocks to exterminate those titans of terrible exploits.

Having thrown back the enemy forces, Hanuman said to his troops :—" We have acted in order to please Rama at the risk of our lives but she, for whom we have fought, the daughter of Janaka, is dead ! Having informed Rama and Sugriva of this on our return, we will do whatever they command ".

Thus spoke that monkey general and heroically calling in his troops, he returned slowly with them.

Meanwhile, seeing Hanuman going to rejoin Raghava, the wicked Indrajita, desiring to offer oblations, went to the sacrificial altar of Nikumbhila and, reaching that place, he invoked the God of Fire, Pavaka. Having entered the place of sacrifice at the instance of the titans, Indrajita began to pour on the libations, and the fire blazed up, consuming the oblations and blood, and Agni, effulgent, sparkling and satisfied, resembled the setting sun.

Thereafter Indrajita poured libations on the earth for the prosperity of the titans, according to the rites in which he was well versed and, beholding this, the titans, instructed in what was fitting and unfitting, stood round in great numbers.

CHAPTER 83

Lakshmana's Speech

MEANWHILE in that fight between the titans and the monkeys, Raghava, hearing the formidable tumult, said to Jambavan :—

" O Friend, to judge by the fearful uproar and the clamour of the combatants, Hanuman is performing an exceedingly difficult feat at this moment. Go, attended by thine army, O Leader of the Bears, and lend thine aid to that Prince of Monkeys who is engaged in combat ! "

" Be it so ! " said the King of the Bears, and thereafter, surrounded by his troops, he advanced to the western gate to join Hanuman and that Lord of the Bears beheld Hanuman returning amidst his monkeys who had given up the fight and were lamenting. Beholding the host of bears, resembling a dark and fearful cloud, Hanuman caused them to halt and retrace their steps. Then that illustrious warrior, in company with those troops, speedily returned to seek out Rama and, full of grief, addressed him saying :—

" Whilst we were fighting, under our very eyes, Indrajita, born of Ravana, slew Sita who was weeping, O Destroyer of thy Foes and, my mind being afflicted by this spectacle, in despair I have come to inform thee of what has taken place ! "

Hearing these tidings, Raghava, overcome with sorrow, fell to the earth like a tree whose roots have been severed and, beholding the son of Raghu, who was like a God, lying on the ground, the monkey leaders from all sides rushed towards him as he lay consumed with the violence of his grief, resembling a fire that has suddenly been ignited ; and they sprinkled him with water that was fragrant with the scent of blue and white lotuses.

Then Lakshmana, full of anguish, pressed him in his arms and addressed the half-conscious Rama, in words pregnant with reason and penetration, saying :—

" O Thou who walkest in the path of virtue, O My Noble Brother, though thou hast mastered thy senses yet righteousness

242

has not been able to preserve thee from misfortune! I see the form of that which is animate and inanimate but not the form of dharma, hence in mine opinion, it does not exist! Inanimate objects may be seen and also those which are animate but the spiritual law is not manifest, else the virtuous such as thou would not suffer adversity! If unrighteousness brought evil in its train, then Ravana would now be in hell and thou, who art virtuous, wouldst not be afflicted by ill-fortune. Meanwhile calamity spares the titan in order to strike thee down, which proves the consequences of righteousness and unrighteousness to be reversed! If virtue produced good results and unrighteousness evil ones, then those (like Ravana), who have forsaken virtue, would suffer evil consequences. Those who never take pleasure in ill-doing should not be robbed of felicity since their every delight is in doing good; those who follow righteousness should pluck the fruits thereof. Since prosperity attends on those in whom unrighteousness abides and those, who make virtue their way of life, are afflicted, these words (vice and virtue) have no meaning! O Raghava, if the evil-doer perished through his own unrighteousness, unrighteousness itself would perish through its own evil and, it being destroyed, how could it destroy? If it be through the decree of destiny that a man is slain or slays another, then it is destiny and not the slayer who is at fault. O Thou, Slayer of thy Foes, since one is unable to discern the law of dharma meting out retribution or behold its form and it is as if it were not, how is it possible to attain the highest by means of dharma? If dharma truly existed, O King, O Most Virtuous of Men, then thou wouldst not have suffered this misfortune; it is therefore manifest that this law is meaning-less! Dharma, being weak and powerless, attaches itself to the strong and, because of its weakness, rubs out any difference between itself and vice, therefore, in mine opinion, one should disregard it. If unrighteousness is merely the result of strength, then abandon it since might is right. But if, as some hold, dharma is loyalty to one's word, O Scourge of thy Foes, then thy sire is guilty of adharma in the duplicity and cruelty he meted out to thee without reason! If one accepts the existence of righteousness, then Indra, the Bearer of the Thunderbolt, God of a Hundred Sacrifices, was not justified in performing a sacrifice after slaying the Ascetic Vishvarupa. If righteousness gives birth to unrighteousness, it must perish, O Raghava! Men will act accordingly to their whim, O Kakutstha. In mine opinion, O beloved Raghava, dharma has indeed been destroyed; thou hast severed its roots by abandoning thy kingdom! Like streams from the mountains, all success is brought to birth by material prosperity. The man of small intelligence, without resources, sees all his deeds come to nought as trickles of water drying up in the hot season. Renouncing wealth when one is accustomed to the advantages in which one is reared, is an error of judgment and is setting out on the wrong path. He who has wealth has friends and kinsfolk; he who has wealth is verily a man of importance; he who has wealth is a wise man. The wealthy man is brave, the wealthy man is wise, the wealthy man is powerful, above all the wealthy man is a man of worth! O Hero, I have pointed out the disadvantages that result from giving up one's good fortune, I see no reason for thy determination to abandon the crown.

" He who possesses a fortune finds virtue, pleasure and prosperity to be at his disposal; the poor man who seeks wealth, cannot attain it and merely dreams of it. Wealth is the creator of joy, pleasure, pride, anger, and inner and outer control; all these come from wealth, O Foremost of Men! Prosperity eludes virtuous men and those who pursue the path of duty in this world, nor can it be discerned any more than the stars in a stormy sky! Whilst, in accordance with thy sire's command, thou didst live in exile, O Hero, a titan bore away thy consort who is dearer to thee than life itself.

" O Hero, by my valour I shall be able to dissipate this great grief that Indrajita has caused thee to-day, O Raghava, arise therefore, rise up, O Lion among Men, O Long-armed Warrior, who art fixed in thy vows! Dost thou not know that thou art the Self, the Highest Self?

" Here am I, O Irreproachable Hero, at thy command! The tidings of the death of the daughter of Janaka enrages me! With my shafts I shall overwhelm Lanka, its chariots, horses, titans and its king."

CHAPTER 84

Bibishana consoles Rama

WHILST Lakshmana, in his fraternal affection, was consoling Rama, Bibishana, who had been restoring order in the ranks, came to that place.

Four warriors, armed with various weapons, escorted him and they resembled heaps of black collyrium and were like unto the leaders of elephant herds. Then that hero approaching, beheld Raghava plunged in affliction, as also the monkeys themselves, whose eyes were full of tears, and he saw the great-souled Raghava, the joy of the Ikshvaku Race, stunned with burning grief, whereupon Bibishana, his heart pierced with anguish, enquired :—" How is this ? "

Then Lakshmana, seeing Bibishana, Sugriva and the monkeys, uttered these impetuous words :—

" Indrajita has slain Sita ! Hearing these tidings from Hanuman's lips, Raghava has been overwhelmed with despair, O My Friend ! "

As Saumitri was still speaking, Bibishana interrupted him and addressed Rama, whose mind was agitated, in words fraught with good sense, saying :—

" O Indra among Men, that which thou hast heard spoken by Hanuman with a sorrowful mien, seems to me as probable as the drying up of the sea ! I am fully conversant with the wicked Ravana's design ; assuredly he would never permit Sita to be ill-treated, O Long-armed Warrior ! Though constantly pressed by me, who desired his welfare, to release Vaidehi, he would never listen to me. Neither by persuasion nor threats, conciliation nor gifts nor by sowing dissension, has anyone been able to behold Sita, how much less by force of arms ? It was in order to deceive the monkeys that Indrajita set out to meet them again ; this seeming daughter of Janaka is the effect of illusion, O Long-armed Warrior.

" To-day Indrajita is going to the sacrificial ground of Nikumbhila to offer an oblation. Having performed the sacrifice, on leaving, the son of Ravana will be invincible in battle even to the Gods led by Vasava. It is he, in the role of a skilled magician, who has made use of this illusion in order to undermine the courage of the monkeys. Let us leave now with our forces ere he accomplishes his object. Shake off the distress that has visited thee on this account, O Lion among Men ! The whole army is dispirited on beholding the grief that overwhelms thee. Come, pluck up courage, rise, call up thy valour and command Lakshmana to join with us and the troops which we command.

"With his whetted shafts, that lion among men will compel Ravani to break off his sacrifice, after which he may be slain. Thy brother's sharp and penetrating arrows, that fly on wings and resemble birds of prey, will drink his blood. O Long-armed Warrior, let Lakshmana, who is endowed with auspicious marks, bear down on that titan in order to destroy him, as Indra looses his thunderbolt. O Best of Men, it is not fitting to defer the slaying of a foe ; now suffer Lakshmana to fall on thine adversary speedily in order to slay him, as Mahadeva looses his thunderbolt on the enemies of the Gods in order to exterminate them."

CHAPTER 85

Lakshmana goes to the Nikumbhila Grove to fight Indrajita

THUS did the titan speak, but Raghava, who was overwhelmed with grief, did not fully comprehend what was said to him. Thereafter, having regained his strength, Rama, the Conqueror of Hostile Citadels, answered Bibishana, who was seated at his side, saying :—

"O Bibishana, Prince of the Nairritas, I desire to hear once more what thou hast said to me ; do thou repeat what I long to know."

Hearing these words of Raghava, Bibishana, skilled in discourse, repeated that which he had already told him, saying:—

"The behests thou didst lay upon me, O Long-armed Warrior, regarding the disposal of the forces, have been carried out scrupulously; the divisions of the army are drawn up on all sides and the leaders have each had their posts allotted to them. O Mighty Lord, now hear what I have to impart further.

" O Prince, beholding thee afflicted, we are discouraged; abandon thy distress, that grief which conduces to the joy of the foe afar off! Take courage, O Hero, and destroy the rangers of the night! May felicity be thine, since thou art to be re-united with Sita! O Joy of the House of Raghu, listen to my sage counsel! Let Saumitri set out bravely at the head of a considerable force and converge on the Nikumbhila Grove, in order to slay Ravani in combat by the aid of arrows, resembling venomous snakes, loosed from his bow!

" That warrior,[1] on account of his asceticism received a marvellous boon, the Brahmashira Weapon, from Swyambhu and also steeds that course at his will; he has undoubtedly reached the Nikumbhila Grove with his forces! If he succeeds in carrying through the sacrifice, know that we are lost!

" ' The foe who strikes thee ere thou hast reached the Nikumbhila Grove and ignited the fire, armed as thou art, will bring about thy death, O Enemy of Indra! ' Such were the words pronounced by the Lord of the World and thus was the end of that crafty titan ordained! O Rama, send thy powerful brother to slay Indrajita and, he being slain, Ravana with his friends is also slain! "

Bibishana having spoken thus, Rama answered him saying :—

" O Thou, whose prowess is truth, I know the magic power of that barbarian; his knowledge of the Brahma Weapon endows that skilful and great magician with immense power so that he is able to deprive the Gods and Varuna himself of consciousness in combat! While he ranges the sky in his chariot, O Illustrious Prince, one is no more able to follow his course than that of the sun in the midst of heavy cloud! "

Then Raghava, who was conversant with the magic power of that crafty foe, said to Lakshmana who shone with effulgence :—

" Go with the entire army of the Lord of the Monkeys with its generals and Hanuman at their head, O Lakshmana; take the army of the bears with their leader Jambavan, and destroy the titan possessed of the power of magic. This magnanimous

[1] Indrajita.

night-ranger[1] will follow thee with his ministers in order that thou mayest fall upon that master of illusion."

Hearing these words of Raghava, Lakshmana of redoubtable courage, who was accompanied by Bibishana, took up his rare bow, the foremost of all, and donning his mail, furnished with a sword and arrows, and full of joy, addressed him thus :—

" To-day the arrows loosed from my bow, having pierced Ravani, will lay Lanka waste as herons ravage a lotus pool ! This very day the shafts speeding from my bow will pierce the body of that barbarian ! "

Having spoken thus to his brother, the illustrious Lakshmana, eager to slay Ravani, departed with all speed and, having paid obeisance to the feet of his elder brother and circumambulated him, he set out for the Nikumbhila Grove, the place of sacrifice, where Ravani was to be found. Followed by Bibishana, Prince Lakshmana, burning with courage, with the good wishes of his brother, hastened away. Then Hanuman, at the head of countless monkeys and Bibishana with his counsellors speedily followed in his wake.

Whilst the great hosts of monkeys threw themselves in his train, Lakshmana beheld the forces of the King of the Bears stationed in the way. Thereafter Sumitra's son, the joy of his friends, having already covered a great distance, observed the army of the King of the Titans ranged for battle and, bow in hand, that conqueror of his foes, the joy of the House of Raghu, coming upon that skilful magician, prepared to enter into combat with him in conformity with Brahma's ordinance, and that prince, who was full of ardour, was accompanied by Bibishana, the valiant Angada and also the son of Anila.

Thereafter Lakshmana, as one entering into darkness, penetrated into the ranks of the countless enemy host that was exceedingly formidable, blazing with its glittering weapons and shaded by its dense rows of mighty chariots with their standards.

[1] Bibishana.

CHAPTER 86

Indrajita breaks off his Sacrifice to fight with Làkshmana

As these events were taking place, the younger brother of Ravana[1] gave the following counsel to Lakshmana, which was advantageous to his undertaking but detrimental to his foes, saying :—

"Armed with rocks, throw thyself with thy monkeys on the army of the titan which is now visible and resembles a dark cloud. Seek to overthrow them, O Lakshmana, for the son of that Indra of the Titans will become visible the instant the ranks are broken. With thine arrows, that equal Indra's thunderbolt, assail the enemy ; enter into the fray with all speed ere the sacrifice be completed. O Warrior, triumph over that perverse but skilled magician, the wicked Ravani of ruthless exploits, the terror of the worlds ! "

At these words of Bibishana, Lakshmana, endowed with auspicious marks, let loose a rain of shafts on the son of the Lord of the Titans. Thereafter the bears and monkeys in a body, arming themselves with huge trees, rushed on the army of the titans which was drawn up in battle array and which, with sharp darts, swords, picks and spears hurled itself on the simian battalions eager to overcome them.

Thereupon a desperate struggle ensued between monkeys and titans and the city re-echoed with the mighty tumult. Missiles of every kind, whetted darts, trees and mountain peaks sped through the air in dreadful wise so that the sky was obscured and innumerable titans, possessed of monstrous arms and faces, hurled their weapons on the foremost of the monkeys, creating extreme terror amongst them, whilst, from their side, the monkeys struck the titans with whole trees and crags, crushing them in the struggle. And the foremost of the bears and monkeys, of immense stature, created great terror among the titans with whom they fought. Learning that his army, over-whelmed by their foes, was losing ground, the invincible

[1] Bibishana.

249

Indrajita arose, the sacrificial rites as yet uncompleted and, leaving the Nikumbhila Grove, that was darkened by trees, Ravani, enraged, ascended his chariot that stood ready harnessed and fully equipped ; with his bow and arrows, he was formidable and resembled a heap of black collyrium, terrifying to behold with his reddened eyes, like unto Mrityu the Destroyer.

Beholding him standing in his chariot and the titan host ranged round about him, rushing to attack Lakshmana with fury, Hanuman, the scourge of his foes, who resembled a mountain, uprooted a huge tree, difficult to wield and, like unto Kala's consuming fire, that monkey, with repeated blows, struck down the enemy on the battlefield where they lay insensible.

Seeing the son of Pavana creating confusion in the ranks, thousands of titans attacked him with spears, those bearing lances with lances, those with swords with blows of their swords and those with harpoons with blows of harpoons. Iron bars, maces, sticks in their hundreds, Shataghnis,[1] iron hammers, terrible axes, Bhindipalas, blows from their fists like unto lightning, slaps sounding like thunder, were all delivered at Hanuman, who like unto a mountain in stature, in his rage, created a terrible carnage.

Then Indrajita beheld the foremost of the monkeys, the intrepid son of Pavana, like unto a rock, destroying his adversaries and, addressing his charioteer, he said :—

" Drive towards that monkey ; he will certainly destroy all the titans if he is suffered to do so ! "

At this command, the driver set his course at Maruti and drove the invincible Indrajita, who was standing in the chariot, upon him. Then that redoubtable titan, drawing near, let fall arrows, blows from his sword, harpoons, spears and axes on the head of that monkey, so that those formidable missiles that fell upon him threw Maruti into a transport of rage and he said :—

" O Perverse Son of Ravana, if thou hast any claim to valour, then fight ; with thy two arms strive with me ! O Insensate One, if thou dost withstand my might, thou shalt be accounted as the foremost of the titans ! "

Then Bibishana pointed out the son of Ravana, to Lakshmana, as he, with bow upraised, sought to slay Hanuman, and said :—

[1] See Glossary of Weapons.

" The Conqueror of Vasava, the son of Ravana, standing in his car, is about to slay Hanuman ! O Saumitri, do thou slay Ravani with thy formidable arrows of incomparable workmanship, the destroyers of their foes, that put an end to their lives ! "

Hearing Bibishana's words, that magnanimous one, a veritable Bibishana,[1] looked on Indrajita of dreadful prowess, who, standing in his chariot, was invincible and resembled a mountain.

CHAPTER 87

Indrajita and Bibishana denounce each other

HAVING spoken thus, Bibishana, delighted, taking Saumitri, who bore his bow in his hand, hastened away. Proceeding some distance, they entered a great wood where Bibishana pointed out Indrajita's place of sacrifice to Lakshmana and the illustrious brother of Ravana showed Saumitri a huge Nyagrodha Tree of fearful aspect, resembling a dark cloud, and said :—

" It is here that the powerful son of Ravana offers up his victims and thereafter enters into combat. Becoming invisible to all creatures, the titan overthrows his enemies in the fight, paralysing them with his excellent shafts. Do thou pierce the valiant son of Ravana, his chariot, steeds and charioteer with thy flaming darts ere he reaches the Nyagrodha Tree ! "

" Be it so ! " replied the mighty Saumitri, the delight of his friends and, taking his stand, he drew his marvellous bow.

Thereafter Indrajita, the powerful son of Ravana appeared before them in his chariot, that shone like fire, clad in armour with his sword and banner. Burning with ardour, Lakshmana challenged that invincible descendant of Poulastya, saying :—

" I challenge thee to combat ! Let it be in fair fight ! "

Thus accosted, the brave and exceedingly energetic Indrajita, observing Bibishana, overwhelmed him with reproaches, saying :—

" O Thou, born and bred in this race, the brother of my sire, why dost thou seek to harm his son, O My Paternal Uncle, O

[1] Bibishana—One who inspires terror.

Titan ? For thee, O Wretch, there is neither tradition, brotherly feeling nor a sense of duty ! O Impious One, Thou art to be pitied ! O Perverse Being, thou art the object of reproach to the virtuous, thou who didst abandon thine own kind in order to seek service with the enemy. Is it not a want of intelligence in thee, that thou dost not discern the great difference between living with one's kindred and seeking a miserable refuge with strangers ? Even if a stranger be endowed with every quality and a relation bereft of them all, yet the kinsman, though wanting in all merit, is to be preferred ; a stranger is always a stranger ! He who renounces his own kind to follow another will perish under the blows of the enemy after his own kinsfolk have been destroyed. Thou alone art capable of such ruthlessness and so relentless an attitude to thy kind, O Ranger of the Night, O Younger Brother of Ravana ! "

Thus addressed by his brother's son, Bibishana answered :—

"Art thou ignorant of my character that thou dost reproach me thus, O Titan ? O Perverse Prince, do not insult me but treat me with respect. Albeit I have been born in the race of titans, I possess those principles which appertain to men, my nature is not that of the demons ! Nay, I do not delight in cruelty nor does injustice find favour with me but, even if his character be dissimilar, how can a brother banish his own brother ? The one, who rejects him who renounces his duty and is bent on evil-doing, is assured of good fortune, as one who shakes off a snake from his hand. One is told to fly that perverse wretch who habitually purloins his neighbour's goods and has intercourse with other's wives, as one would flee from a burning dwelling.

" To take possession of another's property or to look with desire on his neighbour's wife or to distrust one's friends are the three faults that lead to destruction ! The ruthless slaughter of the great sages, the war on the Gods, arrogance, anger, hate and self-will are the defects of my brother, who is destroying himself and his empire, obscuring his good qualities as clouds veil the mountains. It is on account of his vices that I abandoned my brother, whose son thou art. Thou, thy father and Lanka are doomed ! O Titan, Thou art a mere boy possessed of an over-weening pride and art ill-mannered ! Say what thou wilt to me, thou art caught in the noose of death ! Thou shalt suffer the penalty thou hast merited for the harsh reproaches thou hast made to me this day! From henceforth thou shalt not be able to approach the Nyagrodha Tree, O Vilest of the Titans! Having outraged Kakutstha, thou canst not survive! Enter into combat with this God among men! Fall on the field of battle and go to the abode of Yama to the satisfaction of the Gods! Display thy prowess, exhaust thy weapons and missiles but if thou approachest within the range of Lakshmana's shafts, thou and thine army shalt not return alive!"

CHAPTER 88

The Combat between Lakshmana and Indrajita

HEARING Bibishana's words, Indrajita, seething with anger, answered him with fresh invectives and advanced upon him in fury. Standing in his richly decorated chariot, that was yoked to black steeds, his weapons and sword upraised, bearing his mighty, pliant and terrible bow and his arrows that were fatal to the foe, he resembled the Destroyer, Death Himself.

Then Lakshmana in all his splendour appeared before that mighty archer standing in his car, decked with ornaments, the slayer of his foes, the valiant son of Ravana, and, transported with fury, Indrajita addressed Saumitri, who was seated on Hanuman's back and resembled the rising sun, and Bibishana also and the foremost of the monkeys, saying :—

"Do ye all behold my prowess! In an instant, a rain of arrows speeding from mine irresistible bow will fall upon you in the fight like unto a shower of rain from the sky! Soon the shafts loosed from my great bow will scatter your limbs as the wind a heap of cotton! Pierced by my sharp darts, spears, lances, daggers and other weapons, this day I shall send you all to the abode of Yama! When, roaring like a thundercloud, I scatter the waves of mine arrows with a steady hand in the fray, who can stand before me?

"Formerly in a night engagement, with my darts that are equal to thunderbolts, I overthrew you both, leaving you unconscious with your escort; hast thou forgotten it? Since thou desirest to measure thy strength with mine, I who in my fury resemble a venomous reptile, I deem thou art anxious to enter the region of death!"

Hearing the taunts of Ravani, that Indra among the Titans, the son of Raghu replied indignantly :—

"It is not easy to succeed in those undertakings of which thou dost boast and, in fact, he who accomplishes his end, alone is skilful! O Thou whose situation is desperate, thou deemest to have attained thy purpose in this enterprise which is untenable from every aspect, merely by saying I have accomplished mine end! O Insensate One, rendering thyself invisible on the field of battle is the procedure of a rogue; honest men do not practice it! Since I am within the range of thy shafts, O Titan, manifest thy prowess; of what use is this bragging?"

Thus addressed, Indrajita who was ever victorious in combat, stretched his dread bow and with a powerful arm let fly his whetted shafts on his adversary. Discharged by him, those swift arrows resembling venomous snakes, struck Lakshmana hissing like serpents, and the impetuous son of Ravana, Indrajita, with those arrows of extreme velocity, overwhelmed Saumitri, who was endowed with auspicious marks, whereupon the fortunate Lakshmana, his limbs pierced by those darts, covered in blood, shone like a smokeless flame!

Meanwhile Indrajita, contemplating his feat, advanced, emitting an exceedingly loud cry and said :—

"O Saumitri, the feathered shafts loosed upon thee from my bow will rob thee of thy life, for their impact is mortal! This very day, O Lakshmana, bands of jackals, eagles and vultures will descend upon thee when thou hast fallen unconscious under my blows! Rama of perverse soul will see thee, his devoted brother, struck down by mine arm, thine armour shattered, thy bow in pieces, thy head severed, thou who art a warrior by birth only!"

To these insolent words of Ravana's son, the sagacious Lakshmana replied in measured and judicious terms, saying :—

"Cease from boasting, O Wretched Titan of crooked ways, what purpose is served by vain speech? Demonstrate thy valour in action; thou dost vaunt thine exploits ere thou hast accomplished them! To what end, O Titan? Act in such a way that

I may believe in thine utterances ! Mark how, without addressing a single word of contempt or provocation to thee and without bragging, I shall slay thee, O Last of Warriors ! "

Thus speaking, Lakshmana, with five Narachas loosed with great force from his bow, which he stretched up to his ear, struck the titan full in the breast and those feathered shafts of swift flight, resembling fiery serpents, shone in the breast of the Nairrita like the rays of the sun.

Struck by those darts, the son of Ravana, enraged, in his turn, pierced Lakshmana with three well-aimed arrows. Thereupon an appalling and fearful exchange of blows ensued between those lions among men and titans, who sought to triumph over each other. Valiant and endowed with strength, both courageous by nature, each found it hard to overcome the other, neither having his equal in energy and prowess. Resembling two planets coursing through the heavens, those two heroes strove, so that they seemed like those two invincible warriors, Bala and Vritra, struggling proudly like two lions, standing immoveable as they showered innumerable darts on each other, and that King of Men and Prince of the Titans fought on with extreme ardour.

CHAPTER 89

Lakshmana and Indrajita continue to fight

MEANWHILE the son of Dasaratha, slayer of his foes, arming himself with arrows, loosed them in fury on that Indra of Titans and at that twanging of his bow-string, the titan leader, his countenance ashen, fixed his gaze on Lakshmana.

Bibishana beholding the blenched features of the son of Ravana, said to Saumitri who was engaged in combat :—

" O Long-armed Warrior, I behold inauspicious signs round Ravana's son, hasten therefore for he is assuredly nearing his end ! "

Thereupon Saumitri, selecting some arrows resembling venomous snakes, let fly those barbed shafts like unto exceedingly poisonous serpents on Indrajita and he, struck by those missiles like unto thunderbolts hurled on him by Lakshmana, was dazed

awhile, his senses stupefied. Thereafter, beholding the valiant
son of Dasaratha standing in the field, he flung himself upon him,
his eyes red with anger and, drawing near, he began to taunt him
afresh, saying :—

" How is it that thou hast forgotten my prowess, when at the
first encounter thou and thy brother were bound and laid low,
thou who dost now seek to enter into combat with me anew ?
In that great struggle under mine arrows resembling thunderbolts, both of you with your followers were first felled to the
earth by me and then deprived of your senses.

" Meseems it has escaped thy memory ! Since thou hast
dared to challenge me, it is clear thou desirest to enter the abode
of Yama ! If, at the first assault thou didst fail to recognize my
superior strength, I shall soon demonstrate it to thee; stay
therefore and face me with resolution ! "

Speaking thus, he pierced Lakshmana with seven arrows and
Hanuman with ten powerful whetted shafts; thereafter with
re-doubled fury, Indrajita pierced Bibishana with a hundred
well-aimed darts. Seeing this, the younger brother of Rama,
unmoved, began to laugh, saying :—

" This is nothing ! " and that lion among men, Lakshmana,
undaunted, taking up some dreadful darts, hurled them in anger
on Ravani in the fight, saying :—

" Nay, it is not thus armed that warriors enter the fray, O
Night Ranger ! Thy darts are trifling and without power,
conducing to mine ease; it is undoubtedly not in this wise that
brave men fight ! "

With these words, he, from his bow, loosed a shower of
arrows on his adversary. Shattered by Lakshmana's shafts, the
heavy golden armour of the titan fell to pieces on the floor of the
chariot, like a mass of stars falling from the sky. His coat of
mail riven, riddled with wounds inflicted by Narachas, the
valiant Indrajita resembled the rising sun and, full of ire, the
courageous son of Ravana of redoubtable valour, struck Lakshmana with a thousand shafts, cleaving his celestial armour.
Then, exchanging blow for blow, they rushed on each other and
breathing heavily, engaged in a terrible struggle and, in the
twinkling of an eye, their limbs were lacerated by arrows and
from every part of their bodies the blood flowed.

For a long time these two valiant warriors tore each other with their sharp weapons and, in their unbridled energy, the two skilled combatants sought to overcome each other. Both riddled with a mass of arrows, their armour and standards shattered, they caused the hot blood to flow, as waterfalls let loose their torrents, and they let a dreadful hail of missiles fly with a great clamour, like unto the dark destructive clouds of doom, loosing their floods from the sky.

For a long time they fought thus without turning back or experiencing any fatigue and those foremost of archers let fly their shafts again and again, and the multi-shaped darts crossed and re-crossed each other in the air. With agility, speed and grace, the struggle between man and titan continued with an appalling din and each, on his side, raised a tremendous clamour inspiring terror, like unto a fearful tempest and the sound of those two redoubtable warriors in desperate combat resembled two clouds clashing in the sky. With golden-footed Narachas, those two warriors, sought to overcome one another, inflicting wounds from which rivers of blood flowed and from their pierced bodies the golden-hafted arrows, covered with blood, fell to the earth in which they buried themselves. By thousands their whetted shafts converged in the sky, cleaving and riving each other, and both let fall a formidable mass of darts in the struggle, so that they appeared like heaps of Kusha Grass destined for two sacrificial fires. The bodies of those illustrious heroes, full of wounds, shone like a Kimshuka or a Shalmali Tree, leaf-less and in full flower in the forest; and the impact was appalling, as Indrajita and Lakshmana fought, each desirous of overcoming the other.

Lakshmana battled with Ravani and Ravani with Lakshmana, each striking the other without ceasing and the streams of arrows buried in their flesh gave those two powerful warriors the appearance of two hills covered with trees, and their limbs streaming with blood, riddled with arrows, shone like two fires.

Thus did they fight for a long time without turning back in combat or giving way to exhaustion. Nevertheless, in order to allow the invincible Lakshmana, ever in the forefront of the fight, to overcome the fatigue of combat, the magnanimous Bibishana threw himself into the fray remaining near him to lend him his support.

CHAPTER 90

Indrajita loses his Charioteer, Chariot and Horses

SEEING the desperate struggle between man and titan, who resembled two elephants with broken tusks desirous of overcoming each other, Ravana's valiant brother, curious to behold the outcome of the duel, stood in the forefront of the battle, his excellent bow in his hand.

Standing erect, he stretched his great bow, letting fly long and pointed arrows on the titans and these shafts of burning impact, falling thick and fast, tore the demons to pieces as a thunderbolt rives the high mountains.

Then, in their turn, Bibishana's followers, the foremost of warriors, arming themselves with maces, swords and harpoons, struck the valiant titans in the fight and, surrounded by his companions, Bibishana resembled a full-grown elephant in the midst of young tuskers pressing close to him.

In order to encourage the monkeys, whose dearest wish was to slaughter their foes, Bibishana, the foremost of the titans, conversant with what was fitting to the occasion, uttered these pertinent words to them, saying :—

" Indrajita is the sole support of the King of the Titans and this is all that is left of his army, why therefore, O Foremost of the Monkeys, have you relaxed your efforts ? This wicked wretch being slain in the fore-front of battle, all the titan warriors, save Ravana, have been slain ! The valiant Prahasta is dead and the all-powerful Nikumbha also, Kumbhakarna, Kumbha, Dhumraksha, Jambumali, Mahamali, Tikshnavega, Ashaniprabha, Suptagna, Yajnakopa, Vajradamshtra, Samhradin, Vikata, Arighna, Tapana and Mainda, Praghasa as well as Prajangha and Jangha, Agniketu, Durdharsha, Rashmiketu who was full of energy, Vidyujjihva, Dvijihva and Akampana, Suparshva, Shakramali, Kampana, Devantaka and Narantaka who was full of valour. By slaying all these countless and exceedingly powerful titans, you have swum the ocean and now it is for you but to cross the hoof mark of a cow. Attack the titans who still remain, O Monkeys ; all these warriors, whose strength has filled them with pride, have perished in the fight. It is not fitting for me to slay my father's son, but, laying aside all pity for Rama's sake, I will put an end to my brother's offspring ; yet though I desire to slay him, tears fill mine eyes and deter me ; the long-armed Lakshmana will best know how to subdue him ! O Monkeys, closing in upon him, place yourselves so that you may wipe out those who stand near to him."

Thus incited by the exceedingly illustrious titan, the foremost of the monkeys demonstrated their delight by lashing their tails, and thereafter those tigers among the Plavamgamas, amidst repeated clapping of hands, emitted every kind of cry, like peacocks on beholding the clouds.

Jambavan too was surrounded by his leaders and their forces and they assailed the titans with their nails and teeth and blows from stones. Thereafter that Lord of the Bears decimated the titans, who, banishing all fear, full of vigour, overwhelmed him with countless missiles such as darts, axes, sharp pikes, lances and spears, striking him, their exterminator, in the fray.

Thereupon a formidable conflict ensued between monkeys and titans, like unto the fearful contest between the Gods and the Asuras fired with wrath, and Hanuman, enraged, broke off a mountain peak and having caused Lakshmana to dismount, slew the titans in their thousands. Meanwhile after a fearful combat with his maternal uncle, the valiant Indrajita, slayer of his foes, threw himself afresh on Lakshmana and a desperate duel arose between those two heroes amidst the general conflict. Then those valiant warriors let loose a rain of missiles with which they overwhelmed each other and, in the twinkling of an eye, they disappeared under a hail of arrows, as the glowing sun and the brightness of the moon under clouds at the end of summer. Their movements were so swift that one was unable to perceive when they took up their bows or stretched them or changed hands or loosed their shafts or selected or separated them or when they closed their fists or took aim and launched a succession of arrows with force, filling the sky on every side, nor was any object distinguishable. Lakshmana struck Ravani and Ravani, in his turn, struck Lakshmana and a general confusion arose between them during the combat. Barbed and pointed shafts, loosed by those two warriors, filled the space in the heavens as it were and those whetted darts, that fell in hundreds, spread over the cardinal points and the intermediate regions, so that everything was engulfed in darkness and extreme terror took possession of all beings.

Then the orb of a thousand rays sank behind the Asta Mountains enveloped in shadow, and torrents of blood flowed that day and fearful beasts of prey emitted full-throated howls.

" May good fortune befall the worlds ! " murmured the great Rishis, whilst the Gandharvas with the Charanas, panic-stricken, fled away.

Meanwhile Saumitri with four arrows pierced the four black steeds caparisoned in gold of that Indra among the Titans, and, with the aid of a sharp, yellow, shining and terrible Bhalla, furnished with beautiful plumes, resembling Mahendra's thunderbolt, resounding like the clang of a gauntlet hurled with full force, that mighty son of Raghu severed the head of the charioteer from his shoulders while he circled round.

Thereupon, his charioteer slain, Mandodari's valiant son seized the reins himself, taking up his bow ; and it was marvellous to behold him driving his chariot as he fought. Yet while his hands were occupied with the steeds, his adversary struck him with pointed darts and while he attended to his bow, the horses were pierced with arrows. Then Indrajita, even though his horses were riddled with darts, caused them to circle bravely under the arrows loosed by Saumitri with exceeding lightness of hand. Seeing his charioteer slain in the fight however, the son of Ravana lost his zest for combat and grew anxious, and observing the titan's countenance change, the monkey leaders began to acclaim Lakshmana in the height of joy. Thereafter Pramathin, Rabhasa, Sharabha and Gandhamadana, eager to bring matters to a close, struck a mighty blow, and those foremost of monkeys, endowed with extreme vigour and remarkable valour, with a rapid bound, threw themselves on the four magnificent steeds of Indrajita.

Under the weight of those monkeys who resembled mountains, the horses threw up torrents of blood and thereafter, crushed and mangled, fell lifeless on the earth. Having slain the titan's steeds and shattered his chariot, the monkeys, with a further bound, returned to Lakshmana's side.

Springing from his car, the horses having perished, and his charioteer being slain, Ravani caused a shower of darts to fall on Saumitri, whereupòn, like unto Mahendra, Lakshmana overwhelmed Indrajita with shafts and he, fighting on foot, his excellent steeds being dead, loosed countless whetted and marvellous darts on Saumitri in the fight.

CHAPTER 91

The Death of Indrajita

THE mighty Ranger of the Night, Indrajita, his horses slain, stood in the field in a paroxysm of fury, flaming with valour, and in their desire to triumph, those two archers, armed with bows, hurled themselves against one another like two mighty elephants in the forest.

Rushing this way and that, titans and monkeys slew each other, not wishing to abandon their leaders. At that moment, the son of Ravana began to encourage the titans and praised and gladdened them by addressing them thus :—

" O Foremost of the Titans, a profound darkness reigns over all regions nor can we distinguish between ourselves and the enemy, therefore fight fearlessly in order to delude the monkeys and I too shall return to enter into combat in another chariot ! O Brave Companions, do not suffer the monkeys to triumph whilst I am in the city ! "

At these words, the son of Ravana, slayer of his foes, eluding the vigilance of the dwellers in the woods, re-entered the City of Lanka, in order to provide himself with a fresh chariot ; and he caused a car embellished with magnificent gilding, furnished with javelins, swords and arrows, harnessed to the most excellent of steeds and driven by a skilful and intelligent charioteer to be made ready, whereafter the illustrious Ravani, victor in combat, ascended it. Surrounded by the foremost of battalions, the valiant son of Mandodari, Indrajita, urged on by the force of destiny, left the city and, drawn by swift steeds, with exceeding courage he rushed on Lakshmana and Bibishana who accompanied him.

Beholding the crafty son of Ravana, mounted in a chariot, Saumitri, the intrepid monkeys and the Titan Bibishana were astonished ; Indrajita, however, struck down the foremost of the monkeys with fury. Under the clouds of arrows falling in hundreds and thousands, Ravani, victorious in combat, stretching his bow to a circle, slew the monkeys in his wrath, displaying his extreme skill, and the monkeys, overwhelmed by the Narachas of dreadful impetus, took refuge with Saumitri, as all beings with Prajapati. Thereupon, inflamed with martial ardour, that descendant of Raghu severed the bow of Indrajita, thus demonstrating his fleetness of hand but he, seizing hold of another, hastened to string it, yet Laksnmana shattered it also with three arrows and, having broken his weapons thus, Saumitri pierced Ravani's breast with five darts like unto venomous snakes. Then these shafts, leaving that great bow, having entered Indrajita's body, fell to the earth like huge red serpents.

His weapon severed, vomiting blood, Ravani took hold of another powerful bow with its stout cord and, aiming at Lakshmana, with extreme speed caused a shower of missiles to fall upon him, like unto Purandara letting loose his floods. Yet, irresistible as that hail of arrows, poured down by Indrajita was, Lakshmana, the Conqueror of his Foes, standing immoveable, repelled them.

Thus did Ravani witness Lakshmana's marvellous prowess, he who was the intrepid and valiant son of Raghu. Thereafter Lakshmana, in fury, pierced each of those titans with three shafts in the fight, manifesting the velocity of his arrows, and Indrajita, on his side, riddled him with a hail of shafts.

Then that Indra among the Titans, grievously wounded by his valiant adversary, the slayer of his foes, loosed a continuous shower of arrows on Lakshmana but, ere they reached him, they were severed by the sharp spear of that warrior, the destroyer of his enemies, and Lakshmana, with a crescent-shaped arrow, cut off the head of Indrajita's charioteer in his excellent car, while he was coursing here and there.

Deprived of their driver, the horses, without deviating from their course, continued to draw the chariot, advancing and describing circles in a marvellous manner. Thereupon Saumitri, of fixed courage, unable to control his anger, let fly his shafts against the titan's steeds causing them to take fright.

Provoked by this action, the son of Ravana struck the terrible Saumitri with his ten arrows and those shafts, equal to lightning, that seemed composed of all the poisons, glanced off his golden armour.

Seeing that his coat of mail was impenetrable, the son of Ravana, Indrajita, in a transport of rage, manifesting his lightness of hand, struck Lakshmana in the forehead with three arrows of graceful joints, and that illustrious warrior, the joy of the House of Raghu, with three shafts embedded in his forehead, shone in the forefront of battle like unto a triple mountain. Albeit thus smitten by the titan's arrows, Lakshmana, in his turn, instantly let fly five shafts which struck Indrajita, who was adorned with lovely earrings, full in the face.

Thereafter Lakshmana and Indrajita, warriors of exceeding prowess, armed with powerful and mighty bows, overwhelmed each other with sharp arrows. With their limbs streaming with blood, those two heroes, Lakshmana and Indrajita, at that instant shone on the field of battle like two Kimshuka Trees in flower and each hurling himself on the other desirous of victory, pierced his opponent's limbs with formidable arrows. Filled with martial ardour, the son of Ravana smote Bibishana's handsome countenance with three darts and, having pierced that Indra of the Titans with three iron-tipped shafts, he struck all the monkey leaders one after the other.

Highly provoked, the exceedingly energetic Bibishana felled the horses of the wicked Ravani with a mace, whereupon the mighty Indrajita, springing down from his car, his horses slain and his charioteer dead, hurled a javelin on his paternal uncle.

Beholding this, the enhancer of Sumitra's delight, with his sharp arrow, severed it in ten pieces in its flight and it fell on the earth. Thereafter Bibishana, his mighty bow in his hand, let fly five Marganas, the impact of which being equal to lightning, and struck Indrajita, whose horses had been slain, in the breast. Having passed through his body, those golden-hafted arrows, that flew straight to their target, were stained with blood so that they resembled huge red serpents.

Then, highly incensed against his paternal uncle, Indrajita, standing in the midst of the titans, selected a marvellous arrow of great power that he had received from Yama and, seeing him place that formidable shaft on his bow, the valiant and intrepid Lakshmana took up one of immeasurable power which had been bestowed on him during sleep by the God Kuvera, and that weapon was irresistible, nor could the Gods nor the Asuras with their leaders stand before it.

And those excellent bows, resembling maces, when stretched by their arms, emitted a piercing sound like unto two ospreys and the two powerful arrows notched on those wonderful bent bows lit up the faces of the two heroes with a vivid glow. Those barbed shafts loosed from the bows illumined the heavens, striking against each other with a violent impact and the shock of those formidable weapons as they struck against each other caused them to burst into flame, emitting sparks and smoke. Like unto two great planets colliding together, they fell shattered in a hundred pieces on the battlefield.

Seeing those weapons severed and broken in the forefront of the battle, Lakshmana and Indrajita were seized with mortification and fury and, in his anger, Saumitri armed himself with Varuna's shaft whilst Mahendra's conqueror, fighting on foot, let fly Rudra's weapon in the fight which shattered Varuna's dart, despite its immense potency. Thereafter, in his ire, the illustrious Indrajita, victorious in combat, as if about to destroy the worlds, took up the flaming Agneya Weapon but the valiant Lakshmana diverted it with the Solar Dart and, seeing his shaft thus baffled, Ravani, maddened with anger, seized hold of the Asura Weapon that was sharp and fatal to its foe. Then from his bow sped shining Kutamudgaras, spears, Bushundis, maces, swords and axes and, beholding that dire and dreadful weapon, irresistible to all beings, the destroyer of every missile, the illustrious Lakshmana arrested it with the aid of the Maheshwara Weapon.

Thereupon a prodigious struggle arose between the rivals, causing the hair to stand on end and, from all sides, Beings, standing in the sky made a circle round Lakshmana and the heavens were filled with a host of Beings overcome with astonishment at the fearful tumult arising from that dread conflict between monkeys and titans. Rishis, Pitris, Gandharvas, Garudas and Uragas with Shatakratu at their head watched over Lakshmana during .the fight and, in that instant, the younger brother of Raghava took up the foremost of shafts, the Avya Weapon of flaming impact, in order to transfix Ravana's son, and also the well-plumed and gilded dart, skilfully fashioned, to which the Celestial Host paid homage and with which Shakra, that mighty Lord of great energy, who is drawn by bay horses, formerly overcame the Danavas in the war between Gods and Asuras. That weapon of Indra's, undefeated in combat, foremost of shafts was placed by Saumitri on the most excellent of bows and the fortunate Lakshmana, in order to achieve his purpose, spoke to the presiding Deity of that weapon, thus :—

" If Rama, the son of Dasaratha, is truly virtuous and loyal and, in feats of heroism has no rival, then slay the son of Ravana ! "

Thus speaking, that warrior, the slayer of his foes, stretched his bow up to his ear and let fly an arrow united to Indra's weapon on Ravani in the fight, that was incapable of missing its target, and it severed the lovely head of Indrajita, graced with earrings and its casque, causing it to roll on the earth. Separated from the body, Indrajita's huge head, streaming with blood, resembled a golden ball thrown on the ground ; and the son of Ravana fell dead on the battlefield with his armour, his helmet and his broken bow.

Then all the monkeys with Bibishana, beholding the corpse, shouted in exultation, as the Gods rejoiced at the death of Vritra, and in the skies, the Bhutas, magnanimous Rishis, Gandharvas and Apsaras, on beholding the leaders of the great titan army scattering on all sides, harassed by the victorious monkeys, emitted shouts of triumph.

Hard pressed by the monkeys, the titans, flinging down their arms, hastily fled in disorder towards Lanka and, in the general stampede the titans, throwing away their weapons, lances, swords and axes, ran in all directions at once. Terror-stricken, harried by the monkeys, some re-entered Lanka, others threw themselves into the sea or took refuge on the mountain. Now that Indrajita lay dead on the battlefield, the titans fled away in their thousands. As the sun withdraws behind the Asta Mountain and its rays disappear, so did the titans vanish from the horizon when Indrajita had fallen. As the solar orb with its rays extinguished or a fire without heat, so did that long-armed warrior lie bereft of life and the world, freed from her sufferings and delivered from her enemy, rejoiced! And the blessed Shakra was exceedingly gratified at the death of that titan of evil deeds and the great Rishis also, whilst in the heavens, the Gods could be heard striking their gongs and the dancing Apsaras and the magnanimous Gandharvas caused a rain of flowers to fall that was marvellous to behold.

On the death of that titan of cruel exploits, peace reigned, the waters became limpid, the air pure and Devas and Danavas rejoiced at the fall of one who was a source of terror to all the worlds. Thereafter a shout of triumph arose from the Devas, Gandharvas and Danavas who said :—

" Now let the Brahmins go about their pursuits without anxiety, their sins removed ! "

Then the monkey leaders, beholding that Bull among the Nairritas slain in battle, whose prowess was irresistible, paid homage to Lakshmana and Bibishana, Hanuman and Jambavan ; and all the Plavamgamas, growling and leaping with chattering of jaws, surrounded that descendant of Raghu, lashing their tails and clapping their hands. ' Victory to Prince Lakshmana ! ' rose the cry and, embracing each other, the monkeys, their hearts filled with joy, hymned the praises of Lakshmana in every way.

Witnessing that difficult feat of Lakshmana's, he who was the delight of his friends and seeing the corpse of Indra's adversary, the Gods, highly gratified, experienced supreme delight.

CHAPTER 92

Rama commends Lakshmana who is cured of his Wounds by the Monkey Sushena

Lakshmana, graced with auspicious marks, his limbs bathed in blood, having slain that conqueror of his foes on the battlefield, experienced supreme satisfaction.

266

Taking with him Jambavan, Hanuman and all the inhabitants of the woods, the valiant and illustrious Lakshmana speedily returned to Sugriva and Raghava, leaning on Bibishana and Hanuman. Thereafter, having circumambulated Rama and paid obeisance to him, Saumitri stood beside his brother as Upendra by Indra.

Then that hero, Bibishana, approaching with a look which itself was eloquent of delight, described Indrajita's fearful end and it was with joy that Rama learned how the head of Ravani had been severed by the great-souled Lakshmana and the tidings that Indrajita had fallen under Lakshmana's blows filled that valiant prince with unequalled felicity so that he cried out :—

" Well done, O Lakshmana, this exceedingly difficult feat pleases me ! Ravani's death means victory, be assured thereof ! "

Thereafter, smelling the head of Lakshmana, who had increased his glory yet who was abashed, the mighty Rama caused him to be seated on his lap and, with gentle strength, having clasped his brother, who was wounded, to his breast, he gazed upon him tenderly again and again. Then Rama, smelling his head once more, passed his hand rapidly over his body and, in order to sooth him, said :—

" Thou hast accomplished an auspicious and highly momentous feat, O Thou whose exploits are beyond the power of others ! Now that his son is slain, I deem Ravana to be defeated. To-day the death of that perverse wretch confers victory over Ravana, the Scourge of Men, upon me, be thou blessed, O Warrior ! Thou hast severed the right arm of the King of the Titans on which he leant for support ! Bibishana and Hanuman too, bore themselves with valour in the great fight. In three days, that warrior was utterly vanquished ; from now I am delivered from my foes, for Ravana will assuredly come forth, setting out with considerable forces. When, on hearing of the death of his son, which will overwhelm him with grief, the King of the Titans advances surrounded by his vast army, I shall encircle him with my powerful forces and slay him, difficult though it be. The conqueror of Indra having fallen in combat with thee, under thy direction, O Lakshmana, neither Sita nor the earth itself would be hard to regain ! "

Having lavished comfort and caresses on his brother, the son of Raghu, Rama, joyfully addressed Sushena, saying :—

"Do thou pluck out the arrows from the highly intelligent Saumitri, who is ever devoted to his friends, and restore him. Speedily heal the wounds of Saumitri, who is attached to his friends, and do thou nurse back to health all those who received blows and wounds in the conflict, those bears and monkeys whose valiant battalions have trees as their weapons."

At these words of Rama, the powerful monkey leader, Sushena, administered a sovereign remedy to Lakshmana's nostrils and having inhaled it, that hero was at once liberated from his darts and wounds. Restored to his normal state and freed from the arrows, his burning pains at an end, his fever suddenly allayed, Saumitri experienced supreme delight. Thereupon Rama, the King of the Plavagas, Bibishana and the valiant Chief of the Bears with their forces, seeing Saumitri standing free from pain, rejoiced exceedingly.

Then that supremely difficult exploit of Lakshmana's was praised by Dasarathi of great soul, and, recollecting that the conqueror of Indra had fallen in the fight, the King of the Monkeys was filled with joy.

CHAPTER 93

Ravana's Grief on hearing of his Son's Death

POULASTYA'S ambassadors, having learnt of Indrajita's death and confirmed it, conveyed the tidings to Dashagriva in all haste, saying :—

"O Great King, Thine illustrious son has been slain by Lakshmana, who was accompanied by Bibishana ; we were witness thereof ! That hero, confronted by a hero, measured his strength with Lakshmana's ! Thy son, undefeated in any combat, he who triumphed over the Gods with Indra at their head, has gone to the Celestial Regions, having been overwhelmed by Lakshmana's shafts ! "

Hearing of the terrible, cruel and grievous end of his son on the battlefield, that bull among the titans swooned away and only came to himself after a long time.

Distracted with grief on account of his son's death, that unfortunate one, beside himself, burst into lamentation, crying:—

" O Thou, the Conqueror of Indra, how hast thou suffered thyself to be overcome by Lakshmana this day ? In thy wrath, wast thou not able to strike down Kala and Antaka themselves with thy shafts, as also the peak of the Mandara Mountain ? How much more was it possible for thee to strike down Lakshmana in the fight ? Hereafter the King of Death will be held in greater reverence by me, since to-day he has brought thee under the sway of destiny, O Long-armed Warrior ! Even among the Celestial Host, this is the path trodden by those skilful warriors who wage a brave fight ! He who is slain in the service of his lord goes to the heavenly regions. Seeing Indrajita slain this day, the Gods and all the Guardians of the World, free from anxiety will sleep in peace ! Now the Three Worlds and the entire earth with its woods appears deserted to me without the only Indrajita. To-day I shall hear the cries of the youthful daughters of the Nairritas in the private apartments, like unto the roar of elephants in a mountain cave. O Hero, where hast thou gone, relinquishing thy right to the throne, to Lanka, the titans, thy mother, myself and thy consorts ? Assuredly, I should have preceded thee to the abode of death so that I might have received those honours due to the departed, offered up by thee, but the contrary has taken place, O Hero ! Why do Sugriva, Lakshmana and Raghava still live and why hast thou deserted me ere thou hadst rid me of this triple thorn ? "

Having first lamented thus, Ravana, the King of the Titans was overcome with a violent rage on account of the death of Indrajita and the grief at losing his son increased the fire of anger within him who was irascible by nature, as in the summer months the rays of the sun become more intense. From his half-opened mouth, he seemed to breathe forth flame and smoke in his rage, as Vritra formerly from his, and his eyes, naturally red, were further inflamed with ire, glowing in dreadful wise. Under the sway of anger, his aspect, ever a source of terror, caused him to resemble the enraged Rudra ! Tears fell from the eyes of that infuriated monster like boiling oil from two flaming lamps.

Grinding his teeth, he made a sound like unto the revolving of the rod[1] with which the Gods and Danavas churned the milky ocean. Mad with anger, like unto Antaka eager to devour all beings animate or inanimate, he allowed his gaze to wander over the four quarters of the horizon nor did any titan dare approach him, and in a transport of rage the King of the Titans, seated amidst his warriors, in order to excite their ardour, said :—

" Having practised penance for thousands of years and gratified Swyambhu on countless occasions, as the fruit of mine austerities, he accorded me complete immunity from Devas and Asuras.

" Brahma bestowed a coat of mail, that gleamed like the sun, on me which, in my conflicts with the Gods and Asuras, none of my foes, though armed with thunderbolts, were able to shatter. To-day, clad in that armour and mounted on my chariot of war, who will dare to withstand me, be it Purandara himself?

" The great bow with its arrows bestowed on me when I gratified Swyambhu, after an encounter with Devas and Asuras, that redoubtable bow will be drawn by me to the sound of countless musical instruments, in a mighty battle, to Rama and Lakshmana's destruction! "

Tormented by the death of his son, the ferocious Ravana, overpowered by anger, having reflected within himself, resolved to slay Sita. Rolling his reddened eyes, that cruel and terrible titan, in his anguish, said in the presence of all the Rangers of the Night, in plaintive tones :—

" My unfortunate son, in order to deceive the monkeys, having had recourse to magic, showed them an illusory corpse, saying :—' This is Sita ! ' Verily it shall become a reality ! I shall slay Vaidehi who is devoted to that evil wretch ! "

Having spoken thus, he seized hold of a sword that was well-tempered and bright as the stainless sky and rushed out in haste surrounded by his wives and counsellors. Ravana, whose heart was torn with grief on account of his son, taking up his sword, rushed out to find Maithili and seeing the king setting out in a great rage, the titans emitted leonine roars and embracing each other, said :—

[1] This refers to the Mountain Mandara which was used by the Gods and Asuras as the churning rod.

" To-day we shall see those two brothers humbled ! In his anger, Ravana has overcome the four Guardians of the World and countless others have fallen under his blows ; the Three Worlds have yielded up their treasure to him whose prowess and valour have no equal on earth ! "

As they were speaking thus, Ravana, in a transport of rage, was rushing to where Sita was to be found in the Ashoka Grove, and, though his friends sought to restrain him, he ran on, as in the sky the planet Rahu bears down on Rohini.

The irreproachable Maithili, in the midst of the female titans who guarded her, beholding that furious titan with a great sword, was seized with terror, and the daughter of Janaka, Sita, seeing him continue to advance with that weapon upraised, though his friends sought to restrain him, in the height of misery, wailing, uttered these words :—

" Beholding that wicked wretch rushing upon me in fury, I, who am defenceless but who yet have a defender, fear that he intends to slay me ! Despite my loyalty to my lord, he entreated me again and again, saying ' Be my consort ' and I constantly repulsed him. My refusal has assuredly caused him to give way to despair and, in a transport of fury, he is preparing to slay me. Or it may be that those two tigers among men, those brothers, Rama and Lakshmana, have, on my account, been cut down to-day on the battlefield. I hear a great clashing of gongs and the exultant shouts of innumerable people rejoicing ! Woe is me, the two princes have died for me or else this titan of cruel intent has come to slay me on account of grief over his son or he has been unable to slay Rama and Lakshmana ! Why did I not follow Hanuman's counsel, miserable creature that I am ! If I had departed, seated on his back, I should now be resting happily in the lap of my lord. Assuredly Kaushalya's heart will break when she learns that her son has perished in the fight and, weeping, she will recollect the birth, childhood, youth, virtuous deeds and beauty of that magnanimous hero. Overcome with despair, having offered up the obsequies in honour of her dead son, distracted with grief, she will ascend the funeral pyre or cast herself into the river. Cursed be that wicked hunch-back Manthara and her sinister counsels ; it is she who is the cause of the sufferings which will overwhelm Kaushalya."

Hearing the unfortunate Maithili lamenting thus, she, who resembled Rohini fallen under the sway of Rahu in the absence of the Moon, a virtuous and honest counsellor, the sagacious Suparshwa, seeking with his companions to restrain Ravana, the King of the Titans, said to him :—

" Why, O Dashagriva, dost thou, the younger brother of Vaishravana himself, seek to put Vaidehi to death in an access of rage, disregarding the law ?[1]   Thou who art a student of the Veda, who hast been purified by pious observances and who delightest in the scriptures, how art thou able to harbour the thought of slaying a woman ?   O Valiant Monarch of the Titans, spare the beautiful Maithili and loose the vials of thy wrath on that man, entering into combat with him with our aid.   This is the fourteenth day of the dark fortnight[2] and to-morrow, on the day of the new moon, march to victory surrounded by thy forces.   Courageous, armed with thy sword, in thine excellent chariot, a mighty car-warrior, thou shalt cut down the terrible Dasarathi and take possession of Mithila's daughter ! "

Thereupon the wicked and powerful Ravana, giving ear to the judicious words of his devoted counsellor, returned to the palace and re-entered the assembly hall surrounded by his friends.

CHAPTER 94

Rama's Exploits

HAVING entered the council chamber, the unhappy king, the mighty Ravana, overwhelmed by the death of his son, seated on his throne, in the depth of affliction, breathing like an enragèd lion, saluted the leaders of his army and addressed them saying:—

" Do ye set out at the head of cavalry with a column of chariots, elephants and horses, with which you are abundantly supplied, and, in the fight, hurl yourselves upon Rama only, overwhelming him with a rain of missiles, like clouds in the rainy

---

[1] The Law of Dharma or Righteousness.
[2] Dark Fortnight—The fortnight of the waning moon.

season. Thereafter when your sharp darts have pierced his limbs in that great battle, to-morrow, I myself will put an end to Rama's life in the presence of all beings."

On this command from their king, the titans set out in their swift-moving chariots followed by innumerable battalions. Armed with maces, harpoons, swords, arrows and life-destroying axes, all those titans struck the monkeys, who countered them with blows from rocks and trees. Then, as the sun rose, a great and terrible struggle ensued between titans and monkeys, fearful to behold and they struck each other with countless shining weapons, javelins, swords and axes in the fray and a prodigious dust storm, arising on account of the battle, was laid again by the rivers of blood from titans and monkeys. With elephants and chariots as the banks, javelins as the fish, standards as the trees, corpses as the floating logs, rivers of blood flowed.

Though soaked in gore, the valiant monkeys, leaping hither and thither in the fight, hacked the banners, armour, chariots, horses and weapons of every kind to pieces. With their sharp teeth and nails the Plavamgamas tore the hair, ears, foreheads and noses of their opponents. A hundred of the foremost of the monkeys leapt on every titan like birds on a felled tree and the titans, like unto hills, struck the redoubtable monkeys with heavy maces, javelins, scimitars and axes. Cut to pieces by their foes, the great army of monkeys sought shelter with Rama, the son of Dasaratha, the only true refuge.

Then that exceedingly energetic hero, taking up his bow, penetrating into the ranks of the titans, overwhelmed them with a hail of darts, and when he entered their lines, like unto the sun entering the clouds, those formidable warriors, whom he was consuming with the fire of his shafts, were unable to discern him. And the titans, beholding the terrible exploits of that hero so disastrous to them, recognized their author to be Rama, and as the passing of a hurricane through a forest becomes patent, so, when innumerable battalions were overthrown and great cars overturned, they perceived it to be his work. And they beheld their army decimated by arrows, battered and crushed by his shafts but, so rapid were his movements, that they could not see Rama and they were no more able to discern Raghava than beings distinguish the soul that governs the senses.

" There is the one who is exterminating our cohorts of elephants ! " " There is he, who with his sharp arrows is destroying cavalry and infantry ! "

Speaking thus, the titans, taking each other to be Rama in the fight, under this delusion, slew each other in anger, and they were not able to see the real Rama, who, nevertheless, was destroying their army, for they had all been thrown into bewilderment by the exceedingly mighty, marvellous and powerful Gandharva Weapon ! And sometimes on that vast battlefield, thousands of Ramas appeared to the titans and sometimes they could only see one ; and the bow of that hero seemed to them to be a myriad golden bows, whirling like a circling torch, while Raghava himself remained invisible !

With his body the pivot, his strength the lustre, his arrows the spokes, his bow the felly, the twanging of the cord and the gauntlet the sound, the force of his intelligence its radiance, its splendour the impetus of his weapon, its circumference the circle traced by Rama, while he was massacring the titans, he resembled the Wheel of Time in the eyes of all beings. And in the eighth part of a day, Rama with his flaming arrows, single-handed, exterminated the army of the titans who were able to change their form at will, which comprised eighteen thousand great elephants, fourteen thousand cavalry and two hundred thousand infantry.

Exhausted, their horses slain, their chariots shattered, their standards broken, those rangers of the night, who had escaped the carnage, took refuge in the City of Lanka.

With the corpses of elephants, infantry and horses, the battle-field resembled the ground where the mighty Rudra, enraged, disports himself.

Then Devas, Gandharvas, Siddhas and Paramarishis cried out :—

" Well done ! Well done ! " lauding Rama's achievement.

And the magnanimous Raghava said to Sugriva who stood near with Jambavan and the foremost of monkeys, Mainda and Dvivida :—

" The power to wield this terrible weapon belongs to me and Tryambaka[1] alone ! "

[1] Tryambaka—A name of Shiva meaning ' Three-eyed '.

Having destroyed the army of the King of the Titans, Rama, the equal of the magnanimous Shakra, who amidst darts and arrows transcended all fatigue, received the delighted homage of the Celestial Host.

CHAPTER 95

The Lamentations of the Titan Women

ALL those thousands of elephants and horses and those mounted upon them with the myriad chariots bright as fire and their flaming banners, as also the innumerable titans who were full of valour, able to change their form at will, armed with maces and axes and wonderful golden pennants, fell under the fiery darts, decorated with fine gold, of Rama of imperishable exploits.

Beholding this and hearing those tidings, the rangers of the night, who had escaped the carnage, were filled with terror and those wretched titans were united in a common misfortune.

The female titans and those who had lost their sons and kinsfolk, overwhelmed with affliction, assembled to wail and lament, crying :—

" How did Shurpanakha, who was old, hideous and of sunken belly, dare to approach Rama in the forest, he who was the equal of Kandarpa himself ? Seeing that handsome youth, full of nobility, ever engaged in the welfare of all beings, that monstrous Rakshasi, who should have been slain by others, was overpowered by lust. How could she, who was devoid of all good qualities, dare to make love to the all-powerful Rama who is possessed of comely features and endowed with every virtue ? To the detriment of her own race, despite her grey hair and wrinkles, through a ridiculous infatuation condemned by all, that hideous creature pursued Raghava with her importunities to the destruction of the Titans, Dushana and Khara.

" It was on her account that Ravana committed this offence, the fatal bearing away of Sita, the daughter of Janaka, and has provoked the enmity of the implacable and powerful Raghava.

" When the Demon Viradha sought to possess Vaidehi, he fell before her under Rama's blows ; this example should have proved sufficient! And fourteen thousand titans of terrible deeds were cut down in Janasthana by Rama's shafts resembling flaming torches, whilst, in the fight, Khara was also slain with Dushana and Trishiras by his darts that glittered like the sun ; this too should have been sufficient to prove his prowess !

" Kabandha too, with his arms four miles in length, who lived on blood, was slain despite his fury and screams ; this too was a manifestation of Rama's might. He slew the powerful son of that God of a Thousand Eyes, the mighty Bali who was as dark as a cloud, this too proved his valour ! And Sugriva, who dwelt disconsolate on Rishyamukha, the vehicle of his hopes shattered, was restored to the throne by Rama, which was a further proof of his power.

" All the titans counselled Ravana to his advantage, and Bibishana, in accord with his duty, offered him good advice in reasonable words but, in his folly, that monarch disregarded them. If the younger brother of Dhanada had given ear to Bibishana, Lanka, which has now become a cemetery, would not have been laid waste.

" When he learnt that the mighty Kumbhakarna had been slain by Raghava and that the invincible Atikaya had fallen under Lakshmana's blows, as also Indrajita, his beloved son, still Ravana remained blind to the truth !

" ' My son, my brother, my lord has perished in the fight ' is the cry heard from the female titans in every family. Chariots, horses and elephants have been struck down in their thousands by the mighty Rama and are lying here and there with the foot soldiers whom he has also slain. He who is destroying us is Rudra or Vishnu or Mahendra or the God of a Hundred Sacrifices, in the form of Rama, unless he be the God of Death himself ! We live bereft of hope ; our warriors slain by Rama ; we see no end to our fears and we lament the loss of our defenders.

" On account of the great boons he has received, Dashagriva seems unaware of the appalling peril that faces him at the hands of Rama. Neither Devas, Gandharvas, Pisachas or Rakshasas will be able to rescue him when he falls into Rama's power. Each time Ravana has entered the lists against Rama, inauspicious omens have appeared foretelling his destruction !

" When the Grandsire of the World was gratified with him

he received immunity from Devas, Danavas and Rakshasas but he did not ask to be protected from man. Here without doubt is one of those who will prove fatal to the titans and Ravana.

" Oppressed by that titan, who was filled with arrogance on account of the boon he had obtained through his severe penances, the Vibudhas took refuge with Brahma and, in order to be of service to them, the magnanimous Grandsire of the World uttered these memorable words :—

" ' From to-day the Danavas and Rakshasas shall not cease to wander through the Three Worlds harried by constant fear ! '

" Meantime the Gods with Indra at their head approached the Destroyer of Tripura, the God whose vehicle is the bull, who received them favourably and, being gratified, Mahadeva said to them :—

" ' For your salvation, a woman will be born who will bring about the destruction of the titans ! This woman, whom the Gods will employ, as formerly hunger was used to wipe out the Danavas, will be the destroyer of the titans and Ravana .' By bearing Sita away in his perversity and misconduct, Ravana has dug a fearful abyss in which all will be engulfed! Who is there in the world who can rescue us ? We have fallen into Raghava's hands, who is the equal of Time, the Destroyer of the Worlds !

"As elephants (that are) trapped in a blazing forest, there is no refuge for us in this extreme peril ! The magnanimous Bibishana chose the fitting moment to take refuge with him from whom he foresaw the danger was to come."

Thus did the consorts of those rangers of the night lament with piercing cries, in despair, plunged in grief and terror, their arms interlaced.

CHAPTER 96

Ravana goes out to fight and encounters ill Omens

FROM every dwelling in Lanka the piercing cries emitted by the female titans and their heart-rending lamentations reached Ravana's ears and, sighing for a long time, that fierce-eyed monarch reflected awhile and thereafter fell into a great rage.

Biting his lips, his eyes red with anger so that the titans themselves were not able to endure his aspect, he resembled the Fire of Dissolution itself. In a voice choking with fury, he issued the following orders to the titans who stood near, consuming them with his glance, as it were, and said :—

" Do you summon Mahodara, Mahaparshwa and Virupaksha speedily and let troops go forth into battle at my command."

At these words, in accord with the king's command, the titans, in fear, called the warriors together and those titans of formidable aspect unanimously cried :—" Let it be so ! " and having performed many benedictory rites and paid obeisance to Ravana, those mighty car-warriors all bowed down with joined palms to their master, whose victory they desired, and set out towards the battlefield.

Then Ravana, agitated with fury, with a sneering laugh, said :—

" To-day with my shafts, loosed from the bow resembling the sun at the end of the world-cycle, I shall send Raghava and Lakshmana to the abode of Yama ! By the death of our foes, I shall avenge Khara, Kumbhakarna, Prahasta and Indrajita this day !

" Neither space nor the cardinal points nor heaven nor the seas themselves will be visible under the cloud of shafts with which I shall cover them. To-day with my bow I shall cut the foremost of the monkey battalions to pieces with a succession of my plumed darts. To-day from the height of my chariot, swift as the wind, I shall submerge the simian army under the rolling waves of mine arrows with the aid of my bow in the guise of the ocean. This day I shall be the elephant who tramples under his feet those divisions resembling lakes, with open lotuses the faces, the glistening stamens the bodies ! This day, with each arrow loosed in the battle, I shall pierce the monkey forces in their hundreds, as they fight furiously with trees. By slaying mine adversary to-day, I shall dry the tears of all those who have lost their brothers or whose sons have perished. To-day, pierced by my shafts, so large a number of monkeys will lie scattered here and there that, through my prowess one will not be able to discern the earth's surface ! To-day the crows, vultures and beasts of prey will be sated by the flesh of the foe struck down by my darts.

278

" Let my chariot be yoked with all speed and let my bow be brought immediately ; let those rangers of the night, who are still here, follow me into battle ! "

At this command, Mahaparshwa gave his orders to the army leaders, who were present, saying :—

" Hasten to assemble the troops ! " On this, the leaders summoned the titans, going from house to house, making the entire circuit of Lanka at a rapid pace. Instantly all the titans of grim aspect ran out with a formidable clamour, carrying every kind of weapon in their hands. Swords, lances, clubs, maces, hammers, Halas, spears with sharp points, huge Kutamudgaras, harpoons of every kind, discus, pointed Parashvas, Bhindipalas, Shataghnis and various other arms. Thereafter four officers under his command, brought a hundred thousand chariots to Ravana and three hundred thousand elephants, sixty kotis of horses, mules and buffalo and innumerable foot soldiers, all hastening there at the king's command.

Whilst the leaders rallied the forces who were to be found in the city, the sovereign's driver prepared his chariot ; and it was superbly furnished with celestial weapons and embellished with every kind of ornament, filled with various arms, adorned with rows of bells, encrusted with pearls, blazing with its jewelled pillars and covered with thousands of golden pinnacles.

Beholding it, all the titans were seized with exceeding admiration and, perceiving it, Ravana, the Lord of the Titans ascended thereon and mounted that car glittering like a myriad suns, blazing like fire itself, and effulgent with its own lustre. Then Ravana drove away immediately surrounded by innumerable titans, bearing down the earth as it were with the weight of his forces ; and, amongst the titans on all sides, there was a great din of shouting and shrilling of pipes accompanied by tabors, war drums and conches.

" There goes the King of the Titans with his fan and canopy, the abductor of Sita, the ruthless slayer of brahmins, that thorn in the side of the Gods, who is setting forth to fight the Prince of the House of Raghu ! " Such were the cries heard on all sides and, at the uproar, the earth trembled whilst the monkeys fled in terror.

Meanwhile, the long-armed Ravana, surrounded by his

ministers, marched on, full of the ardour of combat and certain of victory. At his command Mahaparshwa, Mahodara and the indomitable Virupaksha ascended their chariots and these warriors, in their delight, emitted war cries loud enough to shatter the earth and, with formidable shouts, they set out eager for victory.

The highly effulgent monarch, surrounded by his valiant battalions, rushed into battle, brandishing his bow, like Yama at the dissolution of the world, and that great warrior, mounted on his car harnessed to swift steeds set out through the gate where Rama and Lakshmana were encamped. At that moment the sun lost its brilliance, the quarters were enveloped in darkness, the birds emitted dreadful cries, the earth trembled, the Gods let fall a rain of blood and Ravana's horses stumbled, whilst a vulture alighted on the pole of his banner and sinister jackals howled. Then that titan felt his left eye twitch and tremors pass through his left arm; he grew pale and his voice seemed to die away. As Dashagriva set forth to fight, ill omens appeared presaging his death; a meteor fell from the sky with the crash of thunder and herons and vultures emitted mournful cries. Ravana, however, remained unmoved by the terrible portents that appeared and rushed madly to his doom, urged on by destiny.

At the sound of the titan chariots, the rakshasa host and the monkey army also prepared to give battle and from every side, impatient for victory, challenged one another.

Meanwhile, in his ire, Dashagriva with his golden shafts, created havoc among the monkeys and some among those heroic warriors had their heads severed by him and the hearts of others were pierced or their ears cut off and some fell lifeless, the flanks of others being torn, their heads broken or their eyes put out. Whenever the ten-headed titan, rolling his eyes furiously, turned his chariot in the fight, the ferocity of his assault was irresistible to the leaders of his foes.

CHAPTER 97

The Fight between Virupaksha and Sugriva. Virupaksha's Death

THE mutilated corpses of the monkeys, who had fallen under the shafts of Dashagriva were heaped on the earth, and the Plavamgamas were as unable to endure that irresistible avalanche of darts loosed by Ravana, as butterflies a scorching fire. Tormented by those sharp arrows, they fled screaming like elephants enveloped in flames and Ravana advanced in the fight scattering them with his darts as the wind disperses the clouds.

Having, in his fury, exterminated those inhabitants of the woods, that Indra among the Titans rushed on to find Raghava. Then Sugriva, seeing the monkeys cut to pieces and routed, gave over his position to Sushena and addressed himself for battle. Relinquishing his command to that monkey, who was his equal in valour, Sugriva went out to meet the enemy, a tree in his hand. At his side and following in his footsteps marched all the monkey leaders brandishing enormous rocks and every kind of tree.

Thereafter that royal giant let forth a great shout and fell on that mob of titans, destroying their leaders, and that mighty monarch crushed the titan divisions, as at the end of the world cycle the wind breaks down the great trees ; and he let fall a shower of stones on the titan divisions like a huge cloud letting loose hailstones amidst a flock of birds in a wood. Under the avalanche of stones loosed by the King of the Monkeys, the titans, their heads shorn of their ears, fell like crumbling mountains, and whilst the titans were being overthrown by Sugriva, who was crushing them as they fell, they cried out. Then Virupaksha, armed with his bow, proclaiming his name, leapt down from his chariot and that indomitable titan mounted an elephant and, advancing thereon, and he, full of vigour, let forth a terrible cry and hurled himself on the monkeys. Thereafter he rained a shower of formidable darts on Sugriva in the forefront of battle and arrested the rout of the titans by reviving their courage.

Riddled with wounds from the sharp arrows of the titans, that Indra of Monkeys, howling with rage, resolved to slay him and, brandishing a tree, that valiant and indomitable monkey leapt forward and struck the huge head of his adversary's elephant, and under the virulence of that blow, the great tusker sank down emitting loud cries.

Then the courageous titan jumped down from the back of the stunned beast and, turning on the monkey, threw himself upon him, but he, clad in mail covered with the hide of a bull, unsheathing his sword, with a rapid step, rushed defiantly on Sugriva who stood fast, waiting. Then Sugriva met the impact of Virupaksha and thereafter let fly a great rock like unto a cloud, whereupon that lion among the titans, seeing the stone falling, jumped aside and, full of valour, struck the monkey with his sword. Pierced by the valiant titan's sword, the monkey lay on the ground for a time deprived of consciousness, then, suddenly rising to his feet in the great struggle, he whirled his fist round and round, bringing it down violently on the titan's chest.

Wounded by his blows, the night-ranger, enraged, with his sword severed Sugriva's armour in the forefront of battle and, under the shock, he fell to his knees. Thereupon the monkey, picking himself up, gave the titan a terrific blow that resounded like thunder, but Virupaksha evaded it skilfully and, with his fist, struck Sugriva on the chest.

Thereafter the monkey king waxed even more furious and, seeing that the titan had parried his thrust, sought an opportunity to attack him. In his rage, he struck him a violent blow on the temple like unto Indra's thunderbolt which felled him to the earth, and the blood flowed from his mouth covering him like water from a mountain torrent. Rolling his eyes in fury, foaming at the mouth and bathed in blood, he seemed more misshapen[1] than ever and the monkeys beheld their enemy covered with blood, trembling, and rolling from side to side, emitting plaintive cries.

Meanwhile the two valiant armies of monkeys and titans, who were fighting one another, began to create a terrible uproar like two seas that had burst their banks.

In the presence of the all-powerful titan, who had been slain by the King of the Monkeys, the varied multitude of monkeys and titans resembled the Ganges in flood.

[1] A play on the word Virupaksha, which means ' Distorted '.

CHAPTER 98

Mahodara is slain by Sugriva

IN that fearful struggle, both armies gradually melted away under each others' blows like two lakes drying up under the summer heat. The destruction of his forces and the death of Virupaksha redoubled the fury of the Lord of the Titans. Seeing his army decimated and destroyed by the monkeys, he recognized that destiny was opposing him and he became apprehensive.

Thereafter he addressed Mahodara, who stood near him, saying :—" From now on, O Long-armed Warrior, thou art my only hope of victory ! Go, triumph over the enemy forces ! Display thy heroism to-day ; the time has come to return the favours thy master has bestowed on thee ! Fight bravely ! "

At these words, that foremost of titans, Mahodara replied :— " Be it so ! " and rushed on the enemy's army as a butterfly into a flame. Then that exceedingly powerful titan, whose ardour had been stimulated by the words of his master and also on account of his own native valour, began to create carnage among the monkeys.

From their side, the noble-hearted monkeys, arming them-selves with enormous stones, penetrated into the ranks of the redoubtable titans and slew them all. And Mahodara, at the height of fury, with his golden shafts severed the hands, feet and thighs of the monkeys in the great struggle and they, after a hard fight with the titans, fled to different quarters, some taking refuge with Sugriva.

Witnessing the rout of his powerful army, Sugriva rushed upon Mahodara and the Lord of the Monkeys, seizing a huge and formidable rock resembling a hill, threw it at him with great force, in order to crush him.

Seeing the stone falling, Mahodara, unmoved, cut it to pieces with his arrows. Under the titan's darts, it fell in a thousand fragments on the earth so that it resembled a flock of frightened vultures. Beholding that rock broken, Sugriva, mad with anger, tore up a Sala Tree and flung it at his adversary, who broke it into many pieces. With his shafts, that hero, the scourge of his foes, broke the tree, whereupon Sugriva, observing an iron stake lying on the ground, brandished the flashing bar before the eyes of the titan and, with one exceedingly violent blow, struck down his excellent steeds.

Leaping down from his great car, its team of horses having been slain, the valiant Mahodara, highly provoked, took hold of a mace and the two warriors, one armed with an iron bar and the other with a mace, approached each other, bellowing like bulls, resembling two clouds charged with lightning. In fury, the night-ranger, his lustrous mace glittering like the sun, rushed on Sugriva and, as the terrible club was falling upon him, the extremely valiant leader of the monkeys, his eyes red with anger, lifted up his weapon and struck, whereupon the bar instantly fell shattered to the earth. Then Sugriva, boiling with rage, from the ground picked up a huge club gilded on all sides and, brandishing it, hurled it against the mace, striking it, whereupon, on the impact, the two missiles broke in pieces and fell on the field.

Their weapons shattered, the two warriors attacked each other with blows of their fists and, full of ardour and strength, resembled two lit braziers. Amidst loud cries, they struck each other and, having interchanged blows, rolled on the earth. Leaping up immediately, the two pugilists, great champions, scourgers of their foes, exhausted each other, whereupon each seized hold of a sword that lay within reach and, transported with rage, threw themselves upon each other, their weapons upraised. Then those two spirited and experienced warriors moved rapidly from left to right of one another, each seeking to slay his opponent. Meantime the courageous, impetuous and wicked Mahodara, proud of his strength, pierced Sugriva's heavy mail with his sword whereupon the weapon snapped on the impact. Then that elephant among monkeys, with his own sword, severed the titan's head bearing a helmet and adorned with earrings.

Beholding their leader lying headless on the ground, the whole army of titans melted away and, having slain Mahodara, the monkey with his forces began to cheer, whereupon Dashagriva grew furious and Raghava was filled with joy.

With downcast mien, the titans, overwhelmed, all fled away mad with terror, but the son of Surya,[1] having laid Mahodara low, who resembled part of a great mountain, shone with effulgence like that orb itself with its inextinguishable brilliance. And the hosts of the Gods, Siddhas, Yakshas and also the beings who move on the surface of the earth, gazed with great delight on the King of the Monkeys, who had achieved that supreme victory.

CHAPTER 99

The Combat between Angada and Mahaparshwa

MAHODARA having been struck down by Sugriva, the all-powerful Mahaparshwa gazed on his slayer, his eyes red with anger and, with his shafts, began to sow disorder in Angada's formidable ranks ; and as the wind detaches a fruit from its stalk so did that titan sever the upper limbs of the leading monkeys. With his darts, he cut off the arms of some and, full of ire, pierced the sides of others. Overwhelmed by those shafts, that Mahaparshwa loosed upon them, the monkeys grew pale with fright and lost courage.

Then Angada, wishing to give a little respite to his troops, who had been trampled upon and decimated by that titan, leapt up full of fury like the ocean on the day of the full tide. Seizing an iron bar that shone like the rays of the sun, that Prince of the Monkeys struck Mahaparshwa in the struggle and he, losing consciousness, fell from his chariot, its driver having been slain, and lay senseless on the earth.

Thereupon the mighty King of the Bears who resembled a heap of black antimony and was extremely powerful, arming himself with a huge rock like unto the peak of a mountain, strode ahead of his battalion, which resembled a cloud, and with a furious blow struck down the horses and shattered the chariot of the titan.

Mahaparshwa, however, regaining consciousness, leapt up in an instant and, in his great vigour, riddled Angada with

[1] Sugriva.

innumerable arrows again and again and struck Jambavan, the King of the Bears with three spears full in the chest, wounding Gavaksha with innumerable shafts. Thereafter Angada, who was transported with rage, seized hold of an enormous stake and with that iron bar, bright as the rays of the sun, the son of Bali, his eyes red with anger, taking hold of it with both hands and brandishing it with force, with the intention of slaying him, hurled it on Mahaparshwa, who stood some distance off.

Thrown with force, the bar knocked the bow with its arrows from the hand of the titan and struck off his helmet, whereupon Angada, with a single bound, seething with rage, struck the titan a blow with his clenched fist on the ear, which was adorned with an earring.

Enraged, the valiant and illustrious Mahaparshwa seized hold of a great axe in one hand and with that stainless weapon washed in oil, made of solid stone, that titan, in a paroxysm of fury, struck his antagonist violently, but the blow, falling on the left shoulder, glanced off his armour. Then Angada, the equal of his sire in valour, furious, lifted up his fist which was as powerful as lightning and knowing the vital parts of the body, delivered a blow like unto Indra's thunderbolt on the chest of the titan, close to his heart.

On this the titan, his heart riven by the shock, fell dead on that vast battlefield, and seeing him lying stretched on the earth without life, his army took fright, whilst Ravana fell into a transport of rage.

Thereafter the monkeys with Angada, let forth a joyous roaring that resounded far and wide, shattering the gates and turrets of Lanka as it were. The Gods too with their king let forth a great shout and that enemy of Indra, the Lord of the Titans, enraged on hearing the immense uproar among the inhabitants of the Celestial Regions and the forests, resolved to enter into the lists once more.

YUDDHA KANDA

CHAPTER 100

Rama and Ravana fight with magic Weapons

BEHOLDING Mahodara and Mahaparshwa slain and, despite his great strength, the valiant Virupaksha also struck down, a great rage seized Ravana, who urged on his charioteer with these words:—

" By slaying Rama and Lakshmana I shall remove that double scourge, the cause of the slaughter of my faithful adherents and the siege of the city. In the fight I shall cut down Rama, that tree of which Sita is the flower and the fruit, whose branches are Sugriva, Jambavan, Kumuda, Nala, also Dvivida, Mainda, Angada, Gandhamadana, Hanuman, Sushena and all the leading monkeys."

Thereupon that mighty car-warrior, who caused the ten regions to resound, drove rapidly on Raghava with his chariot, and the earth, with its rivers, mountains and woods, trembled with the uproar, and the lions, gazelles and birds that inhabited it were seized with terror.

Then Ravana employed a dark and magic weapon that was formidable and terrifying and with it he consumed the monkeys, who fled hither and thither. Amidst the dust raised by their battalions, for they were unable to endure that weapon created by Brahma himself, Raghava, seeing those countless divisions taking refuge in innumerable places, pursued by Ravana's powerful shafts, stood ready waiting.

Meanwhile that Tiger among the Titans, having routed the army of monkeys, beheld Rama standing there unconquered with his brother Lakshmana, like unto Vasava with Vishnu, and Rama seemed to touch the sky as it were as he stretched his great bow and those heroes with eyes as large as lotus petals were long-armed and the conquerors of their foes.

From his side the extremely illustrious and valiant Rama, who was accompanied by Saumitri, seeing Ravana overwhelming the monkeys in the fight, joyfully took hold of the centre of his bow and immediately began to bend that excellent weapon that was stout and sonorous, riving the earth as it were.

At the sound of Ravana's loosing a myriad arrows and Rama stretching his bow, the titans fell to the ground in their hundreds! Thereafter Ravana, coming within a bow's length of the two princes, resembled Rahu in the presence of the sun and moon. Desiring to be the first to enter into combat, Lakshmana with his sharp arrows, having placed them on his bow, loosed his shafts resembling flames of fire. Hardly had that archer let fly his darts into the air than the extremely energetic Ravana stayed them in their course, severing one with one, three with three and ten with ten, thus demonstrating his lightness of hand. Leaping over Saumitri, that triumphant warrior, Ravana approached Rama in the conflict, who stood ready like unto an unscalable mountain. Bearing down on Raghava, his eyes red with anger, the Lord of the Titans loosed a rain of shafts upon him but, with the aid of his sharp arrows, Raghava severed those innumerable darts that flamed in formidable wise and resembled venomous snakes.

Thereafter Raghava struck Ravana with redoubled blows and Ravana struck Raghava and they riddled each other with a hail of varied and penetrating missiles and, for a long time, described marvellous circles round each other from left to right, overwhelming each other with swift arrows, each remaining undefeated. And all beings were seized with terror witnessing that desperate duel between those two redoubtable bowmen, the equals of Yama and Antaka. The sky was covered with clouds riven by lightning flashes and the firmament became, as it were, pierced with holes by a rain of whirling arrows of extreme velocity, possessing sharp points, adorned with heron's plumes. With their darts, they first obscured the sky as when the sun withdraws behind the Astachala Mountains and two great clouds suddenly appear.

Thereafter, between those two warriors, each seeking to slay the other, an incomparable and unimaginable struggle ensued like unto the duel between Vritra and Vasava. Both were furnished with excellent bows, both were skilled warriors, both brought exceptional knowledge in the science of arms to the fight. In all their manoeuvrings they were followed by a stream of shafts as the waves in two oceans that are whipped up by a tempest.

Then, with a skilful hand, Ravana, the Destroyer of the Worlds, aiming at Rama's forehead, loosed a formidable succession of iron shafts from his bow, which Rama received unmoved on his head like a garland of lotus leaves. Thereupon, reciting a sacred formula, arming himself with Rudra's weapon and choosing a large number of spears, full of wrath, the illustrious Raghava bent his bow and with force let fly those weapons in rapid succession against that Indra of Titans but those darts fell without breaking through the armour of Ravana, who, like an immense cloud, remained unmoved.

Then Rama, skilled in the use of arms, struck Ravana afresh on the forehead, as he stood in his chariot, with arrows to which he had joined a miraculous weapon, and it appeared as if five-headed serpents in the form of darts were penetrating hissing into the earth repelled by Ravana whom they sought to devour. Thereupon, having rendered Raghava's weapon void, Ravana, in a transport of rage, armed himself in his turn with the dreadful Asura weapon which he loosed joined to sharp and terrible arrows with huge points, having the heads of lions, tigers, herons, geese, vultures, falcons, jackals and wolves or resembling serpents with five heads. Others had the heads of donkeys, boars, dogs, cocks, aquatic monsters and venomous reptiles and those sharp arrows were the creation of his magic power. Struck by the Asuric shafts, that lion among the Raghus, he who resembled the God of Fire himself, responded with the Agneya Dart that was full of power and to it he joined arrows of every kind with points that burnt like fire and which resembled suns, planets and stars in hue or great meteors like unto flaming tongues. Those formidable missiles belonging to Ravana striking against those loosed by Rama, disintegrated in space and were annihilated in their thousands.

Thereupon all the valiant monkeys with Sugriva at their head, able to change their form at will, beholding the titan's weapon destroyed by Rama of imperishable karma, let forth joyous acclamations and made a circle round him.

Then the magnanimous son of Dasaratha, the descendant of Raghu, having destroyed that weapon discharged by Ravana's own arm, was filled with felicity, whilst the leaders of the monkeys joyfully paid homage to him.

CHAPTER 101

Ravana flees from Rama

HIS weapon having been destroyed, Ravana, the King of the Titans, whose fury was redoubled, in his wrath instantly produced another; and he loosed the fearful Rudra Weapon, forged by Maya, on Raghava. Thereafter, from his bow, innumerable spears, maces, flaming bars hard as diamond, mallets, hammers, chains and spiked clubs, like unto fiery thunderbolts, issued forth like the tempests at the dissolution of the worlds.

Then the glorious Raghava, most skilled in the knowledge of excellent shafts, that warrior of great renown, broke that weapon with the aid of the marvellous Gandharva Dart, and when it was shattered by the magnanimous Raghava, Ravana, his eyes red with fury, loosed his Solar Weapon whereupon huge and brilliant discs issued from the bow of the skilful Dashagriva of redoubtable courage, which, falling, lit up the sky on every side and the four quarters were consumed by the fall of those flaming missiles that resembled the sun, moon and stars.

With a mass of arrows Raghava destroyed those discs and darts loosed by Ravana in the fore-front of the battle and, seeing his weapon broken, Ravana, the Lord of the Titans with ten arrows struck Rama in his vital parts. Struck by ten shafts that Ravana had discharged from his great bow, the exceedingly energetic Raghava did not flinch and, in his turn, that victorious prince, in the height of anger, pierced Ravana in all his limbs with the aid of innumerable darts.

At that instant, the younger brother of Raghava, the valiant Lakshmana, slayer of hostile warriors, armed himself with seven arrows and, with those exceedingly swift shafts, that illustrious prince severed Ravana's standard in many places, which bore the image of a man's head. With a single arrow, the fortunate Lakshmana of immense vigour, cut off the head adorned with brilliant earrings of the titan who drove the chariot, and with five sharp arrows severed the bow resembling the trunk of an elephant that belonged to the King of the Titans.

Thereafter Bibishana, bounding forward, with his mace slew Ravana's beautiful horses that were as tall as hills and resembled a dark cloud in hue, whereupon Dashagriva, leaping quickly from his car, the steeds of which having been slain, was filled with exceeding wrath against his brother and that powerful and spirited monarch loosed a flaming spear on Bibishana like unto a thunderbolt, but ere it reached its target, Lakshmana severed it with three arrows, whereupon a great cheer arose amongst the monkeys in that formidable struggle, and that spear, wreathed in gold, fell down shattered in three fragments like unto a great meteor falling from the sky amidst a shower of flaming sparks.

Then the titan, that mighty Ravana of wicked soul, armed himself with another superior and tested spear which Death himself would have found hard to resist and which was of immense size and shone with its own effulgence. Brandished with violence by the mighty Ravana of perverse soul it gave out a lurid gleam so that it appeared like forked lightning.

Meanwhile the valiant Lakshmana, perceiving that Bibishana stood in peril of his life, placed himself quickly in front of him and that hero, stretching his bow, with a rain of darts riddled Ravana, who stood waiting to discharge the weapon he held in his hand. Under the shower of arrows with which the courageous Saumitri overwhelmed him, thus frustrating his design, the titan no longer thought of striking him in return. Seeing that he had preserved his brother's life, Ravana, who was standing before him, addressed him thus :—

" O Thou whose strength renders thee arrogant, since thou hast preserved this titan, my spear shall fall on thee ; having pierced thine heart, this bloodstained weapon that mine arm, equal to an iron bar, will hurl at thee will rob thee of thy life's breath and return to my hand."

Thus did Ravana, speak and in a paroxysm of rage, levelling that pick adorned with eight extremely loud bells, created magically by Maya, that was infallible, the slayer of its foes, the splendour of which flamed up as it were, hurled it at Lakshmana with a mighty shout. Loosed with terrible violence and a sound of thunder, that spear fell with force on Lakshmana in the forefront of the battle.

Then Raghava sought to mitigate the power of that weapon and said :—

" May good fortune attend Lakshmana ! May this mortal impact be rendered void ! "

Released by the enraged titan on that indomitable hero, the spear which resembled a venomous snake, falling with extreme violence, penetrated his great chest and so brilliant was it that it appeared like the tongue of the King of the Serpents. Loosed with force by Ravana, that spear penetrated deep into the body of Lakshmana who, with his heart pierced, fell on the earth.

Beholding Lakshmana in that condition, near to whom he stood, the extremely powerful Raghava, full of solicitude for his brother, felt his heart stricken, but after an instant's reflection, his eyes welling with tears, enraged as is Pavaka at the dissolution of the world, he thought—' This is not the time for lamentation ' and thereafter he entered once more into the fearful conflict, resolved to make a supreme attempt to slay Ravana.

His eyes fixed on his brother, Rama saw how he had been pierced with a spear in the great fight and was covered with blood, resembling a mountain with its reptiles. And the most vigorous of monkeys sought to draw out that weapon loosed by the mighty Ravana, overwhelmed though they were by a hail of shafts discharged by the King of the Titans ; the spear, however, having passed through Saumitri's body had penetrated into the earth. Then Rama, with his powerful hands seized hold of that spear and, in his wrath, snapped it, throwing the fragments to a great distance and, as he drew it out, Ravana penetrated his every limb with his shafts that pierced to his very marrow. Ignoring these darts, Rama embraced Lakshmana and said to Hanuman and that mighty Monkey Sugriva :—

" Ye foremost of the monkeys, gather round Lakshmana ! O King of the Monkeys, the time has come for me to manifest my prowess ! For long I have sought this occasion ! May the wicked Dashagriva of infamous exploits perish ! My longing resembles that of the Chatak bird[1] on beholding the clouds at the end of summer. Ere long, I swear to thee either Ravana or

[1] This bird is said only to quench its thirst at a certain season.

Rama will cease to exist in the world! Ye shall be witness thereof! The loss of the kingdom, my sojourn in the forest and my wanderings in the woods of Dandaka, the insult offered to Vaidehi, my encounter with the titans, the great and terrible misfortune that has visited me, this torment resembling hell will be wiped out this day when I slay Ravana on the battlefield! He on whose account I took the army of monkeys in my train, having installed Sugriva, when I had slain Bali in the open field, and on whose account I crossed the ocean, having thrown a bridge over it, that wretch to-day has come within my range of vision and shall therefore cease to live. Appearing before me, Ravana cannot survive any more than one who comes into the presence of a serpent whose glance is poisonous or a snake falling under Vainateya's gaze. Be tranquil witnesses of my combat with Ravana, O Invincible Ones, Foremost of the Monkeys; seat yourselves on the brow of the mountain. To-day in this duel, the Three Worlds with the Gandharvas, the Siddhas and Charanas will recognize Rama's attributes! I shall accomplish a feat that the world with all beings who move or do not move, as also the Gods, will recount as long as the earth exists!"

Speaking thus Rama began to discharge his penetrating shafts embellished with gold at Dashagriva. From his side, Ravana, like a cloud from which the rain falls, showered down arrows and clubs with violence on Rama. And a mighty uproar arose when, in order to slay each other, those marvellous arrows were loosed by Rama and Ravana. Severed and scattered, the shafts with flaming points discharged by Rama and Ravana fell from the sky on the earth, and the twanging of their bows, causing great terror amongst all beings, was astonishing to hear. Then that amazing hail of missiles, that the mighty hero let fly in continuous streams from his burning bow, overwhelmed Ravana who, terrified, took to flight like a great cloud driven before the tempest.

CHAPTER 102

Lakshmana's miraculous Recovery

SEEING the courageous Lakshmana lying on the battlefield drenched in blood, struck down by the spear discharged by the mighty Ravana, Rama entered into a terrible duel with that cruel titan whom he overwhelmed with a hail of arrows. Then he addressed Sushena and said :—

" The valiant Lakshmana, struck down by the ruthless Ravana, is writhing like a serpent, filling me with anguish! When I behold that hero, dearer to me than life itself, how, in mine affliction, can I find the strength to fight? If my brother, who is endowed with auspicious marks, that proud warrior, returns to the five elements, of what use is life or prosperity to me? My prowess is ebbing away as it were and my bow seems to be falling from my grasp; mine arrows are blunted, mine eyes blinded with tears, my limbs are heavy as when one is overcome by sleep, my thoughts wander and I long to die! In this extreme misfortune in which I am plunged, weeping, my mind distracted on seeing my brother, who is emitting inarticulate cries, lying in the dust of the battlefield, brought low by the wicked Ravana, a prey to suffering and seriously wounded in his vital parts, even victory cannot bring me felicity, O Hero. If the moon is hidden from sight what delight can it give? Of what use is it to fight? What purpose is served by living? The combat has no longer any meaning since Lakshmana is lying dead in the forefront of the battle. As that illustrious warrior followed me when I retired to the forest so will I follow him now to the abode of death.

" Ever affectionate to his kinsfolk, he was undeviatingly devoted to me; I was led to this pass by the titans who have made use of magic in the fight. Wives may be found everywhere and everywhere one may meet with friends but I see no place where one could find so dear a brother. Without Lakshmana of what use will it be for me to rule over a kingdom, O Invincible Warrior? What shall I say to Sumitra who loves her son so tenderly ? I shall not be able to endure the reproaches with which she will address me. What shall I say to my mother Kaushalya or even to Kaikeyi ? What answer shall I give to Bharata and the exceedingly powerful Shatrughna ? Having gone with him to the forest, how can I return without him ? Better were it to die than suffer the censure of my family. What sin did I commit in a former life that my virtuous brother is now lying dead before mine eyes ? O My Brother, O Foremost of Men, O First of Heroes, O Prince, why, forsaking me, wilt thou repair to the other regions ? How comes it that thou dost not answer me who am lamenting ? Rise, look about thee, why dost thou remain lying there ? Witness my grief with thine own eyes ! In my despair, be my comforter, O Long-armed Warrior, overwhelmed as I am with anguish, wandering distracted amidst the woods and mountains."

As Rama was speaking thus, overwhelmed with affliction, Sushena, in order to comfort him, addressed these well-considered words to him :—

" O Tiger among Men, abandon this idea that causes thee pain, this thought that pierces thine heart as a javelin in the forefront of the battle. Nay, Lakshmana, the enhancer of prosperity, has not rejoined the five elements for his features have not changed nor is he pale, rather is his countenance serene and handsome ! Observe how the palms of his hands resemble the petals of a lotus and his eyes are bright. Those who appear thus have not yielded up their lives, O Lord of all Men ! Do not grieve O Hero, Conqueror of thy Foes, Lakshmana lives, and the proofs are the multiple beatings of his heart united with his sighs even though his body lies stretched on the earth."

Thus spoke the extremely sagacious Sushena to Raghava and thereafter he addressed that great monkey, Hanuman, who stood near and said :—

" O Friend, go quickly, repair to the Mountain Mahodaya ! Formerly thou hast heard of it from Jambavan, O Warrior ! On the southern peak grow curative herbs, the plants named Vishalyakarani, Savarnyakarani, Samjivakarani and also Samdhani of great virtue. Bring them back, O Warrior, in order to revive that hero, Lakshmana."

At these words, Hanuman repaired to the Mountain of Herbs

but there he became anxious, for that illustrious monkey could not recognize those remedial plants. Then the thought came to Maruti, whose strength was immeasurable, ' I will carry back the peak of the mountain for it is on the summit that the auspicious herbs are growing, at least I infer so from what Sushena has said. If I return without having picked the Vishalyakarani, the loss of time will prove fatal and a great misfortune will follow.'

Reflecting thus, the mighty Hanuman hastened on his way and when he reached that high mountain, he shook the summit three times and having broken it off, balanced it, with its multitudinous trees in full flower of varying fragrance, in his two hands. Thereafter, like a dark cloud charged with rain, that monkey sprang into the air carrying the mountain peak and returned in great haste setting it down and, having rested awhile, he said to Sushena :—

" I am not conversant with the medicinal plants, O Bull among Monkeys, here is the whole summit which I have brought to thee ! "

At these words of the son of Pavana, Sushena, the foremost of the monkeys, having uprooted the herb, took hold of it and there was great amazement among the monkeys witnessing Hanuman's feat which even the Gods themselves could only have accomplished with difficulty.

Then the foremost of monkeys, Sushena, having crushed that herb, held it to Lakshmana's nostrils and on inhaling it that prince, the scourge of his foes, who was riddled with arrows, instantly rose from the ground released from the darts and his sufferings. Meanwhile the monkeys beholding him standing erect cried out ' Excellent ! Excellent ! and, full of joy, paid homage to him.

Then Rama, the slayer of his foes, said to Lakshmana :—

" Come, Come ! " and, embracing him, pressed him close to his heart, his eyes wet with tears. Thereafter, having embraced him, Raghava said to Saumitri :—" O Hero, what good fortune to see thee return from the dead ! Nay, assuredly neither life nor Sita nor victory had any attraction for me ; in sooth what reason had I for living since thou hadst returned to the five elements ? "

Then Lakshmana, pained, answered the magnanimous Raghava who had spoken thus and, in a voice trembling with emotion, said :—

" Bound by thy vow, O Thou who hast truth for thy prowess, it does not become thee to utter such cowardly words ! Nay, those who speak with sincerity do not render a promise void and the proof they give is the fulfilment of their vow ! Thou shouldst not give way to despair on mine account, O Irreproachable Hero ! Mayest thou redeem thy word by Ravana's death this day. Nay, when he comes within the range of thy shafts, thine adversary must not return alive, as a great elephant may not live when he falls under the sharp tooth of a roaring lion. I desire to see that wretch perish ere the orb of the day withdraws behind the Astachala Mountain, his task accomplished. If thou seekest the death of Ravana on the battlefield, if thou wishest to fulfil thy duty and if thou dost aspire to re-capture the princess, O Illustrious Hero, do what I tell thee without delay."

CHAPTER 103

Rama and Ravana renew their Combat

HEARING Lakshmana's words, the valiant Raghava, the destroyer of hostile warriors, at the head of his forces, took up his bow and stretching it allowed a shower of his formidable shafts to fall on Ravana.

From his side, the Lord of the Titans, mounted on his chariot, rushed on Kakutstha, as Svarbhanu on Bhaskara ; and Dashagriva, standing in his car, assailed Rama with darts like unto lightning, as a great cloud covers a huge mountain with its floods. Then Rama, with his arrows that were decorated with gold and resembled flaming brands, overwhelmed Dashagriva with them on the battlefield.

On this the Gods, Gandharvas and Kinneras declared :— ' This combat is unequal, Rama is on foot whilst the titan is in a chariot ! ' whereupon the foremost of the Gods, the blessed Shakra, having heard the words of the Immortals, called Matali to him and said :—

" With my chariot repair speedily to where the illustrious Raghava is fighting on foot ! Go to the battlefield and invite him to ascend this car ; do thou render this signal service to the Gods ! ' "

On this command from his king, Matali, the celestial charioteer, bowing, made answer, saying :—

" With all speed I go to fulfil my duty as a charioteer ! "

Thereupon he harnessed the bay horses to the most handsome of cars, the body of which being wrought with gold and hung with hundreds of little bells, with its emerald shafts shone like the rising sun, and it was yoked to excellent dappled steeds flecked with white, caparisoned in gold, their coats gleaming like the orb of day. A standard fluttered on a golden staff over that marvellous car belonging to Indra and, under the order of the King of the Gods, Matali ascended it and, leaving the Celestial Regions, went to meet Kakutstha. Armed with a lash, standing in the car, Matali, the charioteer of that God of a Thousand Eyes, having paid obeisance to him with joined palms, said to Rama :—

" Saharaksha,[1] O Kakutstha, O Renowned Destroyer of thy Foes, has lent thee this car so that thou mayest be victorious ! Here too is Indra's great bow, his shield bright as fire, his arrows shining like the sun and his goodly spear well-burnished ! Ascend the chariot, O Warrior, and with me as thy charioteer, triumph over the Titan Ravana, as did Mahendra over the Danavas ! "

Thus addressed, Rama whose splendour illumines the worlds, circumambulated the car and, bowing, ascended it. Thereafter a wonderful combat of chariots ensued between the long-armed Rama and the Titan Ravana, causing the hair to stand on end.

Raghava, skilled in the use of powerful arrows, fought with the King of the Titans, matching Gandharva Weapon against Gandharva Weapon and Celestial Arrow against Celestial Arrow. Then the royal night-ranger, in a paroxysm of fury let fly a formidable missile on his rival, marvellous, dreadful, befitting a demon. Loosed from Ravana's bow, those shafts, decorated with gold, falling on Kakutstha, were transformed into serpents of subtle venom and those fearful monsters with brassy faces, vomiting searing flames from their gaping mouths, sprang on

[1] The Lord of a Thousand Eyes, Indra.

Rama, and those reptiles whose contact was equal to Vasuki of iron coils and violent poison, enveloped all regions on every side filling the whole of space.

Seeing those serpents falling on him in the fight, Rama chose the dreadful and appalling Garuda Weapon and discharged it. Leaving Raghava's bow, those golden-hafted arrows, brilliant as flames, transformed themselves into golden eagles, slayers of serpents, and all the darts in the form of snakes were destroyed by arrows in the shape of birds, that belonged to Rama, who was able to change his form at will.

Enraged at the destruction of his weapon, Ravana, the Lord of the Titans, caused a shower of formidable shafts to fall on Rama and while he was riddling Rama of imperishable exploits with thousands of darts, he wounded Matali with countless others. Thereafter, having aimed at the golden standard, Ravana shattered it with a single shaft and the golden device fell from the height of the chariot to the floor. With a series of arrows he struck Indra's steeds, to the exceeding terror of the Gods, Gandharvas, Charanas and also the Danavas and, seeing Rama wounded, the Siddhas and great Rishis were troubled as also the King of the Monkeys and Bibishana.

When the moon of Rama was concealed from their sight by Rahu in the form of Ravana, Budha, in the constellation of Prajapati, rushed on Rohini, the beloved of Shashin, to the misfortune of all beings. With its mist-wreathed waves, flaming as it were, the ocean, surging up in fury, seemed to touch the orb of day ; and the sun in the grasp of the Planet Dhumak-etu assumed a brassy hue dreadful to behold, its rays extinguished, revealing a headless trunk on its disc ; Angaraka too was in opposition to the brilliant star of the Koshalas, the presiding Deities of which being Indra and Agni ; and in the heavens, that planet tormented Vishaka also, and Dashagriva with his ten faces and twenty arms, equipped with his bow, looked like the Mountain Mainaka.

Meanwhile Rama, overwhelmed by that ten-necked demon, was unable to loose his arrows in the conflict and, knitting his brows, enraged, his eyes inflamed, was transported with anger and it seemed as if he would consume the titan.

On seeing the furious countenance of the virtuous Rama,

all beings were seized with terror, the earth shook, the mountains, frequented by lions and tigers, trembled, the trees swayed to and fro, the Ocean, that Lord of Rivers was agitated and flocks of crows, braying like donkeys, described circles in the sky on all sides.

Beholding Rama wrought up with extreme ire and those fearful portents, all beings were filled with fear and Ravana too felt dismayed. The Gods in their chariots, the Gandharvas, the great Serpents, the Rishis, the Danavas, Daityas and winged creatures of the air gazed down on that conflict between those two warriors, who fought with every kind of dreadful weapon, so that it appeared like the dissolution of the worlds. Suras and Asuras who had come to witness the struggle, with their eyes followed that formidable duel, uttering words of sympathy and encouragement and the assembled Asuras cried out to Dashagriva 'Victory to Thee!' and the Suras addressing Rama reiterated 'Triumph! Triumph!'

At that instant the wicked Ravana, in his fury against Rama whom he wished to slay, took hold of an immense weapon that was as hard as diamond, deafening, the destroyer of its foe, furnished with spikes like unto mountain peaks, dreadful to conceive or behold, and Ravana lifted up that lance with its smoke-wreathed flaming point, like unto the fires at the time of the final dissolution of the worlds, that was greatly to be feared, irresistible and which death itself could not endure, the terror of all beings, whom it was able to crush to fragments. At the height of anger, he raised his strong arm and, surrounded by his brave troops, brandishing his weapon, that colossus, his eyes red with fury, emitted a piercing cry in order to encourage his forces, and earth, sky and the four quarters trembled at that fearful shout of the King of the Titans. With his stout arm, taking hold of that weapon he emitted a great cry and addressed his opponent insolently in these words :—

"This spear, as strong as a diamond, O Rama, that I wield in my wrath, through my prowess will shortly rob thee and thy brother of your lives! Thou shalt share the fate of my brave soldiers whom thou didst massacre in the forefront of the battle. Stay therefore that I may strike thee down with this lance, O Raghava."

At these words, the King of the Titans hurled his weapon at Rama, and loosed by Ravana's hand, that lance wreathed in lightning, deafening with its eight bells, passed through the air with a blinding flash.

Seeing that flaming spear, formidable to behold, Rama stretched his bow and discharged an arrow with force, but as the spear fell, Raghava loosed a mass of arrows to intercept it, so that he appeared like Vasava with his floods seeking to stay the encroachment of the fires at the end of the world period. As butterflies are consumed by flames, so were those shafts consumed by Ravana's huge spear; then Raghava, seeing his aerial shafts reduced to ashes, pulverized by contact with that lance, was transported with anger and furious in the extreme. Thereafter Rama, Joy of the House of Raghu, took up his spear favoured by Vasava, that Matali had brought to him; wielding it with his powerful arm, that lance, the destroyer of the worlds, with its sonorous bells lit up the sky like unto a brilliant meteor. In its flight, colliding with the spear belonging to that Indra of the Titans, it was shattered by the impact and that enormous lance fell bereft of its splendour. Thereafter Rama pierced Ravana's swiftly-moving steeds with shafts loosed with great force that were thunderous and flew straight to their target. Displaying all his strength, he wounded his rival in the breast with penetrating javelins and his brow with three arrows, whereupon Ravana, his whole body pierced with arrows and covered with blood, which flowed from wounds in all his limbs, resembled an Ashoka Tree in full flower. His body riddled with darts loosed by Rama, bathed in blood, feeling himself utterly exhausted, that Lord of the Rangers of the Night, in the midst of his army, was filled with extreme wrath.

CHAPTER 104

Rama arraigns Ravana and reproaches him for his Misdeeds

GRIEVOUSLY wounded by the wrathful Kakutstha, Ravana, that proud warrior fell into a great rage. His eyes flaming with anger, that titan raised his bow in a paroxysm of fury and in that great combat, overwhelmed Raghava with blows. Like unto a heavy shower, Ravana deluged Rama as clouds fill a pond. Drowned in a rain of arrows loosed from the titan's bow in the fight, Kakutstha stood firm like unto a mighty mountain.

Then that hero, resolute in combat, with his shafts deflected the succession of darts which fell upon him like unto the rays of the sun. Thereafter, with a skilled hand, the ranger of the night, in fury, struck the breast of the magnanimous Raghava with thousands of darts and the elder brother of Lakshmana, covered with blood, looked like a huge Kimshuka Tree in flower in the forest. His wrath roused by the wounds he had received, the exceedingly powerful Kakutstha armed himself with shafts the lustre of which resembled the sun's at the end of the world period ; and Rama and Ravana, both transported with anger, became invisible to each other on the battlefield that was darkened by their shafts.

Thereafter at the height of fury, the valiant son of Dasaratha addressed his adversary in these mocking and ironic words :—

" Having carried away my consort against her will in Janasthana, imposing on her ignorance, thou art verily no hero ! Bearing away by force, Vaidehi who was wandering forlornly in the great forest far from me, thou thinkest ' I am a great hero ! ' Because thou hast molested other women who were without a protector, which is the act of a coward, thou deemest thyself to be a hero, O Valiant One ! O Thou who hast overthrown the ramparts of duty, O Arrogant Wretch of fickle nature, in thine insolence, thou hast invited death into thine house, saying ' I am a hero ! ' Is it in the role of the valiant brother of Dhanada that thou, grown presumptuous on account of power, hast accomplished this memorable, great and glorious exploit ? Thou shalt presently receive a fitting recompense for this infamous act. O Wretch, in thine own estimation, thinking to thyself ' I am a hero,' thou wast not ashamed to bear Sita away like a thief. Had I been there when thou didst affront Vaidehi, handling her so brutally, I should have dispatched thee to rejoin thy brother Khara by striking thee down with my shafts. By good fortune, O Insensate One, thou art now before me ; to-day with my penetrating darts, I shall hurl thee into Yama's abode. To-day thy head with its dazzling earrings, severed by my weapon, shall roll in the dust on the battlefield where the wild beasts will devour it. Vultures will swoop on thy breast when thou art lying stretched on the earth, O Ravana, and will drink the blood greedily that flows from the wounds inflicted by my sharp arrows. To-day pricked by my shafts, lying without life, birds of prey will tear out thine entrails as eagles destroy serpents ! "

Speaking thus, the valiant Rama, scourge of his foes, covered that Indra among Titans, who stood near, with a hail of arrows, and his courage, strength and martial ardour in loosing his shafts was redoubled. Then all the celestial weapons belonging to Raghava, versed in the Science of the Self, presented themselves before him[1] and, in his joy, that illustrious hero felt the dexterity of his touch increase.

On these auspicious signs appearing of themselves, Rama, the Destroyer of the Titans, attacked Ravana himself with increasing violence.

Wounded by innumerable rocks thrown by the monkeys and the darts showered upon him by Raghava, Dashagriva's heart fainted within him and, in the agitation of his soul, he neither took up his arrows nor stretched his bow nor sought to oppose Rama's valour, while the arrows and missiles of every kind discharged unceasingly by his adversary had death as their target so that the hour of his doom appeared imminent.

Then his charioteer, observing the peril, drove the chariot calmly and slowly out of the fray and, aghast at the appearance of the king, who had sunk down bereft of energy, he turned that dreadful car, rumbling like a cloud, and left the battlefield in haste.

CHAPTER 105

Ravana reproaches his Charioteer

DISTRACTED with fury, his eyes red with anger, urged on by destiny, Ravana addressed his charioteer, saying :—

"Am I then bereft of valour and strength, deprived of prowess, cowardly, infirm of purpose, weak, without energy, devoid of

[1] That is the Deities presiding over them presented themselves before Rama.

magic powers and debarred from combat, that thou hast failed me and actest on thine own understanding ? How comes it that without respect for me and disregarding my commands, in the presence of the foe, thou didst drive my chariot from the field ! Through thine error this day, O Vile Wretch, that which I had won over a long period, glory, valour, honour and renown, are all lost to me ! Before a foe famed for his prowess, who prides himself on his exploits, thou hast transformed me who delights in battle, into a coward. If it is not through heedlessness that thou hast acted thus, O Villain, my suspicions are well founded and thou hast been bribed by the enemy. Assuredly it was not an act of friendship or devotion ; only a foe would conduct himself as thou hast done. If thou hast any loyalty to me, then return in the chariot instantly ere mine adversary has departed and remember the benefits thou hast received at my hands."

At these reproaches from the insensate Ravana, the sagacious charioteer made answer in words that were moderate and full of good sense, saying :—

" I am neither afraid, nor am I mad, nor do I yield to the solicitations of a foe, nor am I negligent, nor have I ceased to be loyal to thee, nor have I forgotten the benefits I have received from thy hand ! It was through my desire to be of service to thee and to safeguard thy glory and on account of a sincere attachment, that I acted as I thought best ! O Great King, thou shouldst not unjustly regard me as a vile and cowardly wretch, I who seek only to do that which is agreeable to thee. Hear me, I will tell thee the reason why I took thy chariot, resembling a flowing current driven back by the tide, from the field.

" Observing thy fatigue following on the tremendous struggle, I no longer recognized thy proud assurance nor thy superior strength. By drawing the chariot unceasingly, my steeds were overcome with fatigue, they were prostrate and overcome with the heat, like unto kine lashed by the rain ; furthermore amidst the portents that were manifest in great numbers, not one, it seemed to me, was favourable to us.

" One should at the proper time and place observe the characteristics, gestures, facial expression, depression or ex-hilaration and the measure of fatigue of one's master, O Mighty Hero ; also the place where the earth is firm and where it is uneven or level, where it is flat or hilly and the time for combat ; when the enemy lays himself open to attack, how to advance and retire, to halt or go forward, to meet the enemy or retreat to a distance, all this must be known by a charioteer, as he stands in his chariot.

" It was on account of thy prostration and the exhaustion of thy steeds and in order to mitigate this terrible fatigue, that I undertook those specific measures. It was not from caprice, O Warrior, that I drove the chariot away ; it was devotion to my lord that made me resolve to act in this wise. Issue any command thou desirest, O Hero, O Scourge of Thy Foes, and I shall fulfil it implicitly with all my heart ! "

Then Ravana, fully satisfied with the reply of his charioteer, addressed many words of praise to him and, in his martial ardour, said :—

" Speedily drive my chariot towards Raghava, O Charioteer, Ravana is incapable of turning back ere he has destroyed his enemies in battle ! "

Speaking thus, the King of the Titans standing in his chariot, bestowed a brilliant ring of great price on his charioteer and, under his orders, the driver set out to the battlefield. Urged on by Ravana's command, the charioteer whipped his steeds into a gallop and, in an instant, the great chariot belonging to that Indra among the Titans stood before Rama in the field.

CHAPTER 106

The Sage Agastya instructs Rama in the Hymn to the Sun[1]

MEANWHILE, seeing Rama exhausted by the fight, standing absorbed in thought on the battlefield, and Ravana, facing him, preparing to begin the encounter anew, the blessed Agastya who had joined the Gods, and also come there to witness the great combat, approached that hero and said :—

" Rama, Rama, O Long-armed Warrior, hearken to the eternal secret which will enable thee to overcome all thine

[1] Hymn to the Sun, 'Aditya-hridaya ', the designation of a Vedic Hymn.

adversaries. It is none other than the ' Hymn to the Sun,' O Dear Child, it is sacred, capable of subduing the foe and brings victory ; this prayer is eternal, imperishable, exalted and auspicious, the delight of the good, the destroyer of all ills, the allayer of fear and anxiety, the increaser of life and the most excellent of all verses :—

" ' O Thou, who on rising art crowned with rays, to whom the Devas and Asuras pay homage, salutations to Thee ! Thou art Vivisvata, the resplendent Lord of the Worlds, the Soul of the Gods, the Effulgent One, Creator of Light, who sustainest the Hosts of Devas and Asuras and the Three Worlds with Thy rays. Thou art the Creator, Maintainer and Destroyer, Thou art the God of War, the Lord of Creatures, the King of the Celestials, the Distributor of Wealth. Thou art Time and Death, the One possessed of splendour, the Lord of the Waters, the Ancestors, the Vasus, the Sadhyas, the Maruts, Manu, Vayu and the God of Fire. Thou art the Source of Life and of the seasons, Thou art the Great Nourisher of all, the Generator of all, the Courser in the heavens, the Maintainer, the One possessed of rays, the Golden, the Brilliant, the Cosmic Energy, the Maker of Day. Thou art all-pervading, myriad-rayed, the Indicator of all paths, from whom proceed the senses, Thou art the Thousand-beamed One, the Subduer of Darkness, the One from Whom all happiness proceeds, the Remover of the sufferings of Thy votaries, the Infuser of life in the Mundane Egg, the One possessed of rays. Thou art the Cause of the Creation, Preservation and Destruction of the Universe, the Beneficent One, the Possessor of Wealth, the Bringer of Day, the Teacher, the Fire-wombed,[1] the Son of Aditi, Thou art supreme Felicity, the Remover of Nescience, the Lord of the Firmament, the Dispeller of Darkness, the One versed in the Rik, Yajus and Sama (Vedas), the One from Whom floweth the showers, the Friend of Waters, the One Who, with a single bound, crossed the Vindhya Range. Thou art intent on creating the Cosmos ; Thou art adorned with gems ; Thou art the Bringer of Death, the Pingala,[2] the Destroyer of all, the Omniscent One, Whose form is the Universe, of great energy, beloved of all, Lord of all

---

[1] Fire-wombed—Who has the Fire of Doom in his womb.
[2] Pingala—The motive power of the Pingala vein.

actions. O Thou, the Lord of stars, planets and constellations, the Creator of all, the Resplendent among the splendid, the Essence of the twelve forms,[1] salutations to Thee ! Salutations to the Eastern and Western Mountains, salutations to the Lord of the stellar bodies and the Lord of Day ! Salutations to Thee, the bringer of victory and the joy that springeth from victory, O Lord of the Golden Steeds ! Salutations to Thee, O Thousand-rayed One, O Aditya ! Salutations to Thee Who controlleth the senses, to Thee O Hero Who art worthy of the Holy Syllable,[2] salutations to Thee Who awakeneth the Lotus ! Salutations to Thee, O Fierce One, Who art the Lord of Brahma, Ishana and Achyuta ! To Thee, O Sun, Possessor of Light, Thou of illumining power, the Devourer of all, Who assumest the form of Rudra, be our salutations ! Salutations to Thee, the Destroyer of darkness, of cold and of the foe ; salutations to Thee of Infinite Soul, the Destroyer of the ungrateful, the Lord of the Stars ; salutations to Thee, Whose lustre resembles refined gold, the Destroyer of ignorance, the Architect of the universe. Salutations to Thee, the Remover of darkness, the Illuminer, the Beholder of all the worlds. It is Thou Who createst all and destroyeth all, Who dryeth up, consumest and annihilatest all. Thou wakest when all creatures sleep, in whose heart Thou abidest ; Thou art both the Sacrificial Fire and the fruit of sacrifice. Thou art the sum of all action and the Lord thereof.'

" O Raghava, he who recites this hymn in the time of peril, in the midst of the wilderness or in any danger does not succumb to it. Do thou offer a deep devotion to that God of Gods, the Lord of the World ! He who recites this hymn three times will be victorious ! O Long-armed Warrior, the hour has come when thou wilt triumph over Ravana ! "

Having spoken thus, Agastya returned whence he had come. These words dispelled the grief of the illustrious Raghava who felt himself fortified, full of ardour and well pleased. Thereafter meditating on Aditya he recited the hymn and experienced supreme felicity. Having rinsed his mouth three times and purified himself, that hero took up his bow. Seeing Ravana, he

---

[1] Twelve Forms—The twelve months.
[2] The Holy Syllable—The Pranava 'Aum'.

rejoiced and advanced towards him in order to enter into combat, calling up his whole strength with the intention of slaying him.

At that instant the Deity of the Sun, amidst the Host of the Gods, knowing that the destruction of the Lord of the Rangers of the Night was at hand, casting glances of joy and supreme satisfaction on Rama, approached him and said :—" Put forth thine whole strength ! "

CHAPTER 107

Sinister Portents appear

THEREAFTER Ravana's charioteer drove his car forward speedily, with joy, eating up space as it were, and that chariot, capable of crushing hostile armies, bore an immense standard and resembled the City of the Gandharvas. Harnessed to excellent steeds, garlanded with gold, it was filled with implements of war and adorned with flags and banners. The scourge of enemy forces and the joy of its own, Ravana's car was driven with exceeding velocity by its charioteer.

Then that prince of men, Rama, observed the chariot of the King of the Titans, rolling noisily along with its great standard, harnessed to dreadful black horses and resembling a Vimana[1] in space, bright as the sun, dazzling to behold, like unto Indra's bow, and the rain of arrows falling therefrom resembled the waters loosed by a cloud. Seeing the chariot of his adversary, which bore down upon him like a cloud, with a sound resembling a mountain shattered by lightning, Rama instantly stretching his bow, like unto the crescent moon, said to Matali, the charioteer of that God of a Thousand Eyes :—

" O Matali, behold the furious pace of the chariot of mine adversary as he rushes upon me in violent rage ! Be vigilant and drive to meet the car of my foe, I wish to destroy him as the wind scatters a rising cloud ! Without swerving or confusion, thy glance alert, thy mind steady, holding the reins with a firm hand, drive swiftly ! Assuredly thou hast no need of my counsel,

[1] Vimana—A celestial chariot, seat or abode.

accustomed as thou art to drive Purandara's chariot, yet in mine ardent desire to enter into combat, I make appeal to thine experience, I do not instruct thee."

Extremely gratified by Rama's words, Matali, the most excellent charioteer of the Gods increased the speed of his car. Passing Ravana's great chariot on the right hand, he covered it with the dust of his own wheels.

Enraged, Dashagriva, his eyes inflamed with anger, riddled Rama with arrows as he stood before him. Provoked by the blows, Rama, whose strength was redoubled by his fury, armed himself with Indra's extremely powerful bow and his great arrows of exceeding swiftness that glittered like the rays of the sun. Thereupon a fierce combat ensued between the two warriors, who stood face to face like two proud lions, each desirous of destroying the other.

At that moment, Devas, Gandharvas, Siddhas and Paramarishis, hoping for Ravana's downfall, assembled to witness that duel between those chariots.

Thereafter dreadful portents appeared, causing the hair to stand on end, foreshadowing death to Ravana and victory to Raghava. And the Gods caused blood to fall on Ravana's chariot; a great whirlwind blew from left to right whilst, in the sky, a large flock of vultures flew over his head following the evolutions of his car. Though still day, Lanka, enshrouded in the light of dusk, hued like a Japa flower, seemed aglow; great meteors accompanied by lightning fell with the sound of thunder and the titans were seized with terror witnessing those portents so unfavourable to Ravana. In whatever direction the titan drove, the earth shook and the limbs of his soldiers appeared as if paralysed. The rays of the sun falling before Ravana seemed to him coppery, yellow and white, like unto mountain ores, and the vultures and jackals who pursued him, their jaws vomiting flames, began to howl on beholding his lugubrious and downcast mien distorted with anger. Contrary winds blew raising clouds of dust on the battlefield, so that the King of the Titans was unable to distinguish anything. Indra loosed his thunderbolts on all sides on his army with an unendurable sound, without a single threatening cloud appearing; all the cardinal points were enveloped in darkness and a dense cloud of dust hid the sky.

Dreadful birds[1] fought desperately among themselves, falling in hundreds before his chariot, emitting fearful cries. From his horses' flanks sparks flew continually and from their eyes tears fell, fire and water thus issuing from them simultaneously. Many other terrifying portents, foretelling Ravana's death, appeared, whilst omens propitious to Rama, foreshadowing his imminent triumph, could be seen.

Beholding those inauspicious signs, Raghava was greatly delighted and regarded Ravana as already slain. Seeing those portents relating to himself, which he knew how to interpret, Rama experienced supreme felicity and, full of confidence, manifested a matchless energy in the struggle.

CHAPTER 108

The Fluctuations of Combat

THEN the desperate duel of chariots between Rama and Ravana broke out with increased fury so that all the worlds were seized with terror.

The battalions of titans and innumerable companies of monkeys stood motionless with weapons in their hands and, beholding those two warriors, man and titan, all were amazed, their hearts beating rapidly. Ready for combat, their arms filled with every kind of missile, they stood absorbed in the spectacle, forgetting to loose their shafts at one another, and the titans had their eyes riveted on Ravana and the monkeys on Rama so that both armies took on a strange aspect.

Meanwhile, witnessing those portents, both Raghava and Ravana, steady, resolute and full of anger, fought with determined courage. ' I shall triumph ' reflected Kakutstha, ' I must die ' thought Ravana and both displayed their full strength with assurance in the encounter.

At that instant, Dashagriva, in his wrath, placed his arrows (on the bow) and loosed them with force in the direction of the standard on Raghava's chariot but those missiles failed to reach the flag in Purandara's car and, glancing off the support, fell

[1] Sharikas—Turdas Salica or Gracula Religiosa.

on the earth. Meanwhile Rama, enraged, stretched his bow with energy, resolving to return blow for blow and, aiming at Ravana's banner, loosed a sharp arrow resembling a great snake, irresistible, shining in its own lustre; and he let fly his weapon in the direction of Dashagriva's standard, which being severed, fell to the earth.

Beholding his flag torn down and overthrown, the extremely powerful Ravana, inflamed with ire, blazed with wrath and indignation and, under the goad of his fury, let fall a hail of flaming shafts, striking Rama's horses. These celestial steeds, however, did not flinch, remaining motionless as if brushed by lotus stalks and, seeing the horses unaffrighted, Ravana, enraged, discharged a fresh rain of arrows, maces, iron bars, discus, clubs, rocks, trees, spears and axes, and those weapons were all created by magic, and, summoning up all his powers, he loosed them in hundreds and thousands. Appalling and terrible was that unending flood of weapons re-echoing with a sinister sound but Ravana failed to strike Rama's chariot, though his shafts fell on the monkey host on all sides covering the whole of space, and thus Dashagriva, unheeding, fought on.

Seeing him deploying increasing efforts in the struggle, Kakutstha, as if smiling, took up his sharp arrows and loosed them in hundreds and thousands. Observing them fall, Ravana, with his shafts, covered the entire sky and, on account of that rain of dazzling missiles loosed by those two antagonists, it seemed as if a second heaven of weapons had been created and, amongst them, there was not one that did not attain its target, not one, that did not pierce another and not one, that was loosed in vain ; and, having collided with one another, they fell to the ground.

Thus Rama and Ravana fought with an increasing supply of weapons and, in the struggle, they showered down their spears without pause to right and left, so that these formidable weapons covered the firmament ; Rama striking Ravana's steeds and Ravana striking those belonging to Rama ; thus, both exchanged blow for blow and both, in the height of anger, entered upon a tremendous duel causing the hair to stand on end. Then with sharpened arrows Rama and Ravana continued their combat and, contemplating his broken standard, Ravana was consumed with rage.

CHAPTER 109

The Duel continues

WITNESSING the combat between Rama and Ravana, all beings were struck with amazement and those two warriors, assuming a dreadful aspect in the struggle, highly enraged, determined on mutual slaughter and, in their excellent cars, bore down on each other. Thereupon their drivers, parading their skill as charioteers, advanced, circled and manoeuvred in various ways. In their rapid course and swift evolutions, those two marvellous chariots ranged the battlefield, whilst the two warriors discharged countless shafts on each other, like unto clouds letting loose their showers.

Having displayed their immeasurable resource in the use of weapons, those two champions halted face to face, chariot shaft to chariot shaft, their horses' heads touching, their standards intertwined. Then Rama loosed four sharp arrows, driving back Ravana's four spirited steeds and he, furious on beholding them retreat, let fly his penetrating shafts on Raghava.

That hero, however, grievously wounded by the mighty Dashagriva, manifested neither agitation nor emotion and again the Ten-necked One discharged his shafts, that resounded like thunder, aiming at the charioteer of that God who bears the Thunderbolt; and he struck Matali with his arrows with great force without being able to disturb him in any way or cause him to falter. Nevertheless Raghava, indignant at the affront offered to Matali more than if it had been directed at himself, with the aid of a succession of darts, decided to humble his adversary, and the valiant Raghava discharged twenty, thirty, sixty and thereafter hundreds and thousands of shafts on his rival's chariot.

On his side, Ravana, the Lord of the Titans, standing in his car, enraged, overwhelmed Rama with an avalanche of maces and clubs and the struggle became more desperate causing the hair to stand on end.

312

At the sound of the maces, clubs and axes and the loosing of plumed arrows, the seven seas were agitated and the tumult of the oceans sowed terror in the Danavas and Pannagas in their thousands, in the depths of hell. The earth shook with its mountains, forests and jungles; the orb of day lost its brilliance and the wind ceased to blow. Devas, Gandharvas, Siddhas and Paramarishis were wrought up with anxiety as also the Kinneras and Great Serpents.

" May good fortune attend the cows and brahmins! May all the worlds endure forever! May Raghava emerge triumphant in his combat with Ravana, the King of the Titans! "

Offering up these prayers, the Devas accompanied by hosts of Rishis witnessed that duel between Rama and Ravana, a spectacle that caused the hair to stand on end, and the hosts of the Gandharvas and Apsaras, watching that indescribable struggle, cried out :—" The sky resembles the sea and the sea the sky, but the fight between Rama and Ravana resembles nought but itself! "

Thus did they speak on beholding the combat between Rama and Ravana. In his rage, the Long-armed Warrior, the increaser of the glory of the Raghus, Rama, placed an arrow, like unto a venomous reptile, on his bow and cut off one of Ravana's heads, whereupon that glorious head, adorned with sparkling earrings, rolled on the earth in the presence of the Three Worlds. Nevertheless another, equal to the former, grew immediately and Rama, with a steady hand, dexterously sundered the second head with his shafts. Hardly was it eliminated when another head appeared which was severed once more by Rama's darts like unto thunderbolts. Thereafter he struck off a hundred more, being unable to bring Ravana low, and that hero, conversant with every weapon, he the increaser of Kaushalya's delight, who had made use of innumerable missiles, reflected :—

' These were the shafts by the help of which I slew Maricha, Khara, and Dushana as also Viradha in the Krauncha Wood and Kabandha in the Dandaka Forest; these were the shafts wherewith I transfixed the Sala Trees and the mountains and Bali and with which I agitated the ocean! All these weapons found their target, how is it that they have so little power over Ravana? '

Absorbed though he was in his reflections, Raghava, without

ceasing from action, let loose a shower of arrows on the breast of his adversary. On his side, Ravana, the Lord of the Titans, standing in his chariot, enraged, overwhelmed Rama with an avalanche of maces and clubs. Thus the fearful and desperate conflict, causing the hair to stand on end, continued in the air and on the ground and thereafter on the summit of the mountain.

Devas, Danavas, Yakshas, Pisachas, Uragas and Rakshasas watched the dreadful combat that lasted seven days and neither by night nor day for a single hour did Rama and Ravana cease from fighting and the son of Dasaratha and the Indra of the Titans continued to struggle thus. Then the magnanimous charioteer of the King of the Gods, beholding no sign of Raghava gaining the victory, addressed him rapidly in the following words.

CHAPTER 110

The Death of Ravana

At that moment, Matali sought to recall Raghava's thoughts, saying :—" How is it that thou dost act in regard to Ravana as if thou wert unaware of thine own powers ? In order to bring about his end, discharge Brahma's Weapon upon him, O Lord ! Foretold by the Gods, the hour of his doom is at hand ! "

Prompted by Matali, Rama took up a flaming shaft that was hissing like a viper, formerly bestowed on him by the magnanimous and powerful Sage Agastya. A gift of the Grandsire, that weapon never missed its target and it had been created of yore by Brahma for Indra and bestowed on the King of the Gods for the conquest of the Three Worlds. In its wings was the wind, in its point the fire and the sun, in its haft space, and, in size, it resembled the Mountains Meru and Mandara. With its marvellous point, haft and gilding, it was composed of the essence of all the elements and was as resplendent as the sun. Resembling the Fire of Time enveloped in smoke, it was like unto an enormous snake and was capable of riving men, elephants, horses, gateways, bars and even rocks. Dreadful to behold, covered with blood from countless victims, coated with their flesh and of the temper of lightning, it emitted a thunderous sound. The disperser of hosts, it created universal alarm, and hissing like a great serpent, it was exceedingly formidable. In war, it was the provider of nourishment to herons, vultures, cranes and hordes of jackals ; it was a form of death itself, the sower of terror, the delight of the monkeys, the scourge of the titans and its wings were composed of innumerable brightly coloured plumes, like unto Garuda's.

That marvellous and powerful shaft that was to destroy the titan was the object of terror to the worlds, the remover of the fear of the supporters of the Ikshvakus, the depriver of the glory of the foe, and it filled Rama with delight. Having charged it with the sacred formula, the valiant Rama of indescribable prowess placed that excellent weapon on his bow according to the method prescribed by the Veda and, when he made ready, all beings were seized with terror and the earth shook. Enraged, he stretched his bow with force and, deploying his whole strength, discharged that weapon, the destroyer of the vital parts, on Ravana, and that irresistible shaft like unto lightning, irrevocable as fate, loosed by the arm of one equal to the God who bears the Thunderbolt, struck Ravana's breast. Loosed with exceeding force, that missile, the supreme destroyer, pierced the breast of the wicked-hearted titan and, covered with blood, that fatal dart having extinguished his vital breaths, buried itself in the earth. Thereafter, having slain Ravana, that shaft, stained with blood which dripped therefrom, its purpose accomplished, returned submissively to the quiver.

And Dashagriva, who had been struck down suddenly, let his bow and arrow fall from his hand as he yielded up his breath. Bereft of life, that Indra of the Nairritas of redoubtable valour and great renown, fell from his chariot as Vritra when struck by Indra's thunderbolt.

Seeing him stretched on the ground, the rangers of the night who had escaped the carnage, struck with terror, their sovereign being slain, fled in all directions and, from every side, the monkeys who, in the presence of the dead Dashagriva had assumed a victorious air, hurled themselves upon them, armed with trees. Harassed by the monkey divisions, the titans, terror-stricken, took refuge in Lanka and, having lost their lord, in despair, gave way to tears.

In the ranks of the monkeys, however, there arose cries of joy and shouts of triumph proclaiming Raghava's victory and Ravana's defeat, and the skies re-echoed to the music of the drums beaten by the Gods. A rain of flowers fell from heaven on to the earth, covering Raghava's chariot with a ravishing and marvellous shower of blossom. The cry of ' Well done ! Well done ! ' came from the firmament and the celestial voices of the magnanimous Gods were raised in Rama's praise. On the death of that source of terror to all the worlds a great joy filled the Celestial Host as also the Charanas.

The blessed Raghava, by slaying that Bull among the Titans, fulfilled the ambitions of Sugriva, Angada and Bibishana; peace reigned over all ; the cardinal points were stilled ; the air became pure, the earth ceased to tremble, the wind blew gently and the star of the day regained its full glory.

At that instant, Sugriva, Bibishana and Angada, the foremost of his friends, and Lakshmana also, approached that happy conqueror and joyfully offered him due homage. Rama, the delight of the House of Raghu, surrounded by his adherents on the battlefield, having slain his adversary by his extraordinary power, resembled Mahendra amidst the Celestial Host.

CHAPTER III

The Lamentations of Bibishana

SEEING his brother defeated, lying on the battlefield, Bibishana, his heart torn with violent grief, began to lament, saying :—

" O Illustrious Warrior, thou who wert renowned for thy skill, experience and outstanding courage, even among the valiant, O Thou accustomed to a luxurious couch, how is it that thou art lying stiff and motionless, thy long arms adorned with bracelets, stretched on the ground, having suffered thy diadem, the lustre of which equals the sun, to fall on the earth ? O Hero that which I predicted has come to pass ! Carried away by passion, in thy presumption, disregarding my counsel, this fate has overtaken Prahasta, Indrajita, Kumbhakarna, Atiratha, Atikaya, Narantaka, and thee thyself. Alas! The rampart of the virtuous has disappeared, the incarnation of duty has departed, the refuge of the strong and powerful is no more. The sun has fallen to earth, the moon is obscured by darkness; fire has lost its brilliance, energy is bereft of force, since that hero, the prince of warriors, lies stretched on the earth. What remains now that he is deprived of his might and that tiger among the titans lies as if asleep in the dust? That great tree, the Lord of the Titans, whose stability was the foliage, his valour the blossom, his asceticism the sap, his heroism the intertwining roots, has been overthrown on the battlefield by that tempest, Raghava. That elephant in mustha, Ravana, his strength the tusks, his lineage the backbone, his exuberance the trunk, his wrath the limbs, has been seized by the lion, Ikshvaku. That blazing fire, whose prowess and energy are spreading flames, his angry breathing the smoke, his martial ardour the heat, has been extinguished by that cloud, Rama. That bull among the titans with the Nairritas as his tail, hump and horns, his love of pleasure the eyes and ears, he the conquerer of his foes, equal to the wind in swiftness, that tiger of the lords of the earth is lying dead."

Hearing these words, full of good sense and virtue, uttered by Bibishana who was torn with grief, Rama addressed him saying:—

" Nay, this hero has not succumbed on account of his lack of prowess! Endowed with burning courage in battle, having displayed the greatest energy, he fell without yielding. One should not mourn for those who, firm in their duty as warriors, for the sake of renown fall on the field of battle. It is not the time to weep for this brave warrior, the terror of the worlds and their leaders, now that he lies under the sway of death; no one is always victorious in war; sometimes the brave succumb to the blows of the enemy and at other times it is the foe who is overcome by them. This path followed by Ravana was taught to us by the Sages and the warrior class hold it in great honour. The warrior who is slain in battle, should not be mourned, this is the law. In this conviction, do thy duty without further anxiety and consider what action should now be taken."

Then Bibishana, who was overcome with grief, instantly replied to that noble prince who had spoken to him in his brother's interest and said :—

" This valiant one who, in previous battles was never defeated even by the assembled Gods under Vasava's command, assailed by thee on the field, beheld his power shattered as the ocean when coming in contact with its shores. The bestower of gifts on those who desired them, he knew how to enjoy wealth and entertain those who served him. The distributor of treasure amongst his friends, he suffered his wrath to fall on his foes. Feeding the sacred fire, he practiced severe penances, was conversant with the Veda and fulfilled his duty as a real hero. Now, with thine approval, I desire to perform his obsequies."

Touched by these poignant words of Bibishana's, Rama commanded him to perform the funeral rites that lead the soul to heaven, and said :—

" Death has terminated our emnity that now has no reason for its existence. He is as dear to me as thee ; let us therefore perform the obsequies ! "

CHAPTER 112

The Lamentations of Ravana's Consorts

HEARING that Ravana had fallen under the blows of the highly powerful Raghava, the female titans, like unto cows which have lost their calves, overcome with grief, their hair dishevelled, rushed out of the inner apartments and, though restrained, rolled in the dust again and again. Issuing from the northern gateway with their attendants, they entered that dreadful battlefield searching for their dead lord and cried out, ' O Our King, Our Support ', running hither and thither on the ground that was covered with headless trunks, mud and gore. Their eyes full of tears, overcome with grief, they emitted cries like unto female elephants who have lost the leader of the herd.

Then they beheld that great and exceedingly powerful and illustrious Ravana, their lord, lying in the dust and they immediately all fell upon his body like creepers that have been torn down in the forest. In a transport of passion, one embraced him sobbing, one pressed his feet, one hung on his neck, whilst another, beating the air with her arms, rolled on the ground and yet another, gazing on her dead lord, swooned away, and one, laying her head in his lap, wept as she looked on him, her tears bathing his face, as rime covers a lotus flower.

Beholding their lord lying stretched on the earth, in their despair, they emitted continual cries of pain as their lamentations increased—' He of whom Shakra himself stood in awe, he who was the source of terror to Yama, he, by whom the King Vaishravana was dispossessed of his Chariot Pushpaka, he, who caused the Gandharvas, Rishis, and the magnanimous Gods to tremble, is now lying dead on the field. He had nought to fear from Asuras, Suras or Pannagas, for it was in man that the peril lay for him ; he, who could not be slain by Devatas, Danavas or Rakshasas is lying here on the earth, struck down by a mere mortal fighting on foot ; he, who could not be slain by Suras, Yakshas or Asuras, received his death blow from a man, as one who is defenceless.'

Thus did the wretched consorts of Ravana speak amidst their sobs and, overwhelmed with grief, continued to lament without ceasing, saying :—

" Not heeding the advice of thy friend, who ever offered thee prudent counsel, to our destruction thou didst bear Sita away and thus the titans have fallen and we shall perish this day on account of thy fault. Thy beloved brother, Bibishana, speaking to thee in reasonable terms was publicly affronted by thee in thy folly, driven on, as thou wert by destiny ; if thou hadst returned the Princess of Mithila to Rama, this fearful and appalling disaster, that is destroying us to the very root, would never have taken place. The wishes of thy brother, of Rama and of thine innumerable friends would have been fulfilled ; none of us would have been widowed nor the hopes of our enemies accomplished. But, in thy perversity, having retained Sita by force, the titans, we ourselves and thou thyself, are all victims of a triple destruction. Nevertheless, O Bull among the Titans, it is not thy passion that is the cause but destiny ; all that dies is slain by destiny. This destruction of the monkeys and the titans in combat and thine own, O Long-armed Warrior, is the work of destiny. Neither the considerations of wealth, desire, valour nor dominion can avert the course of destiny ! "

Thus the wretched consorts of the King of the Titans lamented like ospreys, overwhelmed by grief, their eyes full of tears.

CHAPTER II3

The Lamentations of Mandodari : Ravana's Funeral Rites

WHILE the consorts of Ravana were lamenting thus, the foremost amongst them steadily fixed on him a tender and sorrowful glance and, in the presence of her lord, Dashagriva, who had been slain by Rama of inconceivable exploits, the unfortunate Mandodari expressed her grief in this wise :—

" O Long-armed Warrior, younger brother of Vaishravana, did not Purandara himself fear to stand before thee in thy wrath and did not the great Rishis and the illustrious Gandharvas as also the Charanas, assailed by thee, flee to every quarter ? Now Rama, who is but a mortal, has defeated thee in combat, thou who didst surpass the Three Worlds in prowess ; thou whose strength rendered thee invincible, how is it that thou hast fallen under the blows of a mere man, a wanderer in the forest ? Thou , able to assume any form at will, living in a place inaccessible to man, how can thy defeat by Rama be explained ?

" Nay, I do not believe that thou wast thus struck down in the forefront of the battle by Rama's action, thou who wert ever wont to be victorious in all circumstances. Rather, having recourse to inconceivable magic, was it destiny in the form of Rama in person or it may be that it was Vasava who slew thee, O Mighty Hero ! But would Vasava have ventured to stand face to face with thee on the battlefield in view of thy great prowess and strength, thou the foe of the Celestials ? Assuredly it was that great Yogi, the Supreme Soul, the Eternal Spirit Who was thy slayer. He who has no beginning, middle or end, the Most High, greater that Mahat,[1] the Support of Nature, He Who carries the conch, the discus and the mace, Whose breast bears

[1] Mahat—Cosmic Intellect.

the Shrivatsa Mark, to Whom prosperity belongs, the invincible, indestructible, everlasting Vishnu, the true Hero assuming human form surrounded by all the Gods in monkey shapes, He, the Lord of the Worlds, has slain thee, thou, the enemy of the Gods, with thy kinsmen and the titans who attended on thee!

" Formerly, having subdued the senses, thou didst conquer the Three Worlds and thereafter thy senses conquered thee in their turn. Rama is no mere mortal; once in Janasthana he slew thy brother Khara and the innumerable titans who followed him; furthermore when Hanuman audaciously penetrated into the City of Lanka, inaccessible to the Gods themselves, we were sorely distressed. How oft did I address thee, saying, ' Have we nought to fear from Raghava ', but thou didst not heed me. These are the consequences! Without cause thou didst cherish a passion for Sita, O King of the Titans, to the destruction of thy kingdom, life and race! By offering insult to the illustrious Sita, who surpasses Arundhati and Rohini, thou didst commit an unpardonable offence! She is more patient than the earth itself, the prosperity of prosperity itself, the beloved consort of Rama, of faultless limbs, who was the splendour of the lonely forest where she dwelt. By bearing that unfortunate one away, assuming a disguise and without being able to enjoy the anticipated delight of union with Maithili, thou hast brought about thine own destruction!

" O My Lord, the asceticism of that lady faithful to her husband, has consumed thee! Since all the Gods and their leaders with Agni at their head feared thee, thou wast not instantly destroyed when thou didst lay brutal hands on that slender-waisted lady. But, O Lord, when the time is ripe, the one who acts wickedly reaps the fruit of his evil actions; of that there is no doubt. He who behaves virtuously culls felicity and he who acts sinfully reaps ill-fortune. Bibishana has found happiness and thou in the same wise has met with disaster. Thou didst possess other women who surpassed Maithili in beauty but in thine infatuation thou didst not perceive it. None dies without a determining cause, for thee it was none other than Sita. Far didst thou go to seek that woman who was to be the reason of thy death; now Maithili, released from all her sufferings, will rejoice with Rama. Trifling indeed is my merit, since I have fallen into this ocean of grief, I who formerly sported on Mount Kailasha, Mandara and Meru and in the woods of Chaitaratha and all the gardens of the Gods with thee, being adorned with marvellous garlands and jewels, roaming at large in a chariot of incomparable magnificence, beholding innumerable countries, whilst now I am deprived of all pleasures and enjoyments by thy death, O Hero! Here am I, transformed as it were into another; condemned on account of the fluctuations of the fortunes of kings. O Prince, how gracious wert thou with thy charming eyebrows, brilliant complexion and arched nose; thou whose beauty, splendour and radiance rivalled the moon, the lotus and the sun; dazzling with innumerable diadems and variegated garlands, thy red lips and brilliant earrings; handsome and pleasing, whose glances, misty with wine, roved here and there in the banqueting hall, conversing with tender smiles! Alas to-day thy countenance has lost its radiance, O King, mutilated as thou art by Rama's shafts, red with blood, covered with flesh and brains and soiled with the dust of chariots. Ah! the final period of my life has come; the sad state of widowhood! Wretched being that I am, I never contemplated this! ' My father is the King of the Danavas, my consort the Lord of the Titans, my son the Conqueror of Shakra! I have nought to fear with such protectors who crush the arrogance of their foes, who are terrible and renowned for their might and courage,' thus did I speak in my pride. With such a power as thou possessed, O Bull among Titans, how has so great a disaster overtaken thee suddenly, through a mere man? Thou wert like a marvellous sapphire, enormous, like unto a mountain and dazzling with thy rings, bracelets, chains of emeralds and pearls and thy flowery garlands; full of gaiety in pastimes and enjoyments. Thy body, that shone with the lustre of thine ornaments, as a cloud riven with lightning, is now pierced by many arrows, ill-fitted to be embraced, without a space that is not bristling with darts, like unto an hedgehog, the muscles torn with shafts loosed with violence on thy vital parts, a corpse, lying on the earth, that was formerly dark in hue and is now the colour of blood, O King! Alas! That which seemed a dream has now become a reality! How was Rama able to strike thee down, thou who wert death to Death himself; whence comes it that thou hast fallen under his sway, thou who enjoyed the wealth of the Three Worlds whom thou didst inspire with a lively fear ; thou who conquered the Guardians of the Worlds, who overcame Shankara with thy shafts, who didst humble the proud and manifest thy great prowess. Thou who didst trouble the universe, the scourge of the virtuous, whose strength inspired thee to utter insolent threats in the enemy's presence ; thou the support of thy family and thine attendants, the slayer of redoubtable warriors, thou who exterminated the leaders of the Danavas and Yakshas in their thousands, thou who triumphed in the fight over those wearing impenetrable armour, thou who many a time obstructed the sacrifices, thou the saviour of thy race, who set at nought the laws of duty, who took refuge in the power of magic in battle, who robbed the Gods, Asuras and men of their daughters from here and there and who didst plunge the wives of thy foes into mourning ; thou, the guide of thy people, who ruled over the Island of Lanka, thou the perpetrator of dreadful deeds, thou who didst prepare for us many a pleasure and enjoyment, thou the foremost of warriors ; beholding thee, O Lord, who despite thy great powers, hast been struck down by Rama, my heart must be hard indeed that I yet live bereft of thee, my Beloved. Having rested on sumptuous couches, O King of the Titans, how is it that thou art now sleeping on the earth, the dust thy coverlet ?

"When mine illustrious son Indrajita was struck down by Lakshmana in the fight, I was deeply distressed but to-day I am undone, I, who, already bereft of parents and kinsfolk, now lose my last support in thee ! Deprived of pleasure and enjoyments, now that thou hast left on the last journey from which none returns, O King, I shall waste away in thy perpetual remembrance. I cannot live without thee ; take me with thee ; why dost thou leave me in my misery ? Art thou vexed to see me unveiled who have crossed the city boundary to run here on foot, O Lord ? Look on thy cherished consorts who have discarded their veils ; seeing them all come forth from the city, art thou displeased ? This company, with whom thou didst disport thyself, is desolate, deprived of its leader and thou dost not comfort them. Hast thou no reverence for us ? Those women whom thou hast widowed, O King, and more than one was of noble lineage, who were devoted to their consorts, firm in their duty and submissive to their Gurus, in their grief have cursed thee and, on this account, thou hast fallen under the blows of thine adversary. Stricken by thee, they have cursed thee and this is the retribution ! O King, the truth of the saying, The tears of women devoted to their husbands do not fall on the earth in vain ', has been proven by thee ! How comes it, O King, that thou, who didst surpass all the worlds in valour, wert so base as to carry off this woman, having lured Rama from the hermitage with the aid of an illusory deer ? In the intoxication of thy strength thou didst bear away Rama's consort after separating her from Lakshmana, and yet, if I reflect carefully, thou wert never a faint-hearted warrior ! This is the manifest proof of the changeability of fortune. Conversant with the past and future and reflecting on the present, that long-armed warrior, my truthful brother-in-law,[1] seeing Maithili, whom thou hadst borne away, sighing deeply, told me what had taken place. The destruction of the foremost of the titans has been brought about by this infatuation which was the source of thy lust and anger. Thou didst sacrifice thy real interests to this violent appetite that destroys everything to its very roots and, by this action, the whole titan race is deprived of its leader.

" Nay, I should not weep for thee, though famed for thy strength and valour but my woman's nature inclines my heart to compassion. Bearing with thee the sum of that which thou hast done, be it good or ill, thou hast gone to the place for which thou wert destined ; it is for myself I should lament, I who am plunged in affliction by thy loss.

" Thou didst not give ear to thy friends who desired thy welfare and, though exceedingly sagacious, thou didst ignore the counsels of thy brothers, O Ten-necked One. Bibishana's words so full of reason, that were measured, prudent, salutory and affectionate were not heeded by thee despite their significance. Drunk with thine own power, the utterances of Maricha, Kumbhakarna and of thy sire also, were not acceptable to thee; behold the consequences !

" O Thou who resemblest a dark cloud in hue, who art clothed in yellow, wearing dazzling bracelets, why are thy limbs stiff

[1] Bibishana.

324

and covered with blood ? Thou feignest sleep ; why dost thou not answer me who am overcome with grief ? Why dost thou not speak to me, the daughter of the supremely powerful Yatudhàna Sumali,. who never retreated in battle ? Rise ! Rise ! Why dost thou remain lying there in the face of this fresh insult ? To-day the rays of the sun fall on Lanka without fear. Thy mace, that brilliant weapon encircled with gold, like unto Surya, with which thou didst exterminate thy foes in battle, resembling the thunderbolt of Indra, which thou didst wield at thy whim to the destruction of the many on the battle-field, now lies shattered in a thousand pieces by Rama's arrows. Why dost thou lie embracing the earth like a loved one ? How is it that thou dost not address a word to me as if I were no longer thy beloved ?

" Woe unto me, whose heart did not split into a thousand pieces, riven by grief, when thou didst return to the five elements!"

Thus did Mandodari lament, her eyes full of tears ; and thereafter her heart overflowing with love, she swooned away, falling unconscious on Ravana's breast, like a flash of lightning striking a crimson cloud at dusk. Thereupon her companions, distressed, raised up her who was lamenting and placing her in their midst, said :—

" O Queen, art thou not conversant with the uncertainty of fate in this world and how, in a moment, the fortune of kings may change ? "

To these words, Mandodari replied with sobs and cries, her pure and lovely face and her breast bathed in tears.

Then Rama said to Bibishana :—

" Proceed with the obsequies of thy brother and offer consolation to his wives ! "

Thereafter the sagacious Bibishana, having reflected within himself, made this answer that was discreet, reasoned and in conformity with duty and understanding, saying :—

" I cannot perform the funeral rites for one who failed to fulfil his responsibilities and his vows, who was cruel, ruthless and disloyal ; a ravisher of others wives ! Under the guise of a brother he was mine enemy and took pleasure in inflicting injury ; Ravana does not merit this homage ! The world may say of me 'he was a barbarian', but when they learn of Ravana's wicked deeds, everyone will approve my conduct."

Thus did he speak, and Rama, full of joy, the foremost of those who are firm in their duty, answered Bibishana, who was skilled in speech, saying :—

" I seek thy welfare, since with thine aid I have been victorious, nevertheless it is essential that I should utter what is fitting, O Chief of the Titans ! Though unjust and wicked, this night-ranger was ever energetic, valiant and courageous in war. It is said that the Gods with Shatakratu at their head were not able to overcome him. He was magnanimous and powerful, this oppressor of the worlds. Death brings emnity to an end ; we have accomplished our purpose, let us perform the obsequies ; it is meet for me, as well as for thee, to do so. In accord with tradition, this ceremony should take place in thy presence. Perform this pious act speedily, thou wilt receive much glory therefrom."

At these words of Raghava, Bibishana hastened to carry out the funeral rites.

Entering the City of Lanka, that Indra among the Titans, Bibishana, began to prepare for the Agnihotra Ceremony in honour of his brother. Carts, wood of varying essences, fire, utensils, sandal, logs of every kind, fragrant gums, perfumes, cloths, jewels, pearls and coral were all assembled by him and he soon returned surrounded by titans, whereupon, accompanied by Malyavan,[1] he initiated the sacrifice.

Having placed Ravana, the supreme Lord of the Titans, wrapped in linen cloths on a golden bier, the Twice-born with Bibishana at their head, their eyes suffused with tears, raised the litter decorated with many fragrant and divine symbols to the sound of innumerable musical instruments and funeral chants, and all, turning their faces towards the south, took up pieces of wood which had been distributed among them.

Then the brahmins, versed in the Yajur Veda, bearing flaming brands went forward and those who had taken refuge with them, and the women of the inner apartments followed sobbing with tottering steps, running hither and thither. And Ravana was placed in a spacious ground, amidst profound lamentation, and a

[1] Malyavan—The brother of Sumali.

great pyre was built with pieces of Sandal and Padmaka Wood and grass, according to tradition; and he was covered with antelope skins.

Thereafter, in honour of the King of the Titans, a rare offering was made to the ancestors and the altar was installed to the south-west with the sacred fire in its proper place. Then curd and clarified butter were poured on Ravana's shoulder and a wooden mortar placed at his feet with one between his thighs; vessels of wood and the lower and upper kindling sticks, with a spare pestle, were set there according to the prescribed rules. Now the titans sacrificed a goat in honour of their king, according to tradition, as taught by the great Rishis, and, having dipped a cloth in butter, they covered the face of their sovereign, who was adorned with garlands and sprinkled with perfumes. Thereafter Bibishana's companions, their faces bathed in tears, covered the body with cloths and every kind of roasted grain, whereupon Bibishana kindled the pyre according to the sacred rites and, having laved him with a cloth which had been previously wetted with water and mingled with linseed and sacrificial grass, he bowed down to him; then he addressed the consorts of Ravana again and again in order to console them, finally entreating them to return home. And when they had all re-entered the City of Lanka, that Indra among the Titans took up his place by Rama in an attitude of reverence.

Rama, however, with his army, Sugriva and Lakshmana, rejoiced at the death of his enemy, as the God who bears the Thunderbolt on the destruction of Vritra.

Having laid aside the arrows and bow that Mahendra had bestowed upon him as also the massive armour, Rama, the slayer of his foes, renounced his wrath, his adversary having been subdued, and once more assumed a gentle mien.

CHAPTER 114

Bibishana is installed as King of Lanka

HAVING witnessed the death of Ravana, the Devas, Gandharvas and Danavas mounted their respective chariots, discoursing on these matters. Conversing of Ravana's fearful end, the heroism of Raghava, the courageous fighting of the monkeys, the great valour of Maruti and Lakshmana and Sita's fidelity to her lord, those blessed ones returned joyfully from whence they had come.

Raghava, however, sent back the celestial chariot blazing like a flame that Indra had lent him and took leave of Matali after offering his thanks to him. Then Shakra's charioteer, dismissed by the mighty Rama, mounting his celestial car, ascended into the sky.

Matali having returned to heaven in his chariot, Raghava, the foremost of car-warriors, in the height of felicity, embraced Sugriva and, having done so, accepted Lakshmana's homage and returned to the camp amidst the acclamations of the monkey ranks.

Thereafter Kakutstha addressed the son of Sumitra, the devoted Lakshmana, the bearer of auspicious marks, who stood near him and said :—

" O Friend, install Bibishana as King of Lanka ! On account of his loyalty, his zeal and the service he formerly rendered to us, my greatest desire is to see Bibishana, the younger brother of Ravana enthroned in Lanka, O Dear One."

At these words from the magnanimous Raghava, Saumitri, full of joy, said :—" So be it ! " and speedily took up a golden jar which he placed in the hands of the foremost of monkeys. Thereafter that warrior commanded water to be drawn from the four seas and the monkeys went there in all haste and, having drawn water from the oceans, returned as swiftly as thought.

Then Saumitri, at Rama's command, lifting up an excellent jar, caused Bibishana to take his place on a high seat and, following the injunctions laid down in the sacred texts, surrounded by a crowd of his friends, with that water installed him as King of Lanka amidst the titans.

All the monkeys as well as the titans assisted at Bibishana's installation and, amidst unequalled transports of delight, they paid tribute to Rama. Bibishana's counsellors were exceedingly happy, as also the titans who were devoted to him and, being enthroned as King of Lanka, he, Raghava and Lakshmana, who accompanied him, experienced supreme satisfaction. Then the new monarch, having spoken graciously to his subjects, went to where Rama was to be found.

Thereafter the people of the city offered him curds, parched rice, sweetmeats, roasted grain and flowers, which he placed at the disposal of Rama and Lakshmana, and Raghava, seeing Bibishana's work accomplished and his purpose attained, accepted all in deference to him.

Then Rama addressed the valiant Hanuman, who resembled a mountain, as he stood before him with bowed head and joined palms, saying :—

" With the approval of the great King Bibishana, O My Friend, do thou re-enter Lanka and enquire for Maithili. Say to Vaidehi that I am well, as also Sugriva and Lakshmana. O Most Eloquent of Speakers, tell her of the death of Ravana on the field of battle. Impart these agreeable tidings to Vaidehi, O Prince of the Monkeys, and having received her commands, return ! "

CHAPTER 115

Hanuman carries Rama's Message to Sita

THUS commanded, Hanuman, born of Maruta, returned to Lanka overwhelmed with honours by the rangers of the night and, entering the city invested with Bibishana's authority which he had sought, Hanuman penetrated to the Ashoka Grove, knowing that Sita was to be found there.

There he beheld Maithili like an anguished Rohini, uncared for, sitting sorrowfully at the foot of a tree surrounded by female titans and, approaching her humbly and gently, Hanuman inclined his head in obeisance to her.

At the appearance of the mighty Hanuman, that Goddess remained silent, but thereafter, having recognized him, she was delighted, and marking her tranquil looks, Hanuman the foremost of monkeys, prepared to relate all that Rama had said :—

" O Vaidehi, Rama is well as also Sugriva and Lakshmana ; he enquires as to thy welfare ! His purpose is accomplished, he, the conquerer of his foes has slain his adversary. Assisted by Bibishana and the monkeys, Rama, with the skill and wisdom of Lakshmana, has slain Ravana despite his prowess, O Goddess ! These are pleasant tidings but I will delight thee still further, O Divinity. In this war, undertaken on thine account, O Virtuous Sita, Rama has achieved a great triumph ! Take heart therefore, have no further anxiety ; Ravana is dead and Lanka subdued. Banishing sleep, I resolved to deliver thee and bridging the sea fulfilled my vow. Do not fear now to be in Ravana's abode since Bibishana has become the Lord of Lanka. Because of this, take courage, thou canst dwell peacefully in the palace ; Rama himself is coming hither with a joyful step eager to see thee."

At these tidings, the divine Sita, her face radiant as the moon on account of joy, was unable to utter a single word and that prince of monkeys enquired of Sita, who remained silent, saying:—

" Of what art thou thinking, O Goddess, since thou dost not answer me ? "

Thus interrogated by Hanuman, Sita, fixed in the path of duty, in the height of joy, said in a voice broken with sobs :—

" Hearing these pleasant tidings of the triumph of my lord, for a moment joy rendered me speechless. Nay, assuredly, reflecting on it, O Plavamgama, I do not know what gift I can offer thee which would be equal to this ! I know nothing on earth comparable to these happy tidings or with what I can recompense thee fittingly. Gold, precious gems of every kind, even a throne or any object in the Three Worlds cannot be measured against thy message ! "

At these words of Vaidehi, the monkey, standing before her with joined palms, joyfully replied :—

" O Thou who art ever engaged in what is pleasant and advantageous to thy Lord and who desirest him to be victorious, thine affectionate speech confers honour on thee, O Irreproachable Lady."

Hearing this, Maithili, the daughter of Janaka addressed these flattering words to the Son of the Wind :—

" Thy speech which is characteristic, urbane and dictated by the eight-fold intelligence is worthy of thee. Thou, the exceedingly virtuous son of Anila art deserving of praise ! Assuredly strength, prowess, knowledge of the scriptures, courage, boldness, superior skill, energy, endurance, steadiness, constancy and humility, these brilliant qualities and many others are all to be found in thee ! "

Unmoved by this praise, Hanuman, standing before her with joined palms, addressed Sita respectfully and said :—

" With thy consent I will slay all those female titans who formerly taunted thee in thy misfortune, O Thou whose lord is a god. I know that those monsters of hideous shape and conduct, those cruel beings of savage looks, those grim-visaged titans, more than once addressed thee in threatening tones at Ravana's command. Grant me permission to strike down those barbarians of distorted features and fearful aspect. I shall beat them with my fists, heels, long arms, thighs and knees ; I shall tear them to pieces with my teeth, chew up their ears, pull out their hair, knock them down and destroy them, since they have caused thee pain, O Illustrious Princess ! I shall exterminate those monsters who formerly insulted thee."

Hearing Hanuman's words, the unfortunate Sita, friend of the distressed, reflecting carefully, said to him :—

" Who would be angry with women, who are dependent on a monarch who is their supporter, and who act on other's advice as mere servants or slaves, O Excellent Monkey ? All that has happened to me is on account of an evil fate and the consequence of some fault committed formerly. One reaps the fruit of one's actions. Do not speak thus, O Long-armed Warrior, the path of destiny is inexorable ! It was inevitable that these circumstances should overtake me and, in this conviction, I wish in compassion to protect the slaves of Ravana. It was under the orders of that titan that these women ill-treated me. He being slain, they will no longer oppress me, O Son of Maruta. There is an ancient saying full of wisdom which a bear uttered formerly in the presence of a tiger, hear it, O Plavamgama !

" 'A superior being does not render evil for evil, this is a maxim one should observe ; the ornament of virtuous persons is their conduct. One should never harm the wicked or the good or even criminals meriting death. A noble soul will ever exercise compassion even towards those who enjoy injuring others or those of cruel deeds when they are actually committing them, who is without fault ? ' "

Hearing these words, Hanuman, who was skilled in speech, said to Sita, the irreproachable consort of Rama :—

" Thou art worthy of Raghava, thou, his chaste wife crowned with many virtues. O Goddess, command me to seek out Rama ! "

On this, Vaidehi born of Janaka, said : —

" I desire to see my lord, the friend of his devotees ! "

Hearing her speak thus, Hanuman, the exceedingly intelligent son of Maruta made this reply to Maithili, causing that princess great delight

" This day shalt thou see Rama, whose countenance resembles the full moon, with Lakshmana and his trusted friends, his enemies slain, as Sachi looks upon Indra, the King of the Gods."

Having spoken thus to Sita, who was as radiant as Shri herself, the exceedingly valiant Hanuman immediately departed to rejoin Raghava. Without delay, the foremost of monkeys, Hanuman, repeated the words that the daughter of Janaka had uttered, in their proper sequence to Rama who was the equal of the Chief of the Gods.

CHAPTER 116

Rama sends for Sita

THAT highly intelligent monkey, having paid obeisance to Rama, whose eyes resembled the petals of a lotus, the most skilled of archers, said to him :—

" It behoveth thee to visit Maithili who is consumed with grief and on account of whom this enterprise, that has been crowned with success, was undertaken. In the distress that overwhelms her, Maithili, her eyes bathed in tears, hearing of thy victory, expressed a desire to behold thee once more. Confiding in me formerly, her glances warm with emotion, she repeated ' I desire to see my lord again ! ' "

These words of Hanuman instantly evoked thoughts in Rama, the first of men, càusing him to shed tears. Sighing deeply, he said to Bibishana standing near, who resembled a cloud :—

" Bring the Princess of Videha, Sita, hither, anointed with celestial unguents, adorned with heavenly jewels, having laved her head ; do not delay ! "

At these words of Rama, Bibishana hastened to the private apartments to fetch Sita with her attendants. Beholding the unfortunate Maithili, Bibishana, the powerful King of the Titans, paid obeisance to her, raising his joined palms to his forehead, and respectfully addressed her, saying :—

" O Vaidehi, sprinkle thyself with celestial unguents, adorn thyself with divine ornaments and ascend this palanquin ! May happiness attend thee ! Thy lord desires to see thee ! "

Then Vaidehi answered Bibishana who had addressed her thus, saying :—" Without having bathed, I wish to see my consort, O Bibishana."

Hearing this, Bibishana replied :—" It behoveth thee to do what Rama commands ! " Whereto the virtuous Maithili, who regarded her husband as a god, filled with conjugal duty, said : ' Be it so ! '

Thereupon Sita, her tresses waved, adorned with priceless ornaments, wearing gorgeous raiment, ascended a palanquin borne by those titans accustomed to do so, accompanied by a large escort under Bibishana's command.

And Bibishana approaching that magnanimous hero, who was merged in meditation, bowing down to him, joyfully announced Sita's arrival.

Hearing that his consort, who had dwelt long in the titan's abode, had come, rage, joy and grief overwhelmed Raghava, the slayer of his foes and, beholding Sita in the palanquin, Rama, in order to test her, dissembling his happiness, said to Bibishana :—

" O Supreme Lord of the Titans, O My Friend who ever rejoiced in my victories, bring Vaidehi nearer to me."

At Raghava's command, the righteous Bibishana caused the crowd to disperse, whereupon titans clad in armour, wearing turbans, with drums and bamboo staves in their hands began to move about driving away the warriors, bears, monkeys and titans, who, scattering, stood apart some way off. And as they were being driven away, a tremendous clamour arose resembling the roar of the sea buffeted by the winds.

Seeing them dispersing, whilst confusion was created amongst them, Rama in affection for them, grew indignant at their departure and, highly incensed, with a glance that seemed as if it would consume him, addressed the exceedingly intelligent Bibishana in terms of reproach, saying :—

" Why, disregarding me, dost thou harass them, are they not my people ? Her conduct, not raiment, walls, seclusion or other royal prohibitions, are a woman's shield. In times of calamity, peril, war, the Swyamvara or the nuptual ceremony, it is not forbidden to behold a woman unveiled. It is not prohibited to look upon a woman who has fallen into distress and difficulty, above all in my presence. Therefore, leaving the palanquin, let Vaidehi come hither on foot so that the dwellers in the woods may see her at my side."

Hearing Rama's words, Bibishana became thoughtful and conducted Sita to him reverently, whilst Lakshmana, Sugriva and also Hanuman, hearing Rama speak thus, were saddened.

Then Maithili, confused and shrinking within herself, approached her lord accompanied by Bibishana ; and it was with astonishment, delight and love that Sita, whose husband was a god, gazed on Rama's gracious appearance, she whose own face was still beautiful. Beholding the countenance of her dearly loved lord, whom she had not seen for so long and which was as radiant as the full moon when it rises, she cast aside all anxiety and her own face became as fair as the immaculate orb of the night.

CHAPTER 117

Rama repudiates Sita

BEHOLDING Maithili standing humbly beside him, Rama gave expression to the feelings he had concealed in his heart, saying :—
" O Illustrious Princess, I have re-won thee and mine enemy

has been defeated on the battlefield; I have accomplished all that fortitude could do; my wrath is appeased; the insult and the one who offered it have both been obliterated by me. To-day my prowess has been manifested, to-day mine exertions have been crowned with success, to-day I have fulfilled my vow and am free. As ordained by destiny the stain of thy separation and thine abduction by that fickle-minded titan has been expunged by me, a mortal. Of what use is great strength to the vacillating, who do not with resolution avenge the insult offered to them?

"To-day Hanuman is plucking the fruit of his glorious exploits, and Sugriva, who is valiant in war and wise in counsel, with his army is reaping the harvest of his exertions! Bibishana too is culling the fruits of his labours, he who cast off a brother, who was devoid of virtue, to come to me."

When Sita heard Rama speak in this wise, her large doe-like eyes filled with tears and, beholding the beloved of his heart standing close to him, Rama, who was apprehensive of public rumour, was torn within himself. Then, in the presence of the monkeys and the titans, he said to Sita, whose eyes were as large as lotus petals, her dark hair plaited, and who was endowed with faultless limbs :—

"What a man should do in order to wipe out an insult, I have done by slaying Ravana for I guard mine honour jealously! Thou wert re-won as the southern region, inaccessible to man, was re-gained by the pure-souled Agastya through his austerities. Be happy and let it be known that this arduous campaign, so gloriously terminated through the support of my friends, was not undertaken wholly for thy sake. I was careful to wipe out the affront paid to me completely and to avenge the insult offered to mine illustrious House.

"A suspicion has arisen, however, with regard to thy conduct, and thy presence is as painful to me as a lamp to one whose eye is diseased! Henceforth go where it best pleaseth thee, I give thee leave, O Daughter of Janaka. O Lovely One, the ten regions are at thy disposal; I can have nothing more to do with thee! What man of honour would give rein to his passion so far as to permit himself to take back a woman who has dwelt in the house of another? Thou hast been taken into Ravana's lap and he has cast lustful glances on thee; how can I reclaim thee, I who boast of belonging to an illustrious House ? The end which I sought in re-conquering thee has been gained ; I no longer have any attachment for thee ; go where thou desirest ! This is the outcome of my reflections, O Lovely One ! Turn to Lakshmana or Bharata, Shatrughna, Sugriva or the Titan Bibishana, make thy choice, O Sita, as pleases thee best. Assuredly Ravana, beholding thy ravishing and celestial beauty, will not have respected thy person during the time that thou didst dwell in his abode."

On this, that noble lady, worthy of being addressed in sweet words, hearing that harsh speech from her beloved lord, who for long had surrounded her with every homage, wept bitterly, and she resembled a creeper that has been torn away by the trunk of a great elephant.

CHAPTER 118

Sita's Lamentations ; She undergoes the Ordeal by Fire

HEARING these harsh words from the wrathful Raghava, causing her to tremble, those fearful utterances, which till that time had never been heard by her and were now addressed to her by her lord in the presence of a great multitude, Maithili, the daughter of Janaka, overwhelmed with shame, pierced to the heart by that arrow-like speech, shed abundant tears. Thereafter, wiping her face, she addressed her husband in gentle and faltering accents, saying :—

"Why dost thou address such words to me, O Hero, as a common man addresses an ordinary woman ? I swear to thee, O Long-armed Warrior, that my conduct is worthy of thy respect ! It is the behaviour of other women that has filled thee with distrust ! Relinquish thy doubts since I am known to thee ! If my limbs came in contact with another's, it was against my will, O Lord, and not through any inclination on my part ; it was brought about by fate. That which is under my control, my heart, has ever remained faithful to thee ; my body was at the mercy of another ; not being mistress of the situation, what could

I do ? If despite the proofs of love that I gave thee whilst I lived with thee, I am still a stranger to thee, O Proud Prince, my loss is irrevocable !

"When, in Lanka, thou didst dispatch the great warrior Hanuman to seek me out, why didst thou not repudiate me then ? As soon as I had received the tidings that I had been abandoned by thee, I should have yielded up my life in the presence of that monkey, O Hero ! Then thou wouldst have been spared useless fatigue on mine account and others lives would not have been sacrificed, nor thine innumerable friends exhausted to no purpose. But thou, O Lion among Men, by giving way to wrath and by thus passing premature judgement on a woman, hast acted like a worthless man.

" I have received my name from Janaka, but my birth was from the earth and thou hast failed to appreciate fully the nobility of my conduct, O Thou who are well acquainted with the nature of others. Thou hast had no reverence for the joining of our hands in my girlhood and mine affectionate nature, all these things hast thou cast behind thee ! "

Having spoken thus to Rama, weeping the while, her voice strangled with sobs, Sita addressed the unfortunate Lakshmana, who was overwhelmed with grief, saying :—

" Raise a pyre for me, O Saumitri, this is the only remedy for my misery ! These unjust reproaches have destroyed me, I cannot go on living ! Publicly renounced by mine husband, who is insensible to my virtue, there is only one redress for me, to undergo the ordeal by fire ! "

Hearing Vaidehi's words, Lakshmana, the slayer of hostile warriors, a prey to indignation, consulted Raghava with his glance and by Rama's gestures he understood what was in his heart, whereupon the valiant Saumitri, following his indications, prepared the pyre.

None amongst his friends dared to appeal to Rama, who resembled Death himself, the Destroyer of Time ; none dared to speak or even to look upon him.

Thereafter Vaidehi, having circumambulated Rama, who stood with his head bowed, approached the blazing fire and, paying obeisance to the Celestials and brahmins, Maithili, with joined palms, standing before the flames, spoke thus :—

"As my heart has never ceased to be true to Raghava, do thou, O Witness of all Beings, grant me thy protection ! As I am pure in conduct, though Rama looks on me as sullied, do thou, O Witness of the Worlds, grant me full protection ! "

With these words, Vaidehi circumambulated the pyre and with a fearless heart entered the flames.

And a great multitude were assembled there, amongst which were many children and aged people who witnessed Maithili entering the fire. And, resembling gold that has been melted in the crucible, she threw herself into the blazing flames in the presence of all. That large-eyed lady, entering the fire, who is the Bearer of Sacrificial Offerings, appeared to those who watched her to resemble a golden altar. That fortunate princess entering the fire, which is nourished by oblations, seemed, in the eyes of the Rishis, Devas and Gandharvas, to resemble a sacrificial offering.

Then all the women cried out :—'Alas ! ' on seeing her, like a stream of butter hallowed by the recitation of mantras, fall into the flames, and she appeared to the Three Worlds, the Gods, the Gandharvas and the Danavas like a goddess smitten by a curse and cast down from heaven into hell. Then, as she entered the flames, a great and terrible cry rose from the titans and the monkeys.

CHAPTER 119

Brahma's Praise of Rama

MEANWHILE the righteous Rama, hearing the lamentation of the masses, afflicted, pondered awhile and his eyes filled with tears.

Then the King Vaishravana and Yama with the Pitris, the Thousand-eyed Lord of the Celestials, Varuna, Lord of the Waters and Mahadeva the blessed Three-eyed God who rides the Bull, as also Brahma the Creator of the World, King of the Learned, all gathered together, having hastened there in their chariots as bright as the sun, coming to the City of Lanka to seek out Rama.

Lifting up their great arms and hands adorned with jewels, they made obeisance with joined palms and the King of the Gods addressing Raghava, said :—

" O Creator of the Universe and foremost of those versed in the spiritual science, how canst thou manifest indifference to Sita falling into the flames ? How art thou unaware that thou thyself art the Chief of the Gods ? Formerly thou wert the Vasu Ritadhaman, the Progenitor of the Vasus ! Thou art the Creator of the Three Worlds, Swyamprabhu, the eighth Rudra and the fifth of the Sadhyas. The Twin Ashwins are thy two ears, the sun and moon thine eyes ; these are the forms at the beginning, middle and end of creation in which thou dost appear, O Scourge of Thy Foes ; and yet thou dost distrust Vaidehi as if thou wert an ordinary man ! "

Thus addressed by the Protector of the Worlds, the Leader of the Gods, Raghava, Lord of Peoples, Foremost of the Pious, answered :—

" I deem myself to be a man, Rama, born of Dasaratha ; who then am I in reality ? From whence have I come ? Let the Grandsire of the World inform me ! "

Thus spoke Kakutstha and Brahma, foremost of those who know the truth, addressed him saying :—

" Thou art the great and effulgent God Narayana, the fortunate Lord armed with the discus. Thou art the One-Tusked Boar, the Conqueror of thy Foes in the past and the future. Thou art the imperishable Brahman, Existence Itself, transcending the three divisions of time ; Thou art the Law of Righteousness, the Four-armed, the Bearer of the Sharnga Bow ; Thou art the Subduer of the senses, the Supreme Purusha ; Thou art invincible, Thou art the Holder of the Dagger, Thou art Vishnu, Thou art Krishna and of immeasurable might ; Thou art Senani and Gramani, the Controller of passions, the Origin and Dissolution ; Thou art Upendra and the Slayer of the Demon Madhu, Thou art the Creator of Indra and Indra Himself ; Thou art the Lotus-navelled One ; Thou dost bring combat to an end. The great and divine Rishis acknowledge Thee as their refuge and protector. Thou art the Himalayas of a hundred peaks, the Essence of the Vedas, the God of a Hundred Tongues, the Great Bull, Thou thyself art the Creator of the

World, Swyamprabhu ; Thou art the Refuge and Elder of the
Siddhas and Sadhyas ; Thou art the Sacrifice, the sacred
syllable ' Vashat ' and 'Aum ', the greatest of the great. None
knows thine origin or end or who Thou really art. Thou art
manifest in all beings, in the cows and the brahmins ; Thou
pervadest all regions, the firmament, the mountains and the
rivers, Thou, the Thousand-footed God, the Thousand-headed
One, Thou of a Thousand Eyes ! Thou art the support of all
beings and the earth. When the earth is withdrawn, under the
form of a great serpent, Thou dost appear on the waters supporting all the worlds and the Gods, Gandharvas and Danavas, O
Rama. I am thy heart and the Goddess Saraswati, thy tongue ;
the Gods are the hairs of Thy body, I, Brahma created them
thus. When Thou dost close thine eyes, it is night and when
Thou dost open them, it is day. The Vedas are Thy Samskaras[1];
nothing exists apart from thee ; the whole universe is Thy
body, the earth Thy forbearance ; Agni Thy wrath, Soma Thy
beneficence, the Shrivatsa Mark, Thy holy symbol.

" Thou didst cover the Three Worlds in three strides ; Thou
didst bind the terrible Bali and establish Mahendra as King.
Sita is Lakshmi and Thou, the God Vishnu, Krishna and
Prajapati. It was in order to slay Ravana that Thou didst enter
a human body. This task that we entrusted to Thee has been
accomplished, O Thou, the foremost of those who observe their
duty. Ravana having fallen, do Thou ascend to heaven joyfully !
Thy might is irresistible, O Rama, and thine exploits are never
fruitless. To behold Thee and offer adoration to Thee is never
unprofitable ! It is not in vain that men are devoted to Thee on
earth. Those who are ever faithful to Thee, attain to Thee who
art the primeval Purusha and their desires will be fulfilled in this
world and the other worlds. Those who recite this eternal,
ancient and traditional theme, transmitted by the Rishis, will
never suffer defeat."

---

[1] Samskaras—Latent Impressions.

CHAPTER 120

Sita is restored to Rama

HEARING those excellent words uttered by the Grandsire, Vibhabasu, who bore Vaidehi in his lap, having extinguished the pyre, rose up, and that Bearer of Sacrificial Offerings, assuming a corporeal form, stood up and took hold of the daughter of Janaka. Then that youthful woman, beautiful as the dawn, wearing ornaments of refined gold, attired in a red robe, having dark and curly hair, wearing fresh garlands, the irreproachable Vaidehi was restored to Rama by the God of Fire.

Thereafter the Witness of the whole world, Pavaka, addressed Rama, saying :—

" Here is Vaidehi, O Rama, there is no sin in her ! Neither by word, feeling or glance has thy lovely consort shown herself to be unworthy of thy noble qualities. Separated from thee, that unfortunate one was borne away against her will in the lonely forest by Ravana, who had grown proud on account of his power. Though imprisoned and closely guarded by titan women in the inner apartments, thou wast ever the focus of her thoughts and her supreme hope. Surrounded by hideous and sinister women, though tempted and threatened, Maithili never gave place in her heart to a single thought for that titan and was solely absorbed in thee. She is pure and without taint, do thou receive Maithili ; it is my command that she should not suffer reproach in any way."

These words filled Rama's heart with delight and he, the most eloquent of men, that loyal soul, reflected an instant within himself, his glance full of joy. Then the illustrious, steadfast and exceedingly valiant Rama, the first of virtuous men, hearing those words addressed to him, said to the Chief of the Gods :—

" On account of the people, it was imperative that Sita should pass through this trial by fire ; this lovely woman had dwelt in Ravana's inner apartments for a long time. Had I not put the innocence of Janaki to the test, the people would have said :— ' Rama, the son of Dasaratha is governed by lust ! ' It was well known to me that Sita had never given her heart to another and that the daughter of Janaka, Maithili, was ever devoted to me. Ravana was no more able to influence that large-eyed lady, whose chastity was her own protection, than the ocean may pass beyond its bournes. Despite his great perversity, he was unable to approach Maithili even in thought, who was inaccessible to him as a flame. That virtuous woman could never belong to any other than myself for she is to me what the light is to the sun. Her purity is manifest in the Three Worlds ; I could no more renounce Maithili, born of Janaka than a hero his honour. It behoveth me to follow your wise and friendly counsel, O Gracious Lords of the World."

Having spoken thus, the victorious and extremely powerful Rama, full of glory, adored for his noble exploits, was re-united with his beloved and experienced the felicity he had merited.

CHAPTER 121

Dasaratha appears to Rama

HEARING those excellent words uttered by Raghava, Maheshvara addressed him with even greater eloquence, saying :—

" O Lotus-eyed One, O Thou the possessor of long arms and a broad chest, O Scourge of Thy foes, fortunate it is that thou hast accomplished this great feat, O Most Pious of Men !

" O Rama, it is well for all beings that thou hast dispelled this deep and dreadful darkness of the whole world, this fear created by Ravana. Go now and console the unfortunate Bharata with thy presence, the illustrious Kaushalya, Kaikeyi and Sumitra, the mother of Lakshmana. Rule over Ayodhya, giving satisfaction to thine innumerable friends and establish the dynasty of the Ikshvaku Race. O Mighty Hero, having performed the Ashvamedha Sacrifice and acquired supreme renown, having distributed wealth among the brahmins, do thou attain the highest state.

" Behold King Dasaratha standing in his chariot, thy sire, thy superior in the world of men, O Kakutstha ! Having crossed the

sea of relativity by thy grace, full of glory he has entered the
region of Indra ; with thy brother Lakshmana pay homage to
him ! "

Hearing the words of Mahadeva, Raghava who was accompanied by Lakshmana, bowed before his sire, who was standing
in his aerial car on high, and that prince with his brother
Lakshmana beheld his sire blazing in his own effulgence, clad
in spotless raiment. With extreme delight, King Dasaratha,
standing in his chariot, once again beheld his son who was as
dear to him as his own life and that long-armed warrior, on his
seat, took him in his lap and embracing him, said :—

" Far from thee I do not prize the heaven in which I dwell
with the Gods, O Rama, this is the truth ! O Most Eloquent of
Men, the words addressed to me by Kaikeyi, which were designed
to effect thy banishment, have never been erased from mine
heart ! Embracing thee and Lakshmana and beholding thee
well and happy, I am delivered from mine affliction as the sun
when the mist has been dispelled. By thy grace, O My Son, thou
who art truly filial and of noble soul, I am redeemed, as was the
virtuous Brahmin Kahola by Ashtavakra. Now it is made clear
to me, O Dear Child, that in order to destroy Ravana, the Gods
determined that the supreme Purusha should become incarnate
as man.

"Assuredly Kaushalya will see all her desires fulfilled, O
Rama, when she beholds thee returning from the forest, O
Slayer of Thy Foes. O Rama, the people, seeing thee returning
to the city and installed as king and ruler of the world, will
indeed be blessed ! I desire to see thee re-united with Bharata,
thy devoted, valiant, pure and loyal brother. Thou hast passed
fourteen years in the forest with my beloved Sita and Lakshmana,
O Dear Child. The term of thine exile is over, thy vows honoured,
and further, by slaying Ravana on the battlefield, thou hast
gratified the Gods. Thy task is accomplished ; thou hast won
infinite renown, O Slayer of Thy Foes ; now, installed as king,
mayest thou with thy brothers live for a long time ! "

With joined palms, paying obeisance to King Dasaratha, who
had thus addressed him, Rama answered :—

" O Virtuous Sire, give thy blessings to Kaikeyi and Bharata !
Thou didst pronounce a terrible curse upon them, saying :—' I

renounce thee and thy son ! ', may this malediction not fall on
Kaikeyi or her son, O Lord." ' Be it so ! ' replied that great
monarch, paying obeisance with joined palms to Rama who had
spoken thus, and thereafter embracing Lakshmana, he said to
him :—

" Thou hast acquired extreme merit, O Pious One, and thy
fame will be great on earth ; by Rama's grace thou shalt attain
heaven and thy power shall be inconceivable. Attend on Rama
and be happy, O Thou who art the increaser of Sumitra's
delight. Rama is ever engaged in the welfare of all beings. The
Three Worlds with their Indras, the Siddhas and the great
Rishis do honour to that great hero and adore him as the
supreme Purusha. He, thy brother, is the invincible, imperishable Brahman, the essence of the Veda, which is secret, and the
Inner Ruler of all, O Dear Child ! Thou hast acquired great
merit and glory in serving him and the Princess of Videha with
devotion ! "

Having spoken thus to Lakshmana, the King paid obeisance
to Sita who stood before him with joined palms, and addressed
her in gentle tones, saying :—

" My Daughter, do not take it ill that Rama renounced thee !
O Vaidehi, he acted thus in thine own interest in order to
demonstrate thine innocence ! The proof of thy chaste conduct,
which thou hast given to-day, places thee above all other women.
O My Daughter, thou hast no need to be instructed regarding
thy duty towards thy husband, nevertheless I must tell thee that
he is the Supreme God."

Having thus addressed his two sons and Sita, King Dasaratha,
the descendant of Raghu, ascended to the region of Indra in his
chariot. Mounted on his aerial car, full of majesty, his body
blazing with effulgence, that foremost of men, having given his
counsel to his two sons and Sita, returned to the abode of the
Sovereign of the Gods.

CHAPTER 122

On Rama's request Indra restores the Army

KING DASARATHA having departed, Mahendra, the Vanquisher of Paka, addressed Raghava, who stood before him with joined palms, and said :—

" O Rama, O Lion among Men, our presence here must not prove unfruitful ; we are pleased with thee ; ask what thou desirest ! "

Hearing these magnanimous words of the blessed Mahendra, Raghava, of compassionate soul, answered him joyfully :—

" Since thou wishest to gratify me, O Chief of the Vibudhas, grant me that which I ask of thee ! O Most Eloquent of Orators, let all the valiant monkeys, who for my sake descended into the region of death, be resuscitated and live again. I wish to see all those monkeys happy, who for my sake left their sons and wives, O Great Lord.

" Those courageous monkeys, those heroes who courted death and, crowning their sacrifice, succumbed, do thou restore to life, O Purandara ! Devoted to mine interests they disregarded death ; be gracious enough to give them back to their families ; I solicit this favour of thee ! I wish to see the Golangulas and the Bears in all their former energy, freed from their sufferings and their wounds, O Munificent God. Let there be flowers, roots and fruits, even though they be out of season, and rivers with pure water in abundance wherever the monkeys are to be found."

Hearing these words of the magnanimous Raghava, Mahendra answered graciously :—

" Hard indeed to fulfil is this boon, thou dost crave, O Dear Prince of the Raghus, but my words never prove vain ; so be it ! May all those who have been slain in battle by the titans, the Bears and the Gopucchas, whose heads and arms have been severed, be resurrected ! May those monkeys rise up exulting, without pain or wounds, in all their natural vigour and courage, like sleepers who wake at the end of night, and let them be reunited with their friends, relatives and tribes ! O Thou, the

Wielder of the Great Bow, may the trees be laden with fruit and flowers even out of season and the rivers be full of pure water."

Thereupon those excellent monkeys, who were formerly covered with wounds, rose up healed, as persons who have been asleep, and there was general astonishment amongst the monkeys, who questioned each other, saying, ' What is this ? '

Seeing his purpose fulfilled, the Gods, in an excess of joy, unanimously addressed Rama, who was accompanied by Lakshmana, praising him and saying :—

" Now return to Ayodhya, O King and disband the monkeys ; do thou console the devoted and illustrious Maithili ! Seek out thy brother Bharata who, in sorrow of thy separation, has given himself up to penances. Approach the magnanimous Shatrughna and all thy mothers, O Scourge of Thy Foes ! Be installed as king and rejoice the hearts of the citizens by thy return ! "

Having spoken thus to Rama who was accompanied by Saumitri, the Gods, paying obeisance to him, joyfully returned to heaven in their chariots blazing like the sun ; and Rama with his brother ordered the encampment of the army.

Thereafter, under Rama and Lakshmana's protection, that great and glorious company of happy people, radiant with splendour, resembled the night illumined on all sides by that orb of cool rays.

CHAPTER 123

Bibishana places the Chariot Pushpaka at Rama's disposal

HAVING passed the night, Rama the conqueror of his foes, rose happily and Bibishana, paying obeisance to him with joined palms, addressed him, saying :—

" Here are various articles for bathing such as unguents, ornaments, sandalwood paste, raiment and celestial garlands of every kind. Lotus-eyed women, versed in the art of applying perfume await thy pleasure, as is fitting, O Raghava ! "

At these words, Kakutstha answered Bibishana saying :—

" Do thou invite the foremost of the monkeys and Sugriva to bathe first, for the pious Bharata, accustomed to happiness, that youthful and loyal hero is suffering on mine account. Far from Bharata, Kaikeyi's son, who has been loyal to his duty, I do not value bathing or raiment or jewels ! Order it so that we may return to Ayodhya soon, assuredly the route is extremely arduous."

Thus did Rama speak and Bibishana answered :—

" I will arrange for thee to reach that city in one day, O Prince ! May happiness attend thee ! There is an aerial car named Pushpaka that shines like the sun, which the powerful Ravana forcibly took from Kuvera, having overcome him in combat. That celestial and marvellous chariot, going everywhere at will, is at thy disposal, O Thou of unequalled prowess ! That car, bright as a cloud, which will transport thee to Ayodhya in perfect safety, is here. But if I am worthy of a boon, if thou dost recall any merit in me, then remain here for at least one day, O Virtuous One. If thou hast any friendship for me, then remain here with thy brother Lakshmana and Vaidehi, thy consort. Having received all possible homage, O Rama, thou shalt depart. I have prepared those honours dictated by mine affection, O Rama, do thou enjoy them with thine innumerable friends and thine army also. I beg thee in all humility, out of my profound esteem and feeling of friendship for thee, O Raghava ; I am thy servant and therefore may not command thee."

Then Rama answered Bibishana, who had spoken thus in the presence of all the titans and monkeys and said :—

" O Hero, Thou hast honoured me with thy friendship with thine whole soul and in all thine actions hast proved thy supreme affection for me. Nevertheless I cannot accept thy request, O King of the Titans, because my heart urges me to see my brother Bharata again, he who came to Chittrakuta in order to bring me back to Ayodhya though, as he bowed before me, I did not listen to his appeal. I wish to see Kaushalya, Sumitra and the illustrious Kaikeyi, as also mine house, my friends, the people of the city and the country. Grant me leave, O Dear Bibishana, Thou hast paid me sufficient honour ! Do not be angry, O My Friend, I beg of thee. O Foremost of the Titans, prepare the aerial car speedily, my task has been accomplished, what justification is there for remaining here longer ? "

Hearing Rama's words, that Indra among the Titans, Bibishana, hastened to order the aerial Chariot Pushpaka, gilded and bright as the sun, with its seats of emerald and pearl, its rooms ranged round about, silvered all over, its white banners and supports and gilded apartments enriched with golden lotuses which were hung with many bells. Round the windows, set with pearls and rare gems, rows of bells were placed giving forth a melodious sound, and that moving palace, resembling the peak of Mount Meru, constructed by Vishvakarma, abounded in rich ornaments, gold and jewels and sparkled with silver, and its floors were inlaid with crystal and the thrones of emerald (displayed there) furnished with rare coverings.

Having prepared that indestructible vehicle, the Chariot Pushpaka, which was as swift as thought, Bibishana stood before Rama, and that aerial car, that went everywhere at one's will and resembled a mountain, having been placed at his disposal, the magnanimous Rama who was accompanied by Saumitri, was astonished.

CHAPTER 124

Rama sets out for Ayodhya

THE Chariot Pushpaka, having been prepared and adorned with flowers, Bibishana, who stood a little way off with joined palms, reverently enquired of Rama with some urgency, saying :—

" What shall I do now, O Raghava ? "

Then the supremely illustrious Raghava, having reflected awhile, in the presence of Lakshmana, made answer affectionately, saying :—

"All the inhabitants of the woods have brought about the fulfilment of my mission by their efforts ; O Bibishana, do thou gratify them abundantly with jewels and riches of every kind. With their support thou hast recaptured Lanka, O Sovereign of the Titans ! Full of ardour, they did not fear to expose their lives nor did they ever retreat in combat. They have fulfilled their task ; now reward them by distributing gold and gems among them. When, in thy gratitude, thou hast loaded them with gifts, the monkeys will be fully satisfied.

" Thou dost know how to give and how to receive, thou art liberal and master of thy senses, all know thee to be a renunciate, it is for this that I address thee and exhort thee, O Prince; a king will wage war in vain and his army abandon him at the first opportunity if he be wholly devoid of those qualities that render him pleasing to all."

Hearing Rama's words, Bibishana bestowed precious gems and riches of every kind in abundance on all the monkeys and, beholding the foremost of the monkeys loaded with jewels and silver, Rama ascended the chariot of his adversary, holding the chaste and illustrious Vaidehi to his breast and accompanied by his brother Lakshmana, that valiant bow-man.

Standing in the chariot, Kakutstha bade farewell to all the monkeys, to the mighty Sugriva and to Bibishana and said :—

" O Foremost of Monkeys, you have accomplished all that could be asked of a friend, now go where you will, I give you all leave to depart. O Sugriva, thou who fearest nought but unrighteousness, thou hast done all that a devoted and loyal companion could do ; return to Kishkinda at the head of thine army. And thou, Bibishana, occupy the throne of Lanka that I have conferred upon thee. Even the inhabitants of heaven and their chiefs will not be able to trouble thee. I go to Ayodhya, that was the royal residence of my sire and wish to take leave of you all and to offer you my salutations ! "

Thus did Rama speak and all the leaders of the monkeys and the monkeys themselves as also the Titan Bibishana, paying obeisance with joined palms, answered :—

" We desire to go to Ayodhya, take us all with thee ! We shall delight in ranging the woods and copses and assisting at thine installation, of which thou art worthy. Having paid obeisance to the Queen Kaushalya, we shall return to our homes without delay, O Greatest of Kings ! "

Thus did they speak and the virtuous Rama answered the monkeys, Sugriva and Bibishana, saying :—

" Nothing would be more agreeable to me, as also to mine innumerable friends, than to return to the capital with you all. Hasten to take thy place with thy monkeys in the chariot, O Sugriva, and thou too, O Bibishana with thy ministers, O King of the Titans."

Thereupon Sugriva with the monkeys and Bibishana with his counsellors, took their places in the celestial Pushpaka Chariot and, all being installed, that marvellous aerial car belonging to Kuvera rose into the air under Raghava's command. In the chariot, which shone brightly, and was harnessed to swans, Rama exulted, overcome with delight, and resembled Kuvera himself, whilst all the monkeys, bears and titans, full of vigour, seated comfortably in that celestial car travelled at ease.

CHAPTER 125

Rama tells Sita of the Places over which they are passing

UNDER Rama's command, that aerial chariot harnessed to swans flew through the air with a great noise, and Rama, the delight of the Raghus, letting fall his glance on every side, said to the Princess of Mithila, Sita, whose face resembled the moon :—

" See how Lanka has been constructed by Vishvakarma on the summit of the Trikuta Mountain, which resembles the peak of Mount Kailasha. Behold the battlefield covered with a mire of flesh and blood; there, O Sita, a great carnage of monkeys and titans took place. There lies the ferocious King of the Titans, Ravana, who, despite the boons he had received, was slain by me on thine account, O Large-eyed Lady.

" Here Kumbhakarna was struck down as also another ranger of the night ; Prahasta and Dhumraksha perished here under the blows of the monkey, Hanuman. Vidyunmalin was put to death at this spot by the great-souled Sushena, and in another, Lakshmana overcame Indrajita, the son of Ravana. Angada struck down the Titans named Vikata and Virupaksha, hideous to look upon, as also Mahaparshwa and Mahodara. Akampana succumbed, as also other valiant warriors, Trishiras, Atikaya, Devantaka and Narantaka, Yuddhonmatta and Matta, both great heroes, Nikumbha and Kumbha, the two sons of Kumbhakarna, who were full of courage ; Vajradamshtra, Damshtra and innumerable other titans perished here and the invincible Maharaksha whom I slew in combat ; and Akampana[1] was slain and the powerful Shonitaksha whilst Yupaksha and Prajangha also succumbed in the great struggle. Vidyujjihva, a titan of fearful aspect fell there and Yajnashatru died also ; the mighty Suptaghna too, as also Suryashatru, were slain with Brahmashatru, who had no equal, and here Mandodari's consort, for whom she wept surrounded by her companions to the number of a thousand or more.

" Here is the place where the ocean was traversed, O Lady of Lovely Looks, and, having passed over the sea, there is the spot where the night was spent. There the bridge that I had thrown over the ocean of salty waves on thine account, O Large-eyed Lady, that causeway, difficult of construction, was built by Nala. Behold the ocean, O Vaidehi, that indestructible abode of Varuna's that seems without bourne, whose thundering waters abound in conch shells and pearls. O Maithili, behold that golden mountain, which, cleaving the waves, rose out of the bosom of the deep in order to allow Hanuman to rest. And here, our headquarters were established ; here, formerly the Lord Mahadeva granted me a boon and there is the sacred and purifying spot known as Setubandha[2] where even the greatest sins are washed away. Here Bibishana, King of the Titans, first came to me. Now we have reached Kishkindha with its beautiful woods, it is Sugriva's capital where I slew Bali."

Then Sita, seeing the City of Kishkindha of which Bali was formerly the support, said to Rama in gentle, loving and wistful tones :—

" I desire to enter thy royal capital, Ayodhya, O Prince, with the beloved consorts of Sugriva, Tara at their head, as also the wives of the other leaders of the monkeys ! "

Thus spoke Vaidehi and Raghava answered, ' So be it ! ', thereafter reaching the heights of Kishkindha, he caused the aerial chariot to halt and said to Sugriva :—

" O Lion among Monkeys, command all the Plavamgamas, accompanied by their wives, to come to Ayodhya with Sita and

[1] Akampana appears twice ; it is not known if it refers to the same warrior or another.
[2] This place is still to be seen near Rameshwara—a place of pilgrimage.

myself. Let all come, O King, and make haste to depart, O
Sugriva ! "

Hearing Rama's command, he whose energy was immeasurable, Sugriva, the illustrious monarch of the monkeys, attended
by his ministers entered the inner apartments and, seeing Tara,
said to her :—

" O Dear One, at the command of Raghava, who wishes to
gratify Vaidehi, do thou speedily assemble the consorts of the
magnanimous monkeys so that they may leave for Ayodhya to
visit the wives of King Dasaratha."

Hearing Sugriva's words, Tara, of beautiful limbs, gathered
all the female monkeys together and said to them :—

" Sugriva commands us to leave for Ayodhya ; do me the
favour of accompanying me and witness the entry of Rama in
the midst of the people from town and country and the splendour
of the wives of Dasaratha."

Thus commanded by Tara, the female monkeys, having first
adorned themselves and circumambulated her, ascended the car,
anxious to behold Sita, and that aerial chariot at once rose into
the air with them.

Then Raghava, gazing down on all sides, having reached the
vicinity of Rishyamuka, once more addressed Vaidehi, saying :—

" O Sita, here is a great mountain resembling a cloud rent by
lightning, abounding in gold and other metals. It is here that I
met that Indra among Monkeys, Sugriva, and entered into an
agreement with him to slay Bali. Here is the Pampa Lake with
its marvellous fields of blue lotuses and here separated from
thee, out of the depth of mine affliction, I wept ! It was on its
banks that beheld the virtuous Shabari.

" Here I slew Kabandha, whose arms extended for four miles !
O Sita, in Janasthana, I came upon that magnificent tree, the
Ashwatta, near which Jatayu, the renowned and valiant Monarch
of Birds perished under Ravana's blows on thine account, O
Lovely One. And there is our hermitage, O Lady of Brilliant
Complexion, where our enchanting leafy hut may be seen. It is
there that thou wert borne away by force by the King of the
Titans.

" There is the ravishing Godavari of transparent waters and
there, the retreat of Agastya can be seen, that is covered with

palms, as also Sharabhanga's hermitage where the God of a Thousand Eyes, the Destroyer of Cities, entered in secret. O Goddess of slender waist, behold the ascetics with Atri at their head, the equal of Surya and Vaishnava ; in that place the Giant Viradha fell under my blows and there, O Sita, thou didst visit the virtuous Sage. See, O Lady of beautiful form, the King of Mountains, Chittrakuta, appears ; it is there that the son of Kaikeya came to crave my forgiveness. Here is the enchanting Yamuna with its ravishing woods and here the retreat of Bharadwaja looms into view, O Maithili. Now we are in sight of the Ganges, that three-branched sacred river. There is the City of Shringavera where my friend, Guha, dwells, and there, the River Sarayu with rows of stone pillars on its banks commemorating the Kings of the House of Ikshvaku ! Behold there the royal abode of my Sire ! O Vaidehi, bow down to Ayodhya, we have returned ! "

During this time the monkeys and the titans were leaping about in delight on seeing that city and, with the palaces with which it abounded, its wide spaces and the elephants and horses that filled it, Ayodhya appeared to the monkeys and titans to resemble Amaravati, the city of the mighty Indra.

CHAPTER 126

Rama's Meeting with the Sage Bharadwaja

HAVING completed the fourteen years of exile, on the fifth day of the lunar fortnight, the elder brother of Lakshmana reached the hermitage of Bharadwaja and bowed low before that Ascetic. Paying obeisance to him, he enquired of the Sage, saying :—

" O Blessed One, dost thou know if all are well and happy in the city ? Is Bharata fixed in his duty ? Do my mothers still live ? "

Thus did Rama question Bharadwaja and that great Sage, smiling, answered the Prince of the Raghus cheerfully and said :—

" Bharata, his locks matted, carrying out thine instructions,

353

awaits thy return. In the presence of thy sandals, to which he pays homage, he rules all in the best interests of thy family and country.

" Beholding thee clad in bark, setting out on foot, thy consort making the third,[1] banished from thy kingdom, entirely devoted to thy duty, obedient to the behests of thy sire, renouncing every pleasure, like unto a God driven from heaven, formerly I was filled with pity for thee; then, O Victorious Warrior, thou, dispossessed by Kaikeyi, nourished thyself on fruits and roots; but now I see thee, thy purpose accomplished surrounded by friends and kinsfolk, having triumphed over thine enemy and my joy is supreme !

" I know all that thou hast experienced of good and ill whilst dwelling in Janasthana, O Raghava, and how, engaged in procuring the welfare of the Sages, seeking to protect them all, thine irreproachable consort was borne away by Ravana. I know of the appearance of Maricha and Sita's delusion; the meeting with Kabandha; thine arrival at Lake Pampa, the alliance with Sugriva when Bali fell under thy blows; the search for Vaidehi and the exploit of the Wind-god's son; the construction of the causeway by Nala and the finding of Vaidehi; how Lanka was set on fire by the foremost of the monkeys whilst he was bound; how Ravana, proud of his strength, fell in the fight with his sons, kinsfolk, ministers, infantry and cavalry; how after the death of Ravana, who was a thorn in the side of the Gods, thou didst meet the Celestials and receive a boon from them; all these things I know by virtue of my penances, O Hero, O Thou who art fixed in virtue.

" Therefore I have sent my disciples to carry the news to the city and I too will grant thee a boon, O Most Skilful of Warriors; but first accept the Arghya, to-morrow thou shalt go to Ayodhya,"

Hearing these words, the illustrious prince, with bowed head, answered joyfully, ' It is well ! ' and made the following request :—

" On the road I take to reach Ayodhya, though it is not the season, yet may all the trees bear honeyed fruits and those fruits have the fragrance of 'Amrita '[2] and may every variety be found there; O Blessed One ! "

[1] Rama and Lakshmana being the other two.
[2] Amrita—Nectar of Immortality.

Thereupon the Sage replied : " So be it ! Thy desire shall be realised immediately ! " Then the trees of that region instantly resembled those of Paradise. Those that had none, grew fruits, and those that had no flowers were covered with blossom ; trees that had withered were enveloped with foliage and all dripped with honey for three leagues along the way.

Meanwhile the foremost of the monkeys regaled themselves on those celestial fruits to the extent of their desire and, transported with joy, imagined they had entered heaven.

CHAPTER 127

Rama sends Hanuman to seek out Bharata

WHEN he beheld Ayodhya, that descendant of Raghu of rapid step full of magnanimity, gave himself up to pleasant thoughts and, having reflected awhile, that fortunate and illustrious hero said to the monkey, Hanuman :—

" Hasten with all speed to Ayodhya, O Foremost of Monkeys, and ascertain if all are happy in the royal palace. Passing Shringavera, communicate with Guha, King of the Nishadas, who dwells in a wooded country, and offer him my salutations. When he hears that I am safe and well, freed from all anxieties, he will be content, for he is my second self and my friend. He will gladly show thee the way to Ayodhya and give thee tidings of Bharata. Do thou enquire of Bharata as to his well-being and inform him that I have returned with my consort and Lakshmana, my mission accomplished. Tell him of Sita's abduction by the ruthless Ravana, of my meeting with Sugriva and the death of Bali in combat ; of how I set out to find Maithili and how thou didst discover her, having crossed the great waters of that domain of the unchangeable Lord of Rivers ! Tell him of our arrival on the shores of the sea, the appearance of Sagara and how the causeway was constructed ; how Ravana perished ; of the boons bestowed on me by Mahendra, Brahma and Varuna and, by the favour of Mahadeva, the meeting with my Sire.

Inform Bharata, O My Friend, that I am coming accompanied by King Bibishana and the Lord of the Monkeys. Say to him, ' Having overcome the army of the enemy and attained a glory without parallel, Rama, his purpose accomplished, is approaching with his valiant friends '. Do thou carefully observe the expression on the face of Bharata when he hears these tidings and how he comports himself. Thou wilt know all by his gestures, the colour of his face, his glances and his words. Whose mind would not be moved by the thought of (ascending) an ancestral throne, fulfilling all one's dreams, and to a kingdom abounding in prosperity, hosts of elephants, horses and chariots ? If the fortunate Bharata wishes to reign in his own right, then, by mutual agreement, let that descendant of Raghu govern the entire earth ! ''

On receiving these instructions, Hanuman, born of Maruta, assuming human form, left in all haste for Ayodhya and advanced with speed, like unto Garuda swooping on a great serpent on which he wishes to lay hold. Traversing the path-way of his sire, the shining abode of great birds and, crossing over the formidable confluence of the Ganges and the Yamuna, he reached the City of Shringavera. Then the valiant Hanuman sought out Guha and said to him, his voice ringing with joy :—

" Thy friend, Kakutstha, that true hero who is accompanied by Sita as also Saumitri, enquires as to thy welfare. Having spent the fifth night of the moon with the Sage Bharadwaja, on his request, Raghava has now taken leave of him and thou wilt see him to-morrow."

Having said this, the illustrious and agile Hanuman, whose hair stood on end with delight, rushed on regardless of fatigue. Thereafter he crossed the river sacred to Parasurama, and the Valukini, Varuthi and Gaumati and the formidable forest of Sala Trees, also many densely populated countries and opulent cities. Having journeyed a great distance that foremost of monkeys came to the flowering trees that grow in the neighbourhood of Nandigrama and resemble those of Chaitaratha, the gardens of the King of the Celestials. There he beheld people who, with their wives, sons and grandsons, well-attired were given up to enjoyment in those pleasant surroundings.

Thereafter, at a distance of one league from Ayodhya, he

observed Bharata, clad in a black antelope skin, sad, emaciated, wearing matted locks, his limbs besmeared with dust, dwelling in a hermitage, afflicted on account of his brother's misfortune. Living on fruit and roots, practising penance, self-controlled, his hair knotted, dressed in bark and a black antelope skin, disciplined, pure of soul, like unto a Brahmarishi in radiance, he, having placed Rama's sandals before him, ruled the earth by protecting the four castes from every peril with the aid of his ministers, and virtuous priests and senior officers wearing red robes surrounded him. And his subjects, faithful to their duty, had resolved not to neglect the welfare of their king, who resembling, righteousness itself, seemed to be the God of Dharma incarnate.

Then Hanuman, paying obeisance with joined palms, said to that loyal prince :—

" Thy brother, Kakutstha, for whose exile to the Forest of Dandaka in robes of bark and matted locks, thou grievest, enquires as to thy welfare. I bring thee good tidings, O Prince, abandon thy despair ; the moment has come when thou wilt be re-united with thy brother Rama. Having slain Ravana and recovered Maithili, Raghava is returning with his valiant friends, his purpose accomplished. The mighty Lakshmana too is coming and the illustrious Vaidehi, Rama's devoted companion, as Sachi is to Mahendra."

Hearing Hanuman's words, Bharata, the son of Kaikeyi swooned with joy, felicity causing him to lose consciousness. In a moment, however, the descendant of Raghu, Bharata, rose up breathing with an effort and addressed Hanuman who had brought him those pleasant tidings. Deeply moved, the fortunate Bharata, embracing the monkey bedewed him with his tears that fell from him in great drops, inspired not by suffering but by joy, and said :—

" Whether thou be god or man who has come hither out of compassion for me, O My Friend, I wish to bestow a gift on thee for the happy tidings thou hast brought me. I offer thee a hundred thousand cows, as also a hundred prosperous villages and sixteen youthful women for thy consorts, possessed of curls, with sweet expressions, golden skins, shapely noses, lovely ankles and gracious mien, resembling the moon, adorned with every kind of ornament, all of noble families."

Hearing from that Prince of Monkeys of the miraculous return of Rama, Bharata, whose desire to behold his brother again threw him into a transport of delight, added joyfully :—

CHAPTER 128

Hanuman tells Bharata of all that befell Rama and Sita
during their exile

" VERILY it is with joy that I learn these tidings of my protector after the innumerable years that he has passed in the forest. How felicitous is the well-known saying, ' Happiness comes to man even if it be after a hundred years ! ' How did Raghava and the monkeys conclude an alliance and for what purpose ? Answer my questions candidly ! "

Thus interrogated by the prince, Hanuman, seating himself on a heap of Kusha Grass, began to describe Rama's life in the forest and said :—

" O Lord, thou knowest how he was exiled on account of the two boons bestowed on thy mother ; how the King Dasaratha died in consequence of his son's banishment ; how the messengers, O Lord, brought thee back from Rajagriha ; how, returning to Ayodhya, thou didst refuse the crown ; how thou didst go to Chittrakuta to appeal to thy brother, the scourge of his foes, begging him to accept the throne, thus conforming to the way of virtuous men ; how Rama renounced the kingdom and how, on returning, thou didst bring back the sandals of that illustrious hero ; all this, O Long-armed Warrior is well-known to thee but what happened subsequent to thy departure, now hear from me !

"After thy return, distress seized the denizens of the forest, creating a great turmoil. Thereupon Rama, Sita and Lakshmana entered the huge, dreadful and lonely Dandaka Forest that was trodden down by elephants and formidable with its lions, tigers and deer. Having penetrated into its depths, the powerful Viradha appeared before them emitting fearful cries. Lifting him up, as he was roaring like a great elephant, those two warriors threw him headlong into a pit and having accomplished that difficult exploit, the two brothers, Rama and Lakshmana, at dusk reached the enchanting hermitage of Sharabhanga. That Sage having ascended to heaven, Rama, a true hero, paid obeisance to the ascetics and thereafter went to Janasthana.

" Fourteen thousand titans, who dwelt in Janasthana, were slain during the time that the mighty Raghava resided there. For having fallen into the hands of the only Rama, during the fourth watch, those demons were wholly exterminated. Taking advantage of their great power, in order to harass the ascetics, those demons, inhabitants of the Dandaka Forest, were slain by Rama in combat. The demons slain and Khara also, Rama then despatched Dushana and subsequently Trishiras. Thereafter a female demon, named Shurpanakha, accosted him and, being ordered to do so, Lakshmana, rising, took up his sword and instantly cut off her ears and nose. Thus mutilated, that titan woman took refuge with Ravana.

" Then a redoubtable titan in Ravana's service, named Maricha, assuming the form of a jewelled deer, beguiled Vaidehi, who, on beholding it, said to Rama :—

" ' O My Beloved, capture it for me, it will enliven our solitude.'

" Raghava, bow in hand, rushed out in pursuit of that deer and destroyed it with a single arrow, O My Friend.

" While Raghava, however, was thus engaged in the chase, Lakshmana too had left the hermitage, and Dashagriva, entering there, speedily took hold of Sita, as Graha seizes Rohini in the sky. Slaying the Vulture Jatayu, who sought to deliver her, the titan, taking hold of Sita, departed in all haste for his capital. Meanwhile some strange looking monkeys, as large as hills, standing on the summit of a mountain, astonished, observed Ravana, the King of the Titans proceeding with Sita in his arms ; and, mounting into the sky with her in the Chariot Pushpaka, which was as swift as thought, the all-powerful Ravana returned to Lanka. There he entered his vast palace decorated with pure gold and, with many words, sought to console Vaidehi but she, regarding his speech and his person with disdain and as less than a straw, was imprisoned in the Ashoka Grove.

" Meantime Rama returned, having slain the deer in the forest and, as he did so, he beheld the vulture so beloved of his sire, dead, at which he suffered extreme distress. Thereafter Raghava with Lakshmana set out in search of Vaidehi and they crossed the Godavari River with its flowering woodlands.

" In the great forest, the two princes met a titan, named Kabandha, counselled by whom that true hero repaired to the Mountain Rishyamuka in order to confer with Sugriva and, even before they met, they were firm friends.

" Sugriva had formerly been banished by his irascible brother Bali and, in consequence of this meeting, a sound alliance was formed between them. Rama, by the strength of his arms established him on the throne, having slain Bali, that giant full of valour, in the field. Regaining his kingdom, Sugriva vowed in return to set out with all the monkeys in order to find the princess and, under the command of their magnanimous sovereign, ten kotis of those Plavamgamas repaired to different regions.

" Whilst, discouraged, we were resting on the lofty Vindhya Mountain, plunged in despair, a long time passed. Meanwhile the powerful brother of the King of the Vultures, named Sampati, informed us that Sita was dwelling in Ravana's palace, whereupon I, whom thou seest here, was able to dispel the grief of my companions and, resorting to mine own prowess, crossed over a hundred leagues of sea and discovered Maithili alone in the Ashoka Grove, clad in a soiled silken cloth, stained with dust, afflicted yet faithful to her conjugal vow. Approaching that irreproachable lady I paid obeisance to her and bestowed a ring on her in Rama's name as a pledge, and she, in her turn, gave me a brilliant jewel.

" My mission accomplished, I returned and gave Rama that token, the bright gem ; and he, receiving tidings of Maithili, regained his zest for life, as one, who in extremity, drinks Amrita. Summoning up his strength, he resolved to overthrow Lanka, as, when the time has come, Vibhabasu prepares to destroy the worlds.

" Reaching the shores of the sea, the Prince commanded Nala to construct a causeway and the army of valiant monkeys crossed the ocean on that bridge.

" Prahasta fell under the blows of Nila, Kumbhakarna under those of Raghava, Lakshmana slew Ravana's son and Rama, Ravana himself. Having been received by the Granter of Boons, Shakra, as also Yama, Varuna and Mahadeva, Swyambhu and Dasaratha, Rama was showered with favours by all the Rishis. The glorious Kakutstha, Scourge of His Foes, was rendered happy by obtaining these boons and returned to Kishkindha accompanied by the monkeys in the Chariot Pushpaka.

" He has reached the Ganges once more and is dwelling with the Sage,[1] where without hindrance, thou shouldst behold him to-morrow, when the Pushya Star is in an auspicious aspect ! "

Thereupon, hearing Hanuman's delightful words, Bharata, full of joy, paid obeisance to him and, in accents pleasing to the heart, said :—

"After a long time my desires are at last fulfilled ! "

CHAPTER 129

Bharata sets out to meet Rama

HEARING those marvellous tidings, Bharata, that real hero, the slayer of hostile warriors, delighted, issued a command to Shatrughna, saying :—

" Let all righteous men, having purified themselves, worship all the Deities and sacred altars of the city with fragrant garlands and diverse musical instruments. Let the bards conversant with the tradition and all the panegyrists, with the queens, ministers, guards, the army, the courtiers, brahmins, nobles and the foremost of the artisans issue forth from the capital in companies, in order to behold the countenance of Rama, which is as lovely as the moon."

At this behest, Shatrughna, the slayer of hostile warriors, called together some thousands of labourers, whom he divided into groups, and he said to them :—

" Fill up the hollows and level the uneven ground from Ayodhya to Nandigrama. Sprinkle every part with water as cold as ice and let others scatter roasted grain and flowers

[1] The Sage Bharadwaja.

everywhere ; set up large standards on all the main highways of the capital. At the rising of the sun, let all the dwellings be adorned with crowns and garlands, with many flowers and decorations in five colours ; let contingents of soldiers stand along the royal highway to keep it free."

At this command from Shatrughna, which filled everyone with joy, Dhristi, Jayanti, Vijaya, Siddhartha, Arthasadhaka, Ashoka, Mantrapala and Sumantra set out. Thousands of elephants intoxicated with ichor and female elephants with golden girths, bearing standards, splendidly adorned, on which illustrious warriors were mounted, issued forth, whilst others set out on horses and in chariots also, and warriors armed with spears, cutlasses and nets, furnished with banners and pennants were escorted by the foremost of their leaders and thousands of infantry.

Thereafter the litters, bearing the consorts of King Dasaratha, with Kaushalya and Sumitra at their head, also set out. And Bharata, ever fixed in his duty, surrounded by the Twice-born, the elders of the city, the merchants and counsellors with garlands and sweetmeats in their hands, rejoiced by the sound of conches and drums, his praises sung by panegyrists, having placed the sandals of the illustrious Rama on his head, took up the white parasol decorated with bright garlands and two golden chowries made of Yaks tails, worthy of a king. Then that magnanimous prince, emaciated by long fasting, pale, wearing robes of bark and a black antelope skin, yet full of joy at the tidings of his brother's approach, set out with his escort to meet Rama and the sound of the horses hooves, the noise of the chariot wheels, the blare of conches and beat of drums, the roaring of elephants, the blast of trumpets and booming of gongs caused the earth to tremble as the whole city proceeded to Nandigrama.

Thereafter Bharata, glancing round, said to Hanuman, the son of Pavana :—

" Is it due to the levity of thy monkey nature that I do not behold Kakutstha, the illustrious Rama, Scourge of His Foes ? Neither are those monkeys, able to change their form at will, to be seen ! "

To these words, Hanuman, testifying to the truth, answered the virtue-loving Bharata, saying :—

" That sylvan army has reached the trees covered with fruit and flowers, flowing with honey, where the humming of bees intoxicated with love can be heard. All this was created by virtue of a boon bestowed by Vasava on the Sage Bharadwaja, as a reward for his great hospitality. One can hear their shouts of delight and, to my mind, those monkeys have crossed the River Gaumati. Observe that immense cloud of dust near the wood ; in mine estimation, the monkeys are shaking the boughs of the Sala Trees; behold that aerial chariot, bright as the moon, which can be seen in the distance, it is the celestial Car Pushpaka created by Brahma's thought and was obtained by that hero after he had slain Ravana and his kinsfolk. Glittering like the rising sun, that celestial chariot, swift as thought, that is bearing Rama, belongs to Dhanada, who received it from Brahma. In it are the two valiant brothers, offspring of the House of Raghu, accompanied by Vaidehi, the supremely illustrious Sugriva and the Titan Bibishana."

At that moment, from women, children, youthful persons and the aged, the joyful clamour ' Rama has come ! ' arose, reaching the skies.

Alighting from their chariots, elephants and horses in order to go on foot, the people beheld that prince standing in his aerial car, resembling the moon in the sky. With joined palms, Bharata advanced joyfully to meet Rama, to whom he paid obeisance, offering him water wherewith to wash his hands and feet, as also the Arghya.

In that chariot, created by Brahma's thought, the elder brother of Bharata with his large eyes, looked as radiant as the God who bears the Thunderbolt. Then Bharata, with a deep bow, paid reverence to his brother Rama, who was seated in the car, like unto the sun on the summit of Mount Meru, and at Rama's command, that swift and excellent vehicle, harnessed to swans, descended to earth. Then the faithful Bharata approaching Rama, full of joy paid obeisance once more, and Kakutstha, drawing Bharata to him, whom he had not seen for a long time, caused him to sit on his lap, embracing him affectionately. Thereafter, Bharata, the scourge of his foes, approached Lakshmana and Vaidehi and saluted them lovingly ; then the son of Kaikeyi embraced Sugriva, Jambavan, Angada, Mainda,

Dvivida, Nila and Rishabha also, and Sushena, Nala, Gavaksha, Gandhamadana, Sharabha and Panasa, clasping them in turn in his arms.

In the form of men, those monkeys, able to change their shape at will, gaily wished Bharata good fortune ; then, after embracing him, that prince, full of valour, said to Sugriva, that lion among monkeys :—

" We are four brothers, thou shalt be the fifth, O Sugriva ; benevolence creates friendship and malevolence enmity ! "

Thereafter Bharata addressed Bibishana in comforting words, saying :—

" Be thou blessed ; thy co-operation ensured the success of this difficult enterprise ! "

At that instant, Shatrughna, having paid obeisance to Rama and Lakshmana, bowed reverently to the feet of Sita. Then Rama approached his mother, who was pale and drawn with grief and, prostrating himself, touched her feet, thus rejoicing her heart, after which he saluted Sumitra and the renowned Kaikeyi, thereafter paying obeisance to the other Queens and his spiritual preceptor.

Then all the citizens, with joined palms said to Rama :— " Be thou welcome, O Long-armed Hero, thou art the increaser of Kaushalya's delight ! "

To the elder brother of Bharata, those thousands of hands joined in salutation caused the inhabitants of the city to appear like a lotus in flower.

Then Bharata, conversant with his duty, himself took Rama's sandals and fastened them on the feet of that Indra among Men and thereafter, with joined palms, said to him :—

" This kingdom that I received in trust, I now render back to thee in its entirety. To-day, since I see thee as Lord of Ayodhya, the purpose of mine existence has been fulfilled and my desires consummated. Now examine thy treasury, thy storehouses, thine house and thine army ; by thy grace, I have increased them tenfold ! "

These words uttered by Bharata out of fraternal love, caused the monkeys and the Titan Bibishana to shed tears. Thereafter, in his joy, Raghava made Bharata sit on his lap and, with his chariot and army, proceeded to the hermitage.

Reaching that place with Bharata and his troops, Rama alighted from his aerial car and thereafter spoke to that most excellent chariot, saying :—

" Now go hence and place thyself at Vaishravana's disposal, I give thee leave to depart."

Thus dismissed by Rama, that excellent car proceeded in a northerly direction and reached Dhanada's abode. The celestial Car Pushpaka, which had been borne away by the Titan Ravana, returned at Rama's command with all speed to Dhanada.

As Shakra touches the feet of Brihaspati, Raghava, having touched the feet of his friend, his spiritual preceptor, seated himself by his side, a little way apart, on an excellent seat.

CHAPTER 130

Rama is installed as King : The Benefits that accrue from the Recitation and Hearing of the Ramayana

RAISING his joined palms to his forehead, Bharata, the increaser of Kaikeyi's delight, said to his elder brother, Rama, that true hero :—

" Thou hast honoured my mother by conferring the kingdom on me ; now I give back to thee that which was entrusted to me. How can I, who am but a young steer, bear the heavy load that one full grown is scarcely able to sustain ? To my mind, it is as hard to preserve the boundaries of this kingdom as to build up a dam which has been swept away by a torrent. How can a donkey outpace a horse or a crow surpass a swan in flight ? Nor am I able to follow in thy footsteps, O Hero, O Scourge of Thy Foes ! As a tree with a vast trunk and branches, planted in a courtyard, that has grown immense and difficult to climb, dries up when it has blossomed without yielding any fruit, so, O Long-armed Prince, if, being our master, thou dost not uphold us all, we thy servants, are in the same case !

" Let the universe to-day witness thine enthronement, O Raghava, thou who art as radiant as the sun at noon in all its effulgence. From henceforth, let it be to the sound of gongs, the tinkling of girdles and anklets and the gentle strains of melodious singing that thou dost wake and fall asleep. Do thou rule the world as long as the sun revolves and the earth endures."

Hearing Bharata's words, Rama, the conqueror of hostile cities, answered ' So be it ! ' and took his place on an excellent seat.

Thereafter, at the command of Shatrughna, skilled and deft-handed barbers quickly surrounded Raghava ; and first Bharata bathed and the mighty Lakshmana also, then Sugriva, that Indra among Monkeys, followed by Bibishana, the Lord of the Titans ; whereupon Rama, his matted locks shorn, performed his ablutions and he was clothed in robes of great price, covered with garlands and sprinkled with every kind of perfume ; thereafter he re-appeared blazing in his own effulgence. The hero, Bharata, attended on Rama's robing and Shatrughna, the upholder of the prosperity of the Ikshvakus, on Lakshmana's, and all the consorts of King Dasaratha attended on Sita. Kaushalya, in love of her son, herself adorned all the consorts of the monkeys with joy.

Then Shatrughna, having issued the command, Sumantra harnessed a magnificent chariot and when that celestial car, bright as flame, had been brought before him, Rama, that long-armed warrior, conqueror of hostile citadels, took his place therein. Sugriva and Hanuman, whose beauty equalled Mahendra's, bathed and attired in robes of divine loveliness and sparkling earrings, followed ; thereafter Sugriva's consorts, as also Sita, advanced eager to behold the capital.

In Ayodhya all the ministers of King Dasaratha, with Rama's spiritual Preceptor Vasishtha, at their head, took counsel as to what ought to be done ; and Ashoka, Vijaya and Siddhartha, with undivided mind, entered into consultation regarding the honours to be paid to Rama by the city and said :—

" Prepare all that is needed for the coronation of the magnanimous Rama, who is worthy of this honour, beginning with the benedictory prayer."

Having issued these orders, the ministers as also the spiritual Preceptor set forth from the city in haste, in order to behold Rama, who resembled the God of a Thousand Eyes in his chariot drawn by bay horses. And Raghava, seated in his car, proceeded along the highway to his capital; Bharata took up the reins, Shatrughna the parasol, Lakshmana the fan and Sugriva one of the chowries, whilst that Indra among the Titans, Bibishana, held the second that was made of Yaks tails of dazzling whiteness and like unto the moon, waving it to and fro over the prince, behind whom he stood. At that instant, the sweet music of Rama's praises rang out in the sky sung by companies of Rishis and Gods with the Marut Hosts.

The illustrious Sugriva, that bull among the monkeys, was mounted on an elephant named Shatrumjaya, as high as a hill, and nine thousand elephants carried the monkeys, who in the form of men, proceeded along the way, adorned with ornaments of every kind.

Then that Lord of Men advanced towards the city encircled with palaces, to the sound of conches and the roll of drums; and the inhabitants of the city beheld Raghava radiant with beauty advancing in his chariot, and, having exchanged salutations, they took up their places behind Kakutstha, the magnanimous Rama, surrounded by his brothers. In the midst of his counsellors, the brahmins and the people, Rama shone with splendour like unto the moon amidst the stars; and, as he advanced along the highway, preceded by the musicians and those who bore the Swastika on the palms of their hands, he was attended by a joyous crowd. Before Rama marched those who carried roasted grain and gold, and virgins and kine were there with the Twice-born and men with their hands full of Modaka.[1]

Meantime Rama informed his ministers of his alliance with Sugriva and of the prowess of the son of Anila; and the monkeys and the inhabitants of Ayodhya were astounded by the narrative concerning the monkeys' exploits and the valour of the titans. Whilst relating these incidents, the illustrious Rama, who was attended by the Vanaras, entered Ayodhya, which was filled with healthy and happy people, and where every house was decorated.

Thereafter they came to the ancestral dwelling, the abode of the descendants of Ikshvaku, and that prince, the delight of the House of Raghu, paid obeisance to Kaushalya, Sumitra and Kaikeyi and thereafter addressed Bharata in gentle and reasonable words saying :—

[1] Modaka—A kind of sweetmeat.

" Let Sugriva stay in the magnificent palace, set amidst the woods in the Ashoka Grove, which abounds in pearls and emeralds."

At these words, Bharata, that true hero, took Sugriva by the hand and led him into the palace. Meanwhile servants bearing oil lamps, couches and carpets entered immediately as commanded by Shatrughna and the exceedingly valiant younger brother of Raghava said to Sugriva :—

" Do Thou, O Lord, issue thy commands for Rama's coronation ! "

On this, Sugriva gave over four golden urns encrusted with gems to the monkey leaders, saying :—

" To-morrow, at dawn, see to it that ye return with your urns filled from the four seas, O Monkeys."

At this command, those powerful monkeys, resembling elephants, immediately rose into the air, so that they looked like swift eagles, and they were Jambavan, Hanuman, Vegadarshin and Rishabha, who brought back their urns filled with water, whilst five hundred other monkeys drew water in their jars from five hundred rivers. The mighty and valorous Sushena returned with his vessel, adorned with every variety of gem, bearing water from the eastern sea ; Rishabha, without delay, brought water from the southern sea ; Gavaya, with his urn powdered with red sandal and camphor, filled it at the vast ocean of the west, and Hanuman, the marvellous son of Anila, who was as swift as the wind, with his huge urn, encrusted with diamonds, drew water from the icy northern sea.

Beholding the water brought by those foremost of monkeys for Rama's coronation, Shatrughna, attended by servants, imparted the tidings to the chief Priest Vasishtha, and his companions, and that venerable one hastened there with the brahmins, whereupon he caused Rama accompanied by Sita, to ascend a throne inlaid with precious gems. Then Vasishtha, Vijaya, Javali, Kashyapa, Katyayana, Gautama and Vamadeva consecrated that lion among men with pure and fragrant water, as the Vasus crowned Vasava of a Thousand Eyes.

Then the Ritvijs and the Brahmins with sixteen virgins, counsellors, warriors, as also the merchants, were full of joy and Rama was sprinkled with pure water, and the Celestial Beings, standing in the firmament with the Lokapalas and the Gods assembled to anoint him with the juice of all the sacred herbs.

And having been crowned by the magnanimous Vasishtha, the priests placed royal vestments upon him ; and Shatrughna bore the immaculate shining canopy, and Sugriva, the King of the Monkeys, the chowry made of Yaks tails, the Lord of the Titans, Bibishana carrying the second, that was as bright as the moon. Thereafter, on Vasava's command, Vayu bestowed on Raghava a brilliant golden garland embellished with a hundred lotuses, and a necklace of pearls enriched with every variety of gem was also conferred on that Lord of Men by Shakra.

The Gods and Gandharvas sang and troops of Apsaras danced at the installation of the virtuous Rama, who was worthy of that honour. The earth too was covered with rich crops and the trees with their fruit and flowers gave forth their fragrance in honour of Raghava. Hundreds and thousands of horses, cows and heifers were distributed amongst the Twice-born by that prince, who had already bestowed hundreds of bulls on the brahmins ; and Raghava gave them thirty crores of gold and rich attire and priceless ornaments.

Then a golden crown encrusted with precious stones, glittering like the sun's rays, was offered to Sugriva by that valiant leader of men, who bestowed two bracelets set with emeralds, the lustre of which rivalled the moon's, on Angada, the son of Bali. And Rama gave unto Sita a necklace of pearls embellished with gems that was without peer and like unto moonbeams, and celestial and immaculate raiment richly embroidered with superb ornaments. Then Vaidehi, the delight of Janaka, prepared to bestow her own necklace on the son of the Wind as a token and, unclasping it from her neck, she looked on all the monkeys and on her lord again and again, whereupon Rama, understanding her gesture and approving it, said to the daughter of Janaka :—

" Give the necklace to whom thou pleaseth, O Lovely and Illustrious Lady ! "

Thereupon the dark-eyed Sita gave the necklace to the son of Vayu, and Hanuman, in whom courage, strength, glory, skill, capability and reserve, prudence, audacity and prowess were ever to be found, that lion among monkeys, adorned with that necklace, looked as radiant as a mountain covered by a white cloud silvered by an aureole of moonbeams.

Thereafter all the elder and leading monkeys received fitting gifts of jewels and raiment, whereupon Sugriva, Hanuman, Jambavan and all those monkeys having been overwhelmed with favours by Rama of imperishable exploits, and received precious gems in addition, according to their merits, with all that their hearts could desire, returned joyfully from whence they had come ; and Rama, the scourge of his foes, lord of the earth, sought out Dvivida, Mainda and Nila and satisfied all their wishes.

Thereupon the festival which they had attended being terminated, the foremost of the monkeys took leave of that lord of men and returned to Kishkindha. And Sugriva, the King of the Monkeys, having assisted at Rama's coronation and being overwhelmed with honours by him, went back to his capital.

Thereafter, Bibishana, that virtuous monarch, having obtained the kingdom of his forbears, returned to Lanka full of glory with the leading titans.

The supremely illustrious and magnanimous Raghava, having slain his foes, ruled his empire in peace, enhancing the joy of his people.

Devoted to virtue, Rama addressed Lakshmana who was fixed in his duty, saying :—

" O Faithful One, aid me in defending the land protected by the ancient kings with their armies. As was the custom of our ancestors in days of yore, do thou share the weight of state affairs with me as heir presumptive."

Yet, despite the earnest entreaties addressed to him, Saumitri did not accept the dignity, and the high-souled Rama conferred it on Bharata. Thereafter that prince performed the Paundarika, Ashvamedha, Vajimedha and other sacrifices of many kinds again and again. Reigning for ten thousand years, he offered up ten horse sacrifices, distributing immense wealth in charity, and Rama, whose arms reached to his knees, the powerful elder brother of Lakshmana, ruled the earth in glory and performed many sacrifices with his sons, brothers and kinsfolk. No widow was ever found in distress nor was there any danger from snakes or disease during his reign ; there were no malefactors in his kingdom nor did any suffer harm ; no aged person ever attended the funeral of a younger relative ; happiness was universal ; each attended to his duty and they had only to look on Rama to give up enmity. Men lived for a thousand years, each having a thousand sons who were free from infirmity and anxiety ; trees bore fruit and flowers perpetually ; Parjanya sent down rain when it was needed and Maruta blew auspiciously ; all works undertaken bore happy results and all engaged in their respective duties and eschewed evil. All were endowed with good qualities ; all were devoted to pious observances and Rama ruled over the kingdom for ten thousand years.

This renowned and sacred epic, the foremost of all, granting long life and victory to kings, was composed by the Rishi Valmiki, and he who hears it constantly in this world is delivered from evil ; if he desires sons he obtains them, if wealth he acquires it.

He who, in this world, listens to the story of Rama's enthronement, if he be a king, will conquer the earth and overcome his enemies. Women will obtain sons as Sumitra and Kaushalya obtained Rama and Lakshmana and Kaikeyi, Bharata.

The hearing of the ' Ramayana ' grants longevity and victory equal to Rama's, he of imperishable exploits. The one who, mastering his anger, listens with faith to this epic, formerly composed by Valmiki, overcomes all obstacles and those who hear this story set forth by Valmiki will return from their journeys in foreign lands and rejoice the hearts of their kinsfolk. They will obtain fulfilment of all the desires they conceive in this world from Raghava, and its recitation will bring delight to the Celestials ; it pacifies the adverse forces in those houses where it is to be found.

Hearing it, a king will conquer the earth ; if he be a stranger he will fare well ; women who hear this sacred epic in their pregnancy, will give birth to sons who are unsurpassed. He who recites it with reverence will be freed from all evil and live long. Warriors should listen to it recited by the Twice-born with bowed heads in order to achieve prosperity and obtain sons.

Rama is ever pleased with the one who hears this epic or who recites it in its entirety and he who does so will obtain a felicity comparable to Rama's, who is Vishnu, the Eternal, the Primeval God, the Long-armed Hari, Narayana, the Lord. Such are the fruits produced by this ancient narrative. May prosperity attend thee! Recite it with love and may the power of Vishnu increase!

The Celestial Beings rejoice in the understanding and hearing of ' Ramayana ' and the Ancestors are gratified. Those who, in devotion, transcribe this history of Rama, composed by the Rishi Valmiki, attain to the region of Brahma.

The hearing of this rare and beautiful poem in this world brings prosperous families, wealth and grain in abundance, lovely wives, supreme felicity and complete success in all undertakings.

This narrative which promotes long life, health, renown, brotherly love, wisdom, happiness and power should be heard in reverence by virtuous men desirous of felicity.

END OF YUDDHA KANDA

BOOK VII.
UTTARA KANDA

CHAPTER I

The Sages pay homage to Rama

WHEN Rama regained his kingdom, having slain the titans, all the Sages came to pay him homage.

Kaushika, Yavakrita, Gargya also, and Kanva, the son of Medhatithi, who dwelt in the eastern region ; Svastiyatreya, the blessed Namuchi and Pramuchi, Agastya and Atri, the blessed Sumukha and Vimukha, led by Agastya, came from the southern region, and Nrishangu, Kavashin, Dhaumya and the great Rishi Kausheya, who inhabited the western region, also presented themselves with their disciples ; and Vasishtha, Kashyapa, Vishvamitra, Gautama, Jamadagni and Bharadvaja came with the seven Rishis who were established in the northern quarter.

Reaching the palace of Raghava, those magnanimous ascetics who shone like Fire, the devourer of offerings, presented themselves at the gate and they were all conversant with the Veda and its component parts and versed in the various traditions.

Addressing himself to the doorkeeper, the virtuous Agastya, Prince of Sages, said to him :—

" Let the arrival of the ascetics be made known to the son of Dasaratha ! "

Thereupon the vigilant guardian of the door, hearing these words from the Sage Agastya, instantly went away and, trustworthy, skilled in the art of procedure, instructed in conduct and gesture, he entered the presence of that magnanimous sovereign, who was as radiant as the full moon, and informed him of the arrival of that Prince of Sages, Agastya.

Learning that those ascetics, who resembled the rising sun, had come, Rama said to the door-keeper :—

" Usher them in with all due respect ! "

Thereafter, when the Sages had entered, Rama rose in deference to them and honoured them with water and the Arghya, bestowing on each a cow.

Then Rama, bowing low, paid obeisance to them and caused raised and costly seats encrusted with gold to be brought, that were covered with cushions of Kusha Grass and antelope skins, and those mighty Sages seated themselves according to rank and, questioned by Rama concerning their well-being, the great Rishis versed in the Veda, who were accompanied by their disciples, replied to him, saying :—

" O Long-armed Hero, Joy of the House of Raghu, all is well with us ! By the grace of heaven we behold thee happy and delivered from thine enemies ! By divine grace, O King, thou hast slain Ravana, that destroyer of the worlds, nor is it any great matter for thee to slay Ravana with his sons and grandsons ! Furnished with thy bow, thou canst undoubtedly destroy the Three Worlds ! By heaven's favour, we behold thee with Sita victorious to-day. We see thee with thy brother Lakshmana, who is devoted to thine interests, in the midst of thy mothers and other brothers, O Virtuous Prince. By the grace of heaven, the Rangers of the Night, Prahasta, Vikata, Virupaksha, Mahodara, Akampana and Durdharsha have perished. By divine grace, O Rama, Kumbhakarna, he, whose monstrous form had no equal in the world, was overthrown by thee in combat. Trishiras, Atikaya, Devantaka and Narantaka, those mighty night rangers, were struck down by thee, O Rama. By the grace of heaven, thou didst measure thy strength against that Indra of Titans whom the Gods themselves were unable to destroy and didst vanquish him in single combat. Assuredly it was no small matter for thee to overcome Ravana in fight but, by divine grace, thou wast able to join issue with Ravani and, in combat, slay him also.

" Once thou wast delivered from his magic bonds, O Long-armed Hero, by heaven's favour, thou didst triumph over that enemy of the Gods who bore down on thee like Time itself ! We marvelled to learn of the death of Indrajita ! By granting us the sacred and agreeable gift of security, thou hast enhanced thy victory, O Kakutstha, O Scourge of Thy Foes ! "

Hearing those pure-souled Sages speak thus, Rama was extremely surprised and, with joined palms, answered them, saying :—

" O Blessed Ones, I vanquished Kumbhakarna and that Ranger of the Night, Ravana, both of whom were filled with valour, why, therefore, do you praise me particularly on account of Ravani ? Since I vanquished Mahodara, Prahasta, the Titan Virupaksha, also Matta and Unmatta who were both invincible, and those great warriors, Devantaka and Narantaka, why this commendation on Indrajita's account ? Did I not overcome those Rangers of the Night, Atikaya, Trishiras and Dhumraksha who were full of courage ? Why, therefore, do you extol me because of Ravani ? In what lay his special power, strength and prowess ? How was he superior to Ravana ? If I may learn it, for this is no command I lay upon you, if it be no secret that you may not reveal, I desire to know it, therefore speak ! Shakra himself was vanquished by him ; in virtue of what boon and from what source did the son derive those powers that his sire Ravana, did not possess ? From whence did this titan gain pre-eminence over his father in combat ? How was he able to triumph over Indra ? Tell me now of all the boons he received, O Foremost of the Sages ! "

CHAPTER 2

The Birth of Vishravas

THUS questioned by the magnanimous Raghava, the illustrious Kumbhayoni answered as follows :—

" Learn, O Rama, of the brilliant exploits of that warrior and how he slew his adversaries without being wounded by them ; but first I shall tell thee of Ravana's birth and lineage, O Raghava, and thereafter of the rare boon accorded to his son.

" In former times, during the Kritayuga, there lived a son of Prajapati, O Rama, and that lord, Poulastya by name, was a Paramarishi equal to the Grandsire of the World Himself. One is unable to enumerate all the virtues he owed to his excellent character and it is sufficient to say that he was the son of Prajapati and, as such, was the favourite of the Gods. He was beloved of the entire world on account of his charming qualities and great wisdom. In order to pursue his ascetic practices, that foremost of Munis repaired to the hermitage of Trinabindu and took up his abode on the slopes of the great Mountain Meru.

There, that virtuous soul, his senses fully controlled, gave himself up to the practice of austerity, but some youthful maidens, whose fathers were Rishis, Pannagas and Rajarishis, wandering in those solitudes, disturbed him. Accompanied by Apsaras, they came to divert themselves in that place and, as it was possible to find fruits in every season and disport oneself in those woods, the young girls constantly went there to play. Attracted by the charms of Poulastya's retreat, they sang, played their instruments and danced, thus in full innocence, distracting the hermit from the exercise of his penances.

" On this, that mighty and exalted Sage cried out in indignation :—

" ' She who falls under my gaze, will instantly conceive ! '

" Thereupon all those maidens, who heard the magnanimous Sage, terrified of the brahmin's curse, left that place ; but the daughter of the Sage Trinabindu had not heard it. Entering the wood, wandering here and there without fear, she was unable to find the companions who had accompanied her.

"At that moment the illustrious and mighty Rishi, born of Prajapati, was concentrating on the sacred scriptures, his soul purified by asceticism. Hearing the recitation of the Veda, that youthful maiden approached, and beholding that treasury of asceticism, she instantly grew pale and manifested all the signs of pregnancy. Thereupon, discovering her condition, she became extremely bewildered and said :—

" ' What has happened to me ? ' Thereafter, realising the truth, she returned to her father's hermitage.

" On seeing her in that state, Trinabindu said :—' What means this strange condition in which thou dost find thyself ? '

" Thereat, with joined palms, the unfortunate girl answered that treasury of asceticism, saying :—

" ' I do not know, Dear Father, what has brought me to this pass. Preceded by my companions, I had gone to visit the sacred hermitage of that great and pure-souled Rishi Poulastya. Thereafter I was unable to find any of those who had accompanied me to the woods but, perceiving the alteration in my body, seized with fear, I returned here.'

" Then that Rajarishi Trinabindu, of radiant aspect, entered into meditation awhile and it was revealed to him that this was the work of the ascetic and, the curse of that great and pure-souled Sage having been made clear to him, he, taking his daughter, went to where Poulastya was to be found and said to him :—

" ' O Blessed One, accept this daughter of mine in all her native perfection as alms spontaneously offered. O Great Rishi, assuredly she will ever be completely obedient to thee who art given to the practice of asceticism and to the mortification of the senses.'

" Hearing the words of the virtuous Rajarishi, that Twice-born One, who was willing to accept the young girl, said :—' It is well ! ' and, having given his daughter to that king of Sages, Trinabindu returned to his hermitage whilst the young wife remained with her consort, gratifying him with her virtue. Her character and conduct so charmed that powerful and exalted Sage that, in his delight, he addressed her, saying :—

" ' O Lady of lovely limbs, I am well pleased with thine outstanding virtues and will confer on thee a son like unto myself who will perpetuate both our houses ; he will be known by the name of Poulastya and, as thou hast listened to me reciting the Veda, he will also be called Vishravas.'[1]

" Thus, his heart filled with delight, did the ascetic speak to his divine consort and, in a short time, she gave birth to a son, Vishravas, who was famed in the Three Worlds and full of glory and piety. Learned, looking on all with an equal eye, happy in the fulfilment of his duty, like unto his sire inclined to asceticism, such was Vishravas.

[1] From the root ' Sru ', to listen.

CHAPTER 3

Vishravas becomes the Protector of Wealth

" THE son of Poulastya, that foremost of Munis, was not long in establishing himself in asceticism like his sire. Loyal, virtuous, devoted to the study of the Veda, pure, detached from all the pleasures of life, his duty was his constant aim.

"Hearing of the life he was leading, the great Muni Bharadwaja gave his own daughter of radiant complexion to him and Vishravas accepted Bharadwaja's daughter with traditional rites and began to consider how he might perpetuate his line and happiness. In extreme delight, that foremost of the ascetics, conversant with his duty, begot with his wife a wonderful child full of vigour, endowed with all the brahmic qualities.[1]

"At the birth of this child, his paternal grandfather was filled with joy, and Poulastya, beholding him, bethought himself how he might make him happy. 'He shall become the " Guardian of Wealth ",' he said in his delight, which was shared by all the Sages, and he gave him a name, saying :—

"'Since the child resembles Vishravas, he shall be known as Vaishravana !'

"Thereafter Vaishravana, retiring to pastoral solitudes, grew up to resemble the mighty Anala, who is invoked at the time of sacrifice and, while he sojourned in that retreat, the thought came to that magnanimous one, 'I will pursue my supreme duty ; the path of duty is the highest path'.

"For a thousand years he gave himself up to asceticism in the great forest and practising severe austerities, performed heavy penances. At the end of a thousand years, he underwent the following discipline—drinking water, he fed on air alone or took no nourishment whatsoever. A thousand ages passed like a single year, whereupon the mighty Brahma, accompanied by the Hosts of the Gods and their leaders, came to the hermitage and said to him :—

"'I am highly gratified with thine accomplishments, O Devoted Son, now choose a boon ! May prosperity attend thee ; thou dost merit a favour, O Sage !'

"Then Vaishravana answered the Grandsire of the World, who stood near and said :—

"'O Blessed One, I desire to be the saviour and protector of the world !'

"In the satisfaction of his soul, Brahma, who was accompanied by the Celestial Host, joyfully answered :—'So be it ! It is my desire to create four Guardians of the Worlds. Now there shall be the region of Yama, the region of Indra, the region of Varuna

[1] Such as self-control, purity, austerity, etc.

and the one sought by thee. Go, O Virtuous Ascetic, and reign over the dominion of wealth! With Shakra, Varuna, the Lord of the Waters, and Yama, thou shalt be the fourth. Receive as thy vehicle this chariot named Pushpaka, which is as bright as the sun, and be equal to the Gods. Be happy, we shall now return from whence we came, having accomplished that which we had to do by conferring this double gift, O Dear Son!'

"With these words, Brahma withdrew to the region of the Gods and when the Celestial Host, with the Grandsire at their head, had gone to the heavenly region, Vaishravana, having become the Lord of Wealth, humbly addressed his sire with joined palms and said :—

"'O Blessed One, I have received a rare boon from the Grandsire of the World, but the divine Prajapati has not assigned me a dwelling place ; do thou therefore counsel me, O Blessed One, O Lord, as to where an agreeable retreat may be found where no suffering comes to any living being.'

"At these words of his son, Vaishravana, the foremost of the ascetics answered saying :—

"'Hear, O Most Virtuous of Men! On the shores of the ocean, to the south there is a mountain named Trikuta. On its lofty summit, which is as great as the capital of the mighty Indra, the ravishing City of Lanka was constructed by Vishvakarma for the Rakshasas and it resembles Amaravati. Do thou dwell in Lanka and be happy! Do not hesitate! With its moats, golden walls, engines of war and the weapons with which it is filled, with its gold and emerald archways, that city is a marvel! The Rakshasas left it formerly in fear of Vishnu and it is deserted, all the demons having gone to the nethermost region. Now Lanka is empty and has no protector. Go and inhabit it, My Son, and be happy! No harm will visit thee there.'

"Hearing the words of his sire, the virtuous Vaishravana went to dwell in Lanka on the summit of the mountain, and soon, under his rule, it was filled with thousands of delighted Nairritas disporting themselves.

"That righteous King of the Nairritas, the blessed Sage Vaishravana, dwelt in Lanka, that city surrounded by the sea and, from time to time, the saintly Lord of Wealth, in the

Pushpaka Chariot, went to visit his father and mother. Hymned by the Hosts of the Gods and Gandharvas and entertained by the dances of the Apsaras, that Guardian of Wealth, radiating glory like unto the sun, went to visit his sire. "

CHAPTER 4

Origin of the Rakshasas and of the Boons they received

THIS discourse of Agastya filled Rama with astonishment. " How was it that the Rakshasas formerly dwelt in Lanka ? ", such was the question that Rama put to the ascetic, shaking his head and casting wondering glances upon him from time to time.

He said :—" O Blessed One, the words ' Formerly Lanka belonged to the Eaters of Flesh ' from thy lips causes me extreme surprise. We have been told that the Rakshasas were the offspring of Poulastya and now, thou affirmest that they owe their origin to a different source. Were Ravana, Kumbhakarna, Prahasta, Vikata and Ravani stronger than they ? Who, O Brahmin, was their first king ? What was the name of that one of terrific strength ? For what fault were they driven out by Vishnu ? Tell me all in detail, O Irreproachable Sage and, as the sun chases away the shade, so dispel my curiosity ! "

Hearing Raghava's fair and eloquent words, Agastya, amazed, answered :—

" Formerly Prajapati created the waters, choosing that element as his source and, thereafter, in order to protect it, that lotus-born One generated all creatures. Then those beings, tormented by hunger and thirst, humbly presented themselves before their author and enquired saying :—

" ' What shall we do ? '

" Whereupon Prajapati, smiling, gave this answer to them all :—

' Protect the waters carefully, O Sons of Manu ! ' Then some said :—' Rakshami ' (we will protect) and others ' Yakshami ' (we will sacrifice). Thus addressed by those afflicted by hunger and thirst, the Creator said :—

" ' Those among you who have said "Rakshami" shall be Rakshasas and those among you who have said "Yakshami" shall be Yakshas.'

" On this, two brothers sprang up, named Heti and Praheti, the equals of Madhu and Kaitabha, who were Rakshasas, oppressors of their foes ; and the righteous Praheti withdrew to the solitudes to practice asceticism, but Heti did all in his power to find a wife and, immeasurably intelligent and of great wisdom, he espoused the sister of Kala, a young girl named Bhaya,[1] who was exceedingly terrifying ; and that foremost of those possessing sons begot a son by the name of Vidyutkesha.

" The son of Heti, Vidyutkesha, was possessed of the splendour of the sun and grew like a lotus in a lake and that ranger of the night, having reached the bloom of youth, his sire resolved that he should wed. In the interests of his son he sought out the daughter of Sandhya, who was his equal in beauty, and Sandhya, reflecting ' a daughter must inevitably be given to some stranger ' gave her to Vidyutkesha in marriage, O Raghava.

" Vidyutkesha, that ranger of the night, having received the daughter of Sandhya, began to divert himself with her as Maghavat with the daughter of Paulomi. After a time, O Rama, Salatantaka was filled with child, as a cloud is charged with water from the ocean.

" Repairing to the Mandara Mountain, the Rakshasi brought forth a child who was as beautiful as a cloud, even as Ganga had been delivered of an infant by the God of Fire. Having given birth to that child, she again desired to disport herself with Vidyutkesha and, forsaking her son, she rejoined her consort. Then the infant who had just been born and was as radiant as the autumnal sun, whose voice resembled the rumbling of a cloud, placing his fist in his mouth cried for a long time, and Shiva, who was following the Path of the Wind, mounted on his bull and accompanied by Parvati, heard the sound of weeping and with Uma beheld the son of the Rakshasi who was crying. Allowing himself to be moved by compassion by his consort, Bhava, the Destroyer of Tripura, made him equal to his mother in age and bestowed immortality upon him. Thereafter the unchanging and imperishable Mahadeva bestowed an aerial car

[1] Bhaya—Fear.

383

upon him that traversed space, in order to gratify Parvati, and she, on her side, also conferred a boon on him, saying :—

" ' The Rakshasas shall conceive instantly and give birth as they conceive ; their children shall at once attain the age of their mothers.'

" Thereafter the highly intelligent Sukesha, proud of the favours he had received, having obtained this great fortune from the Lord Hara, began to range everywhere, displaying himself in his aerial car and resembling Purandara when he obtained heaven.

CHAPTER 5

The Story of the three Sons of Sukesha

" A GANDHARVA named Gramani, who was as effulgent as fire, had a daughter named Devavati in all the beauty of her youth, famed in the Three Worlds, equal to a second Shri,[1] and that virtuous Gandharva, beholding Sukesha to be thus endowed, gave her to him as a second Shri of whom he was the guardian.

"Approaching her beloved consort, who had attained a sovereign state by virtue of the boons he had received, as a mendicant on whom wealth has been conferred, Devavati was highly delighted. United to that woman, the ranger of the night appeared as majestic as a great elephant, the offspring of Aryama. In time Sukesha became a father, O Raghava, and begot three sons, the equals of the Three Sacrificial Fires, Malyavan, Sumali and Mali, the foremost of heroes, rivals of the Three-eyed God ; such were the sons of the Sovereign of the Rakshasas. In repose, they resembled the Three worlds, in action, they were like unto the three Sacrificial Fires,[2] as powerful as the Three Vedas and as formidable as the three humours of the body.[3]

" These three sons of Sukesha, shining like three fires, throve like

---

[1] Shri—The Goddess of Prosperity, Lakshmi.
[2] Three Sacrificial Fires—Garhapatya, Ahavaniya and Dakshina. See Glossary.
[3] Three Humours of the body—Wind, bile and phlegm.

diseases that have been neglected and, learning of the boons their sire had received, which had led him to increased sovereignty and which he owed to his asceticism, the three brothers repaired to Mount Meru in order to practice penance.

" Adopting a rigid and formidable course of austerity, O Foremost of Monarchs, those Rakshasas gave themselves up to fearful mortifications, sowing terror among all beings. On account of their penances, faith, virtue and equanimity, scarce to be witnessed on earth, they agitated the Three Worlds with the Gods, Asuras and men.

" Then the Four-faced Deity,[1] in his marvellous chariot, came to pay homage to the sons of Sukesha and said :—

" ' It is I who am the conferrer of boons ! '

" Whereupon they, recognizing him to be Brahma, the Dispenser of Favours, who was accompanied by the Indras and their Hosts, with joined palms, shaking like trees, answered him, saying :—

" ' If our penance has found favour with thee, O Lord, then grant us the boons of remaining invincible, of destroying our enemies, of living long, of becoming powerful and of being devoted to one another.'

" ' Let it be so ! ' " replied the God, who was a lover of brahmins, to the sons of Sukesha and he returned to Brahmaloka. Thereupon those rangers of the night, O Rama, who had become supremely arrogant on account of the boons they had received, began to harass the Gods and Asuras, and the Celestials with the companies of Rishis and Charanas, being thus persecuted and having no protector with whom they could take refuge, resembled beings in hell.

" Meantime, O Prince of Raghu, the three Rakshasas sought out the immortal Vishvakarma, the foremost of architects and joyously said to him :—

" ' O Thou, who from thine own resources, created the palaces of the great Gods, strong, dazzling and impregnable, do thou in thy transcendent intelligence construct a dwelling for us of our own choosing on the Himavat, Meru or Mandara Mountains. Build us a vast abode equal to that belonging to Maheshvara.'

" Then the mighty-armed Vishvakarma spoke to the Rakshasas

[1] Four-faced Deity—Brahma.

concerning a residence equal to Indra's Amaravati and said :—

" ' On the shores of the southern sea there is a mountain named Trikuta and there is also another named Suvela, O Princes of the Rakshasas. On the central peak resembling a cloud, inaccessible even to birds and which is hewn on four sides, is a city of thirty leagues in extent, covering a space of a hundred leagues in length. Surrounded by golden walls, pierced by gateways and furnished with terraces of gold, it is called Lanka, and was constructed by me at Shakra's command. Go and establish yourselves in that city, O Invincible Rakshasas, as the inhabitants of heaven dwell in Amaravati. When you occupy that Citadel of Lanka with the innumerable Rakshasas who surround you, none will be able to expel you and you will overcome your foes.'

" Thus counselled by Vishvakarma, the foremost of the Rakshasas followed by thousands of their companions went to inhabit the City of Lanka. Surrounded by strong walls and deep moats, it was filled with hundreds of golden palaces and there the rangers of the night began to dwell in great felicity.

" At that time, there lived a Gandharvi named Narmada, O Descendant of Raghu, and she had three daughters born of her own will, who were as lovely as Shri or Kirti. Though not of their race, she gave her three daughters, whose faces were as radiant as the full moon, to those three Indras among the Rakshasas. The youthful Gandharvis of supreme attraction were wedded by their mother under the Uttara Phalguni Constellation, which is presided over by the Deity Bhaga.[1]

" Having accepted their wives, O Rama, the sons of Sukesha diverted themselves with them, as the Celestials sport with the Apsaras. And the consort of Malyavan, Sundari[2] in name and nature, gave birth to many sons—Vajramushti, Virupaksha, Durmukha, Suptagna, Yajnakopa, Matta and Unmatta. Sundari had a daughter also, O Rama, the lovely Anala.

" On her side, the consort of Sumali, whose complexion resembled the full moon, was called Katumati and she was dearer to him than his own life. I will enumerate the offspring that ranger of the night begot with her according to their birth, O Great King :—

[1] Bhaga—An Aditya regarded in the Veda as presiding over love and marriage.
[2] Sundari—The name means ' Beautiful '.

" They were—Prahasta, Akampana, Vikata, Kalikamukha, Dhumraksha, Danda, Suparshwa of great energy, Samhradi, Praghasa, Bhasakarna, Raka, Pashpotkala, Kaikasi of gracious smiles and Kumbhanasi. These, we are told, were the offspring of Sumali.

" Mali's wife was the Gandharvi named Vasuda, who was supremely graceful, whose eyes resembled lotus petals and who rivalled the most ravishing of the Yakshis. Hear, O Lord Raghava, and I will tell thee of the offspring the youngest brother begot with her; they were Anala, Anila, Hara and Sampati; these sons of Mali became the counsellors of Bibishana.

" Meanwhile, those foremost of night-rangers surrounded by hundreds of their sons, in the intoxication of their extreme strength, harassed the Gods and their leaders with the Rishis, Nagas and Yakshas. Ranging the earth, irresistible as the tempest, ruthless as death in combat, overweeningly proud of their boons, they constantly impeded the sacrifices of the Sages.

CHAPTER 6

Vishnu goes to the defence of the Gods

" Thus afflicted, the Gods and Rishis, those treasuries of asceticism, terror-stricken, sought refuge with the God of Gods, Maheshwara, He Who creates and destroys the universe, the Inner Ruler, Who is unmanifest, the substratum of the worlds, the supreme Guru, adored by all. And the Gods, coming to that enemy of Kama,[1] the Destroyer of Tripura, addressed him in a voice shaking with fear, and said :—

" ' O Bhagawat, the sons of Sukesha, wrought up with pride on account of the boons they have received from the Grandsire of the World, those scourgers of their foes, are oppressing the children of the Lord of Creatures. Our dwellings, which should be our refuge, no longer afford us shelter; having driven out

---

[1] Kama—The God of Love, who, having disturbed the meditations of Maheshwara was burnt to ashes by him by a single glance from his third eye.

the Gods from heaven, they themselves assume the rôle of Gods.
" I am Vishnu ", " I am Rudra ". " I am Brahma ". " I am the King
of the Gods ", " I am Yama ", " I am Varuna ", " I am the Moon ",
"Verily, I am the Sun ", thus do Mali, Sumali and Malyavan
speak, those Rakshasas, formidable in combat, who harass us
as also those who precede them. We are terrified, O Lord,
deliver us from fear ; do thou assume a terrible form and subdue
those thorns in the side of the Gods.'

" On this prayer from the united Gods being addressed to
Kapardin,[1] of reddish hue, he, in deference to Sukesha answered
the Celestial Host, saying :—

" ' Nay, I shall not destroy these Rakshasas ; I am not able to
slay them, O Ye Gods, but I shall unfold to you how you may
rid yourselves of them ! This step having been taken, O
Maharishis, go and seek refuge with the Lord Vishnu who will
himself destroy them ! '

" Thereupon, offering obeisance to Maheshwara, with jubilant
cries they presented themselves before Vishnu, though filled with
terror on account of those rangers of the night.

" Bowing down to the God who bears the conch and discus,
they paid him great homage and, in trembling tones, denounced
the sons of Sukesha, saying :—

" ' O Lord, by virtue of the boons they have received, the three
sons of Sukesha, like unto three fires, penetrated into our abode
and took possession of it. Lanka is the name of that inaccessible
citadel built on the summit of the Mount Trikuta ; it is there
that these rangers of the night, our persecutors, have established
themselves. Come to our aid and destroy them, O Slayer of
Madhu ! We take refuge in Thee, be our deliverer, O Lord of
the Gods! Do Thou offer up their lotus-like faces, severed by Thy
discus, to Yama. In time of peril, none but Thee canst give us
shelter, O Lord. As the sun dispels the mist, so do Thou dispel
our terror in regard to these Rakshasas, who, with their adherents
take delight in warfare ! '

" When the Gods had spoken thus, the Lord of Lords, Janardana, who strikes terror in the hearts of his foes, re-assured
them, saying :—

" ' The Rakshasa Sukesha, who, on account of the boons

[1] Kapardin—Wearer of a Kaparda, a particular knot of hair.

received from Ishana, is intoxicated with pride, is known to me and his sons also, the eldest of whom is Malyavan. Those Rakshasas, the vilest of all, exceed all limits and I shall exterminate them in my wrath, O Ye Gods, have no fear ! '

" Hearing the words of the mighty Janardana, Vishnu, each of the Gods returned to his abode, chanting His praises.

" Learning of the intervention of the Gods, that ranger of the night Malyavan, said to his two valiant brothers :—

" ' The Immortals and the Rishis have unitedly sought out Shankara in order to bring about our destruction and addressed Him thus :—

" O Lord, the offspring of Sukesha, intoxicated with pride, by the power they received from those boons torment us without respite. Harassed by these Rakshasas, it is impossible for us, O Prajapati, to remain in our retreats for fear of those wicked ones ; do Thou defend us and subdue them, O Three-eyed God, and, with Thy word of power ' Hum ', burn them up, O Supreme Consumer.

" ' Thus did the Gods speak and the Slayer of Andaka, shaking his head and hands, answered them saying :—

" ' It is impossible for me to destroy the celestial children of Sukesha in the open field but I will tell you the means whereby they may be slain. Let the God who bears the Mace and Discus in His hands, who is clad in yellow, Janardana, Hari, Narayana, the Lord of Shri, be your refuge ! '

" ' Having received this counsel from Hara and taken leave of that enemy of Kama, the Gods went to Narayana's abode and related all to Him. Then Narayana said to the Gods, who had Indra at their head :—

" ' I shall slay all your enemies, O Ye Gods, fear not ! '

" ' O Foremost of the Rakshasas, Hari promised those Gods, who were filled with terror, that He would destroy us. Therefore do what you think fit. Narayana has slain Hiranyakashipu and other foes of the Gods ; Namuchi, Kalanemi, Samrhada that foremost of warriors, and Radheya, Bahumayin, the virtuous Lokapala and Yamala, Arjuna, Hardikya, Shumbha, Nishumbha, all those Asuras and Danavas, full of courage and strength, said to be invincible in the field, who had offered hundreds of sacrifices, were versed in magic and skilled in the use of weapons and who were all a source of terror to their foes. Knowing this, it behoveth us to unite in order to slay the wicked Narayana who wishes to exterminate us.'

" Hearing Malyavan, their elder brother speak thus, Sumali and Mali answered him as the Twin Ashwins address Vasava, saying :—

" ' We have studied the Veda, made charitable gifts, offered sacrifices, safe-guarded our sovereignty, obtained the boon of longevity and freedom from disease and have established righteousness. Plunging our weapons into the bottomless ocean of the Gods, we have explored it ; we have overcome our enemies though their valour was unequalled ; nay, we have nothing to fear from Mrityu, Narayana, Rudra, Shakra and Yama, all hesitate to oppose us ! Since we have come together, let us assist each other mutually and exterminate the Gods, whose perfidy has been revealed to us.'

" Having taken counsel together thus, those huge-bodied and valiant Nairritas hurled themselves into the fray, like unto Jambha and Vritra of yore.

" O Rama, thus resolved, summoning up all their strength, they set out to fight, mounted on their chariots, elephants and horses that resembled elephants, mules, bulls, buffalo, porpoises, serpents, whales, turtle, fish, and birds resembling Garuda, also on lions, tigers, boars, deer and Yaks.

" Intoxicated with pride, all those Rakshasas marched out of Lanka, and those enemies of the Gods determined to lay siege to Devaloka. Perceiving the destruction of Lanka to be at hand, all the beings who inhabited it, recognizing the peril in which they stood, became wholly dispirited, whilst the Rakshasas, borne in marvellous chariots hastened towards Devaloka in hundreds and thousands, but the Gods avoided the path they had taken.

" Thereupon, at Kala's command, terrible portents appeared on earth and in the skies, foretelling the death of the Rakshasa leaders. From the clouds a torrent of hot blood and bones fell, the seas over-passed their bornes and the mountains shook. jackals of formidable aspect howled lugubriously, emitting hoarse laughter that resembled the rumble of clouds. Groups of phantoms passed by in succession, and flocks of vultures, vomiting flames, hovered like fate over the Chief of the Rakshasas. Red-footed pigeons and crows fled in all directions, ravens croaked and two footed cats were seen.

" Disregarding these omens, the Rakshasas, proud of their strength, continued to advance without halting, caught in the noose of death. Malyavan, Sumali and Mali of immense power, preceded the Rakshasas like unto flaming braziers ; Malyavan, who resembled Mount Malyavan, was escorted by all the rangers of the night, as the Gods by Dhatar. That army of the foremost of the Rakshasas, thundering like massed clouds, eager for victory, advanced towards Devaloka under Mali's leadership

" Then the Lord Narayana, learning thereof from a messenger of the Gods, resolved to enter into combat with them. Making ready His arms and quivers, He mounted Vainateya and, having put on His celestial armour which shone like a thousand suns, He strapped on two dazzling quivers full of arrows. Buckling on His stainless sword, that God, Whose eyes resembled lotuses, furnished with His conch, discus, mace, sword, excellent weapons and His bow,[1] fully equipped, mounted the son of Vinata,[2] who was as high as a hill, and thereafter the Lord set out in all haste to slay the Rakshasas.

" On the back of Suparna, the dark-hued Hari, clad in yellow, resembled a cloud transpierced with lightning on the peak of a golden mountain. As He left, with His discus, sword, bow, spear and His conch in His hands, Siddhas, Devarishis, Great Serpents, Gandharvas and Yakshas hymned the praises of the renowned enemy of the Asura Host.

" With the blast of His wings, Suparna struck at the Host of the Rakshasas, bringing down their standards and dispersing their weapons so that they reeled like the dark summit of a mountain whose crags are crumbling away.

" With their excellent shafts however, soiled with flesh and blood, like unto the fires of doom at the end of the world cycle, which they loosed in thousands, those rangers of the night covered and pierced Madhava.

[1] Vishnu's bow, named ' Sharnga '.
[2] Son of Vinata—Garuda.

CHAPTER 7

The Combat between Vishnu and the Rakshasas

" In the midst of rumblings, the clouds in the form of Rakshasas poured down a shower of weapons on the Peak Narayana, as with their torrents they shroud a mountain, and the dark and immaculate Vishnu, surrounded by those swarthy and powerful rangers of the night, resembled Mount Anjana under rain. As locusts in a rice field or gnats in a flame, as flies in a pot of honey, as monsters in the deep, so did the arrows, keen as diamonds, swift as the wind or thought, which the Rakshasas loosed on Hari, piercing him, disappear as the worlds vanish at the time of universal destruction.

" Warriors in chariots or seated on the heads of elephants, soldiers on horseback, infantry stationed in the sky, leaders of the Rakshasas resembling mountains, with their shafts, spears, swords and darts, caused Hari to hold His breath, like unto the Twice-born when practising Pranayama.[1]

" Like an ocean where fishes play, that invincible God, under the countless blows of those rangers of the night, drew His bow and loosed His shafts on them ; then Vishnu with extreme force, like unto lightning, swift as thought, riddled them with His penetrating weapons and spears by hundreds and thousands. Having dispersed them under a load of arrows as the wind a downpour, the Supreme Purusha blew His great Conch Panchajaya, and that king of conches, born of the waters, into which Hari blew with all His strength, re-echoed in such fearful wise that it shook the Three Worlds as it were. The sound of that king of conches struck terror into the Rakshasas, as the King of Beasts in the forest terrorizes the elephants intoxicated with ichor. At the sound of the conch, the horses were no longer able to stand erect, the frenzy of the elephants was subdued, whilst the warriors fell from their cars bereft of strength.

" Loosed from His bow, Vishnu's arrows, possessed of plumed

[1] The science of breath control.

392

hafts, having rent the Rakshasas, penetrated into the earth. Pierced by those darts, which the hand of Narayana loosed in the fight, the Rakshasas fell on the earth like crags struck by lightning, their powerful limbs torn by Vishnu's discus, the blood flowing in torrents, as from mountains secreting gold. The sound of that king of conches, the twanging of the bow-string and the voice of Vishnu stifled the cries of the Rakshasas.

" Then Hari severed their trembling necks, their darts, banners, bows, chariots, pennants and quivers. As the rays fall from the sun, as masses of water spout forth from the sea, as mighty tuskers rush down the mountain side, as torrents of rain fall from a cloud, so did the darts and arrows discharged by Nara-yana from His bow, fall in hundreds and thousands. As a lion before a Sharabha, as an elephant before a lion, as a tiger before an elephant, as a panther before a tiger, as a dog before a panther, as a cat before a dog, as a snake before a cat, as mice before a snake, so did the Rakshasas flee before the mighty Vishnu. Some escaped, others fell in their flight and the rest lay stretched on the earth. Whilst slaying his foes in their thousands, the Destroyer of Madhu filled the conch with his breath, as Indra the clouds with water.

" Put to flight by Narayana's shafts, terrified by the sound of the conch, the army of the Rakshasas, their ranks broken, fled in the direction of Lanka.

" Seeing his troops routed, decimated by Narayana's arrows, Sumali covered Hari with a hail of darts on the battlefield, as the fog obscures the sun, whereupon the valiant Rakshasas plucked up courage. Then Sumali, proud of his strength, rallying his forces, hurled himself forward with a great shout. Shaking his earrings as an elephant his trunk, that night-ranger, in his joy, raised a great clamour like unto a cloud pierced by lightning and, while Sumali cried out thus, Hari cut off the head of his charioteer with its dazzling earrings, and the steeds of that Rakshasa swerved, bearing away Sumali, the leader of the Titans, as those other steeds, the senses, when uncontrolled, bear away man's judgment.

" Thereafter while Sumali was being borne away by the horses of his chariot, Mali, alert, armed with his bow, rushed on the mighty Vishnu who, on his vehicle, had thrown himself into the fray; and he let fly his arrows decorated with gold from his bow, which fell on Hari piercing him, as birds penetrate into the Krauncha Mountain. Assailed by the shafts, which Mali loosed in their thousands in the fight, Vishnu remained as undisturbed as one in full control of his senses in the face of adversity.

" Twanging His bow-string, Bhagawat, the Author of all beings, still bearing his sword and mace, discharged a hail of arrows on Mali, like unto thunder and lightning, penetrating his body, and those shafts drank his blood as serpents a pleasing draught.

" In the confusion into which he had thrown Mali, the God who bears the conch, discus and mace, struck off his diadem and brought down his banner, his bow and his steeds. Deprived of his chariot, that most powerful ranger of the night seized hold of his mace and, with this weapon in his hand, like a lion from a mountain height, hurled himself on the King of the Birds[1] as Antaka on Ishana, striking him on the forehead, as Indra strikes a mountain with his thunderbolt.

" On receiving that violent blow dealt by Mali, Garuda, distracted with pain, carried the God away from the fight, and Vishnu, having turned away through this act of Mali's and Garuda's, a great clamour arose from the Rakshasas shouting in triumph.

" Hearing the Rakshasas shout thus, the younger brother of Harihaya, the blessed Hari, was incensed with that King of Birds who served as his mount and, with the intention of slaying Mali, though his back was turned, He loosed His discus that was as bright as the solar orb, whose radiance illumines the heavens. Like unto Kala's wheel,[2] the discus fell on Mali's head and that terrible head of that leader of the Rakshasas, thus severed, rolled down amidst torrents of blood, as formerly that of Rahu.

" At that instant, the Gods, transported with joy, emitted roars like unto lions, crying with all their strength, ' Victory to Thee, O Lord! '

" Beholding Mali slain, Sumali and Malyavan, in burning grief, took refuge in Lanka with their forces. Meanwhile Garuda

---

[1] King of Birds—Garuda, Vishnu's vehicle.
[2] Kala's Wheel—The Wheel of Time consisting of days, weeks, months, years, decades, centuries and aeons.

having recovered, retraced his steps and, in fury, dispersed the Rakshasas with the blast of his wings. Their lotus faces cut with the discus, their breasts torn by the mace, their necks severed by the ploughshare, their foreheads split open by pikes, some pierced by the sword, some slain by arrows, those Rakshasas began to fall from the skies into the waters of the sea.

" Narayana, like unto a luminous cloud, with his excellent shafts loosed from His bow, as so many lightning strokes, exterminated those rangers of the night with their hair dishevelled and streaming in the wind. Their parasols broken, their rich apparel torn by the shafts, their entrails ripped open, their eyes wide with fear, those warriors, throwing away their arms, fell into a frenzy of terror. Resembling elephants attacked by a lion, those night-rangers with their mounts emitted cries whilst fleeing from that Primeval Lion,[1] who pursued them.

" Overwhelmed by a rain of darts from Hari, they threw away their weapons, and those rangers of the night resembled sombre clouds which the wind drives before it. Their heads severed by the discus, their limbs crushed with blows from the mace, cut in two by strokes of the sword, those foremost of the night-rangers, resembling sable clouds, crumbled like rocks and they stumbled and fell on the earth which they covered completely like dark mountains which have been shattered.

CHAPTER 8

The Combat between Vishnu and Malyavan

" WHEN the army that followed him was destroyed by Padmanabha,[2] Malyavan halted in his flight, as the ocean when it reaches the shore. His eyes red with anger, his head trembling, that ranger of the night said to Padmanabha, the Supreme Purusha :–

" 'O Narayana, Thou art ignorant of the ancient tradition of warriors, since Thou, as if a stranger to their caste, dost slay

---

[1] Primeval Lion—Referring to Vishnu's incarnation as Nrsingha, half man, half lion.
[2] Padmanabha—The Lotus-navelled One.

those who, in their terror, have retreated in the fight. That assassin who commits the sin of slaying a foe who has turned his back on him, O Chief of the Gods, does not attain heaven, as do the virtuous on leaving this world. Assuredly if Thou dost desire to enter into combat, Thou Who art armed with conch, discus and mace, here I stand! Manifest Thy prowess that I may witness it!'

" Seeing Malyavan standing motionless, like unto the mountain of that name, the younger brother of the King of the Gods, in his valour, answered the foremost of the Rakshasas, saying :—

"' I have vowed to the Gods that I will deliver them from the terror thou hast inspired, by slaying thee, I shall honour that pledge. The welfare of the Gods is dearer to me than life itself; therefore I shall destroy you all; now descend into the lowest hell!'

" Thus did the Lord of Lords speak, He Whose eyes resembled crimson lotuses and, filled with fury, the Rakshasa, with his spear, cut open his breast. Wielded by Malyavan's arm, that weapon emitting the sound of a bell, glittered in the breast of Hari like lightning athwart a cloud. Thereafter, He Who is dear to the God Who bears the Spear [2] drawing out that lance, hurled it at Malyavan and, as formerly Skanda loosed it, that weapon, flying from the hand of Govinda, rushed on the Rakshasa like unto a great meteor striking the Anjana Mountain, and it fell on his mighty chest, that was adorned with innumerable diamonds, as lightning strikes a rocky summit. That blow cut his mail asunder and his eyes were veiled but, recovering consciousness, he stood erect once more, like unto an immoveable rock. Armed with an iron club with innumerable spikes, he struck the God violently in the centre of the breast and, in his martial ardour, having wounded the younger brother of Vasava with his fist, that ranger of the night retreated a bow's length. At that moment, the cry ' Excellent, Excellent ' arose in the sky.

" Thereafter the Rakshasa attacked Garuda, and Vainateya incensed, drove him off with the blast of his wings as a violent tempest disperses a heap of withered leaves.

---

[2] The God Who bears the Spear—The God of War, Karttikeya, also called Skanda.

" Seeing his elder brother driven back by the blast of Garuda's wings, Sumali, overcome with confusion, with his troops fled in the direction of Lanka. And thrust back by the violence of the wind produced by those wings, Malyavan also, joined by his forces, fled to Lanka covered with shame.

" O Lotus-eyed Prince, the Rakshasas having been repeatedly defeated in the battle by Hari and having lost the most valiant of their leaders, in their inability to withstand Vishnu, Who was destroying them, abandoned Lanka and went to dwell in Patala with their consorts. O Prince of the House of Raghu, those Rakshasas, renowned for their strength and who were the issue of the Salakatankata Race, remained under the leadership of Sumali. It was Thou Who didst destroy those warriors of the family of Poulastya named Sumali, Malyavan, Mali and their companions, who were all exceedingly resourceful and more powerful than Ravana. None other could have subdued the enemies of the Gods or have weeded out those thorns in the side of the Celestials, save Narayana, the God Who bears the conch, discus and mace. Thou art that Four-armed God, Narayana, eternal, invincible and immutable, Who came to exterminate the Rakshasas. Thou art the Father of all Beings, who, whenever righteousness declines and for love of those who take refuge in Thee, dost appear to wipe out evil-doers.

" O Lord of Men, I have related in detail all that concerns the origin of the Rakshasas. Learn further, O Prince of the Raghus, of the immeasurable power of Ravana and his sons.

" For a long time, Sumali wandered about the nether regions, tormented by the fear of Vishnu, whilst the mighty God of Wealth, surrounded by his sons and grandsons, sojourned in Lanka.

CHAPTER 9

The Birth of Dashagriva and his Brothers

" AFTER a time, that Rakshasa, named Sumali, emerged from the nether regions to range the world of men. With his earrings of pure gold, he, like unto a dark cloud, took with him a young girl who resembled Shri without her lotus and, as that Rakshasa wandered about the earth, he beheld the Lord of Wealth, who in his Chariot Pushpaka was going to visit his sire. Beholding that son of Poulastya, that lord who was as radiant as a God, advancing towards him like unto fire, he, amazed, returned to Rasatala from the world of men.

"Thereafter that exceedingly intelligent Rakshasa reflected 'Which is the best way of increasing our power?' Thus did the foremost of the Rakshasas, who was like unto a dark cloud and was wearing golden earrings, reflect within himself and, having considered awhile, that extremely sagacious Rakshasa said to his daughter Kaikasi, for such was her name:—

"'My Daughter, it is time for thee to wed; thy youth is slipping away and, afraid of being refused, those who are in love with thee do not pay their suit. Striving to fulfil our duty, we seek only thine advantage. Assuredly, thou art endowed with every good attribute and resemblest Shri in person, O Dear Child! A young daughter is a source of anxiety to her father who is concerned for her honour, nor does he know whom she will wed. O Beloved Child, the mother's family, the father's family and the one into which she is received are all three involved in this anxiety. Do thou therefore seek out that blessed ascetic, the foremost of Poulastya's offspring and choose Vishravas, the descendant of Poulastya, O My Daughter. Assuredly thou wilt beget sons equal to that Lord of Wealth, who, in his splendour, rivals the sun.'

"At these words, in filial obedience, that young girl went to seek out Vishravas where he was undergoing penance. At that time, O Rama, that Twice-born, the issue of Poulastya was engaged in the Fire Sacrifice and himself appeared like unto a fourth fire. Heedless of the late hour and, in obedience to her sire, she presented herself before the ascetic and, halting there with her eyes cast down, fixed on her feet, she scratched the earth from time to time with her toe.

"Beholding that lovely girl, whose face resembled the full moon and who shone in her own radiance, that Muni of exalted lineage, enquired of her saying:—

"'O Fortunate One, whose daughter art thou? From whence dost thou come and for what reason or with what motive? Answer me truthfully, O Beautiful One?'

" Thus questioned, the young girl with joined palms, answered:
' By thine own powers, O Muni, thou must be conversant
with mine intentions ! Learn only, O Brahmarishi, that it is by
the command of my sire that I have come, and Kaikasi is my
name: The rest must be known to thee.' Thereafter the Muni,
reflecting awhile, uttered these words :—

" ' I know well, O Fortunate One, what brings thee here, thou
art desirous of having sons by me, thou whose gait is like unto
an intoxicated elephant ! But, having presented thyself at this
hour,[1] hear me, O Fortunate One, thou shalt bring forth offspring of a dark aspect delighting in the companionship of doers
of evil deeds. O Lady of Lovely Form, thou shalt beget
Rakshasas of cruel exploits.'

" At these words, Kaikasi prostrated herself, saying :—

" ' O Blessed One who recitest the Veda, I do not desire such
sons whose nature is depraved, from thee, be gracious unto me !'

" Thus besought by that youthful maiden, Vishravas, foremost
among Munis, like unto the moon in the presence of Rohini,
added :—

" ' O Lady of Lovely Face, the son thou shalt bring forth last
will be like unto me, assuredly he will be virtuous.'

" Thus did he speak to that young girl, O Rama, and after some
time she gave birth to a hideous child with the face of a demon,
exceedingly dark ; and he had ten necks and great teeth and
resembled a heap of collyrium ; his lips were of the hue of copper,
he had twenty arms and a vast mouth and his hair was fiery red.
At his birth, jackals and other wild beasts with flaming jaws
circled from left to right. The God Parjanya let loose a rain of
blood whilst clouds emitted harsh sounds ; the sun ceased to
shine, fierce winds blew and the unchanging ocean, Lord of the
Rivers, was agitated.

" His father, who resembled the Grandsire of the World, thereupon conferred a name upon him and said :— ' This child with
ten necks shall be called Dashagriva.'

" After him the mighty Kumbhakarna was born, that giant who
was unequalled on earth, and a daughter of hideous aspect,
named Shurpanakha, while Kaikasi's last child was named
Bibishana.

[1] That is at dusk, interrupting the Evening Devotions, which was inauspicious.

" When this great being was born, a rain of flowers fell and, in the heavens, celestial gongs resounded whilst an aerial voice cried, ' Excellent ", " Excellent '.

" Thereafter Kumbhakarna and Dashagriva throve in that vast forest and each was exceedingly powerful and they were scourgers of the worlds. The insensate Kumbhakarna ranged the Three Worlds devouring the great Rishis who were fixed in their duty, and yet he remained unsatisfied.

" As for the virtuous Bibishana, ever vowed to righteousness, the study of the Veda being his chief nourishment, he lived as the subduer of his senses.

" After a time Vaishravana, the Lord of Wealth, went to visit his sire in his Chariot Pushpaka and, seeing him flaming with effulgence, the Rakshasi sought out Dashagriva and said to him :—

" ' My Son, behold Vaishravana, thy brother, blazing with glory and behold thy state, who art of the same family, O Dashagriva. Thou who art of immeasurable might, strive to be like Vaishravana himself.'

" Hearing his mother's words, the arrogant Dashagriva experienced a wave of overpowering bitterness, whereupon he formulated this vow.

" ' I swear to thee in truth that I shall become my brother's equal if not his superior in power ; banish any fears that may have entered thine heart ! '

" Thereafter, in his spleen, Dashagriva, accompanied by his younger brother,[1] began to undertake an exceedingly difficult task, undergoing a rigid penance.

(He thought) ' I shall accomplish mine end by asceticism ' and having thus resolved, he went to the lovely hermitage of Gokarna in order to purify his soul. There that Rakshasa with his younger brother performed unsurpassed austerities. Such were his mortifications that he gratified the Lord, the Grandsire of the World, who, in his satisfaction, granted him those boons that would assure him of victory. "

[1] Kumbhakarna.

CHAPTER 10

Concerning the Penances practised by Dashagriva and his Brother

THEN Rama enquired of the Muni :—" How did those highly powerful brothers practice penance, O Brahmana, and of what nature was it ? "

Then Agastya of tranquil mind answered Rama and said :—

" Various were the pious observances of each of them ; Kumbhakarna too, putting forth all his strength, constantly pursued the path of duty. In the heat of summer he stood amidst five fires and, in the rainy season, he took up the Vira posture,[1] whilst in the winter season he remained plunged in water.

" Thus two thousand years passed during which he applied himself to piety and remained on the righteous path.

" On his side, Bibishana, who was virtue itself, intent on duty and of pure soul, stood on one leg for five thousand years. This penance accomplished, troops of Apsaras danced and a rain of flowers fell, whilst the Gods hymned his praises. During another five thousand years, he stood facing the sun, his head and arms raised, his mind fixed in contemplation of the Veda. In this wise, Bibishana, like an inhabitant of heaven in the Nandana Gardens, dwelt for ten thousand years. And Dashagriva deprived himself of nourishment for the same period and every thousand years sacrificed one of his heads to the God of Fire. Thus nine thousand years passed and nine of his heads had been sacrificed to Fire ; when ten thousand years had gone by, Dashagriva prepared to sever his tenth head when the Grandsire of the World appeared, and He, with the Gods, highly gratified, presented Himself before Ravana and said to him :—

" ' I am pleased with thee, what boon shall I confer on thee this day ? Thou shalt not have undergone these austerities in vain. O Thou who art conversant with dharma, speedily choose what boon will most please thee ; thou hast found favour with me, O Dashagriva ! '

[1] Vira posture—The posture which is favourable to the regulation of breath.

" Thereupon Dashagriva, delighted, bowing down to that God, answered in a voice trembling with joy :—

" ' O Bhagawat, for living beings there exists no fear like that of death ; there is no foe comparable to Mrityu, therefore I choose immortality ! '

" Thus spoke Dashagriva and Brahma answered him saying :-

" ' It is not possible to grant thee immortality, choose some other boon ! '

" At these words of Brahma, the Creator of the World, O Rama, Dashagriva replied with joined palms :—

" ' May I not be slain by Suparnas, Nagas, Yakshas, Daityas Danavas, Rakshasas nor by the Gods, O Eternal One, O Lord of Beings. I do not fear other creatures, who, with men, I look upon as mere straws, O Thou who art adored by the Celestials.'

" Thus spoke the Rakshasa Dasaratha, and the Lord, the Grand-sire of the Worlds, who was accompanied by the Gods, said to him :—

" ' It shall be as thou desirest, O Foremost of the Rakshasas ! ' Then, having answered Dashagriva thus, O Rama, the Grand-sire added :—

" ' Hear what great favour I shall grant thee further in my satisfaction. The heads that formerly were sacrificed by thee into the fire, O Irreproachable One, will now grow again as they were before and, O Rakshasa, I will finally confer another boon on thee that is hard to obtain, O My Friend, thou shalt be able to assume any form thou desirest at will.'

" As soon as the Grandsire had spoken thus, the heads of the Rakshasa Dashagriva, that had been consumed by fire, grew again.

" O Rama, having spoken thus to Dashagriva, the Grandsire of the Worlds said to Bibishana :—" ' O My Dear Bibishana, thou whose intellect is fixed on virtue, I am gratified with thee, choose a boon, O Righteous and Pious One.'

" Then the pure-souled Bibishana, who radiated good qualities as the moon her beams, spoke with joined palms, saying :—

" ' O Bhagawat, I have endeavoured to do that which I ought to do. Thou art the Guru of the World ; if, in thy satisfaction, thou dost accord me a boon, then hear me, O Blessed Lord. May my soul ever be fixed in righteousness in the midst of the greatest adversity. Without being instructed, may I be able to use the Brahma Weapon. May whatever thoughts come to me, wherever or in whatever state I find myself, always conform to virtue and may I fulfil my duty! O Most Exalted of Beings, these are the boons I consider to be the most precious ; for those who follow dharma nothing is impossible ! '

" Then Prajapati, full of joy, again addressed Bibishana saying :–

"' O Most Virtuous and Dear Child, let it be as thou sayest, though thou wast born in the Rakshasa Race, O Slayer of Thy Foes, no evil ever enters thy heart ! I grant thee immortality ! '

" Having uttered these words, as Prajapati was preparing to accord a boon to Kumbhakarna, all the Gods, with joined palms, addressed him thus :—

"'As for Kumbhakarna, do not grant him any boons! Thou knowest well how the Three Worlds fear this perverse wretch ! In the Nandana Gardens, seven Apsaras and ten servants of Mahendra were devoured by him, O Brahma, as also Rishis and men. Such are the deeds of this Rakshasa before receiving a boon ; if one is conferred on him, he may consume the Three Worlds ! O Thou whose splendour is immeasurable, feigning to grant him a boon cause him to become bemused ; in this way, the worlds will live in peace and he will receive his just deserts.'

" Thus did the Gods speak, and Brahma, born of the lotus, thought on the Goddess, his consort, and, as soon as he called her to mind, Saraswati appeared at his side and, with joined palms said to him :—

" ' O Lord, I am here, what shall I do ? '

" Then Prajapati answered that Goddess, who had come there, saying :—

"' O Thou who art Speech, be thou in the mouth of that Indra among the Rakshasas and utter that which the Gods desire.'

"' So be it ! ' " she answered and, having entered his mouth, Kumbhakarna said :—

"' To sleep for innumerable years, O Lord of Lords, this is my desire ! '

"' May it be so ! ' " answered Brahma and, with the Gods, he departed.

"The Goddess Saraswati then left the Rakshasa, while Brahma, with the Gods ascended to the heavenly region.

"When Saraswati had departed, Kumbhakarna came to himself and that perverse wretch, in his misfortune, reflected :—

"' How can such words have passed my lips? I must have been bemused by the Gods who came hither.'

"Having received those various boons, the three brothers of flaming energy, returned to the Sleshmataka Forest where they dwelt happily.

CHAPTER 11

Dhanada cedes Lanka to Dashagriva

"SUMALI, having learnt of the boons that the rangers of the night had received, abandoning his fear, emerged from the nether regions, and the companions of that Rakshasa, Maricha, Prahasta, Virupaksha and Mahodara rushed out also full of fury.

"Thereafter Sumali with his friends, surrounded by the foremost of the Rakshasas, sought out Dashagriva and, embracing him, said :—

"' By the grace of heaven, O Dear Child, the desire of my heart has been fulfilled since thou hast received these excellent boons from the Lord of the Three Worlds. The great fear that forced us to abandon Lanka in order to take refuge in Rasatala, into which we were precipitated by Vishnu, has now been dissipated ! Many and many a time, under the threat of that terror, we abandoned our retreat but, being pursued, together we plunged into hell. Thy brother, that crafty Lord of Wealth, took possession of the City of Lanka, the abode of the Rakshasas. If it be possible by conciliation, gifts or force, to regain the possession of it, then do so, O Irreproachable Hero ! Thou wilt then become the sovereign of Lanka and, by thy grace, the Rakshasa Race, that has been disestablished, will be reinstated; thereafter thou wilt reign over us all, O Lord.'

"Then Dashagriva answered his maternal grandfather who stood near and said :—

" ' The Lord of Wealth is mine elder brother ; it is not fitting that thou shouldst speak thus.'

" Quietly rebuked in this wise by that Indra of the Rakshasas, the most powerful of them all, Sumali, being aware of his intentions, did not insist further.

" Some time later, as Ravana continued to reside in that place, Prahasta addressed these significant words to him :—

" ' O Valiant Dashagriva, such a speech is not worthy of thee ; brotherly love is not the concern of heroes ! Hear me ! There were two sisters who loved each other and who were supremely fair ; they were wedded to that Lord of Creatures, the Prajapati Kashyapa, and with him Aditi begot the Gods, those Lords of the Three Worlds, whilst Diti begot the Daityas. To the Daityas, those virtuous heroes, the earth, with its mountains, surrounded by the ocean, formerly belonged. They waxed exceedingly strong, nevertheless they were slain in war by the mighty Vishnu, who gave over the imperishable Triple World to the Gods. Thou art therefore not the only one to act in opposition to a brother, which was done by the Gods and Asuras. Follow my counsel therefore ! '

" Dashagriva, hearing these words was filled with joy and, having reflected a moment, he said, ' It is well ! ' and, in his delight, that same day the valiant Dashagriva with his rangers of the night repaired to the wood bordering on Lanka. Stationed on the Trikuta Mountain, that ranger of the night sent out Prahasta, who was skilled in speech, as his ambassador, and said to him :—

" ' Go speedily, O Prahasta, and speak to the foremost of the Nairritas, addressing him in conciliatory words, saying :—

" ' This City of Lanka, O King, belongs to the magnanimous Rakshasas ! O My Friend, thou didst take possession of it ; it is not just, O Thou who art beyond reproach ! If thou dost restore it to us now, O Hero of unrivalled exploits, I shall be gratified and justice will have been maintained. '

" Then Prahasta repaired to the City of Lanka, whose strong support was Dhanada, and addressed that Lord of Wealth of illustrious lineage in the following words :—

" ' I have been deputed by thy brother Dashagriva, who is near at hand, that long-armed hero who is pious and the foremost of

warriors, to come hither and my words are those of Dashanana,
O Lord of Wealth !

" ' This ravishing city, O Large-eyed Hero, was formerly held
by the Rakshasas of terrible exploits, whose chief was Sumali.
It is on this account, dear son of Vishravas, that Dashagriva asks
thee to restore it to them ; this request is made in all friendliness.'

" Having heard Prahasta, Vaishravana replied in words worthy
of one who is skilled in speech and said :—

" ' Lanka was bestowed on me by my sire when it had been
abandoned by the rangers of the night ; I have peopled it by
inducements of gifts, honours and every kind of privilege. Now
go and bring this answer to Dashagriva—" The city and the
kingdom under my dominion are thine also, O Long-armed
Hero, enjoy this realm without restriction; share this dominion
and its riches with me without division." '

" Having spoken thus, that Lord of Wealth went to visit his
sire and paying obeisance to him related the nature of Ravana's
request, saying :—

" ' O My Father, Dashagriva has sent a messenger to me,
saying, " Give up the City of Lanka that was formerly occupied
by the Rakshasa Race." What shall I do now, O Blessed One,
tell me ? '

" On this enquiry, the Brahmarishi Vishravas, foremost of the
ascetics, said to Dhanada who stood before him with joined
palms :—

" ' Hear me, O My Son, the long-armed Dashagriva has spoken
of this matter in my presence and I have often rebuked him ; he
is exceedingly wicked and, in my wrath, I said to him " Thou
wilt be destroyed ; it were better for thee to listen to my words
which are fraught with reason and integrity ". He is perverse
however, and the boons he has received have so intoxicated him
that he can no longer discriminate between what is just and
unjust. It is on account of my curse that he has fallen into this
lamentable condition. Do thou therefore retire to Mount
Kailasha, that support of the earth, O Long-armed Hero, and
leave Lanka with thy followers at once. In that place the enchanting Mandakini, the most excellent of rivers flows, whose
waters are covered with golden lotuses radiant as the sun, and

Kumuda, Utpala and other varieties of water-lilies of sweet fragrance. Devas, Gandharvas, Apsaras, Uragas and Kinneras sojourn there, constantly disporting themselves. It is not fitting, O Dhanada, that thou shouldst enter into combat with that Rakshasa, for thou art conversant with the special boons he has received.'

" Hearing this reply and obedient to the counsel of his venerable sire, Dhanada left Lanka with his consort, his sons, his ministers, his vehicles and his wealth.

" Meantime Prahasta had sought out the mighty Dashagriva and, with a joyous heart, said to him in the midst of his counsellors :—

" ' The City of Lanka is now free, Dhanada has abandoned it and has departed. Do thou establish thyself therein so that, with us, thou canst fulfil thy duty.'

" Thus did Prahasta speak, and the all-powerful Dashagriva invaded Lanka with his brothers, his army and his court. As the Gods enter heaven, so did that enemy of the Celestials enter that city that Dhanada had just deserted and which was divided by well-planned highways. Enthroned by the rangers of the night, Dashanana installed himself in that city, which was filled with Rakshasas resembling dark clouds.

" The Lord of Wealth, however, in reverence for his father's words, built a city on Mount Kailasha which was immaculate as the moon, adorned with splendid palaces sumptuously decorated, as Purandara constructed Amaravati.

CHAPTER 12

The Marriages of the Rakshasas

" THE foremost of the Rakshasas, having been anointed king, with his brother began to consider giving his sister in marriage. He therefore gave that Rakshasi to the King of the Kalakas and the Lord of the Danavas himself presented Shurpanakha, his sister, to Vidyujjihva.

" This being accomplished, that night-ranger left for the chase and thereafter he beheld the son of Diti, Maya, O Rama. Seeing him accompanied by a young girl, that Rakshasa, Dashagriva said to him :—

" ' Who art thou wandering in the forest that is devoid of man or beast ? How is it that thou art in the company of this youthful maiden whose eyes resemble a doe's ? ' "

"O Rama, to this question, put to him by that ranger of the night, Maya replied, saying :—

" ' Hear me and I will tell thee the truth ! There was a nymph named Hema of whom thou hast already heard. The Gods bestowed her on me, as Pauloma was given to Shatakratu. Full of love for her, I passed centuries at her side when she was taken from me by the Gods. Thirteen years passed and in the fourteenth, I built a golden city which I decorated with diamonds and emeralds by the aid of my magic powers. There I dwelt, deprived of Hema, sad, dejected and extremely wretched. Thereafter, taking my daughter with me, I left that city in order to retire to the forest. This is my child, O King, who was brought up in Hema's lap and here I am seeking a husband for her. A daughter is a great calamity, at least for all those who have regard to her honour. In truth, she is a source of anxiety to the family of her father and that of her mother.

" ' Two sons were also born to me by my wife ; the first was Mayavi, O Dear Friend, and Dundubhi followed immediately. I have told thee the whole truth in accordance with thy wish ! And now, My Dear Son, I would know something of thee, who art thou ? '

" At these words the Rakshasa answered respectfully :—

" ' I am of Poulastya's race and my name is Dashagriva, my father was the Sage Vishravas, who was the third son of Brahma.' "

" On hearing these words of that Indra among the Rakshasas, O Rama, indicating that he was the son of a great Sage, Maya, the foremost of the Danavas wished to give his daughter to him. Taking her hand in his, Maya addressed that King of the Rakshasas, saying :—

" ' O King, this child, whose mother was the nymph Hema, the youthful Mandodari, for such is her name, do thou accept as thy consort.'

" ' Let it be so ! ' answered Dashagriva, whereupon igniting a fire there, he took her hand in his, O Rama. Maya was conversant with the curse that Dashagriva's sire, that treasury of asceticism had pronounced, nevertheless he bestowed his daughter in marriage on him, knowing him to be the offspring of the Grandsire of the World. At the same time, he gave him a marvellous spear which he had obtained through his supreme penances. It was with this weapon that Ravana wounded Lakshmana. Then, having brought about this marriage, the Lord of Lanka returned to that city.

" There, with their consent, he chose two wives for his two brothers ; the daughter of Virochana, named Vajravala, was given by him to Kumbhakarna, and Bibishana received as wife the virtuous Sarama, the daughter of the King of the Gandharvas, the magnanimous Shailusha, and she had been born on the shores of the Lake Manasa.

" At that time in the rainy season, the waters of the Manasa Lake were swollen and the mother of the girl cried out affectionately, ' Do not overflow, O Lake ! [1] ' Thereafter the girl was called Sarama.[2]

" These alliances having been concluded, the Rakshasas gave themselves up to pleasure, each with his own consort, as the Gandharvas in the Nandana Gardens.

" And Mandodari gave birth to a child with the voice of a thunder-cloud, he who is known to thee as Indrajita. Scarcely had he been born than that son of Ravana began to roar with a terrible voice, like unto thunder, and the city was deafened, O Raghava. His father therefore called him Meghanada ;[3] and he grew up in the magnificent private apartments, hidden in the lap of the foremost of women, as a fire is concealed under shavings ; and that son of Ravana filled his mother and father with joy.

---

[1] Saranariddhata—O Lake (Saro), do not overflow'
[2] Sarama—The wife of Bibishana who befriended Sita when in captivity.
[3] Meghanada—The name means ' The roar of a thunder-cloud '.

CHAPTER 13

Ravana's Crimes

" SOME time later, the Lord of the Worlds sent Nidra[1] to Kumbhakarna in the form of overpowering sleep and Kumbhakarna said to his brother, who was present :—

"'O King, sleep holds me in thrall, prepare a refuge for me.'

" Therefore the king selected some artisans, like unto Vishvakarma, who constructed a splendid dwelling for Kumbhakarna, a league in expanse and two in length which was exceedingly sumptuous and secluded. On every side, it was decorated with columns of crystal encrusted with gold ; the stairways were made of emerald with rows of small bells hanging from the carved ivory galleries, the floors being of diamond and crystal.

" All should have been constantly and wholly happy in that place, which was enchanting and luxurious in every way, and which was built by the Rakshasas and resembled a sacred cave in the Meru Mountain. It was there, overcome by slumber, that the mighty Kumbhakarna rested innumerable years without waking.

"Whilst his brother, the mighty Kumbhakarna, overcome by Nidra, slept for thousands of years without waking, Dashanana, of unbridled passions, harassed the Devas, Rishis, Yakshas and Gandharvas and overran their beautiful parks and groves like a madman, laying them waste ; and that Rakshasa churned up the rivers, like an elephant disporting itself, agitating the trees like a violent tempest and striking the hills as if by lightning.

" Hearing of Dashagriva's exploits, the virtuous Lord of Wealth, reflecting that he was his own brother, for the honour of his race and desirous of manifesting fraternal affection, sent a messenger to Lanka in Dashagriva's interests.

" Then the messenger, entering the city, approached Bibishana

[1] Nidra—The Personification of Sleep.

who received him with honour and enquired concerning his visit. After asking about the welfare of Dhanada and his kinsfolk, Bibishana brought him to Dashanana in the assembly hall where he was resting.

"Beholding the king blazing in his own effulgence, the messenger said :—' Hail to thee, O King ' and having paid obeisance with these words, stood silent awhile. At that time Dashagriva was reclining on a sumptuous couch adorned with rich coverings whereupon the messenger addressed him saying :—

"'O King, I bring thee the words uttered by thy brother in their entirety—' Between us two, equality of conduct should exist as among others of our race. A truce to these evil deeds ! From now on comport thyself in a seemly manner and, if possible, take righteousness as thy guide ! I have seen the Nandana Gardens laid waste and, it is said, that the Rishis have been persecuted ; the measures that the Gods are taking against thee are known to me. I have been disregarded by thee on countless occasions, but even if a youthful person err, he should be protected by his relatives.

"' Having repaired to the Himavat Plateau to practice dharma and subjugate my senses, I forced myself to undergo penance in order to gratify the Lord Mahadeva ; there I beheld that divine God accompanied by Uma and a glance from my left eye fell on the Goddess ! "Who is this woman ? " I asked myself, desiring this knowledge and for no other reason, for Rudrani had assumed an unparalleled form. Then the Goddess, by her celestial power, consumed my left eye, which grew yellow and the light became obscured as if by dust.

"' Thereupon I repaired to another vast mountain plateau and remained there eight hundred years observing silence. Having completed that penance, the God Maheshwara came to me and, highly gratified, said :—

"" "I am satisfied with thine austerities O Virtuous and Saintly Ascetic. This vow has been fulfilled by me and by thee, O Lord of Rishis ; none other could have observed a similar mortification. These practices are extremely rigid and I myself formerly followed them also. Grant me thy friendship therefore, O Sinless One, thou hast conquered me and thy penance has been fruitful. As the Goddess, whose form thou didst look upon, burnt up thy left eye, turning it yellow, thou shalt be named Ekakshipingali.[1] "

" ' Having thus contracted a friendship with Shankara, I took leave of him and, on my return, learnt of thine evil conduct. Abandon this impious course that will bring dishonour on our race. The Gods with the hosts of Rishis are considering how they may destroy thee.'

" Hearing these words, Dashagriva, his eyes red with anger, clenching his fists and teeth, answered him thus :—

" ' O Messenger, I knew what thou wast about to utter ! Neither art thou my brother nor is he who sent thee ; for the Lord of Wealth is not speaking in mine interests ! That fool forces me to hear of his friendship with Maheshwara ! This speech of thine is intolerable. I have borne it till now, for he is mine elder brother and, as such, it is not fitting that I should slay him. Now, hearing thine address, this is my resolve—' By the strength of mine arms, I shall conquer the Three Worlds. Solely on his account, I shall dispatch the Four Guardians of the World to the region of Yama ! '

" Having spoken thus, the Lord of Lanka, Ravana, slew the messenger with a single stroke of his sword and gave him to the wicked Rakshasas to devour. Thereafter, ascending his chariot amidst acclamations, in his eagerness to subdue the Three Worlds, he set out to seek the Lord of Wealth.

CHAPTER 14

The Combat between Ravana and the Yakshas

"RAVANA, proud of his strength, surrounded by his six ministers, Mahodara, Prahasta, Maricha, Shuka, Sarana and Dhumraksha, those heroes, who dreamt only of war, departed, as if in his fury he would consume the worlds.

" Then he traversed cities, rivers, mountains, forests and woods and soon came to Mount Kailasha. Hearing that the Lord of the Rakshasas, eager to fight, full of insolence and wickedness

[1] Ekakshipingali—Yellow-eyed.

412

accompanied by his counsellors, had established himself on the mountain, the Yakshas dared not remain there for fear of him. Then they said to each other, ' This is the brother of our King ' and, knowing this, they approached Dhaneshwara and, coming into his presence, they imparted his brother's intentions to him. Thereupon, with Dhanada's permission, they set out joyfully in order to give battle.

" The impact of those valiant troops of the King of the Nairritas was as violent as the sea ; and the mountains seemed to be riven asunder, whilst a furious struggle ensued amongst the followers of the Rakshasas and, seeing his army thrown into disorder, Dashagriva, the ranger of the night, after many encouraging shouts, flew into a rage. Then the companions of the King of the Rakshasas of redoubtable valour, each took on a thousand Yakshas. Smitten with blows from maces, iron bars, swords, picks and darts, Dushana, scarcely able to breathe, was overwhelmed by a rain of weapons which fell thick and fast like hail from the clouds. Nevertheless he remained unmoved under the shafts of the Yakshas, as a mountain that the clouds flood with innumerable showers.

" Thereafter, that hero, brandishing his mace like unto Kala's sceptre, flung himself on the Yakshas whom he hurled into Yama's abode. Like unto fire, flaming up on account of the wind, consuming a heap of grass or dried faggots which are scattered about, so did he destroy the army of the Yakshas.

" And his ministers, Mahodara, Shuka and the others, only suffered a few of the Yakshas to escape, who resembled clouds dispersed by the wind. Overwhelmed with blows and broken, they fell in the fight, filled with fury, biting their lips with their sharp teeth. And some of the Yakshas, exhausted, clung to each other, their weapons broken, and sank down on the battlefield as dykes give way before a surge of waters. With those who were slain ascending to heaven, those who fought rushing hither and thither and the companies of Rishis witnessing the scene, there was not a single space left anywhere.

" Beholding the foremost of the Yakshas scattered despite their valour, the mighty Lord of Wealth despatched other Yakshas and, at his call, O Rama, a Yaksha named Samyodhakantaka instantly rushed out at the head of a large force. Struck by him in the fight, as by a second Vishnu with his discus, Maricha fell to the earth like a star falling from the heights of Mount Kailasha, ts merits exhausted.

"Thereafter, that Ranger of the Night, regaining consciousness, gathered up his strength in a moment and entered into combat with the Yaksha, who having been defeated, fled. Meantime Dashagriva, his limbs loaded with ornaments of gold, silver and emerald, advanced to the very portals of the outer defences and, seeing that Ranger of the Night enter, the doorkeeper sought to prevent him ; but the Rakshasa forced his way in, whereupon the Yaksha seized hold of him. Seeing himself checked, O Rama, he was not discouraged and began to break down the door, whilst the Yaksha, overwhelmed by his blows, streaming with blood, looked like a mountain from which minerals are pouring.

" Though struck by the Yaksha with the door-post, that hero was not slain on account of the rare gifts received from Swyambhu, and in his turn, arming himself with the same post, he struck the Yaksha who, his body reduced to dust, disappeared, leaving no trace.

" Thereupon, witnessing the strength of the Rakshasas, a general stampede took place among the Yakshas, who, mad with terror, sought refuge in the rivers and the caves, throwing away their arms, exhausted, their features distorted.

CHAPTER 15

The Combat between Ravana and Dhanada. Ravana seizes Pushpaka

" SEEING the foremost of the Yakshas fleeing in their thousands, the Lord of Wealth said to the powerful Manibhadra :—

" ' O Prince of the Yakshas, slay that wicked Ravana of evil ways and deliver the valiant and heroic Yakshas ! '

"At this command, the long-armed and invincible Manibhadra set out to fight surrounded by four thousand Yakshas and they hurled themselves on the Rakshasas, whom they struck with blows from maces, bars, javelins, lances, swords and clubs. And they entered into a violent struggle, falling on the foe with the swiftness of birds of prey, crying 'Advance! Advance!' 'Yield!' 'Never!' 'Fight!'

"Beholding that formidable combat, the Devas, Gandharvas, Rishis and Chanters of the Veda were extremely astonished. A thousand of the Yakshas fell under Prahasta's blows in the conflict and that irreproachable Hero Mahodara slew a further thousand, whilst, in his fury, O Prince, Maricha, thirsting to fight, slew two thousand of the enemy in the twinkling of an eye.

"On their side, the Yakshas fought valiantly but the Rakshasas called upon their powers of magic and thus gained ascendancy in the combat, O Lion among Men. While wrestling with Dhumraksha in the great struggle, Manibhadra received a violent blow in the chest from a pike but remained unmoved, and he, in his turn, struck the Titan Dhumraksha on the head whereupon he fell senseless.

"Seeing Dhumraksha wounded and covered with blood, Dashanana hurled himself on Manibhadra in the thick of the fray and, while he was rushing on him in fury, the foremost of the Yakshas, Manibhadra, pierced him with three darts. Wounded, Dashagriva struck a blow at Manibhadra's diadem which fell to one side and, from that day, he was known as 'Parshvamauli'.[1]

"Manibhadra, having been put to flight despite his valour, a great clamour arose on the mountain, O King. From afar, the Lord of Wealth, who was armed with a mace and surrounded by Shukra, Prausthapada, Padma and Shakha, beheld Ravana, and, seeing his brother in the field, having lost all dignity, deprived of his glory on account of the curse, the sagacious Kuvera addressed him in words worthy of the House of his Grandsire, saying:—

"'As despite my warning, thou dost not desist, O Perverse Wretch, thou shalt recognize the consequences in the future, when thou hast fallen into hell. He who through heedlessness drinks poison and when he realises it, in his delusion, does not refrain, will know the results of his act in its effects. The Gods do not necessarily approve even dharmic actions, how much

[1] Parshvamauli—'One whose diadem is awry'.

less those that bring about such a condition as thine; it is because of this that thou art reduced to this state and thou dost not appear to be aware of it. He who does not honour his mother, father, a brahmin or a preceptor, will reap the fruit of his fault when he falls under the sway of the Lord of Death. That fool who does not mortify his body will suffer hereafter, when after death he enters the region that his deeds have merited. No wicked man sees his designs fulfilled as he would have wished; as he sows so shall he reap. In this world, prosperity, beauty, power, sons, wealth and prowess are all attained by pious acts. Given over to such iniquitous deeds, thou wilt go to hell. I will not parley with thee further; thus should one act in respect of evil-doers!'

" At these words of Dhanada, which were addressed to Ravana's counsellors led by Maricha, they being struck, turned and fled. Dashagriva, however, who had received a blow on the head from the mace of that powerful Lord of the Yakshas, did not move. Thereafter Yaksha and Rakshasa entered into a fierce and prolonged duel, experiencing no fatigue, and Dhanada loosed the Fire-weapon on the Lord of the Titans, who parried it with the Varuna weapon. Then Ravana, having recourse to magic, natural to a Rakshasa, transformed himself in a thousand ways in order to slay his adversary, and that Ten-necked One assumed the form of a tiger, a boar, a cloud, a mountain, an ocean, a tree, a Yaksha and a Daitya. Thus, though wearing many forms, his own remained hidden. Thereafter seizing hold of a mighty weapon, Dashagriva, whirling it round, brought that enormous mace down on the head of Dhanada and the blow knocked the Lord of Wealth senseless, who fell covered with blood, like unto an Ashoka Tree whose roots have been severed.

" Then Padma and other Rishis surrounded Dhanada and bore him through the sky to the Nandana Wood.

" Having vanquished Dhanada, the foremost of the Rakshasas, with a joyful heart, as a sign of victory, seized the Chariot Pushpaka, that was furnished with golden pillars and doors of emerald, hung with strings of pearls and planted with trees bearing fruit in all seasons; swift as thought, it ranged everywhere at will in its aerial flight. Possessed of golden stairways, encrusted with gems and with floors of refined gold, that indestructible vehicle of the Gods, a perpetual joy to the eyes and heart, that masterpiece created by Vishvakarma at Brahma's command, with its countless ornaments, was indeed a marvel. All that could be desired was to be found therein and it was of a magnificence nothing could surpass ; neither too hot nor too cold, it was pleasantly temperate at all seasons.

"Ascending that chariot, which he had acquired by his prowess, coursing wheresoever he would, the King Ravana, in his pride and wickedness, deemed himself to have overcome the Three Worlds. Having conquered Vaishravana, he descended from Mount Kailasha and, having by his prowess obtained this great victory, that Ranger of the Night, dazzling in his diadem and necklace of flawless pearls, in his marvellous chariot, blazed like fire.

CHAPTER 16

The Origin of Ravana's Name

" O RAMA, having vanquished his brother, the supreme Lord of the Rakshasas went to the great fen where Mahasena was born ; and Dashagriva beheld that vast and golden expanse of reeds sending forth shafts of light like unto a second sun. Ascending the mountain which rose in the centre of that fen, O Rama, he observed that the Chariot Pushpaka was suddenly deprived of motion.

" Thereupon that King of the Rakshasas, surrounded by his attendants, reflected :—' How is this, the chariot has halted ? Why is it not still moving since it was created to follow its master's will ? Wherefore does the Pushpaka Car not go wheresoever I desire ? Is this not the doing of some inhabitant of the mountain'?

" Then, O Rama, the intelligent Maricha said to him :—

" ' It is not without reason, O King, that the Chariot Pushpaka moves no longer. Without doubt it is only able to serve Dhanada and, since it is separated from that Lord of Wealth, it has become motionless ! '

" As he spoke thus, a fearful yellow and black-hued dwarf appeared, who was extremely stout and possessed a shaven head and short arms; it was Nandi. Approaching that Indra among the Rakshasas, that servant of Bhava, Nandi, fearlessly addressed him, saying:—

" ' Begone, O Dashagriva, the Lord Shankara is disporting himself on this mountain; it is forbidden to birds, serpents, Yakshas, Devas, Gandharvas and Rakshasas to come hither!'

" Hearing Nandi's words, Ravana, with his earrings trembling in his wrath, his eyes red with fury, leapt down from the Pushpaka Chariot and approaching the foot of the peak, demanded:—

" ' Who is this Shankara?'

" Then he beheld Nandi standing at the side of that God, supporting himself on his gleaming trident, blazing in his own effulgence, like unto a second Shankara.

" Beholding that monkey-faced One, the Rakshasa, in his contempt laughed derisively, roaring like a thunder-cloud. Highly provoked, the blessed Nandi, Shankara in another form, said to Dashagriva, who stood near:—

" ' Since thou hast derided me in my monkey form, O Dashanana, by bursting into loud laughter resembling thunder, monkeys, like unto myself in form, endowed with prodigious strength, shall be born to destroy thee and thy race. Armed with nails and teeth, O Barbarian, they will descend like an avalanche of rocks, and swift as thought, thirsting to fight and, proud of their strength, shall crush thy great pride and thy high prowess with that of thine adherents and thy sons. I am well able to slay thee now, O Ranger of the Night, but it is no longer necessary to put thee to death since thy previous acts have already overtaken thee.'

" Hearing these prophetic utterances of that magnanimous God, the celestial gongs resounded and a rain of flowers fell from the sky. Disregarding Nandi's words, the extremely powerful Dashanana drew nearer to the mountain and said:—

" ' As it is on thine account that the course of Pushpaka, in which I was travelling, has been arrested, I shall uproot the mountain, O Cowherd! What is the nature of the power which enables Bhava to sport here continually like a king? He is not aware of what should be known to him and that the moment for him to tremble has come.'

" Speaking thus, O Rama, he seized the mountain in his arms

and shook it violently so that the rocky mass vibrated. In consequence of the mountain quaking, the attendants of the God were troubled and Parvati herself, terrified, clung to the neck of Maheshwara.

" Then, O Rama, Mahadeva, the foremost of the Gods, as if in sport, pressed the mountain with his great toe and, at the same time, he crushed Ravana's arms, that resembled pillars of granite, to the great consternation of all the counsellors of that Rakshasa. And he, in pain and fury, suddenly let forth a terrible cry, causing the Three Worlds to tremble, so that his ministers thought it to be the crash of thunder at the dissolution of the worlds ! Thereupon the Gods, with Indra at their head, stumbled on their way ; the oceans became agitated, the mountains shook, and the Yakshas, Vidyadharas and Siddhas cried out :—' What is this ? Do thou pacify Mahadeva, the Blue-throated One, the Lord of Uma; apart from Him, there is no refuge in the world, O Dashanana ! By hymns and prostration seek refuge with Him, propitiated and gratified, Shankara will look on thee with favour.'

" Hearing the words of his ministers, Dashanana, bowing before Him, worshipped the God Whose standard bears the bull, by the recitation of hymns and innumerable sacred texts. Thus did that titan lament for a thousand years.

" Thereafter the Lord Mahadeva, propitiated, released the arms of Dashanana from under the mountain and addressed him saying :—

"'I am gratified with thy courage and endurance, O Dashanana ! When thou wast imprisoned under the rock, thou didst emit a terrible cry, striking terror in the Three Worlds. For this reason, O King, from now on thy name shall be Ravana, and Celestials, Men, Yakshas and other Beings in the universe shall call thee " Ravana "—" He who causes the worlds to cry out ". O Poulastya,[1] follow the path that pleases thee without fear, thou hast my sanction to depart.'

" Thus spoke Shambhu to the Lord of Lanka and he, in his turn, said :—

"'O Mahadeva, if thou art satisfied, then I pray thee, grant me a boon ! I am not able to be slain by Gods, Gandharvas,

[1] Mahasena—The Lord of War, Karttikeya.

Danavas, Rakshasas, Guhyakas or Nagas nor by any other great Beings, I do not take man into account deeming him to be too insignificant. I have been granted a long life by Brahma, O Destroyer of Tripura, but I desire a further lease of life ; do thou confer this upon me, as also a weapon.'

" Thus spoke Ravana, and Shankara bestowed an exceedingly bright sword upon him, famed as Chandrahasa.[1] Thereafter the Lord of Creatures accorded him a further lease of life and, handing him the weapon, Shambhu said :—

" ' Never treat this weapon with contempt, if thou dost disregard it, it will assuredly return to me ! '

" Having received his name from that great God Maheshwara, Ravana paid obeisance to him and re-ascended his aerial Car Pushpaka. Thereafter, O Rama, he began to range the entire world subduing the foremost of warriors, irresistible in combat and those who were filled with courage and boiling with ardour, who dreamt only of war and who perished with their troops by refusing to submit to him. But those, who knew Ravana to be invincible, showed themselves to be more wary and said to that titan, proud of his strength, ' We have been vanquished ! '

CHAPTER 17

The Story of Vedavati

" O KING, when the long-armed Ravana was ranging the earth, he came to the Himalayan Forest and began to explore it. There he beheld a young girl, radiant as a goddess, wearing a black antelope skin and matted locks, leading the life of an ascetic. Seeing the youthful and lovely girl who was given over to austere practices, he was overcome by desire and enquired of her laughingly :—

" ' Why, O Blessed One, hast thou adopted a life so ill-fitted to thy years ? Assuredly such vagaries do not agree with thy beauty, O Timid Lady, a beauty that nothing surpasses, and which inspires others with desire, should not be hidden.

[1] He being a descendant of Poulastya.

" 'Whose daughter art thou, O Fortunate One? From whence springs thy way of life? Who is thy consort, O Youthful Lady of lovely looks? He with whom thou art united is fortunate indeed! I beg of thee to tell me all; why these mortifications?'

" Being thus questioned by Ravana, that young girl, radiant with beauty and rich in ascetic practices, having offered him the traditional hospitality, replied :—

" 'My Sire is named Kushadwaja, a Brahmarishi of immeasurable renown, the illustrious son of Brihaspati, whom he equals in wisdom. I, his daughter was born of the speech of that magnanimous One, whose constant pursuit is the study of the Veda; my name is Vedavati. At that time, the Devas, Gandharvas, Yakshas, Rakshasas and Pannagas approached my sire to ask for my hand but my father did not wish to give me in marriage to them, O King of the Rakshasas, for the reason which I shall now unfold to thee; listen attentively, O Lion among Heroes!

" ' My Sire had chosen Vishnu, Chief of the Gods, Lord of the Three Worlds Himself, to be my consort and on this account he would not permit me to wed any other. Hearing this the King of the Daityas, Shumbhu, proud of his strength, was highly provoked and, during the night, while my father slept, he was slain by that wicked one. My unfortunate mother, who till then, had been so happy, embracing my father's body, entered the fire.

" ' Now I desire to fulfil his will regarding Narayana; it is He to whom I have given my heart. With this intention I am undergoing a rigid penance. I have told thee all, O King of the Rakshasas; Narayana is my lord; I desire no other than the Supreme Purusha. For the sake of Narayana, I have undergone these severe mortifications. Thou art known to me, O King, go hence, thou the offspring of Poulastya. By the grace of mine austerities I know all that has taken place in the Three Worlds.'

" Thereupon Ravana, dismounting from his chariot, overcome by the darts of the God of Love, once more addressed that young girl of severe penances, saying :—

" ' O Lady of Lovely Hips, thou art presumptuous in harbouring such an ambition; it is to the aged that the accumulation of merit accrues, O Thou whose eyes resemble a fawn's. Thou art possessed of the beauty of the Three Worlds, O Timid Lady, but thy youth is passing away; I am the Lord of Lanka and am called Dashagriva ! Become my consort and enjoy every delight according to thy whim. Who is this whom thou callest Vishnu ? In valour, asceticism, magnificence and strength, the one thou lovest cannot compare with us, O Fortunate and Youthful Lady ! '

"As he spoke thus, Vedavati cried out ' For shame ! For shame ! ' and thereafter addressed that Ranger of the Night further, saying :—

" ' Who, had he any wisdom, would fail to pay homage to the Supreme Lord of the Three Worlds, Vishnu, Who is universally revered, save thou, O Indra among the Rakshasas ? '

"At these words of Vedavati, that Ranger of the Night seized hold of the hair of that young girl, whereupon Vedavati, in indignation, cut off her hair with her hand which had been transformed into a sword. Burning with anger, she, as if she would consume that night-ranger, kindled a brazier and, in her eagerness to yield up her life, said to him :—

" ' Soiled by thy contact, O Vile Rakshasa, I do not desire to live and shall throw myself into the fire before thine eyes. Since thou hast affronted me in the forest, O Wretch, I shall be reborn for thy destruction. It is not possible for a woman to slay an evil man and, if I curse thee, my penances will be rendered void ; if, however, I have ever given anything in charity or offered any sacrifice, may I be of immaculate birth and the noble daughter of a virtuous man.'

" So speaking, she threw herself into the fire that she had ignited, and straightway a rain of flowers fell.

" Vedavati is the daughter of Janaka, her supposed father, O Strong-armed Lord, and thy consort, for thou art the eternal Vishnu. That woman, who, in anger, formerly cursed the enemy who resembled a mountain, destroyed him by appealing to thy supernatural power. Thus that goddess was reborn among men, springing up like a flame on the altar, from a field which was turned by the blade of a plough. First she was born as Vedavati in the Golden Age and subsequently, in the Silver Age, she was re-born in the family of the magnanimous Janaka in the race of Mithila, for the destruction of that Rakshasa."

CHAPTER 18

The Gods assume a thousand Forms in fear of Ravana

" VEDAVATI having entered the fire, Ravana remounted his chariot and began to range the earth once more. Having reached Ushirabija, he beheld the King Marutta performing a sacrifice in company with the Gods.

"A Brahmarishi named Samvarta, the brother of Brihaspati himself, conversant with the tradition, was assisting amidst the Celestial Host. Perceiving the Rakshasa, rendered invincible on account of the boons he had received, the Gods, fearing an outrage on his part, assumed the shape of animals.

" Indra became a peacock, Dharmaraja a crow, Kuvera a chameleon and Varuna a swan. The other Deities having escaped in a like manner, O Slayer of Thy Foes, Ravana penetrated into the place of sacrifice like an unclean dog.

"Approaching the king, Ravana, the Lord of the Rakshasas said to him :—

" ' Fight or submit ! '

" Then the monarch replied, ' Who art thou ? ' to which Ravana, with a sneering laugh, answered :—

" ' I am charmed with thy simplicity, seeing thou dost not flee before me, Ravana, the younger brother of Dhanada. In the Three Worlds can there be any other who is ignorant of my strength, I who vanquished my brother and carried off his aerial car ? '

" Then the King Marutta answered Ravana, saying :—

" ' Forsooth thou art highly fortunate that thou hast triumphed over thine elder brother in combat. None in the Three Worlds can equal thee in glory, yet unrighteous deeds can never be commended. Having committed this foul act, thou dost preen thyself on having vanquished thy brother ! What course of asceticism didst thou follow formerly that has earned thee this boon ? I have never heard aught equal to that which thou hast related to me. Halt where thou standest ; never shalt thou approach me alive! This very hour, with my sharp arrows, I shall send thee to the abode of death!'

"Speaking thus, the king, armed with his bow and arrows, in the height of anger, rushed out, but Samvarta barred the way; then the great Rishi said to Marutta:—

"'Hear the words inspired by my attachment for thee! Thou shouldst not enter into combat. If this sacrifice in honour of Maheshwara remain uncompleted, thy race will be destroyed. How can one, who has undertaken a sacrifice, fight? How can he show anger? Further, it is doubtful that thou wilt triumph; the Rakshasa is difficult to overcome.'

"Hearing the words of his Guru, Marutta, that Lord of the Earth, throwing away his bow and arrows, grew calm and gave himself wholly to the ceremony.

"Then Shuka, deeming he had accepted defeat, proclaimed with shouts of triumph, 'Ravana is the victor!'

"Having devoured the great Rishis, who were present at the sacrifice, Ravana, gorged with their blood, began to range the earth once more. When he had departed, the Celestials with Indra at their head returned and spoke to those creatures whose forms they had borrowed.

"In his delight, Indra said to the peacock, whose tail was dark blue:—

"'I am pleased with thee, O Virtuous Bird, thou shalt have nothing to fear from serpents; thou shalt bear a thousand eyes on thy tail and shalt manifest thy joy when it rains, as a testimony of my satisfaction.'[1]

"Such was the boon conferred on the peacock by that great lord. O Monarch, the tails of peacocks, which were dark blue formerly, have become brilliantly hued on account of this boon.

"O Rama, Dharmaraja then said to the crow, who had perched on the sacrificial post:—

"'O Bird, I am gratified with thee, listen to mine auspicious words. Thou shalt not be visited by the various diseases to which all beings are subject, for thou hast gratified me, be assured thereof! Through the grace of the boon I shall confer on thee, O Bird, thou shalt have no need to fear death and shalt

[1] Indra being the 'Bringer of Rain'.

live long, till thou art slain by man. Those inhabiting my empire, who are tormented by hunger, shall be satisfied, as also their kinsfolk when thou hast fed.'

" Varuna, in his turn, said to the swan, the King of Winged Creatures, who was disporting itself in the waters of the Ganges :-
" ' Thou shalt appear in a ravishing and graceful form, radiant as the lunar orb, supremely beautiful, white as pure foam. In contact with mine element,[1] thou wilt rejoice continually. Thou shalt taste a happiness that is unparalleled, which will be the mark of mine approval ! '

" O Rama, formerly swans were not wholly white, their wings were dark at the tips and their breasts were the colour of emerald.

" In his turn, Kuvera addressed the chameleon who was resting on a rock and said :—

" ' I confer on thee a golden hue on account of the pleasure thou hast given me. Thy head will be of an unalterable golden colour as a mark of my favour.'

" Such were the boons conferred on those creatures after the sacrifice of the Gods, who, when the ceremony had been completed, returned with their king to their abode."

CHAPTER 19

*Ravana fights with Anaranya who dies prophesying
the Rakshasa's End*

" HAVING triumphed over Marutta, the Lord of the Rakshasas, Dashanana, ranged the royal cities thirsty for combat and, approaching the mighty monarchs who were the equals of Mahendra and Varuna, that Lord of the Titans said to them, ' Fight or submit ! Thus have I resolved, there is no escape for you ! '

" Thereupon, though not faint-hearted, those sagacious monarchs, fixed in their duty, took counsel together and, despite their great strength, recognizing the superior power of their foe, O Dear Child, all those princes, Dushkanta, Suratha, Gadhi, Gaya and the King Pururava, said to him :—' We are defeated ! '

[1] Literally ' My body '—water, Varuna being the Lord of Rivers.

"Then Ravana, the Lord of the Rakshasas approached Ayodhya, which was as strongly fortified by Anaranya as Amaravati by Shakra. Presenting himself before that lion among men, a king who was equal to Purandara in valour, Ravana said :—

" ' Enter into combat with us or admit defeat, such is our mandate ! '

" The King of Ayodhya, Anaranya, hearing that wicked Monarch of the Rakshasas speak thus, answered indignantly :—

" ' O Lord of the Titans, I accept thy challenge, stay and make thy preparations speedily as I too shall make mine.'

" Thereafter, though already overcome by that which he had heard related and despite his great prowess, the king with his army set out, in an attempt to slay Ravana, with his elephants numbering ten thousand, his horses a million, his chariots in their thousands and his infantry, which, O Prince, covered the whole earth. And that force rushed out to fight with its infantry and cavalry and a terrific and extraordinary struggle ensued between the King Anaranya and the Lord of the Rakshasas.

" In the grip of Ravana's forces, the army of that monarch, having fought for a long time and manifested supreme courage, was entirely destroyed as a libation poured into a fire is wholly consumed. Coming in contact with those ranks projecting flames, the remaining battalions were completely annihilated like moths that enter a brazier.

" Beholding his vast army obliterated as hundreds of streams disappear in the sea in which they empty themselves, the king, transported with fury, stretching his bow, that resembled Shakra's, advanced in the height of anger towards Ravana whereupon his followers, Maricha, Shuka and Sarana, fled like deer. Then that descendant of Ikshvaku loosed eight hundred arrows on the head of the Sovereign of the Rakshasas but, as showers loosed from the clouds on the summit of a mountain, those shafts fell upon him without inflicting a single wound.

" Meantime the Lord of the Rakshasas, provoked, struck the face of Anaranya, unseating that king from his chariot so that the monarch, trembling convulsively, fell to the earth helpless, as a Sala Tree struck down in the forest by a lightning stroke. Then the Rakshasa mockingly enquired of that descendant of the Ikshvaku Race, saying :—

" ' What hast thou gained by entering into combat with me ?
In the Three Worlds, none can stand against me, O Chief of
Men ! I deem that thou art immersed in pleasure and hast not
even heard of my prowess ! '

" Thus spoke Ravana and the king, scarcely breathing,
answered :—

" ' What can I do now ? Assuredly fate is inexorable ! It is
not thou who hast conquered me, O Rakshasa, despite thy boast-
ings, it is Time that has overwhelmed me ; he is the true
author of death ! What can I do, now that I have come to the
end of my days ? Nay, O Rakshasa, I did not turn back in this
fight with thee in which I am about to succumb but, on account
of thy disregard for one of the magnanimous Ikshvakus, I tell
thee this, O Rakshasa:—if I have ever given anything in charity,
if I have ever undertaken a sacrifice, if I have ever practiced a
rigid penance, if I have protected my subjects, may my words
prove true—in the House of the magnanimous Ikshvakus will be
born a warrior named Rama, the son of Dasaratha, who will
extinguish thy vital breaths ! '

"As this curse was being pronounced, the sound of celestial
gongs could be heard and, from the cloud-covered sky, a rain of
flowers fell. Thereafter the king, that Indra among Monarchs,
ascended to the region of Trivishtapa, and that sovereign having
entered heaven, the Rakshasa went away."

CHAPTER 20

Ravana's Meeting with the Sage Narada

"As the King of the Rakshasas was ranging the earth, sowing
terror amongst its inhabitants, he beheld Narada, that foremost
of Munis, riding on a cloud and, having paid obeisance to him
and enquired as to his welfare, Dashagriva questioned him
concerning his presence there. Then Narada, the supremely
illustrious and celestial Rishi of immeasurable effulgence,
stationed on the peak of a cloud, replied to Ravana who stood in
the aerial Car Pushpaka, saying :—

" ' O King of the Rakshasas, O My Friend, stay a moment ! O Son of Vishravas, Offspring of a noble Race, I am gratified by thy valiant exploits. Vishnu, overcoming the Daityas, pleased me and thou also hast filled me with delight by harassing the Gandharvas and Uragas and exterminating them. I will tell thee something that should be known to thee if thou art willing to hear it ! Pay attention to my words, My Dear Son !

" ' Why destroy the world, O Dear Child, thou whom the Gods cannot slay ? This world passes away and is under the power of Mrityu ; it is not worthy of thee to harass the world of mortals, thou who may not be destroyed by Suras, Danavas, Daityas, Yakshas, Gandharvas and Rakshasas. Who would slay creatures who are ever bewildered in respect to their welfare and a prey to great calamities ? Who would strike a world such as this which is overcome by age and disease ? What wise man would enjoy making war on this world of men amidst a perennial stream of every kind of affliction that visits it on all sides ? How can one torment this world which is perishable, smitten by divine forces, hunger, thirst and old age and assailed by misfortune and disappointment ?

" ' Sometimes, full of joy, men give themselves up to music and dancing, whilst others are crying out in distress, their faces streaming with tears that fall from their eyes. Through attachment to mother, father, children or in affection for their consorts, they rush into ills they know not, then why torment a world already brought low by nescience ? Assuredly thou hast heretofore subdued the world of men, O Dear One ! Thou shouldst undoubtedly descend to Yama's abode ; it is Yama whom thou shouldst overcome, O Poulastya,[1] O Thou the penetrator of hostile citadels. When death is subdued, verily the whole universe is subdued.'

" Thus spoke Narada, radiant in his own effulgence, whereupon the Lord of Lanka began to laugh and paying obeisance to him, replied :—

" ' O Great Rishi, thou who findest felicity in the company of the Gods and Gandharvas and who takest delight in warfare, I am resolved to descend into Rasatala for the purpose of conquest and, having triumphed over the Three Worlds and placed the

[1] Ravana is here addressed as a descendant of Poulastya.

428

Serpent Race and the Gods under my yoke, I shall churn up the ocean containing the Nectar of Immortality.'

" Thereafter, the blessed Rishi Narada asked Dashagriva :—

" ' Why therefore dost thou remain here engaged in another path ? ' Assuredly the way that leads to the City of Yama, the King of the Dead, is extremely hard, O Invincible Hero, O Scourge of thy Foes.'

" Thereat, bursting into laughter, like unto the crash of thunder in autumn, Dashanana cried out: —

" ' Verily it is accomplished ! ' Then he added, ' Resolved to slay Vaivasvata, O Great Brahmin, I shall go to the southern region, where that king, born of Surya, dwells. Truly, O Most Blessed One, in mine anger and martial ardour, I swear I shall overcome the four Guardians of the World ! Here am I, ready to march against the city of the King of the Pitris. I shall compass the end of Mrityu, he who plunges all beings into mourning.'

" Having spoken thus to the Muni and taken leave of him, Dashagriva went away and entered the southern region accompanied by his ministers.

" Narada however, filled with brahmanic ardour stood awhile plunged in thought and, as he pondered, that Indra among ascetics resembled a smokeless fire.

" He reflected :—' How can death be overcome, he who afflicts the Three Worlds with their rulers and all animate and inanimate beings, visiting them with just retribution at the termination of their lives ? He, the witness of their offerings and sacrifices, like unto a second Pavaka ; he, whose power energises the worlds when beings attaining consciousness put forth their activity, and in fear of whom the Three Worlds are disturbed. He before whom the Three Worlds flee in terror, how dare that foremost of Rakshasas stand before him ? He who is Vidhatar and Dhatar, the distributor of rewards and punishments in accordance with men's deeds; he the conqueror of the Three Worlds, how can Ravana overcome him ? And if he does subdue him, what other order will he establish ? Curiosity urges me to descend into Yama's abode in order to witness the duel between Yama and that Rakshasa in person.' "

CHAPTER 21

Ravana goes to the Nether Regions to challenge Yama

" Reflecting thus, the foremost of the ascetics departed with a light step for Yama's abode in order to acquaint him with what had taken place and there he found the God Yama before a fire, dealing out justice to every being according to his deserts.

" Then Yama, becoming aware of the presence of that great Rishi Narada, offering him a comfortable seat and the Arghya, according to tradition, said to him :—

" ' O Devarishi, is all well or is righteousness in jeopardy ? Wherefore hast thou come hither, thou who art revered by the Gods and Gandharvas ? '

" Thereupon Narada, that blessed Rishi, answered him saying :—

" ' Hear what I have to tell thee and do what thou considerest fitting ! That ranger of the night, named Dashagriva, is coming here to overthrow thee by the force of his will, though thou art invincible. It is on this account that I have come hither in all haste, fearing what would befall thee, O Lord Who bearest the Rod.'[1]

"At that instant, they beheld the Rakshasa's chariot, bright as the sun, approaching in the distance ; and the mighty Dashagriva advancing in the dazzling Pushpaka Car dispelled the darkness of the region of death.

" On all sides that long-armed hero beheld those who were eating the fruit of their good and evil acts and he observed the soldiers of Yama and his attendants, ferocious beings of formidable and hideous aspect. He saw those undergoing torment emitting loud cries, giving themselves up to bitter lamentations, devoured by worms and fierce dogs, uttering shrieks that rent the ears, filling all with terror ; and those who were crossing the Vaitarani River, which flowed with blood, sinking at each step into the burning sands which scorched them ; and malefactors

[1] The Rod of Punishment.

being cut to pieces in the Asipatra Wood[1] or plunged in the Raurava region[2] or the Ksharanadi[3] or slashed with Kshuradharas[4], crying out for water, tortured by hunger and thirst, emaciated, afflicted, pale, their hair in disarray, besmeared with mud and filth, stricken and demented, running hither and thither. And Ravana beheld them in hundreds and thousands on the way, and he saw others in palaces, where songs and musical instruments could be heard, disporting themselves as the result of their good deeds. And milk was supplied to those who had given kine in charity and rice to those who had distributed rice, and dwellings to those who had bestowed dwellings on others ; each reaping the fruit of his own deeds. Others among the virtuous were surrounded by youthful women adorned with gold, precious gems and magnificent pearls, resplendent in their own radiance ; all these appeared to the long-armed Ravana, Lord of the Rakshasas.

" Then those who were in torment as a punishment for their evil deeds, were audaciously liberated by the Rakshasa who was powerful and valiant, and those phantoms, suddenly receiving that unexpected clemency, set free by that mighty monarch, rushed upon him, and a great clamour arose, whereupon the soldiers belonging to Dharmaraja, who were full of courage, ran to that spot.

"Armed with arrows, iron bars, spears, maces, lances and picks in their hundreds and thousands, they attacked the Pushpaka Car bravely. Seats, upper galleries, floors and arches were rapidly demolished by those warriors who fell upon it like a swarm of bees ; but the celestial aerial car, though broken, was indestructible and resumed its former shape through Brahma's power. That great army of the magnanimous Yama was not to be counted and the advance guard alone numbered a hundred thousand warriors.

" Trees, rocks, missiles in their hundreds were thrown in profusion with all their strength by those valiant followers of Dashanana and by the king himself. Although their limbs were covered with blood and lacerated by every kind of missile, the

[1] Asipatravana—A wood in hell where the leaves are as sharp as swords.
[2] Raurava—Another hell.
[3] Ksharanadi—A river in hell, the waters of which were said to be corrosive.
[4] Kshuradhara—A sharp razor-like instrument.

ministers of the foremost of the titans fought like giants and the foremost of warriors, the intrepid soldiers of Yama and Ravana's followers struck each other with redoubled blows, O Prince. Thereafter, leaving their adversaries, Yama's forces rushed on Dashanana with their spears, and the King of the Rakshasas, his body streaming with blood, shone like an Ashoka Tree in flower.

" Meantime, spears, maces, javelins, lances, darts, arrows, rocks and trees poured from the mighty bow of that courageous warrior. A formidable shower of trees, stones and weapons of all sorts fell on the forces of Yama and thereafter on the earth.

" Having severed all those missiles and repelled that hail of projectiles, the soldiers of Yama struck that redoubtable titan, who fought single-handed against hundreds and thousands and they all surrounded him like a mass of clouds round a mountain and, with their Bhindipalas and their spears, they assailed him with such force that he could scarcely breathe. His coat of mail severed, cut to pieces midst rivers of blood flowing from his person, full of rage, he abandoned Pushpaka and leapt to the earth. Furnished with his bow and arrows, he expanded in energy in the combat and speedily regaining his senses, full of fury, he stood there like a second Antaka. Placing the celestial shaft, Pashupata[1] on his bow and bending it, he cried ' Stay ! Stay ! ' and, stretching the cord up to his ear, he loosed that missile in the fight, as Shankara when attacking Tripura.

"And that dart with its circle of fire and smoke resembled a blazing fire that, growing, consumes a forest during the summer season. With its crown of flames, that shaft, loosed by that eater of flesh, ranged the field of battle freely, reducing the bushes and trees to ashes. Then the soldiers of Vaivasvata fell like the standards of the Great God Indra, consumed by the violence of the blaze, and that Rakshasa of formidable prowess, with his companions uttered a great roar which convulsed the earth."

[1] The weapon of Shiva.

CHAPTER 22

The Duel between Ravana and Yama; Brahma intervenes

" HEARING that great tumult, the Lord Vaivasvata realised his enemy had triumphed and that his army was destroyed. Knowing his forces were slain, his eyes red with anger, he addressed his charioteer, saying :—

" ' Take my chariot there speedily ! '

" Thereupon the driver brought the vast celestial car of his most powerful master and that exceedingly energetic one ascended it. And Mrityu, the destroyer of the Triple World of perpetual change, with a lance and mallet in his hand and Time as his Rod, stood at Yama's side ; and that divine weapon blazed like fire.

" Beholding Kala[1] highly enraged, inspiring terror in the whole universe, the Three Worlds were agitated and the inhabitants of heaven were seized with fear. Thereafter the charioteer urged on his steeds that were the colour of blood, and drove his thundering chariot to meet the Lord of the Rakshasas ; and, in an instant, his horses, the equals of those belonging to Hari, carried Yama with the speed of thought to the scene of the combat.

" Seeing that terrible chariot that Mrityu accompanied, the followers of the foremost of the Rakshasas took to their heels, saying :—

" ' It is impossible for us to contend with him ! ' In their cowardice, beside themselves with terror, they fled away, Dashagriva, however, in the presence of that chariot that spread terror in the Universe, remained unmoved and experienced no fear.

" Coming within range of his adversary, Yama, in fury, loosed arrows and darts piercing Ravana's vital parts but he, master of himself, let fly a hail of shafts on Yama's chariot, as a cloud lets fall its waters, and though the Rakshasa was unable to repel those

[1] Kala—Time as Death.

433

great shafts that fell in hundreds on his mighty breast, yet he experienced no ill effect ; nevertheless, after a fight lasting seven days, and all those missiles of various kinds that Yama, the Scourge of his Foes, loosed upon him, Ravana, averting his face, became distraught and a terrible struggle ensued between Yama and the Rakshasa, each eager to triumph and neither turning back in the fight.

"At that time, Devas, Gandharvas, Siddhas and great Rishis with Prajapati at their head, assembled on the field of battle, for the duel taking place between the Lord of the Rakshasas and the King of the Dead appeared like the dissolution of the worlds.

" Ravana, stretching his bow, like unto Indra's thunderbolt, filled the whole of space with his shafts and he struck Mrityu with four barbed arrows and his driver with seven, thereafter with his swift arrows piercing Yama in his vital parts a hundred thousand times.

" Then, from the mouth of the enraged Yama, a circle of flame issued, accompanied by wind and smoke, verily a fire of wrath. Beholding that marvel in the presence of Gods and Danavas, both Mrityu and Kala were transported with rage and Mrityu, in a paroxysm of anger, said to Vaivasvata :—' Suffer me to destroy this wicked Rakshasa ! This very day, in accord with the natural law, this Rakshasa shall cease to be ! Hiranya-kashipu, the fortunate Namuchi, Shambara, Nishandi, Dhuma-ketu, Bali, Virochana, the Giant Shambhu, mighty monarchs, Vritra and Bana, the Rajarishis versed in the Shastras, Punnagas, Daityas, Yakshas and troops of Apsaras, with the earth and its mountains, rivers and trees and the great ocean, have all been destroyed by me at the end of the World cycle, O Great King. Those beings and others in great numbers, who were powerful and invincible, have been annihilated by my glance, how much more easily can I bring about the death of this ranger of the night? Let me go therefore, O Virtuous Lord, that I may destroy him ! No creature, however powerful he may be, can survive if my glance falls upon him. This power is not mine own ; it is a natural law that on whosoever I cast my glance, O Kala, he does not live even for an instant.'

" Thus spoke Mrityu and the illustrious Lord of Justice answered :—

434

" ' Calm thyself, I shall slay him ! ' Then the Lord Vaivasvata, his eyes red with anger, lifted up the Rod of Death that
never misses its target, that Rod to the sides of which the snares
of destruction are attached, and he seized hold of a hammer like
unto a flash of lightning, which, by its aspect alone, extinguishes
the breath of living beings, how much more when it falls on
them ! That weapon surrounded by flames, that huge mace,
that seemed to consume the Rakshasa, emitted sparks when that
mighty being took hold of it. Then, as the God prepared to
smite Ravana, the Grandsire of the World appeared suddenly
and said :—

" ' O Great-armed Vaivasvata, O Thou, whose courage is
immeasurable, know that thou must not strike the ranger of the
night with thy Rod. I have bestowed a boon on him, O King
of the Gods, thou must not render it void for I have pledged my
word ! Verily he who makes me appear as a deceiver, whether
he be God or a mere mortal, renders the Triple World guilty of
deceit ! That terrible weapon, if loosed in anger, will strike
down all beings, irrespective if they are dear to me or no.
Inevitable destruction and death to all follows on that Rod of
Death of immeasurable splendour created by me ! Undoubtedly,
O My Friend, thou shouldst not let it fall on Ravana's head, for
once it falls, none will survive even for an instant. Should it
fall on the Rakshasa Dasbagriva, whether he die or does not die,
either way, deceit will have been practised ! Therefore turn
aside that uplifted Rod from the King of Lanka and confirm my
good faith in deference to the worlds ! '

"Thus addressed, the virtuous Lord of Death, Yama
answered :—

" ' I shall restrain the Rod as thou art our Master, but, as I
may not slay mine adversary who is protected by thy boon, what
shall I do now in the fight ? I shall render myself invisible to the
Rakshasa ! '

" So speaking, he vanished with his chariot and horses.

" Thereafter, Dashagriva, master of the field, proclaimed his
name and, re-mounting Pushpaka, emerged from Yama's abode.
Vaivasvata, however, with the Gods, preceded by Brahma,
joyfully returned to the Celestial Region, as did the great Muni
Narada also."

CHAPTER 23

Ravana's Struggle with the Sons of Varuna

" HAVING overcome Yama the foremost of the Gods, the Ten-necked Ravana, proud warrior, went to seek out his followers. Beholding him with his limbs covered with blood, riddled with wounds, they were amazed. With Maricha at their head, they offered felicitations to him on his victory and re-assured by him, they all took their places in the Pushpaka Chariot. Thereafter the Rakshasa descended into the watery region[1] inhabited by Daityas and Uragas under the powerful protection of Varuna. From there he went to the Capital Bhogavati, where Vasuki reigns, and, having subjugated the Nagas, he joyfully entered the city made of precious stones. There the Nivatakavachas[2], Daityas protected by Brahma dwelt, and the Rakshasa, approaching them, challenged them to fight. Instantly those intrepid Daityas, full of valour, armed with every weapon in their martial ardour, rushed out joyfully.

" Then the Rakshasas and Danavas struck each other furiously with spears, tridents, Kalishas, harpoons, swords and Parash-vadhas and, while they fought thus, a whole year passed away without either side being victorious or suffering defeat.

"At the end of that time, the Grandsire, Lord of the Three Worlds, the imperishable God, appeared in his marvellous chariot and, in order to bring the bellicose activities of the Nivatakavachas to a close, that Ancient One made known to them the purpose of his intervention, saying :—

" ' Ravana cannot be overcome in battle by the Gods or Asuras and you yourselves cannot be destroyed even by the Immortals and Danavas together. It would find favour with me, if the Rakshasas were joined with you in friendship ; undoubtedly all benefits are shared by friends.'

---

[1] Watery Region—Lit: Rasatala, the hell said to be situated at the bottom of the sea.
[2] A race of giants.

" Thereupon, in the presence of fire, Ravana concluded an alliance with the Nivatakavachas and became their friend.

" Honoured by them according to tradition, he sojourned in that place for a year, where he passed his time exactly as in his own city. There, having studied a hundred forms of magic he became proficient in one, then he set out to explore Rasatala in order to discover the capital of the Lord of the Waters, Varuna. Reaching the City of Ashma, he slew all the inhabitants and, with his sword, pierced his powerful brother-in-law, Vidyujjihva, the consort of Shurpanakha, who was proud of his strength and who, with his tongue, was licking a Rakshasa, preparatory to devouring him. Having slain him, Ravana thereafter, in an instant, destroyed four hundred Daityas. It was then that the celestial abode of Varuna, resembling a cloud, dazzling as Mount Kailasha, appeared to that monarch, and he beheld there the Cow, Surabha, from whom milk ever flows which forms the Ocean Kshiroda.

" Ravana saw Vararani, Mother of cows and bulls also, from whom is born Chandra of cooling rays, who ushers in the night, taking refuge under whom, the great Rishis subsist on the froth of that milk from which the Nectar of Immortality, the food of the Gods sprang, as also Svadha, the food of the Pitris. Having circumambulated that wonderful Cow, known to men as Surabha, Ravana penetrated into a formidable region defended by troops of every kind. It was then he beheld the splendid residence of Varuna, abounding in hundreds of cataracts, ever wearing a delightful aspect and resembling an autumn cloud.

" Having struck down the leaders of the army in battle, whom he riddled with blows, Ravana said to those warriors :—' Speedily inform the King that Ravana has come hither seeking battle, saying "Accept this challenge if thou art not afraid, otherwise, paying obeisance to him declare, ' I am defeated ! ' " '

" Meantime, the sons and grandsons of the magnanimous Varuna, provoked, set out with Go and Pushkara.[1]

" Those valiant beings, surrounded by their troops, harnessed their chariots that coursed wheresoever they desired and shone like the rising sun.

[1] Two Generals.

" Thereafter a terrible struggle ensued, causing the hair to stand on end, between the children of the Lord of the Waters and the crafty Ravana. The brave companions of the Rakshasa Dashagriva, in an instant, destroyed Varuna's entire army.

" Seeing their army struck down in the fight, the sons of Varuna, overwhelmed by a hail of missiles, broke off the conflict and, as they were escaping underground, they beheld Ravana in the Pushpaka Chariot and hurled themselves into the sky in their fleet cars. Having attained an equally advantageous position, a desperate fight broke out afresh and a terrible conflict arose in the air like unto that between the Gods and the Danavas. With their shafts, like unto Pavaka's, they put Ravana to flight and, in their joy, emitted countless shouts of triumph.

" Then Mahodara, provoked, on seeing Ravana thus sore pressed, banished all fear of death and, in his martial ardour, casting infuriated glances round about, with his mace struck the chariots that were coursing at will with the speed of the wind, causing them to fall on the earth. Having slain the soldiers and destroyed the chariots of Varuna's sons, Mahodara, seeing them deprived of their cars, emitted a loud shout. The chariots with their steeds and their excellent drivers, destroyed by Mahodara, lay on the earth and, though bereft of their vehicles, the sons of the magnanimous Varuna, by virtue of their natural prowess, remained courageously in the sky without being perturbed. Stretching their bows, they pierced Mahodara and, gathering together, they surrounded Ravana on the battle-field and, with their formidable shafts, like unto thunderbolts loosed from their bows, they overwhelmed him in their rage, as clouds rain down on a great mountain.

" On his side, the irascible Dashagriva, like unto the fire of dissolution, showered down a fearful hail of missiles on their vital parts with irresistible and uninterrupted force, and there were maces of every kind, Bhallas in their hundreds, harpoons, lances and huge Shataghnis. Then Varuna's sons, reduced to walking on foot, saw themselves restricted like unto sixty-year old elephants who have entered a great morass and, beholding the sons of Varuna thus stricken and exhausted, the supremely powerful Ravana emitted shouts of joy like unto an immense cloud, and letting forth those loud roars, he struck Varuna's offspring with shafts of every kind which he showered down upon them like a cloud.

" Thereupon they turned back and fell headlong to the ground and their followers carried them hastily from the battlefield to their homes, whilst the Rakshasa cried out ' Carry the tidings to Varuna ! '

" Thereafter one of Varuna's counsellors, named Prahasta, answered him saying :—

" ' Varuna, the Lord of the Waters, that mighty monarch, whom thou art challenging to combat, has gone to Brahmaloka to hear the Gandharva music. Why exhaust thyself in vain, O Hero, since the King is not here ? '

" Then the Lord of the Rakshasas, having heard this, proclaimed his name and emitted joyful cries ; thereafter, issuing out of Varuna's abode and returning from whence he had come, Ravana ascended into the sky and directed his course to Lanka."

SOME COMMENTATORS CONSIDER THE FOLLOWING
FIVE CHAPTERS TO BE INTERPOLATIONS.

FIRST OF THE INTERPOLATED CHAPTERS

Ravana's Meeting with Bali

" THEREAFTER Ravana's war-intoxicated followers ranged the City of Ashma and Dashanana beheld there a great palace, the archways of which were set with emeralds and adorned with a network of pearls. Abounding in golden pillars and sacred altars, the stairways, made of gold, were studded with diamonds and hung with small bells and delightful seats placed here and there, so that it resembled the palace of Mahendra.

" Beholding that beautiful dwelling, the supremely powerful Ravana reflected within himself :—' Whose is this marvellous mansion like unto the peak of Mount Meru ? Go, O Prahasta and ascertain speedily to whom this residence belongs ! '

" Thereupon Prahasta entered that excellent abode and, finding no one in the first apartment, he went to another, penetrating into seven rooms till at last he observed a fire burning, in the flames of which he beheld a man seated, laughing aloud ; and, hearing that dreadful laughter, Prahasta's hair stood on end. The man thus seated as if unconscious in the fire, blinding to look upon as the sun and like unto Yama himself, was wearing a golden chain. Beholding this, that night-ranger speedily left the house and communicated all to Ravana.

" O Rama, Dashagriva, resembling a piece of collyrium, alighting from Pushpaka, sought to enter that dwelling but a huge-bodied person, moon-crested, barred the door. His tongue resembled a flame, his eyes were red, his teeth dazzling, his lips like the Bimba Fruit, his nose dreadful and he was handsome of form with a neck curved like a conch, marked with three lines, his jaws enormous, his beard thick, his bones well covered with flesh, possessing large fangs, his whole aspect terrible, causing the hair to stand on end ; and he held a mace in his hand as he stood at the door; then as Ravana beheld him, his hair rose on end, his heart beat furiously and his body trembled.

" Perceiving these inauspicious omens, Ravana began to ponder within himself and while he was reflecting thus, that Being addressed him, saying :—

" ' Of what art thou thinking, O Rakshasa ? Tell me without fear ! I shall confer the pleasure of combat on thee, O Hero, O Night-ranger ! '

" Thereafter he spoke again to Ravana, saying :—

" ' Dost thou desire to enter into conflict with Bali or hast thou some other intention ? '

" Hearing these words, Ravana was overwhelmed with fear so that his hair stood on end but, recollecting himself, he answered:-

" ' O Thou, the foremost of those skilled in speech, who resideth in this mansion? I would enter into combat with him if thou counsellest me to do so ! '

" Then that Being answered him, saying :—

" ' The Lord of the Danavas lives here ; he is supremely magnanimous, valiant, possessing truth for his prowess, endowed with many qualities, resplendent, like unto Yama bearing a noose in his hand, bright as the rising sun, incapable of being defeated in combat, impetuous, invincible, victorious, a veritable ocean of accomplishments, soft-spoken, the support of those who depend on him, devoted to his preceptor and the brahmins, conversant with the proper time (for executing actions), gifted with great powers, truthful, handsome, skilful, heroic, ever engaged in the study of the Veda ; though walking on foot, he moves like the wind, he shines like fire, radiating heat like the sun, he stands in awe of neither Gods, spirits, snakes nor birds, fear is unknown to him. Dost thou wish to fight with Bali, O Lord of the Rakshasas, O Thou gifted with supreme energy ? Then enter this abode speedily and engage in the encounter ! '

" Being thus addressed, the Ten-necked Titan went in to where Bali was, and that foremost of the Danavas, who resembled a flame of fire and was as hard to gaze upon as the sun, beholding the Lord of Lanka, burst into laughter and, taking the Rakshasa by the hand placed him on his lap, saying :—

" ' O Ten-necked Lord of the Rakshasas, O Long-armed One, what desire of thine shall I gratify ? Say what has brought thee hither ? '

" Being thus addressed by Bali, Ravana answered :—

" ' O Illustrious One, I have heard that formerly thou wert imprisoned by Vishnu, verily I have the power to release thee from these bonds ! '

" Hearing these words of Ravana, Bali laughed and said :—

" ' Hear and I will tell thee, O Ravana ! The Dark-hued One Who stands at the door, formerly subdued all the Danavas and other powerful Lords and I also was imprisoned by Him. He is as invincible as Death ; none in the world can delude Him. He, Who stands at the entrance, is the Destroyer, Creator and Preserver, Lord of the Three Worlds. Neither thou nor I know Him ; He is the Lord of the past, present and future, He is Time, He is the Kali Yuga, He overthrows all beings ; He is the Creator and Destroyer of the Three Worlds and of all animate and inanimate things ; that great God of all Gods creates and re-creates the universe again and again for ever. O Night-ranger, He is the Dispenser of the fruits of sacrifices, gifts and oblations, verily He is the Creator and Preserver of the entire Universe, there is none in the Three Worlds comparable with Him in majesty and glory. O Scion of the House of Poulastya.

He has the Danavas, our forbears, and thee, under His control, like beasts bound with ropes.

" 'Vritra, Danu, Shuka, Shambu, Nishumbha, Shumbha, Kalanemi, Prahlada and others, Kuta, Virochana, Mridu, Yamala, Arjuna, Kansa, Kaitabha and Madhu all radiated heat like the sun and were as resplendent as its rays, all moved like the wind and showered down rain like unto Indra, all celebrated sacrifices and underwent severe penances, all were exalted of soul and followers of the Path of Yoga, all acquired wealth and enjoyed many pleasures, all distributed gifts abundantly, studied the Veda and protected their subjects, all were defenders of their kinsfolk and slayers of their foes, none could stand against them in the Three Worlds and they were powerful, thoroughly conversant with the Shastras and all branches of learning and were never known to retreat in battle.

" 'They ruled the kingdoms of the Gods, having overcome them a thousand times, and they were ever engaged in harassing them and protecting their own followers. Inflated with pride and arrogance, given to attachment, they were as effulgent as the newly risen sun, but the glorious Hari, the Lord Vishnu knows how to bring about the destruction of those who perpetually trouble the Gods. He creates them all and Himself constantly brings about their end ; existing by Himself at the time of dissolution.

" 'These highly powerful and illustrious Danava Chiefs, able to assume any form at will, were destroyed by that glorious God, and further, all those heroes, said to be invincible and irresistible in warfare, have been discomfited by the wondrous power of Kritanta.'[1]

" Having spoken thus to Ravana, the Lord of the Danavas again addressed the King of the Rakshasas, saying :—

" ' O Hero, O Thou gifted with great strength, take up this shining disc that thou seest and draw near to my side ; I shall then tell thee how I have broken my bonds forever. Do what I have told thee, O Long-armed One, delay not ! '

" O Descendant of Raghu, hearing this, the highly powerful Rakshasa, laughing, proceeded to where that celestial disc was. Proud of his strength he deemed himself able to lift it with ease

[1] Kritanta—The incarnation of the force of destiny, lit: ' Bringer to an end

but, taking hold of it, he could not move it by any means and, being ashamed, that highly powerful one again attempted it and barely raising it, that Rakshasa immediately fell to the earth unconscious, bathed in a pool of blood, like unto a Sala Tree that has been felled.

" Meantime the counsellors of the Lord of the Rakshasas, who were in the Pushpaka Chariot, cried out loudly 'Alas ! Alas ! ' and thereafter, the Rakshasa, regaining his senses, rose up, his head bowed in shame and Bali said to him :—

" ' Draw near, O Foremost of the Rakshasas, and listen to my words, O Hero ! This disc encrusted with gems, which thou didst seek to lift, was an ornament for the ear belonging to one of my forbears and has remained here where it fell, look upon it ! O Thou, endowed with great strength, the other fell on the summit of a mountain and, besides these two, his crown also fell on the earth before an altar during the encounter. Formerly neither time, death nor disease could overcome mine ancestor Hiranyakashipu, nor could he be visited by death during the day, at dawn or dusk. O Foremost of the Rakshasas, neither a dry nor a wet object nor any weapon could encompass his end.

" ' It came about that he entered into a dreadful quarrel with Prahlada[1] and antagonism having grown up between him and the defenceless and courageous Prahlada, the Lord appeared in the form of Nrsingha, he of dreadful aspect who was the cause of terror to all beings. O Foremost of the Rakshasas, that awful Being, casting glances here and there, overwhelmed the Three Worlds and, taking up Hiranyakashipu in his arms, he tore his body open with his nails ; that same Being, the supreme and taintless Vasudeva stands at the door ! I shall now tell thee of that supreme God, do thou hear me, if my words have any significance for thee. He who stands at the door has subdued thousands of Indras and hundreds and thousands of great Gods and Rishis.'

" Hearing these words, Ravana said :—

" ' I have beheld Kritanta, the Lord of Spirits and Death Himself ! His hair is formed of serpents and scorpions, he bears a noose in his hand, his tongue is like unto a flame of fire darting like lightning, his jaws dreadful, his eyes red; he is endowed with

[1] Prahlada his son, a devotee of Vishnu.

immense speed and is the terror of all beings, like unto the sun incapable of being looked upon. Unconquerable in combat, the chastiser of evil-doers, yet even he was overcome in conflict, nor did I experience the least fear of him, O Lord of the Danavas. I do not know this person (at the door), it behoveth thee to tell me who he is.'

" Hearing these words of Ravana, Bali, the Son of Virochana, answered :—

" ' He is the Lord Hari, Narayana, the Protector of the Three Worlds. He is Ananta, Kapila, Vishnu and the highly effulgent Nrsingha ; He is Kratudhama and Sudhama who bears the dreadful mace in his hands. He resembles the Twelve Adityas, He is the first Man, the primeval and excellent Purusha ; He is like unto a dark blue cloud and is the first Lord of the Gods. O Long-armed One, He is encircled by flame ; He is the supreme Yogi, beloved of His devotees ; He projected the universe, preserves it and destroys it, assuming the form of Time endowed with great power. This Hari, bearing the discus in His hand, is the sacrifice and is worshipped in the sacrifice, He is the one great form of all the Gods, all beings, all worlds and all knowledge ; He is Baladeva, O Mighty-armed One, the Slayer of Warriors ; He has the eye of a hero and is the eternal Guru, the Father of the Three Worlds. All Sages, desirous of liberation, meditate on Him. He who knows Him thus, is freed from sin ; he, who remembers, adores and worships Him, attains all.'

" Hearing these words of Bali, the highly powerful Ravana, his eyes red with anger, went out with uplifted weapons.

" Beholding him thus inflamed with fury, the Lord Hari, Who bore a club in His hand, reflected, ' In deference to Brahma, I shall not slay this sinner yet,'[1] and making himself invisible, He vanished.

" Then Ravana, not beholding that Purusha there, rejoiced, and, shouting exultantly, issued out of Varuna's abode and departed by the same way by which he had come."

---

[1] Since Brahma had granted him the boon of invulnerability.

UTTARA KANDA

Ravana challenges the Sun God

"AFTER reflecting awhile, the Lord of Lanka went to the Solar Region, passing the night on the enchanting summit of Mount Sumeru. Riding in the Pushpaka Chariot, which was endowed with the speed of the sun's steeds, he, by various ways advanced, and beheld the glorious and resplendent Sun, the purifier of all, adorned with golden bracelets and crowned with a halo encrusted with gems. His lovely countenance was graced with a pair of brilliant earrings, his person embellished with Keyuras,[1] golden ornaments and garlands of crimson lotuses. His body was annointed with red sandalwood and he was blazing with a thousand rays.

" Beholding the Sun, foremost of the Gods, Surya, that primeval Deity without end or middle, having Uchhaisravas as his steed, He the Witness of the World, Lord of the Earth, Ravana was overwhelmed by His rays and said to Prahasta :—

" ' O Counsellor, do thou go at my behest and apprise the Sun of mine intention saying, ' Ravana has come hither to challenge thee, do thou fight or admit defeat; do one or the other speedily !'

" Hearing these words, that Rakshasa advanced towards the sun and beheld two door-keepers named Pingala and Dandi and, having communicated Ravana's resolutions to them, he stood silent, being overpowered by the sun's rays.

"Approaching the Sun, Dandi related the matter to him and, hearing of Ravana's intention, the sagacious Surya, that enemy of the night, said to him :—

" ' O Dandi, either subdue Ravana or say to him " I have been defeated, do as thou deemest best ! "

"At this command, Dandi approached the high-souled Ravana and informed him of what the Sun had said.

" Hearing Dandi's words, the Lord of the Rakshasas proclaimed his victory by a roll of drums and went away."

[1] Keyuras—Bracelets worn on the upper arm.

THIRD OF THE INTERPOLATED CHAPTERS

1st SERIES

Ravana's Encounter with the King Mandhata

" HAVING passed the night on the enchanting summit of Mount Sumeru and deliberated for some time, the mighty Lord of Lanka went to the region of the moon. There he beheld one sprinkled with heavenly unguents, seated in his chariot attended by Apsaras and being embraced by them, proceeding on his way, worn out by the gratification of desire. Seeing such a person, his curiosity was aroused and, observing a Rishi, named Parvata, there, he said to him :—

" ' Thou art welcome, O Blessed Sage, verily thou hast come at a fitting moment ! Who is this shameless being proceeding in a chariot attended by Apsaras ? He appears to be unaware of his peril ? '

" Thus addressed by Ravana, the Rishi Parvata, said to him :—

" ' O Child, O Thou gifted with high intelligence, hear me and I will tell thee the truth. By him all these worlds have been subdued and Brahma propitiated, and he is on his way to a blissful place. As thou, by virtue of asceticism, hast conquered the worlds, O Lord of the Rakshasas, so has he ; and, having drunk the Soma-juice and performed many pious acts, he has set forth on his journey. O Foremost of the Rakshasas, thou art valiant and hast truth for thy prowess ; the mighty are never offended by the virtuous ! '

" Then Ravana beheld a large and excellent car, radiant and effulgent, from which the sound of music and singing issued and he said :—

" ' O Great Rishi, who is that person endowed with radiance who proceeds surrounded by charming singers, dancing girls and Kinneras ? '

" Hearing these words, Parvata, the foremost of Sages, again replied :—

" ' He is a hero, a mighty warrior, who has never retreated in battle. Having performed innumerable heroic feats in combat and slain many adversaries, he has received countless wounds and finally sacrificed his life for his master. Having destroyed a myriad people in battle, he has at last been slain by his enemies. He is now to be a guest of Indra or, it may be that he is going to some other auspicious region. This foremost of men is being entertained by singing and dancing.'

" Then Ravana enquired once more :—

" ' Who goeth yonder shining like the sun ? '

" Hearing Ravana's words, Parvata said :—

" ' That person, resembling the full moon, adorned with various ornaments and robes, O Mighty King, whom thou beholdest in a great chariot accompanied by troops of Apsaras, has distributed much gold, therefore he proceedeth in supreme effulgence in a swiftly coursing car.'

" Hearing Parvata's words, Ravana said again :—

" ' O Foremost of Rishis, do thou tell me which of these kings proceeding here, if entreated, will grant me the pleasure of battle ? Verily thou art my father ; do thou point out to me such a one, O Thou conversant with piety.'

" Thus addressed, Parvata, once more replied to Ravana, saying :—

" ' O Great King, all these monarchs desire heaven not conflict, but, O Mighty One, I shall indicate to thee one who will enter into combat with thee.

" ' There is a supremely powerful king, the Lord of the Seven Islands, well known by the name of Mandhata, who will do battle with thee.'

" Hearing these words of Parvata, Ravana said :—

" ' Do thou tell me where this king doth dwell, O Thou of great devotion, I shall go to where that foremost of men resides.'

" Hearing Ravana's words, the Sage said again :—

" ' The son of Yuvaneshwa, having conquered the world consisting of the Seven Islands, from sea to sea, Mandhata, the foremost of kings is coming here.'

" Thereupon the long-armed Ravana, proud of the boon conferred upon him in the Three Worlds, beheld the heroic Mandhata, the Lord of Ayodhya and the foremost of monarchs. The Lord of the Seven Islands was proceeding in a gilded and decorated car resplendent as that of Mahendra, radiant in his own beauty, sprinkled with celestial unguents, and the Ten-necked One said to him :—' Do thou give me battle ! '

" Being thus addressed, he, laughing, said to Dashanana :—

" ' If thy life is not dear to thee, then enter into combat with me, O Rakshasa ! '

" Hearing these words of Mandhata, Ravana said :—

" ' Ravana has experienced no harm from Varuna, Kuvera or Yama, what should he fear from a mere man ? '

" Having spoken thus, the Lord of the Rakshasas issued orders to the titans who were invincible in battle, whereupon, in fury, the counsellors of the wicked-souled Rakshasa, well skilled in the art of warfare, began to discharge a hail of arrows.

" Then the mighty monarch, Mandhata, with golden feathered shafts, assailed Prahasta, Shuka, Sarana, Mahodara, Virupaksha, Akampana and other generals, and Prahasta covered the king with arrows but, before they reached him, that foremost of men shattered them to pieces. As grass is consumed by fire so was that host of Rakshasas consumed by the King Mandhata by means of hundreds of Bushundis, Bhallas, Bhindipalas and Tomaras.[1] As Karttikeya sundered Mount Krauncha with his shafts, so did Mandhata, full of rage, pierce Prahasta with five Tomaras endowed with supreme velocity and, brandishing his mace, resembling Yama's, again and again he struck Ravana's chariot violently and that club resembling lightning, fell with force so that Ravana was thrown down like unto Shakra's banner. Thereafter the joy of King Mandhata was increased, as the waters of the salty ocean at the time of the full moon, but the entire Rakshasa Host, shrieking with terror, stood round the unconscious Lord of the Rakshasas. Speedily regaining his senses, Ravana, the terror of all beings, Lord of Lanka, showered missiles on the person of Mandhata and, beholding that king falling unconscious, the highly powerful rangers of the night were greatly delighted and emitted leonine roars.

" Regaining his senses in a moment, the King of Ayodhya, beholding his adversary acclaimed by his followers and ministers, was enraged, and assuming a dazzling form like unto the sun or moon, instantly began to slay the titans with a dreadful hail of

[1] See Weapons Glossary.

shafts ; and his arrows and the noise thereof overwhelmed the entire Rakshasa Host, that resembled a tempestuous ocean.

" Thereupon a fearful conflict arose between man and demon and those two heroic and high-souled leaders of men and Rakshasas, like persons possessed, taking up the attitude of warriors, entered the field with swords and bows and, highly enraged, began to assail each other with shafts, wounding each other in the attack. Then, setting the Raudra-weapon on his bow, Ravana discharged it, but Mandhata turned it aside with the Fire-weapon. Thereafter Dashanana took up the Gandharva weapon and King Mandhata the Brahma-astra, a source of terror to all. And Ravana took up the Celestial and dreadful Pashupata-weapon, the increaser of fear in the Three Worlds, obtained from Rudra, by virtue of his rigid penances.

" Beholding this, all moveable and immoveable beings were stricken with terror and the Three Worlds, including all that was animate and inanimate, Gods and Serpents, together took refuge in their abodes under the earth.

" Meantime, by virtue of their meditation, the two foremost of ascetics, Poulastya and Galava, aware of the conflict, remonstrated with these two warriors in various ways and restrained the King and the Lord of the Rakshasas. Thereafter the man and the Rakshasa were reconciled and, highly delighted, returned from whence they had come."

FOURTH OF THE INTERPOLATED CHAPTERS
1st SERIES

Ravana visits the Moon Region and is given a Boon by Brahma

" THE two Rishis having departed, Ravana, the Lord of the Rakshasas, proceeded for forty thousand miles in the upper air, whereupon he reached that excellent higher sphere where swans, endowed with every virtue, dwell. And, having gone on, he ascended yet higher for ten thousand leagues, where on all sides, the clouds, Agneya, Pakshana and Brahma[1] are eternally

[1] Agneya—Clouds produced by fire.
Pakshana—Winged Clouds.
Brahma—Those created by Brahma.

established. Thereafter, he proceeded to an excellent airy region where the high-souled Siddhas and Charanas ever abide, which is ten thousand leagues in extent.

" O Slayer of thy Foes, he then passed to a fourth region, where the Bhutas and Vinayakas perpetually sojourn and thereafter, he went to the fifth aerial realm, which extends over ten thousand leagues, where Gunga, the foremost of rivers is to be found, and the elephants headed by Kumuda, from whose bodies, drops pour down constantly as they sport in the waters, spout forth the sacred stream which they sprinkle in all directions. Here the waters fall down in rain and snow under the rays of the sun, purified by the wind, O Raghava.

" Then that Rakshasa went to the sixth aerial region, O Thou endowed with great radiance, where Garuda dwells, ever revered by his kinsfolk and friends, and, thereafter, ascended to the seventh aerial region, lying ten thousand leagues higher, where the Seven Rishis dwell.[1] And again proceeding ten thousand leagues higher he reached the eighth aerial region where Gunga, known as the Ganges of the sky, having strong currents, is found in the path of the sun and, who, upheld by air, sends forth a great roaring.

" Now I shall describe the region yet higher than these, where the Moon-god dwells and the extent thereof is eighty thousand leagues. There the Moon encircled by stars and planets, from whom hundreds and thousands of rays stream forth, illumines the world, bringing happiness to all beings.

" Thereupon, beholding Dashagriva, the Moon, blazing up as it were, consumed him with its cold fires and, stricken with fear of those rays, his counsellors were unable to withstand them and Prahasta, uttering the words ' Let victory be thine ! ' thereafter said :—

" ' O King, we are being destroyed by the cold and must leave this place ! O Foremost of Monarchs, the icy rays of the moon have the property of fire.'

" Hearing the words of Prahasta, Ravana, beside himself with wrath, lifted his bow, twanging it and began to assail the Moon with Narachas, whereupon Brahma speedily went to that lunar region and said :—

[1] The Plough of which the Seven Rishis are said to be the Regents.

" ' O Ten-necked One, O Mighty-armed One, O Son of Vishravas, O Gentle One, do thou go hence from here speedily ; do not oppress the Moon, for that highly effulgent King of the Twice-born desireth the well-being of all. I will bestow a mystical formula on thee ! He who recollects it at the hour of death, does not succumb ! '

" Thus addressed, the Ten-necked Rakshasa, with joined palms, said :—

" ' O God, if I have found favour with thee, then, O Lord of the Worlds, O Thou of great penances, impart that sacred mantra to me, O Thou truly Pious One, reciting which, O Great One, I shall be liberated from fear of the Celestials. Verily, by Thy favour, O Lord of the Gods, I shall become invincible to all the Asuras, Danavas and Birds.'

" Thus accosted, Brahma said to Dashanana :—

" ' O Lord of the Rakshasas, do not repeat this mantra daily but only when thy life is in danger. Holding a string of Rudraksha beads and repeating it, thou shalt become invincible ; but if thou dost not recite it, thou shalt not meet with success. Hear and I shall communicate this sacred formula to thee, O Foremost of the Rakshasas, reciting which thou shalt obtain victory in the encounter :—

" ' Salutations unto Thee, O God, O Lord of Lords, O Thou worshipped by the Celestials and Asuras. O Thou, the same in the past, present and future, O Great God, O Thou having tawny eyes, O Thou, a boy assuming the form of an aged Being, O Thou who wearest a tiger skin. O God, Thou art worthy to be worshipped and art the Lord of the Three Worlds. Thou art Ishwara, Hara, Haratanemi, the Fire at the end of the World Cycle, Yugantadahaka ; Thou art Baladeva, Thou art Ganesha, Lokashambu, and Lokapala, Thou art endowed with huge arms, Thou art blessed, the Bearer of the Trident ; Thou art possessed of dreadful teeth and jaws, the greatest of the Gods, Thou art Time, Thou art Power, Thou art the Blue-throated[1] and possessed of a huge belly, Thou art Devantaka, the foremost of the ascetics and the Lord of all creatures. Thou art the Leader, Protector, Hari-Hara, Destroyer and Preserver, Thou wearest

---

[1] Blue-throated—Shiva who drank the poison churned from the ocean and became blue-throated. The story is told in the classics.

matted locks, art clean-shaven and wrapped in a loincloth,
Thou art mighty and illustrious, Thou art the Lord of
Spirits and Goblins, the Support of all, Protector of all, Destroyer
of all, the Creator and the Eternal Preceptor, Thou art the Bearer
of the Kamandalu,[1] the Wielder of the Pinaka Bow and the
Dhurjata.[2] Thou art worthy of veneration, Thou art Aum, the
highest of all, the First Chanter of the Sama-Veda. Thou art
Death and the nature of death, Pariyatra[3] and the Observer of
great vows ; Thou art a brahmachari dwelling in a cave bearing
a Vina, Panava and quiver in thine hands ; Thou art immortal,
lovely to look upon as the newly risen sun ; Thou dwellest in
the crematorium ; Thou art the illustrious Lord of Uma, transcending all taint ; Thou didst pluck out the eyes of Bhagadeva
and the teeth of Pusha. Thou art the overcomer of fever and
bearest a noose in Thy hand, verily Thou art Dissolution and
Time of the flaming mouth, fire being Thy symbol, Thou art
highly effulgent and the Lord of men. Thou art demented and
causest people to tremble ; Thou art the Fourth and deeply
venerated of men, Thou art the Holy Dwarf, Vamanadeva, and
the Dwarf who circumambulates the East. Thou wearest the
semblance of a beggar with three locks, and art crafty by nature.
Thou didst stay the hand of Indra and of the Vasus, Thou art the
Seasons, the Creator of seasons ; Thou art Time, Honey and the
One of honey eyes. Thou art the Lord of herbs, a lordly tree
bearing fruit and flowers ; Thy seat is made of arrows ; Thou
art ever worshipped by people in all conditions ; Thou art the
Creator and Protector of the Universe, the Eternal and true
Purusha ; Thou art the Controller of Righteousness, Virupaksha,
the Three Dharmas, the Protector of all beings. Thou art the
Three-eyed One of many forms blazing like a million suns, Thou
art the Lord of the Celestials, the foremost of the Gods, bearing
matted locks and the crescent moon, Thou art worthy of being
approached and art one with created beings ; Thou art the Player
of all musical instruments, ever creating and binding all, and dost
bring about the liberation of all beings. Thou art Pushpadanta,

---

[1] Kamandalu—The coconut loshtha used by ascetics who may not touch
metal.
[2] Dhurjata—Lit: a burden, ' He whose matted locks are a burden ', or He who
bears the burden of the Three Worlds.
[3] Pariyatra—The name of a well-known mountain in the Vindhya Chain.

indivisible, the foremost of Destroyers; Thou hast tawny beards, bearest a bow and art fearful and endowed with terrible might.'

" ' These hundred and eight sacred and excellent names, uttered by me, destroy all sins, bestow merit and give refuge to those who seek it. O Dashanana, if thou dost recite them, thou shalt be able to overcome thy foes ! ' "

FIFTH OF THE INTERPOLATED CHAPTERS

1st SERIES

Ravana and the Maha-Purusha

" HAVING conferred that favour on Ravana, the Grandsire, sprung from the lotus, speedily went to his own region and Ravana, having obtained the boon, departed.

"After a few days, that Scourge of the Worlds, the Rakshasa Ravana with his counsellors reached the banks of the western ocean and, on an island, a person was seen seated there alone, bright as fire, named Mahajambunada. His form was dreadful like unto the Fire of Dissolution and, beholding that highly powerful Being resembling Mahendra, the Chief of the Gods among the Celestials, or the sun among the planets, a lion among the Sharabhas, Airavata among elephants, Sumeru among mountains and Parijata among trees, Dashagriva said :—

" ' Enter into combat with me ! ' and his eyes flickered like a cluster of planets.[1] Gnashing his teeth, he made a sound like a grinding mill and the highly powerful Dashanana amidst his counsellors, roared aloud. Thereafter with darts, Shatis, Rishtis and Pattikas, he assailed that highly effulgent Being of long arms, dread aspect, huge teeth, grim form, conch-like neck, broad chest, frog-like belly, leonine countenance, feet like unto the summit of Mount Kailasha, the palms of his hands and the soles of his feet like unto red lotuses, endowed with the swiftness of thought and the wind, terrifying, bearing a quiver, adorned with bells and chowries, encircled by flames, emitting

[1] Lit: Grahamala—A cluster of planets or meteors.

a sweet sound like a net-work of Kinkinis,[1] wearing a garland of golden flowers round his neck, noble, like unto the Rig-Veda and resembling the Anjana or Golden Mountain.

"As a lion remains unmoved by the attack of a wolf or an elephant, or Mount Sumeru by the King of the Serpents, or the vast ocean by the current of a river, neither was that great Being perturbed, but addressing Dashagriva, said :—

" ' O Vicious-minded Night-ranger, I shall soon rid thee of thy desire for combat.'

" O Rama, the might of that Being was a thousand times greater than Ravana's, which was a source of terror to the worlds. Piety and asceticism, which are the roots of attainment of everything in the world, are in his thighs, desire is in his male-organ, the Vishvadevas are at his waist and the winds at the side of his intestines ; the eight Vasus dwell in his middle, the oceans abide in his belly, the quarters are his hips, the Maruts his joints, the Pittris are at his back and the Grandsire has taken refuge in his heart. Charitable acts of making many gifts of kine, gold and land are the hair in his armpits ; the Mountains, Himalaya, Hemakuta, Mandara and Meru are his bones, the thunderbolt is in his palm, the sky in his frame, the evening rain-clouds are on his neck ; the Creator and Preserver and the Vidyadharas are his arms ; Ananta, Vasuki, Vishalaksha, Iravat, Kamvala, Asvatara, Karkotaka, Dhananjaya, the veno-mous Takshaka and Utpatakshaka[2] have taken shelter under his nails in order to vomit forth their poison. Fire is in his mouth, the Rudras on his shoulders ; the fortnights, months, years and seasons in his jaws, the lunar fortnight and the dark half of the month are his nostrils, the airy currents are the pores of his body, Saraswati with her Vina is in his throat, the Asvins are in his ears and the sun and moon in his two eyes.

" O Rama, all the branches of the Veda and the sacrifices, the whole galaxy of stars, sweet speech, good deeds, energy and asceticism are supported by his body in human form.

" Then that Purusha struck Ravana playfully with his hands, which were as powerful as lightning and, thus assailed, Ravana fell to the ground immediately and having put that Night-

[1] Kinkinis—Small bells.
[2] Great Serpents.

ranger to flight that great Purusha, like unto the Rig-Veda, resembling a mountain be-decked with lotus wreaths, entered the region under the earth.

" Then Ravana addressed his counsellors thus :—

" ' O Prahasta, O Shuka, O Sarana and ye other ministers, where has that Purusha suddenly gone ? Do ye tell me ! '

" Hearing the words of Ravana, the Night-rangers said :— ' That Purusha, who crusheth the pride of Devas and Danavas, has entered into that place ! '

"As Garuda swoops on a serpent so did that wicked-minded Ravana speedily approach the entrance of that cave and entered it fearlessly. Penetrating there, he beheld three warriors, dark like unto collyrium, wearing Keyuras,[1] adorned with red garlands, besmeared with sandalpaste, bedecked with diverse golden ornaments set with gems ; and he saw three crores of exalted beings, fearless, pure, radiant as fire, intent on dancing.

" Beholding them, Dashagriva was not in the least afraid but watched them gyrating whilst he stood at the entrance ; and they all resembled the Maha-Purusha, who had previously been seen by him, and all were of similar colour, dress, form and all equally endowed with energy. Then the hair of Dashagriva stood on end as he gazed upon them but, on account of the boon he had received from the Self-born, he issued out of that place alive. Thereafter he saw the Maha Purusha lying on a couch, and his dwelling, his seat and his bed were all white and costly and he slept there enveloped in flames.

"And there, with a fan in her lotus-like hands sat the Goddess Lakshmi, most beautiful in all the Three Worlds and their decoration, as it were ; chaste, adorned with celestial garlands, sprinkled with excellent sandal-paste, bedecked with rich ornaments and clad in costly robes. And the wicked Ravana, Lord of the Rakshasas, having entered there without a counsellor, beholding that chaste damsel of sweet smiles, seated on a royal throne, became filled with desire and wished to hold her by the hand, as one under the sway of death fondles a sleeping serpent.

" Beholding that Lord of the Rakshasas with a loosened garment and knowing him desirous of taking hold of her, the huge-armed Deity, sleeping, enveloped in flames, laughed aloud

---

[1] Keyuras—An ornament used at the waist.

and suddenly by his power began to consume Ravana, the harasser of his foes, who fell down on the earth like an uprooted tree. Beholding that Rakshasa fallen, the Purusha addressed him saying :—

" ' Rise up, O Foremost of the Rakshasas, thou shalt not meet with death to-day ! Thou shalt live protected by the Grandsire's boon. Do thou therefore go hence without fear, O Ravana, thy death is not yet decreed ! '

" Regaining consciousness after a while, Ravana was seized with fear and being thus addressed, that enemy of the Gods rose up, his hair standing on end and said to that highly resplendent Deity :—

" ' Who art thou endowed with great energy and like unto the Fire of Dissolution ? Say who art thou, O God and from whence hast thou come hither ? '

" Being thus accosted by the wicked-minded Ravana, the God, smiling, replied in accents as deep as the muttering of clouds, saying :—

" ' What hast thou to do with me, O Dashagriva, thou shalt be slain ere long ! '

" Being thus addressed, the Ten-necked Rakshasa, with joined palms, said :—

" ' On account of Brahma's boon, I shall not tread the path of death ; there is none born amongst men or Gods who can equal me or, in virtue of his prowess, disregard the Grandsire's boon. His words may never prove vain nor can any, howsoever he exert himself, prove them to be false ; I do not see any in the Three Worlds who could render his boon to me void. O Great God, I am immortal, I do not fear Thee and even were I to meet with death, may it be through thee and none other, O Lord; death at Thy hands will bring me glory and renown ! '

" Then Ravana endowed with dreadful prowess saw the Three Worlds with all the animate and inanimate creatures within the body of the Deity. The Adityas, the Maruts, the Sadhyas, the Vasus, the Twin Ashvins, the Rudras, the Pittris, Yama, Kuvera, the seas, mountains, rivers, all the branches of learning and of the Veda, Fire, the planets, the stars, the sky, the Siddhas, Gandharvas, Charanas and the Maha Rishis conversant with the knowledge of the Veda, Garuda, the Nagas, the other Gods, Yakshas, Daityas and Rakshasas were all seen in their subtle forms in the limbs of that Purusha lying there. "

On this, the virtuous-souled Rama said to Agastya, the foremost of Munis :—" O Lord, tell me who was that Maha Purusha on that island ? Who were those hundreds and thousands of beings ? Who is the Purusha who humbles the pride of Daityas and Danavas ? "

Hearing Rama's words, Shri Agastya answered :—

" O Thou existing eternally, O God of Gods, hearken and I will tell thee. That Purusha on the island was the illustrious Kapila and all those who were dancing are the Deities equalling that intelligent Kapila in energy and power. And that Rakshasa, bent on sin, was not looked on by Him with a wrathful glance, therefore he was not immediately reduced to ashes, but Ravana, who resembled a mountain, with his person pierced, fell to the ground. As a crafty man penetrates a secret, so did that Purusha pierce Ravana's person with his arrow-like words.

" Thereafter that Rakshasa of great prowess, having regained his senses after a long time, returned to where his counsellors were."

CHAPTER 24

Ravana carries off a number of Women and is cursed by them

"WHILE Ravana of perverse soul was returning in the height of joy, continuing his journey, he bore away the youthful daughters of Kings, Rishis, Gods and Danavas. Whenever he met a young maiden of remarkable beauty, he slew all her kinsfolk and friends and took her into his chariot. Thus the daughters of Pannagas, Rakshasas, Asuras, men and Yakshas were compelled to enter his equipage and all these unfortunate beings, under the sway of fear, in their grief, shed burning tears like unto fire.

" The youthful daughters of Nagas, Gandharvas, great Rishis and Danavas lamented in their hundreds in the aerial Car Pushpaka, and those charming women with long tresses, graceful limbs and faces as radiant as the full moon, with their rounded breasts gleaming like an altar and decorated with diamonds, their hips like unto the axles of a chariot, who resembled the consorts of the Gods with their elegant waists and their complexion like unto refined gold, were mad with fear and grief. The breath of their sighing scorched the ear, lending the Pushpaka Chariot the appearance of a fire ceremony that is lit on all sides.

" Fallen into the power of Dashagriva, those women were overcome with affliction and the sadness expressed in their looks and mien caused them to resemble black antelopes that have become a prey to a lion. And one asked herself ' Is he not going to devour me ? ' whilst another, in the despair that overwhelmed her, thought ' He is about to slay me ! ' Recollecting their mothers, fathers, husbands and brothers, plunged in grief and affliction, those women, thus assembled began to lament, saying :—

" 'Alas ! What will become of my son without me ? What will become of my mother ? ' And, submerged in an ocean of grief, they cried ' What can I do now far from my lord ? O Death, I call upon thee to bear me away for affliction is now my portion. Have I committed some misdeed formerly in another body ? '

" Then all those wretched women, sunk in an ocean of despair exclaimed :—' We see no end to our misery ! Woe unto the world ! Assuredly none is more vile than the mighty Ravana, since under his blows our helpless consorts have perished, as stars disappear on the rising of the sun. Ah ! That powerful Rakshasa takes delight in devising the means of our destruction ! Alas ! He gives himself up to evil without scruple, he is indifferent to every condemnation ; till now none has been able to put an end to the exploits of this wicked wretch, yet it is a great sin to lay hands on other men's wives ; this Rakshasa is the vilest of all since he seeks enjoyment with them. Because of this, a woman will be the cause of the death of this wicked being ! '

" When those virtuous and noble women had uttered these words, celestial gongs sounded and a shower of blossom fell. Cursed by his captives, Dashagriva seemed to lose all his power and glory and, hearing those women, who were chaste and devoted to their consorts, lamenting in this wise, that bull among the Rakshasas became distracted.

" Thereafter he made his entry into the City of Lanka to the acclamations of the rangers of the night and, at that time, the fierce Rakshasi, who was able to change her form at will, the sister of Ravana, suddenly sank down on the earth before him, and Ravana, helping her to rise and comforting her, said :—

" ' O Dear One, what is this ? Why dost thou seek speech with me so urgently ? '

" Thereupon, her eyes inflamed and suffused with tears, she said to him :—

" ' O King, I have been widowed through thy ruthless conduct ! O Lord, thy valour in combat has cut down those Daityas called Kalakeyas to the number of fourteen thousand and, in addition, my valiant lord who was dearer to me than life itself. He was slain by thee, his foe, a brother in name only and, by thee, I myself am slain, O Prince, thou my kinsman ! From now, I shall bear the title of widow through thy fault ! Was it not for thee to spare a brother-in-law in the fight ? '

" Hearing those indignant words from his sister, Dashagriva, in order to appease her, spoke soothingly, saying :—

" ' Dry thy tears, my dear sister and fear nothing ! I shall load thee with gifts, homage and favours. In the heat of battle, being carried away by a desire to triumph, I loosed my shafts without being able to distinguish mine own people from others and did not recognize my brother-in-law whom I struck in the height of the conflict. That is how thy consort fell under my blows in the fight. O My Sister, whatever presents itself at this time, I will do for thy pleasure. It is for thee to go and live near thy kinsman, Khara, who enjoys sovereignty. Fourteen thousand Rakshasas will be made subject to that powerful Prince in the expeditions and distribution of spoils. There, that son of the sister of thy mother, thy cousin Khara, the Ranger of the Night, will ever be obedient to thy commands. Let that warrior speedily go and guard the Dandaka Forest ; Dushana shall be his commander ; great is his valour. The courageous Khara shall ever obey thy will and be the leader of the titans able to change their form at pleasure.'

" Having spoken thus, Dashagriva placed an army of fourteen thousand Rakshasas, full of valour, under Khara's command. Surrounded by all those titans of redoubtable appearance,

Khara set out fearlessly at once to the Dandaka Forest. There
he established his authority without hindrance and Shurpanakha
dwelt near him in the forest."

CHAPTER 25

Dashagriva allies himself to Madhu

" DASHAGRIVA, having given over that redoubtable army to
Khara and consoled his sister, became master of himself once
more and was freed from anxiety.

" Thereafter that powerful Indra among the Rakshasas
penetrated into the marvellous Nikumbhila Grove where he
beheld hundreds of sacrificial posts and altars and, as if blazing
in brilliance, a sacrifice was being performed.

" There, clad in a black antelope skin, holding a coconut
loshta and staff, he beheld his own son, Meghanada of dread
aspect. Approaching him, the Lord of Lanka, clasping him in
his arms, enquired of him :—

" ' What art thou doing here, O Child, tell me truly ! '

" Then that excellent Twice-born of rigid penances, Ushanas,[1]
in order that the sacrifice should prove auspicious,[2] answered
Ravana, saying :—

" ' I shall tell thee myself, O King, listen to all that has taken
place. Seven sacrifices with countless preparatory rites have been
undertaken by thy son, the Agnisthoma, Ashvamedha, Bahus-
varnaka, Rajasuya, Gomedha and the Vaishnava and, having
engaged in the Maheshvara sacrifice, difficult for men to undertake, thy son, on its completion, received gifts from the Lord of
Creatures Himself : a stable and celestial chariot coursing at will
in the sky, the power of illusion by which darkness is created on
the field of battle so that even the Gods and Asuras can no
longer find their way, and, in order to exterminate the foe in
combat, O King, he has also been granted two inexhaustible

---

[1] Ushanas—another name of the Sage Sukra.
[2] Meghanada having taken the vow of silence till the ceremony was
completed.

quivers, a bow that no weapon can shatter and a powerful arrow. Having received these gifts, thy son, O Dashanana, wishes to meet with thee on the completion of the sacrifice and will soon present himself before thee.'

" Then Dashagriva said :—

" ' This is not well done, since our enemy, Indra, has been worshipped with these offerings. However, what is done is done and doubtless thou wilt acquire merit thereby, let us now return, My Friend, and enter our abode.'

" Thereafter Dashagriva with his son and Bibishana returned to his dwelling and caused all the captives, who were crying and sobbing, to be brought down ; and the virtuous Bibishana, being aware of his intention regarding those women, who were noble and veritable pearls, the offspring of the Gods, Danavas and Rakshasas, said to his brother :—

" ' It is practices such as these, which thou dost follow with deliberate intention despite thy knowledge of the causes of destruction of beings, that are ruinous to thy good name, thy family and fortune ! After ill-treating their relatives, thou hast carried away these high-born women, whilst Madhu affronts thee by carrying off Kumbhinasi,'

" Then Ravana answered :—' I was not aware of this ; who is this Madhu of whom thou speakest ? ' and Bibishana replied to his brother indignantly and said :—

" ' Learn the consequences of thine evil karma ! The elder brother of our maternal grandfather, Sumali, that virtuous old man named Malyavan, Ranger of the Night, the father of our mother, is the grandfather of Kumbhinasi, so that we are virtually her brothers. She has been borne away by Madhu, a Rakshasa of superior power, while thy son was engaged in the sacrifice and I was bathing in the waters. Kumbhakarna, on his side, was still under the influence of sleep. Having slain the aged ministers, that foremost of night-rangers instantly carried away the princess most ruthlessly, though she was in the precincts of the inner apartments. Though these ill-tidings were known to us, we did not slay the ravisher since it is imperative that a young girl be provided with a consort by her brothers. This is the fruit of thy perverse and wicked conduct which, as thou seest, thou art now reaping in this world itself.'

" Hearing these words of Bibishana's, that Indra of the Rakshasas, Ravana, wrought up through the wickedness of his soul, like unto an ocean with surging waves, his eyes red with anger, said :—

" ' Let my chariot be harnessed speedily, let my warriors stand ready with my brother Kumbhakarna and the foremost of the rangers of the night in their conveyances heaped with every weapon. To-day, having slain Madhu, who dares to defy Ravana, I shall go to the region of the Gods, burning to fight, surrounded by my companions.'

" Four thousand Akshauhinis of the foremost of the titans, armed from head to foot with various weapons, instantly rushed out, eager for hand to hand encounter, and Indrajita marched in the advance guard with his warriors. Ravana occupied the centre and Kumbhakarna the rearguard. As for the virtuous Bibishana, he remained in Lanka, faithful to his duty. All the other warriors advanced against Madhu's city and they were mounted on mules, buffalo, fiery steeds, porpoises and great serpents, covering the sky and, beholding Ravana on the march, hundreds of Daityas, who were at emnity with the Gods, followed him.

" Meanwhile Dashanana, having reached Madhupura, entered it, yet he did not find Madhu there but his own sister, who, paying obeisance to him, with a deep bow cast herself at his feet, for Kumbhinasi feared the Lord of the Rakshasas.

" Then he, raising her up, said to her :—

" ' Do not tremble ! ' and the King of the Rakshasas added ' What dost thou desire of me ? ' Then she replied :—' O Long-armed Prince, if I find favour with thee, then, O Proud Hero, do not slay my lord ; it is not fitting to reduce women of nobility to such affliction. Of all ill-fortune, to become a widow is the greatest. Be true to thy word, O Indra of Monarchs, and receive my supplication with favour. Thou hast thyself said " Thou hast nothing to fear ! " '

" Then Ravana, in cheerful tones, answered his sister, who stood near him, saying :—' Where is thy husband, tell me quickly ! I shall go with him to conquer the region of the Gods. I shall not slay Madhu because of my tender affection for thee.'

"At these words, Kumbhinasi roused her lord, that Ranger of

the Night, who was sleeping profoundly and, in the height of joy, said to him :—

" ' My powerful brother, Dashagriva, is here, who desires to vanquish the world of the Gods ; he has chosen thee as his ally, therefore go, O Titan, with thy kinsmen and lend him thy strong support. It is fitting that thou shouldst assist him in this matter on account of his magnanimity and the honour which he has paid thee.'

" On hearing this, Madhu answered, ' So be it ! ' and beholding Ravana, the Lord of the Rakshasas, he approached him according to tradition and paid him due tribute.

" Thus honoured, Dashagriva passed a night in Madhu's abode and then started on his way. Having reached Kailasha, that mountain that served as Vaishravana's retreat, the Indra among the Rakshasas, like unto Mahendra, caused his army to set up camp."

CHAPTER 26

Nalakuvara curses Ravana

" It was on Kailasha, the sun having withdrawn behind the Astachala Range, that Dashagriva, full of vigour, chose to encamp the army.

" When the immaculate moon rose over the mountain with a splendour equal to his, the vast host that composed the army, furnished with diverse weapons, lay sleeping.

" The mighty Ravana, resting on the summit of the mountain, surveyed the splendour of the forests in the light of the moon, the flaming Karnikara Woods, the Kadambas and Vakulas, pools covered with lotuses in bloom, the waters of the Mandakini, the Champaka, Ashoka, Punnaga, Mandara, Cuta, Patala, Lodhra, Priyanga, Arjuna, Ketaka, Tagara, Narikela, Priyala, Panasa and other trees. Sweet-throated Kinneras, transported with love, sang melodies that ravished the soul with delight ; there the Vidyadharas, intoxicated, their eyes inflamed, diverted themselves with their consorts. Like unto a carillon of bells, sweet music was heard from the troops of Apsaras who were singing in Dhanada's abode. Trees, shaken by the wind, covered the mountain with a shower of blossom, distilling the perfume of honey and mead, and a balmy breeze, laden with the enchanting aroma of nectar and pollen, blew, enhancing Ravana's voluptuous desire. The songs, the myriad flowers, the freshness of the breeze, the beauty of the mountain in the night, the moon at its zenith, threw Ravana, that mighty warrior, into a ferment of passion.

" Meanwhile, Rambha, loveliest of nymphs adorned with celestial ornaments, was on her way to a sacred festival and her face was like unto the full moon, her limbs smeared with sandal-paste, her hair sown with Mandara flowers, and she was garlanded with celestial blooms. Her eyes were beautiful, her waist high, adorned with a jewelled belt, and her hips were shapely, the gift of love as it were. She was enchanting with her countenance embellished with the marks of flowers[1] that bloom in the six seasons and, in her beauty, stateliness, radiance and splendour, she resembled Shri. Swathed in a dark blue cloth, like unto a rain cloud, her countenance bright as the moon, her eyebrows resplendent arches, her hips like the tapering trunks of elephants, her hands like two fresh buds, under Ravana's eyes she passed through the ranks of the army.

" Thereupon he, rising, pierced by the shafts of love, with his hand stayed the course of that nymph who was abashed and, smiling, enquired of her :—

" ' Where art thou going, O Lady of lovely hips ? What good fortune art thou pursuing ? For whom has this auspicious hour dawned ? Who is about to enjoy thee ? Who, this day, will quaff the elixir of thy lips exhaling the perfume of the lotus that rivals nectar or ambrosia ? Who will caress those two breasts like unto twin goblets, rounded, blooming, that touch each other, O Youthful Woman ? Who will stroke thy large hips shining like refined gold covered with dazzling garlands, celestial to look upon ? Is it Shakra or Vishnu or the Twin Ashvins ? O Lovely One, if thou dost pass me by in order to seek out another, it will not be a gracious act ! Rest here, O Lady of lovely limbs, on this enchanting mountain side, it is I, who

---

[1] It was customary for women to use flower dyes to trace patterns on their skin.

exercise dominion over the Three Worlds, who with joined palms address this humble request to thee, I, Dashanana, Lord of the Three Worlds and their Ordainer, therefore grant my request.'

"Hearing these words, Rambha, trembling, with joined palms, replied :—' Look on me with favour, it is not fitting that thou shouldst address me thus, thou who art my superior ! Rather is it thy duty to protect me from others if I should be in danger of suffering violence at their hands, for apart from duty, I am virtually thy daughter-in-law, I speak truth ! '

"Then Dashagriva answered Rambha, who had prostrated herself at his feet and whose hair stood on end merely on beholding him, and said :—

"' Hadst thou been my son's consort, thou wouldst in effect be my daughter-in-law ! ' Thereupon she answered :—

"' Truly it is so, by law, I am the wife of thy son and dearer to him than his life's breath, O Bull amongst the Rakshasas ; he is the son of thy brother Vaishravana, who is renowned in the Three Worlds, and is named Nalakuvara, an ascetic in virtue, a warrior in respect of valour and, in wrath he resembles Agni ; in forbearance he is like unto the earth ! I was going to meet that son of the Guardian of the Worlds ; it is for his sake that I am adorned with these ornaments so that he and no other should enjoy me. For these reasons, let me go hence, O King, O Subduer of thy Foes, for that virtuous prince awaits me impatiently. It is not for thee to thwart his desires, let me go ! Do thou follow the path of the virtuous, O Bull among the Rakshasas ! It is for me to pay thee homage and for thee to protect me ! '

"Thus did she address Dashagriva, who answered her in smooth accents, saying :—

"' Thou hast said thou art my daughter-in-law ! For those who have but one husband, this argument is valid but in Devaloka, the Gods have established a law that is said to be eternal, that Apsaras have no appointed consorts nor are the Gods monogamous ! '

"Thus speaking, the Rakshasa, who had stationed himself on the mountain ridge, inflamed with desire, ravished Rambha and, when she was released from his embrace, her garlands and her ornaments spoiled and torn away, she resembled a river where a great elephant, disporting himself, muddying the waters, has borne away the banks. Her hair in disorder, her hands clenched, like unto a creeper with its flowers shaken by the wind, trembling with terror, she sought out Nalakuvara and, with joined palms, fell at his feet.

" Then he enquired of her saying :—

" ' What is this, O Blessed One ? Why dost thou prostrate thyself at my feet ? '

" Thereupon she, sighing deeply, trembling, with joined palms began to tell him everything and said :—

" ' O Lord, this night, Dashagriva scaled the Trivishtapa Peak while he was encamped on that mountain with his army and I was observed by him as I came to meet thee, O Conqueror of Thy Foes ! That Rakshasa seized hold of me and questioned me saying " To whom dost thou belong ? " Then I told him all, verily the whole truth, but he, intoxicated with desire, would not listen to me when I pleaded with him, saying " I am thy daughter-in-law ! " Refusing to listen to mine entreaties, he assaulted me ruthlessly ! This is mine only fault, O Thou of firm vows, thou shouldst therefore pardon me. O Friend, verily there is no equality of strength between man and woman ! '

" These words filled the son of Vaishravana with indignation and hearing of this supreme outrage, he entered into meditation and having ascertained the truth, the son of Vaishravana, his eyes inflamed with anger, instantly took water in his hand and sprinkled his whole person in accord with tradition, after which he pronounced a terrible curse on that Indra of the Rakshasas, saying :—

" ' Since, despite thy lack of love for him, he ravished thee thus brutally, O Blessed One, on this account he will never be able to approach another youthful woman unless she shares his love ; if, carried away by lust, he does violence to any woman who does not love him, his head will split into seven pieces.'

" Having uttered this curse like unto a scorching flame, celestial gongs resounded and a shower of flowers fell from the sky. All the Gods with the Grandsire at their head were filled with joy, conversant as they were with the whole course of the world and the future death of the Rakshasa.

"When Dashagriva learnt of the curse, however, his hair stood on end and he ceased to indulge in uniting himself with those who had no affection for him. Thereafter, among those who had been borne away by him and remained faithful to their consorts, there was great rejoicing when they heard of the curse uttered by Nalakuvara, which was pleasing to their heart."

CHAPTER 27

The Fight between the Gods and the Rakshasas. The Death of Sumali

"HAVING crossed Mount Kailasha with his infantry and cavalry, the extremely powerful Dashanana reached Indraloka and, like an ocean that overflows, the tumult of the Rakshasa army, approaching on all sides, reverberated in Devaloka.

"Hearing of Ravana's advent, Indra trembled on his throne and addressed the assembled Gods, Adityas, Vasus, Rudras, Sadhyas and Hosts of Maruts, saying :—

"'Prepare to fight against the wicked-minded Ravana!'

"At Shakra's command, the Gods, his equals in war, endowed with great valour, boldly armed themselves for combat. Mahendra however, who feared Ravana extremely, profoundly perturbed, sought out Vishnu and spoke to him thus :—

"'O Vishnu, how shall I withstand the Rakshasa Ravana, whose strength is formidable and who, alas, is advancing to attack me? He owes his power to the boon he has received from Brahma and to nought else and the words uttered by that Lotus-born God must be carried into effect! Do Thou grant me such assistance again which Thou didst accord me when I destroyed Namuchi, Vritra, Bali, Naraka and Shambara! O Lord, O God of Gods, Slayer of Madhu, there is no refuge save Thee in the Three Worlds with all the animate and inanimate beings. Thou art the blessed Narayana, the eternal lotus-born One; Thou art the Sustainer of the Worlds and of myself, Shakra, the King of the Gods; Thou hast created the Three Worlds with all the moving and unmoving objects and, at the end of the world cycle, all is withdrawn into Thee, O Bhagawat;

therefore, O God of Gods, tell me truly if Thou wilt arm Thyself with sword and discus in order to enter into combat with Ravana ? '

" Thus spoke Shakra, the King of the Gods, and that sovereign Lord, Narayana, answered him saying :—

" ' Fear not ! Hear me ! On account of the boon he has received which renders him invincible, this wicked wretch may not be overcome by the Gods and Asuras combined ! Intoxicated with his power, that Rakshasa, accompanied by his son, will certainly achieve a great feat. As for thy request, that I should enter into combat with him, I shall certainly not meet the Rakshasa Ravana in fight, for Vishnu never leaves the battlefield without laying his adversary low ; it is not possible to accomplish this to-day since Ravana is protected by the boon, but I swear to thee, O King of the Gods, Shatakratu, that I myself will become the cause of that titan's death. The Gods shall rejoice when I make known to them that the hour has struck ! I speak the truth, O Mighty Lord of the Gods, Consort of Sachi, therefore fight with the assistance of the Gods and banish all fear ! '

" Then the Rudras with the Adityas, Vasus, Maruts and the two Ashvins, assembling, advanced to meet the Rakshasa. At that instant, the end of the night having come, a great clamour arose from Ravana's army as they took the field on all sides, and those valiant warriors, wrought up with excitement, on seeing each other, eagerly rushed on the foe. Thereafter confusion was sown amongst the ranks of the Daivatas by the presence of that indomitable and vast army in the forefront of battle and a terrible struggle ensued between the Gods, Danavas and Rakshasas, amidst a fearful tumult and under a hail of missiles of every kind.

" Then those valiant Rakshasas of grim aspect grouped themselves round Ravana in the fight, and Maricha, Prahasta, Mahaparshwa, Mahodara, Akampana, Nikumbha, Shuka, Sarana Dhumaketu, Mahadamshtra, Ghatodara, Jambumalin, Maharada Virupaksha, Saptaghna, Yajnakopa, Durmukha, Dushana, Khara, Trishiras, Karaviraksha, Suryashastru, Mahakaya and Atikaya, Devantaka, Narantaka and the highly powerful Sumali, Ravana's maternal grandfather, all those warriors, encircling their valiant leader, entered the battlefield.

"And with whetted shafts, enraged, he began to assail the Celestial Host, as a tempest scatters the clouds ; and the forces of the Gods were overthrown by the rangers of the night, O Rama, and scattered in all directions, like unto a herd of deer before lions.

" Meantime the courageous Savitra, the eighth Vasu, entered the battlefield surrounded by soldiers, full of martial ardour, furnished with every kind of weapon and he began to sow terror in the enemy ranks when he appeared in the midst of the fight. Thereafter the two Adityas, full of valour and intrepidity, Twastar and Pushan, at the head of a division, entered the lists in their turn, whereupon a fearful struggle ensued between the Rakshasas and the Gods, who never retreated in battle and were jealous of their good name. And the Celestials there present fell in hundreds of thousands under the blows of the Rakshasas, who were formidable and armed with weapons of every kind. On their side, the Gods, redoubtable in their vigour and extreme valour, with the help of faultless arrows, despatched their foes to the region of Yama. Thereupon O Rama, the Rakshasa Sumali, fully armed, hurled himself on the foe in fury and scattered the entire Celestial Host with his innumerable and penetrating missiles, as a violent hurricane, the clouds, and with formidable blows from spears and javelins, decimated them, so that the Gods were unable to stand.

" The Immortals having thus been put to flight by Sumali, the eighth Vasu, Savitra, enraged, stood fast, and surrounded by his forces, full of energy and courage stayed the onrush of that Ranger of the Night, whereupon a fearful duel, causing the hair to stand on end, ensued between Sumali and the Vasu, both warriors who did not know what it was to retreat in battle. Under the powerful missiles of his adversary, the chariot of the Rakshasa, that was harnessed to serpents, suddenly fell to pieces ; and having shattered his chariot in the fight with his countless darts, the Vasu seized hold of his mace with the intention of slaying him. Brandishing that weapon with its flaming point, resembling the Rod of Death, Savitra brought it down on Sumali's head and the mace fell upon him with the flash of a meteor, so that it appeared like a great thunderbolt hurled by Indra on a mountain. Thereafter nothing of the Rakshasa could be seen, neither bone nor head nor flesh, for that mace, by overthrowing him on the battle field, had reduced him to dust.

" Then the Rakshasas, beholding that Sumali had fallen in the fight, questioning each other, all fled, routed by that Vasu who had overcome them."

CHAPTER 28

The Duel between Indra and Ravana

" SEEING Sumali overthrown and reduced to dust by Vasu and beholding his army in flight harassed by the Gods, the valiant son of Ravana, whose voice resembled the muttering of a thundercloud, provoked, rallied the Rakshasas and, mounted on an excellent chariot that coursed wheresoere he willed, that great warrior hurled himself on the Celestial Host. Like unto a fire that consumes the forests, he entered the field armed with every weapon, and when the Gods beheld him, a general stampede followed, none daring to face such a combatant. Then Shakra stayed all those fugitives by admonishing them thus :—

" ' Neither should you tremble nor flee, return and fight, O Ye Gods ! Behold my son, who is invincible, entering the lists ! '

"At that moment the son of Shakra, the illustrious God Jayanta, mounted on his chariot, that was marvellously constructed, turned towards the battlefield. Thereafter the Gods, surrounding the son of Sachi, turned back to fight Ravani and a well-matched contest ensued between Gods and Rakshasas. Then Ravani loosed his golden shafts on Gomukha, the son of Matali, Jayanta's charioteer, whilst Sachi's son, in his turn, in wrath harassed Ravani's driver on every side. His eyes dilated with the fury that possessed him, the mighty Ravani covered his opponents with darts and thereafter, in his ire, he let fly innumerable extremely sharp weapons on the Celestial Host and Shataghnis, pikes, javelins, maces, swords, axes and huge crags were all discharged by him upon them. Then the worlds became agitated and while Indrajita decimated the enemy battalions the quarters were enveloped in darkness.

" Meanwhile the army of the Gods deserted Jayanta and, in

confusion broke their ranks, being overwhelmed by the shafts of their rival.

" Rakshasas and Gods could not distinguish each other and the forces thrown into disorder on every side, fled in all directions.

" The Gods struck the Gods and the Rakshasas the Rakshasas, bewildered by the darkness that enveloped them, whilst others ran away. At that instant, a warrior, full of valour, named Puloman, the foremost of the Daityas, seized Jayanta and bore him away. Taking hold of his daughter's son, he dived into the sea for he was his maternal grandfather and Sachi's sire.

" Learning of Jayanta's disappearance, the Gods, cast down and discouraged, dispersed. Then Ravani, enraged, emitting loud cries, surrounded by his forces rushed on the Gods.

" Not beholding his son and observing the flight of the Gods, the Lord of the Celestials said to Matali :—' Bring me my chariot ! ' and Matali harnessed the divine, powerful and huge car, bringing it in all haste to his master. Thereupon, above the chariot and before him, clouds, riven by lightning, driven by the tempest emitted formidable mutterings and the Gandharvas struck up every kind of musical instrument while troops of Apsaras danced at the departure of the King of the Gods, and Rudras, Vasus, Adityas, the two Ashvins, as also the Hosts of the Maruts, armed with every kind of weapon, formed the escort of the Lord of the Thirty, as he started out.

"As Shakra advanced, a bitter wind blew, the sun ceased to shine and a great meteor fell. At the same time, the courageous Dashagriva, burning with ardour, himself ascended the divine Pushpaka Car constructed by Vishvakarma and harnessed to huge serpents, who, as it were causing the hair to stand on end, consumed everything with the wind of their breath.

" Daityas and titans surrounded the celestial car that was rolling towards the field of battle, advancing to meet Mahendra, and Dashagriva, having dismissed his son, took his place himself, whilst Ravani left the field and remained a tranquil witness.

" Then the struggle was resumed between the Rakshasas and the Gods, who like unto clouds, caused a shower of missiles to fall in the fight. And the wicked Kumbhakarna, brandishing weapons of every kind, came there, O King, unaware with whom the conflict was taking place ; using his teeth, his feet, his hands, lances, picks, mallets or anything whatsoever in order to assail the Gods in his fury. Having attacked the formidable Rudras, it went ill with that Ranger of the Night, who, in an instant, was riddled with wounds ; and the army of the Rakshasas, hard pressed by the Gods, assisted by the Hosts of Maruts and armed with every weapon, were completely routed and, in the struggle, some fell on the earth mutilated and palpitating, whilst others remained clinging to their mounts. Some titans twined their arms round their chariots, elephants, donkeys, buffalo, serpents, horses, porpoise and boars with heads of goblins, where they lay motionless, whereupon the Gods pierced them with their shafts and thus they died. The sight of all those Rakshasas lying here and there in the sleep of death on that vast battlefield looked passing strange and, at the forefront of the battle, a river flowed, blood being its waters, weapons its crocodiles, in which vultures and crows abounded.

" Meantime Dashagriva, seething with anger on seeing his army entirely overthrown by the Gods, hurled himself with one bound into that sea of warriors, slaying the Celestials in the fight and challenging Shakra himself.

" Thereupon Shakra stretched his great bow that gave forth a thunderous noise and, when he drew it, the twanging of that weapon caused the quarters to resound. Then Indra, bending that great bow, let fall his flaming arrows like unto fire or the sun on Ravana's head and, on his side, that powerful titan covered his rival with a hail of arrows loosed from his bow and both showered down missiles on every side so that nothing could be distinguished and the whole firmament was enveloped in darkness."

CHAPTER 29

Ravani takes Indra captive

" IN the darkness that had supervened, the Gods and the Rakshasas engaged in a terrible struggle, slaying each other in the intoxication of their strength and, in the obscurity that enveloped them like a great veil, the supremely intrepid Indra, Ravana and Meghanada alone were not deluded.

"Beholding that army wholly annihilated, Ravana was suddenly seized with violent rage and emitted a great roar. In his fury that invincible warrior addressed his driver, who stood near with the chariot, saying, ' Take me through the enemy ranks from one end to the other ! This very day, with mine innumerable and powerful weapons, all the Gods in my path will be despatched by me to the region of Yama. I myself shall slay Indra, Dhanada, Varuna, Yama and all the Gods and shall soon strike them down and trample them under my feet. Do not delay, drive the car on speedily, and again I say to thee, " Drive through the enemy ranks from end to end ! We are now in the Nandana Gardens therefore take me to the Udaya Mountain ! " '

"At this command, the charioteer drove his steeds, who were as swift as thought, through the enemy ranks.

" Divining Ravana's intention, Shakra, standing in his chariot on the battlefield, addressed the Gods, whose sovereign he was, saying :—

" ' O Ye Gods, hear me, this is what I consider expedient—Dashagriva should without delay be captured alive. That extremely powerful Rakshasa will enter our ranks in his chariot with the speed of the wind, like unto an ocean whose waves are overflowing on the day of high tide. He may not be slain for a special boon protects him but seek to make him captive in the struggle ! It was by taking Bali prisoner that I was able to enjoy the Three Worlds ; for this reason let us do the same to this wicked wretch.'

" Thus speaking, Shakra left Ravana and went to another part of the field, sowing terror among the Rakshasas whom he assailed, O Great King.

"While the indefatigable Dashagriva went to the left, Shatakratu penetrated the right wing of his adversary's forces. Having advanced a hundred leagues, the King of the Rakshasas covered the entire Host of the Gods with a shower of arrows.

" Seeing the carnage that was being created in his army, the intrepid Shakra stayed Dashanana by encircling him, whereupon the Danavas and Rakshasas beholding Ravana overcome by Shakra, cried out ' Alas ! We are lost ! '

" Standing in his chariot, Ravani, who was transported with rage, penetrated into the ranks of the redoubtable Celestial Host and routed the army by resorting to the power of illusion that had been conferred on him by Pashupati. Then, leaving the Gods aside, he rushed on Shakra himself, and the highly energetic Mahendra did not observe the son of his adversary. The Gods, however, whose strength was immeasurable, severed Ravani's armour, even wounding him, but he remained unperturbed and with his excellent shafts pierced Matali who was advancing towards him, covering Mahendra afresh with a hail of missiles.

" Thereupon Shakra descended from his chariot dismissing his charioteer, and mounting Airavata, he pursued Ravani, who had made himself invisible through his magic power, but he, springing into the sky, assailed him with arrows. Seeing that Indra was exhausted, Ravani bound him by his magic and led him to the side where his own army was. Beholding Mahendra borne away by force from the fight, all the Celestials enquired ' What has taken place ? One cannot discern the magician who has triumphed over Shakra, that victorious warrior, who, by the aid of magic, has carried Indra away despite his skill.' Then all the divisions of the Gods, in their wrath, overwhelmed Ravana with a hail of shafts and forced him to retreat, whilst he, worn out in the encounter with the Adityas and the Vasus was unable to continue the fight.

" Beholding his sire harassed and assailed with shafts in the encounter, Ravani, remaining invisible in the struggle, said to him :—

" ' Come, O Dear Father, let us give up the fight, know that victory has been obtained, therefore abandon thy feverish activity! The King of the Gods and of the Three Worlds has been taken captive ! The Gods have seen the pride, which inspired their forces, humbled. Enjoy the Three Worlds at thy pleasure, having overcome the foe by thy valour, why fatigue thyself further with combat ? '

" Hearing Ravani's words, the battalions of the Gods and the Immortals deprived of Shakra, who had led them, gave up the fight. And the all-powerful enemy of the Gods, the illustrious Sovereign of the Rakshasas, thus entreated to cease from further fighting by his son, whose dear voice he recognized, answered him with deference, saying :—

" ' Thy valour is equal to the greatest of heroes, thou in whom my family and race find their increase, O Prince, since this day thou hast overcome the one whose strength is immeasurable, he, the Sovereign of the Gods. Ascend Vasava's chariot and proceed towards the city with thine army as an escort ; I, on my side, with my companions, will follow joyfully with all speed.'

" On this the valiant Ravani, surrounded by his forces with the Chief of the Gods in chains, set out towards his abode, thereafter dismissing the Rakshasas who had fought in the campaign."

CHAPTER 30

Telling of the Curse pronounced by the Sage Gautama on Shakra

" WHEN the all-powerful Mahendra had been overcome by the son of Ravana, the Gods with Prajapati at their head went to Lanka and, approaching Dashagriva, who was surrounded by his brothers, Prajapati, from the sky where he was stationed, addressed him in conciliatory tones, saying :—

" ' My Dear Ravana, I am pleased with thy son's bearing on the battlefield ! Assuredly in valour and heroism, he is thine equal if not thy superior ! Thou hast overcome the Three Worlds by thy prowess and fulfilled thy vow ; I am gratified with thee and thy son. He, standing there full of strength and energy, will become renowned in the worlds under the name of Indrajita[1] and that Rakshasa, with whose support the Gods have been brought under thy subjection, shall become powerful and invincible. O Long-armed Hero, do thou release Mahendra, the Chastiser of Paka and say what the inhabitants of heaven shall bestow on thee as ransom ? '

" Then that victorious warrior, Indrajita, answered saying:—

" ' O Lord, if that God is to be set free, then grant me immortality ! '

[1] Conqueror of Indra.

" Thereupon the all-powerful Prajapati replied to Meghanada, saying :—

" ' There is none immortal on earth, whether it be beast, bird or any other mighty being.'

" Hearing this irrevocable decree of the Grandsire, the Lord, Indra's vanquisher, the courageous Meghanada, said to him :—

" ' Then hear me , and may it come to pass in this wise on the release of Shatakratu ! This is my desire, I, who constantly worship Pavaka with oblations and mantras and who delight in fighting and overcoming my foes, let the chariot of Vibhabasu harnessed to steeds, be placed at my service and may death be unable to strike me down when I am mounted upon it ! This is my request, but, should I engage in combat without having completed my prayers and offered my oblations to the God of Fire, then may I perish ! All, O Lord, seek immortality by means of penances ; I wish to acquire immortality through valour ! '

" ' Let it be so ' said the Blessed Grandsire and thereafter Shakra was set free by Indrajita and the Gods returned to their own abode.

" Meantime, O Rama, the wretched Indra, his glory dimmed, his heart full of anxiety, was plunged in melancholy and, beholding him in that plight, the Grandsire enquired of him, saying :—

" ' O Shatakratu, didst thou not formerly commit some great sin ? O Chief of the Gods, O Lord, when in my wisdom I created men, they were all possessed of the same colour, shape, language and appearance, there was no difference between them in form or aspect, nevertheless my mind was pre-occupied when I reflected on those beings and, I created a woman as distinct from them, modifying each of the male characteristics. Thus I made a female, who on occount of the grace of her limbs became known as Ahalya ; " Hala " meaning ugly, from which " Halya " is derived, and she in whom " Halya " does not appear is named Ahalya; this was the name I called her. When I fashioned that woman, O Chief of the Gods, O Bull among the Celestials, I reflected, " To whom shall she belong ? " This is how, O Lord Shakra, O Destroyer of Cities, thou didst come to know this woman and, in thine heart, being the Lord of the Worlds, thou didst resolve " she shall be mine ".'

" ' Meantime I placed her under the protection of the

magnanimous Gautama and he, having taken care of her for many years, gave her back to me, whereupon I, having tested the absolute self-control of that illustrious ascetic and recognizing the height of his austerity, gave her to him in wedlock. That virtuous and renowned Muni was gratified with her company but the Gods were in despair because she had been given to Gautama and thou, enraged, thy heart filled with desire, went to the hermitage of the Sage and beheld the woman who was as radiant as a flame in a brazier, whereupon thou didst ravish her in the heat of thy passion. Thereafter thou wert observed by that high-born Rishi in the hermitage and, in his indignation, that extremely powerful ascetic cursed thee, due to which, O King of the Gods, thou hast just suffered this change of circumstance. And that ascetic addressed thee, saying :—

" ' " Since thou hast wantonly ravished my spouse, O Vasava, thou shalt fall captive to thine enemy on the field of battle ! This vile passion that thou hast manifested, O Perverse Wretch, will undoubtedly spread among men and women and whosoever shall be guilty of it shall bear half the responsibility, whilst the other half shall be thine ; nor shall thy state be permanent, for the sovereignty of whoever the Gods choose as their King shall not endure ; this is the curse I pronounce on thee ! "

" ' Thus spoke Gautama and thereafter he reproached his spouse, and that exalted ascetic addressed her, saying :—

" ' " O Shameless One, leave my hermitage ! Though young and lovely, since thou art inconstant, thy beauty shall no longer belong to thee alone in the world and shall assuredly be shared by all beings, since on thine account, this mischief has been perpetrated by Indra ! From now on, all beings shall partake of thy beauty ! "

" ' Then Ahalya sought to propitiate the great Rishi Gautama, saying :—

" ' " It was in ignorance that I suffered myself to be seduced by Indra, O Great Ascetic, for he assumed thy form, nor was it by giving way to desire, O Rishi, therefore forgive me, it is thy duty ! "

" 'At these words of Ahalya's, Gautama answered :—

" ' " In the House of Ikshvaku there will be born a mighty warrior named Rama, renowned in the universe and he will repair to the forest for the sake of the brahmins. That long-armed hero will be none other than Vishnu in human form; thou shalt behold him, O Blessed One, and, seeing him, thou shalt be purified, for it is he who can efface the sin thou hast committed. Having offered him the traditional hospitality, thou shalt return to me once again and we shall resume our common life, O Lady of fair countenance!"

"'Having spoken thus, the Rishi re-entered his hermitage, while his consort gave herself up to rigid penances. It is on account of this Sage's curse that all this has taken place; therefore, O Mighty Hero, call to mind the sin thou didst commit. This is why thou didst fall a victim to thy foes, O Vasava, and for no other cause, therefore, with thy senses fully controlled, speedily offer up a sacrifice to Vishnu. Purified by this propitiatory rite, thou shalt return to the Celestial Region. Thy son, O Lord, did not perish in the fight but was borne away to the ocean by his maternal grandfather.'

"Hearing Brahma's words, Mahendra undertook a sacrifice in honour of Vishnu and thereafter the Lord of the Gods ascended to heaven, reigning there as king.

"I have described to thee, how great was the power of Indrajita, who overcame the King of the Gods, how much more therefore was he able to triumph over other beings!"

Hearing these words of Agastya, Rama and Lakshmana as also the monkeys and titans, exclaimed "How wonderful!" and Bibishana, who stood at Rama's side, said :—

"I remember that remarkable feat now, I was formerly witness thereof."

Then Rama addressed Agastya saying :—"All thou hast said is true!"

"This, O Rama, is the narrative of the origin and progress of Ravana, the thorn in the side of the worlds, who, like his son, bore away Shakra, the King of the Gods, in the fight."

CHAPTER 31

Ravana goes to the Banks of the Narmada River

THE all-powerful Rama, in his astonishment, bowed low to that excellent Rishi Agastya and again enquired of him, saying :—

" O Blessed One, O Best of the Twice-born, when that cruel Rakshasa began to range the earth, were the worlds bereft of warriors ? Was there no prince, no being, able to oppose him, since that Lord of the Titans met with no resistance, or had the rulers of the worlds lost their power or were the many kings he overcame, without weapons ? "

Having listened to the words of that son of Raghu, the blessed Sage answered him smiling, as the Grandsire of the World addresses Rudra, and said :—

" It was destroying the rulers thus that Ravana ranged the earth and, O Rama, Lord of the Worlds, he came to the city of Mahishmati which rivalled that of the Gods, where the Deity of Fire dwelt perpetually. There a monarch reigned, named Arjuna, in effulgence like unto the fire which was kept there ever concealed in a pit covered by reeds.[1]

" On that day, the powerful Sovereign of the Haihayas, Lord Arjuna went to the River Narmada to sport with his wives and at that time, Ravana approached Mahishmati and that Indra among the Rakshasas enquired of the King's counsellors, saying :—

" ' Tell me quickly, where is the Lord Arjuna, speak truly ; I am Ravana who have come to measure my strength with that most powerful of monarchs. Do you announce mine arrival to him ! '

" Hearing Ravana's words, the sagacious ministers informed the King of the Rakshasas of the absence of their sovereign and the son of Vishravas learning from the people of the city that Arjuna had departed, went away in the direction of the Vindhya Range, which like unto a cloud floating in space, appeared to him to resemble Himavat and, springing from the earth, it

---

[1] Agni Kunda—A pit or hole in the ground where the sacred fire is kept.

seemed to lick the skies and was possessed of a myriad peaks. Lions frequented its caverns whilst its crystalline cataracts, falling over the cliffs, resounded like peals of laughter, and Gods, Gandharvas as also the Apsaras and Kinneras with their consorts, disporting themselves there, transformed it into a paradise. Its rivers flowed in translucent waves and that Vindhya Range, like unto Himavat, with its peaks and caves resembled Shesha with his hoods, his tongues darting forth.

" Gazing upon it, Ravana reached the Narmada River, whose pure waters flowed over a bed of stones and which emptied itself into the western sea. Buffalo, Srimaras, lions, tigers, bears and elephants, tormented by heat and thirst, agitated the waters, whilst Chakravakas, Kavandas, Hamsas, Sarasas and other waterfowl, with their impassioned warbling, abounded there. The flowering trees formed its diadem, the pairs of Chakravaka birds its breasts, the banks of sand its thighs, the flocks of swans its bright girdle ; the pollen of the flowers powdered its limbs, the foam of the waves was its immaculate robe ; sweet was its contact for whoever entered it and it was lovely to look upon with its flowering lotuses.

" Dismounting from the Chariot Pushpaka, close to the Narmada, that most beautiful of streams, Dashanana, a bull among titans, accompanied by his ministers, went towards it as towards a lovely and attractive woman and seated himself on the enchanting sandy banks that were frequented by Sages.

" Beholding the Narmada, the ten-necked Ravana, transported with delight, exclaimed ' It is the Ganges herself ! ' Thereafter he addressed his ministers Shuka and Sarana and others, saying :—

" ' Surya of a thousand rays seems to have changed the world to gold and, in the sky, that orb of the day whose beams were just now intense, having observed me seated here, has grown as cool as the moon. Anila, who, refreshed by the waters of the Narmada, inspired by fear of me, blows softly diffusing a sweet perfume, that marvellous stream, the Narmada, increaser of felicity, in whose waters crocodile, fish and birds abound, appears like a timid girl. You who were wounded by the weapons of kings equal to Shakra in combat and who were covered with blood like unto the sap of the Sandal Tree, now plunge into the beautiful and hospitable Narmada as elephants intoxicated with ichor and led by Sarvabhauma immerse themselves in the Ganges. Bathing in that great river will free you from all ills ! As for me, I shall presently offer up flowers in tranquillity to Kapardin on this sandy bank that shines like the autumn moon.'

" Hearing these words of Ravana, Prahasta, Shuka and Sarana with Mahodara and Dhumraksha dived into the Narmada River and, agitated by those titan leaders resembling elephants, the stream appeared like unto the Ganges when Vamana, Anjana, Padma and other great tuskers disport themselves therein.

" Thereafter, emerging from the waters, those highly powerful Rakshasas soon gathered heaps of flowers that they placed on the sandy bank, whose enchanting radiance rivalled that of a dazzling cloud and, in a moment, those titans had heaped up a mountain of flowers, whereupon the King of the Rakshasas entered the river to bathe, like unto a great tusker entering the Ganges.

" Having bathed and recited the most excellent of prayers according to tradition, Ravana emerged from the waters and divested himself of his wet garments, clothing himself in a white robe. Then the Rakshasas followed their king, who advanced with joined palms, so that they appeared like moving hills. Wherever the Lord of the Rakshasas went, a golden Shiva-Linga was borne before him and he placed it on a sandy altar and worshipped it with flowers, perfumes and sandal-paste. Having paid homage to that symbol that delivers all beings from their sufferings and which was large and exceedingly beautiful, adorned with a crescent moon, that Ranger of the Night, with uplifted arms, danced and sang before it."

CHAPTER 32

Arjuna captures Ravana

" NOT far from where the dread Lord of the Rakshasas was making his offering of flowers on the sandy banks of the Narmada, Arjuna, the foremost of conquerors, supreme sovereign of Mahishmati, was sporting with his wives in the waters of that river. In their midst, that monarch looked like a great tusker surrounded by innumerable female elephants. Then he, desiring to measure the great strength of his thousand arms, stayed the rapid course of the Narmada and, the waters thus arrested by the myriad arms of Kartavirya, flowed towards its source bearing away its banks. With its fishes, crocodiles and sharks, its carpet of flowers and Kusha Grass, the current of the Narmada grew turbulent, as in the rainy season, and, as if purposely released by Kartavirya, that flood bore away all Ravana's floral offerings, whereupon he, leaving the sacrifice only half performed, cast his glance on the river that appeared to him to resemble a cherished consort who is overwrought.

" Having surveyed the waters rising like waves in the sea, rushing from the west to overwhelm the eastern shore, Ravana observed that, in a little while, the birds no longer shunned it and it had returned to its natural state, like a woman who is pacified.

" Pointing with the finger of his right hand, Dashagriva signalled to Shuka and Sarana that they should seek out the cause of the rising current and, at this command from their king, the two brothers, Shuka and Sarana rose into the air and turned westward. Having traversed two miles, those Night-rangers observed a man in the river sporting with some women and he resembled a huge Sala Tree, his hair floating in the stream and the corners of his eyes were inflamed by the desire which agitated his heart. And that Scourge of his Foes blocked the river with his myriad arms, as a mountain the earth with its countless slopes and foot-hills, and innumerable fair women surrounded him, as a tusker in rut is encircled by female elephants.

" Beholding that prodigious sight, the two Rakshasas, Shuka and Sarana returned together to Ravana and said to him :—

" ' O Prince of the Rakshasas, an unknown person, like unto an enormous Sala Tree, in order to amuse his consorts, is staying the course of the Narmada like a dyke. Restrained by his myriad arms, the river is throwing up great waves like unto the sea ! '

" Hearing these words from Shuka and Sarana, Ravana said, ' It is Arjuna ' and rushed away, eager to enter into combat with him. And, as Ravana, the Lord of the Rakshasas, set forth to meet Arjuna, a fierce dust storm arose accompanied by muttering clouds raining drops of blood and that Indra among the Rakshasas, escorted by Mahodara, Mahaparshwa, Dhumraksha, Shuka and Sarana, proceeded in the direction where Arjuna was. Soon that mighty Rakshasa, of the hue of antimony, reached the waters of the Narmada and there, surrounded by his wives, as a tusker by female elephants, the foremost of monarchs, Arjuna appeared before him. Then the Lord of the Rakshasas, who was intoxicated with power, his eyes red with anger, said to Arjuna's ministers in stentorian tones :—

" ' O Counsellors of the Lord Haihaya, inform him speedily that he who is called Ravana has come to fight with him ! '

" When they heard these words of Ravana, Arjuna's ministers raised their weapons and answered him saying :—

" ' O Ravana, thou hast indeed chosen an excellent moment for combat ! Wouldst thou fight a prince who is drunk and who is, further, amidst his consorts ? Dost thou really desire to fight with our king whilst he is surrounded by his wives ? Possess thyself in patience to-day, O Dashagriva, and when the night is over, if thou still wishest to do so, then challenge Arjuna, O Dear Friend. If, however, thou art bent on combat, O Thou sated with war, then overcome us here and thereafter meet Arjuna and fight with him.'

" Then Ravana's ministers slew some of Arjuna's counsellors and devoured them avidly, and a great uproar arose on the banks of the Narmada, from the followers of Arjuna and Ravana's ministers. The soldiers of the King of the Haihayas assailed Ravana and his ministers, on whom they hurled themselves with appalling fury with arrows, darts, javelins and tridents that pierced like lightning, and they created a tumult like unto the sea with its crocodiles, fish and sharks.

" Meanwhile the ministers of Ravana, Prahasta, Shuka and Sarana, enraged and full of valour, decimated the army of Kartavirya, and Arjuna's followers, mad with terror, informed him of the attack by Ravana and his ministers.

" On these tidings, Arjuna addressed the concourse of women, saying :—' Have no fear ', and rushed out of the water, like another Pavaka emitting terrible flames, so that he resembled the Fire of Dissolution at the end of the World Period. Adorned with bracelets of refined gold, he at once seized hold of a mace and hurled himself on the Rakshasas, whom he dispersed as the sun the darkness. With his arms, Arjuna, having brandished the huge mace, let it fall with the force of Garuda's flight.

" Then Prahasta, unshakeable, like unto a hill, mace in hand, stood barring his path, like unto the Vindhya Range obstructing the sun, and he hurled that dreadful weapon bound with copper, emitting a great shout like unto Antaka. At the tip of the pike, loosed by Prahasta's hand, a brilliant flame appeared like the point of an Ashoka Tree that seemed to glow, but the son of Kritavirya, Arjuna, without being perturbed, skilfully deflected that mace that was falling upon him, with his own weapon. Then the supreme Lord of the Haihayas hurled himself on his adversary with his heavy weapon which he brandished in his five hundred arms.

" Struck by that powerful blow of the mace, Prahasta, who had confronted him, fell like a mountain that has been riven by Indra's thunderbolt.

" Seeing Prahasta lying there, Maricha, Shuka and Sarana, as also Mahodara and Dhumraksha fled from the battlefield.

" His ministers routed and Prahasta struck down, Ravana threw himself on Arjuna, the foremost of monarchs, and a formidable duel ensued between that king of a myriad arms and the twenty-armed Ravana causing the hair to stand on end. Like unto two oceans that overflow, two mountains shaken to their foundations, two flaming suns, two blazing fires, two elephants intoxicated with their own strength, two bulls fighting for a heifer, two muttering clouds, two lions proud of their strength, like unto Rudra and Kala enraged, so did the Rakshasa and the King Arjuna, armed with maces, assail each other with fearful blows. Resembling mountains, able to withstand the dreadful lightning strokes, so did man and Rakshasa endure the blows of the mace. As the noise of thunder creates reverberations, so the impact of those weapons resounded in every quarter. Arjuna's mace, falling on his opponent's breast, lent it the appearance of gold or a cloud illumined by lightning. In the same way, each time Ravana's mace fell on Arjuna's breast, it resembled a meteor falling on a high mountain. Neither Arjuna nor the Sovereign of the Rakshasas wearied in the struggle, which remained undecided as formerly the duel between Bali and Indra. As two bulls struggle with their horns or two elephants with their sharp tusks, so did those two most valiant of men and Rakshasas fight. Finally Arjuna, in fury, with all his strength struck the huge chest of Ravana with his mace, but, protected by the armour bestowed on him by Brahma as a boon, that weapon was rendered impotent and fell cloven on the earth. Under the blow dealt by Arjuna, however, Ravana fell back a bow's length and sank down groaning.

"Perceiving him to be overcome, Arjuna immediately rushed on Dashagriva and seized hold of him as Garuda did a serpent. With his myriad arms, that mighty king took hold of Dashanana and bound him as Narayana had bound Bali.

"Ravana, having been made captive, all the Siddhas, Charanas and Devatas cried out, 'Well done! Well done!' and showered flowers on Arjuna's head. As a tiger who has captured a gazelle or a lion an elephant, so did the King of the Haihayas emit loud roars like unto a cloud.

"Thereafter the night-ranger, Prahasta, having recovered consciousness, seeing Dashanana bound, rushed on Arjuna in fury and the forces of the Rakshasas assailed him with extreme violence as, at the end of the hot season, the rain-clouds break over the ocean.

"'Release him! Release him!' they cried unceasingly, attacking Arjuna with iron bars and spears but, entirely unmoved by the hail of weapons, ere they could reach him, the intrepid King of the Haihayas, Scourge of his Foes speedily took hold of those projectiles hurled at him by the enemies of the Gods, and by means of many a dreadful and irresistible missile, he put them to flight as the wind disperses the clouds.

"Having scattered the Rakshasas, Arjuna, the son of Kritavirya, surrounded by his friends, bearing Ravana, bound, returned to his city. Then the Twice-born and the people scattered flowers and rice upon him, as he made his entry into the capital, resembling the God of a Thousand Eyes when he captured Bali."

CHAPTER 33

Arjuna releases Ravana on the request of Poulastya

"HEARING from the Gods in heaven of Ravana's capture, which resembled the binding of the wind, Poulastya, despite his self-mastery, was moved by tender affection for his offspring and approached the Lord of Mahishmati. Entering the path of the wind, whom he equalled in velocity, that Twice-born One, with the swiftness of thought, reached the City of Mahishmati and, as Brahma enters Indra's capital, he penetrated into that city that resembled Amaravati and was full of prosperous and cheerful people.

" Walking on foot, he advanced like unto the sun with such effulgence that the eye could scarcely rest upon him and, beholding him, the inhabitants hastened to inform Arjuna.

" ' It is Poulastya ', said that Sovereign of the Haihayas on perceiving him, whereupon, with joined palms, he touched his forehead in salutation as he went forward to meet the ascetic. Like Brihaspati before Shakra so did the Purohita precede the king, bearing the Arghya and also the Madhuparka offerings.

" Thereafter the Rishi drew near like unto the rising sun, and Arjuna, deeply moved on beholding him, paid obeisance to him as Indra offers reverence to Brahma. Presenting him with the Madhuparka, a cow, and water wherewith to wash his feet, as also the Arghya, that Indra among Monarchs addressed Poulastya in a voice trembling with delight and said :—

" ' Since I behold thee, O Thou whose sight is hard to obtain, to-day Mahishmati has become the equal of Amaravati, O Foremost of the Twice-born ! To-day I am happy, O Lord, to-day, my desires are consummated ; to-day my birth is rendered fruitful ; to-day, my penance has been blessed since I now embrace thy two feet that are worshipped by the Celestial Host. Here is my kingdom and here my sons and my consorts at thy service ; what are thy commands ? '

" Then Poulastya, having enquired concerning his welfare, the discharge of his duty and the sacrificial fires and his offspring, said to the Sovereign of the Haihayas :—

486

" ' O Foremost of Kings, whose eyes are as large as lotus petals, whose face shines like the full moon, none is equal to thee in strength since thou hast conquered Dashagriva, he, before whom, the ocean and the wind are stayed and remain motionless in fear, he, my grandson whom thou didst make captive on the battlefield, who till now was invincible. Thou hast swallowed his glory and rendered thy name illustrious. O Dear Friend, on my request, now release Dashanana ! '

" Thereupon Arjuna, without uttering a word, having listened to Poulastya's appeal, cheerfully released the foremost of the Rakshasas and, having set that enemy of the Gods free, Arjuna honoured him with jewels, garlands and celestial raiment and contracted an alliance with him in the presence of fire, then, prostrating himself at the feet of Brahma's son,[1] he returned to his abode.

" Thereafter Poulastya himself dismissed the powerful Lord of the Rakshasas after embracing him and he, having received hospitality, departed, ashamed at his defeat, whilst Poulastya, the son of that Grandsire of the World, he the foremost of Munis, who had just delivered Dashagriva, returned to Brahma-loka.

" Thus, despite his immense strength, was Ravana, who had been defeated by Kartavirya, released at Poulastya's request. So are the mighty overcome by those who are still mightier than they, O Thou, who increaseth the felicity of the Raghavas ! He who desires his own happiness should not despise his adversaries.

" Meanwhile the Lord of those eaters of flesh, having contracted a friendship with that thousand-armed monarch, began to range the earth full of arrogance, overcoming its rulers."

CHAPTER 34

Bali hangs Ravana on his Girdle

"RELEASED by Arjuna, Ravana, the Lord of the Rakshasas, unwearyingly ranged the earth and whenever he heard of any who was possessed of extraordinary strength, whether man or titan,

---

[1] Poulastya.

in his arrogance he sought him out in order to provoke him to combat.

" One day he came to the city of Kishkindha and challenged King Bali of the golden diadem. There he found the kinsfolk of that monkey only, Tara, her father Sushena and the Lord Sugriva, who answered that belligerent one, who had just come, saying :—

" ' O King of the Rakshasas, Bali, who would have accepted thy challenge, is not here, what other Plavamgama is able to meet thee in combat ? Bali has gone to the four oceans to perform the Sandhya Ceremony, O Ravana, he will soon return, have patience awhile ! That heap of bones, white as conch shells, belongs to those who desired to measure their strength in combat with the Lord of the Vanaras, O Prince. Even hadst thou sucked the nectar of immortality, O Ravana, thy meeting with Bali would put an end to thine existence. O Son of Vishravas, look upon this marvellous universe once more for soon it will no longer be possible for thee to do so. Since thou art in haste to die, however, go to the southern sea where thou wilt behold Bali who resembles the Deity of Fire.'

" Thereupon, having inveighed against Tara and the others, Ravana, that Ravana of the Worlds,[1] remounted his Chariot Pushpaka and drove towards the southern sea. There he beheld Bali, like unto a mountain of gold, absorbed in the performance of Sandhya.

" Descending from the Pushpaka Car, Ravana of the hue of collyrium, stole upon Bali silently in order to seize him, but by chance, he was observed by him who had no doubts as to his fell design, though Bali remained unmoved like a lion in the presence of a hare or Garuda before a serpent, and he was in no wise perturbed by Ravana of malevolent intent.

" He reflected, ' This is Ravana, who with malice in his soul, approaches in order to seize hold of me. I shall hang him on my girdle and go to the three other oceans, then all will behold mine adversary, Dashagriva, his arms and limbs and his raiment dangling, hooked to my side like a snake caught by Garuda.'

" Thinking thus, Bali remained there reciting his Vedic Mantras in a low voice, like unto the King of the Mountains.

[1] Ravana meaning " The One who causes others to cry out '.

Each desiring to lay hold on the other, in the pride their strength inspired in them, the Sovereign of the Monkeys and the Lord of the Rakshasas sought to realise their design.

" Perçeiving by the sound of his footsteps that Ravana was about to place his hands upon him, Bali, though his back was turned, caught hold of the titan as Garuda a serpent and, having seized the Lord of the Rakshasas, hooked him to his girdle, thereupon that monkey, with one bound, sprang into the air, and though lacerated and torn by his nails, Bali carried off Ravana as a tempest propels a cloud.

" Meantime the ministers of Dashanana, whom he was bearing away, fell upon Bali emitting loud cries in order to make him release him. Pursued by them, Bali, in his aerial course, shone like the sun that is followed by a drift of clouds in space. Those foremost of the Rakshasas, exhausted by the wind that caused their arms and thighs to shake, were stayed in their course, and the mountains themselves made way for Bali, how much more those who, made of flesh and blood, sought to survive. With a speed impossible to flocks of birds, that Indra among monkeys, in great haste, paid obeisance to all the oceans in turn and, at dusk, received the homage of all winged creatures on the way, he, the foremost among them ; thereafter with Ravana he finally reached the Western Sea. There that monkey performed the Sandhya Ceremony and, having bathed, still bearing Dashanana, went to the Northern Sea. Thereafter that great monkey with his adversary traversed thousands of leagues, swift as the wind or thought. Having observed the Sandhya Ceremony at the Northern Sea, Bali, carrying Dashanana, went to the Eastern Sea. There, Vasavi, the Lord of the Monkeys, performed his evening devotions and, still bearing Ravana, he returned to Kishkindha. Having performed the Sandhya at the four oceans, that monkey, weary of supporting Ravana, halted in a wood near Kishkindha and that King of the Monkeys, unhooking Ravana from his girdle, with a mocking laugh, said :—' Whence art thou ? '

" Greatly astonished, the King of the Rakshasas, whose eyes were half-closed with fatigue, addressed the Lord of the Monkeys thus :—

" ' O Foremost of Monkeys, O Thou who resemblest Mahendra, I am the Lord of the Rakshasas, Ravana, who came in the hope of entering into combat with thee and here I am, thy captive! What strength, what energy, what inner power has enabled thee to bind me thus without fatigue and with such speed, O Valiant Monkey? Assuredly there are only three beings who could have acted thus, the mind, the wind and Suparna. Having witnessed thy power, O Bull among Monkeys, in the presence of fire I wish to enter into an alliance of sincere and enduring friendship with thee! Consorts, sons, city, kingdom, pleasures, raiment and food will all be shared by us, O King, O Foremost of the Monkeys!'

"Thereupon, lighting a fire, monkey and titan became brothers and embraced each other. Clasping hands, the monkey and the titan joyfully entered Kishkindha, like unto two lions into a rocky cavern. Resembling another Sugriva, Ravana sojourned there for a month and thereafter his ministers desirous of overcoming the Three Worlds, led him away.

"Thus did Ravana act with Bali formerly and, although humbled by him, swore to be his brother in the presence of fire. Bali's strength was unequalled, O Rama, it was immeasurable ; yet thou didst consume him as the fire a cricket."

CHAPTER 35

The Story of Hanuman's Childhood

THEN Rama made a further enquiry of that Sage, whose hermitage was in the southern region and, paying obeisance to him in great reverence, with joined palms addressed him in pregnant terms, saying :—

"Assuredly the prowess of Bali and Ravana was incomparable, yet, to my mind at least, it was never equal to Hanuman's! Courage, skill, strength, tenacity of purpose, sagacity, experience, energy and prowess are all to be found in Hanuman!

"When beholding the Ocean, the army of the monkeys was in despair, that long-armed hero consoled them, traversing a hundred leagues and destroying the City of Lanka. Entering Ravana's inner apartments, he discovered Sita and encouraged her by his words. Single-handed, Hanuman slew those who marched at the head of the enemy forces, the sons of Ravana's ministers, the Kinkaras, and thereafter, when he had broken his fetters and admonished Dashanana, he reduced Lanka to ashes as Pavaka the world. Such feats were never surpassed by Indra, Varuna, Vishnu or Kuvera. By the might of his arms, I have conquered Lanka and regained Sita, Lakshmana, my kingdom, friends and kinsfolk. Who but Hanuman, the companion of the King of the Vanaras, would have been capable of obtaining tidings of Janaki ? But how comes it, that in his devotion to Sugriva, he did not consume Bali at the time of the quarrel, as a fire a shrub ? It seems to me that Hanuman was not yet aware of his powers when he witnessed the King of the Monkeys, whom he loved as his own being, set at nought ! Recount to me in detail and candidly everything concerning Hanuman, O Blessed and Illustrious Ascetic, O Thou whom the Gods revere ! "

Hearing these sagacious words, the Sage, in Hanuman's presence, answered :—

" What thou hast said regarding Hanuman is true, O Prince of the Raghus ! I deem none is equal to him in strength or surpasses him in swiftness and intelligence but formerly an irrevocable curse was pronounced on him by the Sages, on account of which, that hero was made unconscious of his great power, O Scourge of thy Foes.

" In his childhood, O Mighty Rama, he did something of which I cannot speak, so puerile was it, but if thou so desirest, O Raghava, I will disclose it to thee.

" There is a mountain named Sumeru that Surya gilds as a boon ; there Kesharin, the sire of Hanuman, dwells. Vayu begot a wonderful child on his cherished and illustrious consort, Anjana, and she brought that son, whose colour was like unto an ear of corn, into the world. Wishing to pluck some fruits, that lovely woman penetrated into a thicket, and the child, who in his mother's absence suffered greatly from hunger, began to emit piercing cries, like unto Karttikeya in the Shara Wood.

"At that moment, he observed the sun rising like unto a bunch of Java flowers,[1] and, eager for food, he imagined it to be a fruit

[1] China Roses

and rushed towards it. Turning to the rising sun, the child, himself like unto the dawn, wishing to lay hold of it, sprang into the sky. And Hanuman's bounds, he being but a child, greatly astonished the Devas, Danavas and Yakshas who reflected, ' Neither Vayu, Garuda nor even thought itself have the velocity of this son of the Wind who has leapt into the sky. If, whilst still a child, the speed of his flight is such, what will it not be when he attains his youthful strength.'

" Now Vayu followed in his son's wake lest the sun should scorch him and protected him with his cooling breath. Thus Hanuman, rising in space, traversed thousands of leagues and, on account of his sire's power and his own guilelessness, drew near to the sun.

" ' That little One is not conscious of his error ' reflected Surya, ' we must act accordingly ', and he refrained from consuming him.

" Now on that very day that Hanuman sprang into the sky to seize hold of the solar orb, Rahu[1] had prepared to take hold of it himself and, coming in contact with that child in the sun's chariot, Rahu sprang away in fear, he, the scourge of the sun and moon. Provoked, that son of Simhika went to Indra's abode and, scowling, said to that God, who was surrounded by the Celestial Host :—

" ' O Vasava, in order to satisfy my hunger, thou didst bestow the sun and moon on me, why hast thou made a present of them to another, O Slayer of Bali and Vritra ? To-day, which is the time of the conjunction, I had gone to lay hold of the sun when another Rahu approached and seized it.'

" Hearing these words of Rahu, Vasava, astonished, rose up from his throne and bearing his golden diadem, went out. Thereafter he mounted Airavata, foremost of elephants, who was as high as a hill or the peak of Mount Kailasha with his four tusks, running with mada juice, enormous, richly caparisoned and whose golden bells rang merrily.

" Then Indra commanded Rahu to precede him and directed his course to where Surya and Hanuman were. Thereupon Rahu set out with all speed leaving Vasava far behind and the child, Hanuman, beheld him as he drew near, whereupon he

[1] The demon who causes the sun's periodic eclipse.

let go of the sun and, taking Rahu to be a fruit, once more bounded into the sky to seize Simhika's son.

" Observing that Plavamgama loosing his hold on the sun in order to throw himself upon him, the offspring of Simhika, of whom the head alone remained visible, taking refuge under Indra's protection, in his terror, cried out ' Indra, Indra ' without ceasing, and Indra, recognizing the voice of Rahu ere he was able to discern him, answered his appeal, saying ' Have no fear, I am about to slay him ! '

" Meantime, beholding Airavata, Maruti reflected ' O, the lovely fruit ! ' and threw himself on that Lord of Elephants and while he sought to take hold of Airavata, his form fearful to behold suddenly appeared over Indra and his followers. Thereafter as he rushed on Sachi's consort, Indra, not unduly angered, with his finger loosed a thunderbolt that struck Hanuman and, at the impact, the child fell on a mountain, in his fall breaking his left jaw. Seeing his son lying inanimate under the stroke of the thunderbolt, Pavana was enraged against Indra, and the God Maruta, who penetrates and infuses all beings, withdrew into a cave to which he bore his child. Thereafter, as Vasava restrains the floods, he caused immense sufferings to all beings by preventing the passage of excreta and urine in them.

" On account of Vayu's wrath all creatures on every side were deprived of their breath so that their joints were dislocated and they became as blocks of wood. All sacred studies, the holy syllable ' Vashat ', religious ceremonies and duties being suspended by Vayu's displeasure, the Three Worlds became a hell.

" Then all creatures with the Gandharvas, Devas, Asuras and men, in their affliction and the desire to become happy once more, hurried to Prajapati ; and the Gods, their bellies swollen, with joined palms, said to him :—

" ' Thou hast created four kinds of beings, O Blessed One, Thou art their protector. Thou hast given us Pavana as the Lord of our lives, why nevertheless, has he who had become the Ruler of the Vital Breaths, now brought about this misfortune in the manner of a woman in the inner apartments ? '

" Hearing these words of all the beings, Prajapati, who was their protector, said to them, ' It is true ! ' and added ' Learn the reason which incited Vayu to anger and has caused this impediment. O Beings, this I have probed for myself. The Foremost of the Gods, this day, caused his son to fall at Rahu's instigation, whereupon that God of the Wind became enraged and Vayu, though bodiless, circulates in every body. A body bereft of Vayu is like a piece of wood, Vayu is the vital breath, Vayu is felicity itself, Vayu is the universe ; without Vayu, the whole world cannot be happy ; now that the universe is bereft of Vayu it is deprived of life ; all creatures without breath are as boards. For not having honoured the son of Aditi, we must seek out Maruta, the author of our ills, lest we perish ! '

" Thereupon, accompanied by all beings, Prajapati with the Devas, Gandharvas, Serpents and Guyhakas approached Maruta in the place to which he had borne his son, whom the King of the Gods had struck down.

" Meanwhile, perceiving the offspring of Sadagati,[1] radiant as the sun, fire or gold, in that dark cave where he had been withdrawn, the Four-faced God was moved with compassion as also the Devas, Gandharvas, Rishis, Yakshas and Rakshasas."

CHAPTER 36

The Boons bestowed on the Child Hanuman and how he was cursed by the Ascetics

"As soon as he beheld the Grandsire of the World, Vayu, taking his young child, for whom he had wept as one dead, rushed towards Dhatar. With his waving locks, his diadem and the garlands with which he was adorned, Vayu, having bowed three times, fell at the feet of Brahma.

" Then he, who was conversant with the Veda, his arms decorated with dazzling bracelets, touched the child as if in play , thereupon, that God sprung from the lotus, merely by caressing the child, revived him as seed that is watered.

[1] Sadagati—A name of Vayu, the God of the Wind, meaning 'Ever-going ', his son being Hanuman. The Wind God is also known as Vayu, Kesarin and other titles.

" Beholding his son restored, the Wind-god, blowing auspiciously, began to circulate in all beings as erstwhile and, freed from the obstructions caused by Maruta, all creatures became happy, like lakes covered with lotuses over which an icy wind has ceased to blow.

" Then Brahma, who possesses the three pairs of qualities,[1] who is Himself the essence of Trimurti, having his abode in the Three Worlds,[2] He who is revered by the Gods, said to the Celestials, in his anxiety to propitiate Maruta :—

" ' Know the truth, I will impart it to you for it is important ! Hear all of you, Mahendra, Agni, Varuna, Maheshwara, Dhaneshwara and others—this child will carry out all you have to accomplish, therefore grant him every boon in order to gratify his sire.'

" Thereupon the God of a Thousand Eyes, delighted, his brow radiant, took off his garland of lotuses and spoke thus :—

" ' Since the thunderbolt escaped from my grasp and shattered his jaw, this child shall be called Hanuman. I shall bestow an excellent boon upon him ; from to-day, he will be invulnerable to thunderbolts ! '

" Then Martanda, in his turn, that blessed One who dispels the darkness, said :—

" ' I will bestow a hundredth part of mine effulgence upon him and when he is able to learn the Shastras, I will endow him with eloquence ! '

" Thereafter Varuna accorded him the following boon, saying :—

" ' Innumerable years shall pass, yet shall my noose and my waters never be used against him ! '

"After this, Yama granted him the boon of invulnerability and immunity to disease and said :—

" 'As a sign of my satisfaction, I shall grant him the further boon of never being slain in battle ! '

" Then the red-eyed Dhanada spoke thus :—

" ' This mace held by me shall protect him in combat ! '

---

[1] The three pairs of qualities—Renown and Virility ; Majesty and Beauty ; Knowledge and Detachment.
[2] The three worlds—Bhur ; Bhuvah ; Swah.

" Thereafter the God Shankara, bestowing the foremost of favours upon him, said :—

" ' I shall restrain my shafts from wounding him ! '

" Then Vishvakarma of the great Car, casting his eyes on the child, said :—

" ' He will be invulnerable to the celestial weapons forged by me and his life shall endure ! '

" Finally the magnanimous Brahma spoke thus :—

" ' None of my weapons shall be able to harm him ! '

" Beholding the child enriched by the boons of the Gods, the Four-faced Lord, Guru of the Worlds, in his satisfaction addressed Vayu, saying :—

" ' Thy son, Maruti, will be the terror of his foes, the support of his friends and invincible ! Able to change his form at will, he will accomplish all he desires and go wheresoever he pleases with unimaginable velocity. In order to destroy Ravana and gratify Rama, he will perform such feats of arms that will cause every being to tremble ! '

" These words pacified Vayu, as also the Immortals and, with the Grandsire at their head, they all departed to the place from whence they had come.

" Vayu, the Bearer of Perfume, taking his son, returned home and, telling Anjana of the boons he had received, went away.

" O Rama, receiving these favours which filled him with power, and with the temerity natural to him, Hanuman resembled the ocean that is overflowing.

" In his intemperate ardour, that bull among monkeys shamelessly began to create trouble in the hermitages of the great Rishis. Scattering the spoons, jars, sacrificial fires, and heaps of bark used by those peace-loving Sages, overturning and shattering them, by such exploits, he, who had been rendered invulnerable to all brahmanic weapons by Shambhu, distinguished himself.

" Knowing from whence his power was derived, the great Rishis bore with him, nevertheless, despite the warnings of his sire, Kesharin, the son of Anjana exceeded all bounds, whereupon highly indignant, those mighty Rishis, born in the line of Bhrigu and Angiras, cursed him, O Prince of the Raghus, without, however, giving rein to their full anger and irritation.

" They said :— ' Since, in the knowledge of thy power, O Plavamgama, thou dost harass us, by the adverse effect of our curse thou shalt become unaware of it for a long time, but, when it is remembered by thee, thou shalt be able to wield it effectively. '

" Thereafter, the knowledge of his powers was taken from him in virtue of the great Rishis' words and, from that moment, Hanuman ranged the solitudes in a placid mood.

" At that time, Riksharajas, full of effulgence, like unto the sun, the father of Bali and Sugriva, ruled over all the monkeys and after a prolonged reign, that Sovereign of the Monkeys succumbed to the natural law of time and, having died, the ministers, learned in the sacred formulas, installed Bali in his father's stead and Sugriva as heir-apparent.

" Hanuman and Sugriva were as one and there was no difference between them ; they loved each other as do Agni and Anila but when the quarrel between Bali and Sugriva arose, Hanuman, on account of the brahmins' curse, was unaware of his powers, nor, in the terror in which Bali had thrown him, did Sugriva call them to mind, O Lord. The curse of the brahmins having robbed him of that knowledge, the foremost of Monkeys, supported Sugriva as an ally in the fight, who resembled a lion that a great elephant subdues. For valour, energy, intelligence, strength, amiability, sweetness of disposition, knowledge of what is fitting and not fitting, steadfastness, skill, courage and audacity, who can surpass Hanuman in the world ?

" That Indra among monkeys, in order to acquire grammar took refuge with the Sun-god and, in his spirit of enquiry that was without equal, he travelled from the mountain where he rises to the one where he sets, with a large book, a vast encyclopedia comprising the Sutras, their Commentaries, their meaning and the synthesis.

" That Prince of Monkeys became an accomplished scholar and none equalled him in the Shastras nor in the interpretation of the Prosody. In all the sciences and in the rules of asceticism, he rivalled Brihaspati. By thy grace, he will become a very brahmin conversant with the meaning of the most recent grammatical systems. Like unto an ocean, eager to engulf the worlds, like unto Pavaka desirous of consuming them at the final dissolution, who is able to challenge Hanuman, that second Antaka ?

" O Rama, on thine account, the Gods created Hanuman and the other foremost of monkeys, Sugriva, Mainda, Dvivida as also Nila, Tara, Tareya, Nala, Rambha, Gaja, Gavaksha, Gavaya, Sudamshtra, Prabhojya, Atimukha and Nala as also the bears with those leading monkeys who were all created by the Gods, O Rama.

" I have answered thy question fully and have just told thee of Hanuman's exploit accomplished in childhood."

Agastya's tale greatly amazed Rama, Saumitri, the monkeys and the Rakshasas, and Agastya addressed Rama, saying :—

" Thou hast learnt all that I have to tell ; now that we have beheld thee and received thine hospitality, we crave leave to depart ! "

Hearing the words of the supremely pious Agastya, Raghava with joined palms, bowing to that great Rishi, said :—

" To-day the Gods, my parents, ancestors and my family have been blessed by thy holy sight, yea, sanctified for ever. In the joy of my return, this is what I have to ask of thee. It is for thee in thine affection to concede it.

" I, who came to establish the inhabitants of the city and the country in their personal duties, desire thy co-operation in the sacrifice that I now wish to perform, O Thou who belongest to the virtuous. Wilt thou, whose asceticism eliminates all faults, not assist me in these ceremonies, for then shall I be welcomed by mine ancestors and my felicity be complete ? Do ye all assemble here ! "

On this request, Agastya and the other Rishis of rigid penances, answered, " Let it be so ! " and went to their hermitages.

Having spoken thus, all those ascetics departed in the order in which they had come.

Raghava, having reflected on the utterances of the Sage, was greatly astonished, and the orb of the day having withdrawn behind the Asta Mountain, he dismissed the monkeys and the kings; thereafter that foremost of men, having performed his evening devotions and the night having come, retired to the inner apartments.

CHAPTER 37

Homage is paid to Shri Rama

THE installation of Kakutstha, who was versed in the science of the Self, having taken place, the following night was spent by his subjects in rejoicing and when it had passed, at dawn, those who were charged with waking the king assembled at the palace. Thereafter these sweet-voiced minstrels, like unto the learned Kinneras, chanted pleasantly to that valiant prince as to a cherished son :—

" O Gentle Hero, awake ! O Thou who increaseth the felicity of Kausbalya, when thou dost sleep the whole universe is wrapped in slumber, O Monarch ! Thine heroism is equal to Vishnu's and thy beauty to the Ashvins. Thou, the rival of Brihaspati in wisdom, art a second Prajapati. Thy life's span is like the earth's, thy radiance like the sun's, thou art endowed with the swiftness of the wind and thy profundity is like the deep. Thou art unshakable like unto Sthanu[1] and thy charm rivals the moon. No king was ever like unto thee in the past nor shall there ever be such a monarch in time to come, O Sovereign. O Lion among Men, since thou art invincible, firm in thy duty and ever seeketh the welfare of thy subjects, glory and prosperity will never desert thee. Humility and piety ever reside in thee, O Kakutstha ! "

These and similar praises were addressed to him by the bards as also the Sutas,[2] who, with divine hymns, sought to rouse Raghava, and it was amidst these melodious chants that he woke from sleep and rose from his couch, that was covered with white stuffs, like unto Vishnu when he leaves the snake that has served as his bed.

Then that magnanimous hero stood up and countless attendants approached him, bowing with joined palms, offering him beautiful ewers for washing and, having bathed and purified himself, he went at the appointed hour to kindle the sacrificial

---

[1] Sthanu—Shiva.
[2] Sutas—A class of personal attendants.

499

fire and thereafter with swift steps, he entered the sacred pavilion reserved for the Ikshvakus. There for a long time Rama paid homage to the Gods, his ancestors and the brahmins, according to tradition, then, coming forth surrounded by his people, he went to the outer court of the palace accompanied by his counsellors and also the family priests, who shone in their own effulgence, led by Vasishtha. Wealthy Kshatriyas, Lords of countless provinces walked at Rama's side, as the Celestials by Shakra. Bharata, Lakshmana and Shatrughna, of great renown, joyfully formed an escort of honour round him, like unto the Three Vedas at the Adhvara Sacrifice.[1] At his side walked innumerable attendants with joined palms and radiant countenance, named Muditas. Twenty monkeys full of energy and prowess led by Sugriva followed Rama, and Bibishana between four Rakshasas walked beside that hero, as Guhyakas by the Lord of Wealth. Elders, and merchants and those of noble families, bowing to the king, followed him with dignity, and that Sovereign, surrounded by the blessed and illustrious Rishis, mighty kings, monkeys and Rakshasas, like unto the Chief of the Gods, received continual homage from the ascetics; and the countless praises of those who entered Rama's presence, and traditions, full of eloquence and piety, were constantly recited by the magnanimous brahmins versed in the Scriptures.

FIRST OF THE INTERPOLATED CHAPTERS

2nd SERIES

ON having heard the whole story, that descendant of the House of Raghu addressed the Sage Agastya and said :—

" Revered Lord, Riksharajas was the name of Sugriva and Bali's sire but what was the name of their mother ? From whence did she come and why were Bali and Sugriva so called ? Do thou tell me all concerning this matter."

Thereupon the Sage Agastya answered :—

" O Rama, I shall relate everything briefly that I heard from Shri Narada when he visited my hermitage.

---

[1] Adhvara—A religious sacrifice, especially the Soma Sacrifice.

" Once, when that highly virtuous ascetic was journeying through the world, he came to my retreat and I paid him due homage and made him welcome. When he was seated at his ease, being curious, I put this same question to him and he answered me, saying :—

" ' Hear me, O Great Ascetic, Foremost of the Pious, there is a mountain named Meru, which is all golden, enchanting and most beautiful. Its central peak is greatly revered by the Gods and the marvellous assembly hall of Brahma is situated there, which extends over a hundred leagues. The Four-mouthed Deity, sprung from a lotus, ever resides there and, on a certain occasion while he was practising Yoga, a few tears fell from his eyes, whereupon the Patriarch, with his hand, brushed them away allowing them to fall on the earth and from them a monkey was born.

" ' O Foremost of Men, as soon as that monkey appeared, the high-souled Brahma instructed him in sweet accents, saying :—

" ' " Do thou proceed to that foremost of the mountains where the Gods perpetually dwell, O Chief of Monkeys, and subsist there on the various fruits and roots. On that enchanting mountain, thou shouldst live depending on me, O Foremost of Monkeys, living in this wise for some time, thou shalt attain prosperity." '

" O Rama, that great monkey, offering salutations to the feet of Brahma, said to the Creator of the World :—

" ' O Lord, I shall execute thy behest and live depending on Thee ! '

" Thereafter that forest dweller immediately proceeded to the wood abounding in fruit and blossom, and there he lived on fruits, gathering honey and various blooms, returning to Brahma each evening with an offering of the most excellent fruit and flowers, which he placed at the feet of that God of Gods. In this way he spent a long time on that mountain.

" O Rama, once that great monkey, Riksharajas, was afflicted by thirst and went to the northern peak of Mount Meru where he beheld a lake ringing with the songs of a myriad birds. Shaking his neck in delight, he observed his reflection in the waters and, beholding that image, the monkey chief filled with anger and anxiety asked himself, ' What arch enemy of mine dwells in these waters? I shall destroy the excellent abode of that vicious-souled one!' Thinking thus within himself, that monkey, in his impetuosity, plunged into the lake and with a bound emerged once more, but as he rose from the waters, he found himself transformed into a woman, who was extremely charming, graceful and fair.

" Her waist was wide, her eyebrows symmetrical, her hair black and curly, her countenance fair and smiling, her bosom high and her beauty matchless. On the banks of that lake, she appeared enchanting, illumining the four quarters, agitating the minds of all beings and, in the Three Worlds, she was as beautiful as any. O Rama, she resembled the simple creeper, Sastilata, or Lakshmi bereft of her lotus or the pure rays of the moon or Parvati.

"At that time, Indra, the Lord of the Celestials, having worshipped the feet of Brahma, was returning by that way and the Sun-god also came thither.

" Simultaneously beholding that lovely female form, they were overcome with desire, and, their minds being in a ferment, they were wholly swept away.

" Thereupon Indra begot a son on that woman, named Bali, so-called because his seed fell on the hair of that beauty, and the Solar Deity begot another son on her, named Sugriva, who sprang from her neck.

" Those two powerful monkeys being born, Indra conferred a lasting golden chain on Bali and returned to his own abode and, having engaged Hanuman, the Wind-god's son, in the service of Sugriva, the Sun-god too returned to the Celestial Region.

" O King, when the sun rose after that night had passed, Riksharajas resumed his own monkey shape and he gave his two highly powerful sons, those foremost of monkeys possessed of yellow eyes, able to change their shape at will, some honey like unto nectar to drink. Thereafter, taking them with him, he went to the abode of Brahma and that God, beholding Riksharajas with his two sons, consoled him in diverse ways and issued a command to his messenger, saying :—

" 'At my behest, O Messenger, proceed to the beautiful City of Kishkindha, that large, golden and enchanting capital is worthy of Riksharajas. There thousands of Vanaras dwell, besides those who are endowed with magic powers. Inaccessible and abounding in gems, those of the four castes inhabit it, and it is pure and sacred.

" 'At my command, Vishvakarma created that celestial and enchanting City of Kishkindha, do thou find an abode for Riksharajas, the foremost of the Monkeys and his sons there, and, having called the leading Plavamgamas together and received them courteously, install him on the throne. On beholding this monkey chief, gifted with intelligence, they will all become subject to him.'

" Brahma having spoken thus, the celestial messenger with Riksharajas proceeded to that most beautiful City of Kishkindha with the speed of the wind where, as commanded by Brahma, he installed Riksharajas as king.

" Thereafter, having bathed and being adorned with a crown and various ornaments, Riksharajas, with a joyful heart began to rule over the monkeys, and all the Vanaras residing on the earth, comprising the Seven Islands and bounded by the sea, became subject to him.

" Thus Riksharajas was both father and mother to Bali and Sugriva ; may prosperity attend thee ! The learned, who listen to and cause others to hear this narrative, enhancing their delight, obtain all their desires.

" O Lord, I have duly described at length all that concerns the birth of the monkey kings and the Rakshasas."

SECOND OF THE INTERPOLATED CHAPTERS

2nd SERIES

SHRI RAMA with his brothers, hearing that ancient and wonderful tale, was astonished and, having listened to the Rishi Agastya's narrative, said :—

" By thy favour, O Rishi, I have heard this highly sacred theme ! O Great Muni, I am filled with amazement on hearing the story of Bali and Sugriva. O Blessed One, I am not surprised that those two sons of the Gods should be so powerful since their origin was divine ! "

Rama, having uttered these words, Agastya said :—

" O Long-armed One, even thus was the birth of Bali and Sugriva brought about in days of yore. I shall now relate another ancient legend to thee, O Rama, as to why Ravana bore Sita away, hear me with attention !

" In the Golden Age, Ravana offered reverence to the Grandsire's offspring, that truthful Rishi Sanatkumara, who, shining in his own effulgence, was as resplendent as the sun and who was seated in his own retreat, and paying homage to him, Ravana said :—

" ' O Lord, who is there now among the Gods, who is brave and powerful and by whose aid the Celestials can overcome their foes, one whom the Twice-born worship daily and upon whom devotees constantly meditate ? O Thou, whose wealth is thy piety and who art possessed of the sixfold riches, do thou graciously tell me in detail.'

" Being conversant with Ravana's intentions, the glorious Sage Sanatkumara, having knowledge of all things through his meditations, said to him affectionately :—' Hear me, O My Son, the wise, in their sacrifices, duly pay homage to the Lord of the Universe, whose origin is unknown to us, who is daily worshipped by the Celestials and Asuras, He is the supremely powerful Narayana from whose navel, Brahma, the Creator of the World has sprung and from whom, all things animate and inanimate are born. Yogis meditate upon Him and offer sacrifices in His honour according to the Puranas, Vedas, Pancharatras and other rituals. In combat, He is ever victorious over the Daityas, Danavas, Rakshasas and other enemies of the Gods, all of whom ever worship Him.'

" Hearing the words of the great Ascetic Sanatkumara, Ravana, the Lord of the Rakshasas, making obeisance to him, answered :—

" ' Being slain by Hari, to what state do the Daityas, Danavas and Rakshasas attain and why does Hari destroy them ? '

" Thereupon Sanatkumara replied :—' They who are slain by the Gods abide in Swarga but are born again on earth when their merit is exhausted. They are born and they die, they suffer and enjoy according to the merits of their previous births, but those who are slain by the Wielder of the Discus, the Lord of the

Three Worlds, Hari, attain to His region, since even His wrath is like unto a boon, O King ! '

" Hearing the words spoken by that mighty Ascetic Sanat-kumara, that night-ranger, Ravana, filled with delight and wonder, began to reflect on how he might enter into conflict with the Lord."

THIRD OF THE INTERPOLATED CHAPTERS

2nd SERIES

"As the vicious-souled Ravana was reflecting thus, the great Ascetic Sanatkumara said to him :—

" ' O Long-armed Warrior, what thy mind has conceived will be accomplished in a great encounter ! Rejoice and wait awhile ! '

" Hearing these words, the long-armed Ravana addressed the Sage and said :—

" ' O Foremost of the Rishis, do thou tell me in detail what are His distinguishing characteristics ? '

" Having listened to the Lord of the Rakshasas, the ascetic replied :—

" ' Listen and I will tell thee all :—O Foremost of the Rak-shasas, in the universe of animate and inanimate beings, that great God is all-pervading, subtle, eternal and omnipresent. He is present in the Celestial Region, on earth and in the region under the earth, on the mountains, in the forests and all stationary objects, rivers and cities ; He is " Aum ", He is Truth, He is Savitri and the earth ; He is the supporter of the earth and the Serpent Ananta ; He is day and night, morning and evening, death, the moon, time, the wind, Brahma, Rudra, Indra and Varuna. He causes the worlds to appear and shine forth ; He creates them, destroys them, rules over them and sports therein. He is eternal, the Lord of Men, He is Vishnu, the Ancient Purusha and the only Destroyer. What more is there to say, O Dashanana ? He pervades the Three Worlds, the moving and unmoving. Wearing yellow raiment like unto the filaments of a lotus, Narayana resembles the lightning flashes. Bearing the

Shrivatsa Mark on His breast, that cloud-coloured Lord, like unto the moon, is pleasing to look upon. Lakshmi resides in His body in the form of warfare, as lightning in the clouds. Neither Devas, Asuras nor Nagas are able to look on Him but the one, with whom He is pleased, alone beholds Him. O My Son, neither by the fruits of sacrifice, penance, self-control, gifts nor rituals nor by any other means can one behold that Supreme God. Those alone see Him who have surrendered their whole life and being to Him and who, by virtue of discriminative knowledge, have burnt up all their sins. If thou desirest to behold Him, hear me and I will tell thee all.

" ' At the close of the Golden Age and the beginning of the Silver Age, the Lord Narayana will assume human form for the sake of men and the Gods. A son, named Rama, will be born to Dasaratha of the Ikshvaku Race, who will rule on earth. Rama will be highly effulgent, powerful and as forbearing as the earth nor shall his enemies in combat be able to look on him, as one is unable to gaze upon the sun.

" ' His consort, the gracious Lakshmi shall be renowned under the name of Sita and be born as the daughter of Janaka, King of Mithila ; she will issue from the earth. In beauty, she will be unequalled in the world, endowed with auspicious marks she will ever follow Rama like a shadow, as the moon is accompanied by its beams; of virtuous conduct, she will be chaste and patient. Sita and Rama will always appear together as the sun and its rays. O Ravana, I have now related to thee all that concerns Narayana, the great, eternal and incomprehensible·Brahman.'

" O Raghava, on hearing these words, the mighty Lord of the Rakshasas began to devise means whereby he might enter into combat with thee. Meditating again and again on the words of Sanatkumara, he began to wander here and there."

Listening to this narrative, Rama, his eyes wide with wonder, was greatly astonished and, being delighted, he again addressed Agastya, the foremost of the wise, saying :—

" Do thou recount the ancient traditions further, O Lord."

THE illustrious Rishi Agastya, sprung from a vessel,[1] paying obeisance to Rama, as Brahma pays homage to Shiva, addressed that hero whose prowess was truth, saying :—

" Do thou hear me ! "

Thereafter the highly effulgent Agastya began to relate the subsequent events in that legend, and the blessed Sage with a delighted heart described to Rama all he had heard narrated, saying :—

" O Illustrious and Long-armed Rama, it is on this account that the vicious-souled Ravana stole Sita, the daughter of Janaka, away. O Thou who art possessed of long arms, O Great Warrior, O Thou who art invincible, Narada recounted this tale to me on the summit of the Meru Mountain. O Raghava, the highly effulgent One told me this story in the presence of the Devas, Gandharvas, Siddhas, Ascetics and other great Beings. O Lord of Monarchs, O Conferer of Honours, do thou hear this tale which removes great sins ! Listening to it, O Thou of long arms, the Rishis and the Devas, with delighted hearts, their eyes shining with the splendour of lotus flowers, said to the Ascetic Narada :—

" ' He, who listens to or relates this story with faith and devotion, shall be blessed with sons and grandsons and, after his death, be honoured in the Celestial Region.' "

FIFTH OF THE INTERPOLATED CHAPTERS

2nd SERIES

" O RAMA, Ravana, the Lord of the Rakshasas, proud of his strength, accompanied by his warriors, began to range the earth desirous of conquest. Whenever he heard of any among the

---

[1] Agastya was said to have been born in a water jar.

Daityas, Danavas or Rakshasas who were powerful, he challenged them to fight.

" O Lord of the Earth, having traversed the whole world, the Ten-necked Rakshasa beheld the Sage Narada returning from Brahmaloka to his own abode, like unto a second sun, passing through the clouds. Then Ravana, with a cheerful heart, approached him and, with joined palms, addressed the Sage, saying :—

" ' O Thou gifted with the six kinds of wealth, many times thou hast beheld all creation from Brahma down to an insect. Do thou tell me, O Great One, in which region the inhabitants are the most powerful, I wish to challenge them to combat according to my whim.'

" Thereupon, reflecting an instant, the divine Sage Narada answered him saying :—

" ' O King, there is a large island in the Milky Ocean, where all the inhabitants are endowed with great strength and are of enormous stature, as effulgent as the moon's beams, possessing fair complexions, voices as deep as the muttering of clouds and who are extremely valiant. Their arms are long and like iron bars, O King of the Asuras, such are the people of that island, who are as powerful as thou wouldst wish to see on earth.'

" Hearing the words of Narada, Ravana said :—

" ' O Divine Sage, why are the people of that island so strong and how did such mighty beings come to live in that place ? O Lord, do thou relate everything to me at length. The whole world is ever seen by thee like a fruit in the palm of the hand ! '

" Hearing the words of Ravana, the blessed Sage said :—

" ' O Lord of the Rakshasas, the people of that island constantly worship Narayana with their whole being. Their hearts and minds are ever set on Him and, having given their lives and souls to Narayana alone, they have been blessed with that abode and dwell on Sweta-dwipa. Those who die in battle at the hands of Shri Narayana, Bearer of the discus and Preserver of the World, go to the celestial region. O Friend, neither by sacrifice, penance, excellent gifts nor by any other pious act does one attain to that region full of bliss.'

" Hearing these words of Narada, Ravana was amazed and

reflecting awhile, said :—' I will enter into conflict with these people ! '

" Thereafter, taking leave of Narada, he proceeded to Sweta-dwipa and Narada, pondering for a long time, curious to witness that encounter, speedily left for that island, he being fond of mischief and conflict.

" O Prince, Ravana, with his Rakshasas, advanced on Sweta-dwipa, rending the four quarters with his leonine roars, and Narada preceded him to that island that was difficult of access even to the Devas.

" There the Pushpaka Car of the mighty Ravana was assailed by adverse winds so that it was unable to stand against them and was tossed about like a straw, nor could it remain stationary on account of the furious blasts. Then Ravana's counsellors said to him :—

" ' O Lord, we are beside ourselves and overcome by fear ; it is not possible for us to remain here, how then shall we be able to fight ? '

" Speaking thus, the Rakshasas fled away in all directions ; then Ravana sent away his aerial car decorated with gold with the Rakshasas and, assuming a terrible form, entered the island alone.

" Thereafter, as he was approaching, he was observed by many women of that white island, who, drawing near, took hold of his hand and smiling, said :—

" ' Why hast thou come hither ? Who art thou ? Who is thy sire ? Who has sent thee, tell us all candidly ? '

" Than Ravana, enraged, answered :—

" ' I am the son of the Sage Vishravas and my name is Ravana ! I have come hither in order to fight but I see no warrior here ! '

" When the wicked-minded Rakshasa had spoken thus, the maidens laughed gently, but one of them, incensed, suddenly took hold of Ravana as one would a child and, as if in play, tossed him to and fro to her companions, saying :—

" ' See, I have caught an insect, how wonderful it is with its ten hands, twenty arms and its colour resembling a heap of antimony ! '

" Thereafter, they passed him from hand to hand in play, each spinning him with her fingers and Ravana, worn out by being handled thus, grew exceedingly angry and bit the hand of one of those fair ones, who, being in pain, let him go, whereupon another, seizing the powerful Rakshasa, rose into the sky. Then Ravana, in fury, tore her with his nails and being dropped by that damsel, the night-ranger, terrified, fell into the waters of the sea, as a mountain peak when shattered by a thunderbolt.

" O Rama, those youthful women of Sweta-dwipa again caught hold of the Rakshasa and began to fling him to and fro. At that moment, the illustrious Sage Narada, observing Ravana's plight, was astonished and, laughing loudly, began to dance with delight.

" O Great King, desirous of receiving death at thy hand, the wicked Ravana bore Sita away. Thou art Narayana, the Wielder of the Conch, discus and mace. Thou dost bear the lotus, the thunderbolt and the bow in thine hands. Thou art Hrishikesha and art adorned with the Shrivatsa Mark, Thou art the Maha-Yogi, ever worshipped by the Devas and Thou dost confer fearlessness on Thy devotees. Thou hast assumed a human form in order to slay Ravana. Dost Thou know thy Self to be Narayana, O Blessed One, do not forget thy real Self, recollect that Thou art the true Self ; Brahma Himself has declared Thee to be the Mystery of all mysteries !

" O Prince of the Raghus, Thou art the Three Gunas, the Three Vedas, The Three Regions, that of the Celestials, of men and the region under the earth, Thou dost sport in the three divisions of time, Thou art conversant with the science of archery, music and medicine, Thou art the Destroyer of the enemies of the Gods. In days of yore, Thou didst traverse the Three Worlds in three strides. Thou art born of Aditi and art the younger brother of Indra, born to bind Bali. O Fore-most of the Gods, the purpose of the Devas has been accomplished ! The wicked Ravana with his sons and kinsmen has been slain ; the Rishis, who have piety as their wealth, and all the Gods are gratified. O Chief of the Immortals, all this has been brought about by Thy grace !

" Sita is the personification of Lakshmi and arose from the earth ; for thy sake, she was born in the House of Janaka. Bringing her to Lanka, Ravana protected her with care as his own mother. O Rama, I have related the whole story to thee, the immortal Narada described it to me, having heard it from the Rishi Sanatkumara; Dashanana followed the instructions of Sanatkumara faithfully.

"Whoever listens to this narrative in faith and knowledge at the time of sacrifice, his offerings of food, becoming imperishable, reach the ancestors."

Hearing this divine theme, the lotus-eyed Rama, with his brothers, was greatly astonished and the monkeys, their eyes wide with delight, with Sugriva, the Rakshasas, Bibishana, the kings, their counsellors and the assembled Brahmins, Kshatriyas, Vaishyas and Shudras gazed on Rama with joy.

Then the highly effulgent Agastya said to Rama :—

"O Rama, we have all looked on Thee and been honoured by thee and now beg leave to depart."

Speaking thus and having received due homage, they returned whence they had come.

The sun having set, Rama, the foremost of men, bade farewell to the monkeys and their Sovereign and duly performed the Sandhya Rites; thereafter night having gradually set in, he entered the inner apartments.

CHAPTER 38

Rama takes leave of his Allies

HAVING been duly installed as king, Raghava spent his days directing all those things pertaining to the inhabitants of the city and country. After some time, he, with joined palms, addressed the King of Mithila in these terms :—

"O Lord, now that our happiness is assured by thy support, it being by virtue of thy great prowess that I have been able to slay Ravana, all those of the Houses of Ikshvaku and Mithila, everywhere, enjoy a felicity without parallel. Do thou return to thy capital after accepting these jewels; Prince Bharata will attend thee as thine escort."

"Be it so !" replied Janaka and prepared to depart, thereafter adding :—

" I am pleased with thee and thy conduct ; as for the gems that thou hast heaped upon me, I bequeath them all to my daughter, O Prince ! "

Janaka having departed, Raghava, with joined palms, respectfully addressed the son of Kaikeyi, his maternal uncle, the Prince Yudajita, saying :—

" This empire, I myself, Bharata and Lakshmana also, are at thy disposal, O Lion among Men. The King, thine aged sire may be grieving on thy behalf and thy return this day will delight him, O Lord. Lakshmana will follow thee as thine escort after thou hast accepted wealth and gems of every kind."

Acquiescing to his request, Yudajita answered " It is well! As for the pearls and gold, do thou retain them forever ! " Thereafter, the son of Kaikeya paid obeisance to Rama, keeping him on his right hand and after receiving homage, he departed, followed by Lakshmana as Vishnu by Indra at the time of the destruction of Vritra.

Having bade farewell to his maternal uncle, Rama embraced his friend, Pratardana, the King of Kashi, and addressed him in these words :—

" Thou hast proved thy friendship and devotion to the full, O Prince, as witnessed by the campaign undertaken with Bharata.[1] Now return this day to the enchanting City of Benares of which thou art the support and which is surrounded by great walls and magnificent gateways."

Speaking thus, the virtuous Kakutstha, rising from his throne, held him in a close embrace for a long time, thereafter permitting him to take his leave. Bidding farewell to the King of Kashi, Raghava, the increaser of Kaushalya's joy, speedily returned to his own city in safety.

Having dismissed Kasheya, Raghava smilingly addressed courteous words to the hundred monarchs present and said to them :—

" Your loyalty has been unshakable and your affection enduring ; through the grace of your devotion and the prowess of magnanimous warriors such as you are, that insensate and perverse wretch, Ravana, has been slain ! It is your prowess that

---

[1] A commentator explains that at the time Rama was fighting with Ravana, the King of Kashi and Bharata went to his aid.

has destroyed him, I was merely the occasion of his destruction
in the fight with his forces, his sons, his ministers and his kinsfolk. Hearing that the daughter of King Janaka had been borne
away in the forest, the great-hearted Bharata summoned you all.
Your devotion has been unanimous, O Princes of great soul, but
your stay here has been prolonged and I now wish to assure
myself of your safe return."

Then the kings, greatly delighted, answered him saying :—

" By the grace of heaven thou hast triumphed, O Rama, and
hast regained thy kingdom ! By divine grace, thou hast recovered Sita ! By divine grace, thy foe is vanquished ! To
behold thee victorious and delivered from thine enemies, O
Rama, was our most ardent desire and is now our supreme
satisfaction ! The praises thou hast heaped upon us are natural
to thee, O Thou whose merits are such that we cannot match
them with our tributes. We are about to take leave of thee but
thou wilt ever remain in our thoughts ! O Long-armed Warrior,
we shall return full of devotion to thee. Mayest thou, O Great
Prince, ever hold us in affection."

" Be it so ! " replied Rama and the kings, highly delighted paid
obeisance to Raghava with joined palms, eager to return home
and, having been duly honoured by him, went to their own
countries.

CHAPTER 39

Rama loads his Allies with Gifts

THOSE magnanimous princes departed joyfully on their countless
elephants and horses whose tread shook the earth. Many army
divisions, full of ardour, had come to the aid of Raghava under
Bharata's command with their regiments and squadrons.
Thereafter, in the pride of their strength, those monarchs
said :—

" We did not see Rama's adversary, Ravana, on the battlefield ;
Bharata called on us too late or those Rakshasas would assuredly
soon have fallen under our blows. With the protection of the
valiant Rama and Lakshmana we should have striven successfully
without anxiety on the shores of the ocean."

Conversing on this and other matters, those kings, full of joy returned to their kingdoms, those mighty empires that were prosperous, happy, abounding in silver and grain and overflowing with treasure. Reaching their capitals safely, those monarchs, anxious to gratify Rama, paid him homage by sending him every kind of precious object : horses, carriages, jewels, elephants intoxicated with ichor, rare sandalwood, celestial ornaments, gems, pearls, coral, lovely slave girls, coverings made of goats skin and a variety of chariots.

The mighty Bharata, Lakshmana and Shatrughna, having accepted those gifts, took their way back to the capital and, returning to the ravishing City of Ayodhya, those lions among men handed all those objects of great price to Rama, who, receiving them, joyfully bestowed them on Sugriva, who had fulfilled his duty, and also on Bibishana and the other Rakshasas and the monkeys, by whose aid he had attained victory, and those monkeys and titans decorated their heads and arms with the jewels that Rama had given them.

Thereafter, the Sovereign of the Ikshvakus, that warrior of the great car, he whose eyes resembled the petals of the lotus, Rama, seating Hanuman and Angada on his knees, said to Sugriva :—

" This Angada, thine illustrious son, and the Son of the Wind, thy minister, O Sugriva, both of whom are endowed with wisdom and devoted to our interests, merit every kind of honour and, on thine account also, O King of the Monkeys."

With these words, the illustrious Rama took off some extremely rare ornaments from his breast and decorated Angada and Hanuman with them.

Thereafter Raghava addressed the foremost of the monkey leaders—Nila, Nala, Kesharin, Kumuda, Gandhamadana, Sushena, Panasa, the valiant Mainda and Dvivida, Jambavan, Gavaksha, Vinata and Dhumra, Balimukha, and Prajangha, Samnada of great valour, Darimukha, Dadhimukha and Indrajanu, and in a sweet voice, consuming them with his glance as it were, in gentle accents said :—

" You are my friends, my brothers, my very Self ! It is you who have saved me from misfortune, O Dwellers in the Woods ! Happy is King Sugriva to possess such excellent friends ! "

Uttering these words, that lion among men bestowed jewels upon them in accord with their desserts as also diamonds of great price and then embraced them all. Thereafter they drank of fragrant honey and partook of choice viands, roots and fruits and, sojourning there for a month, such was their devotion to Rama, that it seemed to them that but an hour had passed. Rama too spent the time happily in the company of the monkeys, who were able to change their form at will, and the extremely powerful titans and bears of great energy.

In this way the second month of autumn passed and the monkeys and titans savoured delights of every kind in that city belonging to the Ikshvakus that was full of allurements and, during the time they were thus entertained, by the grace of Rama's affectionate regard, the hours flew by happily for them.

CHAPTER 40

Rama takes leave of the Bears, Monkeys and Titans

IN this way, the bears, monkeys and titans passed their time with Rama, and thereafter the mighty Raghava said to Sugriva :—

" Return to Kishkindha, My Friend, which may not be conquered by the Gods or Asuras themselves. With thy ministers, rule over thine empire without hindrance. O Mighty King, thou shouldst look on Angada with supreme affection as also Hanuman and the great-hearted Nala, Sushena thy valiant father-in-law, and Tara the foremost of warriors, the invincible Kumuda and Nila who is full of strength, the energetic Shatabali, Mainda, Dvivida, Gaja, Gavaksha, Gavaya, the mighty Sharabha and the King of the Bears the indomitable Jambavan. Look also with affection on Gandhamadana, the agile Rishabha, the Plavamgamas Suptala, Kesharin, Shumbha and Shankashuda, all these magnanimous ones, who in order to serve my cause were ready to give up their lives ; look on them always with friendliness and never cause them pain."

Having spoken thus to Sugriva, whom he embraced again and again, Rama said affectionately to Bibishana :—

" Do thou rule Lanka faithfully ; thou art conversant with

thy duty, this is my conviction and also of those in the capital, the Rakshasas and thy brother Vaishravana. Give no place in thy soul to evil, O King! Just monarchs are assured of earthly prosperity. Think ever of me and Sugriva, mine ally, O Prince, and in perfect contentment go hence without anxiety!"

Hearing Rama's words, the bears, monkeys and Rakshasas cried, "Excellent! Excellent!" praising Kakutstha again and again, saying :—

" Thy wisdom, O Long-armed Hero, thy wonderful valour, thine extreme goodness, O Rama, has ever rendered thee the equal of Swyambhu!"

While the monkeys and the titans were speaking thus, Hanuman, bowing to Raghava, said :—

" I shall ever hold thee in the greatest affection, O Prince, my devotion is thine forever, O Hero, nor shall I give mine allegiance to any other object. As long as thy story is told in the world, assuredly life will remain in my body, O Valiant Rama. The Apsaras will recount thine history and all thy divine exploits to me, O Joy of the Raghus, O Lion among Men, and, listening to them, O Great Hero, the nectar of thy deeds will dispel all mine anxieties, as the wind chases away a flock of clouds."

As Hanuman was speaking, Rama rose from his marvellous throne and, embracing him tenderly, said to him :—

" Undoubtedly so will it be, O Best of Monkeys, as long as my story is current in the world, so long will thy fame endure and life remain in thy body. For every service thou hast rendered me, I would give up my life and still remain thy debtor, O Monkey. In mine heart, the memory of what thou hast done for me will ever abide, O Hanuman ; it is in times of misfortune that one has recourse to those whom one has benefited."

Thereafter, taking from his neck a string of pearls from which an emerald as bright as the moon hung, Raghava placed it round Hanuman's and, with that rope of pearls falling on his breast, the monkey appeared as radiant as Mount Sumeru when the moon passes over the summit of that golden peak.

At a signal from Hanuman, those powerful monkeys, having placed their heads at the feet of Raghava, rising one after the other, went away.

Sugriva, who held Rama in a firm embrace, and the virtuous Bibishana were shaking with sobs and all were weeping, their eyes brimming with tears, beside themselves, distracted with grief as it were, on leaving Raghava. Overwhelmed with gifts by the magnanimous Rama, each returned to his own country, as souls leave the body. Titans, bears and monkeys, after bowing to Rama, the Increaser of the glory of the Raghu Race, their eyes filled with tears, caused by that separation, took the road to their own countries.

CHAPTER 41

Rama dismisses the Pushpaka Chariot

HAVING said farewell to the bears, the monkeys and the titans, the long-armed Rama began to live happily with his brothers.

One day, at noon, that great Prince Raghava heard a melodious voice speaking from the sky, saying :—

" O My Friend Rama, look on me and know, O Prince, that it is I, Pushpaka, who come from Kuvera's abode. At his command I have returned from his palace ; it is he, O First of Men, who has told me to place myself at thy service, saying :—

" ' Thou hast been won by the magnanimous Prince Raghava in the fight when he struck down Ravana, that invincible Monarch of the Titans. I experienced supreme felicity on the slaying of that wretch with his forces, sons and kinsfolk. Having been made captive in Lanka by Rama, the Paramatman, do thou go and serve him as a vehicle, O Friend ! It is I who command thee ! It is my supreme desire that thou shouldst carry that hero, the Joy of the Raghu Race, round the world ; go without anxiety ! '

" Obedient to the behests of the illustrious Dhanada, I have reached thee without difficulty and place myself at thy disposal. Inaccessible to all beings, at Dhanada's will, in obedience to thy commands I come to surrender my power to thy service."

Hearing these words, the valiant Rama answered the Pushpaka Car in the sky, that had returned to him, saying :—

" O Most wonderful of chariots, O Pushpaka, welcome to thee ; Dhanada's generosity must not find me wanting ! "

Thereafter the long-armed Raghava paid homage to Pushpaka with roasted grain, flowers and fragrant perfumes, saying :—

" Go now, O Pushpaka, wherever thou desirest but come again whenever I call thee to mind ! Go by the path of the Siddhas, O Friend, and let no harm come to thee. Mayest thou not suffer any collision in thy fantastic journeyings in space, such is my will ! "

Rama, having dismissed the aerial car with due homage, Pushpaka replying ' So be it,' went wheresoever it desired and, when that chariot of pure soul had disappeared, Bharata, with joined palms, addressed his elder brother, the Joy of the House of Raghu, saying :—

" O Hero, thou who hast the soul of a God, under thy rule one beholds beings who are not of the human race speaking frequently, nor is there any disease among men and their days are passed in peace ; even the aged do not die and women give birth without pain, whilst all enjoy good health. A real felicity is to be seen among the citizens and, in the rainy season, Parjanya lets loose the nectar of immortality; soft auspicious and balmy breezes blow and the people of town and country all exclaim ' May such a king reign over us long ', O Prince ! "

Hearing these gracious and flattering words spoken by Bharata, Rama, the foremost of monarchs, was supremely gratified.

CHAPTER 42

The Felicity enjoyed by Rama and Sita

HAVING dismissed the Pushpaka Chariot, which was encrusted with gold, the long-armed Rama entered the Ashoka Grove that was rendered beautiful by Sandal, Agallocha, Mango, Tunga and Kalakeya Trees with groves of Devadaru on all sides, whilst Champaka, Aguru, Punnaga, Madhuka, Panasa and Asana Trees adorned it and radiant Parijatras blazed like smokeless fires. Lodhra, Nipa, Arjuna, Naga, Saptaparna, Atimuktaka,

Mandara and Kadali Trees screened it with a web of thicket and creepers ; Priyangu, Kadamba, Bakula, Jambu, Dadima and Kovidara Trees embellished it on every side with their magnificent flowers, marvellous fruits of celestial fragrances, divine nectar, tender shoots and buds. Heavenly trees of graceful shape, thick with heavy foliage and enchanting blossom were humming with intoxicated bees. Kokilas, Bhringarajas and other birds of varied plumage, their heads crowned with pollen from the Mango Trees, added to the beauty of those marvellous woods. Some of the trees had the brilliance of gold or resembled tongues of flame, others were as dark as collyrium and everywhere only flowers of sweet fragrance and wreaths of blossom of all kinds were to be found.

Pools of various shapes, filled with limpid water on which tufts of flowering lotus and water-lilies floated, were approached by steps made of rubies. Trees in full flower adorned the banks which re-echoed to the call of Datyuhas and Shukas and the cries of geese and swans. That grove was enclosed by flat rocks of differing forms within which were many grassy glades of the sheen of emerald and pearl, and these were adorned by trees rivalling each other in the profusion of their blossom, the earth beneath being heaped with flowers, resembling the sky full of stars, so that it appeared like the garden of Indra or Chaitaratha created by Brahma.

Such was Rama's pastoral retreat with its arbours filled with countless seats and grassy couches inviting one to rest ; and the Increaser of Raghu's joy entered that magnificent Ashoka Grove and seated himself on a throne of great splendour which was decorated with innumerable flowers and covered with a carpet of Kusha Grass.

Taking Sita by the hand, Kakutstha gave her delicious wine made of distilled honey to drink, as formerly Purandara had offered to Sachi. Thereafter pure viands and fruits of every kind were brought by servants, whilst lovely Apsaras, skilled in the arts of singing and dancing, began to perform in the Prince's presence and troops of Nymphs and Uragas, surrounded by the Kinneris intoxicated with wine, danced before Kakutstha, and the virtuous Rama, the most captivating of warriors, delighted those ravishing and charming women.

Seated by Vaidehi, he was radiant with splendour and resembled Vasishtha at the side of Arundhati. In this way, in the joy that possessed him, Rama, like unto a God, each day prepared some new delight for Sita, the Princess of Videha, who was like unto the daughter of a Celestial Being.

While Sita and Raghava sported thus for a long time, the flowery season, that yields perpetual enjoyment, passed away and, as those two tasted every kind of felicity, Spring appeared once more. One day, having fulfilled the functions of state, that virtuous Prince returned to his palace where he spent the rest of the day. On her side, Sita, having worshipped the Gods and performed her morning duties, offering her services to all her mothers-in-law without distinction, thereafter adorned herself with marvellous jewels and re-joined Rama, like unto Sachi when re-united with that God of a Thousand Eyes as he returns to his City Trivishtapa.

Beholding his consort glowing with beauty, Raghava experienced an unequalled delight and exclaimed " It is well ! " then he addressed the lovely Sita, who resembled a daughter of the Gods, and said :—

" Now, O Vaidehi, that thou dost bear a child in thy womb, what dost thou desire, O Lady of lovely hips ? What pleasure can I prepare for thee ? "

Smiling, Vaidehi answered Rama, saying :—

" O Raghava, I wish to visit the sacred retreats of the Rishis of rigid penances, who dwell on the banks of the Ganges where they subsist on fruit and roots, and there I will throw myself at their feet, O Lord. O Kakutstha, it is my supreme desire even to pass a night in the hermitage of these ascetics who live on fruit and roots."

Then Rama of imperishable exploits gave her permission to do so, saying :—

" Be at peace, O Vaidehi, to-morrow without fail, thou shalt go there ! "

Having answered Maithili, born of Janaka, in this wise, Kakutstha went to the central court surrounded by his friends.

520

CHAPTER 43

Rama informs himself concerning current Rumours from his Friends

HAVING entered there, the King was surrounded by entertaining companions accustomed to the exchange of humorous experiences, Vijaya, Madhumatta, Kashyapa, Mangala, Kula, Suraji, Kaliya, Bhadra, Dantavakra and Sumagadha, and they beguiled the magnanimous Raghava with amusing tales of every kind amidst great merriment.

Raghava, however, during some narrative, enquired of Bhadra, saying :—

" O Bhadra, what do they say of me in the town and country ? What do they say of Sita, Bharata and Lakshmana ? What do they say of Shatrughna and Kaikeyi our mother ? Kings are always the subject of criticism whether they are in the forest or on the throne."

On hearing Rama's enquiry, Bhadra, with joined palms, answered :—

"Amongst the inhabitants of the city, nought but what is good is spoken of thee, O King, above all they tell of thy victory over Dashagriva, whom thou didst slay, O Dear Prince ! "

At these words of Bhadra, Raghava said :—

" Tell me all truthfully without reserve, what reports, good or ill, do the people of the city circulate regarding me ? When I learn of them, I shall endeavour to do what is meet in the future and eschew what is evil. Tell me all in full confidence without fear. Laying aside every scruple, relate all the rumours current about me in the kingdom ! "

Thus exhorted by Raghava, Bhadra, with joined palms, in profound reverence, addressed that mighty hero in measured tones, saying :—

" Hear, O King, what the people are saying, be it good or ill, in the highways, markets, streets, woods and parks—' Rama has achieved the impossible by throwing a bridge over the sea which to our knowledge was never done by his predecessors nor even by the Gods and Danavas together. With his foot-soldiers and cavalry, he has destroyed the invincible Ravana and has made the monkeys, bears and Rakshasas subject to him. Having slain Ravana in the fight and recovered Sita, Raghava, having mastered his anger, has taken his spouse into his house again. What pleasure can his heart experience in possessing Sita, whom Ravana formerly held in his lap, having borne her away by force? How is it that Rama was not filled with aversion for her after she had been taken to Lanka and conducted to the Ashoka Grove, where she was left to the mercy of the titans? We shall now have to countenance the same state of affairs regarding our own wives, since what a king does, his subjects follow!'

" These are the sayings current everywhere among the people of town and country, O King."

At these words, Raghava, stricken with grief, asked, " Is it thus that they speak of me ? "

Then all, bowing to the ground in reverence, answered the unfortunate Raghava and said :—

" It is true, O Lord of the Earth ! "

Having heard their unanimous testimony, Kakutstha, the Scourge of His Foes, dismissed his companions.

CHAPTER 44

Rama summons his Brothers

HAVING dismissed his companions, Raghava began to ponder within himself and thereafter said to the doorkeeper who stood near :—

" Go speedily and seek out the son of Sumitra, Lakshmana of auspicious marks and the fortunate Bharata and the invincible Shatrughna."

At Rama's command, the janitor paid obeisance with joined palms and went to Lakshmana's abode which he entered unchallenged and there, having saluted the magnanimous prince, he said :—

" The King desires to see thee, do thou go to him without delay ! "

" It is well ! " answered Saumitri and, in obedience to Raghava's command, he ascended a chariot and hastened to the palace. When he had departed, the doorkeeper approached Bharata and, saluting him in a like manner, said :—

" The king respectfully requests thy presence ! "

Hearing these instructions issued by Rama, Bharata, rising swiftly from his seat, started out hurriedly on foot. Beholding the virtuous Bharata going away, the messenger speedily approached Shatrughna's abode and, with joined palms, addressed him, saying :—

" Go quickly, O Prince of the Raghus, the king wishes to see thee ; Lakshmana has already preceded thee as also the renowned Bharata."

At these words, Shatrughna descended from his throne and, bowing to the ground, went to rejoin Raghava.

Meantime the messenger having returned, paid obeisance to Rama and made it known to him that his brothers had come. Learning of the youthful princes' arrival, Rama, who was deeply troubled, with a downcast mien, sad at heart, said to the doorkeeper :—

" Make haste and usher them into my presence ! Mine existence depends on them, they are my very life's breath ! "

At this command from that Indra of Men, the princes, attired in white, bowed with joined palms and entered respectfully. On beholding Rama, who resembled the moon in eclipse or the sun that the dusk robs of its splendour, whose eyes were filled with tears and who looked like a lotus bereft of its brilliance, they placed their heads at his feet and then stood silent. Thereupon the mighty Rama, shedding tears, having raised them up, clasped them in his arms and said to them :—

" Be seated ! You are my whole wealth, you are my very life ! It is with your assistance that I attained a kingdom and now rule, O Princes ! "

Thus spoke Kakutstha and all, attentive and deeply moved, wondered what words he might be about to address to them.

CHAPTER 45

Rama commands Lakshmana to take Sita to the Hermitage

ALL having taken their places full of sadness, Kakutstha, his features stricken, said to them :—

" Hear me all of you, may good betide you ! Do not let your attention wander ! This is what people are saying about me concerning Sita ! The inhabitants of the city as also those of the country censure me severely and their criticism pierces my heart ! I am born in the Race of the illustrious Ikshvakus and Sita belongs to the family of the great-souled Janaka. My Dear Lakshmana, thou knowest how, in the lonely forest, Ravana bore Sita away and that I destroyed him. It was then that the thought came to me regarding the daughter of Janaka, ' How can I bring Sita back to Ayodhya from this place ? ' Thereupon, in order to re-assure me, Sita entered the fire in my presence and that of the Gods, O Saumitri ! Agni, the Bearer of sacrificial offerings, witnessed to Maithili's innocence and Vayu also, who was then journeying through space, and Chandra and Aditya proclaimed it formerly before the Gods and all the Rishis, that the daughter of Janaka was without fault. The Gods and Gandharvas testified to her pure conduct in Lanka, where Mahendra placed the proofs in my hand, further I knew from my own inner being that the illustrious Sita was innocent. It was then that I took her back and returned to Ayodhya. Since then a great sadness, on hearing the censure of the people of town and country, has filled my heart. Whoever it may be, if his ill fame be current in the world, he falls to a lower state, so long as the defamatory rumours exist. Dishonour is condemned by the Gods ; honour is revered in the world and, it is on account of fair repute, that great souls act. As for me, so greatly do I fear dishonour that I would renounce my life and you yourselves on its account, O Bulls among Men, how much more therefore is it incumbent on me to separate myself from the daughter of Janaka. See therefore in what an ocean of grief I have fallen ! There is no misfortune greater than this ! To-morrow, at dawn,

O Saumitri, take my chariot with Sumantra as thy charioteer and, causing Sita to ascend it, leave her beyond the confines of the kingdom.

" On the further side of the Ganges, the magnanimous Valmiki has his hermitage of celestial aspect situated by the Tamasa ; it is in a solitary spot that thou shouldst leave her, O Thou who art the Joy of the House of Raghu. Go quickly, O Saumitri, and carry out my behest. Do not discuss it in any way ; go therefore, O Saumitri, it is not the time for observations. Any resistence on thy part will cause me extreme displeasure. Yea, I swear to thee by my two feet, by my life, that those who seek to make me alter my resolve in any way or oppose my desire, I shall deem to be mine enemies. If you are subject to me and hold me in reverence, then obey me and take Sita away from here this very day. Formerly she appealed to me saying, ' I wish to visit the sacred retreats of the banks of the Ganges ', let her wish be fulfilled ! "

Having spoken thus, the virtuous Kakutstha, his eyes filled with tears, re-entered his apartments escorted by his brothers, his heart riven with grief, sighing like an elephant.

CHAPTER 46

Lakshmana takes Sita away

WHEN the night had passed, Lakshmana, with a sad heart and downcast mien, said to Sumantra :—

" O Charioteer, harness swift horses to the most excellent of cars and, by the king's orders, prepare a comfortable and luxurious seat for Sita, she, in accord with the king's wish, under my charge, is to visit the retreats of the great Rishis of pious practices, therefore bring hither the chariot with all speed ! "

Then Sumantra saying, " Be it so ! " yoked some superb horses to a splendid chariot that was well furnished with cushions and, approaching Saumitri, the heaper of honours on his friends, he said :—

" The car is ready, let what must be accomplished be done, O Lord ! "

At these words of Sumantra, Lakshmana re-entered the King's palace and, having approached Sita, that Bull among Men addressed her thus :—

"According to the wish that thou didst express to him, that Lord of Men, the king, has charged me to take thee to the desired retreats. At the request of our sovereign, I will conduct thee without delay to those excellent solitudes of the Rishis on the banks of the Ganges, O Divine Vaidehi. I shall take thee to those hermitages inhabited by the Sages."

At these words of the magnanimous Lakshmana, Vaidehi experienced supreme felicity, so greatly did the thought of the expedition please her and, having furnished herself with costly raiment and jewels of every kind, she prepared to depart, saying :—

" I shall give these jewels as also the excellent robes and various treasures to the wives of the ascetics."

" It is well ", said Saumitri, causing Maithili to ascend the chariot and, recollecting Rama's command, he went forward drawn by swift horses.

Thereafter Sita said to Lakshmana, the increaser of prosperity :

" I behold countless inauspicious omens, O Joy of the House of Raghu, observe how my left eye twitches and all my limbs tremble, further my mind is confused and I feel extremely restless whilst all my courage has ebbed away, O Saumitri. The earth appears deserted, O Large-eyed Prince, can thy brother be happy, O Thou who art so devoted to him ? May all be well with my mothers-in-law without distinction, O Hero ! May all beings in town and country be happy ! "

Thus, with joined palms, Sita, the divine Maithili prayed, and Lakshmana listening, bent his head and, though his heart was contracted with grief, he cried in joyous accents, " Mayest thou too be happy ! "

Meantime they reached the banks of the Gaumati and rested in a hermitage, and the following day, at dawn, Saumitri, rising, said to the charioteer :—

" Harness the car speedily ! To-day, with great strength, I shall bear the waters of the Bhagirathi on my head, as did Tryambaka."[1]

[1] Tryambaka—the Lord Shiva.

Thus commanded, the driver with joined palms, said to Vaidehi :—

" Mount ! " and he gave rein to the horses yoked to the chariot, who were as swift as thought, whereupon she, hearing the voice of the charioteer, ascended that excellent car. Thereafter the large-eyed Sita accompanied by Saumitri and Sumantra reached the Ganges, that destroys all sin and, arriving there at noon, beholding the waters of the Bhagirathi, the unfortunate Lakshmana began to weep openly in his profound distress and the virtuous Sita, in her extreme solicitude, observing Lakshmana's misery, enquired of him, saying :—

" Wherefore art thou groaning ? We have reached the banks of the Jahnavi, the object of my desires for a long time and, at the moment of rejoicing, why dost thou cause me pain in this wise, O Lakshmana ? O Bull among Men, is thy grief on account of these two days absence from Rama, thou who art ever in attendance on him ? Rama is dearer to me than life, O Lakshmana, yet I do not distress myself ; do not behave like a child ! Let us cross the Ganges and visit the Sages so that I may distribute the raiment and jewels. Having paid homage to the great Rishis, which we owe to them and, passing one day there, we shall return to the city. My heart is impatient to see Rama again, whose eyes are like the petals of a lotus, whose chest is like a lion's, that foremost of men ! "

At these words of Sita's, Lakshmana, wiping his beautiful eyes, hailed the ferrymen and they, with joined palms, said " The boat is ready ! "

Eager to cross over that splendid river, Lakshmana boarded the skiff, and his mind pre-occupied, took Sita across the Ganges.

CHAPTER 47

Lakshmana tells Sita she has been repudiated

THE younger brother of Raghava, having first assisted Maithili to board it, entered the well-furnished boat ready to depart, thereafter he said to Sumantra, " Wait here with the chariot " and, overcome with grief, he commanded the craft to set sail.

Arriving at the farther bank of the Bhagirathi, Lakshmana, with joined palms, his face bathed in tears, said :—

"A stake has been driven into my heart by the noble and virtuous Rama, which will bring universal censure upon me. Death were better for me this day, verily death would be preferable to the mission on which I am engaged, which the world will condemn. Forgive me and do not impute this offence to me, O Illustrious Princess."

Thereafter, making obeisance, Lakshmana threw himself on the earth. Seeing him weep, paying her homage and calling on death, Maithili, alarmed, said to Lakshmana :—

" What is this ? I do not understand anything ; tell me the truth, O Lakshmana, why art thou agitated ? Is the king well ? Tell me the cause of thy grief ! "

Thus questioned by Vaidehi, Lakshmana, his heart filled with anguish, with bowed head, choked with sobs, addressed her saying :—

" Having learnt in open council that he was the object of severe censure in the city and country on thine account, O Daughter of Janaka, Rama, his heart riven, returning home told me of it. I am unable to repeat the things spoken in confidence to me, O Queen. Although thou art blameless in mine eyes, the king has repudiated thee. Public condemnation has perturbed him ; do not misunderstand the matter, O Goddess. I am to leave thee in the vicinity of the sacred hermitages. The king has commanded me to do so on the pretext of satisfying thy desire. The ascetics' retreats on the banks of the Jahnavi are sacred and enchanting, do not give way to grief, O Lovely One. The foremost of Rishis, the supremely illustrious Sage Valmiki was a great friend of thy sire, King Dasaratha. Taking refuge under the shadow of the feet of that magnanimous One and living in chastity, be happy, O Daughter of Janaka. It is by remaining faithful to thy Lord and practising devotion to Rama in thine heart that thou shalt, by thy conduct, acquire supreme felicity, O Goddess."

CHAPTER 48

Lakshmana leaves Sita on the Banks of the Ganges

HEARING Lakshmana's harsh words, the daughter of Janaka overcome with despair, fell to the ground but, regaining consciousness after a time, her eyes bathed in tears, she addressed him in broken accents, saying :—

"Assuredly this body of mine has been created for misfortune and is its supporter from this time forward. What sin can I have committed in days gone by or whom did I separate from her husband, that I, who am virtuous and chaste, should be cast off by the king?

" Formerly I lived in the forest following in Rama's footsteps and was content in the misfortune in which I found myself, O Prince, now, how can I, abandoned by all, live in solitude, O dear Lakshmana? To whom shall I confide the affliction that has overwhelmed me? What can I say to the ascetics, O Lord? For what sin, for what reason, am I repudiated by the magnanimous Raghava? I may not yield up my life in the waters of the Ganges, lest I bring the royal line to an end! Therefore do what thou hast been commanded, O Saumitri, leave me to my wretched plight! It is for thee to carry out the king's behests, yet hear me—do thou with joined palms pay homage to all my mothers-in-law and, having worshipped his feet, address the king. With bowed head, speak to them all, O Lakshmana, and do thou also say to the king, who is ever fixed in his duty, ' O Raghava, thou knowest I am truly pure and that I have been bound to thee in supreme love, yet thou hast renounced me in fear of dishonour, because thy subjects have reproached and censured thee, O Hero. Thou shouldst, however have spared me, since thou art my only refuge.' Further, thou shouldst say to the king who is established in righteousness, 'As thou dost act in regard to thy brothers, so shouldst thou act in regard to thy subjects; this is pre-eminently thy duty and will bring thee immeasurable renown; by its observance thou wilt enjoy the fruits of the earth! As for me, I am not distressed on mine own account, O Prince of Raghu, it is for thee to keep thy fair name untarnished ! The husband is as a God to the woman, he is her family, and her spiritual preceptor, therefore, even at the price of her life, she must seek to please her lord.'

" Repeat these words to Rama, it is all I ask of thee. Having borne witness that I am far advanced in pregnancy, do thou depart."

So did Sita speak and Lakshmana, sad at heart, bowed to the earth without being able to answer her. Thereafter he circumambulated her sobbing aloud and, after reflecting awhile, said :—

" What hast thou said, O Beautiful Princess, I have never ráised mine eyes to thy face and have ever but looked on thy feet, O Irreproachable One. How should I, in his absence, dare to gaze upon the one Rama has abandoned in the lonely forest ? "

With these words, he paid obeisance to her and re-entered the boat. Boarding the skiff, he urged the ferryman on, saying :—

" Cross to the farther shore."

Beside himself with grief, in deep affliction, he, having reached the other bank proceeded in his swiftly moving chariot, turning round again and again to gaze on Sita, who, as if bereft of all support, was wandering about distraught on the farther side of the Ganges. Her eyes fixed on the chariot and on Lakshmana, now far distant, Sita was overcome with grief, and, crushed by the weight of her misfortune, the illustrious, noble and virtuous woman, seeing herself without a protector in the forest, that re-echoed to the cry of peacocks, a prey to despair, burst into loud sobs.

CHAPTER 49

Valmiki offers Sita his Protection

BEHOLDING Sita who was sobbing, the sons of the Rishis ran to seek out the blessed Valmiki of rigid penances and, having paid obeisance to the feet of that great ascetic, the children of the Sages informed him that a woman was weeping nearby, saying :—

" O Lord, a lady resembling Shri, whom we have never before

seen and who must be the consort of some great man, her
features distorted, is lamenting in the vicinity of the hermitage !
O Blessed One, thou wilt surely deem her to be a goddess fallen
from heaven ! Verily the most lovely of women, in deep
distress, appeared before us on the bank of a river, shedding
scalding tears, overcome by grief. In this misfortune that was
assuredly not merited, she is alone and without a protector. We
do not know the lady but do thou receive her with kindness for
she is close to this retreat and has come to take refuge with thee."

Valmiki, that Prince of Sages, being aware of everything by
virtue of his asceticism, ascertaining the truth of their words,
with rapid steps went to where the Queen was weeping, and, as
he strode forward, the disciples followed that illustrious Muni.

Bearing the Arghya in his hands, proceeding on foot, the
sagacious Valmiki reached the banks of the river and beheld
Raghava's beloved consort lamenting like one bereft. Thereafter,
having consoled her by virtue of his holiness, the great ascetic
addressed her in a sweet voice, saying :—

" O Virtuous Lady, thou art the daughter-in-law of King
Dasaratha, Rama's beloved consort, the daughter of Janaka ! O
Faithful One, by virtue of my meditations, the cause that brings
thee here has been revealed to me. O Auspicious One, I am
fully aware of thy purity, for all that comes to pass in the Three
Worlds is known to me. By my spiritual vision, I am convinced
of thy chaste conduct, O Daughter of Janaka ; thou art under
my protection, O Vaidehi, take comfort ! Not far from mine
hermitage there are many female ascetics established in pious
practices, they will care for thee as for their own daughter, O
Dear Child. Now accept the Arghya and trust in me, giving up
all anxiety. Do not grieve but look on this as thine abode."

Hearing these excellent words from the Sage, Sita, paying
obeisance to his feet, with joined palms, accompanied the
ascetic.

Beholding the Sage approaching, followed by Vaidehi, the
female ascetics came out to meet them and, filled with delight,
said :—

" O Foremost among the Sages, be thou welcome ; it is long
since thou hast visited us, we bow down to thee, what are thy
commands ? "

Hearing their words, Valmiki answered :—

"This lady is Sita, the consort of the virtuous Rama, she is the daughter-in-law of King Dasaratha, the chaste daughter of Janaka. Though innocent, her husband has renounced her, we should all therefore protect her ; she is worthy of our affection ! Such is my wish, who am your spiritual preceptor ; at my behest, do ye pay her every honour."

Having placed Sita in the charge of those female ascetics, the great and illustrious Sage Valmiki, followed by his disciples, returned to his hermitage.

The following Traditional Verses appear here in the original text

THUS has this ancient tale been narrated in its entirety, may good betide you ! May the might of Vishnu increase !

Those who have installed Shri Rama, who is the colour of a blue lotus, in their heart, will achieve success, nor will they ever experience defeat !

May the rains come when they are needed ; may the earth bring forth a rich harvest of grain and may the land be free from disorders. May the brahmins be without anxiety and just.

May prosperity reign in due time and the monsoons never fail. May Raghunath ever triumph and Shri ever reign.

May the kings of the earth protect their subjects in accord with justice. May the cows and the brahmins prosper. May all the worlds be happy.

May good fortune attend the King of Koshala, who is an ocean of virtue ; may good fortune attend on that monarch born of the Sovereign of the World.

May good fortune attend on Punyashloka,[1] the Knower of the Veda and the Vedanta, who appears in the form of a dark-coloured cloud causing delusion to human beings.

May good fortune attend the King of the City of Mithila, the close companion of Vishvamitra, the personification of prosperity in a gracious form.

May good fortune attend on the Blessed Rama, whose subjects

[1] Vishnu.

are full of joy, who is, with his brothers and Sita, ever devoted to his sire.

May good fortune attend on the One who is constant and noble, who dwelt in and abandoned Saketa (Ayodhya) and wandered about Chittrakuta worshipped by the self-controlled.

May good fortune attend on my Guru, who, bearing the bow, the arrow and the sword, was ever worshipped with devotion by Janaki and Lakshmana.

May good fortune attend on that King of the Vultures who dwelt in the Dandaka Forest, who is the enemy of those who oppose the Gods, who is a great devotee and a granter of liberation.

May good betide him who is exalted by Sattwa, who is extremely approachable, who is perfect in virtue and who desired to partake of the roots and fruits offered to him in reverence by Shabari.

May good fortune attend on the destroyer of Bali, he of supreme steadfastness, the fulfiller of the desire of the Monkey King, whose companion was Hanuman.

May good fortune attend him who is resolute in combat, the foremost of the conquerors of the Rakshasas, the blessed Hero of the Raghus, who passed over the ocean by a causeway.

May good fortune attend on the Blessed Rama, King of Kings and Princes, who returned to the celestial city and was installed there with Sita.

May good fortune attend on him who was honoured by the foremost Acharyas and all the great Sages of old engaged in prayer, benediction and blessings.

CHAPTER 50

Sumantra seeks to console Lakshmana

HAVING seen the Princess of Mithila conducted to the hermitage, a profound anguish seized the unfortunate Lakshmana, and that hero said to Sumantra, who drove his car repeating the sacred formulas[1] :—

---

[1] Literally " The Mantra Charioteer ".

" See into what affliction Sita's plight has thrown Rama !
What could be sadder for Raghava than to have to renounce the
daughter of Janaka, a chaste wife ? It is evident to me that fate
has separated Raghava from Vaidehi ! O Charioteer, destiny is
inexorable ! Raghava, who, in his wrath, slew the Gods,
Gandharvas, Asuras and Rakshasas, is under the sway of destiny.
Formerly Rama, at his father's command, dwelt in the vast and
lonely Dandaka Forest for fourteen years, but more painful and
cruel to me seems the repudiation of Sita through listening to the
calumny of the people. What justification was there, O Suta,
for this dishonourable procedure consequent on the ill-considered
reports regarding Maithili ? "

Hearing these words uttered by Lakshmana, the loyal and
sagacious Sumantra answered :—

" Do not grieve about Maithili, O Son of Sumitra, O Lakshmana, it was formerly predicted by the brahmins to thy Sire.
Assuredly Rama is destined to become extremely unhappy ;
misfortune is his lot ! Undoubtedly that long-armed hero will
be separated from all those he loves. Under the sway of destiny,
that great man will renounce thee, Shatrughna and Bharata. Do
not repeat to Bharata or Shatrughna what Durvasa uttered in
reply to the king who was questioning him. It was in the
presence of a large assembly when I was present, O Bull among
Men, that the Rishi uttered these words, Vasishtha himself,
with others, being there.

" Hearing the words of the Rishi, the foremost of men,
Dasaratha, then charged me saying, ' Do not repeat anything
that thou hast heard to others '—I have kept his command
scrupulously and, as I see it, under no circumstances should I
divulge the matter to any, yet, if I can trust thy discretion, O
Dear One, then hear me, O Joy of the Raghus. If I repeat the
secret formerly confided to me by King Dasaratha then it is fate
and inevitable. It is on account of fate that a similar misfortune,
the source of thy present distress, took place. Do not speak of
it before Bharata or in Shatrughna's presence either."

When he heard those grave and portentous words of Sumantra's, Saumitri said to the charioteer, " Tell me the whole truth !"

CHAPTER 51

Vishnu is cursed by Bhrigu

THUS requested by the high-souled Lakshmana, the charioteer began to relate what the ascetic had said.

" Formerly a great Sage, named Durvasa, the son of Atri, passed the rainy season in Vasishtha's hermitage. Thy supremely illustrious Sire went there himself, desirous of beholding the magnanimous family priest and he observed the great ascetic, Durvasa, bright as the sun, radiant in his own effulgence, seated by the side of Vasishtha. Those two Sages, the foremost of ascetics, saluted him with respect and bade him welcome, honouring him with a seat, fruit and roots, and water wherewith to wash his feet. Thereafter he dwelt in their company and the illustrious Rishis there present, at noon, used to recount pleasing traditions, and once during their recital, the king, with joined palms, said to the magnanimous ascetic, the son of Atri :—

" ' O Blessed One, how long will my dynasty endure ? To what age will Rama live ? And my other sons, how long will they survive ? How long will the sons of Rama live ? Be so good as to tell me the destiny of my race, O Blessed Lord.'

" Hearing the words of King Dasaratha, the highly effulgent Durvasa began to speak thus :—

" ' Learn, O King, what happened formerly during the conflict between the Devas and Asuras. The Daityas, whom the Suras threatened, took refuge with the consort of Bhrigu and she, having given them a haven, they dwelt there in safety. Seeing them thus succoured, the Chief of the Gods, enraged, with his sharp-edged discus severed the head of Bhrigu's wife.

" ' Beholding the murder of his consort, Bhrigu, in his wrath, instantly cursed Vishnu, the destroyer of enemy hosts, saying :—

" ' " Since in thine insensate fury, thou hast slain my spouse, who should never have died thus, thou shalt take birth in the world of men, O Janardana, and there thou shalt live separated from thy consort for many years."

"'Having pronounced this curse, Bhrigu was overcome with remorse and his merits being exhausted by the malediction he had uttered, he began to propitiate that God, paying homage to the One who delights in penance and protects his devotees. Thereafter that God spoke, saying, "For the good of the worlds, I will be subject to thy curse."

"' This is how the illustrious Vishnu was cursed by Bhrigu in days of yore and descended on earth, becoming thy son, O Foremost of Monarchs. Renowned in the Three Worlds under the name of Rama, he has to undergo the dire consequences of Bhrigu's curse. He will reign in Ayodhya for a long time. Those who follow him will be happy and prosperous and, having reigned for eleven thousand years, Rama will go to Brahmaloka. Having performed many great sacrifices, distributing costly gifts, he, who may not be overcome by the most powerful beings, shall establish many dynasties and he will beget two sons by Sita.'

" Having related all concerning the past and future of his race to King Dasaratha, Durvasa fell silent, whereupon the king paid obeisance to the two magnanimous ascetics and returned to the city.

" This is what I was formerly told by the Rishi and I have kept it in my heart ; none of these things could have happened otherwise. Sita's two sons will be installed in Ayodhya by Raghava, the words of a Sage never fail to be fulfilled. It being so, do not grieve either for Sita or for Rama, O Son of Raghu. Take courage, O Prince."

Hearing this remarkable speech of the charioteer's, Lakshmana experienced unsurpassed felicity and cried out, " Excellent ! Excellent ! "

Meantime while Lakshmana and the charioteer were thus conversing on the way, the sun set and they halted on the banks of the Keshini River.

CHAPTER 52

Lakshmana seeks out Rama

HAVING passed the night by the Keshini, Lakshmana, the Joy of the House of Raghu, rose at dawn and continued on his way.

At noon, that Prince of the Great Car entered the opulent City of Ayodhya, crowded with happy people. The extremely sagacious Saumitri, however, became exceedingly apprehensive, reflecting " On mine arrival, when I fall at Rama's feet, what shall I say to him ? " As he was thus anxiously pondering, Rama's residence, bright as the moon, rose before him, and the prince, dismounting at the door of the palace, his heart contracted, with bowed head entered without hindrance. Seeing his elder brother, Rama, seated on his throne in deep distress, Lakshmana's eyes were filled with tears and, seizing hold of his feet, his soul afflicted, with great reverence he offered obeisance to him and addressed him in plaintive accents, saying :—

" In accord with thy command, O Lord, I left the daughter of Janaka on the banks of the Ganges near the splendid retreat of the Sage Valmiki, following the counsel given to me. It is there at the entrance of the hermitage that I abandoned the chaste Sita and have returned to serve thee. Do not grieve, O Foremost of Men, it has been decreed by destiny. Assuredly those like thee, who are intelligent and wise, do not give way to despair. All growth ends in decay, those who rise high, fall, and all meetings end in separation ; death is the end of life. Therefore in regard to sons, wives, kinsfolk and wealth, detachment should be practised, for separation from them all is certain. Thou who art able to control the spirit by the spirit and the mind by the mind and all the worlds, O Kakutstha, how much more art thou able to control grief. Nay, nay, in similar circumstances, the foremost of men, like thyself, do not distress themselves. Assuredly thou wilt be censured anew, O Raghava, for giving way to grief on account of calumny. Undoubtedly the people will condemn thee. O Best of Men, thou who art so well endowed with firmness of purpose, give up this faint-heartedness and cease to grieve."

Hearing the words of the magnanimous Lakshmana, the son of Sumitra, Kakutstha, beloved of his friends, answered him in cheerful tones, saying :—

" It shall be as thou sayest, O Best of Men, O Valiant Lakshmana, I am gratified by the execution of my behests, O Hero. O Gentle Prince, my distress has been assuaged by thy felicitous words ; I shall be guided by them, O Saumitri."

CHAPTER 53

Rama tells Lakshmana the Story of Nriga

HEARING Lakshmana's remarkable speech that filled him with amazement, Rama replied :—

"Assuredly it would be difficult in these times to find a relative like thee, O Dear Brother! O Thou who bearest auspicious marks, who art gifted with intelligence and art one with me in thought, now learn all that is passing in my heart and, knowing it, do what I command thee.

" O Dear Saumitri, four days have gone by since I concerned myself with the interests of my people and my soul is tormented ; now call together my subjects, the family priests and also the ministers with all those to whose affairs attention must be given ! The king who does not fulfil his duties in regard to his people each day, undoubtedly falls into the darkest hell.

" It is related that formerly a monarch named Nriga reigned, who was illustrious, truthful, pure-hearted and devoted to the brahmins. Once at the time of a sacred pilgrimage to Pushkara, that monarch bestowed on the brahmins hundreds and thousands of kine with gilded horns, accompanied by their calves.

"And it came about that one cow with its calf, belonging to a poor brahmin, was accidentally given away and he, hungry and thirsty, searched in vain here and there for that cow for a long time. Finally, having reached Kankhala, he observed his cow in the abode of a brahmin and, though in good health, it had grown old. Thereupon that brahmin called the cow by name crying ' Shabali, come ' and the beast, hearing him, recognized the voice of that one who was stricken with hunger and followed him.

" Then the ascetic, in whose house the cow had been retained, speedily pursued him and, reaching that Rishi, addressed him in harsh tones, saying ' That cow belongs to me and was given me by the foremost of monarchs ; it was Nriga who bestowed her on me as a gift.'

" Thereupon a great quarrel ensued between those two learned brahmins, and wrangling, they both approached the one who had given away that cow, but though they waited there a long time, they were unable to gain admission to the palace. Having tarried there many days and nights, they became greatly enraged and those two illustrious ascetics, furious at not achieving their purpose, uttered the following dreadful malediction :—

" ' Since thou hast refused to grant us audience in order to settle our dispute, do thou become a lizard and remain invisible to all beings ; in that state thou shalt pass hundreds and thousands of years in a ditch ; when Vishnu, in human form, descends to earth among the Yadus, whose glory he will enhance, thou shalt be liberated from the curse ! He shall be named Vasudeva. When the Kali Yuga has come, Nara and Narayana will descend on earth to relieve her of her burden.'

" Having pronounced this curse on the king, the two brahmins fell silent and they both agreed to bestow the cow, who had become old and weak, on another brahmin.

" O Lakshmana, King Nriga is still suffering under that dreadful curse. The folly of not attending to the dispute between contestants is to be attributed to the king. Therefore let all those who have come for reasons of arbitration be ushered into my presence , though a king does not seek the fruit of duty fulfilled. Go now personally and see if anyone seeks audience with me."

CHAPTER 54

The End of the Story of Nriga

HEARING the words of the supremely effulgent Rama, the exceedingly sagacious Lakshmana, with joined palms, replied :—

" O Kakutstha, it was for a very trivial fault that the Twice-borns struck down Nriga, that royal Sage, with that dreadful curse like unto the Rod of Yama. O Foremost of Men, what did King Nriga reply to those enraged ascetics when they condemned him to such suffering? "

Thus questioned by Lakshmana, Raghava took up the tale again, saying :—

" O Gentle One, hear what that prince first did when he was struck down by the curse. Learning that the two Sages had departed, the king called together his ministers, citizens and chief priests and, in the presence of his subjects, said :—

" ' Hear me carefully! Having pronounced a dreadful curse upon me, the Rishis Narada and Parvata have, with the speed of the wind, returned to the Region of Brahma. Let the youthful Prince Vasu, here present, be installed on the throne to-day. Let artisans construct three ditches, where I shall expiate the curse laid upon me by the brahmins, one proof against the rains, one against the cold and a third against the heat; let this habitation be made comfortable and trees laden with fruit and bushes covered with flowers be planted round about, as also shrubs of every kind to lend shade. The precincts of these ditches should be pleasant and I shall pass the time agreeably there till the termination of my sufferings. Let flowers with a sweet fragrance be sown frequently for half a league on all sides! '

" Having made these arrangements, he installed Vasu on the throne and addressed him, saying :—

" ' My Son, be ever fixed in thy duty and rule thy subjects in accord with the laws of the Kshatriyas. Keep before thine eyes the curse the two brahmins pronounced upon me. Do not grieve on my account, O Foremost of Men. Destiny is just, O My son, it is destiny[1] that has plunged me in this affliction. What must happen will happen; what we must pursue will be pursued; what is to be attained will be attained, whether good or ill, according to the acts of a previous existence. Do not grieve, O My Son.'

" Having spoken thus to his son, the highly illustrious King Nriga descended into the constructed ditch in order to take up his abode there. Having entered that deep hole adorned with precious gems, the magnanimous Nriga suffered the curse that the two brahmins had pronounced on him in their anger."

[1] Karma—See Glossary.

CHAPTER 55

The Story of Nimi

" I HAVE related the cursing of Nriga in detail but, if thou so desireth, listen to the following story ! "

On this, Saumitri said :—

" I never tire of hearing these marvellous tales, O King ! "

Thus spoke Lakshmana, and Rama, the Joy of the Ikshvakus, began to recount many exceedingly instructive legends, saying :-

" There was once a king named Nimi, the twelfth son of the magnanimous offspring of the Ikshvakus and he was full of courage and truth. That highly valorous monarch founded a beautiful city, resembling that of the Gods, in the vicinity of Gautama's hermitage, and the name of that city was Vaijanta ! It served as the residence of the royal Sage Nimi and, while he dwelt in that vast capital, he reflected ' I will perform a great sacrifice to gratify my sire ! '

" Having invited his father, Ikshvaku, the son of Manu, he first welcomed Vasishtha, the foremost of Rishis ; thereafter the Rajarishi Nimi, the Joy of Ikshvaku, invited Atri, Angira and also Bhrigu, that treasury of asceticism.

" Meanwhile Vasishtha said to Nimi, the foremost of royal Sages :—' I am already pledged to Indra, therefore wait for me till his sacrifice is completed.'

" Soon afterwards, the great ascetic Gautama undertook the sacrifice[1] whilst the mighty Vasishtha was officiating at Indra's ceremony.

" King Nimi, that foremost of men, having assembled the brahmins, celebrated a sacrifice in the vicinity of his city on the side of the Himavat Mountain, its term exceeding five thousand years.

" Indra's sacrifice being completed, the blessed and irre-proachable Sage Vasishtha returned to the king and offered himself as officiating priest. Observing that Gautama had, in the interval, filled that office, Vasishtha was transported with

[1] In Vasishtha's place.

541

rage and, anxious to behold the king, sought out the monarch, but that day he lay in a deep sleep and the fury of the magnanimous Vasishtha burst forth anew, so that he began to curse the king, who was unaware of his presence there, saying :—

" ' Since thou didst choose another and have failed to treat me with due respect, O King, thy body will be rendered lifeless ! '

" Thereupon the king awoke and, hearing the curse pronounced against him, in a transport of rage, said to the son of Brahma :—

" ' When I was unconscious and asleep, thou, beside thyself with anger, hast subjected me to the fire of thy wrath like unto the Rod of Yama ! For this, be assured thy body too, O Brahmarishi, shall be bereft of sensation for a long time.'

" Thus both dominated by anger, the foremost of kings and the chief of the ascetics, mutually cursed one another and they, whose powers were equal to the Gods, were both instantly deprived of their bodies."

CHAPTER 56

The Cursing of the Nymph Urvashi

HAVING heard this story, Lakshmana, the Slayer of His Foes, with joined palms, addressed the effulgent Rama, saying :—

" O Kakutstha, how did that Twice-born One, worshipped by the Celestials, and the king, having cast off their bodies, regain them once more ? "

Thus questioned by Lakshmana, Rama, having truth for his prowess, answered :—

" Following on their mutual cursing, those two virtuous Ones, that Sage among monarchs and the foremost of ascetics, having discarded their bodies, lived in their subtle forms. Thereafter, the great Rishi Vasishtha, desirous of regaining his physical shape, sought out his sire, and that virtuous Sage in his subtle body, paid obeisance to the feet of that God of Gods, the Grandsire, and addressed him, saying :—

" ' O Lord, through King Nimi's curse, I am deprived of my physical body, O Lord of Lords, O Mahadeva, I am merged in air ! Those deprived of a body suffer great misfortune ; many righteous deeds may not be performed without a body, O Lord, by thy favour grant me another form ! '

" Then Brahma Swyambhu, whose powers are immeasurable, said to him :—

" ' Do thou enter the vital seed of Mitra and Varuna, O Thou illustrious One ! Thou shalt then be born without a mother, O Foremost of the Twice-born, and, endowed with great virtue, shalt regain thy state.'

" Thus spoke the divine Grandsire, and Vasishtha, circumambulating him, instantly left for Varuna's abode. At that time, Mitra, being worshipped by the foremost of the Celestials was reigning over Varuna's kingdom and the chief Apsara, Urvashi, came there by chance in company with her friends.

" Beholding the lovely Urvashi sporting in the waters, Varuna was seized with extreme delight and desired to unite himself with that nymph, whose eyes are as large as lotus petals and whose face was as radiant as the moon, but she, with joined palms, answered him saying :—

" ' Mitra has already invited me for this purpose, O Chief of the Gods ! '

" Then Varuna, being stricken with desire, said :—' Since thou dost not wish to be united with me, I shall loose my vital seed in the vessel created by Brahma, O Thou of lovely hips and beautiful complexion, thus shall my desire be satisfied.'

" Hearing this amiable speech, Urvashi was highly gratified and said to him :—

" ' Be it so, for my mind is fixed on thee, though my body belongs to Mitra, O Lord ! '

"At these words of Urvashi, Varuna discharged his powerful vital seed, that shone like fire, into the vessel. Then the divine Urvashi immediately sought out Mitra and he, in the height of anger, said to her :—

" ' Why didst thou desert me, who first chose thee ? For what reason hast thou taken another, O Thou without moral sense ? For this misdeed, I condemn thee to live in the world of men for a time ; thou shalt be united with the son of Budha, the royal Sage Pururavas, who rules over Kashi ! Go to him, O Sinful One ! '

" Then Urvashi, under the influence of that curse, went to Pratisthana to Pururavas, the beloved son of Budha, and she bore him a lovely child, Ayu, who was full of valour and became the father of Nahusha, the equal of Indra in glory, and when the Lord of the Celestials loosed his thunderbolt on Vritra and suffered eclipse,[1] Nahusha reigned in his stead for thousands of years.

" In consequence of this curse, Urvashi, of charming teeth, beautiful eyes and graceful brows, descended on earth where she passed many years and, the period of the curse having expired, she returned to the Region of Indra."

CHAPTER 57

The End of the Story of Vasishtha and Nimi

HEARING that wonderful and divine theme, Lakshmana, highly delighted, said to Raghava :—

" O Kakutstha, how did that Twice-born One and the king, adored by the Gods, who had been deprived of their physical bodies regain them again ? "

Thus questioned, Rama, that true hero began to relate the history of the magnanimous Vasishtha, saying :—

" O Prince of the Raghus, from that vessel in which the two mighty Gods had emptied their vital seed, two Sages were born, who were the foremost of Rishis. First Agastya appeared, that blessed ascetic, and he said to Mitra, ' I am not thy son ' and went away. O Lakshmana, the seed of Mitra formerly received by Urvashi, was to be found in the same vessel as that of Varuna's

"After a time Vasishtha was born in his turn, he who is worshipped by the Celestials, he is a God to the Ikshvakus and the mighty and highly effulgent Ikshvaku chose the irreproachable Vasishtha as his family priest for the good of our race, O My Friend ! I have thus described to thee how the magnanimous Vasishtha, who was previously bodiless, was re-born, now hear of the history of Nimi.

[1] Being overwhelmed by the sin of slaying a brahmin.

" Beholding the king deprived of his body, all the sagacious Rishis assisted him by the celebration of a sacrifice and the foremost of the Twice-born preserved the body of that first of monarchs by means of unguents, cloths and herbs with the help of the citizens and servants. At the conclusion of the sacrifice, Bhrigu said to Nimi, ' I shall restore thee to life, O King, I am gratified with thee.'

" Thereafter the Gods in their delight said to him :—' Choose a boon, O Royal Sage, where shall thy consciousness be set ? '

" Thus spoke the Gods and Nimi's spirit answered :—

" ' I wish to live in the eyes of all beings, O Illustrious Gods ! '

" ' So be it ', said the Celestials, ' Thou shalt dwell in the eyes of all beings in the form of air. By thy grace, O Lord of the Earth, their eyes shall close again and again for rest when thou dost move about in the form of air.'

" Having spoken thus, the Gods returned to their own region and the magnanimous Rishis bore away Nimi's body to the sacrificial ground and began to rub it with great energy to the accompaniment of sacred formulas. And from the Arani,[1] thus violently agitated, a great and highly ascetic Being arose and, on account of him being born from an inanimate body, he was called Mithi, the King of Videha, and through this birth, he became the ancient Janaka.[2] It was from that Being of severe penances, who was called Mithi, that the race of Mithila originated. O Friend, I have told thee all without omitting anything concerning the curse and of the wonderful birth of that royal Sage and the foremost of kings."

CHAPTER 58

Shukra curses Yayati

THUS spoke Rama, and Lakshmana, the Slayer of His Foes, said to his mighty brother who was blazing with effulgence :—

" O Lion among Monarchs, this ancient history of the King

---

[1] Arani—The sticks used to light the sacred fire made of wood from the sacred fig-tree.

[2] Some Commentators explain that the name ' Janaka ' meaning ' Sire ' was given to the father or begetter of that great Race.

of Videha and the Sage Vasishtha is astonishing and wonderful, but why was King Nimi, a warrior full of valour, who had received initiation, unable to forgive the Rishi Vasishtha ? "

Thus questioned by Lakshmana, who was conversant with the Shastras, Rama, the foremost of warriors, answered his illustrious brother, saying :—

" O Valiant One, forgiveness is not always shown by men ! O Saumitri, hear with what resignation King Yayati bore the injuries done to him !

" King Yayati, the prosperity of his people, was the son of Nahusha—he had two wives, whose beauty was unequalled on earth. One was his favourite, Sharmishtha, born of Diti and the Daitya Vrashparvan, the other consort of Yayati was the daughter of Shukacharya and called Devayani, who was not beloved of her husband.

" Two sons of great beauty and amiability were born to them, Sharmishtha begot Puru and Devayani, Yadu. Puru was the favourite of his sire on account of his good qualities and also because of his mother, whereupon Yadu, much distressed, said to Devayani :—

" ' Thou, who art born in the family of the divine son of Bhrigu of imperishable exploits, art exposed to misery and contempt. It is intolerable, let us both enter the fire, O Queen, and let the King amuse himself for innumerable nights with the daughter of the Daitya. Or, if thou art able to endure it, then allow me to go my way. Do thou suffer this for I shall not brook it and have resolved to put an end to my life.'

"At these words from her son, who was weeping, Devayani, overcome by grief, highly indignant, called her Sire to mind and being thought upon, Bhargava instantly appeared before his daughter and, beholding her perturbed and beside herself, he enquired of her saying :—

" ' O Child, what is the matter ? ' Then Bhargava, his heart wrung, questioned her again and again, whereupon Devayani, enraged, answered her father, saying :—

" ' I shall enter the fire or drink poison or cast myself in the waters for I will not continue living. Thou dost not know to what misery and contempt I am subject ! When a tree is neglected, those who live thereon suffer. The king disregards me and treats me with disdain, therefore thou too art disregarded ! '

"At these words, which filled him with fury, the descendant of Bhrigu began to curse the son of Nahusha, saying :—

" ' O Nahusha, since in the wickedness of thy heart, thou hast looked upon me with contempt, old age shall come upon thee and thou shalt become senile.'

" Having spoken thus and comforted his daughter, the descendant of Bhrigu, that highly illustrious Brahmarishi returned to his own abode.

" Having solaced his daughter, Devayani, and pronounced that curse on the king, the foremost of the Twice-born, Shukra, radiant as the sun, departed."

CHAPTER 59

Puru takes the place of his Father cursed by Shukra

"At these words of the enraged Shukra,[1] the unfortunate Yayati, overtaken by old age, said to Yadu :—

" ' O Yadu, My Son, Thou art conversant with dharma, do thou take mine old age upon thyself and give me back my youth so that I may continue to give myself up to various enjoyments. O Foremost of Men, I am not yet sated with pleasures ; once I am satisfied, I will resume my senility.'

" Hearing these words, Yadu answered that foremost of monarchs, saying :—

" ' Thou hast excluded me from all matters, O King, and deprived me of thy proximity, let Puru, who feasts with thee, take this upon himself ! '

" Hearing the words of Yadu, the king addressed Puru, saying :—

" ' O Hero, do thou take mine old age upon thee.'

" On this, Puru, with joined palms, cried out :—

" ' What good fortune is mine ! Do thou favour me, I am at thy command ! '

[1] Also called Bhargava.

" This response from Puru filled Nahusha with exceeding joy and, seeing himself freed from senility, he experienced an unequalled satisfaction. Thereupon, regaining his youth, he performed thousands of sacrifices and ruled the earth for innumerable years. After a long time, the king said to Puru :—

" ' Give me back mine old age, my Son, that I deposited with thee ! I placed this decrepitude upon thee and that is why I now reclaim it. Fear not, I am pleased with thy submission to my will and shall install thee as king in token of my satisfaction.'

" Having spoken thus to his son, Puru, King Yayati, born of Nahusha, addressed the son of Devayani harshly, saying :—

" ' Thou art an intractable Rakshasa born to me as a warrior, O Thou who dost disregard my behests ! Thou shalt never be king ! Since thou hast set me at nought, who am thy sire and thy spiritual director, thou shalt beget terrible Rakshasas and Yatudhanas ! Assuredly, O Thou of perverse soul, thy race shall not intermingle with the issue of the lunar race and will resemble thee in conduct.'

" Having spoken thus for the good of his realm, that royal Sage invested Puru with the supreme dignity and himself withdrew to the forest.

"After a long time, when the hour fixed had struck, he went to the Celestial Abode. Thereafter Puru ruled the empire with great equity and glory in the City of Pratishthana in the kingdom of Kashi.

" Yadu however begot thousands of Yatudhanas in the inaccessible City of Durga. In this wise, Yayati endured Shukra's curse in accord with the traditions of the Kshatriyas but Nimi never exercised forgiveness.

" I have related everything to thee, let us follow the example of those who accept all, so that we do not fall like Nriga."

As Rama, whose face resembled the moon, was speaking thus, the heavens were spangled with stars and the east became a roseate golden colour as if she had donned a robe covered with the pollen of flowers.

IN the clear light of dawn, the lotus-eyed Rama performed the morning rites and took his seat in the council chamber on the royal throne in the company of the brahmins and citizens engaged in affairs of state. And the Priest Vasishtha with the Sage Kashyapa and others well versed in the rules of government, ministers conversant with the law, scriptures and ethics were of the assembly, which resembled Indra's Hall of Justice or Yama's or Kuvera's.

Then Rama said to Lakshmana, who was endowed with auspicious marks :—

" O Saumitri, O Long-armed Warrior, do thou go out to the city gate and summon those who have come here as petitioners."

Thereupon, according to Rama's command, Lakshmana, endowed with auspicious marks, went to the gate and called upon those who had come as complainants, but no one presented himself, for, under the rule of Ramachandra, there was neither poverty nor disease and the earth was filled with grain and herbs. Neither children nor the young nor those of middle age met with death, the kingdom was ruled with equity and there was no adversity. Thus during Rama's administration none was to be seen who was in need of justice.

Then Lakshmana, with joined palms, said to Rama :—" None has come as complainant," whereupon Rama, with a delighted heart, answered :—

" Do thou go once more, O Saumitri, and see if any presents himself! Under royal decree, unrighteousness must not prevail. Though laws inaugurated by me protect my subjects from harm, like the arrows I discharge, yet, O Long-armed One, do thou engage thyself in vigilance on their behalf."

Thus addressed, Lakshmana went forth from the palace and observed a dog sitting at the gate. Fixing its gaze steadfastly upon him, that dog was howling unceasingly and the valiant Lakshmana, beholding it in that plight, said :—

" O Fortunate One, what has brought thee hither, speak without fear ? "

Hearing the words of Lakshmana, the dog replied :—

" I wish to communicate something to Rama of imperishable exploits, who is the refuge of all beings and who confers fearlessness on all."

Hearing the dog's words, Lakshmana entered the beautiful palace to inform Rama and, having reported the matter to Ramachandra, he went out and said to the dog :—

" If thou hast anything true to say then come and inform the king ! "

Hearing the words of Lakshmana, the dog said :—

" Since we are vilely born, we may not enter the temple of a God, the palace of a king or the abode of a brahmin, nor may we go where there is fire, Indra, the sun or the wind ! The king is the personification of virtue ; Shri Ramachandra is truthful, well versed in the science of warfare and is ever engaged in the welfare of all beings ; he is perfectly cognisant of the time and place to exercise the six qualities, a master of ethics, omniscient, all-seeing and is the delight of his subjects. He is the moon, the sun, Agni, Yama, Indra, Kuvera and Varuna. O Saumitri, do thou go and communicate to the king, the protector of his subjects, that without his permission I may not enter."

Thereupon the highly effulgent and noble-minded Lakshmana went into the palace and said to Rama :—

" O Long-armed One, the enhancer of Kaushalya's joy, I have carried out thy behests and shall relate everything to thee, hear me ! As a petitioner, a dog is at the gate awaiting thy pleasure."

Then Rama answered, saying :—

" Whosoever it may be, speedily bring him in ! "

SECOND OF THE INTERPOLATED CHAPTERS

3rd SERIES

HEARING the words of Rama, the sagacious Lakshmana immediately sent for the dog who stood before Rama, and he, beholding it, said :—

" Come, communicate what thou hast to say without fear ! "

Thereupon the dog, whose skull was gashed, said :—

" The king is the protector of animals and their lord ! He is awake when others sleep ; by administering the law, the king protects dharma ; without his support, his people perish. The king is the lord, the king is the father of all the world ! He is Kala,[1] He is Yuga,[2] He is the creation which comprises all animate and inanimate beings ; He is dharma because He supports all, for it is dharma that sustains the worlds, by dharma the Three Worlds are upheld ; it is dharma that restrains the wicked ; it is for this he is called Dharana ;[3] dharma is greater than all and confers benefits after the death of the body ; nought is superior to dharma in the world. O King, charity, compassion, reverence for the wise and absence of guile are the chief virtues that constitute dharma. They who follow dharma are happy in this life and in the next. O Raghava, O Thou of firm vows, thou art the authority of authorities. Thou art well known for such conduct as is followed by the pious. Thou art an ocean of good qualities and the abode of righteousness. O Foremost of Kings, if in mine ignorance I have said many things to thee, with bowed head I crave thy forgiveness ; be not angry with me."

Hearing these words from the dog, that were full of wisdom, Rama said :—

" What shall I do for thee, speak without fear ! "

Then the dog answered :—

" O King, it is by dharma that a king rules, it is by dharma that a king protects his subjects and becomes a refuge, delivering men from fear. Bearing this in mind, O Rama, do thou hear me. There is a brahmin named Sarvatha-siddha who lives on alms and who has all his desires satisfied. Through no fault of mine he has inflicted a wound on my head."

Hearing these words, Rama sent forth a messenger who brought Sarvartha-siddha there, and he, beholding Rama in the assembly of those effulgent and leading Sages, said :—

---

[1] Kala—Time.
[2] Yuga—The World Cycle.
[3] Dharana—The Supporter, Upholder.

" O Sinless King, for what purpose hast thou sent for me ? "
Then the king answered, saying :—

" O Brahmin, thou hast injured this dog. What offence did
it commit that thou didst strike it severely with thy staff?
Anger is a mortal foe ; anger is a sweet-spoken enemy in 'the
garb of a friend ; anger is the first of passions and like unto a
sharp sword ; anger bears away the essence of good ; it carries
away all that is acquired by asceticism ; sacrifices, gifts and
charity are all destroyed by anger, therefore it is proper to
banish anger by every means. Passion runs wild on all sides
like exceedingly wicked steeds. Satiated with all the objects of
enjoyment, it is better to govern these appetites with patience.
By mind, speech and sight, a man should engage himself in the
well-being of others. He should give up aversion and injure no
one. The harm that an uncontrolled mind can accomplish is
beyond the range of a sharp sword or a serpent that has been
trodden underfoot or a foe who has been provoked. Even the
nature of one who has learnt humility cannot always be trusted ;
a study of the Scriptures does not alter the innate character of a
man, he who conceals his nature, will reveal his true self at a
given moment."

Rama of imperishable exploits, having spoken thus, Sarvatha-
siddha, the foremost of the Twice-born, said :—

" O King, wandering about the whole day in search of alms,
I became angry and struck the dog. It was seated in the centre
of a narrow street and I requested it to move away ; thereupon
moving with reluctance, it stood by the roadside. O Descendant
of Raghu, at that time I was overcome with hunger and struck
it for its perverse conduct. I am guilty, O King, do thou punish
me, O Lord of Monarchs, do thou administer correction and I
shall be released from the fear of hell."

Then Rama enquired of all his ministers, saying :—

" What shall be done now ? What punishment should be
inflicted on him ? By administrating justice in accord with the
crime, our subjects are protected."

Thereupon Bhrigu, Angiras, Kutsa, Vasishtha, Kashyapa and
the other Rishis, ministers, leading merchants and Sages
conversant with the Shastras, who were present there, said, "A
brahmin is exempt from punishment," and the Sages, conversant

with the law, having spoken thus, those ascetics addressed Rama, saying :—

" O Raghava, a king is the ruler of all and thou above all, for thou art the Chastiser of the Three Worlds, the Eternal Vishnu."

They, having spoken thus, the dog said :—

" Thou didst solemnly enquire ' What shall I do for thee ? ' therefore if thou art pleased with me and dost wish to bestow a favour on me, do thou appoint this brahmin to be head of the holy assembly of the Kalanjava Monastery."

Thereupon the king instantly sanctioned the appointment, and the brahmin, honoured and gratified, mounted on an elephant, proceeded to occupy his new and dignified status.

At this Rama's counsellors were astonished and said :—

" O Thou of great effulgence, this brahmin has not been punished, rather hast thou favoured him with a boon ! "

Hearing the words of the ministers, Rama said :—" You do not know the secret of the matter, the dog knows it well ! " Thereafter, questioned by Rama, the dog said :—

" O King, I was formerly the head of the assembly of Kalanjava and after worshipping the Gods, feeding the brahmins and feasting the servants, male and female, I used to take my food. I duly administered all things and my mind was untouched by sin. I protected the articles belonging to the tutelary Deities carefully, cultivated virtue, followed dharma and engaged in the welfare of all beings. In spite of this, I have fallen into this wretched state. O Raghava, this brahmin is given to anger and impious, he injures others and is harsh and cruel, he will dishonour seven generations of his race He will by no means be able to discharge the duties of the head of an assembly.

" He who wishes to see his children, friends and beasts fall into hell, is made chief of the Gods, cows and brahmins ! O Raghava, he perishes who deprives the brahmins, women or children of their legitimate possessions; one who misappropriates the offerings of the brahmins or the Gods, goes to the lowest hell."★

Hearing the words of the dog, the eyes of Rama opened wide

★ This story seems to imply that if a man is appointed to a position of authority and does not discharge his responsibilities faithfully, he is in grave danger in future incarnations.

in astonishment. Thereafter the dog departed from whence it had come.

In its former birth it had been high-minded but was born in a degraded state in that existence. Repairing to the holy City of Kashi, that dog, desiring to leave its body in a sacred spot, thereafter undertook a waterless fast.

THIRD OF THE INTERPOLATED CHAPTERS

3rd SERIES

FOR a long time a vulture and an owl dwelt near the City of Ayodhya in a forest on a mountain, that was intersected by many streams, where cuckoos called and which abounded in lions, tigers and birds of every kind.

One day, the wicked vulture alleging that the owl's nest was his, began to quarrel with him, whereupon both said :—

" Let us seek out the lotus-eyed Rama, who is the king of the people and let him decide to whom the nest belongs."

Having thus agreed, the vulture and the owl, wrangling with one another, wrought up with ire, came before Rama and touched his feet. Beholding that Lord of Men, the vulture said :—

" O Preserver of humanity, thou art the foremost of the Devas and Asuras, O Resplendent One, in hearing and intelligence thou art superior to Brihaspati and Shukracharya. Thou art conversant with the good and evil karma of all creatures. In beauty thou resemblest the moon, in splendour the sun, in glory the Himalaya, in profundity the ocean, in prowess the Grandsire, in forbearance the earth, in speed the wind ; thou art the Spiritual Preceptor of all animate and inanimate beings and art endowed with every kind of wealth ; thou art illustrious, forgiving, invincible, victorious and master of all the scriptures and laws. O Foremost of Men, hear my plea ! O Lord of Raghu, I had built a nest for myself and this owl is now occupying it as his own, therefore, O King, do thou protect me ! "

The vulture, having said this, the owl spoke, saying :—

" True it is that in a king, there is to be found a portion of the moon, of Indra, the sun, Kuvera and Yama but there is also a measure of man in him. Thou, however, art the all-pervasive Narayana Himself, Thou, impelled by thine own Self dost judge all creatures impartially, yet a certain gentleness is manifest in thee and therefore people say thou art endowed with a portion of the moon. O Lord, by anger, punishment and reward, thou dost remove the sins and dangers of thy subjects ; it is thine to give and withdraw, thou art the dispenser, destroyer and protector and art as Indra to us. In energy thou art as fire, irresistible to all creatures and, since thou dost spread thy lustre on all beings, thou art like the sun ! Thou resemblest the Lord of Wealth and art even superior to him, for prosperity resides in thee. Thou lookest on all creatures whether animate or inanimate with the same eye, O Raghava, and dost regard foe and friend alike, duly protecting thy subjects. O Raghava, those who have incurred thine anger are already slain, therefore thou art praised as Yama. O Foremost of Kings, since, in human form, thou art merciful and beneficent, people sing thy glory, thou who art intent on not harming men. The king is the strength of the weak and helpless, the eye of the blind and the refuge of those who seek shelter in him. Thou art also our Lord, therefore hear our plea! O King, entering into my nest, this vulture is oppressing me ; thou alone, O Foremost of Men, art the divine chastiser of creatures ! ''

Hearing these words, Rama called for his ministers with those of King Dasaratha, Vrishti, Jayanta, Vijaya, Siddhartha, Rashtravarddhana, Ashoka, Dharmapala and the highly powerful Sumantra and others, who were well versed in the law, highminded and conversant with the Shastras, intelligent, nobly born and skilled in counsel.

Thereafter summoning both, Rama, descending from his throne, enquired of the vulture :—" How long has this nest been made ? Tell me if thou dost remember it ! "

Then the vulture replied :—" From the time men were first born on earth and spread over the four quarters of the globe, I have been living in this nest."

Thereupon the owl said :—

"At the time when trees first covered the earth, this nest of mine was constructed."

Hearing these words, Rama said to his counsellors :—

" That assembly is not an assembly where there are no wise and elderly men, nor those who do not dwell on righteous topics. That religion is no religion where truth is not to be found and that truth is no truth where there is guile. Those counsellors are liars, who remain silent when they are well informed in any matter. He who does not speak either on account of passion, fear or anger, binds himself with a thousand nooses of Varuna and, at the expiration of a full year, is only released from a single sin."

Hearing these words, the ministers said to Rama :—

"O Thou of great intellect, what the owl has said is true, the vulture has spoken falsely. Thou art proof of this, O Great King, since the king is the final refuge of all, the root of the people and eternal dharma itself. Those punished by the king do not fall into a lower state, they are saved from hell and expand in virtue."

Hearing these words of the ministers, Rama said :—

" Hear what is related in the Puranas ! Formerly the sun, moon and firmament with its stars, the earth with its mountains and forests, the Three Worlds with all that moves and does not move were merged in the waters of the great ocean.

"At that time, Narayana existed as a second Sumeru and, in his belly, lay the earth with Lakshmi. Having destroyed the creation and entered the waters, the highly effulgent Vishnu, identical with the souls of creatures, lay asleep there for many long years. Beholding Vishnu asleep after the destruction of the worlds and, knowing all the entries to be obstructed, the great Brahma entered his belly. Thereupon a golden lotus sprang from Vishnu's navel, and that great Lord, the Creator, Brahma, rose therefrom and engaged in severe penances for the purpose of creating the earth, air, mountains, trees, men, reptiles and all other life-forms from the womb or egg.

" Thereafter, from the wax in the ears of Narayana, two valiant and dreadful Daityas, Madhu and Kaitabha were born. Beholding the Grandsire, they were greatly enraged and rushed upon him, whereupon Brahma, the Self-born cried out loudly.

"Awakened by that sound, Narayana engaged in combat with

Madhu and Kaitabha and slew them with his discus and the earth was drenched with their blood. Then, purifying it once more, Vishnu, the Preserver of the World covered it with trees and created medicinal herbs. Thus filled with the marrow of Madhu and Kaitabha, the earth was called Medini. It is for this that I hold this abode does not belong to the vulture but to the owl, O Counsellors, the owl having maintained that he built the nest when trees were first created, that is, before men appeared. This vicious vulture should therefore be punished, for this evil-minded one, having robbed another of its nest, is now oppressing him."

At that moment a voice was heard in the sky, saying :—

" O Rama, do not slay the vulture for it has already been reduced to ashes by the power of Gautama's asceticism. O Lord of Men, this vulture in a former birth was an heroic, truthful and pure king, by the name of Brahmadatta. One day a brahmin called Gautama, the very personification of Time, came to the house of Brahmadatta for food and said :—

" ' O King, I shall feed in thy house for more than a hundred years ! '

" Thereupon, with his own hands offering that effulgent brahmin water to wash his feet, the King Brahmadatta entertained him with due hospitality. Once, accidentally, flesh was mixed with the food of the high-souled Gautama and he, enraged, uttered a terrible curse, saying :—' O King, do thou become a vulture ! '

" The monarch thereupon replied :—' O Thou of great vows, do not curse me thus, be propitiated, it was in ignorance that this offence was offered by me, O Great One ! O Blameless One, do thou so act that this curse be rendered void ! '

" Recognizing that the offence had been unwittingly committed by the king, the ascetic said :—

" ' O King, a monarch shall be born under the name of Rama in the Race of Ikshvaku. O Foremost of Men, thou shalt be released from the curse when he touches thee.' "

Hearing these words from the sky, Rama touched Brahmadatta and he, giving up his vulture's form, assuming a beautiful body sprinkled with celestial perfumes, worshipped Rama and said :—

" O Thou conversant with piety, by thy grace I have been
saved from a dreadful hell, thou hast verily brought the curse to
an end for me ! "

CHAPTER 60

The Ascetics seek out Rama

As Rama and Lakshmana passed the time conversing thus, the
temperate spring night drew on and, when the stainless dawn
broke, Kakutstha, having performed his morning worship, went
to the audience chamber to attend to affairs of state.

Then Sumantra approached him and said :—

" O King, there are some Sages who are waiting at the gate
with Chyavana, the descendant of Bhrigu, at their head ; these
illustrious Rishis seek audience with thee, O Great King, and,
eager for thy sight, those dwellers on the banks of the Yamuna
have sent me to announce their arrival."

Hearing these words, the virtuous Rama, conversant with his
duty, said :—" Let those blessed ascetics, whose leader is
Bhargava, enter." Thereupon, in deference to the king's
summons, the chamberlain, with joined palms, bowing low,
ushered in those eminent ascetics, numbering over a hundred,
who were blazing in their own effulgence. Thereafter those
magnanimous Sages, entering the palace, with their loshtas
filled with holy water drawn from sacred places, carried various
kinds of fruit and roots as an offering to the king, which Rama
accepted with delight.

Then that long-armed prince said to those illustrious Sages :—

" Do you occupy these seats according to your pleasure."

Thus invited by Rama, those great Rishis took their places on
the brilliant golden seats and, seeing them installed, Rama, with
joined palms, paying obeisance to them, enquired of them
saying :—

" For what reason have you come ? In my devotion I would
feign know what I may do for you ? I am at your command O
Illustrious Ones, and shall carry out all you desire with great
delight. My whole kingdom and the life in my breast and all

that I am is at the service of the Twice-born ; this is the truth
that I speak ! ''

Hearing this speech, the magnanimous Rishis of severe
penances, who dwelt on the banks of the Yamuna, cried out :—
" Excellent ! " and with extreme delight, they added :—

" O Thou, the best of Men, none other on this earth would
speak as thou hast done. Many monarchs, though supremely
courageous and powerful, dare not engage themselves in an
undertaking when they consider the difficulties ; thou, however,
without even knowing in what the matter consists, in thy
reverence for the brahmins, dost pledge thy word which thou
wilt undoubtedly honour. It behoveth thee to deliver the Sages
from a great peril, O Lord."

CHAPTER 61

The Story of Madhu

THEN Kakutstha enquired of those ascetics, who had spoken
thus, saying :—

" Say what shall I do, O Munis, in order to dispel this danger
for you ? "

At these words from Kakutstha, Bhargava replied :—

" Learn the cause of our fears and from whence they spring,
O Prince ! Formerly in the Krita-yuga, a highly intelligent
Daitya, the great Asura Madhu, the eldest son of Lola, who was
well-disposed to the brahmins and protected all those who
sought refuge in him, was united in an unequalled friendship
to the supremely illustrious Gods. And Madhu, who was
endowed with valour and ever fixed in his duty, received a
marvellous weapon from Rudra, who held him in high esteem.
Taking from his own trident, another of great power and beauty,
that magnanimous One, well pleased, conferred it upon him and
said :—

" ' Thou hast fulfilled thy duty in a remarkable degree, which
has evoked my grace ! In the supreme delight that I now experience, I confer this excellent weapon upon thee. As long as thou
dost not attack the Gods or the brahmins, O Great Asura, this

559

spear will remain with thee, otherwise it will vanish. Whoever rashly provokes thee to combat will be reduced to ashes by this weapon which, thereafter, will return to thine hand ! '

" Having received this rare gift from Rudra, the great Asura prostrated himself before Mahadeva and said :—

" ' O Lord, Thou who art the Chief of the Gods, O Blessed One, may this weapon ever remain in my family.'

" Thus spoke Madhu, and the Lord of all beings, Shiva, that great God, anwered him saying :—

" ' Nay, that may not be, nevertheless since thy plea finds favour with me, it shall not have been uttered in vain ; thy son shall inherit this weapon. As long as it is in his hand, he will be invulnerable to all beings, but only if it remains there.'

" Then Madhu, the foremost of the Asuras, having received that great and marvellous gift from the God, built himself a magnificent abode. He had a beloved wife, the fortunate and illustrious Kumbhinasi, who was born of Vishvasu by Anala, and she bore him a son full of vigour named Lavana. Cruel and perverse from infancy, he was ever engaged in harming others and, seeing the iniquitous conduct of his son, Madhu was incensed and grieved but he said nothing. After a time he left this world and entered Varuna's abode, having bequeathed the weapon to Lavana and instructed him in the nature of the gift.

" Now Lavana, due to the power of that weapon and his natural perversity, has become the scourge of the Three Worlds and particularly of the Sages, his might being equalled by the power of that weapon. Thou hast heard all, now it is for thee to decide, O Kakutstha, for thou art our supreme refuge.

" Many monarchs, O Rama, have been solicited by the Sages to deliver them from fear, but, O Valiant Prince, we have not found a protector. Learning that thou hadst destroyed Ravana with his infantry and cavalry, we have recognized thee as our saviour, O Dear Son. We know of no other king on earth capable of delivering us ; we entreat thee to free us from the terror which Lavana inspires in us. This, O Rama, is the cause of our present fear ; thou art able to dispel it ; fulfil our desire, O Thou whose valour is unconquerable."

CHAPTER 62

Shatrughna asks permission to fight Lavana

SUCH was the speech of the ascetics, and Rama, with joined palms, enquired of them, saying :—

" On what does he live ? How does he conduct himself ? Where does he dwell ? "

Raghava, having questioned them thus, all the ascetics informed him as to how Lavana sustained himself and said :—

" His food consists of all creatures, particularly the ascetics, his manner of life is savage and he constantly roams in Madhu-vana. Having slain thousands of lions, tigers, antelopes, birds and even men, his daily food is their flesh, and that monster, like unto Antaka at the dissolution of the worlds, also devours all beings."

Hearing these words, Raghava said to those great Sages :—

" I shall slay that demon, have no fear." Having given his word to the ascetics of great effulgence, Rama, the delight of Raghu said to his three brothers who were present :—

" Who is brave enough to slay this Asura ? On whom shall the choice fall, on the valiant Bharata or the sagacious Shatrughna ? "

Listening to Raghava's words, Bharata answered :—" It is I who will slay him ! Let the task be entrusted to me ! "

Hearing Bharata, full of energy and courage, speak thus, Shatrughna, the younger brother of Lakshmana, rose from his golden seat and, bowing before that Lord of Men, said :—

" The long-armed Bharata has already proved his fortitude ; let him remain amongst us, O Joy of the Raghus. When Ayodhya was previously deprived of thy noble person, Bharata, concealing his sorrow in his heart, ruled the kingdom till the return of his lord. Undergoing innumerable hardships, O Prince, lying on a hard couch in Nandigrama, the supremely illustrious Bharata lived on fruit and roots, his hair matted and clothed in bark. Having endured such a test, that son of Raghu should not have to undergo further trials since I, thy servant, am here."

Thus spoke Shatrughna and Raghava said :—

" Be it so, O Descendant of Kakutstha, carry out my commands and I will install thee as king in the splendid capital of Madhu. O Long-armed Warrior, let Bharata stay here as thou wishest ; thou art brave and experienced and well able to establish a kingdom with its flourishing provinces and a capital that is washed by the Yamuna, for he who, having destroyed a dynasty, does not install a king, goes to hell. As for thee, when thou hast slain the son of Madhu, Lavana of perverse ways, do thou govern his kingdom righteously if thou desirest to carry out my wishes. Do not question what I have said, O Hero, the younger brother should undoubtedly obey the elder. O Descendant of Kakutstha, receive the consecration at my hands with the traditional blessings pronounced by Vasishtha and the other brahmins."

CHAPTER 63

The Installation of Shatrughna

THESE words of Rama filled the valiant Shatrughna with confusion and he spoke with exceeding diffidence, saying :—

" O Lord of Men, these measures do not seem to me to be justified ! How may a younger brother be installed when his elders yet live ? Still it is imperative that I should submit to thy will, O Fortunate Prince, for it would be impossible for me to disregard any order of thine. I have heard from thy lips, O Hero, and the scriptures have taught me that one should never oppose the one in authority once he has spoken. My words were ill-advised when I said ' I will slay the redoubtable Lavana in the open field.' This unfortunate utterance places me in a serious dilemma, O Foremost of Men. One should not add anything when one's elders have spoken, for this is a moral taint and, in the next world, proves a cause of retribution. I shall not speak again, O Lord Kakutstha, for fear that a second observation draw punishment upon me. I shall do thy pleasure, O Foremost of Men, O Joy of Raghu, but do thou so order it that in mine interest this improper act be erased."

562

Thus spoke the brave and high-souled Shatrughna and Rama, greatly delighted, said to Bharata and Lakshmana :—

" Prepare everything for the installation with care. This very day I shall install that tiger among men, issue of the House of Raghu. At my command, summon the Purodhas, O Offspring of Kakutstha, and the citizens, Ritvijs and ministers."

Hearing the king's command, the great car-warriors, under the direction of the Purodhas, began the ceremony. Thereafter, the lords and brahmins entered the king's palace and the enthronement of the magnanimous Shatrughna was solemnly performed, to the great delight of Raghava and the city.

The fortunate Shatrughna, son of Kakutstha, having received the divine anointing, resembled a second sun, as Skanda when he was formerly enthroned by the inhabitants of heaven led by Indra.

Meanwhile Shatrughna being installed by Rama of imperishable exploits, the inhabitants of the city were highly delighted as also the illustrious brahmins, and Kaushalya, Sumitra and also Kaikeyi, who with the other queens, rejoiced in their royal residence.

Thereafter the Rishis, who dwelt on the banks of the Yamuna, on account of Shatrughna's enthronement, prophesied the death of Lavana.

Clasping the newly crowned one to his heart, Raghava, in caressing tones, thus enhancing his courage, said to him :—

" Here is an infallible shaft that overthrows hostile citadels ; by means of this thou shalt destroy Lavana, O My Dear Brother, Joy of the House of Raghu. It was fashioned, O Descendant of Kakutstha, when Swyambhu, the divine Ajita reposed on the waters out of sight of the Gods and Asuras, invisible to all beings. That God fashioned this arrow, the foremost of all, in order to slay those two perverse beings, Madhu and Kaitabha, for he was enraged against them, when he desired to create the Three Worlds despite all the Rakshasas.

" Having destroyed Madhu and Kaitabha, for the good of all beings with this marvellous weapon, Brahma created the worlds. I did not loose this dart formerly on Ravana, whom I wished to slay, O Shatrughna, for all creatures would have been greatly diminished thereby.

"As for the superior weapon bestowed on Madhu by the magnanimous Tryambaka for the destruction of his foes, Lavana, while he is ranging the regions in search of his favourite nourishment, leaves it in his dwelling where he honours it in various ways ; but when the desire for combat rises in him or he is challenged, that demon lays hold of that weapon and reduces his foes to ashes. O Foremost of Men, ere he returns to the city and while he is without his weapon, place thyself at the entry furnished with thy powerful shaft. Before he regains his abode, challenge that demon to combat, O Long-armed Warrior, and thou shalt overcome him. If thou actest in any other way, thou canst not slay him ; whereas using these means, O Valiant One, thou wilt exterminate him. Thou knowest all and how to eschew that weapon of irresistible force belonging to the ancient Shitikanta."[1]

CHAPTER 64

Shatrughna sets out to meet Lavana

HAVING spoken thus to Shatrughna, the offspring of Kakutstha, and encouraged him again and again, Rama, the Joy of the House of Raghu continued :—

" Here are four thousand horses, two thousand chariots, a hundred selected elephants and stalls furnished with every provision, also singers and dancers. O Foremost of Men, I give thee gold and silver coins; take with thee a quantity of gold and set out, having furnished thyself with supplies of weapons, food and conveyances.

" By words and gifts, do thou satisfy that well-nourished army that is cheerful, contented and disciplined, O Valiant Prince. Where there are neither riches, women nor kinsfolk, devoted servants will not be found, O Shatrughna. Having marshalled thy great army composed of people full of ardour, do thou go alone, bow in hand to the Madhu Wood. Act in such a manner that Lavana, the son of Madhu, is not aware that thou art approaching, seeking to enter into combat with him, that he may

[1] Shitikanta—The Lord Shiva.

be without suspicion ; there is no other means of slaying him. O Foremost of Men, he who approaches him with that purpose inevitably perishes under his blows. The summer having passed and the rainy season being at hand, thou shalt destroy the wicked Lavana for the hour will have struck !

" With the great Rishis at their head, send the troops forward so that they profit by the summer for crossing the waters of the Jahnavi. There thou shouldst take care to encamp the whole army on the river and thou, who art fleet of foot, shouldst go ahead with thy bow. Halt at the place indicated to you and establish the camps without obstruction so that no-one may have cause for complaint."

Having thus issued his orders and marshalled his army, Shatrughna circumambulated Rama, bowing to him, with joined palms, and in great humility, paid obeisance to Bharata and Lakshmana as also the family priest, Shri Vasishtha.

Having received permission from Rama to depart, that hero, the Scourge of His Foes, circumambulated him and went away. Ordering his army, comprising innumerable elephants and well-bred steeds to advance, that descendant of Raghu took leave of the king and set out on his mission.

CHAPTER 65

The Story of Saudasa who is cursed by the Sage Vasishtha

HAVING caused his army to halt after a month's march, Shatrughna started out alone with a rapid step. Two days later, that hero, the Joy of the Raghus reached the sacred hermitage of Valmiki, the foremost of retreats, and, with joined palms, paying obeisance to that magnanimous Sage, spoke thus :—

" O Blessed One, I desire to spend the night here where the mission of my elder brother has led me ; to-morrow, at dawn, I shall set out for the west."

Thus spoke the great-souled Shatrughna, and the foremost of Sages, smiling, answered him, saying :—

" Be thou welcome, O Illustrious Prince ! This hermitage, O dear Friend, belongs to the descendants of the Raghu Race also;

without hesitation, do thou accept a seat from me and water for thy hands and feet ! "

Thereupon, Shatrughna, being honoured, accepted the fruits and roots for his repast and, being fed thereon till he was fully satisfied, then enquired of the great Rishi, saying :—

" Whose is this fertile area to the east of the hermitage, that has been created by sacrifice ? "[1]

To this enquiry, Valmiki replied :—

" O Shatrughna, hear to whom this region formerly belonged ! One of thine ancestors was the King Saudasa and, of that monarch was born Mitrasaha,[2] who was full of vigour and extremely virtuous. One day the valiant and righteous Saudasa, having followed the hunt, observed two Rakshasas wandering here and there, in the form of tigers, and those monsters were devouring thousands of antelopes in order to appease their insatiable appetites. Seeing those two Rakshasas, who had denuded the forest of deer, Saudasa was seized. with violent anger and pierced one of them with a long dart. Having slain it, that foremost of men recovered his composure and, his anger dissipated, he gazed on the dead Rakshasa. Observing him contemplating his companion thus, the surviving demon, filled with a burning grief, said to him :—

" ' Thou hast slain my companion who had done thee no harm, I shall revenge myself on thee one day, thou wretch ! '

" Speaking thus, the Rakshasa disappeared.

" In the course of time, the son of Saudasa, Mitrasaha, came to the throne, and Saudasa undertook the Ashwamedha Sacrifice in the vicinity of this ashrama with Vasishtha as the officiating priest. This continued for many years and was of exceeding splendour so that it resembled one offered by the Gods. At the close of the rites, the Rakshasa, calling to mind his past grievance, assumed the form of Vasishtha and said to the king :—

" ' Now the sacrifice has been completed, let flesh be brought speedily that I may eat without delay ! '

" Hearing that Rakshasa, transformed into a brahmin, speaking thus, the king addressed his cooks, who were skilled in their art and said :—

[1] That is by the grain scattered during the sacrifice.
[2] In some versions, Viryasaha.

" ' Speedily prepare Havis[1] and such savoury dishes of flesh that will please my Guru ! '

" This command of that monarch bewildered the cooks, whereupon the Rakshasa, assuming their form, prepared a dish of human flesh which he brought to the king, saying, ' Here is a savoury dish made of flesh ! '

" O Foremost of Men, the king, with his consort, Madayanti, presented those dishes brought by the Rakshasa, that were composed of flesh, to the Sage Vasishtha, and that ascetic, perceiving he had been offered human flesh, was transported with rage and began to pronounce a curse upon him, saying :—

" ' Since it has pleased thee, O King, to offer me a repast of this nature, it shall assuredly become thy food.'

" Thereupon Saudasa, incensed, in his turn took water in his hand and was about to curse Vasishtha when his wife restrained him, saying :—

" ' O King, since the blessed Sage is our spiritual Preceptor, it is not proper for thee to pronounce a curse upon him, a priest is like unto a God.'

" Then that virtuous monarch poured out that water charged with power and some fell on his feet, which became stained and, from that time the illustrious Saudasa became known as Kalmashapada.[2] Then that monarch, with his consort, having prostrated themselves before Vasishtha again and again, informed him of what the Rakshasa, under the shape of a brahmin, had done.

" Hearing from that foremost of monarchs of the vile act of the Rakshasa, Vasishtha addressed the king once more, saying :—

" ' The words that I have pronounced in anger may not be uttered in vain but I will grant thee a boon. Thou shalt be freed from the curse in twelve years and, by my favour, shall not remember what has passed, O Foremost of Men.'

" Having suffered the consequences of that curse, Saudasa, the Slayer of His Foes, recovered his kingdom and ruled over his subjects. O Descendant of Raghu, this is the beautiful site of that sacrifice performed by Kalmashapada about which thou hast enquired."

[1] Havis—Anything offered that has been cooked in ghee.
[2] Kalmashapada—Spotted Feet.

Having heard the dreadful story of that monarch, Shatrughna, paying obeisance to that great Rishi, entered the leaf-thatched hut.

CHAPTER 66

The Birth of Kusha and Lava

Now, during the night that Shatrughna passed in the leaf-thatched hut, Sita gave birth to two children and, at midnight, the youthful ascetics brought the pleasant and auspicious tidings to Valmiki, saying :—

" O Blessed One, Rama's consort has given birth to twin sons, do thou perform the rites that will preserve them from evil forces."

Hearing these words, the great Rishi went to see those newly-born Ones, who were as effulgent as the new moon and full of vigour, like unto twin offspring of the Gods.

Coming to where Sita was, on beholding those two infants, his heart was filled with delight and he performed the Rakshasa Rite.[1] Taking a handful of Kusha Grass with its roots, that Twice-born One, Valmiki, pronounced the formula of protection for the destruction of evil forces, saying :—

" Since they will rub the first born of the children with the Kusha Grass[1] blessed by the aid of Mantras, his name shall be Kusha and, as the last born will be carefully dried by the female ascetics with the roots of the grass, he shall be called Lava. Therefore those two shall be called Kusha and Lava and, by these names that I have given them, they will become renowned."

Thereafter, the female ascetics purified themselves and reverently received the grass from the hands of the Muni, applying it to the two children. The rite having been performed in the night, Shatrughna hearing the pleasant tidings, the names the children would bear, and Rama's praises, also that Sita had undergone this double and fortunate birth, approached the leaf-thatched hut where Sita lay and said :—

" O Mother, be thou happy ! "

Thus, for the magnanimous Shatrughna, that night of the

[1] To avert evil.

rainy season in the month of Shravana passed joyfully and
rapidly and, the next day at dawn, that great hero, having offered
up his morning devotions, with joined palms paid obeisance to
the Sage and resumed his journey.

After a march of seven days, reaching the banks of the
Yamuna, he halted at the hermitage of Rishis of great renown,
and that illustrious Prince listened to the pleasant and ancient
legends of Chyavana of the line of Bhrigu and of other Sages.
In this way, Shatrughna, the son of that foremost of monarchs,
King Dasaratha, in great delight, passed the night conversing
with the ascetics, of whom Kancana was the leader, on various
themes.

CHAPTER 67

The Story of Mandhata

THE night having come, Shatrughna enquired of the son of
Bhrigu, Chyavana, concerning the strength of Lavana, saying :—

" O Brahmin, how powerful is his weapon ? Who did Lavana
formerly slay with that splendid shaft in combat ? "

Thus questioned by him, the extremely virtuous Chyavana
answered the magnanimous Shatrughna, the Joy of the Raghus,
saying :—

" O Son of Raghu, innumerable are his exploits ! Hear what
befell a descendant of Ikshvaku. Formerly there reigned in
Ayodhya, the valiant son of Yavanashwa, Mandhata, who was
renowned in the Three Worlds for his prowess.

" Having placed the entire earth under his yoke, that monarch
sought to conquer the Celestial Realm. Great was the fear of
Indra and the Gods on beholding Mandhata's preparations, who
wished to conquer the region of the Devas. Learning of his
intention to share Indra's throne and kingdom, the God, who
chastised Paka, addressed Yuvanashwa's son in propitiatory
accents and said :—

" ' Thou dost not yet rule over the entire earth, not having
wholly subjugated it, O King, yet thou aspirest to the celestial
throne. When the whole earth is under thy dominion, then,

with thy servants, thine army and thy chariots, do thou take possession of the kingdom of the Gods.'

" Thus did Indra speak, and Mandhata answered him, saying :

" ' Who on the face of the earth has contested my domination ? ' Then the God of a Thousand Eyes said :—

" ' The Rakshasa named Lavana, son of Madhu, who dwells in the forest, has not recognized thine authority, O Irreproachable Warrior ! '

"At these extremely unpleasing words uttered by Indra, the king hung his head in shame, being unable to answer him. Thereafter, paying obeisance to the Thousand-eyed God, he departed with bowed head and returned to earth.

" Then that Prince, the Slayer of His Foes, concealing his anger, placed himself at the head of his servants, infantry and cavalry and marched against the son of Madhu in order to conquer him. And that foremost of men sent a messenger to Lavana to challenge him to combat, who, coming before him, covered the son of Madhu with abuses and, while he was still speaking, the Rakshasa devoured him.

"As his envoy failed to return, the king, enraged, assailed Lavana with a hail of arrows, whereupon the Rakshasa, taking up his trident, mockingly hurled it upon him in order to exterminate him and his followers, and the flaming trident, that formidable weapon, reduced the king, his servants, his infantry and cavalry to ashes and returned to the hand of its master.

" Thus did that great monarch perish with his footsoldiers and chariots. O My Friend, it was through the power of that trident, which is unsurpassed ! To-morrow at dawn thou shalt without doubt slay Lavana ere he has taken up his weapon ; thy victory is assured ! The worlds will be freed as a result of thine exploit. O Foremost of Men, I have now told thee all concerning the wicked Lavana ; it is on this account that Mandhata succumbed in his undertaking. To-morrow at dawn, O Magnanimous One, thou shalt undoubtedly slay him ! He will have set out in search of food without his trident. Thy victory is therefore assured, O Foremost of Men."

CHAPTER 68

Shatrughna encounters Lavana

WHILST Chyavana was recounting this story and all were wishing him an overwhelming victory, the night speedily passed away for the magnanimous Shatrughna.

Meantime as the cloudless dawn broke, the bold Rakshasa set out from the city eager to find food and, during this time the intrepid Shatrughna crossed the Yamuna and, bow in hand, took up his position at the gate of Madhupura.

At noon, that Rakshasa of evil karma returned laden with countless living beings and, beholding Shatrughna standing at the gate with his weapon, the demon enquired of him :—

" What wilt thou do with that weapon ? In my wrath, O Least of Warriors, I have devoured thousands of men like thee with their weapons ; it is death that brings thee here. I am not yet fully fed, O Vilest of Men, why hast thou come to cast thyself into my mouth, thou fool ! "

Thus did he speak, laughing loudly, and the courageous Shatrughna shed tears of rage and, in his fury, sparks of fire issued from all his limbs. Thereafter, in a transport of anger, he said to that ranger of the night :—

" I shall enter into single combat with thee ! I am the son of Dasaratha, the brother of the sagacious Rama, my name is Shatrughna, a veritable Shatrughna,[1] and it is my desire to slay thee that has brought me hither ! I wish to fight with thee, therefore be on thy guard ! Thou art the enemy of all beings ; thou shalt not escape me alive ! "

At these words the Rakshasa, sneering, answered the prince, saying :—

" It is my good fortune that has brought thee to me, O Insensate One. Rama slew my maternal aunt's brother, Ravana, on account of a woman, O Wretch. O Lord of Men, I have suffered the entire destruction of Ravana's family and it is because I have neglected to avenge them that thou art over-confident. I shall exterminate you all, O Vilest of Men, I shall

---

[1] Shatrughna—' Slayer of his Foes '.

sweep you all away like straws, both those who are already born and those still to be born. O Thou of vicious intellect, I accept thy challenge ! Stay but a moment till I fetch my weapon, one suited to thy destruction ! "

Thereupon Shatrughna instantly answered saying :—

" What, shalt thou escape me alive ? He who has any wit does not allow a foe to go free who has come forth of his own accord. He, who, in his stupidity, suffers a foe to escape, perishes. Look long on the world, for, with my whetted shafts, I shall despatch thee to Yama's abode, thou the enemy of the Three Worlds and of Raghava."

CHAPTER 69

The Death of Lavana

AT these words from the mighty Shatrughna, Lavana fell into a violent rage and cried out :—" Stay ", striking his hands together and grinding his teeth, thereafter assailing that Lion of the Raghus with redoubled blows.

Thereupon Shatrughna, the Slayer of His Foes, answered Lavana of formidable aspect, who had addressed him thus, saying :—

" When others were slain by thee, I was not yet born, but to-day, pierced by my darts, do thou enter the region of Yama ! May the Rishis and learned brahmins this day be witness of thy death in combat, O Wretch ! When my shafts have consumed thee in the fight, thou who art a ranger of the night, the city and the country too will be at peace. As the rays of the sun penetrate the lotus, so shall the dreadful pointed arrows, loosed by mine arm, pierce thy heart."

Then Lavana, beside himself with anger on hearing these words, hurled a great tree on Shatrughna striking his breast, but he severed it into a hundred pieces, and the Rakshasa, finding himself foiled, seized hold of a large number of trees and hurled them on his adversary; then Shatrughna, burning with ardour, severed those innumerable trees, one by one, with three or four well-seasoned crescent-shaped arrows and, thereafter, he let a shower of darts fall on the valiant Rakshasa without causing him to retreat. With a mocking laugh, Lavana, brandishing a tree, struck the head of that hero so that he fell insensible, and when that warrior fell, a great cry of "Ah! Ah!" arose from the Rishis, Devas, Gandharvas and also Apsaras.

Thereupon the Rakshasa, thinking Shatrughna to be slain, did not enter his house, though the opportunity presented itself and, seeing him lying on the earth, he did not go in search of his trident, but, reflecting, " He is dead," he began to collect his food.

Shatrughna, however, regaining his senses, in an instant took hold of his weapon and went to his place at the city gate once more, amidst the acclamations of the Rishis ; and he selected a celestial, infallible and marvellous arrow that illumined the ten regions with its brilliance and resembled lightning in its velocity. That shaft, smeared with sandalpaste of the colour of blood, wonderfully plumed, was greatly feared by the leaders of the Danavas, the mountains and also the Asuras, and, beholding that dreadful weapon, flaming like Time at the end of the world period, all beings were seized with terror. Then Devas, Asuras, Gandharvas and troops of Apsaras and the whole universe trembled and took refuge with the Grandsire of the worlds. Thereafter the Gods, beside themselves with fear, enquired of that Lord of Lords, the Bestower of Grace, the Grandsire of the Worlds, whether the universe were about to be destroyed. Hearing them speak thus, Brahma, the Grandsire, addressed them in soothing accents, that restored their serenity, saying :—

" Hear me, O Ye Gods, it is in order to destroy Lavana in combat that Shatrughna is armed with that weapon. O Foremost of the Gods, all are overwhelmed by the power of this eternal weapon forged by the primeval God, the Creator of the World. O My Children, that effulgent shaft which causes such terror was fashioned for the destruction of the demons, Madhu and Kaitabha, by the magnanimous God, Vishnu, who alone understands it. In reality, it is the primeval form of Vishnu Himself, therefore go and witness the death of the foremost of the Rakshasas, Lavana, under the blows of that valiant warrior, the younger brother of Rama."

At these words of that God of Gods, the Devas went to the place where the combat between Shatrughna and Lavana was in progress and that weapon of celestial effulgence, which Shatrughna held in his hand, appeared to all beings like the Fire that blazes forth at the dissolution of the worlds !

Beholding the firmament filled with the Celestial Host, the descendant of Raghu emitted a leonine roar and, thereafter, looked on Lavana again and again. On this renewed provocation from his adversary, the Rakshasa, enraged, stretched his bow up to his ear and that most skilled of archers discharged his great arrow on the breast of the enemy, that piercing it, entered the lower regions. Having penetrated into Rasatala itself, the celestial weapon, honoured by the Gods, immediately returned to that hero, the Joy of the Ikshvakus, and, pierced by Shatrughna's arrow, Lavana, that ranger of the night, fell like a mountain struck by lightning.

Thereafter, Lavana being slain under the eyes of the Gods, the mighty celestial trident returned to Rudra. When, with a single shaft, that hero of the Raghus destroyed the terror of the Three Worlds with his bow and marvellous arrow, he resembled that orb of a thousand rays which dispels the darkness.

Then the Devas, great Rishis, Pannagas and Apsaras cried out in chorus :—

" By good fortune, the son of Dasaratha has triumphed ; fear is banished and, like a great reptile, Lavana lies stretched on the earth."

CHAPTER 70

Shatrughna establishes himself in the City of Madhu

LAVANA being slain, the Gods with their leaders, led by Agni, spoke to Shatrughna in affectionate terms, saying :—

" By good fortune, O Dear Child, thou art victorious ; by good fortune, Lavana the Rakshasa is destroyed ! O Lion among Men, O Pious One, do thou ask for a boon. The distributors of boons, those who desired thy triumph, are assembled here, O Long-armed Warrior, let not our presence prove fruitless ! "

Hearing these words of the Gods, that long-armed warrior, Shatrughna, placing his joined palms to his forehead, answered humbly :—

" That I may enter into possession of this ravishing and picturesque city, constructed by the Gods, is my dearest wish ! "

Then the Celestials answered with delight, " Be it so ! this charming city shall assuredly become Shurashena ! "[1]

At these words the high-souled Celestials returned to their abode ; the valiant Shatrughna, however, summoned his army that was encamped on the banks of the Yamuna and the troops immediately came to that place, having learned of his victory, and he established himself there in the month of Shravana.

The inhabitants of that region of celestial aspect lived there for twelve years in peace and happiness, and the fields abounded in grain. Under the aegis of Shatrughna's arms, Indra sent rain in the proper season and the city was full of healthy and happy people. That capital had the brilliance of the crescent moon and rose in splendour on the banks of the Yamuna ; and it was magnificent with its buildings and squares, markets and highways and the inhabitants who belonged to the four castes.

Shatrughna had embellished the magnificent and vast edifices that Lavana had formerly constructed and painted in various colours. Parks and places of entertainment were to be found in all parts of that city, which was also adorned with works of art both human and divine. Of a celestial aspect, it was filled with different kinds of merchandise, and traders from every country came there. Looking on that opulent city, Shatrughna, the younger brother of Bharata, at the height of prosperity and happiness, experienced supreme satisfaction.

After twelve years while he yet dwelt in that enchanting abode, the thought came to him, " I desire to behold Rama again," thereupon, while residing in that city full of people of every condition, the prince resolved to look on the feet of the Chief of the Raghus once more.

[1] Shurashena—' Worthy of Heroes '.

CHAPTER 71

Shatrughna seeks out the Sage Valmiki

Now in the twelfth year, Shatrughna, with a small escort of servants and soldiers, desired to return to Ayodhya where Rama reigned. Having dissuaded his leading counsellors and chief warriors from accompanying him, he set out on his most excellent steed with a hundred chariots.

That descendant of Raghu, having covered fifteen stages (of the journey) reached Valmiki's hermitage where he halted. Thereafter that foremost of men paid obeisance to the ascetic, who, as host, with his own hands offered him water to wash his feet and the Arghya. Then the Sage recounted the most agreeable and varied traditions to the magnanimous Shatrughna and, speaking of the death of Lavana, he said :—

" Thou hast accomplished a difficult feat in slaying him ! O Valiant Youth, many mighty monarchs with their troops of infantry and cavalry succumbed in their struggle with Lavana. Thou hast slain him as it were in sport, O Foremost of Men! By thy valour, the fear of the worlds has been terminated. The death of Ravana was brought about with great difficulty by Rama, but this marvellous feat of arms has been accomplished by thee without any trouble whatsoever ! At the fall of Lavana, great joy broke out amongst the Celestials and happiness now reigns amidst all beings in the whole world, O Prince of the House of Raghu ! Being present in Vasava's assembly, I witnessed thy combat, and my heart too was filled with a keen felicity ; now by smelling the crown of thy head, I testify to the great affection I bear for thee."

With these words, the illustrious Valmiki smelt the crown of Shatrughna's head and offered him and his followers the traditional hospitality.

Having eaten, Shatrughna, the foremost of men, listened to the sweetest chants which told the history of Rama and how all had taken place. Stringed instruments accompanied the singing in the triple mode[1] which was expressive and melodic ; and he

---

[1] That is sung from the heart, throat and head.

heard the story of Rama and what had formerly been achieved by him ; his imperishable exploits as they had taken place in time gone by, and that foremost of men, Shatrughna, was transported, his eyes full of tears, and he remained absorbed, sighing again and again. It seemed to him that this song made the past live once more, and Shatrughna's companions, overcome, listened to the enchanting symphonic poem with bowed heads.

Thereafter, those warriors cried out, " Wonderful ! " and began to question each other, saying :—

" What is this ? Where are we ? Is it a vision or a dream ? Are we seeing that marvellous epic in a dream ? " In their extreme astonishment, they said to Shatrughna :—

" O Prince, do thou interrogate Valmiki, that foremost of Sages," for they were all struck with amazement, but Shatrughna answered them, saying :—

" O Ye Soldiers, it is not fitting to interrogate such a person. Many miracles take place in this hermitage, nevertheless, it does not become us to question a great ascetic out of curiosity."

Having spoken thus to his troops, the son of Raghu paid obeisance to that illustrious Rishi and entered his own quarters.

CHAPTER 72

Shatrughna returns to see Rama

THOUGH that lion among men had laid himself down, he was unable to sleep and his mind was absorbed in the marvellous epic of Rama, and while he listened to those ravishing strains accompanied by stringed instruments, the night passed quickly for the magnanimous Shatrughna. The night being over, that prince, having performed his morning devotions, with joined palms addressed the foremost of ascetics, saying :—

" O Blessed One, I desire to behold the one who is the Joy of the Raghu Race and crave permission to take leave of thee and the other acetics of rigid penances."

Hearing the petition of Shatrughna, the Scourge of his Foes, offspring of the Raghu Race, Valmiki embraced him and granted him permission to depart. Thereupon that prince, having paid obeisance to the foremost of the ascetics, ascended a magnificent chariot and, in his eagerness to see Rama, soon reached Ayodhya.

Having entered that charming city, the long-armed and fortunate descendant of the Ikshvakus sought out Rama of great renown and beheld him seated amidst his counsellors, his countenance as radiant as the full moon, and he resembled the Thousand-eyed God surrounded by the Immortals.

Paying obeisance to the resplendent and magnanimous Rama with joined palms, he addressed that hero, whose prowess was truth, saying :—

" O Great King, all that thou hast commanded has been carried out by me ; the wicked Lavana is dead and his city is occupied. Now twelve years have been passed far from thee, O Joy of the Raghus, and I can no longer live separated from thee, O Prince. Be gracious to me, O Kakutstha, thou whose valour is immeasurable ; do not ask me to remain there longer like a calf separated from its mother."

As he spoke thus, Kakutstha embraced him and said :—

" Do not give way to despondency, O Valiant One, such conduct is not worthy of a warrior. Kings do not withdraw to foreign lands, O Raghava, the duty of a king is the protection of his people. O Virtuous Shatrughna, do thou visit me from time to time in Ayodhya, then thou must return to thy capital. I too cherish thee more than life itself yet it is essential to look to the security of thy kingdom. Meantime remain here with me for seven days, O Kakutstha, and thereafter return to Madhura with thine escort of servants and cavalry."

Hearing Rama's words that were pleasing to the heart and in conformity with dharma, Shatrughna answered sorrowfully, " So be it ! "

Thereafter, having passed a week in Rama's proximity, that skilful archer, Shatrughna, in accord with his brother's will, made preparations to depart. Paying obeisance to that true hero, the magnanimous Rama, and to Bharata and Lakshmana, he ascended his chariot and, being accompanied for a great distance by Lakshmana and Bharata, he hastened to regain his capital.

CHAPTER 73

The Death of a Brahmin's Son

HAVING said farewell to Shatrughna, the fortunate Rama found satisfaction in ruling his kingdom in equity.

Now some time after, an aged peasant, a brahmin, bearing his dead child in his arms came to the palace gate, weeping and crying out again and again :—

" What sin did I commit in a previous existence ? "

Overcome with paternal grief, he repeated unceasingly, " O My Son, My Son ! Ah ! Of what fault was I formerly guilty in another body that I should see mine only son meet with death ? This boy had not yet reached adolescence, his fourteenth year not having been completed ! To my misfortune, before his time, this dear child has been struck down by death ! In a few days, I and thy mother too will die of grief, O Dear Child ! I do not recollect ever to have uttered a lie ; I do not remember ever inflicting an injury on any animal or doing harm to any person ! For what misdeed has this child, born to me, gone to the abode of Vaivaswata this day, ere he had performed a son's duties to his sire ? Never before have I witnessed or heard of such a dreadful thing as, in Rama's reign, for people to die prematurely. Rama must have committed a serious fault since in his kingdom, children succumb. Assuredly the young who inhabit other countries need not fear death ! O King, give me back the life of my child, who has fallen under the sway of death ! With my wife, I shall yield up my life at the gate of the king as if I were without a protector ! Thereafter, having been guilty of Brahmanicide, O Rama, be happy ! Mayest thou live long with thy brothers ! O Mighty Monarch, under thy rule, after a period of prosperity in thine empire, misfortune has now overtaken us, placing us under death's dominion, O Rama ! From now on we shall not enjoy the least felicity since the empire of the magnanimous Ikshvakus no longer has a support. With Rama as its protector, the death of children is certain. People perish under the unrighteous rule of an impious monarch. The

579

evil conduct of a king brings about the premature death of his subjects. When, in the cities and country, crimes are committed and no supervision is exercised, then death is to be feared! Undoubtedly the king will be held to be at fault in city and country, hence the death of this child."

Such were the countless recriminations that the unfortunate father addressed to the king whilst he clasped his son to his breast.

CHAPTER 74

Narada's Discourse

THE piteous lamentations of that unfortunate brahmin reached the ears of the king and he, in the profound distress he experienced, called together his ministers, Vasishtha and Vamadeva, with his brothers and the elders of the city also.

Then eight brahmins were ushered into the king's presence by Vasishtha, who resembled a God, and they said :—

" May prosperity attend thee ! "

Thereafter those foremost of the Twice-born, Markandeya, Maudgalya, Vamadeva, Kashyapa, Katyayana, Javali, Gautama and Narada took their seats, and those Rishis being assembled, Rama paid obeisance to them with joined palms. Then the ministers and citizens received a cordial welcome, as was fitting, and all those highly effulgent persons being seated near him, Raghava informed them of the reproaches of that Twice-born One.

Hearing the words of the prince, who was filled with distress, Narada himself made this memorable reply in the assembly of the Sages :—

" Learn, O King, what has caused the untimely death of this child ! When thou art conversant therewith, do what thou considerest to be thy duty !

" O Prince, Joy of the Raghus, formerly in the Krita Yuga, the brahmins alone practised asceticism ; he who was not a brahmin in no wise undertook it. At the close of that age, all was consumed and absorbed into Brahman. Thereafter the

brahmins were re-born enlightened and endowed with the gift
of immortality. In that age, none died prematurely and all
were wise.

" The Treta Yuga followed when the sons of Manu were
born,[1] who practised austerities ; these noble men were the
rulers, and full of power and heroism. In that era, Brahmins and
Kshatriyas were equal in power nor could any distinction be
found amongst them ; it was then that the four castes were
established.

" When that Yuga, which had been free from nescience, was
consumed in the Fire,[2] unrighteousness placed one foot on the
earth and, on account of wrong-doing, glory waned and the span
of life was diminished, O Best of Monarchs. Flesh that had
been formerly eaten,[3] became impure food throughout the
whole world and, in these conditions, men gave themselves up
to good deeds, taking refuge in purity and justice to rid themselves of evil.

" In the Treta Yuga, brahmins and warriors practised
asceticism and the rest were under the supreme obligation of
obedience, proper to the Vaishya and Shudra classes ; the
Shudras' duty being to serve the other three.

" O Great King, in the Dwapara Yuga, untruth and evil
increased, unrightousness having placed a second foot on the
earth, and then the Vaishyas began to practice penance, so that
dharma, in the form of asceticism, was performed by the three
castes, but the Shudras were not permitted to undertake it during
that time, O Foremost of Men.

" O Prince, a man of the lowest caste may not give himself up
to penance in the Dwapara Yuga ; it is only in the Kali Yuga
that the practice of asceticism is permitted to the Shudra caste.
During the Dwapara Yuga it is a great crime for one of Shudra
birth to perform such practices.

"At this time, in thine empire, a rigid penance is being undertaken by a wretched Shudra, O Prince, and this is the cause of
the death of that child.

" The practice of unrighteousness, be it in the city or the

---

[1] The Kshatriyas or Warrior Class.
[2] The Fire of Dissolution that destroys the worlds at the end of a Cycle.
[3] Men lived on flesh by hunting before agriculture was known.

country, brings about misfortune and the monarch who does not mete out an immediate punishment, goes to hell, of this there is no doubt.

"An act of mortification that is prescribed is well done and a sixth of the merit goes to the king who rules with justice. But how should he, who does not protect his people, enjoy the sixth portion ? O Lion among Men, thou shouldst investigate the happenings in thy kingdom and put down evil wherever it is practised, so righteousness may flourish, man's life be prolonged and the child be revived."

CHAPTER 75

Rama makes a Tour of Inspection of his Kingdom

HEARING the nectar-like words of Narada, Rama was delighted and said to Lakshmana :—

" O Dear Friend, thou who art faithful to thy vows, go and console that leading brahmin and cause the body of the child to be placed in a jar of oil with precious unguents and fragrant salves so that it is covered and does not suffer decomposition. Act in such a way that the body of the child does not dissolve or decay."

Having issued this command to Lakshmana, who was endowed with auspicious marks, the highly illustrious Kakutstha thought of Pushpaka, and said " Come hither ! " Conscious of his intention, the golden chariot[1] appeared before him in the same hour and bowing, said to him :—

" Behold, I am here at thy service, O Long-armed Prince ! "

Listening to the gracious words of Pushpaka, Rama paid obeisance to the great Rishis and ascended the chariot. Armed with his bow, his two quivers and his glittering sword, Raghava left the city in the charge of his two brothers, Saumitri and Bharata, and thereafter that monarch directed his course to the western region which he explored on every side ; then he went to the northern region bounded by the Himalayas, but found no

[1] The golden chariot that is the presiding Deity of Pushpaka.

trace of evil-doing there ; later the eastern region was carefully searched by him and that long-armed Prince, from on high in his chariot, beheld people of pure morals there, as stainless as a mirror. Then he, who causes felicity to the great Rishis, ranged the southern region and, on the side of the Shaivala Mountain, a vast lake appeared to him, on the banks of which the blessed Raghava beheld an ascetic practising an extremely rigorous penance, his head hanging downwards.

On this that Prince born of Raghu approached the one who had given himself up to rigorous practices and said :—

" Blessed art thou, O Ascetic, who art faithful to thy vows ! From what caste art thou sprung, O Thou who hast grown old in mortification and who art established in heroism. I am interested in this matter, I, Rama, the son of Dasaratha. What purpose hast thou in view ? Is it heaven or some other object ? What boon dost thou seek by means of this hard penance ? I wish to know what thou desirest in performing these austerities, O Ascetic. May prosperity attend thee ! Art thou a brahmin ? Art thou an invincible Kshatriya ? Art thou a Vaishya, one of the third caste or art thou a Shudra ? Answer me truthfully ! "

Then the ascetic, who was hanging head downwards, thus questioned by Rama, revealed his origin to that Prince born of Dasaratha, the foremost of kings, and the reason why he was practising penance.

CHAPTER 76

Shambuka is slain by Rama

HEARING the words of Rama of imperishable exploits, that ascetic, his head still hanging downwards, answered :—

" O Rama, I was born of a Shudra alliance and I am performing this rigorous penance in order to acquire the status of a God in this body. I am not telling a lie, O Rama, I wish to attain the Celestial Region. Know that I am a Shudra and my name is Shambuka."

As he was yet speaking, Raghava, drawing his brilliant and stainless sword from its scabbard, cut off his head. The Shudra being slain, all the Gods and their leaders with Agni's followers, cried out, " Well done ! Well done!" overwhelming Rama with praise, and a rain of celestial flowers of divine fragrance fell on all sides, scattered by Vayu. In their supreme satisfaction, the Gods said to that hero, Rama :—

" Thou hast protected the interests of the Gods, O Highly Intelligent Prince, now ask a boon, O Beloved Offspring of Raghu, Destroyer of Thy Foes. By thy grace, this Shudra will not be able to attain heaven ! "

Hearing the words of the Gods, that hero of the region of truth, with joined palms, addressed Purandara of a Thousand Eyes, saying :—

" Since the Gods are gratified with me, let the son of that brahmin be resuscitated ! Accord me this, the greatest of all favours ! It is on account of my negligence that this child, the only son of that brahmin, has died before his time. Give him back his life ! May prosperity be yours ! I have promised that I would restore his son to this Twice-born, do not let my words prove false ! "

Thus spoke Raghava and the foremost of the Celestials, full of joy, gave him this reply, enhancing his felicity :—

" O Kakutstha be happy ! This very day that child has received new life and has been restored to his parents. The child was resuscitated at the instant that the head of the Shudra fell. Be happy ! May prosperity attend thee ! Now let us go, O Raghava, O Foremost of Monarchs, we desire to visit Agastya's hermitage. The hour of consecration is at hand for that great Rishi ! O Illustrious Prince, for twelve years, he has lived in the water. O Kakutstha, let us go together to offer felicitations to that ascetic. Do thou come and visit the foremost of Rishis also and be happy."

" Be it so ! " said the enhancer of the Raghus' joy and ascended the gold-encrusted Chariot, Pushpaka. Meantime, the Gods had left in their vast chariots and Rama followed them without delay to the hermitage of Kumbhayoni.

Beholding those Gods come to meet him, the virtuous Agastya, that treasury of asceticism, paid obeisance to all without distinction and, having received his homage and offered salutations to him, the Gods joyfully returned to their abode with their attendants. When they had departed, Rama descended from the Pushpaka Plane and offered obeisance to that illustrious Rishi.

Agastya, radiant in his own effulgence, returned the salutation of his magnanimous Sovereign, who, having received supreme hospitality, seated himself, whereupon the illustrious Kumbhayoni of rigid penances said to him :—

" O Foremost of Men, be thou welcome ! O Raghava, it is my good fortune that brings thee here ! O Rama, thou art worthy of the highest respect on account of thine outstanding and innumerable attributes, O Prince ! Thou art a guest worthy of honour and abidest in mine heart. The Gods tell me that thou hast come here after slaying the Shudra and, by this act of justice thou hast restored the son of a brahmin to life ! Pass the night here with me, O Raghava, for thou art Narayana, the Blessed Lord and all is to be found in Thee ! Thou art the divine Purusha ! To-morrow at dawn thou canst return to the city in the Pushpaka Chariot.

" O My Friend, here is an ornament wrought by Vishvakarma, which is of divine origin and glows by its own light. Be pleased to accept it, O Kakutstha. To give again what one has received is said to be of the greatest profit. Thou art worthy of this ornament and also of the highest rewards since thou hast protected the Gods and their leaders. I have therefore a right to offer this to thee, do thou accept it, O Prince."

NOTE :

THE FOLLOWING FOURTEEN VERSES ARE CONSIDERED TO BE INTERPOLATIONS.

Then that great warrior of the Ikshvakus, pondering on the duties of the Kshatriyas, answered that magnanimous ascetic, saying :—

" O Illustrious Rishi, only brahmins may accept gifts, it is censurable for a Kshatriya to do so. It is not fitting for a Kshatriya to accept a gift from a brahmin. Do thou tell me therefore how I may do so ? "

On this, the Rishi Agastya replied, saying :—

" O Rama, O Son of Dasaratha, at the beginning of the Golden Age, the human race had no king, only the Celestials had Vasava as their ruler. To obtain a king, therefore, men approached Brahma, the God of Gods and said :—

" ' O Lord, thou hast made Indra ruler over the Celestials, therefore do thou confer a sovereign upon us who shall be the foremost of men ; we cannot live without a king, this is our firm conviction ! '

" Then the Grandsire of the World sent for Indra and the other Gods and said :—

" ' Do ye all sacrifice a portion of your welfare ! ' and the Celestials surrendered part of their power and a king was born, whereupon Brahma named him Kshupa.[1] In his person, Brahma placed an equal proportion of the powers of the Gods and appointed him as ruler of men. By virtue of the portion of Indra's energy, the King Kshupa brought the earth under his control ; by the portion of Varuna's energy, he fostered health in his body ; by the power of Yama, he ruled the people. O Rama, by virtue of Indra's portion, thou art the Ruler of the earth, do thou accept this jewel and confer thy grace on me."

Hearing the words of the Sage, Rama accepted the brilliant and celestial gem sparkling like the rays of the sun and, having taken that excellent ornament, Dasarathi enquired of the great Sage Kumbhayoni, saying :—

" Whence hast thou obtained this divine ornament of celestial workmanship ? Who has given it to thee , O Brahmin, I ask thee out of curiosity , Thou art an ocean of marvels ! "

Then Agastya answered :—

" Hear, O Rama, how I obtained this ornament in the Treta-Yuga."

CHAPTER 77

The Story of Swargin

" O RAMA, formerly in the Treta-Yuga, there was a vast wilderness some four hundred miles in extent where there was neither beast nor bird and there I was undergoing a rigid penance. O My Friend, I began to range that uninnabited solitude ! I cannot describe its beauty with the fruits, roots of exquisite savour and the trees of varying essences.

[1] Kshupa—A shrub or small tree with roots.

" In the centre was a lake some four miles in extent, abounding in swans and waterfowl, Chakravakra birds being its ornament. It was covered with lotuses and waterlilies, no weed or moss grew there and its waters were deep, tranquil and sweet. Near that wonderful lake, I found a spacious hermitage which was of great antiquity and devoid of man or beast. It was there I spent a summer night, O Foremost of Men. At dawn, I rose to perform my morning devotions and directed my steps to the lake. There I beheld a dead body, plump and spotless, shining in splendour in the water. This sight caused me to reflect awhile, O Raghava, and I stood on the banks of the lake asking myself, ' What can this be ? '

" O Lord, a moment later a wonderful celestial chariot came into view, which was magnificent, and harnessed to swans that were as swift as thought. In that chariot I beheld a man of extraordinary beauty, O Joy of the House of Raghu, who was surrounded by thousands of Apsaras adorned with celestial ornaments. Some were singing enchantingly whilst others played on musical instruments such as Mridangas, Vinas and Panavas ; some were dancing and some, with the aid of Chanwaras gleaming like the moon's rays, possessing ornate handles, were fanning the face of that lotus-eyed youth. Then he, who was as radiant as the peak of Mount Meru, leaving his seat, descended from the chariot and, under my gaze, devoured that corpse. Having satisfied his hunger with abundant flesh, he plunged into the waters and after washing his hands and rinsing his mouth according to tradition, he re-ascended his chariot.

" Beholding that heavenly being about to depart, I spoke to him thus, O Prince :—

" ' Who art thou who resemblest a God ? Why hast thou partaken of this forbidden flesh, O My Friend ? Tell me how does this loathsome nourishment benefit thee, O Thou who art the equal of the Celestials ? There is some mystery in this, O Friend, I wish to know what it is ; I cannot believe a corpse to be fitting food for thee.'

" Thus, out of curiosity, in friendly accents, did I speak to that Nakin,[1] O Prince and having listened to me, he told me all."

---

[1] Nakin—One dwelling in ' Naka ', the sky, a divine Being.

CHAPTER 78

Shveta tells his Story

" HAVING listened to these auspicious words, that Celestial Being, with joined palms answered me in this wise, O Rama, Joy of the House of Raghu.

" ' Hear, O Brahmin, of what happened to me formerly, bringing about my felicity and also my suffering. Learn of the inexorable fate about which thou hast questioned me.

" ' In times gone by, my illustrious Sire, the mighty Sudeva reigned over the Vidarbhas. He had two sons by his two queens, O Brahmin, I was named Shveta and my younger brother Suratha. My father having ascended to heaven, I was installed as king by the people, and accordingly applied myself to rule with equity.

" 'A thousand years passed whilst I governed the empire piously and protected my people according to dharma. Knowing by certain indications that I was ageing, O Foremost of the Twice-born, I reflected on the laws of time and went to the forest. There I penetrated into an inaccessible grove, where there were neither beasts nor birds, in order to practise penance on the banks of this beautiful lake, having first placed my brother Suratha on the throne as lord of the empire.

" ' Near this lake, I gave myself up to severe mortifications and practised austerities for thousands of years in the great forest. This excessively rigid penance caused me to attain Brahmaloka, which nothing transcends. Having ascended to heaven, extreme hunger and thirst assailed me, O Foremost of the Twice-born, whereupon, my mind troubled, I approached the Lord of the Three Worlds, the Grandsire, and said to him :—

" ' " O Blessed One, in Brahmaloka one should not be subject to hunger and thirst ; from what act of mine does this desire to eat and drink, spring ? What should be my food, tell me, O Divine Grandsire ? "

" ' Then the Grandsire answered me, saying :—

" ' " O Son of Sudeva, thine own flesh shall be thy savoury nourishment and thou shalt feed on it daily. Thou didst ever nourish thy body well when thou wast performing an excellent penance. That which is sowed ever flourishes, O Virtuous Shveta. Without making any gifts, thou didst practise asceticism ; it is on this account that thou art subject to hunger and thirst in heaven, which thou hast attained. Therefore, thine own body that has been well nourished shall be thy food in heaven, and it shall be converted into Amrita, but when the great and invincible Rishi Agastya comes to the forest, he will deliver thee from this bondage, O Shveta ! My Friend, he can save the hosts of the Gods themselves, how much more is he able to save thee from the domination of hunger and thirst to which thou art subjected, O Long-armed Hero."

" ' O Lord of the Twice-born, since the decree of Bhagawat, that Lord of Lords, I have been nourishing myself miserably on mine own body ! For innumerable years I have fed upon it without it diminishing, O Brahmarishi, and my appetite is excessive. Do thou deliver me from this painful pass ; release will not come to me from any other than the Ascetic Kumbhayoni ! O Dear and Excellent Sage, do thou accept this gift, may good betide thee, accord me this favour ! I will bestow gold, possessions, raiment, savoury food and much. else besides, as also ornaments on thee, O Foremost of Sages, I offer thee all that is desirable and all felicity, as the price of my deliverance, O Grant me that grace ! '

" Hearing these words of that unfortunate Celestial Being, I accepted the rare jewel in order to save him and, as soon as I received that magnificent gem, the mortal body of that Royal-Rishi melted away. His body being thus dissolved, that Rajarishi experienced supreme satisfaction and joyfully ascended to Swarga. This is why that Celestial Being, who resembled Shakra, gave that divine gem, wonderful to look upon, to me, O Kakutstha."

CHAPTER 79

The hundred Sons of Ikshvaku

HAVING heard Agastya's marvellous story, Raghava, full of reverence and admiration, began to question him, saying :—

" O Blessed One, why are there no wild beasts or birds in this

forest where the King of Vidarbha, Shveta, used to practise that
rigid penance ? Why did that prince enter this deserted and
uninhabited wood in order to give himself up to the performance
of asceticism ; I wish to know all in detail ? "

Hearing this question inspired by curiosity, that foremost of
ascetics began to speak thus :—

" In ancient times in the golden age, O Rama, the Lord
Manu was the ruler of the earth. His son was Ikshvaku, the
enhancer of the felicity of his race. Having placed his eldest
son, the invincible Ikshvaku on the throne, Manu said :—

" ' Become the founder of royal dynasties in the world ! '

" O Rama, Ikshvaku promised to follow his injunctions and
Manu, greatly delighted, added :—

" ' I am pleased with thee, O Noble One, undoubtedly thou
shalt found a dynasty but, whilst ruling thy subjects with firmness, never punish any who is without fault ! A punishment
meted out to the guilty according to the law is instrumental in
conducting a monarch to heaven, therefore, O Long-armed Hero,
O Dear Child, exercise extreme care in wielding the sceptre,
this is thy supreme duty on earth.'

" Having counselled his son repeatedly in this wise, Manu
joyfully repaired to the eternal abode of Brahma.

" His Sire having ascended to the Celestial Region, Ikshvaku
of immeasurable glory reflected anxiously within himself as to
how he should create progeny. Having performed many
sacrifices and charitable deeds, he was blessed with a hundred
sons like unto the offspring of the Gods. The youngest of all, O
Descendant of Raghu, was stupid and ignorant nor would he
listen to the advice of his elders. On account of his lack of
virtue, the king named him Danda, thinking that the rod
(Danda) would inevitably fall on him.

"As the monarch was unable to find a province suitable for
his son, O Raghava, Conqueror of Thy Foes, he carved out a
territory for him between the Vindhya and Shaivala Mountains.
Danda became king and there built an incomparably beautiful
city on that charming site surrounded by mountains. He named
that city Madhumanta, O Lord, and chose Shukra Deva of pious
practices as his spiritual preceptor. Danda with his Guru ruled
over that city inhabited by happy people as the King of the Gods

in heaven. That monarch, the son of the foremost of men, with the help of Shukra Deva ruled as the great and magnanimous Shakra in heaven under the guidance of Brihaspati."

CHAPTER 80

Danda insults Aruja

HAVING related that story to Rama, the great ascetic, born from a jar, continued :—

" Danda, O Kakutstha, fully self-controlled, continued to rule for innumerable years, overcoming all obstacles. One day, in the delicious month of Chaitra, the king went to the ravishing hermitage of Bhargava and he beheld the daughter of that ascetic, who was walking in the woodland glade, and she was unrivalled in beauty on earth so that he was seized with desire. Pierced by the darts of the God of Love, he approached that youthful maiden and enquired of her, saying :—

" ' From whence art thou, O Lady of graceful hips ? Who is thy father, O Beautiful One ? Being afflicted with passion, I make these enquiries of thee, O Fair Lady ? '

" Thus did he speak in his agitation and the daughter of the ascetic answered sweetly :—

" ' I am the eldest daughter of Shukracharya of imperishable deeds, know that my name is Aruja, O Foremost of Kings, and I dwell in this hermitage. Do not force thine attentions upon me, O King, for I am a girl still under my father's authority. My Sire is thy Guru, O Great Prince, thou art the disciple of that magnanimous ascetic ; that great Sage will inflict a terrible punishment on thee in his wrath. It is for thee to act honestly regarding me, in accord with the law of dharma, O Prince. Do thou first approach my father and ask for my hand or fearful consequences will follow thine act. In his wrath, my father will consume the Three Worlds themselves, O Thou of faultless form ; if, however, thou ask for my hand, he will bestow it on thee.'

" Thus spoke Aruja, but Danda, who had fallen under the sway of desire, with joined palms, answered her in his frenzy, saying :—

" ' Grant me thy favours, O Charming One, do not delay, on thine account my breath is being extinguished, O Thou of lovely countenance. Having united myself with thee, what care I if death or the most terrible retribution follow ? Respond to my love, O Timid One, that love that overwhelms me.'

" Speaking thus, he seized that youthful woman roughly in his powerful arms and sated his lust on her. Having committed this monstrous outrage, Danda returned to the unrivalled city of Madhumanta with all speed. Aruja however, sobbing near the hermitage, terrified, awaited her father who resembled a God."

CHAPTER 81

The Destruction of Danda's Kingdom

" HAVING heard what had taken place, the blessed and illustrious Rishi, surrounded by his disciples, returned to the hermitage, tormented with hunger. Like unto the moon that has been devoured by the planet Rahu at dawn and is deprived of its radiance, he beheld the unfortunate Aruja besmeared with dust ; and that brahmin, being already consumed with hunger, fell into a transport of rage, so that it seemed he wished to destroy the Three Worlds. Thereafter he addressed his disciples, saying :—

" ' Witness the terrible calamity born of my wrath, like unto fire, that will befall that evil-doer, Danda ! The time has come for the destruction of that wretched monarch and his court, he, who has dared to place his hand in the flame of the sacrificial fire, will soon reap the fruit of his evil act ! In seven nights, he will perish with his children, infantry and cavalry. Pakashana[1] will destroy the territory of that wretch with a rain of dust for a distance of a hundred leagues in extent. In the kingdom of Danda, in seven days, all things animate and inanimate will perish utterly and everything that grows will vanish entirely under the rain of ashes ! '

" Having spoken thus to the inhabitants of the hermitage, his eyes red with anger, he added :—

[1] Pakashana—' Punisher of the Demon Paka , a title of Indra.

" ' Take up your abode beyond the confines of this region ! '

" Hearing the words of Shukracharya, all those who dwelt in the hermitage, left that place to establish themselves elsewhere, and Shukracharya, having spoken thus to that company of Sages, addressed his daughter Aruja and said :—

" ' Remain in this hermitage, O Foolish One, and give thyself up to meditation. O Aruja, awaiting the time of thy deliverance, enjoy carefree this lake of enchanting aspect four miles in extent ! Those creatures that take refuge with thee at that time will in no wise suffer from the rain of dust ! '

"At the command of the Brahmarishi, her Sire, Aruja, who was overcome with grief, answered ; ' So be it ! '

" Having spoken thus, Shukracharya found a dwelling elsewhere.

" Meantime the kingdom of that foremost of men with his servants, his army and his chariots was reduced to ashes on the seventh day, as predicted by that interpreter of the Veda. O Prince, that empire situated between the Vindhya and the Shaivala Mountains, its sovereign having ceased to uphold dharma, thus cursed by the Brahmarishi, has since been known as the Desert of Dandaka, O Kakutstha, and the place where the ascetics dwelt became known as Janasthana. I have now replied fully to all that thou hast asked, O Raghava. The hour for the evening devotions is passing, O Hero; from all directions, the great Rishis with their loshtas filled, having bathed, O Prince, are now worshipping the Sun-god. The sun has withdrawn behind the Astachala Mountains while these learned interpreters of the Veda were reading the Brahmanas together ; do thou also perform thine ablutions, O Rama."

CHAPTER 82

Rama takes leave of Agastya

FOLLOWING the behest of the Rishi, Rama, in order to perform his evening devotions, approached the sacred lake frequented by troops of Apsaras. Having completed his ablutions and the evening rites, he returned to the hermitage of the magnanimous Kumbhayoni. Thereupon Agastya, for his repast, prepared many kinds of fruits and roots with rice and pure ingredients, and the foremost of men partook of that food resembling Amrita and passed the night there happily.

At dawn, that Subduer of His Foes, the Prince of the Raghus, having performed the morning rituals, approached the Sage before his departure and, paying obeisance to that great ascetic, born from a jar, said to him :—

" Suffer me to return to this retreat, I beg of thee ! Happy am I to have received the favour of looking on such a great ascetic whom I shall visit again for my sanctification ! "

Listening to the words of Kakutstha, wonderful to hear, he, whose vision was righteousness, in great delight, answered :—

" O Rama, O Joy of the Raghus, thy speech, brilliantly expressed, is of great eloquence. Thou thyself art the sanctity of all beings ! O Rama, whoever casts a single glance of love on thee is purified ; he goes to paradise where he receives the homage of the Lords of the Third Heaven ; but those who look on thee with a malevolent eye are suddenly struck down by the Rod of Death and fall into hell ! O Prince, Issue of the Raghu Race, thou art the salvation of all beings on earth and those who even speak of thee acquire perfection. Do thou go in peace ! Govern thine empire with equity ; thou art the path of the world ! "

Thus did that Muni speak and the virtuous prince with joined palms, paid obeisance to that ascetic and, having offered salutations to that foremost of Sages and the other Munis, tranquilly ascended the golden Pushpaka Chariot. As he was leaving, the companies of Sages showered blessings of every kind upon him, he who was equal to Mahendra, as the Devas acclaim that God of a Thousand Eyes.

Standing in space, Rama, in his golden Chariot Pushpaka, resembled the moon encircled with clouds. Thereafter, at noon, Kakutstha entered Ayodhya amidst continuous acclamations and, having reached the central court, he dismounted from the car. When the prince left Pushpaka, that magnificent chariot, which coursed wheresoever one willed, dismissing it, he said :—
" Go, may good betide thee ! "

Thereafter Rama issued this command to the doorkeeper who was in the courtyard and said :—

" Go and announce mine arrival to Lakshmana and Bharata, those two swift-footed heroes, and summon them here without delay."

CHAPTER 83

Bharata persuades Rama not to perform the Rajasuya Sacrifice

AT this command from Rama of imperishable exploits, the guard summoned those two youthful princes and came back to inform his master. Then he, seeing Bharata and Lakshmana, embraced them both and said to them :—

" I have faithfully carried out the task of the excellent Twice-born, now I wish to perform the Rajasuya Sacrifice, which to my mind is indestructible and unchangeable, the support of the law and the destroyer of all evil. Accompanied by you both, who are parts of myself, I wish to prepare for this sacrifice based on eternal dharma, for it is an unwritten duty. It was after performing the Rajasuya Sacrifice that Mitra, the Scourge of His Foes, obtained Varuna-hood by means of this rich offering. Having celebrated that sacrifice according to the tradition which was well-known to him, Soma acquired an imperishable state and renown in the world. Do you therefore tell me what is now best, and considering the matter with me, say candidly what is of the greatest profit for the future."

Thus spoke Raghava, and Bharata, a skilful debator, with joined palms made answer, saying :—

" O Dear Brother, in thee the highest sense of duty is to be found ! It is in thee that the world finds her support ; in thee, all glory resides, and also immeasurable valour, O Long-armed Hero. All the kings of the earth, and we too, regard thee as the protector of the universe, as do the Gods and Prajapati. Children look on thee as their father, O Valiant Prince, thou hast become the salvation of living beings also, O Raghava ; how shouldst thou perform a sacrifice of such a nature, O Lord, in which the destruction of many royal Houses is involved ? Further O King, it means the total annihilation of those warriors who have become the heroes of the earth, which will prove a cause of universal condemnation. O Lion among Warriors, O Thou whose virtues render thee unequalled in power, do not destroy the world that is wholly subject to thee."

When Rama heard Bharata speak thus, in words sweet as nectar, he experienced an extreme delight and addressed this benign response to the enhancer of Kaikeyi's joy, saying :—

" I am happy and delighted with what thou hast said, O Irreproachable Hero, this resolute discourse, in accord with righteousness, that thou hast uttered, O Lion among Heroes, has preserved the earth ! The resolve I made to proceed with the great Rajasuya Sacrifice, I now renounce on thine excellent counsel, O Virtuous Bharata. The wise should never commit any act detrimental to the world. Contrariwise one should be willing to receive good advice even from a child, O Thou, the elder brother of Lakshmana ; I am pleased with thy counsel which is wise and considered, O Valiant Prince ! "

CHAPTER 84

The Story of Vritra

THUS spoke Rama to the great-souled Bharata, and thereafter Lakshmana addressed this eloquent discourse to the One who enhanced the felicity of the Raghus, saying :—

" The great Sacrifice Ashwamedha removes all sins and is the infallible means of purification ; may it please thee to undertake it, O Joy of the Raghus !

" It is said in the Puranas that the magnanimous Vasava, sullied by the sin of brahmanicide, was cleansed by performing the Horse-sacrifice. O Long-armed Warrior, in former times when Devas and Asuras were united, there lived a universally honoured Daitya named Vritra. The width of his body was an hundred leagues and he was three times as tall. In his loving-kindness, he cast his beneficent glance in all directions on the Three Worlds. Loyal, grateful, highly intelligent, he ruled his fertile territory with care and integrity and, under his dominion, the earth produced all that could be desired—flowers, roots and delicious fruits. Without being cultivated the earth was abundantly fruitful and for many years that magnanimous prince enjoyed a rich empire marvellous to behold. Then the thought came to him : ' I ·shall perform a rigid penance ; in truth, asceticism is a great joy, all other happiness is a mere illusion.'

" Having established his eldest son over his people as King of Madhura, he gave himself up to a rigid penance that caused terror among the Gods. As Vritra was mortifying himself thus, Vasava, in his extreme affliction, sought out Vishnu and spoke to him as follows :—

" ' On account of his asceticism that long-armed hero, Vritra, has conquered the worlds ; he is powerful and virtuous ; I shall not be able to overcome him. If he continues with these austerities, O Chief of the Gods, we shall be subject to him as long as the worlds endure. Thou hast overlooked the extremely illustrious Vritra or he would not live an instant in the face of thy wrath, O Lord of the Gods. From the moment he succeeded in propitiating thee, O Vishnu, he has taken over the direction of the worlds. It is for thee in thy great solicitude to befriend the universe, then by thy favour, the worlds will live in peace, free from affliction. All the inhabitants of the celestial region have fixed their gaze on thee, O Vishnu. Slay Vritra and by this great feat deliver them ! Thou hast ever lent support to the magnanimous Gods which cannot be withstood by their adversaries ; be the refuge of those who have no other refuge ! ' "

CHAPTER 85

The Death of Vritra

HEARING Lakshmana speak thus, Rama, the Slayer of His Foes, said to him :—" O Thou faithful to thy duty, do thou relate the rest of the history of Vritra's destruction ! "

At these words of Raghava's, the virtuous Lakshmana, increaser of Sumitra's delight, continued his exalted theme, saying :—

" Such was the entreaty addressed by all the inhabitants of

heaven led by that Lord of a Thousand Eyes, to Vishnu, who answered all those Gods with Indra at their head, saying :—

" 'An ancient tie binds me to the magnanimous Vritra, therefore I am unable to favour you by slaying that great Asura ; it is not possible for me to grant you that supreme felicity but I will indicate the means whereby the Thousand-eyed God may destroy him. I shall divide my natural essence into three parts, O Foremost of the Gods, and by these means, that God of a Thousand Eyes can undoubtedly slay Vritra. A third of my being will enter Vasava, a second part into the thunderbolt and a third will enter the bosom of the earth, thus Vritra will perish ! '

" Thus spoke the Lord of the Gods, and the Deities answered him saying :—

" ' O Slayer of Daityas, assuredly what Thou hast uttered will come to pass ! May victory be Thine, we shall now take our leave infused by Thy power in order to slay the Asura Vritra, O Lord ! '

" Then all the magnanimous Gods with Sahasraksha at their head went to the great Asura Vritra's retreat. There they beheld the most powerful of Asuras, effulgent in his own radiance that seemed to consume the worlds and space itself. Beholding the foremost of the Asuras, the Gods were seized with terror and reflected, ' How shall we kill him?' ' How may we avoid defeat!'

"As they were thinking thus, Sahasraksha, the Destroyer of Cities, taking the thunderbolt in his hands, hurled it at Vritra, striking his head. Like unto the Fire of Time, formidable, blazing with its wreath of flame, that thunderbolt falling on Vritra's head caused terror to all the worlds.

" Then the extremely illustrious King of the Gods, reflecting on the iniquity he had perpetrated in slaying his enemy, fled in all haste to the ends of the world ; and the sin of brahmanicide pursued him in his flight and entered into him, so that Indra was subject to great affliction.

" The enemy destroyed, but deprived of their leader, the Gods with Agni at their head, lavished homage on Vishnu, Lord of the Three Worlds, saying :—

" ' Thou art the way, O Supreme Master, the First-born, Father of the Universe ! For the protection of the world thou hast assumed the form of Vishnu. By thy favour, Vritra is slain, but the sin of brahmanicide holds Vasava in bondage, do thou liberate him ! '

" Then Vishnu answered the Gods who had spoken thus and said :—

" ' Let Shakra, he who bears the thunderbolt, perform a sacrifice in mine honour and I will cleanse him of his sin. Let him who destroyed Paka, offer up the sacred Horse-sacrifice and he will become King of the Gods once more, without having anything to fear.'

" Having thus addressed the Gods in these words like unto Amrita, Vishnu, the Lord of the Celestials, while they were yet acclaiming him, returned to Trivishtapa."

CHAPTER 86

Indra is liberated by means of the Ashwamedha Sacrifice

HAVING thus described the slaying of Vritra at length, Lakshmana, the foremost of men, continued :—

" The extremely valiant Vritra, who inspired terror in the Gods, being destroyed, Shakra, his slayer, filled with the guilt of brahmanicide, failed to return to his senses and, having taken refuge at the end of the worlds, his mind confused, distracted, he remained there for some time, resembling a serpent that is casting its slough. And the Thousand-eyed God, having disappeared, the whole world was agitated and the earth seemed to be lost, bereft of its humidity, its forests dried up.[1] There were no running waters to feed the lakes and rivers and a great desolation seized all beings on account of the lack of rain.

" Then the Gods seeing the decay of the world, which filled them with distress, began to prepare for the sacrifice according to the words Vishnu had formerly uttered, and all the Hosts of the Gods accompanied by their spiritual preceptors and the Rishis sought out the terror-stricken Indra in his retreat.

" Beholding Sahasraksha assailed by the guilt of brahmanicide, O Foremost of Men, and having paid homage to the Chief of the Gods, they performed the Ashwamedha. O Foremost of

[1] He being the sender of rain.

Men, thereafter the great Horse-sacrifice took place, which was offered by the magnanimous Mahendra in order to cleanse himself of the sin of brahmanicide, and the ceremony being completed, the spirit of brahmanicide issued out of Indra's body and approaching the Gods enquired of them saying :—' Tell me, where shall be my abode ? ' and the Gods in delight, answered :— ' Divide thyself into four parts, O Evil One ! '

" Hearing the words of the mighty Gods, the spirit of brahmanicide did so, varying his habitation, he with whom co-habitation is a disaster, and said :—

" 'Restraining egoity and following mine own whim with a quarter of myself I shall inhabit the rivers in flood in the rainy season. With another quarter undoubtedly I shall dwell perpetually in the earth as Ushara.[1] I speak the truth ! For the third portion I shall live for three nights each month with radiantly youthful women, whose pride I shall humble ; with my fourth portion I shall live in those who by false report cause the death of innocent brahmins, O Mighty Deities.'

" Then the Gods answered, saying :—' O Thou, to live with whom is a calamity, do as thou sayest, accomplish thy design ! '

" Full of joy, the Gods then paid homage to Vasava of a Thousand Eyes, who was cleansed of his sin and delivered from his affliction. And Sahasraksha, having been installed on the throne, peace came to the whole world and Indra paid homage to that wonderful sacrifice.

" Such is the pre-eminence of the Ashwamedha Ceremony, O Joy of the Raghus ! Do thou perform the Horse-sacrifice ! " Hearing these exalting words of Lakshmana, whose charm touched his heart, that magnanimous sovereign, the equal of Indra in strength and prowess, experienced supreme satisfaction.

CHAPTER 87

The Story of Ila

HAVING listened to Lakshmana, the eloquent and powerful Raghava answered with a smile :—

" O Best of Men, Lakshmana, that which thou hast related

[1] Ushara—Saline soil.

regarding the slaying of Vritra and the fruits of the Horse-sacrifice are wholly true, O Gentle One. It is said that formerly Kardama, the son of Prajapati, the extremely virtuous and blessed, Ila, reigned over the province of Bahlika. That highly illustrious monarch, O Lion of Men, having made the entire earth subject to him, reigned over his subjects as his own sons.

"The magnanimous Gods, the wealthy Daityas, the Nagas, Rakshasas, Gandharvas and Yakshas, inspired by fear, constantly worshipped him, O Dear Friend, O Joy of the Raghus, and the Three Worlds trembled before that irascible potentate. Such was that prince, the illustrious Sovereign of the Bahlikas, full of energy, highly intelligent and fixed in his duty.

"During the lovely month of Chaitra, that long-armed warrior went hunting in the enchanting forest with his attendants, infantry and cavalry, and that magnanimous prince, in that wood, slew wild beasts in their hundreds and thousands, yet was not sated. Countless animals of all kinds had already perished when he reached the country where Karttikeya had been born. There the foremost of the Gods, the invincible Hara, was sporting with the daughter of the King of the Mountains, and, having trans-formed himself into a woman, the Lord of Uma, whose emblem is the bull, sought to entertain the Goddess in the midst of the waterfalls. Wherever there were male beings or trees in the forest, whatsoever there was, assumed a female form. King Ila, the son of Kardama penetrated into that place slaying innumer-able beasts and he observed that they were all female, thereafter he became aware that he too was changed into a woman, as also his followers. His distress was great on this metamorphosis and he recognized it to be the work of Uma's consort and was seized with terror. Thereupon that monarch, with his attendants, his army and his chariots, took refuge with that mighty blue-throated God, Kapardin, and the magnanimous Maheshwara, laughing with that Goddess, the bestower of grace, said to the son of Prajapati :—

"' Rise, rise, O Royal Rishi, O Valiant son of Kardama, except manhood, ask what thou wilt !' The king was sorely disappoin-ted by this reply of the magnanimous Shiva. Transformed into a woman, he did not wish to accept any other boon from the foremost of the Gods and, in his profound distress, that prince, falling at the feet of the daughter of the King of the Mountains, Uma, with his whole heart entreated her, saying :—

" ' O Thou who distributest thy favours in all the worlds, O Lovely Goddess, whose sight is never fruitless, cast thy merciful glance upon me ! '

" Knowing what was passing in the heart of the Rajarishi, that Goddess, who stood before Hara, she, the consort of Rudra, made this reply :—

" ' Half the boon, that thou dost beg of us both, shall be granted by Mahadeva and the other half by me, therefore receive this half from man and woman according to thy desire ! '

" Hearing that remarkable and unparalleled boon bestowed by that Goddess, the king, overcome with joy, said :—

" ' If I have found favour with thee, O Goddess, whose beauty is unrivalled on earth, may I be a woman during one month and, in the second month, assume the form of a man ! '

" Then that Goddess of gracious mien, understanding his desire, answered amicably :—

" ' It shall be so, O King, and when thou art a man, thou shalt not remember thou wast ever a woman and, in the succeeding month, having become a woman, thou shalt forget thou wast ever a man ! '

" That is how that king, born of Kardama, being a man for one month became a woman the following month under the name of Ila, the most lovely female in the Three Worlds."

CHAPTER 88

Budha encounters Ila

THE story of Ila, related by Rama, greatly astonished Lakshmana and Bharata, and both, with joined palms, requested him to recount further details of that magnanimous King and his transformations, saying :—

" What did that wretched king do when he was transformed into a woman and how did he conduct himself when he became a man once more ? "

Hearing these words inspired by curiosity, Kakutstha told them what had happened to that monarch, saying :—

" Having been transformed into a woman, he passed the first month amidst his female attendants, his former courtiers, and that lady, the most beautiful on earth, whose eyes resembled lotus petals, entering a deep forest, wandering on foot amongst the copses, bushes and creepers, having given up all conveyances, sported in the winding vale. Now in that wooded region, not far from the mountain, lay a charming lake frequented by birds of every kind ; there Ila beheld Budha,[1] the son of the Moon, who was as radiant as that orb on rising.

" Budha, who remained inaccessible in the waters, had given himself up to a rigid penance, and that illustrious Sage was benevolent and extremely compassionate. In her astonishment, Ila agitated the waters with her companions, and beholding her, Budha fell under the sway of the God of Love with his shafts and, no longer self-controlled, became restless, as he stood in the lake. Seeing Ila, whose beauty was unsurpassed in the Three Worlds, he reflected :—' Who is this lady, more lovely than the Celestials ? I have never before beheld such radiance amongst the wives of Devas, Nagas, Asuras or Apsaras. If she is not already wedded to another, she is worthy of me ! '

"As he delayed, thinking thus, the company left the water and Budha, pondering, emerged therefrom. Thereafter those women having been summoned by him went to his retreat and they paid obeisance to him, whereupon that virtuous ascetic enquired of them, saying :—

" ' To whom does this lady, the most lovely in all the world, belong ? Why has she come here ? Tell me all without hesitation.'

" Hearing these fair words spoken in gentle tones, all those women answered with sweet voices, saying :—

" ' That lady is our mistress, she has no husband and wanders in the woods in our company.'

" Hearing the reply of those women, that Twice-born called to mind the science by which all may be perceived,[2] whereupon he became conversant with all that had passed regarding King Ila, and that foremost of Sages said to those women :—

[1] Budha—The planet Mercury.
[2] The sacred formula of Avartani.

" ' Here on the mountainous region you shall dwell as Kimpurushis ![1] Make your home on this mountain ; you shall feed on roots, leaves and fruits and shall have Kimpurushas as your consorts ! '

"At this command of the son of Soma, those women, who were men, having been transformed into Kimpurushis, took up their abode on the slopes of the mountain."

CHAPTER 89

The Birth of Pururavas

HEARING of the origin of the Kimpurushis, Lakshmana and Bharata both said to Rama, that Lord of Men, " How wonderful ! "

Thereafter the illustrious and virtuous Rama continued the story of Ila, the son of Prajapati, saying :—

" When he saw that all those troops of Kinnaris had departed, the foremost of the Rishis said to the beautiful Ila with a smile :—

" ' I am the beloved son of Soma, O Lady of gracious mien, do thou look on me with favour ! '

" Thus did he speak in that lonely forest deserted by the others, and that gracious and beautiful solitary One answered him, saying :—

" ' O Dear Son of Soma, I range where I will, I am at thy service, do whatsoever pleaseth thee ! '

" Hearing this charming reply, the son of the moon was overjoyed and united himself with her in love. Thereafter the enamoured Budha passed the month of Madhu,[2] that vanished like a moment, in dalliance with Ila, and, the month having expired, that moon-faced one awoke from her couch and beheld the son of Soma given over to the practice of penance in the waters, supportless, his arms upstretched, and said to him :—

" ' O Blessed One, I came to this inaccessible mountain with

---

[1] Kimpurushis—The females of the Kimpurushas, beings who are half human, sometimes identified with the Kinneras.

[2] Madhu—The month that is part of February and March.

my train of attendants, I do not see them anywhere, where have they gone ? '

" Hearing the words of the Rajarishi, who had lost all knowledge of the past, Budha, in order to re-assure him, said in friendly tones :— ·

" 'A great hailstorm overwhelmed thy attendants whilst thou wast asleep, having taken refuge in the hermitage in fear of the wind and rain. Be happy, banish all anxiety and calm thyself ! O Hero, live here in peace, nourishing thyself on fruit and roots.'

" The King, comforted by these words, then made this noble reply, in the distress that the loss of his people caused him :—

" ' I cannot abandon my kingdom, though deprived of my servants ; I must not delay an instant, O Illustrious Ascetic, permit me to depart. I have an elder son fixed in his duty and extremely illustrious, O Brahmin, his name is Shashabindu ; he shall succeed me. Nay, I cannot abandon my consorts and my good servants, O Illustrious Ascetic, do not reproach me.'

" Thus spoke that Indra among monarchs and Budha, who first consoled him, then addressed these astonishing words to him, saying :—

" ' Be pleased to remain here ; do not grieve, O Mighty Kardameya ; at the end of the year I will grant thee a boon.'

" Hearing these words of Budha of imperishable deeds, who was conversant with the Veda, Ila resolved to remain there. The following month, becoming a woman, he spent in dalliance with Budha and, thereafter, becoming a man once more, he passed the time in the exercise of duty. In the ninth month the lovely Ila gave birth to a son, the mighty Pururavas and, after he was born, she gave the child into the paternal hands of Budha, whom he resembled."

CHAPTER 90

Ila regains her natural State through the Performance of the Ashwamedha Sacrifice

RAMA having related the story of the marvellous birth of Pururavas, the illustrious Lakshmana and Bharata enquired of him once more, saying :—

"After Ila had passed a year with the son of the Moon-god, what did she do ? O Lord of the Earth, tell us all ! "

Thus questioned by his two brothers in affectionate tones, Rama continued to relate the story of Ila, the son of Prajapati, and said :—

" That hero, having recovered his manhood, the extremely intelligent and illustrious Budha called together the Sages, the extremely noble Samvarta, Chyavana the son of Bhrigu, the Ascetic Arishtanemi, Pramodana, Modakara and the Hermit Durvasa. When they were all assembled, the eloquent Budha, able to discern the truth, said to those Sages, his friends, who were endowed with great power :—

" ' Learn what has happened to that long-armed king, the son of Kardama, so that his happiness may be re-established !'

" While those Twice-born were conversing thus, Kardama came to that forest accompanied by Poulastya, Kratu, Vashatkara, and Omkara of great effulgence. All those ascetics, happy to find themselves together and wishing to be of service to the Lord of Bahli, each voiced their views about him ; Kardama, however, expressed himself with extreme wisdom for the good of his son, and said :—

" ' O Twice-born Ones, hear what I have to say for the happiness of the prince. I see no remedy apart from the God who has the bull as his emblem. There is no sacrifice greater than the Ashwamedha, which is dear to the heart of the mighty Rudra. Let us therefore perform this mighty sacrifice.'

" Thus spoke Kardama and all the foremost of Sages approved these means of propitiating Rudra.

" Thereafter a Rajarishi, the disciple of Samvarta, the Conqueror of Hostile Citadels, whose name was Marutta, performed that great sacrifice which took place near Budha's hermitage, whereupon the glorious Rudra was extremely gratified and, the ceremony being accomplished, the consort of Uma, in an excess of joy, addressed all those Sages, in Ila's presence, saying :—

" ' I am pleased with your devotion in the Ashwamedha Sacrifice. O Illustrious Brahmins, what shall I do for this King of the Bahlis ? ' Thus did the Lord of the Gods speak, and the Sages, in deep recollection, caused the Lord of the Gods to look upon them with favour so that Ila might regain his manhood. Then Mahadeva, gratified, gave him back his virility and having conferred that favour on Ila, the mighty God disappeared.

" The Horse-sacrifice being complete and Hara having rendered himself invisible, all those Twice-born, of penetrating gaze, returned whence they had come. The king, however, renouncing his capital, founded the city of Pratishthana in the central region, which was unsurpassed in splendour, whilst Shashabindu, that Rajarishi, Conqueror of Hostile Cities, dwelt in Bahli. From that time Pratishthana became the residence of King Ila, the valiant son of Prajapati, and, his time having come, he went to Brahma's abode.

" The son of Ila, the King Pururavas succeeded him in Pratishthana. Such is the merit of the Ashwamedha Sacrifice, O Bull among Men. Ila, who was formerly a woman, became a man again, which would have been impossible by any other means."

CHAPTER 91

Rama gives the command for the Ashwamedha Sacrifice to be performed

HAVING related this history to his two brothers, Kakutstha of immeasurable glory, addressed these pious words to Lakshmana, saying :—

"Assemble for counsel, Vasishtha, Vamadeva, Javali, Kashyapa and all the brahmins learned in the Ashwamedha Sacrifice. O Lakshmana, I shall loose the caparisoned steed in accord with tradition ! "

On this command being communicated to him, Lakshmana, of swift step, assembled all those Sages and ushered them into Rama's presence. When they beheld Rama, who resembled a God, paying obeisance to their feet, they showered blessings upon him. Having performed the Pranjali,[1] Raghava addressed those Sages on the Ashwamedha Sacrifice, in a speech inspired by dharma.

[1] Pranjali—A gesture of respect. See Glossary.

Hearing the words of Rama and having offered homage to the God, whose emblem is the Bull, all those Twice-born praised the Ashwamedha highly, and that eulogy greatly delighted Kakutstha, who seeing them ready to perform the ceremony, said to Lakshmana :—

" O Long-armed Hero, make known to the magnanimous Sugriva that he should come here with his great monkeys and the innumerable dwellers in the woods in order to enjoy this great festival and be happy. Let Bibishana, he who has no rival in valour, come surrounded by his host of Rakshasas, moving where they will, in order to assist me in the great Ashwamedha Sacrifice. Let wealthy monarchs, who wish to render me a service, come in all haste with their retinues to see the place of sacrifice and all the virtuous Twice-born, who have gone to foreign lands, summon them all to the Ashwamedha Sacrifice, O Lakshmana. Invite all the Rishis, those long-armed warriors, mines of asceticism, who live in distant parts with their wives, as also the players on the cymbals, jugglers and dancers.

" Let a vast structure be set up near the Gaumati River in the Naimisha Wood, O Long-armed Warrior, it is pre-eminently a sacred spot. Let propitiatory rites be performed everywhere and hundreds of brahmins, conversant with the law, assist in the Naimisha Wood at this great sacrifice, the highest of all and which is unsurpassed, O Joy of the Raghus. Assemble all the people speedily, O Virtuous Prince, and do not let them depart ill-contented, unsatisfied or without having been loaded with favours according to tradition. O Hero, send out in advance a hundred thousand loads of rice in good condition and an ayuta of sesamum seed and beans as well as chick-peas, lentils, quantities of salt, oil of good quality and innumerable perfumes.

" Let Bharata first carefully furnish a hundred kotis of gold and as much silver, and go before. In the centre, the merchants, all the jugglers, dancers, cooks and women should be ranged, let them be numerous and young in heart ; the troops, however, should go in advance with Bharata. Shopkeepers, children, the aged, the Twice-born in profound meditation, the masons, carpenters, agents and also the mothers and women of the Princes apartments with the golden statue of my consort for consecration, as also skilled sacrificers, should be first assembled by the illustrious Bharata, who will precede them.

" O Prince, he will cause pavilions to be set up worthy of the mighty kings and their suites. Food, drink and raiment should be supplied for those brilliant escorts."

Thereafter Bharata went away followed by Shatrughna and the magnanimous monkeys who surrounded Sugriva, accompanied by the leading priests. Bibishana, at the head of the Rakshasas and women in great numbers, provided an escort for the Rishis of rigid penance.

CHAPTER 92

Description of the Ashwamedha Sacrifice

HAVING arranged everything in detail with dispatch, the elder brother of Bharata loosed the horse marked with black spots, adorned with his own insignia. Placing Lakshmana, assisted by the priests, in charge of the steed, he himself went to the Naimisha Wood with his army.

That long-armed prince, beholding the vast and beautiful sacrificial spot, was greatly delighted and exclaimed, "How wonderful ! " During his sojourn in the Naimisha Wood, the kings brought all their gifts to Rama and he, in his turn, provided for them abundantly with food, drink and provisions of every kind. Bharata and Shatrughna were in the service of the king ; the magnanimous monkeys, who accompanied Sugriva, attended on the priests with humility ; Bibishana with his innumerable titans became the most diligent servitors of those Rishis of rigid penance. Sumptuous pavilions set up for the powerful monarchs and their retinues were under the orders of that most valiant prince. Such were the excellent arrangements devised for the Ashwamedha Sacrifice.

Meantime Lakshmana carefully watched over the comings and goings of the horse. Thus did that magnanimous Lion among monarchs proceed with the utmost punctiliousness in this foremost of sacrifices, during which nothing was heard but ' Give lavishly of all that is sought,' and, in the Ashwamedha

Sacrifice, that liberal Prince furnished all that everyone required till they were fully satisfied. Sweet dishes of every kind, confections, till they were no longer in demand, were distributed by monkeys and titans, and no-one was seen in rags or afflicted or hungry, but, in that splendid royal feast, only those who were happy and satisfied could be observed. Amongst the venerable Sages present, the oldest could not remember a sacrifice where such prodigious liberality had taken place.

Those who desired gold received gold, those who preferred possessions received them, those who coveted jewels had jewels bestowed upon them ; and one beheld silver, gold, gems and raiment being distributed continually in great quantities.

' Neither Shakra, nor Soma, nor Yama, nor Varuna have ever achieved anything of such magnitude ' proclaimed the ascetics ; and, on every side, monkeys and titans stood distributing raiment, silver and rice in profusion to those who sought them.

This sacrifice of that foremost of monarchs was carried out in accord with every tradition and, at the end of a whole year, it still had not come to a close, nor was the treasury exhausted.

CHAPTER 93

Valmiki commands Kusha and Lava to recite the Ramayana

As this most wonderful sacrifice was proceeding, the disciples of Valmiki, that blessed Sage, suddenly came there and, having witnessed the divine festival, admirable to behold, that company of Rishis constructed some comfortable huts a little way off. Innumerable bullock carts full of provisions, with excellent fruit and roots were heaped in Valmiki's charming grove, and thereafter that Sage said to his disciples, Kusha and Lava :—

" Go, and with great enthusiasm sing the Epic Ramayana, cheerfully and carefully, in the sacred enclosures of the Rishis, the dwellings of the brahmins, along the roads and highways and in the residence of princes, and especially it should be sung at the gate of Rama's pavilion, where the sacrifice is taking place and also before the priests.

" Here are savoury fruits of every kind that grow in the

mountainous regions, eat and then sing. You will not experience any fatigue, O Dear Ones, on account of these roots and succulent fruits that will preserve the purity of your voices. If Rama, the Lord of the Earth, indicates that you should be heard by the assembled Sages, act accordingly. Each time you will have twenty Sargas[1] to sing, which you have previously learnt from me. Above all, do not entertain the least desire for reward ! Of what use is gold to ascetics who live on fruit and roots ? If Kakutstha questions you, saying ' Who is your Master ? ' answer the king in this wise, ' We are both the disciples of the great Sage Valmiki ! ' Sing without fear to the accompaniment of these stringed instruments of a tone unknown heretofore, that you have tuned sweetly. Sing the poem from the beginning without showing any lack of respect to the king, who is the Father of all beings according to the law.

" To-morrow therefore, at dawn, with a cheerful heart and taking care to sing with sweet voices, accompany yourselves on these stringed instruments of harmonized intervals."

Having repeatedly issued these instructions, that ascetic born of Pracetas,[2] of noble birth, the illustrious Sage Valmiki, became silent.

On receiving the commands of that Sage, the two sons of Maithili humbly answered " We will act in accord with thy behests ! " and those Conquerors of Hostile Cities then took their leave.

Those youthful boys allowed the excellent counsels of the Rishi to enter their hearts, as the Ashwins receive the teachings of Bhargava and, eager to put them into practice, they whiled away that auspicious night.

CHAPTER 94

Kusha and Lava chant the Ramayana

WHEN the dawn appeared, those two youthful ascetics, having bathed and ignited the sacred fire, began to sing, as the Rishi had previously instructed them to do.

[1] Sargas—Chapters or divisions.
[2] Pracetas—A name of the God Varuna.

Kakutstha listened to that poem, composed by the aged Valmiki, unheard till then, set to music in multiple cadences, accompanied by stringed instruments, in measured rhythm, and, hearing those youthful musicians, Raghava was greatly mystified.

During an interval in the sacrifice, that foremost of monarchs called together the great Sages, Kings, Pundits, Naigamas,[1] aged Grammarians, venerable brahmins and those versed in music, the Twice-born, those learned in omens and the citizens specially instructed in aesthetics, those who had knowledge of metres, words and accents, those who knew the different rhythms and measures, those versed in astronomy, those skilled in the science of sacrifices and rituals and experienced liturgists, those versed in discerning cause and effect, philosophers, scholars, teachers of hymns and legends and the Veda, those conversant with the Vrittas and Sutras, and also singers and dancers.

Thereafter, having assembled them all, Rama ushered in the two singers to that vast and murmuring throng of listeners for his own great pleasure. The two youthful disciples of the Sage began that recitation that unrolled melodiously, like unto the singing of the Gandharvas, nor could the company be sated with listening to so beautiful a song. In their delight, ascetics and great potentates, seemed to consume those musicians with their gaze, whom they looked upon again and again, and the whole assembly having centred its attention upon them, each said to his neighbour :—' Both resemble Rama, like twin representations of the same planet. If they did not wear matted locks and bark robes, we should see no difference between the singers and Raghava ! '

As the people of town and country spoke thus, Kusha and Lava, having introduced the first part according to Narada's instructions, continued up to the twentieth Sarga[2] during the afternoon, then Raghava, having heard the twenty Sargas, said to his beloved brother, " Give these two musicians eighteen thousand gold pieces immediately with aught else that they may desire, O Kakutstha ! "[3] Thereupon Saumitri instantly offered

[1] Naigamas-Interpreters of the Veda.
[2] Chapter.
[3] This title being used for Lakshmana also.

this to those youthful boys, one after the other, but the great-souled Kusha and Lava would not accept the gold that was presented to them, enquiring in astonishment, " What good is this ? Grain, fruit and roots suffice ascetics like ourselves, what should we do with gold or silver in the forest ? "

These words amazed all Rama's assistants extremely and, desiring to know the origin of the poem, that illustrious prince enquired of those two disciples of the ascetic, saying :—

" What is this poetical composition ? Where is the residence of the sublime author of this great epic ? Where is this bull among the ascetics ? "

On this enquiry from Raghava, the two disciples of the Sage answered, saying :—

" The blessed Valmiki, who is attending the sacrifice, is the author of the poem in which thine whole life is told. Twenty-four thousand verses and a hundred Upakhyanas[1] have been used by that ascetic, the son of Bhrigu.[2] Five hundred Sargas divided into six Kandas, together with the Uttarakanda, O King, are the work of that magnanimous Rishi, our Guru. Thy conduct, thy circumstances, thine entire life is unrolled with its vicissitudes. If thou desirest it, O King, thou mayest hear it from us in the intervals of the sacrifice, in thy moments of leisure.

Thereafter Rama, accompanied by the Sages and magnanimous monarchs, having heard that melodious chant, returned to the sacrificial pavilion.

That recitation accompanied by Talas and Layas,[3] divided into Sargas in harmonious notes and tones, in which the scansion was stressed by the stringed instruments, was heard by the King from the lips of Kusha and Lava.

CHAPTER 95

Rama sends for Sita

SURROUNDED by the ascetics, kings and monkeys, Rama listened during many days to the sublime and wonderful epic, and while

[1] Upakhyanas—Episodes or Tales.
[2] Really in the line of Bhrigu.
[3] Talas and Layas—Musical modes.

the two sons of Sita, Kusha and Lava, were singing, he recognized them. Having reflected deeply, he summoned messengers of virtuous conduct and in the assembly spoke to them of that princess, saying :—

" Go and repeat my words to that Blessed One and say :—

" ' If she be irreproachable in her conduct and without sin, then, should she so desire it and has the approval of the Rishi, let her prove her good faith ! ' Do you then return and inform me concerning this matter. To-morrow at dawn, let Maithili, the daughter of Janaka attest her purity on oath in my presence, before the assembly ! "

At this extremely significant command from Raghava, the messengers straightway went to seek out the foremost of the ascetics and, bowing to that Sage, who shone with infinite effulgence, they, with humility, communicated Rama's words to him.

Hearing them, the extremely illustrious ascetic, learning of Rama's wish, said " Be it so ! May prosperity attend you ! "

Thereafter those royal messengers returned with the Muni's answer and repeated it faithfully to Raghava and he, being informed of the decision of that magnanimous Sage, full of joy, addressed the Rishis and the assembled kings, saying :—

" O Blessed Ones, with your disciples, the kings and their attendants and whosoever may wish to do so, bear witness to the vow that Sita will make ! "

These words of the magnanimous Raghava were praised by all the leading Rishis and those mighty kings who addressed the monarch saying :—

" Such conduct is only possible in Thee and is found nowhere else in the world, O Prince ! "

Having resolved thus, Raghava, the Scourge of his Foes, said :—

" To-morrow this shall take place," whereupon he dismissed the assembly.

The trial by oath being fixed for the following day, the magnanimous and illustrious Rama gave leave to all the great Sages and Kings to depart.

CHAPTER 96

Valmiki leads Sita before Rama

WHEN the night had passed, the great descendant of Raghu went to the place of sacrifice to which he had summoned all the Rishis : Vasishtha, Vamadeva, Javali, Kashyapa, Vishvamitra, Dirghatmas and Durvasa of rigid penances, also Poulastya and Shakti, Bhargava, Vamana, Markandeya, Dhirghayus and the highly renowned Maudgalya, Garga, Chyavana, the virtuous Shatananda, the far-famed Bharadwaja, the illustrious Agniputra, Narada, Parvata and Gautama of great glory, all these ascetics and others of austere observances, in great numbers.

Inspired by curiosity, they all assembled, as also the intrepid titans ; and the valiant monkeys and kings, intrigued, gathered there in like manner, with the warriors, merchants and thousands of the lower caste. Brahmins of rigid penances arrived from every region and all met together to be present at the taking of the oath by Sita ; and that immense multitude stood absolutely motionless, as if turned to stone.

Knowing that all were come, the foremost of Sages immediately approached with Sita following him, her head bowed, her palms joined, choked with sobs, her mind absorbed in Rama.

Beholding Sita walking behind Valmiki, like unto the holy Shruti following in Brahma's footsteps, there arose a great clamour with cries of " Halahala ! " from all those who were oppressed with profound sorrow on account of the unfortunate princess. And some cried " Hail, O Rama ! " and some " Hail, O Sita ! " while the rest acclaimed both. Thereafter, advancing amidst that multitude, the foremost of the ascetics, accompanied by Sita, addressed Raghava, saying :—

" I am Valmiki, and here, O Dasarathi, is Sita of virtuous ways and conduct, who, on account of calumny, was abandoned near mine hermitage, the censure of the people having inspired thee with fear, O Virtuous One ! Sita will prove her innocence ; it is for thee to issue the command. These two sons of Janaki, twin brothers, invincible heroes, are thy sons also ; I speak the truth to thee ! I am the tenth son of Pracetas, O Joy of the Raghus, I do not recollect ever having uttered a lie ; truly these are thy two children. During countless years I have practised asceticism, may I never reap the fruits thereof if Maithili be guilty ! I have nothing wherewith to reproach myself regarding thought, word or deed ; if Maithili be guilty, may I never gather the fruits thereof ! With my five senses and the mind as the sixth, meditating amidst the forest waterfalls, Sita's innocence was revealed to me. That lady of irreproachable and pure conduct, to whom her lord is a God, will give proof of her good faith, O Thou who didst fear public condemnation ! O Foremost of Men, here is that lady whom I proclaim to be essentially chaste, I whose vision is divinely illumined and who, though she was supremely dear to thee and her innocence well known, thou didst repudiate when thy spirit was troubled by the censure of the people ! "

CHAPTER 97

Sita descends into the Earth

THUS spoke Valmiki, and Raghava, on seeing that fair-complexioned princess, with joined palms, answered in the presence of the assembly :—

" O Fortunate and virtuous Brahmin, may it be so ! I fully concur in thine irreproachable words. This assurance was formerly given to me by Vaidehi in the presence of the Gods and, believing in that oath, I reinstated her in my house, but great indeed was the public condemnation, therefore I sent Maithili away. O Brahmin, though wholly convinced of her innocence, it was from fear of the people that I cast off Sita, do thou pardon me ! I acknowledge these twins, Kusha and Lava, to be my sons ! I desire to make my peace with the chaste Maithili amidst the assembly."

Hearing of his intention, the foremost of the Gods, led by Brahma, all assembled there to witness Sita's defence, and Adityas, Vasus, Rudras, Vishvadevas, the hosts of the Maruts and all the great Rishis, Nagas, Sadhyas, Suparnas and Siddhas gathered with delight. Beholding the Gods and the Sages, the foremost of men, Raghava, once more affirmed : " I am in agreement with the irreproachable words of the Rishi Valmiki ! I wish to be reconciled with the chaste Vaidehi in the presence of this assembly."

The defence of Sita filled all who witnessed it with emotion and, at that moment, Vayu, the foremost of the Gods, sent forth a pure and fragrant breeze to the great delight of the assembly, as formerly in the Golden Age, and, it appeared marvellous to all those people from many lands who experienced it !

Beholding that assembly, Sita, attired in a yellow robe, with joined palms, her head bowed, her eyes lowered, said :—

" If, in thought, I have never dwelt on any but Rama, may the Goddess Madhavi[1] receive me ! "

As Vaidehi was still speaking, a miracle took place and, from the earth rose a marvellous celestial throne supported on the heads of Nagas of immeasurable power, their bodies adorned with divine gems. The Goddess Dharani, bidding her welcome, took Maithili in her arms, causing her to be seated on that celestial seat and, while she occupied the throne, a shower of blossoms fell without ceasing from the sky. Then the Gods burst into loud acclamations, crying " Excellent ! Excellent ! O Sita, thy virtue is supreme ! "

From the heavens, the Gods, with delighted hearts, beholding Sita descend into the earth, praised her again and again, and at the place of sacrifice, where all were assembled, Sages, kings and the foremost of men were unable to recover from their astonishment. In the sky, on earth and in the nether regions, all beings, animate and inanimate, Danavas of vast stature and the foremost of the Pannagas cried out in delight, whilst others remained absorbed in their thoughts or gazed on Rama and on Sita in ecstasy. The entire assembly witnessed Sita's descent into the earth and, at that moment, a great tremor passed through the whole world.

---

[1] The Earth Goddess, also called Dharani.

CHAPTER 98

Rama's Anger and Grief, Brahma appeases him

WHEN Vaidehi had descended into the earth, all the monkeys
and Sages cried out in Rama's presence, " Excellent ! Excellent"
but Rama, deeply distressed, supporting himself on a staff
employed in the sacrifice, his eyes veiled with tears, his head
bowed, was overcome with grief. Sighing again and again,
letting fall many tears, a prey to pain and wrath, he said :—

" Beholding Sita, the personification of Shri, vanish in my
presence, my soul experiences an agony hitherto unknown.
Formerly, when she was in Lanka, on the further side of the
vast ocean, I brought her back, how much more easily shall I
be able to wrest her from the bosom of the earth ! O Goddess
Vasuda, give me back my Sita, whom thou retainest, or thou
shalt witness my wrath ! Thou shouldst know me since thou
art assuredly my mother-in-law and Maithili rose from thee
when Janaka was following the plough. Therefore let Sita go or
open thyself to me that I may dwell with her in Patala or else in
Nakaprishtha ! Bring back Maithili on whose account I am
distraught ! If thou failest to return Sita to me in her original
form, I shall plough thee up with thy mountains and forests and
shall destroy thee so that nothing but water remains ! "

Thus spoke Kakutstha, full of wrath and grief, and Brahma,
accompanied by the Hosts of the Gods, addressed the son of
Raghu, saying :—

" O Rama, virtuous Rama, do not be incensed, recollect thy
divine origin and nature, O Scourge of Thy Foes ! Assuredly,
O Prince, I do not need to remind thee that no-one is superior
to thee ! Now recall that thou art Vishnu, O Invincible Hero !
The chaste and virtuous Sita, who was wholly absorbed in thee
formerly, has happily reached the region of the Nagas, by virtue
of her ascetic practices. Thou wilt undoubtedly be re-united
with her in the Celestial Realm. O Rama, hear, in the assembly,
what I relate in this poem, the most beautiful of epics, recited in
thine honour, I will make all known to thee in detail, do not

doubt it. In this poem of Valmiki all is included from the time of thy birth, O Hero, the good and evil that has visited thee and what will happen in the future. That great poet, O Rama, is wholly devoted to thee, none other is worthy of the honour bestowed by poets save Raghava. Formerly, in company with the Gods, I heard the entire classic ; it is divine, marvellously beautiful, true, and the remover of nescience. O Foremost of Men, O Supremely Virtuous Kakutstha, listen to the conclusion of the Ramayana and what concerns the future. Listen now with the Rishis, O Doughty and Illustrious Prince, to the end of this sublime poem entitled 'Uttara'. Assuredly, O Kakutstha, this excellent epilogue may not be heard by any other save thee, who art the supreme Sage, O Hero, O Joy of the House of Raghu."

Having spoken thus, Brahma, the Lord of the Three Worlds, returned to his abode with his followers, the Gods.

Meantime the magnanimous and high-souled Rishis, whose abode was Brahmaloka, at Brahma's command, remained, desirous of hearing 'Uttara kanda' and what should happen to Raghava.

Having listened to the significant words of that God of Gods, the illustrious Rama said to Valmiki :—

" O Blessed One, the Rishis of Brahmaloka desire to listen to ' Uttara kanda ' and all that shall happen to me; to-morrow let it be narrated by thee ! "

Having resolved thus, Rama sought out Kusha and Lava and, dismissing the company, returned with them to the leaf-thatched hut of the Rishi Valmiki, where he passed the night lamenting for Sita.

CHAPTER 99

The Death of the Queens

WHEN night had given way to dawn, Rama called together the great ascetics and said to his two sons :—

" Now sing without anxiety," and when those great and magnanimous Sages were seated, Kusha and Lava sang the epilogue to the 'Ramayana.'

Sita, having re-entered the earth, thus proving her fidelity, and the sacrifice being completed, Rama, in the extremity of grief, not beholding Vaidehi, regarded the world as a desert, and he dismissed the kings, bears, monkeys and titans and the host of leading brahmins, having loaded them with treasure.

Taking leave of them, the lotus-eyed Rama, who was ever absorbed in the thought of Sita, returned to Ayodhya. The Joy of the House of Raghu never sought another consort but, in every sacrifice, he set up a golden image of Janaki in her stead. For ten thousand years, Rama performed the Vajamedha Sacrifice and the Vajapeya, ten times more, distributing quantities of gold, and that fortunate One also performed the Agnisthoma, Atiratra and Gosava Sacrifices, giving away abundant charity.

For a long time, the magnanimous Raghava occupied the throne, his heart fixed in his duty ; bears, monkeys and titans were subject to his rule and monarchs came daily to pay him homage. Parjanya sent rains in the proper season and it was abundant, the skies were clear, the regions sinless, the city and country abounding in cheerful and satisfied people. None died prematurely nor was there any disease, and in Rama's reign, none were destitute.

After many years however, Rama's aged mother, surrounded by her sons and grandsons, passed away and she was followed by Sumitra and the renowned Kaikeyi, who having performed many righteous acts went to the celestial region, where those happy Ones were re-united with Dasaratha and received the fruit of their merit in heaven.

From time to time, in memory of his mother, Raghava distributed gifts to the brahmins vowed to asceticism, and the virtuous Rama offered up obsequies accompanied by gifts of gems to the Sages and performed incomparable austerities in honour of his ancestors.

Thus thousands of years passed happily during which, with the aid of sacrifices, that prince promoted the execution of duty in all its aspects.

CHAPTER 100

Rama sends Bharata to conquer the Gandharvas

ONE day, Yudhajita, the King of Kaikaya, sent his spiritual Preceptor, Gargya, the son of Angiras, a Brahmarishi of immeasurable glory, to the magnanimous Raghava, with ten thousand horses as a token of his unsurpassed affection, and also carpets, gems, diverse splendid stuffs and brilliant ornaments ; such were the gifts bestowed on Rama by that monarch.

Hearing of the arrival of that great Rishi Gargya with those magnificent presents from Ashwapati, his maternal uncle, the virtuous Raghava went out with his suite to meet him to the distance of a mile, and he offered homage to him, as Shakra pays obeisance to Brihaspati.

Having paid salutations to the Rishi and accepted the gifts, he enquired of him fully regarding the welfare of his mother's brother and family. Ushering the blessed Rishi into his palace, Rama began to question him, saying :—

" What message has my uncle confided to thee in sending thee hither ? "

Having come there, that great Rishi, hearing Rama's words, unfolded his mission in eloquent terms, saying :—

" This, O Long-armed Hero, is what thy maternal uncle, Yudhajita, in his affection for thee, requests thee to hear. There is a country of the Gandharvas, rich in fruit and roots, situated on the banks of the Sindhu River ; that country is extremely fertile. The Gandharvas, armed and skilful warriors, defend it. When thou hast conquered them, O Virtuous Kakutstha and destroyed their magnificent citadels, take possession of their cities, which are well constructed. None other can achieve this ; the country is extremely beautiful ; do thou follow my counsel, it is to thine advantage."

This speech of his uncle's, conveyed by the great Rishi, pleased Raghava who replied " So be it ! " and he glanced at Bharata ; thereafter, delighted, Raghava, with joined palms, spoke again to that Twice-born, saying :—

" These two youthful princes will explore the country, O

621

Brahmarishi! Bharata is the father of these valiant youths, Taksha and Pushkala. Under the protection of my uncle, they will show themselves to be devoted in the discharge of their duty. With Bharata at their head, those two youthful princes, accompanied by their troops, will slay the sons of the Gandharvas and take possession of the two cities. Having subdued those two great capitals and installed his two sons, my very virtuous brother will return once more."

Thus did Rama speak to that Brahmarishi, and thereafter issued orders to Bharata to start out with his army, having first installed those youthful princes.

Under the constellation Saumya,[1] preceded by the son of Angiras, Bharata set out with his troops and his two sons, and it seemed as if that army, leaving Ayodhya, followed to a great distance by Raghava, could not have been approached even by the Gods themselves. Then those beings who live on flesh, and titans of colossal stature, followed in Bharata's train, thirsting for blood, and the redoubtable Bhutagramas, in their desire to devour the corpses of the Gandharvas, came in hundreds and thousands, and lions, tigers, boars and birds in countless numbers preceded the troops. In a month and a half, that army composed of cheerful and healthy warriors reached the Kingdom of Kaikeya.

CHAPTER 101

The slaying of the Gandharvas and the conquest of their Country

HEARING of the arrival of Bharata at the head of a vast army accompanied by Gargya, the King of the Kaikeyas, Yudhajita, experienced supreme joy and set out in all haste with a great company against the Gandharvas.

Bharata and Yudhajita, having joined forces, approached the City of the Gandharvas with their swift troops and followers, whereupon, learning of the invasion, the Gandharvas assembled, eager for combat, full of vigour and shouting on every side.

Then a terrible battle of appalling violence ensued, lasting seven days, without victory being decisive for either army.

[1] The planet Mercury.

Rivers of blood, floating with corpses, streamed on every side, scimitars and spears being the crocodiles. Thereafter Bharata, the younger brother of Rama, enraged, loosed a terrible shaft propelled by mantras, named Samvarta,[1] on the Gandharvas. Caught in the noose of destruction, three hundred thousand Gandharvas were slain in an instant, cut to pieces by that hero. The inhabitants of the Celestial Region were unable to remember such a fearful conflict in which, in the twinkling of an eye, so vast a number of warriors perished.

The Gandharvas all being slain, Bharata, the son of Kaikeyi entered those two opulent and magnificent cities, and there, Bharata established Taksha in Takshashila and Pushkala in Pushkalavata, in the country of the Gandharvas, in the ravishing region of Gandhara. Overflowing with treasure and precious gems, adorned with groves, they seemed to vie with each other in magnificence.

For five years the long-armed Bharata, son of Kaikeyi, occupied those capitals of supreme beauty, whose inhabitants were of irreproachable conduct, and thereafter he returned to Ayodhya. Those cities with their innumerable parks, filled with vehicles and well-stocked markets, enchanting beyond imagining, were embellished by fabulous buildings and countless palaces, resplendent with a multitude of magnificent temples and adorned with Tala, Tamala, Tilaka, and Bakula Trees.

Then the fortunate Bharata paid obeisance to the magnanimous Raghava, who was Dharma personified, as Vasava offers salutations to Brahma, and Raghava listened with satisfaction when Bharata told him of the total extermination of the Gandharvas which had taken place and of the occupation of their territory.

CHAPTER 102

Rama bestows Kingdoms on Lakshmana's Sons

HEARING those tidings, Rama with his brothers rejoiced and he uttered these memorable words in their presence :—

" Thy two youthful sons, Angada and Chandraketu, are

---

[1] Samvarta—A weapon with which Kala or Time destroys the worlds.

worthy to reign, O Saumitri, for they are strong and energetic ,
I shall install them both as kings ! Come, find these two valiant
Ones a pleasant region which is not confined, where there is no
danger of treachery from hostile monarchs, where they may live
at ease and where the ascetics' retreats are not despoiled! O
Friend, seek out such a country without causing injury to any ! "

Thus spoke Rama, and Bharata answered :—

" There is a charming and healthy region named Karupatta ;
let two cities that are salubrious and beautiful be established
there for the magnanimous Angada and Chandraketu which
shall be called Angadiya and Chandrakanta."

These words of Bharata were approved by Raghava, and he
brought that country under his rule and established Angada
therein. The City of Angadiya was built for Angada by Rama of
imperishable deeds and it was splendid and well fortified. As
for Chandraketu, who was a giant, his uncle built Chandrakanta
for him in the country of the Mallas,[1] and that capital was
celestial and equal to Amaravati.

Thereafter, greatly delighted, Rama, Lakshmana and Bharata,
those invincible warriors, attended the installation of those two
youthful princes who, having received the divine unction, fixed
in their duty, divided the territory, and Angada had the western
and Chandraketu the northern region. Angada was accompanied
by Sumitra's son,[2] whilst Lakshmana and Bharata followed in
Chandraketu's train.

His sons being firmly established on the throne, Lakshmana
took the road back to Ayodhya, having sojourned in Angadiya
for a year. On his side, Bharata remained with Chandraketu
one year more, thereafter returning to Ayodhya to take up his
place again at Rama's feet.

Both Saumitri and Bharata, in their love for him and their
extreme piety, forgot that time was passing and thus ten thousand
years went by while they devoted themselves to affairs of state.
Employing their days in this wise, their hearts satisfied, surrounded with splendour, dwelling together in that righteous
city, they resembled the Three Fires whose flames are fed with
abundant libations amidst great solemnity.

[1] Mallas—Giants.
[2] Shatrughna.

CHAPTER 103

Death is sent to seek out Rama

AFTER a long time, Death, in the form of an ascetic, presented himself at the gates of the great and virtuous Rama and said :—

" I am a messenger from an all-powerful Maharishi and have come to see Rama on a matter of great importance."

Hearing these words, Saumitri hastened to announce the arrival of the ascetic to Rama, saying :—

" Mayest thou extend thy dominion over both worlds, O Illustrious Prince ! A Messenger has come to see thee, who, by virtue of his penances, is as radiant as the sun."

Hearing Lakshmana's words, Rama said :—

" Bring in that ascetic of great effulgence, who carries a message from his master, O Dear Brother ! "

Then Saumitri answered : " Be it so ! " and ushered in that Sage, flaming in splendour, surrounded as it were with burning rays. Approaching the foremost of the Raghus, who shone in his own effulgence, the Rishi, in an harmonious voice, addressed Raghava, saying :—" May felicity be thine ! "

Then the supremely illustrious Rama, having paid him the traditional homage and offered him the Arghya, enquired of him concerning his state. Having informed Rama of his well-being, the most skilled of orators, that illustrious ascetic seated himself on a golden throne and thereafter Rama said to him :—

" Be thou welcome, O Great Sage, what message hast thou for me, since thou dost come as an ambassador ? "

On this enquiry from that Lion among Men, the Sage said to him :—

" If thou dost revere the wishes of the Gods, this meeting must take place between us alone ; whoever shall overhear us should be put to death by thee ; the words of the Lord of the Ascetics are secret and should be revered by Thee."

" Be it so ! " replied Rama, and having given this assurance, he issued the following command to Lakshmana :—

" Do thou stand at the door, O Long-armed Warrior and

dismiss the door-keeper. It is for me to slay whoever hears the converse between this Muni and myself, for it must take place between us alone."

Having sent Lakshmana to guard the door, Kakutstha, born of Raghu, said :—

" O Ascetic, thou canst now disclose that with which thou hast been charged, speak without fear, I shall treasure it in my heart !"

CHAPTER 104

Death delivers his Message

" LEARN, O Magnanimous Sovereign, that this is the purpose of my coming ! It is the blessed Grandsire who has sent me, O Mighty Prince. I was his son in a former existence, O Conqueror of Hostile Citadels ! Born of Maya, O Hero, I am Death who destroys all ! The Grandsire, Lord of the Worlds, speaks thus to thee :—

" ' Thy task is accomplished, O Friend, O Protector of the Worlds ! Having formerly destroyed all beings by the aid of Maya, lying amidst the waters of the vast ocean, thou didst give me birth. Thou hadst already created the Serpent of large coils, Ananta, as also two mighty Beings, Madhu and Kaitabha, whose crushed bones covered the earth which appeared at that time with its chain of mountains. From a celestial lotus, bright as the sun, that issued from thy navel, thou didst produce me and give me the task of creating the world. Since thou hast charged me with this burden, I lean on thee for support, O Lord of the Earth ! Do thou watch over all beings, for it is thou who art my strength. By virtue of thine invincible and eternal nature, thou shouldst afford protection to all creation, for thou hast assumed the form of Vishnu ! O Mighty Son of Aditi, thou didst enhance the power of thy brothers and when they sought to accomplish their tasks, thou didst come to their aid. When, O Prince, all creatures were being exterminated by Ravana, thou, desiring to slay him, bethought thyself of men. Then thou didst resolve to dwell among them in person for eleven thousand years and thereafter return to us. Thou, who art mind-born, hast completed thy stay among mortals; it is the hour, O Foremost of Men, to return to us ; if it is thy desire to prolong thy sojourn among creatures, O Great King, do so and be happy ! '

" Such are the words of the Grandsire :—' If thou preferest to enter into possession of the world of the Gods once more, O Raghava, they with their leaders will be freed from all anxiety, since Vishnu will be amongst them.' "

Having heard the words of the Grandsire, which Death communicated to him, Raghava, smiling, answered the Destroyer of the Worlds, saying :—

" These wholly admirable words of that God of Gods assuredly causes me supreme delight, as also thy coming hither. I came for the good of the worlds, this is the purpose of my being ; mayest thou be happy ! Thine advent here has moved my heart ; I shall leave without delay. The Grandsire has uttered what is true, I must attend to all that concerns the Gods under my dominion, O Destroyer of the Universe ! "

CHAPTER 105

The Sage Durvasa comes to visit Rama

As the two were conversing thus, Durvasa, that blessed Sage, who wished to see Rama, came to the gate of the palace and, approaching Saumitri, that illustrious ascetic said :—

" Bring me straightway into Rama's presence, the affair is urgent ! "

So spoke the magnanimous Sage, and Lakshmana, the Slayer of His Foes, bowing low, said to him :—

" What is this matter ? Explain thyself, O Blessed Sage! What can I do for thee ? Raghava is occupied, O Brahmin, have patience awhile ! "

Hearing this reply from that lion among men, the great Rishi, highly incensed, said to Lakshmana, whom he seemed to consume with his glance :—

"Announce my presence here to Rama immediately, O

Saumitri, or I shall pronounce a curse on the kingdom, on thee, the city, on Raghava, Bharata and on thy House ! O Saumitri, I can no longer contain mine indignation ! "

Having heard the mighty ascetic's alarming words, Lakshmana pondered awhile within himself concerning their significance, and reflected :—

" It were better that I should perish than all others be destroyed ! "

On this, he made the arrival of the ascetic known to Raghava and, Rama hearing the tidings, took leave of Death and, in all haste, sought out the son of Atri. Having paid obeisance with joined palms to that great Sage flaming in effulgence, he enquired of him, saying :—

" What may I do for thee ? "

On this enquiry from that King of Ascetics, the Sage Durvasa answered :—

" O Virtuous Rama, hear me, this day I have concluded a fast of a thousand years. O Irreproachable Raghava, now give me what thou hast ready to eat ! "

At these words, the King Raghava, with a delighted heart, offered the foremost of Sages dishes, that had been made ready, and that ascetic, having partaken of that food like unto Amrita, addressed Rama, saying :—

" It is well ! " and returned to his hermitage.

Thereafter Rama called to mind the words of Death at that portentous meeting and, with bowed head, his heart wrung with anguish, he was unable to speak. Reflecting again and again within himself, the illustrious Raghava thought, "All is lost ! " and fell silent.

CHAPTER 106

Rama banishes Lakshmana

SEEING Rama, his head bowed, afflicted and like unto the moon in eclipse, Lakshmana spoke to him in cheerful and affectionate tones, saying :—

" Thou shouldst not grieve on mine account, O Long-armed

Warrior; thus was it already ordained and has its roots in a past cause! Slay me without hesitation, be faithful to thy vow! Those who do not honour their promise, go to hell! If thou hast any affection for me, O Great King, and dost find any merit in me, then slay me and fulfil the law, O Raghava!"

Thus spoke Lakshmana, and Rama, his mind troubled, called his ministers and priests together and told them what had taken place, of the arrival of Durvasa and the vow he had made to the Ascetic. When they had heard these things, the ministers and brahmins became silent, nevertheless the illustrious Vasishtha spoke thus:—

"O Long-armed Prince, I perceive that the separation from Lakshmana is for thee a calamity, causing thy hair to stand on end. O Illustrious Rama, do thou abandon him; death is powerful, let not thy words prove false. When a promise is not honoured and virtue is destroyed, undoubtedly the Three Worlds with all animate and inanimate beings, with the hosts of the Gods and Rishis, perish! Therefore, O Lion among Men, in order to save the Three Worlds and assure the continuance of the universe, banish Lakshmana!"

Hearing these words, which were in accord with duty and righteousness, approved by all, Rama, in the midst of the assembly, said to Lakshmana:—

"Lest righteousness should perish, I banish thee, O Saumitri, a sentence of banishment or death is the same to men of honour!"

At this decree of Rama's, Lakshmana, weeping, his mind distracted, departed in all haste without returning to his home.

Having reached the banks of the Sarayu River, he performed his ablutions and, with joined palms, closing the doors of the senses, he began to meditate. As he was thus restraining his senses, he did not release his breath while given up to contemplation, and the Gods with their leaders, the troops of Apsaras and companies of Rishis covered him with a rain of flowers. Becoming invisible to men, the mighty Lakshmana was borne away in the body by Shakra, who carried him to the Celestial Region. Beholding the fourth part of Vishnu entering heaven, the foremost of the Gods, delighted, joyfully and unitedly offered homage to that descendant of Raghu.

CHAPTER 107

Rama installs Kusha and Lava on the Throne

HAVING banished Lakshmana, Rama, a prey to grief and desolation, said to his priests, ministers and citizens :—

" To-day I shall give the royal annointing to the valiant Bharata, who is faithful to his duty, and make him Lord of Ayodhya ; thereafter I shall go to the forest. Make all preparations, lose no time, for to-day I too shall follow the path that Lakshmana has taken ! "

Thus spoke Raghava and his subjects bowed low as if deprived of all strength. On his side, Bharata, beside himself on hearing his brother's speech, refused the crown and expressed himself thus :—

" I swear in truth, O King, without thee I do not wish to reign, even in Svarga, O Thou, the Joy of the Raghus ! Establish thy two sons, the valiant Kusha and Lava in the Southern Koshalas and the Northern Regions; send swift messengers to Shatrughna to announce our departure, let there be no delay!"

Hearing these words of Bharata and also beholding the citizens who, their heads bowed, were overwhelmed with grief, Vasishtha spoke :—

" O Beloved Rama, see how these people are prostrating themselves, having learnt what they desire, fulfill it, do not grieve them ! "

Thus spoke Vasishtha and Kakutstha, having caused them to rise, said to the people, " What is asked of me ? " and they all said to him :—

" If thou art leaving us, let us accompany thee wheresoever thou goest, O Rama ; if thou dost love thy subjects and that affection is unsurpassed, let us, with our sons and wives, follow the righteous path with thee ; whether it be to an inaccessible retreat, river or ocean, thou shouldst not abandon us ; lead us all wherever thou wilt, O Thou our Master ! This is our supreme desire, our most cherished wish ; it will always be the delight of our hearts to accompany thee, O Prince ! "

Recognizing his people's profound attachment, Rama answered, " So be it ! " and occupied himself in carrying through what he had undertaken that day.

He gave over the Southern Koshalas to the valiant Kusha and those of the north to Lava ; thereafter, placing those two princes on his lap, he enthroned them in Ayodhya and bestowed upon them thousands of chariots and numberless elephants with ten thousand horses. Having furnished them with jewels and treasure in abundance and given them cheerful and healthy people to attend upon them, he sent the two brothers, Kusha and Lava, each to his own capital.

Those two heroes being installed in their respective cities, Rama sent out an emissary to the magnanimous Shatrughna.

CHAPTER 108

Rama issues his last Commands

THE messengers, urged on by Rama's command, swiftly and promptly went to Madhura without halting on the way. After three nights they reached that city where they all informed Shatrughna what had happened ; the banishing of Lakshmana, Raghava's vow, the installation of his two sons and the resolution of his subjects to follow him ; how an enchanting city had been built for Kusha under the name of Kushavati on the high ridge of the Vindhya Mountains by the virtuous Rama, and that Shravasti was the name of the ravishing and famous capital of Lava ; they told him also of the preparations made by Raghava and Bharata to take all the people from Ayodhya and enter Svarga.

Having related all these things to the magnanimous Shatrughna, the messengers became silent and thereafter added, " Make all haste, O King ! "

Hearing these fearful tidings regarding the imminent destruction of his entire House, Shatrughna, the Joy of Raghu, called his people together and summoned his family priest, Kanchana, in order to impart the truth to them of his immediate departure with his brothers.

Thereafter, that valiant prince installed his two sons, having distributed abundant wealth equally amongst them, and Subahu was established in Madhura and Shatrughatin in Vaidisha. This being accomplished, that descendant of Raghu left for Ayodhya in a single chariot.

There he beheld the magnanimous Rama like unto a flaming brazier, clothed in a robe of fine wool, in the midst of the imperishable Sages. Paying obeisance to them with joined palms, his senses under control, he addressed his virtuous brother, whose thought too was ever fixed on his duty, and said :—

" I have enthroned my two sons, O King, and have come hither; know well that I am resolved to follow thee ! Do not oppose me, O Valiant One, for I would not that thy will should be disregarded by one like me."

Seeing his resolve was fixed, Rama said to Shatrughna, " So be it."

Having ceased from speaking, the monkeys, who were able to change their form at will, with the companies of bears and titans came there from all directions with Sugriva at their head, all being united in their desire to behold Rama, who stood with his face turned towards the sky.

Devas, Rishis and Gandharvas with their offspring, hearing of Rama's intended departure, had all assembled, saying :—

" We have come here to follow thee, O Prince ! To leave without us, O Rama is to strike us down with the Rod of Death."

At that instant, the supremely powerful Sugriva, bowing before that hero in accord with tradition, addressed him with humility and said :—

" Having installed the virtuous Angada, O Prince, know that I have come hither with the intention of accompanying thee ! "

At these words, the illustrious Kakutstha smiling, answered :—

" So be it ! " Thereafter he said to Bibishana, the King of the Rakshasas :—

"As long as people exist, O Mighty Lord of the Rakshasas, do thou remain in Lanka. As long as the moon and sun continue to shine on the earth, as long as they speak of me in the world, so long shall thine empire endure; this is the will of thy friend, do thou obey ! Govern thy people according to justice and do not question this further. One thing more I wish to say to thee,

O Mighty Monarch of the Rakshasas, do thou worship the Divinity of the House of Ikshvaku, the Guide of the Universe, Shri Jagannath, whom the Devas themselves with their leaders perpetually adore."

" So shall it be," answered Bibishana, and Kakutstha thereafter addressed Hanuman, saying :—

" Resign thyself to continuing to live, do not render my will void. As long as my story is told in the world, O Foremost of Monkeys, so long mayest thou be happy and remember my words ! "

Thereupon Hanuman, acquiescing in Rama's utterance, in his delight, said :—

"As long as thy purifying history is circulated in the world, so long O Rama, shall I remain on earth submissive to thy will ! "

Then Raghava issued the same command to Jambavan and said :—

" Till the Kali Yuga begins, continue to dwell on earth ! "

Thereafter, addressing all the other bears and monkeys, he said :—

" If it be your desire, then follow me ! "

CHAPTER 109

Rama's Departure for the Mahaprasthana

When the dawn broke, the broad-chested and illustrious Rama, whose eyes were as large as lotus petals, said to his spiritual Preceptor :—

" Let the Agnihotra burning brightly with the Twice-born and also the sacrificial canopy be borne in advance and thou, My Lord, precede them on this great journey."

Thereupon Vasishtha, full of majesty, performed the prescribed rituals related to the Mahaprasthana without omitting anything. Then Rama, clothed in fine silk, invoking Brahma and reciting the Vedic Mantras, taking Kusha Grass in both his hands, set out for the Sarayu River, halting from time to time, silently making his way along the rough path. Radiant as the sun, he issued from his palace barefooted and, on his right, walked Shri Lakshmi with her lotus, on his left, was the great Goddess Vyavasaya[1] and, assuming human form, his innumerable arrows, marvellous bow and all the other weapons accompanied him. The Vedas, in the persons of brahmins, the Holy Gayatri, Protector of the World, the sacred syllable " AUM " and the invocation " Vashat " followed in Rama's train as also the great-souled Rishis, and all the Deities of the Earth accompanied that hero to the open gates of heaven.

In his steps trod the women of the inner apartments with the aged, the children, servants, eunuchs and personal attendants. The faithful Bharata with his wives accompanied by Shatrughna followed in Rama's train, attended by the sacrificial fire. All the magnanimous Sages with the ritualistic articles, having assembled there with their sons and wives, joined the procession of the virtuous Kakutstha. Ministers, groups of servants with their offspring, their kinsmen and their flocks joyfully followed in the footsteps of their master. All the citizens, happy and healthy people, distinguished by their good qualities, joined Raghava's departure and all the men and women with their birds, beasts and friends, purified of their sins, went forward cheerfully. Devoted to Rama, the Monkeys, having bathed, delighted and satisfied, cried out exultantly with all their strength, " Kilakila ! "

In that multitude, none was sad, downcast or unhappy, but a universal felicity filled all to the highest degree. In their desire to behold Rama taking his departure, the people of the country, through which he passed, on seeing him, took their places in his train. Bears, monkeys, titans, citizens, with deep devotion, followed him in the utmost serenity. Even the invisible Beings of the city joined Raghava's procession when he went to heaven. Beholding him, all creatures, animate and inanimate, lovingly accompanied him on that journey. Not a single being, not even the least of them, was to be seen in Ayodhya ; even those born of animals followed in Rama's wake.

[1] The Goddess of the Earth.

CHAPTER 110

Rama ascends to Heaven with the other Beings

WHEN he had proceeded about six miles, the Pride of the Raghus beheld the sacred waters of the Sarayu flowing westwards, eddying and rippling in their course, and he went on further to the Goprataraka Ghata,[1] his subjects thronging round him on all sides.

At that moment, as Kakutstha was preparing to ascend to heaven, Brahma, the Grandsire of the World, surrounded by the Gods and the illustrious Rishis adorned with jewels, appeared seated in their aerial chariots, and the whole firmament glowed with a transcendent splendour, a marvellous radiance emanating from the lustre of those heavenly beings of virtuous deeds. Pure, balmy and fragrant breezes blew, whilst shower upon shower of blossom was scattered by the Gods. Thereafter to the sound of a myriad instruments and the singing of the Gandharvas and Apsaras, Rama stepped into the waters, whereupon the Grandsire, from on high, uttered these words :—

" Hail O Vishnu ! Hail O Raghava ! With thy God-like brothers, now enter thine eternal abode ! Return to thine own body if thou so desirest, O Long-armed Warrior ! Occupy the realm of Vishnu or the shining ether, O Mighty God ! Thou art the support of the world, though there are some who do not recognize Thee without the large-eyed Maya, thine ancient Consort ! Thou art the Inconceivable One, the Great Being, the Indestructible, the Ageless One. Enter into thy real body if Thou so desirest."

Hearing these words of the Grandsire, the supremely virtuous Rama formed his resolution and entered Vishnu's abode in his body with his younger brothers.

Thereupon Immortals began to worship that God who had returned to His form as Vishnu, and the Sadhyas, the hosts of Maruts with Indra and Agni at their head, the celestial companies of Rishis, the Gandharvas and Apsaras, Suparnas, Nagas, Yakshas, Daityas, Danavas and Rakshasas and all the dwellers

[1] Cattle ford.

in heaven felt a supreme delight, their desires fulfilled, their sins washed away, and they cried out " Hail ! All Hail ! "

Then the all-resplendent Vishnu said to the Grandsire :—

" Grant to each of these my subjects a suitable abode. They are my devotees and truly deserving, having sacrificed their lives for me ! "

Thus spoke Vishnu, and the God Brahma, Guru of the Worlds, answered saying :—

"All those who have assembled here shall go to the region called Santanakas ! Yea, even the beasts who die meditating on Thy holy Feet shall live in the vicinity of Brahmaloka where I have united all pleasurable things. The monkeys and the bears, the manifestations of various Deities have already returned to the worlds of the Gods, from whence they came forth, and Sugriva has entered the disc of the sun ! "

Even as the great God was speaking, the monkeys and the bears, having assumed their pristine forms, came to Goprataraka Ghata before the eyes of the assembled Gods. At that time, whosoever entered the waters of the Sarayu River, yielded up their lives gladly, their eyes suffused with tears of ecstasy, and, having abandoned their bodies, took their places in a celestial chariot. As for those in animal form, who entered the waters of the Sarayu in hundreds, they ascended to the Third Heaven in divinely resplendent bodies and they appeared as effulgent as the Gods in their celestial lineaments. All beings, whether animate or inanimate, who entered those waters attained to the region of the Gods, and, in their turn, the bears, monkeys and titans, abandoning their bodies in the river, also attained heaven.

Having granted them all a place in paradise, the Grandsire of the World accompanied by the Gods, in the height of felicity, returned to the Third Heaven, his supreme abode.

CHAPTER III

The supreme Virtue of the Ramayana

THIS then is the whole of the great epic and its sequel called the Ramayana, which was composed by Valmiki and is revered by Brahma Himself.

636

The Lord Vishnu returned to Svargaloka as erstwhile, He Who pervades the Three Worlds and all they contain, both the moving and the fixed. Gods, Gandharvas, Siddhas and great Rishis in heaven, ever listen with delight to the poem 'Ramayana'. This epic, which promotes long life, grants good fortune and destroys sin, is equal to the Veda and should be recited by the wise to men of faith.

On hearing it, he who has no son will obtain a son, he who has no fortune will become wealthy ; to read but a foot of this poem will absolve him from all sin. He who commits sins daily will be wholly purified by reciting a single sloka.

The reciter of this narrative should be rewarded with raiment, cows and gold, for, if he is satisfied, all the Gods are satisfied. He who recites this epic 'Ramayana' that prolongs life, will be blessed with his sons and grandsons in this world and after his death, in the other world. He who, with devotion, recites the 'Ramayana' at the hour when the cows are loosed or at noon or at dusk, will never suffer adversity.

The enchanting City of Ayodhya, having remained deserted for countless years, will be re-peopled by a Prince named Rishabha.

This narrative, that grants longevity, with the 'Bhavishya' and 'Uttara', whose author is the son of Pracetas, has the approval of Brahma Himself.

GLOSSARY

(For Flowers, Trees and Weapons, see separate Glossaries)

A

ABHIJIT. A Constellation which denotes victory when the sun enters it.
>The twenty-second Nakshatra q.v.
>A title and name of Vishnu.

ABHIRAS. A leader of robbers who dwelt in Drumakulya.

ABRAVANTI. A city.

ACHMANA. Purificatory rite at which water is taken in the palm of the hands and poured over the head and breast and the mouth rinsed; it also includes touching various parts of the body.

ACHARYA. A Spiritual Teacher.

ACHYUTA. A title of Vishnu meaning ' Imperishable '.

ADAMBARA. A drum, trumpet or elephant's roar during battle.

ADHVARA. A sacrifice, specially the Soma Sacrifice.

ADHVARYA. An officiating priest.

ADHYAS. A reading, chapter or section of a work.

ADIDEVA. A title given to Rama meaning ' Foremost of the Gods '.

ADITI. Mother of the Gods, who represents space or infinity.

ADITYA-HRIDAYA. ' The Heart of the Sun ', a designation of a Vedic Hymn.

ADITYA-VARCAS. ' That which constitutes the knowledge of Aditya '.

ADRIKRITASTHALI. Apsaras or Nymphs.

AGARU. Agallochum, a species of Sandal or Indian Aloe Exorcaria, used as incense or for perfuming purposes.

AGASTYA. A great Rishi, the reputed author of several hymns in the Rig-Veda. This Sage, whose miraculous powers are described in the great classics, entertained Rama, Sita and Lakshmana in his hermitage during their exile. He was said to have been born in a vessel. (See Uttarakanda Chapter LVII.)

AGNEYA. A mountain.
>The south-eastern quarter of which Agni is Regent.
>A cloud produced by fire.

AGNI. The God of Fire.

AGNIGARBHA. ' Fire-wombed ', a name of Agni who causes the Fire of Dissolution at the end of the World-cycle.

AGNIHOTRA. The Fire-sacrifice.

AGNIKETU. A titan warrior.

AGNIKUNDA. A pit or hole where the sacrificial fire burns.

AGNIPUTRA. A Sage, the title means ' Son of Agni '.

AGNISTHOMA. A series of offerings to the God of Fire celebrated for five days during the Spring.

AGNIVARNA. The son of Sudarshana.

AGRAHAYANA. A feast similar to the Harvest Festival.

AHALYA. The wife of the Rishi Gautama, who was transformed into a rock by him when he cursed her for dalliance with the God Indra ; she was ultimately restored to her own form by Rama.

AHASKARA. ' Maker of Day ', a title of the Sun-god.

AHAVANIYA. See under Three Fires.

AIRAVATA. The sacred elephant that transports the God Indra. One of the elephants supporting the four quarters of the earth.

AJA. A king of the dynasty of Ikshvaku, the father of Dasaratha.

AJAMUKHI. A female titan.

AJAS. A class of hermits, see under ' Ascetics '.

AJITA. ' Invincible ', a name given to Vishnu.

AKAMPANA. The titan who informed Ravana of the destruction of Janasthana and who persuaded him to abduct Sita. He was slain by Hanuman.

AKOPA. A minister in the Court of King Dasaratha.

AKSHA. A son of Ravana who was slain by Hanuman.

AKSHAUHINI. An army consisting of a large number of cavalry, infantry, chariots and elephants.

ALAKA. Kuvera's capital.

ALAKSHITA. A forest where Narada dwelt.

ALAMBUSHA. Mother of Vishala q.v.

ALARKA. A hero renowned for his devotion.

AMARAVATI. Indra's capital which is also called Vitapavati.

AMBARISHA. A king of Ayodhya whose story is told in Balakanda.

AMRITA. The ' Nectar of Immortality ' produced by the churning of the ocean by Gods and Demons.

ANALA. The God of Fire.
The name of one of Mali's sons.
The wife of Kashyapa.
Daughter of Sundari.

ANANGA. ' Bodiless ', a name given to the God of Love after he was consumed to ashes by Shiva.
A Monkey Warrior who was the son of Hutasena, the God of Fire, Agni.

ANANTA. The thousand-headed Serpent, also called Shesha, on which the Lord Vishnu rests during the withdrawal of the worlds. The name means ' Eternal ', ' Endless '.

ANARANYA. A king of the race of Ikshvaku.

ANASUYA. The wife of the Rishi Atri.

GLOSSARY

ANDHAKA. A demon, the son of the Sage Kashyapa and Diti, who was said to have a thousand arms and heads, and was slain by Shiva.

ANGA. The kingdom ruled over by King Lomapada, probably Bengal.

    ' A part or limb; an army is divided into angas which has been translated as divisions in this text.

ANGADA. The son of Bali, a monkey warrior, heir-apparent to the kingdom of the monkey race.

ANGADIYA. The city ruled by one of Lakshmana's sons.

ANGALAPA. A city the monkeys searched for Sita.

ANGARAKA. A female demon.
    The Planet Mars.

ANGIRAS. One of the seven immortal Sages, the father of Gargya.

ANILA. The God of the Wind.
    One of the sons of Mali.

ANJALI. A salutation made with joined palms.

ANJALIPANAS. Ascetics who drink from the hollow of their hands.

ANJANA. A nymph with whom the God of the Wind became enamoured and who subsequently gave birth to Hanuman.

ANSHUMAN. The son of Asmanjas; his story is told in Balakanda.

ANTAKA. A name of Yama, the God of Death.

ANTIGAS. A measure implying a great number.

ANTYA. A Madhya ten times.

ANUHLADA. The son of Hiranya kashipu, a Daitya and the father of Prahlada whose story is told in the Vishnu Purana. Anuhlada bore away Sachi, Indra's consort, and was slain by him.

APARAPARVATAS. A mountain range.

APAS. A title meaning the ' Friend of Water '.

APSARA. A water-sprite or nymph; the word ' Ap ' meaning ' water ' and ' sara ' to ' emerge from '. The Apsaras were the wives of the Gandharvas.

ARANI. The wood of the sacred fig-tree which is used for kindling at sacrifices.

ARANYA. A forest or wood.

ARBUDA. A hundred millions.

ARCHIRMALAYAS. The offspring of the Ascetic Maricha.

ARCHISMAN. A monkey leader.

ARGHYA. A traditional offering of water, milk, Kusha Grass, rice, Durva Grass, sandal-wood, flowers and so forth.

ARIGHNA. A titan warrior.

ARISHTANEMI. A Sage.
    A name of Garuda meaning the ' Felly of whose wheel is unhurt '.

ARJUNA. The King of the Haihayas, the son of Kritavirya who defeated Ravana.
    An Asura.

641

ARKA. A monkey leader.

ARSHISHMAN. A titan, the father of Sumali.

ARTHA. Dharma, Artha and Kama—Duty, prosperity and legitimate pleasure, which are said to be the three ends of life.

ARTHA-SHASTRA. The Science of moral and political government. The Artha Shastras are ancient Hindu Treatises summarizing the main duties of man in the field of politics and economics where the subjects are treated from the individual and not the universal point of view.

ARTHASADHAKA. One of the ministers of Dasaratha's court.

ARUJA. Patronymic of the descendants of Bhrigu.
    The daughter of Shukracharya, the name means 'Purity'.

ARUNA. An Eagle or Jay, the brother of Garuda.

ARUNDHATI. The wife of the Rishi Vasishtha who was a model of conjugal excellence.
    The morning star.

ARYAMA. Chief of the Pitris or ancestors.

ASAVA. Wine made of sugar and honey of the blossom ' Bassia Latifolia '.

ASCETICS. Sages who practiced austerities of which some are :—
    Ajas. Those mentioned in the Veda.
    Ardrapatavasas. Those who practised silent prayer.
    Asmakuttas. Those who lived in stone huts on uncooked food.
    Dantolukhalia. Those who partook of raw food, such as grain, and crushed it between their teeth.
    Gatrasayyas. Those who slept on the ground without making a bed.
    Marichipas. Those who lived by absorbing the rays of the sun or moon.
    Pancagnis. Those who practised asceticism between five fires, that is four fires and the sun above.
    Patraharas. Those who lived on the leaves of trees.
    Samprakalas. Those said to be born of the water in which Brahma's feet are cleansed.
    Vaikhanasas. Those born from the nails of Brahma.
    Valakhilyas. Those born from the body of Brahma.

ASHADHA. A month, part of June and July.
    One born under the Constellation Ashadha.

ASHANIPRABHA. A titan warrior.

ASHMA. The city in Varuna's realm that belonged to Bali.

ASHOKA. One of Rama's counsellors. (For the tree of this name see separate Glossary).

ASHRAMA. A hermitage or forest retreat.

ASHTAVAKRA. A Sage of great spiritual eminence.

ASHVA. A Sage.

GLOSSARY

ASHVAGRIVA. The son of Kashyapa.

ASHVAMEDHA. The Horse-sacrifice of Vedic times performed only by kings.

ASHVAPATI. See Yudhajita.

ASHVATARA. The name of the foremost of the Serpent Race; its meaning is ' Swift ', ' Speedy '.

ASHVAYUJ. The month that is part of September and October.

ASHVINS or ASHVINI-KUMARAS. Celestial Horsemen, precursors of the dawn, twin offspring of the sun and patrons of medicine.

ASHVIPUTRAS. The sons of the Ashvins.

ASI. From ' Asi Pattra Vana ', a hell where the trees have leaves as sharp as swords.

ASITA. The father of Sagara q.v.

ATALA. See Patala.

ATAPIN. A name of the Sun meaning ' Causing Heat '.
A bird ' Falco Cheela '.

ATHARVA VEDA. The Fourth Veda.

ATIBALA. See Bala and Atibala.

ATIKAYA. ' Huge-bodied ', a name of a titan warrior.

ATIRATHA. A great Car-warrior, one who can fight innumerable archers, though less than ten thousand.

ATIRATRA. An optional part of the Jyotishtima-sacrifice; also the commencement and conclusion of certain other sacrifices.

ATODYAS. A musical instrument.

ATRI. One of the seven immortal Sages.

ATYARTHA SADAKA. One of the counsellors of King Dasaratha.

AUM or OM. The sacred syllable said to be the first sound in creation; its import can be studied in the Mandukya Upanishad.

AURVA. A great Rishi, the grandson of Bhrigu; the name is derived from ' uru ' or ' thigh ' as he was said to have been produced from his mother's thigh. His austerities alarmed the Gods and his anger against the warrior class, who had slain his forbears, was unparalleled. Eventually it was mitigated by the intervention of the Pitris and he cast it into the sea where this fire of his wrath became a being with a horse's head named Hayashira.

AVANTI. A city searched by the monkeys for Sita.

AVARTANI. A prayer which is said to induce the descent of the Deity and cause all things to be perceived.

AVINDAYA. A titan.

AVINDHA. A wise and elderly titan.

AYODHYA. The capital of Koshala which was ruled over by King Dasaratha, possibly Oudh.

AYOMUKHI. A female titan.

AYURVEDA. The ' Veda of Life ', a work on medicine attributed to the Sage Dhanvantari, who rose from the ocean when it was churned by the Gods and titans.

AYUS. The son of Pururavas and Urvashi; he was the father of Nahusha.

AYUTA. A number not to be counted, a myriad or sometimes said to be a thousand plus a hundred; also sometimes denoting ten thousand.

B

BAHADUR. A title similar to a knighthood.

BAHLIKA. A country scoured by the monkeys in search of Sita.

BAHLIKAS. Bactrians or People of the north and west of India.

BAHUDAMSHTRA. A titan.

BAHUMAYIN. An asura.

BAHUSUVARNAKA. A sacrifice at which liberal distributions of gold are made.

BALA and ATIBALA. The 'Science of sacred formulas', given to Rama by the Sage Vishvamitra.

BALI. The monkey king of Kishkindha, brother of Sugriva.

BALIMUKHA. A monkey leader.

BANA. A king who was the son of Vikukshi and the father ot Anaranya.

BASAKARNA. A titan leader.

BHADRA. One of Rama's courtiers.

BHAGA. A Deity mentioned in the Vedas; it is the name of an Aditya presiding over love and marriage; the appellation actually means 'Wealthy Master' or 'Gracious Lord' and 'Bestower of Wealth'; this name is also used for the Moon.

BHAGIRATHA. A descendant of King Sagara, who by his penances brought the River Ganges to earth.

BHAGIRATHI. A name given to the River Ganges in memory of the Sage Bhagiratha.

BHANU. A title of the Sun meaning 'Possessed of Brightness'.

BHARADWAJA. A Sage who entertained Rama, Sita, Lakshmana and later Bharata in the forest. (See Balakanda.) Many Vedic Hymns are attributed to him.

BHARATA. The younger brother of Rama and son of Queen Kaikeyi.

BHARATVARSHA. Ancient India.

BHARGAVA. A patronymic of the Sage Chyavana, the offspring of Bhrigu. It is also used for Shukra and others.

BHASAKARNA. A titan slain by Hanuman.

BHASKARA. A name of the Sun-god who was the father of Sugriva.

BHASVAT. A name given to the Sun-god meaning 'Luminous', " Splendid ', ' Possessing Light '.

BHAVA. A name of Shiva.

BHAVISHYA. One of the eighteen Puranas; a revelation of future events by Brahma.

BHAYA. 'Fear', the sister of Kala and consort of Praheti.

BHERI. A kettledrum.

BHOGAVATI. A voluptuous subterranean city belonging to the Serpent Race; it is sometimes called Putkari.

BHRAMARA. A bumble-bee.

    A bird.

BHRIGU. A Vedic Sage, said to be the son of Manu.

BHRINGARAJA. A Shrike or bee.

BHUJAMGAS. Beings of the Serpent Race.

BHUR, BHUVAH, SWAH. The Lower, Middle and Upper Worlds.

BHUTAS. Spirits or ghosts.

BHUTAGRAMAS. The aggregate of living beings or a multitude of spirits or ghosts.

BHUTI. The mother of the Nymph Manu.

BIBHUTAKA. A double ladle made of wood for pouring ghee into the sacrificial fire.

BIBISHANA or VIBISHANA. The younger brother of Ravana but a devotee of Rama; he was installed as King of Lanka on Ravana's death.

BINDUSARA. A lake.

BISHAKA or VISHAKA. A devotee who constantly contemplates the Deity.

    One of the Nakshatras q.v.

BLUE-THROATED ONE. A title given to Shiva, whose throat took on this colour when he drank the poison churned from the ocean by the Gods and Asuras.

BRAHMA. The Creative Aspect of Divinity.

BRAHMACHARI. A religious student living in the house of a spiritual Teacher or Guru, having taken certain vows.

BRAHMACHARINI. The female counterpart of a brahmachari.

BRAHMACHARYA. Religious studentship implying the taking of certain vows.

BRAHMADATTA. A king who was cursed by the Sage Gautama and became a vulture.

BRAHMA JNANA. The Knowledge of Brahman, Truth or Reality through direct perception.

BRAHMA KOSHA. The Abode of Hyranyagarbha q.v.

BRAHMA LAYA. The Abode of the Four-faced Brahma.

BRAHMAN. The Absolute or Highest Reality, attributeless being.

BRAHMANMALAS. A country explored by the monkeys when in search of Sita.

BRAHMAPUTRA. The son of Brahma or a brahmin.

    The name of a river.

    The eastern extremity of the Himalayas.

BRAHMARSHI. A Constellation said by some to be Shravana q.v. The name of a certain class of Rishi, higher than a Maharishi and of the brahmanical order. Sometimes written Brahma-rishi.)

BRAHMASHATRU. A titan warrior.

BRAHMASHIRAS. The Abode of the Deity presiding over the Brahma Weapon.

BRAHMAVADI. One who recites or expounds the Veda, or teaches the Spiritual Knowledge.

BRIHASPATI or VRIHASPATI. The spiritual Preceptor of the Gods, also said to be the Regent of the Planet Jupiter which is called by the same name.

BUDHA. The Planet Mercury.

BULL. The white bull, called Nandi, which is said to be the God Shiva's vehicle and represents the Sattwa-guna. (See under Gunas.)

C

CASTES. There are four castes, the priestly, warrior and merchant class and the one that serves the other three.

CHABANYA. A Sage who entertained Shatrughna in his hermitage.

CHAITRARATHA. The King of the Gandharvas.

CHAITRARATHA GARDENS. The Celestial Gardens belonging to the God Kuvera.

CHAITYA. A tombstone, column, monument or sacrificial pile.

CHAKRACHARAS. Designation of a class of Beings ; the name means ' Moving in a circle '.

CHAKRATUNDA. A fish resembling a wheel.

CHAKRAVAKA. A Brahmany Duck or Ruddy Goose.

CHAMARA. A Chowrie or fan made of Yaks tails, an insignia of royality.

CHANDALA. An outcaste.

CHANDARI. A female titan.

CHANDAS. A sacred hymn or verse distinct from those in the Vedas.

CHANDRA. The Moon

CHANDRACHRITAS. A country explored by the monkeys when they were searching for Sita.

CHANDRAHASA. A glittering scimitar, Ravana's sword, which he received from Shiva as a boon. The name means ' Deriding or shaming the moon '.

CHANDRAKANTA. The city ruled over by the son of Lakshmana.

CHARANAS. The Panegyrists of the Gods.

CHARAVAT. A mountain in the ocean where Vishvakarma forged the discus used by Vishnu.

CHARYAGOPURA. The mountain where Kumbhakarna slept.

CHATAK BIRD. ' Cuculus Melanoleucus ', a bird that according to legend lives only on rain-drops.

CHATURANGA. An army consisting of foot soldiers, cavalry, elephants and chariots.

CHITRA. The Planet Spica.

The month Chitra or Chaitra which is part of February and March.

CHITTRAKUTA. A sacred mountain where Rama and Sita dwelt in exile and is to this day considered a holy retreat.

CHYAVANA. A Sage, the son of the Rishi Bhrigu.

D

DADHIMUKHA. A monkey who guarded a grove and was ill-treated by Angada's victorious troops.

DAITYAS. Giants, titans or demons.

DAKSHA. One of Brahma's sons, whose daughter Uma became the consort of Shiva.

DAKSHAYANI. A female demon named Surasa also.

DAKSHINA. Traditional offering made after a sacred ceremony.

DAMSHTRA. A titan warrior.

DANAVAS. A race of Giants who were enemies of the Gods.

DANDA. A staff or rod.

The name of Sumali's son whose story is told in ' Uttara kanda. '

DANDADHARA. ' Bearer of the Rod ', a name of Death as Bearer of the Rod of Punishment.

DANDAKA. The name of a vast forest lying between the Rivers Godavari and Narmada, the scene of Rama and Sita's exile.

DANDI. One of the Sun-god's doorkeepers.

DANSHIRA. A titan.

DANTAVAKRA. One of Rama's courtiers.

DANU. A name of the Demon Kabandha q.v.

One of Bali's forbears.

DARDURA. A mountain in the south, sometimes associated with Mount Malaya.

DARIMUKHA. A monkey warrior.

DARMAPALA. One of Rama's ministers.

DARSHA. Bi-monthly sacrifice performed at the changes of the moon by those maintaining a perpetual fire.

DASARATHA. King of Koshala and father of Rama, Lakshmana, Bharata and Shatrughna.

DASHAGRIVA. ' Ten-necked One ', a title given to Ravana.

DASHANANA ' Ten-faced One ', a title given to Ravana.

DASYUS. Robbers.

DATYUHA or DATYUHAKA. A small Gallinule resembling a cuckoo.

DEVALOKA. The Celestial Region or the Abode of the Gods.

DEVANTAKA. ' Slayer of the Gods ', the title of a titan warrior.

DEVARISHI. See under Rishi.

DEVAS. The Gods or Shining Ones.

DEVASAKHA. A mountain that was called the ' Refuge of the Gods '.

DEVAVATI. The daughter of the Gandharva Gramani who became the consort of Shiva.

DEVAYANI. The wife of Nahusha.

DEVI. A title given to Parvati, the consort of Shiva.

DHANADA. A name of Kuvera meaning ' Granter of Wealth '.

DHANANJAYA. A title meaning ' Victorious in Battle ', used for the Moon-god, Fire-god and others.

DHANESHWARA. ' Lord of Wealth ', a title given to Kuvera.

DHANURVEDA. The Veda of Archery.

DHANYAMALINI. The mother of Atikaya.

DHARA. One of the wives of the Sage Kashyapa.

DHARANI. The Goddess of the Earth personified as the wife of Dhruva q.v.

DHARMA. Righteousness or duty, the traditionally ordained course of conduct ; one of the four ends of life which are Dharma, Artha, Kama and Moksha—duty, prosperity, legitimate pleasure and liberation. Dharma is personfied as one of the Prajapatis, the God of Moral Law and Spiritual Duty.

DHARMABRIT. A Sage whom Rama encountered near the ' Lake of the Five Nymphs.'

DHARMAPALA. One of Rama's counsellors.

DHARMARAJA. A title of Yama as God of Justice.

DHATAR or DHATRI. ' Creator ', ' Author ', ' Founder ', a name given to Brahma, Vishnu and others.

DHAUMYA. A Sage.

DHRISHTI. One of the chief counsellors at the court of King Dasaratha.

DHRUVA. The Deity of the Pole-star whose story is told in the Vishnu Purana.

DHUMA. The God of Smoke.

DHUMAKETU. A meteor, comet or falling star.
    The personified descending node.
    A titan.

DHUMRA. Lord of all the Bears, an ally of Rama.

DHUMRAKSHA. A titan warrior.

DHUNDHUMARA. A title given to the King Kuvalashwa meaning ' Slayer of the Demon Dhundu '.

DHURJAT. A title meaning ' Having matted locks '.

DHWAJAGRIVA. A titan.

DILIPA. The father of the Sage Bharadwaja.

DINDIMA. A musical instrument.
DIRGHATMAS. A Sage.
DIRGHAYUS. A Sage.
DITI. The daughter of Daksha and wife of Kashyapa ; she became the mother of the Daityas.
DIVAKARA. 'Bringer of Day', a title of the Sun.
DRONA. A measure approximating to ninety-two pounds.
DRUMAKULYA. A sacred spot spoken of by the Lord of the Waters on which Rama was told to loose his destructive weapon.
DUKULA. Woven silk or very fine cloth made of the inner bark of the plant of the same name.
DUNDUBHI. A Son of Maya, a giant who fought with Bali, the King of the Monkeys.
A kettledrum.
DURDHARSHA. A title given to Ravana meaning 'Dreadful', 'Unapproachable' or 'Unassailable'.
DURGAPURA. Yadu's city.
DURMUKHA. A monkey warrior.
DURMUKHI. A female titan.
DURVASA. A Sage.
DUSHANTA. A General in Khara's army who was slain by Rama.
DUSHKANTA. A king who yielded to Ravana without fighting.
DVIJIHVA. A titan warrior.
DVIVIDA. A monkey warrior.
DYUMATSENA. Prince of S'abra and father of Satyavanta.

E

EIGHTFOLD INTELLIGENCE. This includes the quality of accepting the truth and what is right, cherishing it, remembering it, propagating it and the knowledge of the ultimate essence.
EKAJATA. A female titan.
EKAKSHIPINGALA. 'One-eyed', a title given to Kuvera.
EKASHALYA. An aquatic creature ; the word means 'having a tip or point' possibly a swordfish.

F

FIVE ASPECTS. The consideration of (a) time, (b) place, (c) persons and things concerned, (d) provision against mischance, (e) of the possibility of success.
FOUR POWERS. Physical power, mental power, power of resource and the power of making friends.
FOURFOLD DEFENCES. Defence by water, mountain, forest or by artificial means.

GLOSSARY

FOURTEEN QUALITIES. Knowledge of time and place, endurance, empirical knowledge, skill, physical strength, power of concealing one's counsel, the honouring of obligations and promises, heroism, appreciation of the enemy's strength and one's own relation to it, gratitude and beneficence to one's dependents or suppliants, non-acceptance of insult, freedom from uncontrolled movements (poise).

G

GADGADA. The father of Jambavan.

GADHI. The father of the Sage Vishvamitra and the son of King Kushanabha, hence the patronymic ' Kaushika '.
A king who yielded to Ravana without fighting.

GAJA. A monkey leader.

GALAVA. A Sage who prevented Ravana and King Mandhata from using the great destructive weapon and reconciling them.

GANDHAMADANA. A general in the monkey army who was wounded by Indrajita.
A mountain of fragrant forests to the east of Mount Meru, sometimes called the ' Mountain of Intoxicating Fragrance '.

GANDHARA. A region where the cities that were ruled over by the sons of Bharata were established, now Afghanistan.

GANDHARVAS. Celestial musicians.

GANGES or GANGA or GUNGA. The sacred river Ganges known under many other names such as :—
Bhagirathi—after the Sage Bhagiratha.
Harasekhara—the Crest of Shiva.
Khapaga—Three-way flowing.
Mandakini—Gently-flowing.
Jahnavi after the Sage Jahnu and so on.

GANHDARVI. The wife of Kashyapa and mother of horses.

GARGYA or GARGA. A great Sage who is mentioned in the Upanishads.

GARHAPATYA. A perpetual sacred fire maintained by a householder who has received it from his father and passed it on to his descendants. See also ' Three Fires. '

GARUDA. King of the Birds, the vehicle of Vishnu and the destroyer of serpents, sometimes portrayed as an eagle or jay with a human head.

GAUTAMA. A great Sage, the husband of Ahalya.

GAVAKSHA. A monkey leader, King of the Golangulas.

GAVASTHANA. ' Ray-furnished ' or ' Having the merit of Auspiciousness ', a title given to the Sun-god.

GAVAYA. A monkey warrior.

GAYA. A king who yielded to Ravana without fighting.
A monkey warrior.

GLOSSARY

GAYATRI. The most sacred prayer of the Rig-veda which is personified as a Goddess and considered to be the consort of Brahma and mother of the four Vedas.

GEYA. A monkey leader.

GHANAVRISHTI. 'He from whom floweth the fruit of acts', or 'He from whom cometh the showers', a name given to Indra.

GHATODARA. A titan warrior.

GHORA. A titan.

GHRITACHI. A nymph, the wife of Kushanabha and mother of a hundred daughters.

GO. A leader of Varuna's troops.

GODAVARI. A river close to the Dandaka Forest.

GODHA. A piece of leather or metal worn on the left arm to protect it from the bow-string.

GOHA. Soft leather, possible cow or doe-skin.

GOKARNA. A hermitage.

GOLANGULA. A black monkey that has a tail like a cow; also called Gopuccha.

GOLOBHA. A giant.

GOMEDHA. The Cow-sacrifice.

GOMUKHA. The son of Matali and the charioteer of Jayanta.

GOPRATARA. 'A Ford for Cattle', a place of pilgrimage near the River Sarayu.

GOSAVA. The sacrifice of a cow lasting a day.

GRAHA. An inauspicious planet such as Mars, Saturn, Rahu and Ketu.

GRAHAMALA. A cluster or group of inauspicious planets.

GRAMANI. The leader of an army or chief of a village or community.
    A Gandharva who gave his daughter, Devavati, to Sukesha in marriage.

GRANDSIRE OF THE WORLD. A title given to Brahma, the Creator.

GRIDHRAS. Birds of prey.

GRIHI. One who, having completed his education, marries and becomes a householder. See Grihasta.

GUHA. King of the Nishadas, a mountain tribe; he was a great devotee of Rama.

GUHYAKAS. Hidden Beings who were attendants of Kuvera.

GULMA. A body of troops consisting of nine platoons, nine elephants, twenty-seven horses and forty-five foot soldiers.

GUNAS. 'Guna' literally means a thread or strand but is also used for quality, attribute or property; for instance, air has tangibility and sound as its 'guna'.
    According to the Sankhya Philosophy, nature consists of an equipoise of the three 'gunas', tamas, rajas and sattwa or darkness and inertia, passion-struggle and finally goodness; these 'gunas' are the characteristics of all created things.

GURU. A traditional Teacher of the spiritual science, one who dispels ignorance.

GLOSSARY

H

HAHA. A Gandharva.

HALA. 'Ugliness' from which 'Halya' meaning 'Ugly' is derived. See the story of Ahalya.

HAMSA. A swan, heron or flamingo.

HANUMAN or HANUMAT. A monkey who was Sugriva's minister and friend and a great devotee of Rama. He was the son of Pavana, the Wind-god and the Nymph Anjana. The name actually means 'He of the fractured jaw'.

HARA. A name of Shiva.
> A son of Mali.
> A monkey warrior.

HARA-HARI. The name of Shiva and Vishnu conjoined.

HARIDASHVA. A name of the Sun-god and of Indra.

HARIDIKYA. An Asura.

HARI. The name of the Lord Vishnu meaning 'Captivating', 'Pleasing'.

HARIHAYA. 'Having bay horses', a title given to Indra.

HARIJATA. A female titan.

HARILOMAN. A monkey warrior.

HARITANEMI. A Daitya.

HARITAS. The people born of the Cow Shabala.

HARIVAHANNA. The name of Garuda.
> The abode of Indra.

HASTA. A star identified as Corvus.

HASTIMUKHA. A titan.

HASTINAPURA. A city on the Ganges.

HAVIS. A sacred draught or anything offered as an oblation with fire, clarified butter or ghee.

HAVISHPANDA. The son of Vishvamitra.

HAWAN. A particular offering to the Gods in an ancient Fire-ceremony.

HAYAGRIVA. 'Horse-necked', according to one legend, Vishnu himself assumed this form to recover the Vedas which had been stolen by two Daityas, Madhu and Kaitabha.

HAYANANA. The 'Place of the Horse-necked One'.

HEMA. A nymph who was the consort of Maya, the great magician.
> A kind of gold.

HEMACHANDRA. A son of Vishala and father of Suchandra.

HEMAKUTA. A mountain.
> A monkey leader, the son of Varuna.

HETI. Heti and Praheti were titans or Daityas born from the waters at the time of creation.

HIMAPANDURA. One of the elephants of the four quarters who support the earth.

HIMAVAT. 'The Abode of Snows', the Himalayas.
> King of the Himalayas.

HIRANYAGARBHA. The name of Brahma as having been born from the golden Egg, a manifestation of the Supreme Soul.

HIRANYA-KASHIPU. ' Clothed in Gold ', a title given to a Daitya who obtained the sovereignty of the Three Worlds from Shiva for a million years and who persecuted his son Prahlada who was a devotee of Vishnu.

HIRANYARETAS. ' Having golden seed ', a name of Agni and the Sun.

HOMA. The Homa Sacrifice is the act of making an oblation to the Gods by pouring butter into the fire to the accompaniment of prayers and invocations. It is regarded as one of the five great Sacrifices called Deva-yajnas.

HRADINI. A titan.

HRASVAKARNA. A titan.

HRASVAROMAN. The father of Janaka.

HRISHIKESHA. A name of Vishnu meaning ' Lord of the Organs of Sense '.

HUHU. A Gandharva.

HUTASENA. ' Eater of the Sacrificial Offerings ', a name given to the God of Fire, Agni.

I

IKSHUMATI. A river.

IKSHVAKU. The son of Manu, founder of the Solar Race of Kings who ruled over Ayodhya.

ILA. The name of King Kardama when he had been transformed into a woman.

ILVALA. A demon subdued by the Sage Agastya.

INDRA. The King of the Gods who is known under other names such as :—

> Mahendra—Great God.
> Shatakratu—He of a Hundred Sacrifices.
> Purandara—Destroyer of Cities.
> Vajrapani—He of the Thunderbolt Hand.
> Lord of Sachi, (Sachi being his consort).
> Maghavan—Possessor of Wealth, and other titles.

INDRAJANU. A monkey general.

INDRAJITA. The son of Ravana, also called Ravani and Indra-shatru.

INDRALOKA. Indra's abode, the Celestial Realm.

INDRA'S BOW. The rainbow.

INDRASHATRU. See Indrajita.

INDRAYANU. A monkey leader.

INDU. A Constellation.

> A name used for the Moon and the Planet Mercury.

IRAVAT. A title meaning ' Granter of Enjoyment or Refreshment '. The name of one of the great Serpents.

IRAVATI. The mother of the elephant Airavata q.v.

ISHANA. ' Ruler ', ' Master ', a name of Shiva.

ITHASA. Legend or tradition, history or traditional account of former events.

J

JABALI or JAVALI. A brahmin at King Dasaratha's court.

JAGANATHA. ' Lord of the World ', a title given to Vishnu, Rama and Dattatreya.

JAGARI. Coarse brown sugar made of Palm sap.

JAHNAVI. A name given to the sacred River Ganges.

JAHNU. The Sage who drank up the sacred River Ganges.

JALADA. A sea that was considered a source of terror to all beings into which the Rishi Aurva had cast his anger.

JAMBAVAN or JAMBAVAT. The King of the Bears, one of Rama's allies.

JAMBHA. A demon slain by Indra.

JAMBHUMALI. A titan.

JAMBU. A fabulous river, said to flow from Mount Meru from the sap of a giant Jambu Tree, which was supposed to be a landmark similar to the Pole-star.

JAMBUDWIPA. One of the seven continents of which the world was said to be composed.

JAMBUNADI. Gold taken from the River Jambu.

JANAKA. King of Mithila and father of Sita.

JANARDANA. ' Exciter or Agitator of Men ', a name given to Vishnu.

JANASTHANA. The colony of titans in the Dandaka Forest. The name means ' Resort of Demons '.

JANGHA. A titan.

JAPA. The silent repetition of a prayer or sacred formula.

JATAPURA. A city, searched by the monkeys for Sita.

JATARUPA. Gold in its original purity.

JATARUPASHILA. North of the Svadu Sea is this mountain of the splendour of gold where Ananta sleeps.

JATAYU. The King of the Vultures who attempted to prevent Ravana carrying off Sita and was slain by him.

JATI. One of the great Serpents.

JAVA. The father of the Demon Viradha.

JAYA. A Goddess, the producer of weapons ; she was the daughter of Daksha.

JAYANTA. One of King Dasaratha's ministers.

Indra's son, who entered into a duel with Indrajita and was saved by being borne away by his maternal Grandsire.

GLOSSARY

JISHNU. A title meaning ' Victorious ', ' Triumphant ' given to Vishnu.

JUTA. The matted locks of a devotee.

JYOTIRMUKHA. A monkey warrior.

JYOTISHOMA. A sacred ceremony, really the Soma Ceremony with either four or seven sub-divisions.

K

KABANDHA. An Asura or demon who was slain by Rama.

KADAMVARI. Natural wines which require no preparation.

KADRU. A daughter of Daksha who became the wife of the Rishi Kashyapa and the mother of the many-headed Serpents including Shesha and Vasuki.

KAHOLA. The father of the Sage Ashtavakra, who cursed his son while he was in the womb causing him to be born with eight humps.

KAIKASI. The consort of Vishravas and mother of Ravana, Kumbhakarna, Bibishana, Shurpanakha and other Rakshasas.

KAIKEYA. The kingdom ruled over by King Kaikeya who was the father of Kaikeyi.

KAIKEYI. The favourite consort of King Dasaratha and mother of Bharata.

KAILASHA. A sacred mountain which was said to be the abode of Shiva.

KAITABHA. A Daitya slain by Vishnu.

KAKUTSTHA. A title used for the descendants of Kakutstha in the House of Ikshvaku, also for Puranjaya, a Prince of the Solar Race whose story is told in Vishnu Purana. The word comes from ' Kakud ' an emblem of royalty and ' Stha ' meaning a prince or grandson of Ikshvaku.

KALA. Time and sometimes Time as Death.
The daughter of Bibishana.
A mountain searched by the monkeys for Sita and Ravana.

KALAGURU. Aloes or Agallochum, a species of Sandal.

KALAHAMSA. Gallinule Porphyria, a species of duck or goose.

KALAKA. The wife of the Rishi Kashyapa and mother of the Danavas.
The daughter of Kashyapa and Kalaka.

KALAKEYAS. Giants or Danavas born of Kalaka.

KALAMAHI. A river.

KALANEMI. An Asura, the enemy of the Gods.

KALAPAS. A string of pearls or a band woven of pearls or small bells.

KALA'S WHEEL. The ' Wheel of Time. '

KALIKAMUKHA. A son of Mali.

KALINDI. The wife of King Asit, mother of Sagara.
A river.

KALIYA. One of Rama's courtiers.

KALMASHAPADA. The name of King Saudasa, whose story is told in Uttarakanda.

KALMASHI. A titan, demon or goblin.
Animals that are spotted or of a variegated colour.

KALPA. A Day, and Night of Brahma, a thousand Yugas. A tree of Paradise.

KAMA. The Indian Cupid or God of Love, also called by other names.
See also under Artha.

KAMADHUK. The wish-fulfilling cow which belonged to the Sage Vasishtha.

KAMPANA. A titan.

KAMPILYA. The city ruled over by Brahmadatta.

KAMVALA. A woollen cloth or upper garment.

KANAKA. A kind of gold.

KANAKHALA. A mountain.

KANCANA. A kind of gold.
A Sage in the line of Bhrigu.

KANCHANA. Shatrughna's family priest.

KANDA. A monkey warrior.

KANDARPA. Another name of the God of Love.

KANDU. A Rishi who cursed a forest.

KANSA. A forbear of Bali.

KANVA. A great Rishi, the son of Medhatithi, the father of Kandu.

KAPALASHIRAS. A Sage.

KAPARDIN. ' Wearing a Kaparda ', a special knot of hair ; a name given to Shiva.

KAPATHA. A titan.

KAPI. A monkey.

KAPILA. A great Sage, founder of the Sankhya System of Philosophy, who was said to be an incarnation of Vishnu. He destroyed the sons of Sagara whose story is told in Balakanda.

KAPIVATI. A river.

KARALA. A titan, one of those whose dwelling was burnt down by Hanuman.

KARANDA or KARANDAVA. A species of duck.

KARAVIRAKSHA. A titan.

KARDAMA. The son of Prajapati, a Sage.

KARDAMEYA. The son of Kardama, see under Ila.

KARENU. An elephant.

KARKA. The Sign of Cancer.

KARKOTAKA. The name of a great Serpent.

KARKUTAKA. The name of a city.

KARMA. The law governing the behaviour of matter in all its gross and subtle forms in accord with the divine purpose.

KARTAR. The Sun.

KARTASVARA. A kind of gold.

KARTAVIRYA. A title of Arjuna, the King of the Haihayas.

KARTÌKA. October, when the sun enters Libra.

KARTTIKEYA. The God of War who is also called Skanda and Mahasena. He was the son of Shiva.

KARUSHAS. A people.

KASHI. The modern Benares, a sacred city. The King of Kashi was Rama's ally.

KASHIKOSHALAS. A region explored by the monkeys for Sita.

KASHYA. An ascetic.

KASHYAPA. The great Vedic Sage, grandson of Brahma, who was the father of Vivasvata.

KATYAYANA. A Sage and Writer of great celebrity, the author of Dharmashastra.

KAUPIN. A loin cloth.

KAUSHALYA. Dasaratha's chief queen and the mother of Rama.

KAUSHEYA. A Rishi.

KAUSHIKA. A title of Vishvamitra after his grandfather.
The name of a devotee who went to hell for having pointed out a road to robbers by which they pursued and killed some persons who were fleeing from them.

KAUSHIKI. The sister of Vishvamitra who became a river.

KAUSTUBHA. The celebrated jewel that was churned from the ocean and later adorned the breast of Vishnu.

KAVANDHAS. Headless spirits or ghosts.

KAVASHIN. A Sage.

KAVERI. A river, the resort of Apsaras.

KAVYAHANAS. A class of Celestial Beings.

KESARIN. The father of Hanuman, a monkey warrior.

KESHINI. A river.

KESIINI. King Sagara's chief queen.

KETUMATI. The consort of Sumali.

KEYURA. A bracelet worn on the upper arm.

KHAGA. 'Coursing in the highest heaven', a title of the sun.

KHARA. A titan, the brother of Ravana, who was slain by Rama.

KHIVA or KHEEVA. Frumenty; hulled wheat boiled in milk and sweetened.

KILA-KILA. The monkeys' cry.

KIMPURUSHAS. Beings, half human, half animal, sometimes identified with the Kinneras.

KINKARAS. Titans sent out by Ravana to capture Hanuman after he had destroyed the Ashoka Grove.

KINKINI. A small bell or woven band of small bells.

KINNERAS. Celestial Beings with horses heads who attend on the God Kuvera.

KIRATAS. A race of hunters.

KIRTI. A celestial nymph personifying fame and glory.

KISHKINDHA. The country ruled over by Bali, possibly Mysore; this kingdom was handed on to Sugriva by Rama.

KNOWER OF SELF. A knower of Truth or Reality—an illumined being.

KOSHALA. The kingdom ruled over by King Dasaratha.

KOTI. Ten millions.

KOYASHTIKA. A lapwing.

KRATHANA. A monkey warrior.

KRATU. A great Sage, one of the seven immortal Sages, Regents of the stars of the constellation of the Plough.

KRATUDHAMA. 'Protector of sacrifices', a title of Vishnu.

KRAUNCHA. A species of heron, Ardea Jaculator.
A mountain.

KRAUNCHACHARYA. A Sage.

KRAUNCHARANYA. A forest.

KRAUNCHAVATA. A mountain.

KRAUNCHI. A daughter of Kashyapa and Tamra; she became the mother of owls and birds of prey.

KRIKARA. A partridge.

KRISHNAGIRI. A mountain.

KRISHNAVARTMAN. Father of Krathana, a monkey leader.

KRISHNAVENI. A river.

KRITANTA. Destiny, fate or death. The name means 'Bringer to an end'.

KRITAYUGA. The Golden Age.

KRITTIKAS. The Pleiades, nurses of the God of War, Karttikeya.

KRODHAVASHA. One of the wives of Kashyapa.

KROSHA. A distance equal to the distance the voice carries.

KSHARANADI. The Kshara River, said to be in hell, its waters are corrosive.

KSHATRAVEDA. A treatise in the Veda relating to a warrior's duties.

KSHATRIYAS. Those of the warrior class.

KSHIRODHA. The ocean of milk.

KSHUPA. The name of one of the kings of the Ikshvaku Race; the word means a bush or shrub, lit.: 'having roots'.

KSHURADHARA. A sharp razor-like instrument.

KUKSHI. Son of Ikshvaku, the father of Vikukshi.
A region explored by the monkeys in search of Sita.

KULA. One of Rama's courtiers.

KULINGA. A city.
A river.
A bird.

KUMBHA. A titan, a son of Kumbhakarna.

KUMBHAHANU. One of Prahasta's companions.

KUMBHAKARNA. The brother of Ravana, a monster slain by Rama.

KUMBHAYONI. A name given to the Sage Agastya referring to his birth in a jar.

KUMBHINASI. The consort of Madhu.

KUMUDA. A monkey leader.

One of the elephants of the four quarters.

KUNJARA. The father of Anjana and maternal grandfather of Hanuman.

The place where Vishvakarma constructed an abode for Agastya.

KURARI. An osprey.

KURUS. A tribe.

A forest.

KUSHA. One of the sons of Rama and Sita.

KUSHADVAJA. The brother of Janaka and father of the wives of Shatrughna and Bharata.

KUSHAMBHA. The son of Kusha and grandson of Brahma.

KUSHANABHA. The son of Kusha and brother of Kushambha; his daughters married Brahmadatta.

KUSHAPARVA. A monkey, the son of Vivasvata.

KUSHASHVA. The son of Sahadeva and father of Somadatta.

KUSHAVATI. The city built by Rama for his son Kusha.

KUSHIKAS. The descendants of Kusha.

KUTIKA. A river.

KUTIKOSHTIKA. A river.

KUTSA. An ascetic.

L

LAGNA KARKA. The sign of Cancer.

LAGNA MEENA. The sign of Pisces.

LAGNAS. The twelve signs of the Zodiac are considered as rising above the horizon in the course of the day. The Lagna has the name of the sign, its duration is from the first rising of the sign till the whole is above the horizon. Lagna literally means the point where the horizon and the path of the planet meet.

LAKSHMANA. The son of King Dasaratha and Queen Sumitra and the favourite brother of Rama, who accompanied him in his exile. Lakshmana was said to be the incarnation of the Serpent Shesha who upholds the world, and also an aspect of Vishnu.

LAMBA. A mountain.

LANKA. The kingdom ruled over by Ravana, King of the Titans, or what is now Ceylon.

LAVA. The son of Rama and Sita.

LAVANA. The son of Madhu and Kumbhinasi who was slain by Shatrughna.

LAYAS. Time in regard to music, quick, moderate, slow.

LOHITANGA. The Planet Mars.

LOKAPALAS. The Guardians of the four quarters who were Gods.

LOKASHAMBHU. ' Creator of Joy ', ' Bringer of Happiness ', a title given to Brahma or Shiva.

LOLA. A Danava, the father of Madhu.

LOMAPADA OR RAMAPADA. A king whose story is told in Balakanda.

LOMASA. A titan.

LOPADMUDRA. The wife of the Sage Agastya.

LOSHTA. A vessel of coconut or metal used for begging and ceremonial purposes.

M

MADA. The temporal juices of an elephant in rut.
The frenzy of intoxication.

MADANA. The God of Love, Kama or Kandarpa.

MADAYANTI. The wife of King Saudasa.

MADGU or MADGUKA. Water-fowl.

MADHA. Spiritous liquor made of honey and molasses and the blossom of Bassia Latifolia.

MADHAVA. A name of Vishnu.

MADHAVI. A name of the earth meaning ' Vernal Beauty ' or ' Drinker of Soma '.

MADHU. A demon, slain by Vishnu

MADHUCCHANDA. Vishvamitra's son who was cursed by his father for disobedience.

MADHUMANTA. A city founded by Danda.

MADHUMATTA. One of Rama's courtiers.

MADHUPARKA. A mixture of curds, butter, honey and the milk of coconut, a traditional offering.,

MADHUPURA. The city of Madhu taken by Ravana.

MADHUSHPANDA. A son of Vishvamitra.

MADHUSUDANA. A name of Vishnu meaning the ' Destroyer of Madhu '.

MADHUVANA. The wood devastated by the monkeys.

MADHYA. A number equal to ten Arbudas.

MAGADHA. A kingdom, now South Bihar.

MAGADHAS. The people of Magadha.
The country of the Magadhas.
Panegyrists.

MAGDHA-PHALGUNI. The season from the middle of January to the middle of March.

MAGHAVAN. A title of the God Indra.

MAHADAMSHTRA. A titan who fought against the Gods.

MAHADEVA. ' Great God ', a title of Shiva.

MAHAKAYA. A titan warrior.

MAHANADA. ' Loud-throated ', the name of a titan warrior.

MAHAPADMA. One of the elephants supporting the four quarters.

MAHAPARSHWA. ' Mighty-flanked ', a titan warrior.

MAHAPRASTHANA. Death, the word means ' Setting out on the great journey ' or ' Departure from life '.

MAHARADA. A titan 'warrior.

MAHARAKSHA. A titan, the son of Khara.

MAHARATHA. A son of Vishvamitra.

MAHARATHAS. Car-warriors, those who can take on ten thousand archers single-handed.

MAHARATHRAS. Great warriors.

MAHARSHIS. Great Rishis, also spelt Maharishis.

MAHARUNA. A mountain.

MAHASENA. The God of War, Skanda or Karttikcya.

MAHASHALA or MAHASHAILA. A mountain where the sun was said to rise.

MAHAT. Cosmic Intellect.

MAHATEJAS. ' Of great energy or lustre ', a title.

MAHATMA. ' Great soul ', a title given to a Rishi or Sage.

MAHAVANA. Great forest.

MAHENDRA. A name of Indra.

   A mountain in the centre of the sea visited by Indra at the time of the new moon.

MAHESHWARA. A name of Shiva.

MAHII. The Earth Goddess.

MAHIMATI. The city ruled over by Arjuna, King of the Haihayas.

MAHISHA. A ' Great or powerful animal ', a name given to Dundubhi, the buffalo slain by Bali.

MAHISHMATI. A city ruled over by the God of Fire.

MAHODARA. The name of a son of Vishvamitra.

   A general in Ravana's army. The name means ' Huge-bellied '.

MAHODAYA. An ascetic who was transformed into one of the lowest caste by Vishvamitra's curse. The mountain where the sacred herbs that revived Lakshmana grew.

MAINA. A small percher about the size of a swallow which can be taught to repeat words. Also called Mina or Mynah.

MAINAKA. A golden mountain north of Kailasha.

   A nymph who tempted Vishvamitra.

MAINDA. A monkey leader.

MAIREYA or MIREYA. Liquor extracted from the blossom of ' Lythrum Fructicosum '.

MAITHILA or MITHILA. The capital of Videha, a kingdom ruled over by King Janaka.

MAITHILI. A name of Sita as daughter of the King of Mithila.

MAITRA. The period of early morning.

GLOSSARY

MAKARA. A kind of sea-monster, sometimes confounded with a shark, crocodile or dolphin.

MALAVANA. A country.

MALAYA. A mountain on the summit of which Agastya dwelt.

MALI. One of the sons of Sukesha.

MALYAVAN or MALYAVAT. Ravana's father-in-law, the brother of Sumali and father of Mandodari.

MANASA or MANASAROVA. A lake on Mt. Kailasha, said to be hollowed out of the mind of Brahma. The name means ' Lake of the Mind '; it is still considered a sacred place.

MANDAKINI. A river near Mount Chittrakuta.

A treeless mountain where Kama practised austerities.

MANDALA. A circle.

MANDARA. A mountain used in the churning of the ocean by the Gods and Asuras.

MANDARKANI. A Sage.

MANDAVI. Bharata's wife, the daughter of King Kushadwaja.

MANDEHAS. Terrible demons that hung suspended from rocks in Garuda's abode.

MANDHATA or MANDHATRI. A king of the race of Ikshvaku, the son of Yuvaneshwa.

MANDODARI. Ravana's consort and the mother of Indrajita.

MANGALA. A monkey warrior.

MANIBADRA. One of Kuvera's warriors who was slain by Prahasta.

MANIBHADRA. A Yaksha defeated by Dashagriva; see under Parshva-Mauli.

MANKUKA. A musical instrument.

MANMATHA. A name of Kama, the God of Love.

MANTHARA. The hunch-backed maid of Kaikeyi, who inspired her mistress to exact the fulfilment of the boons King Dasaratha had conferred on her.

MANTRA. A sacred formula.

MANTRAPALA. A minister of Dasaratha's court.

MANU. The first man, who was given the holy truth by his father Vivasvata. See Bhagavadgita Ch. IV, opening verses.

MARICHA. A demon who, disguised as a deer, lured Rama from his hermitage, thus leaving Sita alone and allowing Ravana to bear her away.

MARICHAS. Offspring of the Ascetic Maricha.

MARICHIMAN. ' Having rays ', a title given to the Sun.

MARKANDEYA. A Sage who was remarkable for his austerities. A Purana is named after him.

MARTANDA. A name of the Sun.

MARTANDAKA. ' He who infuses life into the Mundane Egg ', a name of the Lord.

MARU. A desert that arose from a rift made by Rama's arrows in Drumakulya.

MARUKANTARA. The place on which Rama loosed an arrow on the request of the Ocean.

MARUTAS. Lords of the Tempest.

MARUTI. A name of Hanuman as son of Maruta, the Wind-god.

MARUTTA. A king who encountered Ravana while sacrificing to the Gods.

A Sage, disciple of Samvarta. Marutta officiated at the Ashvamedha Sacrifice for King Ila.

MASHAS. A class of Sage or Hermit.

A measure.

MATALI. Indra's charioteer.

MATANGA. A Sage.

A forest or wood.

MATANGAS. Elephants.

MATARISHVAN. An aerial Being mentioned in the Rig Veda as bringing down fire to earth.

MATHURA. A sacred city.

MATTA. A titan warrior.

MAUDGALYA. A Sage.

MAYA. The deluding power of the Lord by which the universe has come into existence and appears as real.

The son of Diti, a giant who created a magical cave for the Nymph Hema, his consort. Maya was the artificer of the Gods.

MAYAVI. A giant slain by Bali.

MEDINI. A name of the earth on account of it having been covered by the marrow of Madhu and Kaitabha after they had been slain by Vishnu.

MEGHA. The Regent of the clouds.

MEGHANADA. A name of Indrajita meaning ' The Roar of a thunder-cloud '.

MEGHAS. Musical instruments.

One of the ' ragas ' or musical scales.

MEKHALA. An ornament worn round the waist.

MERU. A sacred mountain said to be the abode of Celestial Beings.

MERUSAVARNI. A great ascetic.

MITRAGHNA. A titan warrior slain by Rama.

MITRASAHA. The son of King Saudasa, a king of the Raghu Race.

MLECCHAS. Foreigners, barbarians, eaters of flesh ; a people said to have been born of the sacred cow Shabala for her protection.

MODAKA. A kind of sweetmeat.

MODAKARA. A Sage.

MONKEYS. Sometimes called Vanaras or Forest Dwellers or Deer of the Trees, etc. See also Viharas, Valimukhas.

MRIDANGA. A kind of drum.

MRIDU. One of Bali's fortresses.

The Planet Saturn.

A Danava.

MRIGI. The daughter of Krodavasha, the mother of elephants.

MRITASAMJIVANI. See under FLOWERS and TREES GLOSSARY.

MRITYU. The God of Death, another name of Yama, meaning ' Bringer of Death '.

MUDITAS. A class of servants.

MUHURTA. An instant, a moment, an hour according to the context.

MUNDI. ' Shaven ' or ' bald '.

MUNI. A holy Sage, a pious or learned person, a title given to a holy man.

MURACHAPATTNA. A country.

MURAGA. A tambourine.

MUSHTIKAS. People cursed by Vishvamitra who subsequently assumed the lowest caste.

N

NABHAGA. The son of Yayati and father of Aja.

NAGABHOGAS. Sea-serpents.

NAGAS. Those of the Serpent Race.

NAHUSHA. The father of King Yayati. Nahusha's curious story is found in the Mahabharata and the Puranas.

NAIGAMAS. Interpreters of the Veda.

NAIMISHA WOOD. A wood so-called because Gauri-mukha destroyed the army of Asuras there in the ' twinkling of an eye ', ' nai-misha ' meaning '. twinkling '. It was in this wood that Rama celebrated the Ashvamedha Sacrifice.

NAIRRITA. The ruling star of the titans.

NAIRRITAS. A name given to the titans as offspring of Nairrita.

NAKIN. One dwelling in the sky or ' Naka ', a divine being.

NAKSHATRA. The Hindus, in addition to the common division of the Zodiac into twelve signs, divided it into twenty-seven Nakshatras, two in each sign. Each Nakshatra has its appropriate name :—

    1. Ashwini. 2. Bharani. 3. Krittika. 4. Rohini. 5. Mrgashiras. 6. Ardea. 7. Purnavasu. 8. Pushya. 9. Alesha. 10. Magna. 11. Purva Phalguni. 12. Uttara-Phalguni. 13. Hasta. 14. Chitra. 15. Svati. 16. Vishaka. 17. Anuradha. 18. Jyasatha. 19 Mula. 20. Purvashadha. 21. Uttarashraddha. 22. Abijit. 23. Shravana. 24. Shravishtha or Dhanishta. 25. Shatabhishaj. 26. Purva Bhadrapada. 27. Uttara Bhadrapada. 28. Revati.*.

    * The last is used if Abijit is omitted.

NALA. A monkey chief, general in Sugriva's army.

NALAKUVERA. The son of Vaishravana who was wedded to Rambha and cursed Ravana for his assault on her.

NALINI. A river.

NAMUCHI. A demon slain by Indra by means of the foam on water.

A Sage.

NANDANA. The celestial Gardens of Indra.

NANDI. The sacred bull that is Shiva's vehicle and which symbolizes the Sattwa-guna.

NANDIGRAMA. The city from which Bharata ruled in Rama's absence.

NANDISHVARA. A Sage who cursed Ravana.

NARADA. A divine Sage who appeared to Valmiki and told him the history of Rama's life. See Balakanda.

NARAKA. Hell, of which Manu enumerates twenty divisions, some being the abode of serpents or demons. The seven best known are : Atala, Vitala, Sutala, Rasatala, Talatala, Mahatala and Patala.

The name of a demon slain by Indra.

A son of Kashyapa and Kalaka.

NARANTAKA. 'Destroyer of man', a son of Ravana.

NARAVAHANA. The King of Kailasha who was vanquished by Ravana.

NARAYANA. A name of Vishnu, so called because the waters (Nara) were his first place of motion.

NARMADA. A river.

A Gandharvi, whose daughters married Sumali, Mali and Malyavan.

NARTAKAS. Dancers, actors, bards, mummers or heralds.

NATAS. Dancers.

NATYUHA or NATYUHAKA. A small gallinule.

NIDHIS. The personified treasures of the God of Wealth.

NIKUMBHA. A titan, the son of Kumbhakarna.

NIKUMBHILA. A grove on the outskirts of Lanka.

NILA. A monkey chief, general in Sugriva's army.

NISHADAS. A mountain tribe dwelling in the Vindhya Range who lived by hunting.

NISHAKARA. An ascetic, friend of animals and of the vultures Sampati and Jatayu.

NISHKA. A gold piece or nugget, sometimes worn as an ornament.

NISHUMBHA. See Shumbha.

NIVATAKAVACHAS. A race of giants. The word means 'Whose armour is impenetrable'.

NIYUTA. A hundred thousand.

NRIGA. A king whose story is told in Uttarakanda.

NRISHANGU. A Sage.

NRISNGHA. An Incarnation of Vishnu as half-man, half-lion.

O

OM. See under Aum.

OMKARA. The sacred syllable ' OM ' or ' AUM '.

OSHADHI-PRASTHA. The ' Place of medicinal herbs ', a city in the Himalayas mentioned in the ' Kumara Sambhava ' a poem, on the God of War by Kalidasa.

P

PADMA. A measurement, a thousand billions.
  A Yaksha.
  An elephant.
  A lotus.

PADMACHALU WOODS. Woods where the monkeys sought Sita.

PADMANABHA. The ' Lotus-navelled One ', a name of Vishnu.

PADMAPRABODHA. ' He who awakens the lotus ', a title of the Sun.

PADMAVANA. ' The Lotus-forest ', a celestial retreat.

PAHLAVAS. Warriors born of the sacred cow Shabala, for her protection. A name possibly given to the Persians.

PAKA. A demon slain by Indra.

PAKASHASANA. ' The Punisher of Paka ', a title given to Indra.

PAKSHAJA. The moon.
  Winged clouds.

PALVALA. A lake.

PAMPA. The lake by which Rama and Lakshmana rested in their exile.

PANASA or PANASHA. A monkey leader.
  A titan who was one of Bibishana's counsellors.

PANCHAJANA. A Danava slain by Vishnu.

PANCHAJANYA. Vishnu's conch.

PANCHAPSARAS. The ' Lake of the Five Nymphs ', created by the Sage Mandarkani.

PANCHARATRA. The name of the Vaishnava Sect.

PANCHAVATI. A district near the source of the Godavari River.

PANDU. A mountain.

PANNAGAS. Celestial Serpents, the offspring of Kadru.

PARADHA. A Samudra thirty times.

PARAGAS. Winged creatures.

PARAMARISHIS. Great or Supreme Rishis.

PARAMATMAN. The Absolute, Brahman.

PARANTAPA. A title meaning the ' Oppressor or Subduer of a foe '.

PARASURAMA. ' Rama with the Axe ', the sixth Incarnation of Vishnu, as the son of Yamadagni and Renuka.

PARATPARA. A title meaning ' Greater than the Great '.

PARIHARYAS. Bracelets.

PARIPLAVA. A spoon used in sacrifices.

PARISHTARANIKA. A funeral couch or pyre.

PARIYATRA. One of the principal mountain ranges in India, said to rise from the sea.

PARJANYA. A Vedic Deity or Rain God. Sometimes used as a title for Indra.

PARSHVA-MAULI. 'One with his diadem awry', a name given to the Yaksha Manibhadra after being struck by Dashagriva in combat.

PARUSHA. A titan.

PARVAN. The period of the moon's change.

PARVATA. A Sage who cursed King Nriga.

PARVATI. Shiva's consort; also known under many other names such as :—
Devi, Girija, Kanya, Sati, Padma-Lanchana, Shiva-Duti, Uma and so on.

PASHPOTKALA. Son of Sumali and Ketumati.

PASHUPATI. 'Lord of Creatures', a title given to Shiva.

PATAHA. A war-drum.

PATALA. See under Naraka.

PATTIKAS. Plates of metal (usually copper) inscribed with royal edicts

PAULASTYA. See Poulastya.

PAULOMA. The wife of Kashyapa and mother of the Danavas.

PAULOMI. The consort of Indra, also known as Sachi.

PAUNDARIKA. The Soma Sacrifice lasting twelve days.

PAURNAMASA. A sacrifice performed at the full moon.

PAVAKA. A name of Agni, the God of Fire.

PAVAKAKSHA. A monkey warrior.

PAVAKI. The 'Son of Fire', a name of Skanda, the God of War.

PAVANI. A river.

PAYASA. A preparation of rice and milk.

PHALGUNI. A Nakshatra q.v.

PHANA. A titan.

PINAKA. Shiva's sacred bow.

PINDA. A funeral cake or offering.

PINGAS. 'Tawny Ones', a name given to the monkey race.

PISACHAS. Ghosts or evil spirits.

PISHITAKASHANAS. Flesh-eating imps or goblins, a name also given to the titans.

PITRIS. Ancestors or Manes.

PLAVAGAS or PLAVAGAMAS. 'Those who move by leaps or bounds', the monkeys.

POULASTYA. One of the Seven Immortal Sages and the grandfather of Ravana.

PRABHA. The consort of the moon and sometimes said to be the personification of the light of the sun.

PRABHAKARA. A name of the sun.

PRABHAVA. A minister of Sugriva.

PRABHAVISHNU. A name of Vishnu.

PRABHOJYA. A monkey leader.

PRACANDA. 'The Fierce One', a name of the sun.

PRACETAS. The eleventh Prajapati, Guardian of the West. The father of Valmiki.
A name given to Varuna and Agni.

PRADAKSHINA. A salutation which consists of circumambulating a person keeping him on the right hand.

PRAGHASA. A titan slain by Hanuman.

PRAHASA. One of Varuna's ministers.

PRAHASTA. A titan, the father of Jambumalin and Ravana's counsellor. He was the conqueror of Manibhadra and was later slain by Nila.

PRAHETI. A Daitya, see Heti.

PRAHRADA. A Daitya.

PRAJANGHA. A monkey warrior.

PRAJAPATI. 'Lord of Beings', a name given to Brahma and other Gods.

PRAJAPATIS. The sons of Brahma.

PRAJYOTISHA. A city.

PRALAMBA. A mountain.

PRALAYA. The time of dissolution of the world at the end of a world cycle.

PRAMATHA. A titan.

PRAMATHIN. A monkey renowned for his courage.

PRAMATI. One of Bibishana's ministers.

PRAMODANA. An ascetic.

PRAMUCHI. An ascetic.

PRANA. Vital air or breath.

PRANAYAMA. The Practice or Science of breath control.

PRANJALI. A gesture of respect, holding the hands slightly hollowed, side by side as if presenting an offering.

PRASABHA. A monkey warrior.

PRASENAJIT. The son of Susamdhi and brother at Dhruvasamdhi.

PRASRAVANA. A mountain.

PRATAPANA. A titan.

PRATARDANA. The King of Kashi, also called Kasheya, an ally of Rama.

PRATHISHTHANA. A city founded by King Kardameya.

PRATIHARA. A doorkeeper.

PRATYAKSTHALI. A sacred grove or a site facing the west.

PRAUSTHAPADA. The month which is part of August and September.

PRAYAGA. The confluence of the Ganges and the Yamuna, which is considered a sacred spot.

PRETAS. Ghosts.

PRISHATA. A spotted deer or piebald horse.

PRITHIVI. The earth.

PRITHU. The son of Anaranya and the father of Trishanku.
A monkey warrior.

PRITHUGRIVA. A titan.

PRIYAKA. A dappled deer.

PULAHA. The twelfth Prajapati.

PULOMA. The daughter of the Demon Vaishvanara who became
the wife of Kashyapa.

PUNARVASU. The seventh and considered the most auspicious
Nakshatra q.v.

PUNDARIKA. A nymph.

PUNDRAS. A country.

PUNTIKASTHALA. A nymph outraged by Ravana.

PUNYASHLOKA. 'Well spoken of', 'Famed', a title of Vishnu.

PURANAS. Legends and tales of ancient times in epic form ; there
are eighteen main Puranas.

PURANDARA. 'Destroyer of Cities', a title of Indra.

PURODHAS. See Purohita.

PUROHITA. A family priest.

PURU. The son of Yayati.

PURURAVA. A king who yielded to Ravana without fighting.

PURURAVAS. The son of Budha and Ila. Pururavas married the
Nymph Urvashi and their son was Ayus.

PURUSHA. The Supreme Spirit, the Soul of the Universe, the
original man.
A measurement, said to be twelve span.

PURVAJA. 'Appearing before creation', a title applied to ancestors.

PUSHA or PUSHAN. The sun or 'Newly-risen Sun' or 'Maintainer',
a Vedic Deity, brother of Surya, personified as a herdsman in
the heavens.

PUSHKALA. Bharata's son.

PUSHKALAVATA. The City of the Gandharvas ruled over by
Bharata's son.

PUSHKARA. A general in Varuna's army.

PUSHPADANTA. 'Flowery-toothed', the name of one of Shiva's
attendants.
A Sage.

PUSHPITAKA. A mountain in the sea where Celestial Beings
dwelt.

PUSHPOTAKA. A female titan, the daughter of Sumali.

PUSHYA. A constellation of three stars considered to be auspicious.
When the moon is in a certain degree of the Sign Cancer,
it is said to be under the Pushya Asterism.

PUTRA. A son, who is said to deliver his father from hell or 'Put'.

PUTTRESTI. A ceremony for extending the race by the birth of
sons.

RABHASA A titan warrior.

RABHRU. A Gandharva, one of the guardians of the sandalwood forest.

RAGHAVA. A title of those belonging to the House of Raghu to which King Dasaratha and his forbears belonged.

RAGHU. The son of Kakutstha and father of Pravriddha.

RAHU. A mythical demon said to cause the eclipse of the sun or moon by assuming a meteor's shape.

RAJAGRIHA. The city ruled over by Bharata's maternal uncle, from which Bharata was brought home on the occasion of Rama's exile.

RAJAHAMSA. A royal swan or flamingo.

RAJARISHI. A royal Rishi. See also under Rishi.

RAJAS. See under Gunas.

RAJASUYA SACRIFICE. A great sacrifice performed in ancient times at the installation of a monarch.

RAJATALAYA. The ' Place of the Silver-navelled One ', a mountain near Mount Kailasha.

RAKA. One of Sumali's sons.

RAKSHA RITES. Rites to avert evil.

RAKSHASAS. Titans or demons.

RAKSHASI. A female titan or demon.

RAKTA. ' Of a red or crimson colour ', a name of the Sun.

RAMA or RAMACHANDRA. The Incarnation of Vishnu who appeared as the eldest son of King Dasaratha. It is round this great figure that the Ramayana is written.

RAMA-KAʃHA. The recitation of ' Ramayana ' which has been a tradition in India for thousands of years.

RAMBHA. A nymph who symbolized the perfection of beauty and who was often sent from Indra's realm to distract Sages from their pious practices.
    A monkey leader.

RAMYA. A mountain.

RASALA. A preparation of buttermilk.

RASATALA. A hell, said to be at the bottom of the sea ; it was explored by the sons of Sagara and is often mentioned.

RASHMIKETU. A titan warrior slain by Rama.

RASHTRAVARDHANA. One of Rama's ministers.

RATALAYA. ' Silver-navelled ', the abode of a form of Hiranya-garbha.

RATHA. A chariot.

RATNA. A necklace.

RAURAVA. One of the hells.

RAVANA. A titan who became King of Lanka and after countless wicked deeds, carried off Sita and was ultimately slain by Rama.

RAVI. The Sun.

RENUKA. The wife of Yamadagni and the mother of Parasurama.

RICHIKA. An ascetic who gave his second son Shunashepha to be sacrificed.

   The son of Bhrigu to whom Vishnu gave his bow.

   The husband of Satyavati.

RIG or RIG-VEDA. The original Veda, a collection of hymns.

RIKSHABHA. A mountain.

RIKSHAS. The bears.

RIKSHAVAT. A mountain.

RIKSHYA. A monkey.

RISHAKHA. A monkey leader.

RISHI. A great Sage or illumined Being of which there were four classes :—

   Maharishi—A great Rishi.

   Rajarishi—A royal Rishi.

   Brahmarishi. A sacred Rishi.

   Devarishi. A divine Rishi.

RISHYAMUKA. The mountain on which Sugriva took refuge and where he met Rama.

RISHYASHRINGA. The ' Deer-horned ', the son of Sage Vibhandaka, who married the daughter of King Lomapada, Shanta, and later performed the Puttresti ceremony for King Dasaratha.

RITADHAMAN. A title of Vishnu meaning ' Of true and pure nature '. It is also used for the thirteenth Manu.

RITU. Any fixed time appointed for regular worship or sacrifice such as Vasanta, the Spring; Grishna the hot season; Sarad, the Autumn; Hemantashishshira, the cold and dewy season.

RITVIJS. The priests officiating at an installation ceremony.

ROD OF BRAHMA. See also WEAPONS Glossary.

ROHI. A fish—Cyprynus Rohita Ham.

   A deer.

ROHINI. The Star Aldebaran.

ROHITA. A species of deer.

   A Gandharva who guarded a sandalwood forest.

ROHITAS. The name of the steeds of the Sun-god.

   The name of a Deity celebrated in the Atharva Veda probably a form of the Sun or Fire-god.

ROMASHA. A monkey.

RUDHIRASHANA. A titan.

RUDRA. A name of Shiva.

RUDRAS. The sons of Kashyapa and Aditi.

RUDRASHARAPRAMOKSHA. A place sacred to Shiva where he discharged the arrow at Tripura the Demon.

RUMA. Sugriva's consort.

RUMANA. A monkey warrior, general in Sugriva's army.

GLOSSARY

RUPAYAKA. An island full of gold mines where the monkeys searched for Sita.
RURU. A deer.
RUSHIRAS. A class of Yatudhanas.

S

SACHI. Indra's consort who was said to be the daughter of the Daitya Puloman.
SADAGATI. ' Ever-going ', a name of Vayu, the Wind-god.
SADHYA. The daughter of Daksha.
SADHYAS. The personified rites and prayers of the Vedas, who dwell between heaven and earth and are classes as Deities.
SADIN. A titan.
SAGARA. A king whose history is recorded in Balakanda.
SAHASRADHARA. The discus of Vishnu that was forged by Vishvakarma.
SAHASRAKSHA. The ' Thousand-eyed God ', a title of Indra.
SAHASRARCHIS. ' Thousand-rayed ', a title of the Sun.
SAHIRA. A mountain.
SAHYA. A mountain passed by the monkeys on their march to the sea.
SAKATA. A wooden mortar for cleaning rice.
SALAKATANTAKA. The daughter of Sandhya and the consort of the Titan Vidyukesha.
SALAKATANKATA. A race of giants to which Malyavan, Mali and Sumali belonged.
SALVEYAS. The mountains where the Monkey Sharabha lived.
SAMHRADA. One of Sumali's sons.
     A titan warrior.
SAMIDH The fuel, wood, logs or grass in a sacrificial offering.
SAMNADA. A monkey chief.
SAMNADANA. Grandsire of the monkeys.
SAMNUNATA. A titan.
SAMPATI. The vulture, brother of Jatayu, who told the monkeys where Sita was held captive.
SAMROCANA. A mountain.
SAMSKARAS. Latent impressions.
SAMUDRA. A measure, a Madhya twenty times.
     The waters as a whole, the ocean.
SAMVA. The mountain on which Hanuman alighted on his flight to Lanka.
SAMVARTA. The brother of Brihaspati.
SAMVASADANA. A titan slain by Hanuman's father, Kesarin.
SAMYODHAKANTAKA. A Yaksha, one of Kuvera's warriors.
SANATKUMARA. One of the mind-born sons of Brahma.
SANDHANA. A mountain.

GLOSSARY

SANDHYA. The Goddess of the dawn and dusk.
Devotions undertaken at dawn and dusk.

SANKU. A measure, a thousand Arbudas q.v.

SANTANAS or SANTANAKAS. A region near or the extension of Brahmaloka where the bears and monkeys went on leaving their bodies.

SANU. A monkey warrior.

SANUPRASTHA. A monkey warrior.

SAPINDI. The Sapindi Ceremony was undertaken for the establishing the connection with kindred through funeral offerings.
One of the titan generals.

SAPTAJANAS. The hermitage of the seven Sages.

SAPTAGHNA. A titan warrior.

SAPTARSHI. The seven Rishis who are said to be the Regents of the Seven Stars of the Plough.

SAPTA-SAPTI. 'He from whom proceed the seven senses' or 'Who has seven steeds', a title of the Sun-god.

SARAMA. The daughter of the King of the Gandharvas Shailusha; she was the consort of Bibishana.

SARANGA. A bird or animal of variegated colour such as the peacock or spotted deer.

SARASA. A goose.

SARASWATI. The Goddess of speech and learning.
A river.

SARAYU. The sacred river, the Sarju.

SARGA. A chapter

SARVABHAUMA. The elephant that carried Kuvera.
One of the elephants of the four quarters.

SARVANSHADI. Consists of 'Mura Valerian' and such drugs.

SARVASAU VARNA. A mountain.

SARVATHASIDDHA. A brahmin who ill-treated a dog, his story is told in Uttarakanda.

SARVATMABHUTI. All beings collectively.

SATARHADA. The mother of the Demon Viradha.

SATATAGA. The Wind-god.

SATYAVATI. The sister of the Sage Vishvamitra, who assumed the form of the River Kaushika.

SATYA YUGA. The Golden Age. There are four Yugas that make up the World cycle :—

Satya Yuga. Golden Age.
Treta Yuga. Silver Age.
Dwapara Yuga. Copper Age.
Kali Yuga. Black or Iron Age.

SAUDASA. A king of the Ikshvaku Race.

SAUMANASA. One of the elephants of the four quarters.
A mountain where the Ascetics or Vaikhanasas performed their austerities.

SAUMITRI. A name of Lakshmana as son of Sumitra.

SAUMYA. The Planet Mercury.

SAURA. A divine potion; the name means ' relating to the Sun '.

SAURASHTRAS. A country where the monkeys searched for Sita.

SAUVARCALA. Sochal Salt or alkali.

SAVITA or SAVITRI. The sun, the producer of heat and the spiritual faculties of heat.

SENANI. The leader of an army.
> A name for the God of Love.

SETUBANDHA. The sacred spot where Rama threw the bridge over the sea to Lanka.

SHABALA. The wish-fulfilling cow belonging to Vasishtha.

SHABARI or SHIBRI. A female ascetic whom Rama visited while in exile.

SHADVALA. A grassy spot.

SHAILA. A mountain.

SHAILODA. A river.

SHAILUSHA. A Gandharva, guardian of a sandalwood forest.

SHAIVALA. The mountain where Rama found the Shudra ascetic and slew him.

SHAKAS. A people.

SHAKRA. A name of Indra, King of the Gods.

SHAKRADHWAJA. A standard or flag set up in honour of Indra.

SHAKRALAYA. The abode of Shakra.

SHAKRAMALI. A fabulous thorny rod of the cotton tree used for torturing the wicked in hell.

SHALYAKA. A porcupine. See also WEAPONS GLOSSARY.

SHAMBARA. The Demon of Drought represented in the Rig-veda as the enemy of Indra.

SHAMBARAKARMOKA. The place of Shambara's bow.

SHAMBHU. ' Bringer of Felicity ', the name of a Vedic Deity, later associated with Shiva.

SHAMBHUININ. The ' Soul of the Universe ' in its cosmic form of the eleven Rudras.

SHAMBUKA. A Shudra who sought to become a brahmin and was slain by Rama.

SHAMKHA. One of the Great Serpents.

SHANKHAS. A measure, a hundred billions or a hundred thousand crores.

SHANKHASHUDA. A monkey warrior.

SHANKU. A measure, ten billions.

SHANTA. The daughter of King Lomapada who was wedded to the Sage Rishyashringa.

SHARABANDA. The mother of the Demon Viradha.

SHARABHA. The Chief of the Bears.

SHARABHANGA. A Sage who was visited by Rama and Sita in the Dandaka Forest.

SHARABHU. 'Reed-born', a name of Karttikeya.

SHARABI. A monkey warrior.

SHARAGULMA. A monkey leader.

SHARDULA. One of Ravana's spies.

SHARIKA. A bird, 'Turdas Salica' or 'Gracula Religiosa'.

SHARMISHTA. The daughter of Diti and wife of King Yayati.

SHARNGA. The 'Bow of Time' belonging to Vishnu.

SHASHABINDU. The son of Kardameya.

SHASHANKA. The consort of Rohini, a name of the moon.

SHASHI. 'Hare-marked', a name of the Moon-god.

SHASHTRAS. Teachings of divine and recognized authority.

SHATABALI. A monkey leader.

SHATAGULMA. A monkey warrior.

SHATANANDA. The son of the Sage Gautama and the Spiritual Director of King Janaka.

SHATAPATRA. A title meaning 'Having a hundred petals'.

SHATAVALA. A monkey leader.

SHATAVALI. A monkey warrior.

SHATHA. A titan.

SHATRUGHATIN. A son of Shatrughna.

SHATRUGHNA. 'Slayer of Enemies', the fourth son of King Dasaratha.

SHATRUMJAYA. The elephant that carried Sugriva in Rama's coronation procession.

SHIKHIN. The God of War, Karttikeya is called by this name as the offspring of Shikhin or Shiva.

SHIRIRANASHANA. 'Remover of intellectual arrogance or evil-mindedness', a title.

SHISHIRA. 'Benevolent, cool-rayed', a title.

SHISHUMARA. 'Child-killer', a word used for a crocodile, a por-poise or a dolphin.

SHITIKANTHA. Shiva, the name means 'bark-throated'.

SHIVA. The Lord in the aspect of 'Destroyer of Ignorance' and 'Lord of Bliss'.

SHIVI or SHIVYA. A king of the Raghu dynasty who rescued the God Agni when he had transformed himself into a pigeon and was pursued by Indra in the form of a hawk.

SHONA. A sacred river.

SHONITAKSHA. A titan warrior.

SHRAVANA. The month which is part of July and August. A Nakshatra q.v.

SHRAVASTI. The city ruled over by Lava, Rama's son.

SHRI. The consort of Vishnu, Lakshmi who is the Goddess of Prosperity. A title of courtesy.

SHRIMATI. The wife of the Sage Kapila.

SHRIVATSA. The mark or curl that Vishnu bears on his breast.

SHRUTA-KIRTI. The consort of Shatrughna.

SHRUTI. The Vedas severally.

SHTANU. 'The Firm', a name of Shiva.

SHUDRA. One of the lowest caste.

SHUKA. One of Ravana's spies.
>> A Gandharva.
>> A Parrot.

SHUKRA. The Planet Venus.
>> A great Sage, Shukracharya who was said to be the son of Bhrigu and whose patronymic was Bhargava.

SHUMBHA. Shumbha and Nishumbha were two Asuras and brothers who warred against the Gods and were slain by the Goddess Durga.
>> A monkey warrior.

SHUNAKA. The son of the Sage Richika.
>> An Asura.

SHUNASHEPHA. The second son of the Sage Richika who was offered as a human sacrifice but saved by the Sage Vishvamitra.

SHURA. A Gandharva, guardian of a sandalwood forest.

SHURASHENA. The region round Mathura. The word means 'Worthy of Heroes'.
>> A city ruled over by Shatrughna.

SHURPANAKHA. The sister of Ravana, a female titan who was mutilated by Rama and Lakshmana.

SHVASANA. A name of the Wind-god.
>> A name for the Demon of Drought.

SHVETA. A mountain.
>> The Planet Venus.
>> The King of Vidarbha.
>> A monkey warrior.
>> A son of King Sudesa.

SHYENI. The daughter of Kashyapa and Tamra, mother of birds of prey.

SIDDHARTHA. One of King Dasaratha's counsellors.

SIDDHAS. Semi-divine Beings who dwell between the earth and the sun.

SIDHU. A kind of rum distilled from molasses.

SIKHANDI. 'Overcomer', a title.

SINDHU. The River Indus.
>> A country east of Koshala.

SINGHIKA or SIMHIKA. A female demon who caught hold of Hanuman's shadow when he was crossing the ocean.

SINHAS. 'Flying Lions', probably eagles.

SITA. The daughter of King Janaka, King of Mithila, and Rama's consort.

SIX KINDS OF TASTE. Sweet, bitter, acid, salt, pungent, acrid and harsh.

SKANDA. The God of War who was the son of Shiva, also called Karttikeya.

SLESHMATAKA. A kind of wood taken from the Cordia Myxa Trees. A forest.

SMRITI. Literally ' What is remembered ', tradition or laws given by Manu and others.

SOMA.' The Moon-god, said to be a son of the Sage Atri.
　　The juice that is fermented from Asclepias-acida ; it is used as a beverage or libation in sacred ceremonies.

SOMADATTA. The daughter of Urmila and mother of Brahmadatta.

SOMAGIRI. A mountain.

SOURA SOURAHTRA. Countries east of Koshala.

SRIMARA. A marine monster.
　　A species of deer.

STHULASHIRA. A Sage who was harassed by the Demon Kabandha.

STONE OF HIMAVAT. The stone on which Rudra sat to practice asceticism.

SUBAHU. A son of Shatrughna, who was installed in the City of Madhava.
　　A monkey warrior.
　　A demon who disturbed the sacrifices of the Sage Vishvamitra.

SUBHADRA. A sacred tree.

SUCHENA. A son of Varuna.

SUDAMSHTRA. A monkey leader.

SUDANANA. One of King Janaka's ministers.

SUDARSHANA. A lake covered with silver lotuses.
　　An island where the sun is said to rise.
　　An elephant ridden in battle by Mahadeva.

SUDESA. A king of the Vidarbhas.

SUDHAMA. The name of one of the guardians of the four quarters.
　　A name of Vishnu.
　　A mountain.

SUGRIVA. The King of the Monkeys, an ally of Rama.

SUHOTRA. A monkey warrior.

SUKANABHA. A titan.

SUKESHA. A Daitya, the son of Vidyutkesha ; his story is told in Uttarakanda.

SUMAGADHA. One of Rama's ministers.

SUMALI. The son of Sukesha and father of Mandodari, Ravana's consort.

SUMANTRA. One of the ministers at Dasaratha's court.

SUMATI. The younger wife of King Sagara who gave birth to six thousand sons.

SUMERU. A sacred mountain.

SUMITRA. The mother of Lakshmana and Shatrughna.

SUMUKHA. A Sage.

SUN. The Sun appears under countless names such as :—Anshuman, Ahaskara, Bhanu, Bhaskara, Divakara, Dinakara, Gavasthana, Prabhakara, Surya, Savita, Sura, Suvarnasdrisha, Twasta, Vyomanatha and others.

SUNABHA. 'Having a beautiful navel', a name given to the Mountain Mainaka.

A name given to the son of Garuda.

SUNDA. The father of Maricha.

SUNDARI. A name meaning 'Beautiful' the consort of Malyavan.

SUPARNA. A name of Garuda, King of the Birds.

SUPARSHVA. A son of the Vulture Sampati.

SUPATALA. A Titan warrior.

SUPRABHA. A Goddess who created celestial weapons; she was a daughter of Daksha.

SUPTAGNA. A monkey warrior.

SURA. The Sun.

SURABHI. The daughter of Krodhavasha; she became the consort of Kashyapa.

SURAJI. One of Rama's courtiers.

SURAMUKRA. A titan general.

SURAS. A name of the Gods; in the Veda it is applied to the offspring of the Sun.

SURASA. A female demon who sought to obstruct Hanuman when he was traversing the ocean.

SURASHENA. The country round Mathura.

SURASHTRAS. One of King Dasaratha's ministers.

SURATHA. A king who yielded to Ravana without fighting.

A son of King Sudesa, King of the Vidarbhas.

SURYAKSHA. A monkey warrior.

SURYANANA. A monkey warrior.

SURYANBANDANA. The place where the suns meet.

SURYAPRABHA. The abode of Surya, the Sun-god.

SURYASACHU. A titan.

SURYASHATRU. A titan general.

SURYAVANA. A mountain.

SUSHENA. A monkey general, the father of Tara, Bali's consort.

SUTA. Khara's charioteer.

SUTAGNA. A son of Malyavan and Sundari.

SUTAS. A class of personal attendants.

SUTIKSHNA. A Sage who lived in the Dandaka Forest and entertained Rama, Lakshmana and Sita during their exile.

SUTRAS. Verses expressed in brief and technical language; poetical rhythms and stanzas. There are Sutras on innumerable subjects beginning with the Vedas.

SUVARCHALA. The consort of the Sun-god.

SUVARNA. One of the gold and silver islands rich in gold mines.

SUVARNASADRISHA. 'Of golden aspect', a name of the Sun.

SUVARNIMERU. One of the so-called ' Golden Mountains ' of which there were sixty thousand.

SUVASASUVARNA. A mountain.

SUVELA. A mountain near Lanka where Rama stationed His troops.

SUYAJNA. ·One of King Dasaratha's spiritual Directors.

SVADAMSHTRAS. Ornaments worn in the ears.

SVADHA. An oblation offered to the Pitris. The word means ' Inherent power or strength '.

SVADU. A sea out of which the Jarupashila Mountain rose.

SVAHA. The consort of Agni.
A word of power used in invocation and sacrifices.

SVAHAKARAS. The utterance of ' Svaha ' at ceremonies.

SWAMPRABHA. The daughter of the Sage Merusavarni.

SWAMPRABHU. ' Self-shining ', a title.

SWARGA. The Celestial Region.

SWARGIN. An inhabitant of the celestial Region.

SWYAMBHU. The ' Self-existent ', a name of the Creator.

SWYAMVARA. A ceremony where the bride chooses her own consort.

SVASTI. A benediction.

SVASTIVACHANA. A religious rite preparatory to a sacrifice.

SVASTIYATREYA. A Sage.

SYANDARA. A river.

SYRYAVAM. A mountain in the sea.

T

TAITTIRYA. One of the Upanishads.

TAKSHA. A son of Bharata.

TAKSHAKA. A name of Vishvakarma.
A name of one of the Great Serpents.

TAKSHASHILA. The city ruled by Taksha, Bharata's son, said to be identified with Taxila that was occupied by the Greeks and barbarians.

TALA. A leather strap used by archers.
A clapper used in music.

TAMABHEDA. ' Dispeller of darkness ', a name of the Sun.

TAMAS. See under GUNAS.

TAMRA. One of the wives of Kashyapa.

TAMRAPARNI. A river reputed to be abounding in crocodiles.

TAPANA. ' Possessor of Wealth ', a title associated with the Sun, a Star and a Titan.

TAPAS. Penance or austerity.

TAPOVANA. A forest.

TARA. The consort of Bali.
A monkey general.

TARAKA. A meteor.

TARASA. A monkey warrior.

TAREYA. A monkey leader.

TARKSHYA. In ancient times considered the personification of the Sun in the form of a bird, later it became the name of Garuda.

TARKSHYAS. The father of the monkeys.

TATAKA. A Yakshini, the mother of Maricha.
    A lake.

TEJAS. Lustre, energy or effulgence and spiritual power.

THIRTY, The. This title 'TRI-DASA' applies to the Gods; in round numbers thirty-three—twelve Adityas, eight Vasus, eleven Rudras and the two Ashvins.

THREE DIVISIONS OF TIME, The. Past, present and future.

THREE FIRES, The. The Ahavaniya Fire in the east for offerings to the Devas, the Dakshina Fire in the south for offerings to the Pitris and the Gahapatya Fire in the west which is perpetually maintained and passed on from father to son and from which the other sacrificial fires are lit.

THREE HUMOURS OF THE BODY, The. Wind, bile and phlegm.

THREE KINDS OF ACTION. Trivial, common or ordinary, important and urgent.

THREE PAIRS OF QUALITIES. Renown and virility, majesty and beauty, knowledge and dispassion.

THREE SACRED ABODES, or The THREE WORLDS. Bhur, Bhuvah, Swah, the lower, middle and upper worlds, also called Tri-loka and Tri-bhuvana, that is heaven, earth and the lower worlds.

TIKSHAVEGA. A titan.

TILAKA. A mark of auspiciousness placed on the forehead.

TIME. See KALA.

TIMI. A whale or large fish.

TIMIDHVAJA. The father of Indra and also of the Danavas and Shambara.

TIMINGILA. 'Swallowing even a 'Timi' or fabulous fish', a name given to describe a sea-monster.

TIMIRONMATHANA. 'Lord of the Welkin', the Sun.

TISHYA. An asterism shaped like an arrow containing three stars, also called Pushya and Sidhya.
    The Kali Yuga.

TRETAYUGA. The Silver Age.

TRI-BHUVANA, TRI-DASA. See under The THIRTY.

TRIDIVA. The Region of the Gods.

TRIJATA. A brahmin whose story is told in Balakanda.
    A female titan who spoke in defence of Sita.

TRIKUTA. 'Three-peaked', the mountain on which Lanka was built.

TRINABINDU. A. Sage whose daughter became the consort of the Sage Vishravas.

TRIPATHAGA. 'Three-way-flowing', the 'Traverser of the Three Worlds', a name of the Ganges.

TRIPURA. A demon slain by Shiva.
A city put to fire by the Gods.

TRISHANKU. A king of the Solar Race whose story is told in Bala-kanda.
A constellation.

TRISHIRAS. Also called 'Trimurdhana', a three-headed titan slain by Rama.

TRIVARSHA. Three consecutive showers favourable to crops.

TRIVISHTAPA. The City of Indra also called Amaravati.

TRYAMBAKA. 'Three-eyed', a name of Shiva. This title can also mean 'Uttering the three Vedas or the three mystical Syllables'

TUMBURU. A Gandharva cursed by the God Kuvera and born as the Demon Viradha.

TVASHTA or TVASHTRI. A name connected with the Sun, with one of the Adityas and also Vishvakarma; The meaning is 'One who shines'.

TWICE-BORN. Only a brahmin can be strictly termed 'Twice-born', but the title came to be extended later to the warrior and the agricultural classes.

U

UCCHAISHRAVAS. The white horse of Indra produced from the churning of the ocean by Gods and Asuras. It is said to be fed on ambrosia and be the foremost of steeds.

UDAYA. A golden mountain.

UDGATAR. One of the four officiating priests at a sacrifice.

UGRA. 'Powerful', 'Formidable', 'Terrible', a name given to Rudra or Shiva and also the Sun.

UKHARA. The earth when impregnated with salt or sterile.

UKTHYA. The second day of the Ashva-medha Sacrifice.

ULKAMUKHA. A monkey, the son of Hutashana, the God of Fire.

UNMATTA. A titan warrior.

UPAKHYANAS. Episodes or tales, traditional recitations.

UPA-NAYA. The ceremony of the investiture of the sacred thread by which act spiritual birth is conferred on a youth and he becomes a member of the Brahmin or Twice-born class. The age at which this ceremony takes place is between eight and sixteen years.

UPANISHAD. Esoteric doctrine. The third division of the Vedas, forming part of the revealed Word.

UPASUNDA. A titan warrior.

UPATAKSHARA. A Great Serpent.

UPENDRA. A name of Vishnu and later of Indra.

URAGAS. Great Serpents, those of the Naga Race.

URMILA. The consort of Lakshmana.

URVASHI. A nymph mentioned in the Rig-Veda. Many legends are told of her in the classics.

USHANAS. Another name of Shukra, the Guru of the Asuras and Daityas. This Sage assisted Indrajita in his sacrifices.

USHARA. Saline soil. (See Uttarakanda, Ch. LXXXVI.)

USHIRABIJA. The mountain that is also called Mandara where King Marutta performed his sacrifice.

USHIRAS. A hair-like grass growing on the golden trees of hell. See also FLOWERS and TREES Glossary.

UTTARAGA. A river.

UTTARA KANDA. The seventh and supplementary book of 'Ramayana'.

UTTARA KURUS. A race said to befriend spiritual persons.

UTTARA PHALGUNI. A constellation under which Sita was said to have been born.

V

VACHASPATI. The Mother of the Gods and Goddess of speech and learning. She is also called Saraswati.

VADABA or VADAVA. 'Mare's Fire', the subterranean fire or the fire of the lower regions, fabled to emerge from a cavity called the 'Mare's mouth' under the sea.

VADAVAMUKHA. 'Mare's mouth', the entrance to the nether region said to be found at the south pole where the submarine fire is found.

VAGADEVA. One of the Adityas presiding over wealth.

VAGHRINASAKA. A dark-throated, white-winged bird.
A species of goat.

VAHNI. 'Bearer of Brightness', a title.
A monkey warrior.

VAHNYALAYA. The abode of the Fire-god.

VAHUDAMSHTRA. A titan.

VAIDEHA or VIDEHA. The kingdom ruled over by Janaka.

VAIDEHI. The name of Sita as daughter of Janaka, King of Vaideha.

VAIDISHA. The city where Shatrughna's son ruled.

VAIDYA. A physician.

VAIDYUTA. A mountain.

VAIJANTA. A city founded by King Nimi.

VAIKHANASA. A class of Rishi or Hermit who dwelt on Mount Saumanasa.

VAINATEYA. A name of Garuda.

VAIROCHANA or VIROCHANA. A name of the Sun and Moon, meaning ' Illumining '.
>One descended from Virochana.
>A patronymic of Bali.
>The Son of Prahlada.

VAISHNAVA. Relating to Vishnu or a sacrifice in his honour.
>The Vaishnavas are devotees of Vishnu.

VAISHRAVANA. A name of Kuvera, Ravana's brother.
>The name of the daughter of the Sage Bharadwaja.

VAISHRAVANAVANLAYA. The abode of Kuvera.

VAISHVADEVAS. Relating to all the Divinities or Vaishvas or Vishvas.

VAISHVANARA. The God of Fire, Agni.
>The Zodiac.

VAISHYAS. Those of the merchant or agricultural classes.

VAITARANI. A river in hell.

VAIVASVAT. See Vivasvat.

VAIVASVATA. A name of the God of Death, Yama.

VAJAPEYA. A sacrifice at which an acetous mixture of meal and water is offered to the Gods.

VAJI-MEDHA. The Horse-sacrifice. ' Vaji ' meaning ' swiftness ' or ' strength ' as applied to horses.

VAJRA. A mountain.

VAJRABANU. A titan.

VAJRADAMSHTRA. ' With teeth like thunderbolts ', the name of a titan slain by Angada.

VAJRADHARA. ' Wielder of the Thunderbolt ', a title of Indra.

VAJRAHANU. A powerful titan.

VAJRAKAYA. A titan warrior.

VAJRAMUSHTI. A titan warrior.
>A son of Malyavan and Sundari.

VAJRAVALA. The daughter of Virochana who married Kumbha-karna.

VALAKHILYAS. Divine Beings, the size of a thumb, sixty thousand of whom sprang from the body of Brahma and are said to surround the chariot of the Sun.

VALI. Offerings to the Spirits of the air.

VALIMUKHAS. ' Wrinkled-faced Ones ', the monkeys.

VALLAKA. A small crane.
>An Indian lute.

VALMIKI. Poet, Sage and author of 'Ramayana'.

VALUKINI. A river.

VAMADEVA. A great Rishi who was present at Rama's installation.

VAMANA. The Holy Dwarf, the fifth Incarnation of Vishnu.

VANA. A forest.

VANAPRASTHA. A festival similar to a Harvest Festival.

VANARAS. ' Dwellers in the forest ', a name given to the monkey race. A special breed of elephants.

VANARIS. Female monkeys.

VANCHULAKA. A mythical bird.

VARANA. A mountain.

VARARANI. The mother of kine and bulls.

VARUNA. The Indian Neptune, Lord of the Waters.

VARUNI. The daughter of Varuna who was the personification of wine. Wine prepared from Hogsweed distilled with date or palm juice.

VARUTHI. A river.

VASAVA. A name of Indra.

VASAVI. A name of Bali, as son of Indra or Vasava.

VASHAT. A word of power, a holy Syllable.

VASHATKARA. The utterance of ' Vashat ' at ceremonies. A Sage.

VASISHTHA. A great Sage, the spiritual Preceptor of King Dasaratha and Rama's own Guru.

VASTUPATI. ' Abiding Lord ', a title.

VASU. The son of King Nriga, whose story is told in 'Uttarakanda.' One of the Seven Immortal Sages.

VASUDA. ' One who grants wealth or treasure ', a name of the earth. A Gandharvi who married Mali.

VASUDEVA. A name of the Lord.

VASUDHA. ' Containing wealth ', a name of the earth.

VASUKI. The Serpent King.

VASURETAS. A name of Agni.

VASUS. The sons of Kashyapa and Aditi. The eight Vasus were originally personifications of natural phenomena, they were Apa, Dhruva, Soma, Dhara, Anila, Anala, Pratyusha and Prabhasa.

VASVOKARA. Another name of Amaravati, the City of Indra.

VATA. A name of Vayu, the Wind-god.

VATAPI. A demon consumed by the Sage Agastya.

VAYU. The God of the Wind.

VEDANGAS. A sacred science considered subordinate to and in some sense a part of the Vedas. Six subjects come under the denomination :—Siksha—pronunciation, Kalpa—religious rites, Vyakarana—Grammar, Chandas—Prosody, Jyotish—Astronomy, Nirukti—Explanation of difficult words.

VEDAS. The Holy Scriptures of the Hindu religion, the fountain of divine knowledge.

VEDAVATI. The daughter of the Brahmarshi Kushadwaja.

VEGADARSHIN. A monkey leader.

VEDHAS. ' Arranger ', ' Disposer ', ' Creator ', a name of Brahma.

VEDI. An altar of Kusha Grass or a place of sacrifice.

VENA. A river.

VIBHABASU. ' Abounding in light ', a title of the God of Fire.

GLOSSARY

VIBHANDAKA. The son of the Sage Kashyapa and the father of Rishyashringa.

VIBHUDAS. Celestial Beings or Gods.

VIBISHANA. See Bibishana.

VIBUDHA. A Deity or Teacher of the spiritual truth.
The Moon.

VIDARBHA. A country, probably Birar, whose capital was Kundipura.

VIDHATAR. A name of Brahma, the Creator.

VIDYADHARAS. 'Magical-knowledge Holder', a particular class of good or evil spirits attendant on the Gods.

VIDYUDRUNA. A titan.

VIDYUJJIHVA. A titan skilled in magic who created an illusory head of Rama and his bow to deceive Sita.

VIDYULDAMSHTRA. A monkey warrior.

VIDYUNMALI. A monkey warrior.

VIDYUNMALIN. A titan warrior.

VIDYUTKESHA. A Daitya, the son of Heti.

VIGHANA. A titan.

VIHARA. A pleasure garden or recreation ground, temple or sanctuary.

VIHARAS. 'Those who roam about at pleasure', a name given to the monkeys.

VIJAYA. A minister at King Dasaratha's court.

VIJIHVA. A titan.

VIKATA. A titan.

VIMPAKSHA. A titan.

VIMUKHA. A Sage.

VINA. An Indian lute.

VINATA. The mother of Garuda.
A monkey warrior.

VINAYAKAS. A class of Beings, sometimes malevolent.

VINDHA. The hour that is auspicious for finding what has been lost.

VINDHYA. A mountain ordered by Agastya not to increase in height.

VIPAGA. A river.

VIPANCI. An Indian lute.

VIRA. A name of the Sun.

VIRA POSTURE. The posture which is favourable to the regulation of breath.

VIRABANU. A monkey warrior.

VIRADHA. A demon, the son of Java and Shatarada who was slain by Rama and had formerly been the Gandharva Tumburu.

VIROCHANA. See Vairochana.

VIRUPAKSHA. A titan, also called Virupanetra. The word Virupaksha means 'Of distorted eyes', it is a name also given to Shiva who is said to have three eyes.
The son of Malyavan.
One of the Elephants of the Four Quarters.

VIRYASANA. The son of King Saudasa who became known as Kalmashapada on account of a curse.

VISHAKA. A lunar asterism.

A month in the flowering season.

VISHALA. A titan.

VISHALAKSHA. 'Having beautiful eyes', a name of Shiva, Garuda and a Great Serpent.

VISHAMPATI. 'Lord of Men', a title.

VISHNU. The Lord in the aspect of 'Maintainer of the Universe'.

VISHRAVAS. A great Sage born of Prajapati. The name comes from the root 'Sru' to listen, as his mother conceived when listening to the Veda being recited. He is said to be the son of Poulastya in 'Ramayana' and was the father of Ravana and Kuvera.

VISHVA. The daughter of Daksha.

A title meaning 'He who pervades all'.

VISHVAS or VISHVADEVAS. All the Gods who are said to be the 'Preservers of Men' and 'Bestowers of Rewards'. They are the sons of Vishva.

VISHVAKARMA. The architect of the Gods. The 'Maker of Weapons'.

VISHVAKRITA. Another name for Vishvakarma.

VISHVAMARA. 'Possessed of all desirable things' or 'Granting all boons' or 'Adored or cherished by all', a title.

VISHVAMITRA. A great Sage whose story is told in Balakanda.

VISHVANATHA. 'Lord of the Universe', a name of Shiva.

VISHVARUPA. A title of Vishnu meaning 'Omnipresent' or 'Wearing all forms'.

VISHVATAM. The God of the Wind.

VITAPAVATI. The City over which Kuvera ruled.

VITARDANA. A titan warrior.

VITTAPA. A name of Kuvera.

VIVASVAT. 'The Brilliant One', the Sun. Vivasvat was said to be the father of Manu.

VRANA. The well of the waters of hell.

VRASHPARVANA. A Daitya, father of Sharmishta, the consort of King Yayati.

VRINDA. A large number, a multitude.

VRISHA. The Bull of Shiva, also called Nandi.

VRISHABHA. A monkey warrior.

VRISHADWAJA. An appellation of Shiva 'Having the Bull as his vehicle'.

VRISHTI. A minister at Rama's court.

VRITRA or VRITASURA. A demon slain by Indra.

One of Bali's forbears.

VYAVANAYAKAS. Servants of Queen Kaushalya.

VYAVASAYA. The power of withdrawal.

A name of Vishnu.

VYOMANATHA. 'Lord of the Welkin', the Sun.

GLOSSARY

W

X

Y

YADU. The son of Yayati and Devayani. Yayati was the founder of the Yadavas in which line Krishna was born.

YAJNA. A sacrifice or penance.

YAJNAKOPA. A titan warrior slain by Rama.

YAJNASHATRU. A titan warrior.

YAJURVEDA. The part of the Veda that treats of rituals.

YAKSHA. A minister of Sugriva.

YAKSHAS. Supernatural Beings, attendant on Kuvera.

YAKSHINIS. Female Yakshas.

YAMA. The God of Death.

YAMALA. An Asura, enemy of the Gods.

YAMALA-ARJUNA. Enemies of Krishna who in the form of trees he uprooted as a child.

YAMUNA. A sacred river.

YATUDHANAS. Evil Spirits that assume various forms. The name is also given to the Rakshasas.

YAVA. An island searched by the monkeys for Sita and Ravana.

YAVAKRITA. A Rishi.

YAVANAS. A people said to have been born of the sacred cow Shabala.

YAVANTA. One of Rama's ministers.

YAYATI. The son of Nahusha, a forbear of King Dasaratha, his story appears in the ' Mahabharata ' and the ' Vishnu Purana '.

YOGA. 'Union' : the methods (of meditation, mind-control, self-discipline etc.) through which man came to realise the identity of his own essential being with God.

YOGANDHARA. ' The United ', a title.

YOJANA. A measurement approximately four or five miles.

YUDDHONMATTA. A titan warrior.

YUDHAJITA. Prince of Kaikeya, Bharata's maternal uncle.

YUGA. A world Age or period. The Yugas are four in number and their duration several thousand years. Between each of the periods there is a time called Sandhya or Twilight when creation is withdrawn and lies latent in the Supreme Spirit, Brahman.

YUGANTADAHAKA. The 'End of Time', or the 'Consumer of the Worlds Cycles,' a name of Vishnu.

YUPAKSHA. A titan slain by Hanuman.

YUVANASHVA. The son of Dhundhumara and father of Mandhata.

FLOWERS AND TREES

(Wherever possible Latin or English derivatives are given but in some cases no equivalent has been traced.)

A

ADUMBARI. A species of Fig.

ADUMVARI. Agaru Amyris Agallochum, a species of Sandalwood.

AGNIMUKHA. Semicarpus Anacardium Zeylanica, Plumbago.

AGNIMUKHYA. The Marking Nut Plant.

AMLAKA. Phyllanthus Emblica. A many-branched shrub resembling Hemlock. The fruit is known as Myrabolan and has healing properties; it is often seen in the hand of ' Menhla' the Buddha of Medicine,

AMRA. Mango Mangifera Indica. A short-trunked tree covered with evergreen foliage which flowers from January to March; the blooms are partly white and partly greenish yellow with an orange stripe on each petal. This tree is sacred to Hindus and Buddhists. The wood is used for funeral pyres and the flowers are dedicated to the Moon and the God of Love.

ANKOLA or ANKOTA or ANKOLATA. Alangium Hexapetalum. A small or medium sized, partially deciduous tree with branches armed with spines that grows throughout India in dry regions. The wood is olive brown, hard and close grained, the leaves oblong, glabrous and dark green. The flowers single or in clusters are white and scented; the fruit, a berry, is purplish red. Roots and fruit are used medicinally. Said to be a cure for snake and rat bite and also to alleviate colic and diseases of the blood. It is used as a substitute for Ipecacuanha.

ARAVINDA. Nymphoea Nelumbo, a water lily.

ARISTA. Sapindus Saponeria, the Soap Plant.

ARJUNA or ARJUNAKA. Terminalia Arjuna. A species of Nimba or Neem Tree. A tall evergreen tree usually found on the banks of streams. The leaves cluster at the end of the branches and the flowers forming tassels are tiny.

ARJUNA JARUL. The Queens Flower or Crêpe Flower. An important timber tree which has medicinal value. The flowers that are pinky mauve or white appear in April and last throughout the hot season.

ASANA. Terminalia Tormentosa. A common forest tree yielding excellent timber similar to the Arjuna Tree and rarely seen outside forest areas.

ASHOKA. Saraca Indica. A small evergreen tree which produces a profusion of orange and scarlet clusters of blossom in January and February and has deep dark green shining foliage. Buddha is said to have been born under an Ashoka Tree and Sita was kept prisoner by Ravana in an Ashoka Grove. Both Hindus and Buddhists regard it as sacred and it is said to flourish where a womah's foot has trod. The bark is astringent and bitter, cooling and refrigerant, useful in colic, emaciation and certain venom poisoning ; it is highly beneficial in vaginal disorders and effective in hæmorrhages and ulcers.

ASHVAKARNA or ASHWAKARNA. Vatica Robusta, the Sal Tree, a large tree that grows in the eastern districts of central India. The wood, which ranks with teak is in general use in Bengal. The flowers are abundant and whitish or pale rose in colour.

ASHVALAGNA. The Saul Tree.

ASHVATTHA or ASHWATTHA. The Fig Tree of which there are many varieties :—

> Ficus Bengalensis—The Banian Tree.
> Ficus Religiosa—The Pipal or Peepal Tree.
> Ficus Glomerata—The Rumbal or Umbar Tree.
> Ficus Elastica—The India Rubber Tree.

ATIMUKHA. Premna Spinoza. The wood of this tree is used for kindling.

ATIMUKTA. Dalbergia Oujeinensis. Grows in the hilly tracts of N. India twenty to thirty ft. high. The flowers are abundant and whitish or pale rose.

ATIMUKTAKA. Mountain Ebony. This tree is commonly known as Harimantha.

B

BADRI or VADRI. Ziziphus Jujuba. The Jujube Tree, an attractive small or medium tree which flowers in April, its blossom forming pale green stars. The pulp of the fruit is eaten with sugar and the kernel raw. Sherbet is made from it and the Lac-insect feeds on this tree ; its secretions are used for dyes, lacquer, ink and polishes.

BAKULA or VAKULA. Mimisops Elengi. A tree with fragrant flowers from which a drug of the same name comes. The flowers are white but change to a dull yellow ; the fruit is an ovoid berry, yellow when ripe. The bark, that is pungent and sweet, is used for diseases of the gums and teeth and makes a good gargle.

BALALAKA. Flacourtia Cataphracta. A shrub with hairy leaves and edible fruit ; it flowers in March and April. The fine-grained wood is used for combs and turnery.

BANDHUJIVA. Pentapetes Phoenicia. A plant with a red flower which opens at midday and withers away next morning at sunrise.

BANJULA or VANJULA. Hibiscus Mutabilis. Changeable Rose. Blooms in September and October and possesses large heart-shaped leaves; the flowers are three or four inches across, pure white in the morning, gradually changing to pale pink and red by evening.

BHADRA. The name of various plants and also a tree.

BHANDIRA. Mimosa Seressa, a lofty Fig Tree.

BHANDUKA. Calosanthes Indica. This tree that grows to 40 ft. in height is found throughout India. The bark is thick, the leaves smooth, hairless and glabrous.

BHAVA. Indian Laburnum. Monkeys are particularly partial to the sweet pulp of the pods in which the seeds lie; it is also used for flavouring tobacco and as a purgative. The wood is good for fuel and charcoal.

BHAVYA. Dillenia Indica or Dillenia Elliptica Speciosa. A tree that grows to forty feet; it is an evergreen; the flowers are large and white with yellow antlers and appear at the end of the branches. This tree is found in dense forests and is much cultivated round temples. The bark and leaves are medicinal and the juice from the acid fruit mixed with sugar makes a cooling drink. There is another small fruit tree allied to the Mangolia Speciosa of this name.

BHAYA. Trapa Bispinosa. A floating herb, that grows throughout India and Ceylon, the velvety flowers have four small white petals.

BIBHITAKA or BIBHIDAKA or VIBHIDAKA. Terminalia Bellerica. The Belleric Myrabolan, an important forest tree, though not considered useful for timber, being subject to insect attack. Its fruit however, which appears as a grey velvet ball, is used for medicinal purposes as also for dyes and tanning. The kernels yield oil and, if taken in excess, are said to produce intoxication. A favourite food of monkeys, squirrels, deer and other animals. The flower sprays, in creamy tassels, appear from March to June. The fruit is known as Myrabolan and this name is also used for the fruit of the Amlaka (Phyllanthus Emblica) and Terminalia Chebula, the three making a tonic called 'Trefala Churan'.

BIJAPURA. Citrus Medica. The Citron Tree.

BILVA. Aegle Marmelos, commonly called Bel. The Wood-apple which bears a delicious fruit that, unripe, is used for medical purposes. Its leaves are used in ceremonies in the worship of Shiva.

BIMBA or VIMBA. Momordica Monadelpha. A plant bearing a bright red gourd.

GLOSSARY

C

CHAMIKARA. A species of Thorn-apple.

CHAMPAKA. One of the Magnolias that grows wild in the Eastern sub-Himalayan tract and lower hills, also in Assam, Burma and Southern India; it is much cultivated. A tall, handsome, quick-growing tree that is evergreen, the flowers are deep yellow or orange and very fragrant. The root, bark, flowers and seeds are used for various purposes. The bark has stimulant, expectorant and astringent qualities, the flowers yield a fragrant oil used in opthalmia and gout.

CHANDAKA. The dried buds of this tree are the pungent and aromatic clove.

CHANDANA. Sirium Folium. The sweet-scented Oleander Rosebay which grows in rocky stream-beds on the lower Himalayas. It has evergreen foliage and flowers throughout the year. The blooms are deep rose, pink and white in sprays and are offered to Shiva. The poison, contained in the leaves, when made into a paste, is used for leprosy and skin diseases.

CUTA. A Mango Tree.

D

DADIMA or DADIMAH. Punica Grantum. The Pomegranate which grows throughout India and is indigenous to Persia and Afghanistan. A large shrub or sometimes small tree with numerous ascending branches. The flowers are funnel-shaped and orange in colour. The fruit is hard globose and yellow, tinged with red when ripe. The root-bark is a vermicide. The juice is appetizing and tonic, useful in fever, dyspepsia, biliousness and heartburn and has other curative properties.

DARBHA GRASS. Poa Cynosuroides, a grass used at sacrifices.

DEVADARU. A variety of Pine, probably the Mast Tree, so-called on account of its tall straight trunks being ideally suited for the masts of sailing ships. A beautiful tree revered by the Hindus, who plant it near their temples. Bats and foxes appreciate its fruit.

DEVAPARNA. The Divine Leaf, a medicinal plant.

DHANVANA. Grewia Asiatica. A small tree, widely cultivated in India except in East Bengal. The flowers are yellow.
     Various other plants have this name.

DHANWARIA. Echites Antidy Senterio, a twining plant.

DHARA. Woodfordia Floribunda. Red Bell Bush, a small, spreading shrub which flowers from December to May and from which a red dye is obtained from the bright red blossom.

DHATRI. Sterospernum Aciderifolium.

DHATURA. Datura Fastuosa (Solanaceae). An annual poisonous shrub with a strong disagreeable smell that grows throughout India. The flowers, similar to the convolvulus in shape, are purplish white outside and white inside ; the fruit is a small prickly ball 'closely packed with smooth yellowish-brown seeds. The leaves, flowers and seeds are used medicinally and are narcotic and soporific. Fomentations of the leaves are said to relieve the pains and swellings of rheumatism and the dried flowers, when powdered, are inhaled for asthma and bronchitis and coughs.

DHAVA. The shrub, Grislea Tomentosa, which is common throughout India, the scarlet flowers on long spreading branches appear in the hot season.

DHUVA. One of the Acacia family.

DRONA. A small tree bearing white flowers, commonly known as Ghalaghasiya or Halaksiya.

DUKULA. A plant from the stem of which very fine cloth is made.

DURVA. Panicum Dactylon. Bent Grass.

G

GAJAPUSHPI. Elephant Flower, a kind of Arum.

GHALAGHASIYA. See DRONA.

GOSHIRAKA. A Sandal Tree.

GULAR. A resinous tree, fragments of which, put in water in a loshta, are used for ceremonial purposes.

H

HARISHYAMA. See SHYAMA.

HATAKA. A thorn-apple that is golden in colour.

HIJJAL. See NICHULA.

HINTALA. Phoenix Sylvestris. The Wild Date Tree or Toddy Palm. Forests of these trees cover considerable areas in India and the trees give an excellent yield of palm, oil, mats are woven from the leaves and baskets from the stalks as well as ropes.

I

J

JAMBHU or JAMBHUH. Eugenia Jambolanum. The Rose Apple or Java Plum, which is sacred to Krishna and planted near temples. This tree grows throughout India and is a medium sized ever-green. The flowers, that are fragrant and of a whitish colour appear from March to May. Vinegar is distilled from the juice of the fruit, a one-seeded berry, blackish purple when ripe. The bark, leaves and fruit have other medicinal properties.

JAMBUKA.. A kind of grape without pips.

JAMNU. Prunus Padus L. Bird Cherry.

JAPA FLOWER. China Rose or Shoe Plant, which has large single bell-shaped flowers of a rich chinese red. These are used for decoration at festivals. The crushed flowers are used for shoe polish.

K

KADALA or KADALI. Musa Sapientum. The Plantain or Banana Palm, which has a soft perishable stem and is poetically a symbol of the frailty of human existence.

    Several plants such as Pistia Stritiotes and Bombay Hepthyllum.

KADAMBA. The Plant Nauclea Cadamba.

KAHLARA. A white water-lily.

KAKUBHA. See the ARJUNA Tree.

KALAGURU. A species of Sandal Tree.

KALAYAKA. Various leguminous seeds, chiefly Phaseolus. Also some kinds of pulse and vetches.

KALEYAKA. A fragrant Aloes-wood.

    The yellow Sandal Tree.

    A kind of Turmeric.

    The Plant Curcuma Xanthorrhiza.

KAMANARI. A species of Mimosa.

KAMRANGA. Averrhoa Carambola. A small densely branched tree with variegated white and purple flowers and one variety produces an edible sweet yellow fruit.

KANDI. Amorphophallus Campanulatus, a plant having a bulbous root, which is cultivated throughout India. The tuber is astringent and sweet, easily digestible and increases appetite. It is considered useful for abdominal tumours, colic and obesity.

KANYA. Aloe Perfoliata. This tree produces fragrant white flowers in March and April.

    Several other plants, one of which is the Tube-rose.

KAPIMUKA. The Coffee Plant.

KAPITHA. The Jack-fruit, Feronia Elephantum, which is cultivated throughout India and indigenous to Southern India. A moderate sized deciduous tree with spines ; the flowers are numerous, small, dull red, pale pink, changing to greenish yellow. The many-seeded large globose berry is used for innumerable purposes both culinary and medicinal.

KARANJA. Pongamia Glabra. The flowers of this tree in white short sprays appear when the new leaves are developed. It is a medicinal tree from which an embrocation is made for skin diseases. The juice is applied to sores and used for cleaning teeth as it has antiseptic qualities.

KARAVIRA. Another fragrant Oleander that is common to many parts of India in the rocky stream beds of the lower Himalayas, fringing roads and rivers. The foliage is evergreen throughout the year, but at its height during the rains ; the flowers are deep rose and white, single and double. The sap is poisonous.

KARNIKARA. Pterospternum Acerfolium, also called Cassia Fistula. The common name of this tree is Kaniyar and it is one of the Indian Laburnums.

KARPURA. Ficus Glomerata. In April, the new leaves of shining dark red, lend it a beautiful appearance ; its fruit is much relished. This tree is commonly known as Rumbal or Umbar.

KASANARI. Gmelina Arborea. The Liquorice Plant.

KASHAS. Reeds or Rushes.

KASHASTHALI. Bignonia Suavolens. The Yellow Elder.
     A Trumpet Flower, an extensive climber with clear yellow flowers of which there are several varieties.

KEDUMBRA. A tree with orange-coloured fragrant flowers.

KETAKA. Pandanus Odoratissimus. Grows in the hottest parts of India. The leaves are drooping, green and glossy and the flowers crowded as a catkin-like spadix of orange yellow.

KHADIRA. Acacia Catechu. The Areca or Betel-nut Palm which grows in hot damp coastal regions of Southern India and Ceylon. Betel-nut is the fruit universally chewed by Asian people.

KHARJURA. Pheonix Sylvestris. See Hintala.

KICHAKA. Arundo Karka. A reed or hollow bamboo or rattling cane.
     A tree of the same name.

KIMSHUKA or KUMSHUKA. Butea Frondosa. A tree with beautiful orange flowers and a quantity of milky sticky juice. It is called the ' Flower of the Forest ' or ' Parrot Tree '. From January till March it is a mass of orange and vermilion ; the flowers are constantly visited by birds. Dyes are obtained from these flowers, oil from the seeds and gum from the stem.

KOVIDARA. Bauhinia Variegata. A Mountain Ebony. One of the loveliest of Indian Trees ; like the Pariyatra, it is called ' Tree of Paradise '. It has a dark brown smoothish bark ; the leaves fall in the cold season and the large sweetly-scented flowers open on the bare branches. Their colour varies from magenta, mauve, pink with crimson markings or white with a splash of yellow. The tree is useful for its timber and yields oil and gum and has medicinal uses.

KRITAMALA. Another Laburnum.

KSHUPA. A plant or shrub with short branches and roots.

KUANDA. A plant commonly called Sakurunda, the yellow Amaranth or Barleria.

KUAYRAL. Another Mountain Ebony.

KUJAJA. Wrightia Awtidy Senterica, a medicinal plant.

KUMUDA. A white water lily, called the 'Moonlily', the other lotuses opening to the sun.

KUNDA. Jasmine Multiflorum.

KURAKA. Boswellia Thoriflora, the Olivanum Tree.

KURUBAKA DRONAPUSHPI. The Drona Flower; Drona meaning ' vessel ', ' cup ', or ' pot ', it probably produces a gourd.

KUSHA GRASS. Demontachya Bipennata. A sacred grass used for ceremonies it has long stalks and pointed leaves like rushes.

KUVALA or KUVALAYA. A water-lily, the blue species.

L

LAKUCA or LAKUKA. Artocarpus Lacucha. The same genus as the Jack-fruit; it is cultivated in the plains of Northern India.

LOHDRA. Simplocos Racemosa. The bark of this tree is used for a dye.

M

MADHAVA. A Mango Tree.

MADHAVI. The herb Basil.
    A kind of Panic seed.
    A species of leguminous plant.

MADHUKA. The Mohwa or Indian Butter Tree. A large deciduous tree with thick grey bark found in dry rocky hill regions, valuable for its delicious and nutritive flowers which bloom at night and fall on the ground at dawn. They taste something like figs and are much sought after by bears, birds and deer so that the natives, in order to collect the flowers for themselves, have to guard the trees.

MADHURA. Perennial Jasmine.

MADURA. A tree reminiscent of Cassia which has long sprays of pale pink flowers which appear in January and February. The fruit is a long flat bean. This tree does not appear to have any economic or medicinal uses.

MALLIKA. Evening Jasmine.

MANDARA. Erythinia Indica, the Coral Tree of which there are several varieties. It grows along the coasts and blooms from January till March; its rich red flowers make a striking appearance along the bare branches; they are unscented. New leaves are eaten in curries and the wood, which neither splits nor warps, is used for carved articles.

MATULINGA. A Citron or Sweet Lime.

MAUNJA. A kind of grass.

MRITASAMJIVANI. The ' Reviver of the Dead ', a herb.

MUCHUKUNDA. Pterospernum Suberifolium, a white variety of Calotropis Gigantica, a Thorn-apple.

MUCHULINDA. Probably connected with the ' Muchi Wood ' or ' Coral Tree '.

MYRABOLAN. See AMLAKA.

N

NAGA. Mesua Ferres, a small tree.

NAGAVRIKSHA. A mountain Shrub.

NAKTAMALA or NAKTAMALLAKA. Caleduba Arborea or Dalbergia Arborea.

NALINA. Nelumbium Speciosum. A water-lily.

NARCAL GRASS. Phragmites Karka Trin. A species of Reed.

NARIKELA. A tall unbranched tree with a terminal plume of pinnate leaves ; its flowers are yellowish and resemble stiff catkins. The nut is edible and oil is obtained from it which is used for soap, shampoos and culinary purposes ; it is also useful for the manufacture of candles.

NICHULA. Barringtonia Acutangola, commonly called Hijjal.

NILASHOKA. An Ashoka with blue flowers.

NIMBA. Azadirachta Indica. A tree with bitter fruit, the size of an olive ; the leaves are chewed at funerals and are said to ward off sickness and, when dried, keep off insects ; the timber is similar to mahogany.

NIPA or NIPAKA. A species of Kadamba Tree.

NIVARA or NAIVARA. Wild Rice.

NYAGRODHA. Ficus Indica. The Indian Fig Tree.

O

OSHADI. An annual plant that dies after opening.

P

PADMA. A pink lotus, sometimes this flower is used as a symbol of the Goddess Lakshmi, consort of Vishnu, who is often seen carrying this flower.

PADMAKA. Costus Speciosus or Arabicus, a kind of Fir.

PALASHA. Butea Frondosa. A tall straight tree that grows to 40 or 50 feet in the plains from the Himalayas to Ceylon and Burma. The petals of the flowers are bright orange red, covered with a silvery hair.

PANASA. Like the Kapitha, this tree, Artocarpus Intergrifolia is also a Jack-fruit which bears the largest edible fruit in the world, weighing up to 100 lbs, round and irregular; it is in great demand but less favoured than the Mango or Plaintain. This tree grows in the forest in the Western Ghats.

PARABHADRAKA. Erythinia Fulgens. A Coral Tree which bears angular spikes of rich red blooms along its bare branches from January to March.

PATALA. A tropical climbing plant.

PATALI or PATALIKA. Bignonia · Suavolens. A tree with sweet-scented blossom, possibly the red Lohdra.

PINJARA. Mesua Roxburghii. A medium-sized tree found in the mountains of East Bengal and the Eastern Himalayas. The leaves are dark green and glossy and the flowers composed of four pure white petals and large golden antlers.

PIPAL or PIPPALA. The Pipal, a Fig Tree, Ficus Religiosa.

PIYAL or PRIYALA or PRYALA. A tree similar to the Madhuka.
> The common Oil Plant.
> A vine-like plant.

PRIYAKANYA. Known as Saj and Maddi, a common forest tree that yields excellent hard timber.

PRIYANGU. Fragrant seed, Italian Millet.
> Long Pepper.

PRIYANGU KATUKI. Saffron.

PRIYANKARA. Various plants.

PUNNAGA. Rottleria Tinctoria. The flowers of this tree produce a yellow dye.

PURNA. A Cypress.

PURNASA. Sacred Basil.

Q

R

RAJIVA. A red lotus.

RAKTACHANDAN. The red Sandal-tree.

RANJAKA. Barbadoes Pride. The Redwood Coral Pea Tree. This tree grows to the height of ten feet and large sprays of flowers divided into smaller sprays appear at the end of the branches; they are vermilion streaked with yellow, later becoming entirely red. This tree is medicinal and used for healing wounds and as a purgative; the charred wood is employed in the manufacture of ink.
> The Peacock Flower, which is associated with the God Shiva and therefore sacred to the Hindus.

SALA. Shorea Robusta. The Sal Tree.

SALLAKA. Bignonia Indica. The Gum Tree. Deep blue flowers in clusters appear at the beginning of the hot season and fade later to pale silver when golden berries appear. A translucent green resin exudes from this tree, with a pleasant odour. The wood, gum, bark and fruit all have medicinal value. The timber is known as Lignum Vitae or Brazil Wood.

SANDHANI. A medicinal herb. ' That which produces a salve for wounds '.

SAPTACCHADA. Stercula Foetida. Poon or Devil's Tree, a wild Almond. The black seeds of this tree are roasted and eaten like chestnuts but, taken raw, bring on nausea and vertigo.
    Seven-leafed Milk Plant.

SAPTAPARNA. Alstonia or Echites Scholaris, the Seven-leafed Tree.

SARALA. Pinus Longifolia, a species of Pine.

SARJA. White Murdah.

SARPAT GRASS. Saccharum Bengalense Retz (S. Sara Roxb.). One of the sugar canes.

SASTILATA. A long winding creeper.

SHADVALA. Fresh green grass.

SHAIVALA. Vallisneria Octandra or Bexica, an aquatic plant.

SHALMALI. Bombax Malabaricum or Gossampinus Malabaricum or Salmalia Malabarica, the Red Silk Cotton Tree. A tall, handsome tree found all over India except in the driest areas. The large flowers, appearing in January or February, are brilliant scarlet and pink ; they are much sought after by birds of every kind, and village people also consider them edible. In April, the fruit appears like green fingers which later become brown and split open when a fluffy cotton is freed and floats down to earth ; this is used for tinder and stuffing pillows. An astringent gum is also obtained from this tree.
    This is said to be a tree that grows in hell and the fabulous thorny rod from it is used for torturing the wicked.

SHAMI. Acacia Suma. This tree, possessed of very tough and hard wood is supposed to contain fire ; it is employed for kindling by attrition.
    The Shrub Seeratula Anthelmintica.

SHIMSHAPA or SHINGSHAPA. Dattergia Sisu. A species of Ashoka.

SHIRIBILVA. See under Bilva.

SHIRISHA or SIRISHA. Acacia Sirissa. A close relation to the Rain Tree.

SHIRISHKAPIR. Another of the Sirissas. This tree bears a small white flower which is fragrant at night. It also yields a gum similar to Gum Arabic. Its seeds are used in opthalmic diseases and are useful in leprosy.

SHURNAKA. A kind of grain belonging to the variety called Shashtika.
SHYAMA. A sacred Fig-tree at Prayaga.
>The sacred basil.
>A climbing plant, the Ichnocarpus or Echites Frutescens.
SILLEA. Cephalostashum Capitatum Munro, a large bamboo.
>Datura Metel, a Thorn-apple.
SIMHAKESARA. Cassia Sianica. A Cassia with bright yellow flowers.
SINDHUVARA. Vitex Negundo, a small tree.
SLESHMATAKA. Cordia Myxa. Scarlet Cordia or Aloe Wood. This tree produces fragrant white flowers in March and April. The fruit is like a pale cherry, the nut is edible and the pulp makes bird lime ; it is also medicinal.
SUKLADRUMA. Simplocos Racemosa, a tree bearing white flowers.
SURA. Another Sal tree.
SUVARNYAKARANI. A sacred herb ' That which heals the skin '.
SVADAMSHTRA. Astercantha Longifolia.
SYANDARA. Dalbergia Ougeninensis, a tree similar to the ATIMUKTAS.

T

TAGARA. The Shrub Tabaernoemontana Coronaria. The Moonbeam or Waxflower, which has dazzling white flowers which women wear in their hair. The seeds of the three-ribbed fruit make a red dye ; the roots mixed with lime juice are used as a cure for eye diseases ; a fragrant powder and perfume are prepared from the scented wood.
TAKKOLA. Pinieta Acris.
TALA. Borassus Flabelliformis. The Palmyra Palm, one of the most important of Indian trees. A kind of sugar is obtained from it and the intoxicating drink ' Arrack ' is made from the fermentation of this juice. Fans, mats, etc. are made from the leaves which are also used for thatching ; the hard outer wood of the tree is made into posts and other domestic objects and the hollowed out stems used for waterpipes. The jelly-like pulp of the fruit and the soft kernels of the young fruit are cooked and eaten as vegetables. Brushes come from the ribs of the leaves and the stalks are used for torches.
TAMALA. Phyllanthus Emblica. A tree with black bark and very white blossom, beloved of poets such as Jai-deva. The fruit, Myrabolam, with that of another tree makes the tonic called ' Trefala Churan '.
TILAKA. A tree with beautiful flowers similar to the Sesamum Plant.

GLOSSARY

TIMIDA. Sesamum Indica, the Sesamum Plant which bears an oily seed used in cookery.

TIMIRA. An aquatic plant.

TIMISHA or TINISHA. A climbing plant with purple flowers. A kind of Pumpkin or Water-melon.

TINDUKA. Diospyros Glutinosa or Diospyros Embryopteris, a kind of Ebony.

TINDURA. A Persimmon.

TUNGA. Rottleria Tinctoria. A Coconut.

U

UDDALA or UDDALAKA. Paspalum Frumentaceum. ' Uddalaka-pushpa-bhanjika ' or the ' Breaking of the Uddalaka Flowers ', is a game played by the people of the eastern districts of India.

USHIRAS. Spikenard.
A grass, the small Saccharum.
Andropogan Muricatus, a fragrant root.

UTPALA. The blue Lotus.
A water-lily.
Costus Speciosum, a plant.

V

VAMSHAS. Bamboos.

VANDHIRA. Memisa Sirissa.·

VANIRA. Calamus Rotang, a reed.

VANJULA. Hibiscus Mutabilis.

VARANA. Craetova Tapia. A sacred and medicinal tree.

VASANTA DRU. A Mango.

VASANTA DUTA. Gaetnera Racemosa. A creeper.
A Trumpet flower.

VASANTA KUSUMA. Cordia Latifolia. The name means ' Having blossom in Spring '.

VATA. A species of Banian Tree.

VETRA. An ornamental Palm.

VETTAS. Rattan Canes.

VIBHIDAKA. A tree from the nuts of which dice are made.

VIBHITA or VIBHITAKA. The Tree Terminalia Belerica.

VIJAKA. The Citron Tree.

VISHALYAKARANI. A medicinal herb, " Healer of wounds inflicted by darts '.

W

X

Y.

Z

WEAPONS

A

AGNEYA.   The Fire Weapon or Weapon of the Fire-god Agni.
AINDRA.   Indra's Weapon.
AISHIKA.   An Arrow.
AKSHAS.   Part of a wheel, probably the hub.
ALAKSHYA.   A Weapon the course of which cannot be followed.
ANJALIS.   Arrows resembling hands with the palms hollowed as in a salutation.
ANKUSHA.   A Goad.
ARDEA.   A Weapon called the ' Web '.
ARDRA.   A Weapon producing moisture.
ARHANI.   The Thunderbolt.
ASIRATNA.   A kind of Arrow or Dart.
ASURA.   A magic Weapon used by the Asuras.
AVANAGMUKHA.   A Weapon with a bent or curved head.
AVARANA.   The Weapon of Defence, or Protection.
AVYA.   A kind of Dart or Arrow.

B

BHALLAS.   Crescent-shaped Arrows.
BHINDIPALAS.   Short Darts or Arrows thrown by hand or shot through a tube.
An iron Spear or Dart or a stone fastened to a string.
BIBHITAKA.   A Weapon that breaks through or pierces.
BRAHMADANDA.   The Rod of Brahma.
BRAHMAPASHA.   The Noose of Brahma.
BRAHMASHIRA.   ' Brahma-headed ' therefore four-headed.
BUSHUNDI.   A kind of Mace. This name is applied to various Weapons.

C

D

DAITYA.   The Weapon of the Giants or Daityas.
DANDA.   The name means Rod or Staff as for instance the Rod of Death or Punishment belonging to Yama.

GLOSSARY

DARANA or DARUNA. A Weapon that tears or splits asunder.
DARPANA. The Drying-up Weapon.
DASHAKSHA. The Ten-eyed Weapon.
DASHASHIRSHA. The Ten-headed Weapon.
DHANA. The Weapon that robs the enemy of his spoils.
DHANYA. The Weapon that brings good fortune.
DHARMA-ASTRA. The Weapon of Nemesis.
DHARMANABHA. The Sacred-navelled Weapon.
DHARMAPASHA. The Weapon that has the power of entangling the foe.
DHARMASHAKRA. The Weapon of Justice or Virtue.
DHRISHTA. The Active Weapon, a kind of Arrow.
DHRITI. The Weapon of Forbearance.
DITYA. The Titanic Weapon.
DRIDHANABHA. The Weapon of firm Navel.
DUNDUNABHA. A form of the Danda Weapon.

E

F

G

GANDHARVA. The Weapon of the Gandharvas.

H

HALA. A Weapon shaped like a ploughshare.
HAYASHIRA. The Horse-headed Weapon.

I

ISHIKA. The Ardent Weapon.
ISHU. A Mantra-propelled Arrow.

GLOSSARY

J

JAMBHAKA. Weapons in which evil spirits are said to reside.

JRIMBHAKA. Really magical formulas said to exorcise weapons possessing evil spirits.

JYOTISHTA. The Luminous Weapon.

K

KALAPASHA. The Noose of Death.

KALASHAKRA. The Discus of Death or Time as Death.

KALISHA. An Axe or Hatchet.

KAMARUCHI. An Arrow or Dart, one that is bright and able to go where it will.

KAMARUPA. A Weapon able to assume any form at will.

KAMKALA. A Harpoon.

KANDARPA. A Weapon exciting sex-desire, named after the God of Love Kandarpa.

KANKALA. A Weapon protecting the side, possibly a part of the armour.

KAPALA. A Helmet.

KARAVIRA. The Weapon of the Valiant Hand.

KARNIS. Barbed Arrows with two sides resembling ears.

KASHA. A Whip.

KAUMODAKI. The Iron-headed Club belonging to Shri Vishnu.

KINKINI. The word actually means a small bell, hence the weapon may have had bells hung on it.

KOUMADAKI. A Weapon that gives joy to the earth.

KROUNCHA or KRAUNCHA. The Heron's Beak.

KSHAPANI. An Oar or Net; something that destroys the destroyer.

KSHURA. An Arrow with a razor-like edge or a sharp blade attached to a shaft.

KSHURAPRAS. A crescent-shaped Arrow.

KULISHA. See KALISHA.

KUNTALA. A Sickle-shaped Weapon.

KUTA. A Poniard.

KUTAMUDGARA. A concealed Weapon similar to a Hammer.

KUVERA ASTRA. An instrument for showering gold.

L

LAKSHYA. A Weapon that can be followed in its course.

LOHITA MUKHI. The Bloody-mouthed.

M

MADANA. Weapon of Kandarpa.

MAHABAHU. The Great-armed or Great-handed Weapon.

MAHA-MAYA. The Great Magical Illusion or the Lying Weapon.

MAHANABHA. The Large-navelled Weapon.

MAHISHWARA. The Weapon of Shiva.

MALI. The Weapon that holds or binds.

MANADA. A particular magical Weapon employed by the Gandharvas.

MANAVA. The Weapon of Manu.

MARGANAS. The essence of the nature of an Arrow.

MATHANA. A Weapon that inflicts injury or suffering.

MAYADHARA. The Great Deception.

MODAKI. One of two beautiful mythical Clubs.

MODANA. The Weapon of Inebriation.

MOHA. The Weapon that causes loss of consciousness.

MOHAN. The Weapon of Attraction.

MOUSHALA or MUSHALA. A Club.

MURCHANA. One of the five Arrows of Kandarpa.

N

NAIRASYA. Magical Formulas pronounced on Weapons.

NALIKA. An Iron Arrow or Dart and also a Pike or Javelin.

NANDANA. The Joy-producing Weapon employed by the Vidyadharas.

NARACHA. An Iron Arrow.

NARAYANA. A Water-weapon.

NIRASHYA. The Discourager.

NISHKALI. The Peaceful.

NISHTRINSHA. A Sword, Scimitar or Falchion more than thirty fingers in length.

NIVATA KAVADHA. Impenetrable Armour.

O

P

PAINAKA or PINAKA. Shiva's Trident or Bow.

PAISHA ASTRA, PISACHA or PAISHACHA. The Ghostly Weapon used by the Pisachas. Also called the ' Red-flesh-eater ' or ' Devil's Missile '.

PANTHANA. The Moving Weapon.

PARAMO DARA ASTRA. The Supreme Clearing Weapon.

PARANMUKHA. The Great Mouthed Weapon.

PARA VIRA. Slayer of the Brave.

PARASHAVA. An Iron Weapon.

PARASHVADA. An Axe or Hatchet.

PARIGHA. An Iron Bludgeon or Iron-Studded Club.

PASHA. A Rope.

PASHUPATA. A Weapon sacred to Shiva.

PATH. A kind of Sword.

PITRIYA. The Weapon of the Pitris.

PRAMA THANA. The Churner.

PRASHA. A Bearded Dart.

PRASHAMANA. The Weapon of Destruction.

PRASHVAPRANA. A Weapon dealing with the vital airs.

PRASVAPANA. A Weapon causing sleep.

PRATHAMA. Vayu's Weapon.

PRATIHARATARA. That which neutralizes the effects of other weapons.

PURANG MUKHA. A Weapon that has its face averted.

Q

R

RABHASA. The Desolator.

RAKSHAS. The Titan-Astra which destroys the fortune, courage and life of one's foes.

RATI. The Weapon of Enjoyment.

RISHTIS. Swords, Arrows or Spears, Weapons of the Maruts.

RUCHIRA. The Approving Weapon.

RUDRA. The Rudra Weapon sacred to Rudra or Shiva.

S

SALA. An Arrow with short leads.

SAMVARTA. The Covering Weapon belonging to Kala or Time which he uses at the destruction of the worlds.

SANDHANA. The Arm Weapon.

SANTAPANA. The Weapon that burns up or scorches. One of the Arrows of Kama or Kandarpa.

SARCHIMALI. That which has force or power.

SARPANATHA. The Weapon sacred to the Lord of Serpents.

GLOSSARY

SATYA ASTRA. The Weapon of Existence.
SATYA KIRTI. The Justly-famed.
SAUMYA. The Moon's Weapon.
SAURA. The Heroic Weapon.
SHAKTIS. Iron Spears, Lances or Pikes.
SHAKUNA. The Vulture-shaped Weapon.
SHALYA. A Dart, Javelin or Spear tipped with iron.
SHANKARA. A Weapon of Shiva's called the ' Cause of Welfare '.
SHANKAR ASTRA. The Weapon with a flaming mouth.
SHARNGA. The Bow of Vishnu.
SHATAGNI. A spiked Mace or a stone set round with iron spikes ;
    it is named ' Slayer of Hundreds '.
SHATAPATRA. ' Having a hundred Feathers ', probably an Arrow.
SHATAVAKTRA. The Hundred-mouthed Weapon.
SHATODARA. The Hundred-bellied Weapon.
SHIKARI. One of the two beautiful mythical Clubs.
SHILIMUKHAS. Arrows resembling Heron's feathers.
SHITESU. A sharp Arrow.
SHOSHANA. A Weapon used to dry up water and counteract the
    Varshana Weapon.
SHUCHIVANU. The Pure-handed Weapon.
SHUSHKA. The Dry Weapon.
SINHADAMSHTRA. A Weapon resembling Lion's Teeth.
SOMASTRA. The Dew Weapon.
SUNABHAKA. The Fine-navelled Weapon.
SURA ASTRA. A Weapon named ' The Blasting of Enemies ' that
    steals away lustre and beauty.
SOUMANVA. The Weapon of the Controlled Mind.
SVAPANA. A Weapon affecting sleep.
SVANABHAKA. The Richly-navelled Weapon.

T

TAMASA. The Weapon of Inertia.
TEJASPRABHA. The Sun Weapon.
TOMARA. An Iron Bar, Crow-bar, Lance or Javelin.
TRIMBAKA. The Gaper.
TVASHTRA ASTRA. The Chaos-demon Astra, a weapon possessing
    the power of the Architect of the Gods.

U

USIRATMA. A Scimitar.

V

VALLA. See Bhalla.

VARSHANA. The Rain-producing Weapon.

VARUNA PASHA. The Noose of Varuna.

VATRA. The Blower, a Weapon sacred to the Wind-god.

VATSADANTA. A Weapon resembling Calf's Teeth.

VAYAVYA. A Weapon with the power of the Wind.

VIDDANA. The Weapon that rends or tears asunder.

VIDHUTA. The Strongly-vibrating Weapon.

VIDYADHARA. The Delighting Weapon, one belonging to the Vidyadharas.

VIKARNI. An Arrow.

VILAPANA. The Weapon causing lamentation.

VIMALA. The Stainless Weapon.

VINIDRA. The Weapon of Sleeplessness.

VIPATHA. A large Arrow.

VIPATRA. A Weapon resembling the Karavira Weapon.

VISHNUSHAKRA. The Discus of Vishnu.

VRITTIMAT. A Weapon that revolves like a wheel.

Y

YAMYA. The Dual Weapon.

YAUGANDHARA. A particular magic Formula spoken over weapons that belong to a king.